police community RElations: imAges, rolES, REAlities

editEd by

ALVIN W. COHN
Administration of Justice Services

·ANd

EMILIO C. VIANO
The American University

J. B. Lippincott Company
Philadelphia
New York / San Jose / Toronto

4-12-83

Copyright © 1976 by J. B. Lippincott Company

This book is fully protected by copyright and, with
the exception of brief excerpts for review, no part
of it may be reproduced in any form, by print, photoprint,
microfilm, or any other means, without written permission
from the publisher.

ISBN 0-397-47354-0

ISBN 0-397-47352-4 pbk.

Library of Congress Catalog Card Number 76-000180

Printed in the United States of America

1 3 5 7 9 8 6 4 2

Library of Congress Cataloging in Publication Data
Main entry under title:
Police-community relations.
    Bibliography: p. 605.
    Includes index.
    1. Public relations—Police—Addresses, essays, lectures. 2. Police—
United States—Addresses, essays, lectures. I. Cohn, Alvin W. II.
Viano, Emilio.
HV7936.P8P566   363.2'0973   76-000180
ISBN 0-397-47354-0
ISBN 0-397-47352-4 pbk.

TO OUR PARENTS

Nathan and Myrtle Cohn
Giuseppe and Teresa Viano

CONTENTS

v

pREfACE

The mission of a police organization in contemporary America is both simple and complex. It is simple because it remains for everyone the principal unit of government charged with the responsibility for reducing and controlling crime. It is complex because so much more is demanded and without appropriate and consensually understood definitions than could be handled responsibly. Police are called upon to provide social service functions, such as emergency medical care, to regulate traffic, enforce the law, and bring suspected offenders before the bar of justice. They are supposed to accomplish these and other activities in a professional manner, within the context of the community and its values in which they work, and with as little hostility and antagonism from the public as is possible to obtain.

One former chief of police described what the public expects of its police in the following way (Bain, 1939:5):

> The citizen expects police officers to have the wisdom of Solomon, the courage of David, the strength of Samson, the patience of Job, the leadership of Moses, the kindness of the Good Samaritan, the strategical training of Alexander, the faith of Daniel, the diplomacy of Lincoln, the tolerance of the Carpenter of Nazareth, and, finally, an intimate knowledge of every branch of the natural, biological, and social sciences. If he had all these, he might be a good policeman!

If the chief were writing today, he would probably still add something to describe the value of police-community relations.

In one sense, it is all of the above which is the concern of this book, but, more particularly, the focus is that of police-community relations (PCR). PCR is a large and all-encompassing topic, especially when one reviews all that has been written under such a heading. Sociological, psychological, criminological, administrative, and police management science journals are replete with articles on the subject. Numerous books have been written and it is a common topic for discussion and debate at professional meetings.

This book of readings does not attempt to summarize all that has been written on the subject, nor does it attempt to summarize all that might be considered significant. What it does attempt to do is place PCR in a much different perspective, namely, that PCR should be viewed not as an aspect of police work, but as the *outcome* of police work. That is, this book takes the position that PCR should not be treated administratively within a police department as is traffic, vice, juvenile, or patrol work. Instead, it is recommended that every policeman be held accountable for relating to citizens within a community in a manner that not only enhances the police function, but also merits respect from the citizen.

The book takes the position that while public relations should be an important function of a police agency and while a PCR unit is indeed needed for special projects designed to enhance police and community relationships, these should be viewed as complementary to the PCR function of the individual officer—not solely as the responsibility of a separate administrative unit.

The inclusion or exclusion of any selection in a book of readings obviously reflects the biases—and hopefully the insights—of the authors. We claim no exception to the above, but trust that the materials we have chosen will provide the student with greater awareness and sensitivity to the issue than is currently available in most PCR books we have reviewed. We have not concentrated on riots, disturbances, and problems of the inner city. We have not reviewed the subject as a basic problem for police management in terms of recruitment, selection, and training—even though these are important considerations for any effective PCR program. Finally, we have not attempted to engage in any special polemic in defense or criticism of the police.

Instead, we recognize the importance of policing in our society and the nature and consequences of the various interactions between the police and the policed. We have strived to find selections which describe and discuss the interactive process, as well as what policing and what communities might be defined to be. In other words, we have attempted to illustrate PCR in the context of contemporary American law enforcement and community structure.

Part I of the book deals with the context of police-community relations. It looks at how PCR has been defined and operationalized; examines the meaning and complexity of community and society; and discusses the significance of PCR for both law enforcement and the community. Part II addresses the police role and the various activities and responsibilities of urban police departments. It examines selected standards and goals of policing and how police respond to the multitude of demands from the community.

In Part III, we look at the interactions between police and community, including how the community can shape police systems. This part looks at specific kinds of interactions, such as with juveniles and with the black community, a significant group in our society which has been antagonistic toward the police. This part also looks at a relatively recent development in law enforcement, namely that of using women on routine patrol.

Part IV is concerned with the kinds of tensions that accrue to the police function as a result of the previously described interactions. We examine tensions created between the police and other criminal justice agencies, those that are created as a result of political upheaval, and the consequences of police corruption.

How communities and police departments have attempted to disengage themselves from conflict with each other is the topic of the fifth part. Here, we look at typical PCR programs, which have had some claim to "success." We pay special attention to community involvement in setting priorities, standards for policing, the nature of the control process, and some alternative programs that may have some impact at improving police and community relations.

In the sixth and final part, we look at the process of change and the nature of the resistance to it. We examine how police productivity can be measured, which suggests a process of accountability. We also present a selection which argues for a radical departure in the way in which we select policemen.

We want to express our appreciation to A. Richard Heffron at J.B. Lippincott Co., who provided considerable help and guidance in the direction this book has taken. Additionally, Mark Furstenberg provided us with invaluable insights into the concept of PCR as an outcome of policing. Finally, Mark Blessington helped to ensure that the manuscript was completed within the confines of that notorious and hindering culprit, the "deadline."

A.W.C.
E.C.V.

Reference

Bain, Read
    1939   As quoted in Tappan, Paul W. Crime, Justice and Correction.
                New York: McGraw-Hill. 1960:273.

iNTROdUCTiON

Police-Community Relations Development

Not long ago, we became accustomed to "Support Your Local Police" bumper-stickers and to political rhetoric stating "Respect Law and Order." It soon became apparent that those who supported and those who rejected such slogans were typecast as conservatives and liberals, respectively. For many people, the use of such slogans was viewed as a simplistic response to complex issues revolving about the nature of law enforcement in society and communal responsibility for participating in the "war on crime." No one was suggesting that policing be done away with, but most individuals and groups were willing to admit that something had to be done to bring the police and the policed into more meaningful dialogue.

While many police departments had developed public relations (PR) programs to enhance their image, it was not until the mid-1950s that formal police-community relations (PCR) programs were developed by American law enforcement agencies. As such, they were not much more than PR or image-building units, but they did have as their focus the development of two-way processes of communication. That is, some police departments began to realize that if they wanted to be more effective in reducing and controlling crime, they would have to listen to citizens to determine community values and needs. Wasserman, Gardner, and Cohen (1973:1) summarize the developments which occurred subsequently:

> Within ten years, these units (and police departments in general) were obliged to cope with an unprecedented challenge. Social unrest became a

1

fact of American life in the 1960's fueled by racial concerns, an unwanted war, and the affluence that pemitted young people to engage in civil protest almost as a career. By 1968, the police response had become a matter of broad public concern. . . . As a result of . . . . pressure, U.S. police departments began to adopt community-relations programs on a wholesale basis. They established the appropriate bureaucracies, opened storefront offices to reach the public, trained their people in community relations, and generally tried to accommodate their critics.

As these programs proliferated, many antagonists claimed that the PCR units had as their basic purpose not that of reconciling differences, but a disguised form of public relations. They viewed the police as intractable, unchanging, bigoted institutionally, and intolerant of any kind of deviant belief systems. Ethnic minorities, youth, and the poor appeared to be the most vocal in their oppositon to traditional police practices and looked upon the police as their enemy (Cray, 1972).

The police, on the other hand, were struggling to control many societal problems which they believed they had no hand in creating let alone the ability to solve. Many, indeed, accepted the label of an "occupational force" and did little as individuals or as departments to communicate with their detractors. They fought battles on the streets and on campuses, with helmets and occasionally with bayonets, frequently acting in ways that did little to reduce their image as the enemy.

During and subsequent to the riotous summers of the 1960s, many police departments and citizen groups apparently began to realize that more serious dialogue and efforts were needed if conflicting values and behaviors were ever to be ameliorated. This responsible action began to produce a more meaningful kind of police-community relations than had ever occurred before. Simultaneously, the police launched a drive toward professionalization that involved education and exploration of better police techniques. Analyses of their roles (Gabor and Low, 1973) were initiated, with special attention being paid to the service orientation many police departments were beginning to accept. Furthermore, the infusion of millions of dollars into the criminal justice system by the Law Enforcement Assistance Administration (LEAA) not only tended to enhance such professionalization efforts, but also provided the impetus for police and communities to experiment with innovative practices.

Changing Police Practices

Evaluative research, although not commonly found in American policing, has been spurred by LEAA and such groups as the Police Foundation. The evaluation of one experimental project, for example, tested the questions of whether or not routine patrol has any impact on the level of crime, citizens' attitudes toward police services and their fear of crime, and citizens' satisfaction with police response time to calls for service. In this Police Foundation sponsored research (Kelling et al., 1974), it was found that routine, increased, or decreased amounts of patrolling had no appreciable impact on any of the variables just cited. Although considerable caution must be exercised in concluding that routine patrol—the hallmark of policing (Chapman, 1970)—has much less value than previously believed, it nonetheless points out the value of assessing routine operations in law enforcement.

Changing strategies in policing are not always determined as a result of rigorous testing, nor do they come about simply because of internal managerial decision-making. They also occur as a result of pressures placed on police departments by external groups and agencies. Pressure by such groups as the Retail Merchants' Association, banking and industrial organizations, and politically powerful groups has always resulted in responsiveness by the police hierarchy. Demands—or even suggestions—for change by community groups, neighborhood associations, and church organizations did not tend to result in a similar level of reaction. Apparently, these groups were not powerful enough to convince either the politicians or the police administrators that what they wanted was worthwhile, important, or significant enough to bring about the requested changes.

During the 1960s, however, a new level of responsiveness on the part of law enforcement agencies to the demands emanating from the streets began to occur. Riots, demonstrations, and other kinds of militant behavior either convinced the police that they had better listen to these vocal groups or they were told to listen by more politically powerful persons and groups, such as city administrators. While the interaction was marred at times by hatred, hostility, and mutual antagonism, groups opposed to the traditional policing of law enforcement agencies finally convinced the police to talk. It may be fair to conclude that in most cities each "side" talked *at* each other rather than *with* each other; both sides wanted to be heard, but few wanted to listen.

It would appear from the above that the problem was a simple one; namely, a failure to communicate. But the problem of policing in contemporary America cannot be reduced to such simplistics. Needs, desires, cultural differences, and values of groups and individuals all are intertwined in the very fabric of the democratic society we claim to have. The right to representation, the right to be heard, and the right to constitutional freedoms have been called "inalienable" since the founding of the country. Many people were claiming that law enforcement, as it was being practiced, abridged those rights, and during the 1960s, many groups said they would no longer tolerate such abuse.

Resolving differences of opinion is not always an easy task, nor is it one which people with closed minds (Rokeach, 1960) are willing to try. But it becomes even more of a Herculean task when the exact nature of the differences is discussed in terms of slogans rather than in realities. "Support Your Local

Police" is an admirable request, but not if those who are being solicited for such support view the police as their oppressors. The use of such epithets as "pig" can only exacerbate the problem, for what person, including a policeman, wants to have to deal with someone who accuses him of being less than human?

Professor Louis Radelet, a noted authority in the field of police-community relations, states (1973: viii):

> The problems of living together will not go away. In fact, they seem to become increasingly interconnected, therefore more impossible to understand. Bewilderment and frustration thrive until community action to solve problems becomes more personal psychotherapy than a rational, systematic approach to the external matter. Mix politics with this therapy, and it is small wonder that sometimes rationality seems to have so little chance. Responses to social problems involve countless nonscientific factors. But this can hardly be taken as an excuse for resigning from the "human condition."

Enforcement of Laws

All societies, whether primitive or civilized, have rules, regulations, and traditions which govern the behavior of their members. In simple societies, the pressures on each member probably were sufficient to keep most from infracting such rules. But in complex, large, and highly urbanized societies, it is not possible for each person to observe or to control the behaviors of all others. Therefore some policing, by selected persons or groups, necessarily evolved. The police became charged with the responsibility of enforcing the norms of society—the laws by which society decided it would govern itself.

Law enforcement, as it is practiced in America, has its roots in the British model developed by Sir Robert Peel in London in the 1800s. It is a model based on the concept of social control of those persons who violate what is termed substantive law. The problem that develops with such a model, however, is one of determining the boundary between individual and collective rights. Apparently, this conflict was one considered when the first metropolitan police force was established in London. Reith (1938:188) discussed the misgivings the British had and the argument against the creation of a police force:

> The police of a free country is to be found in rational and humane laws— in an effective and enlightened magistracy—and in the judicious and proper selection of those officers of justice, in whose hands, as conservators of the peace, executive duties are legally placed, but above all, in the moral habits and opinions of the people; and in proportion as these

approximate towards a state of perfection, so that people may rest in security; and though their property may occasionally be invaded or their lives endangered by the hands of wicked and desperate individuals, yet the institutions of the country being sound, its laws well adjusted, and justice executed against offenders, no greater safeguard can be obtained without sacrificing all those rights which society was instituted to preserve.

According to Skolnick (1966:2), Sir Robert Peel argued for the creation of a police force on the basis that society needed some organized means of achieving public order, control over crime, and tranquility in the cities. In the United States, law enforcement agencies have proliferated and tend to be directed toward implementing the above goals, but we are without any complete and accurate information concerning their exact numbers at the federal, state, county, and local levels of government. Furthermore, we do not have complete data on the numbers of police personnel or the total costs of operating law enforcement. The President's Commission on Law Enforcement and Administration of Justice in 1967 estimated the number of agencies to be 40,000, including 50 at the federal level, 200 at the state level, and the remaining dispersed among the various counties, cities, towns, and villages in all 50 states. Additionally, there are approximately 4,000 private security or law enforcement agencies, whose goals may be somewhat different from those of public police forces—especially in the area of protecting private property.

With such an array of agencies, programs, and services, it was inevitable that the various standards and operational procedures of the agencies would come under attack for their lack of consistency and relative poor performance. In 1931, a national investigation of policing resulted in a report (Wickersham Commission, p. 125) which stated:

> The multitude of police forces in any State and the varying standards of organization and service have contributed immeasurably to the general low grade of police performance in this country. The independence which police forces display toward each other and the absence of any central force which requires either a uniform or a minimum standard of service leave the way open for the profitable operation of criminals in an area where protection is often ineffectual at the best, generally only partial, and too frequently wholly absent.

In 1967, the President's Crime Commission echoed the same sentiments and urged that American law enforcement become more professionalized in its operations, reduce its fragmentation, and otherwise upgrade its services in order to reduce and control crime. In 1973, the National Advisory Commission on Criminal Justice Standards and Goals reiterated the same concerns, but suggested in its report, *Police* (p. 4), that no changes could possibly come about in American policing without citizen involvement, cooperation, and responsiveness to mutual needs. In creating a set of standards and goals for law enforcement, the Commission stated (1973:5): "The ultimate purpose of creating standards is to provide a means whereby the people ... can move about with the reasonable expectation that the quality of police service will be as good in one place as it is in another."

Police Activities

In a special report for the President's Crime Commission, Professors Lohman and Misner (1966:38) surveyed the literature and commentaries on police management and enumerated the following major activities of a typical law enforcement agency:

1. Prevention and repression of crime
2. Maintenance of the peace (domestic tranquility)
3. Protection of persons and property (security)
4. Enforcement of laws
5. Detection of crime
6. Recovery of lost and stolen property
7. Apprehension of offenders
8. Regulation of noncriminal conduct
9. Protection of individual rights
10. Control of traffic
11. Miscellaneous public services
12. Preparation of cases for presentation in court

This rather traditional listing of police activities, while undoubtedly accurate, does not reveal what to some is the growing trend of the social service function. That is, in spite of increased mechanization and technological developments, the patrolman on the beat is spending more time providing services to citizens than he is in crime fighting. Professor John Webster (1973:1) comments on the changing nature of policing in America with regard to the social service function:

As urban, industrial America undergoes rapid and unprecedented social change, unresolved problems create ever increasing pressures and familiar institutions change their purposes and meanings in the attempt to cope with change. This is ... true of the police.

He goes on to discuss a study he conducted concerning the activities of a police department in which he recorded all of the dispatched calls within a 54-week period. Similar to the findings of the Police Foundation's Kansas City Patrol Experiment, Webster found that patrolling police in this city spent more time on administrative and social service functions than on any other activity. He concludes (1973:6, 13):

> The data indicate that unnecessary and incorrect emphasis is being placed by the public, police administrators and the police themselves on the role of the patrolman as a crime fighter . . . Instead, what the investigation shows is that crimes against persons . . . actually constitute less of the daily realities of police work and consume far less of the patrolman's actual energies than popular conception supposes. . . . We are left with the astonishing discovery that *less* than *one-third* of an urban patrolman's time is involved in dealing with personal or property crimes and *over half*—about *two-thirds*—of his time is spent in administrative or social service tasks.

These findings are also corroborated by McManus et al. (1970) for the New York City police department. This calls for a re-examination of not only the important thrusts of policing in contemporary society, but of how police departments ought to be operationalizing such thrusts to meet the twin mandates of crime control and the provision of social services to the community.

This is not to say that a police department has primary responsibility for providing those social services which welfare, health, and charitable groups have long provided. But it probably represents a recognition that many people in society expect their police agencies to serve the public in ways which the police have not been trained or feel even inclined to provide. Many communities, for example, look to the police for emergency medical care and appreciate such services. As a result of training in family crisis intervention tactics, Bard (1970) found that the police were capable of settling family disputes; that is, they provided emotional first aid or counseling services to families that might not otherwise look for or accept such services.

The late O.W. Wilson, who was considered to be one of the foremost experts on law enforcement in this country, maintained in the third edition of his classic, *Police Administration* (1972:5), that the "primary purpose of a police department is the preservation of peace and protection of life and property against attacks by criminals and injury by the careless and inadvertent offender." However, he also recognized the shifting nature of police responsibilities when he said (1972:6):

> A broadened concept of *social responsibility* on the part of the police has resulted in a more positive philosophy of service . . . Police service today extends beyond mere routine investigation and disposition of complaints; it also has as its objective the welfare of the individual and of society.

Society and Community

We have heretofore used most liberally the words *society* and *community* as though these are consensually defined and understood terms. While all of us would be able to define these two terms in ways that probably would be understandable to others, it is doubtful that we could agree on their precise meanings. That is, each of us would define the terms from a particular frame of reference, but not necessarily agreeable to others.

In defining society, Webster (1968:1352) actually uses the word community:

(1). A group of persons regarded as forming a single community especially as forming a distinct social or economic class; (2) the system or condition of living together as a community in such a group ... (3) all people, collectively, regarded as constituting a community of related, interdependent individuals. ...

In defining community, Webster (1968:288) eventually uses the term society:

(1a). all the people living in a particular district, city, etc. (1b) the district, city, etc. where they live; (2) a group of people, living together as a smaller social unit within a larger one, and having interests, work, etc. in common ... (4) society in general; the public ...

This would suggest that the terms society and community have a great deal of commonality, for both concepts suggest a level of sharing—geographical space, interests, values, and/or attributes. The sociologist whose responsibility it is to study society and community is not as quick as Webster in arriving at acceptable definitions. The fact that there are differences of opinion as to what exactly constitutes a society or a community has tremendous significance for policing. This applies if for no other reason than it is in society or a given community that policing takes place. Therefore, how the terms are defined will undoubtedly have an impact on the nature of law enforcement services. Furthermore, if police-community relations are to be meaningful, then we have an obligation to know and understand just what we mean by police as well as by community.

In an analysis of how sociologists use the term community, Professor Dennis Poplin (1972:1) suggests that three ways are found in the literature. First, community is used as a synonym for such diverse groups as minorities, religious organizations, the military establishment, and professional associations. Second, it is often used to refer to a moral or spiritual phenomenon reflecting a search or quest for belongingness or unity with other people with whom there may be an interdependence. Third is the use of the term to reflect social and territorial organizations or geographical entities otherwise called towns, cities, or metropolitan areas.

Minar and Greer (1969) devote considerable attention to the concept of community as a moral phenomenon. They state (1969:ix):

> . . . it expresses our vague yearnings for a commonality of desire, a communion with those around us, an extension of the bonds of kin and friend to all those who share a common fate with us.

Poplin discusses this notion and proceeds to distinguish it with its opposite, namely mass society—a concept which suggests a state of alienation, fragmentation, and lack of involvement on the part of citizens. He then (1969:6) compares the two kinds of communities according to selected characteristics, as is shown in Table I-1.

Thus Poplin suggests that the concept of community is complex and multidimensional, especially when viewed as a moral phenomenon. Whether or not it is a group identified as a result of territorial occupation, we are led to believe that the concept of community probably involves interpersonal relationships which lead to ". . . a sense of identity and unity with one's group and a feeling of involvement and wholeness on the part of the individual" (Poplin, 1969:7).

TABLE I-1. Selected Characteristics of Moral Communities and Mass Societies

Moral Communities	Mass Societies
Identification Members of the moral community have a deep sense of belonging to a significant, meaningful group.	**Alienation** Members of mass society have a deep sense of being "cut off" from meaningful group associations.
Moral Unity Members of the moral community have a sense of pursuing common goals and feel a oneness with other community members.	**Moral Fragmentation** Members of mass society pursue divergent goals and feel no sense of oneness with other members of the mass society.
Involvement Members of the moral community are submerged in various groups and have a compelling need to participate in these groups.	**Disengagement** Members of mass society have no meaningful group memberships and feel no compulsion to participate in the collective activities of various groups.
Wholeness Members of the moral community regard each other as whole persons who are of intrinsic significance and worth.	**Segmentation** Members of mass society regard each other as means to ends and assign no intrinsic worth or significance to the individual.

If this is so, then we can more easily understand why various groups which have felt neglected and excluded from the mainstream of American life, such as ethnic minorities, have become so vociferous in demanding attention to their needs and situations.

Since law enforcement is a vital part of that mainstream, the relationships between the police and the policed take on a more dynamic meaning. While a definition of community is an important place to start in order to develop action strategies for improving law enforcement, in the final analysis what is needed, by police and citizens, is an understanding of relationships, needs, values, and concerns. Community, then, will be viewed in terms of its dynamic qualities, rather than only for its "academic" components.

Interactionism

Bell and Newby (1972:21) indicate that whatever approach one takes in describing and understanding a community, it is impossible to do so without making value judgments. This is so because one tends to place values on the interactions between people. These values are sometimes good and sometimes bad, but are determined according to the interests, needs, beliefs, and moralities of those who are doing the interacting. Thus, if interaction can be defined ". . . as a face-to-face encounter between two or more people in which each person takes the other into account" (Poplin, 1972:17), then we are confronted with the reality of a process whereby people are constantly making value judgments in their relationships with others.

Interaction occurs not only between individuals, such as a policeman and a citizen, but between individuals and groups, and between groups. To understand the social system of interactions that occur within any given community means that one also has to understand the kinds of individuals and groups that exist in that community and the nature of their interactions. Furthermore, attention must be given to *potential* as well as *existing* patterns of interaction. In law enforcement, therefore, every citizen, regardless of group identification, potentially may have an encounter with the police. At the very least, simply by virtue of membership in a community, every citizen is affected by the quality and scope of police services. This occurs directly when an arrest is made, for example, or indirectly in terms of the fears one has regarding crime.

Interactions between groups frequently become crystallized into patterns of behavior and it is these patterns which must be identified and understood if police-community relations are to have any meaning in society. Because the police have an obligation to "serve" the community, they must appreciate various social processes that occur in as value-neutral a way as possible. That is, the police have a responsibility to enforce and uphold the law, but society does not give each policeman (nor a police department) the right to determine who or what is good or bad. The beliefs and value judgments of the policeman are expected to be held in check as he or she performs his or her duty. It is when the policeman fails to hold such beliefs in check, when he actually discriminates against those with whom he interacts, that hostilities and antagonisms are fostered and nurtured. It is when the interactions between the police and the policed are perceived negatively (by either group) that hostile confrontations are most likely to occur.

Use of Power

In the past and even today, the attempt to resolve conflicts has more often than not been controlled by that group which has had the most power. Traditionally, the police accepted and used that power, occasionally with considerable abuse. Police brutality, including both physical and verbal types, was perceived as traditional police behavior by those who felt oppressed. Such groups also believed that the police were unchangeable. As a consequence, some began to accept the philosophy that the only way to change the police was to overpower them and, unfortunately, this often took the form of militant violence in the streets.

But those who engaged in criminal activity in the streets were not, as commonly believed, thugs, criminals, hoodlums, and delinquents merely on a collective rampage—taking advantage of the social situation. As Thomas Lynch, then Attorney General of California, reported in an analysis of those arrested during the Los Angeles Watts Riots (Lynch et al., 1966:37):

> The relatively minor types of offenses for which the great majority of riot participants were convicted would seem to indicate that this group of individuals was not the same type of persons usually booked on similar felony charges. A review of their prior criminal history fails to show a record as serious as that generally present in many of the nonriot felony bookings usually handled in urban areas by the police and the courts . . . there was little before the court(s) in the form of evidence or positive proof of specific criminal activity.

Thus we are confronted with the fact that many of the people who took to the streets did so in order to redress their grievances about social conditions and/or the ways in which the police and other "establishment" groups were treating them. While much of their behavior could be condemned as being unreasonable, they at least were able to mount a collective force that was powerful enough to get the attention of those who had previously turned deaf ears to their complaints and concerns and who, conceivably, had the power to do something about their problems.

Police-Community Relations

While the police are called upon to quell riots and disturbances, many of which arise out of social conditions beyond their making or control, they nonetheless are on the front-lines in having to deal with real people who are affected by serious social problems (Viano and Cohn, 1975). How the police deal with these people, in large measure, is both the substantive and procedural concern of police-community relations. That is, what actually constitutes the problems these people have and the ways in which the police deal with such people is and should be the very heart of PCR work. The questions that need to be answered, however, are "what kinds of training, what kinds of programs, and what kinds of belief systems are needed by the police and the policed to deal effectively with the issue?" We need to know the extent, nature, and quality of interactions to determine what kind of a police-community relations program is needed.

For too long, police departments have operated at a level of semi-secrecy which has precluded any realistic knowledge by the community with regard to their total activities. Except for appearances before funding sources to obtain budgets or in the courtroom for individual cases, the management and operation of a typical police department take place behind closed doors. Who makes policy and how a policy is to be implemented are important pieces of information generally withheld from the public. This has led to demands for civilian review boards or some kind of community control over law enforcement (Waskow, 1969), which has been resisted most strenuously by police groups. In fact, the strength of such resistance has probably been the most significant factor preventing the development of such boards.

Public Relations Programs

Another approach to ease tensions and to convince the public that "cops aren't all bad" has been the development of public relations programs. Through this model, such activities as school and church programs are created whereby the policeman becomes involved in special functions to demonstrate that he is really "a nice guy" and just another caring individual in the community. "The Friendly Cop" atmosphere is projected so that he can be trusted, appreciated, and accepted in the community. He is pictured as a friend of babies and the elderly, but one who can be firm (and just) in dealing with criminals. These public relations programs seek to project positive images of policing and the police in an effort to enlist greater cooperation and possibly assistance from the public in crime fighting efforts.

While there may be some facetiousness in describing such public relations efforts, there is no reason for denying a police department the opportunity to project itself in such positive terms. If General Motors, IBM, and mayors and governors are permitted to enhance their images, why shouldn't the police? As a matter of fact, a police department should be involved in such activities, if for no other reason than to enlist the support of the public in crime control activities. However, as we have previously indicated, such PR activities should not be confused with PCR responsibilities, nor should they be substituted for meaningful PCR.

PR is image-building. It is an accepted technique to promote the best interests of the group or organization concerned. It is a healthy form of propaganda. It is unhealthy, at least with regard to policing, if it has as a hidden agenda the cooptation of the public or a "one-upsmanship" quality about it that seeks to convince the community that the police do nothing wrong and are themselves the victims rather than the victimizers.

Police-Community Relations: An Outcome

Police-community relations, on the other hand, seeks to bring together law enforcement and the community in an effort to understand mutual problems and concerns. It is a model which has as its basic technique meaningful communication and dialogue. It is not power-oriented in the sense that one side or the other is the superior in the relationship. However, it is power-oriented in the sense that there is recognition and respect for the fact that both the police and the community indeed have power. PCR is an interactive process and, from that point of view, it is both a means and an end. Successful and meaningful interaction is the technique for police and community to work together and it is, at the same time, the hoped-for result of such collaboration.

As a consequence, police-community relations cannot and should not be viewed as a responsibility for a special unit within a police department, much as traffic, juvenile, or patrol responsibilities are treated. It should not be veiwed as an exclusive function of one group within the department. *If PCR is to be meaningful and if it is to be realistic, then it must be viewed as the OUTCOME of the interactions of every officer, regardless of duty or assignment, with the citizenry.* PCR should be viewed as a necessary ingredient to "good policing" in terms of the relationships which occur as a result of every encounter. It is part and parcel of routine policing; it is not an administrative unit with a mission of pacifying upset individuals or groups.

PCR should not be viewed as an aspect of police work; it must be accepted as an *outcome* of police work. If this view were accepted, police administrators would not be called upon to design special units within their organizations to repair the relationship and image damages wrought by the police in other departmental units. It is a view which might help police managers to accept the inevitability of the existence of some friction between the police and the policed.

It might also help them understand that regardless of the circumstances causing an interaction to occur, some people will always be antagonistic toward the police, and that the policeman should not make the situation worse.

An offender is not likely to thank a policeman for having caught and arrested him, nor is a motorist expected to be grateful for having received a ticket for speeding. But how the policeman arrests a suspect and how he issues a ticket can either reduce potential tension or make the situation worse. When a policeman has to deal with a relative of an injured or seriously ill person, with an upset parent whose child is missing, or with a complainant about some victimization, the way he or she deals with such encounters probably will have more impact on the maintenance of positive police-community relations than any expensive and well-planned PCR program could possibly achieve.

While PCR should be viewed as the outcome of individual efforts on the part of police personnel in terms of their daily and routine activities, this does not mean that there should be no organized effort by a department to deal directly with certain groups within the community who may have legitimate and justifiable concerns or criticisms. Groups within the community which have vested interests need to be respected and heard. Such groups, for example, may be the Retail Merchants Association concerned about shoplifting, but they may also be neighborhood or civic associations concerned about street crime in their residential areas. They may be groups of teenagers who engage in recreational activities on the streets or gay activists who are demanding less harassment.

While the individual policeman can help or hinder police-community relationships by the way in which he polices, a department must have some organized process for meeting with various groups in society. From this perspective, a PCR unit can indeed be important and serve a department well as an effective listening post within the community. This also implies that groups must be willing to listen to police and that every group has access to the police, not merely those who are most favored, organized, or labeled as "responsible." A PCR unit can also develop and implement special projects to enhance relationships and dialogue, but such programs would be undertaken as a *complement* to routine police activity, rather than as a displacement of it.

Training and education at the academy and university levels are important to the development of successful PCR operations as we have defined them. Recruitment of qualified manpower is also essential. However, the most important ingredient to meaningful PCR operations, at the individual policeman level, is that of holding the policeman accountable for his or her actions and behavior. This means that there must be a concerted effort on the part of the police administrator to share appropriate values and beliefs with the individual policeman and to insist that what is demanded behaviorally will indeed be expected without exception. Each employee then would have to account for personal behavior and more publicly than ever before. The administrator will also have to account for the entire department. With such accountability and with greater community involvement in setting law enforcement standards, PCR could become an on-going reality, not merely a hoped-for dream.

Police-Community Collaboration

Successful PCR, as well as PR activities, in the final analysis, should be designed to enhance the police mission as it is defined by the police and by the specific community being policed. This is not to say that we should search for more effective means to make the lot of the policeman better. The concern must be for improving life in the community and for recognizing that policing plays a vital role in that regard. How citizens should be interacting with each other (in crime-free ways) and how citizens should be interacting with those most responsible for the control of crime are the important questions.

The police must show greater respect for the needs of the community and the community must appreciate its police. While we can never expect to create utopia, if both groups work together, some improvement can reasonably be expected. Garmire (1972:11) summarizes it this way:

> . . . I do not believe that . . . policemen and the police service (can become) objects of love and endearment; it is not in the nature of men—particularly Americans—to give such affection to those representatives of authority who directly control their lives. And, no matter how we describe the activities of the police, the business of police is policing. The most that we can hope for, police-community relations or public relations notwithstanding, is respect for the police as professionals, confidence in their integrity, and public conviction that the police will perform their mission.

References

Bard, Morton
    1970   Training Police as Specialists in Family Crisis Intervention.
              Washington, D.C.: U.S. Government Printing Office.
Bell, Colin and Howard Newby
    1972   Community Studies: An Introduction to the Sociology of the
              Local Community. New York: Praeger Publishers.
Chapman, Samuel G.
    1970   Police Patrol Readings. 2nd ed. Springfield, Illinois: Charles C.
              Thomas Publishers.

Cray, Ed
      1972   The Enemy in the Streets: Police Malpractice in America.
                  Garden City, New York: Anchor Books.
Gabor, Ivan R. and Christopher Low
      1973   "The Police Role in the Community." Criminology 10 (Febru-
                  ary) 4:383–414.
Garmire, Bernard I.
      1972   "The Police Role in An Urban Society." in Robert F. Steadman,
                  ed. The Police and the Community. Baltimore: The Johns Hop-
                  kins University Press: 1–11.
Kelling, George L., Tony Pate, Duane Dieckman, and Charles E. Brown
      1974   The Kansas City Preventive Patrol Experiment: A Summary
                  Report. Washington, D.C.: Police Foundation.
Lohman, Joseph D. and Gordon E. Misner
      1966   The Police and the Community—The Dynamics of Their Rela-
                  tionship in a Changing Society. Washington, D.C.: U.S. Govern-
                  ment Printing Office.
Lynch, Thomas C. et al.
      1966   Watts Riot Arrests—Los Angeles: Final Disposition. Sacramento,
                  California: Bureau of Criminal Statistics, Department of Justice.
McManus, George P. et al.
      1970   Police Training and Performance Study. Washington, D.C.: Law
                  Enforcement Assistance Administration.
Minar, David W. and Scott Greer
      1969   The Concept of Community: Readings with Interpretations.
                  Chicago: Aldine Publishing Co.
National Advisory Commission on Criminal Justice Standards and Goals
      1973   Police. Washington, D.C.: U.S. Government Printing Office.
Poplin, Dennis E.
      1972   Communities: A Survey of Theories and Methods of Research.
                  New York: The Macmillan Co.
President's Commission on Law Enforcement and Administration of Justice
      1967   Task Force Report: The Police. Washington, D.C.: U.S. Govern-
                  ment Printing Office.
Radelet, Louis A.
      1973   The Police and the Community. Beverly Hills, California: Glen-
                  coe Press.
Reith, Charles
      1938   The Police Idea: Its History and Evolution in England in the
                  Eighteenth Century and After. London: Oxford University
                  Press.
Rokeach, Milton
      1960   The Open and Closed Mind. New York: Basic Books, Inc.
Skolnick, Jerome H.
      1966   Justice Without Trial: Law Enforcement in Democratic Society.
                  New York: John Wiley and Sons, Inc.

Viano, Emilio and Alvin W. Cohn
  1975   Social Problems and Criminal Justice. Chicago: Nelson-Hall
          Publishers.
Waskow, Arthur I.
  1969   "Community Control of the Police." Transaction (December):
          4-7.
Wasserman, Robert, Michael P. Gardner, and Alana S. Cohen
  1973   Improving Police/Community Relations. Washington, D.C.:
          U.S. Government Printing Office.
Webster, John A.
  1973   The Realities of Police Work. Dubuque, Iowa: Kendall/Hunt
          Publishing Co.
Webster's New World Dictionary. 2nd College ed.
  1970   New York: The World Publishing Co.
Wickersham Commission
  1931   Police Conditions in the United States. The National Commis-
          sion on Law Observance and Enforcement. Washington, D.C.:
          U.S. Government Printing Office.
Wilson, O.W. and Roy C. McLaren
  1972   Police Administration. 3rd ed. New York: McGraw-Hill Book
          Co.

PART 1.

THE CONTEXT of police-
COMMUNITY RELATIONS

Introduction

The development of police-community relations programs, although relatively new in terms of organizational functions and services, is a phenomenon which, in one form or another, has received attention since the inception of modern policing. A review of the history of law enforcement suggests that police departments generally have been concerned not only with improving methods of crime control and apprehension of law violators, but with departmental relationships (and images) with various segments of the community being served.

Simultaneously, citizens within the community, to one degree or another, have expressed concern over how they have been and want to be policed. In effect, there have been both overt and covert forms of recognition of the pluralistic nature of society by both community groups and law enforcement agencies. This means that most everyone recognizes the fact that a distinct and total community hardly exists—that various entities, institutions, vested interest groups, and other collectivities all combine to form what we commonly call the community. As a consequence, law enforcement has been forced—and sometimes against its institutional will—to deal with many and varied groups constituting the society which is being policed. This has occasionally led to strife, misunderstanding, inadequate communications, and, frequently, poor relationships among and between all groups vying for attention.

What a given group of people expect in the way of services from a government agency is not always easy to describe, especially when the mission of an agency is not clearly defined, or if defined, not completely understood or accepted. A water department is supposed to make available clean and plentiful supplies of water. Garbage collection is expected routinely, efficiently, and with

The Context of Police-Community Relations

minimum disruption in the community. But law enforcement services are not as easily defined.

Blau and Scott (1962) suggest that one way to understand organizational delivery systems is to categorize them according to the primary beneficiary of services. As examples, a "mutual benefit association" is one where the prime beneficiary is the membership, such as a union or professional association. A "business concern" obviously owes its allegiance to its stockholders, and a "service organization" provides basic services to clients, such as occurs in hospitals and schools. It is the "commonweal organization" which has as its primary beneficiary the public-at-large, and it is in this category that law enforcement falls.

The problem that immediately arises, however, is how the definition of "public-at-large" is to be defined, and who should do the defining. Blau and Scott attempt but basically fail to clarify the problem:

> The distinctive characteristic of commonweal organizations is that the public-at-large is their prime beneficiary, often, although not necessarily, to the exclusion of the very people who are the object of the organization's endeavor. (In these organizations) . . . . the public could be considered the owners as well as the prime beneficiaries. . . . The issue posed by commonweal organizations is that of external democratic control—the public must possess the means of controlling the ends served by these organizations. . . . The challenge facing these organizations . . . is the maintenance of efficient bureaucratic mechanisms that effectively implement the objectives of the community, which are ideally decided upon, at least in our society, by democratic methods (1962:54–55).

What we are left with is a theoretical statement which provides the basis and reason for defining services, but no defined procedure for its accomplishment. Furthermore, while we have some idea of what a law enforcement agency should be (although no consensus on what it ought to do), we are left without any substantial understanding of what the "public-at-large" is or its relationship to "community." The consequence over the years has meant that police agencies have defined for themselves these terms, have operationalized such definitions, and then have been forced to deal with segments of the public and/or community which either object or attempt to qualify police operations. Powerful vested interest groups along with political leaders have indeed influenced both definitions and operations, but this has not been true for the general population.

In Part I, we attempt to provide the reader with some understanding of the context of police-community relations. We give special attention to three basic issues: (1) how the police operate in relationship to community, (2) some of the problems in defining community, and (3) what we seem to know about police-community operations.

In the first article, "Police and Public Cooperation," Chief of Police (Winnetka, Illinois) and Past President of the International Association of Chiefs of

Police, Don R. Derning, argues that in a democratic society, the police and the public must cooperate. He takes an historical perspective and reviews the efforts which are needed in both police-community relations and public relations spheres. He maintains that better services and relations between law enforcement and the community can be enhanced if communications are developed and maintained between the two groups and on an on-going basis.

Professor William Brown examines the role of police as "law" enforcers and how they should respond in "professional" ways to conflicting demands of various segments of society. In a paper entitled "The Police and the Community," he advocates that police must understand their own communities, look to better ways to serve society, and be more sensitive than they currently are to indications of potential lawlessness.

In "Changing Urban Police: Practitioners' View," authors Robert Igleburger, John Angell, and Gary Pence discuss community needs and state it is their opinion that these are defined via political processes. The writers maintain that law enforcement agencies should partcipate with other agencies in meeting citizen demands for police service and security. Additionally, they argue, the police should assist in the process of reconciling diverse and changing community needs, rather than being aloof to the process of helping citizens—the consumers of service.

Professors Colin Bell and Howard Newby, in "Theories of Community," tackle the difficult problem of defining the concept of community by reviewing the various definitions which appear in the literature. They point out that definitions vary according to the orientations of the writers and that in the final analysis it may be impossible to determine with any reasonable degree of consensus just what the term community means. The authors provide an excellent summary of what has been written, from a sociological perspective. They conclude that the only agreement which exists is that communities deal with people.

Alan Altshuler continues to explore the meaning and definition of community, but also examines the concept of neighborhood in his article, "The Definition of Neighborhoods." He raises the question of the relevancy of neighborhoods in contemporary, mobile, urban society, not only for whites, but for blacks, the working class, and for "social elites."

Sociologist James McKee completes this discussion with "Understanding the Community." He states that a community is many things to many people, but always reflecting differing patterns of behavior and belief systems. He maintains that a community generally does not possess a common set of values upon which can be based social policies or action strategies to deal with problems once they are identified. Insofar as police-community relations are concerned, he argues for the involvement of all the diverse segments of society for the development of planning and action strategies.

In "Police-Community Relations," the Sheriff of Riverside, California, Bernard J. Clark, attempts to distinguish the two concepts of police-community

The Context of Police-Community Relations

relations and police public relations. He defines these terms and then describes their essential significance for police operations. He views PCR as organized and constructive action designed to alleviate problems and to establish harmonious working relationships.

Following this article, Dr. Egon Bittner's "Community Relations" is extracted from a monograph published by the National Institute of Mental Health —Center for Studies of Crime and Delinquency, entitled *The Functions of the Police in Modern Society.* Professor Bittner looks at PCR as an important and valuable function of policing and he asks law enforcement agencies as well as communities to continue in their efforts to enhance communications. He states that the police can only deal with the ills of society by working with all the various groups in society. He concludes with a suggestion that the outcome of such interaction, for both society in general and individual citizens in particular, will occur, in part, when policemen and police departments look at the individual's behavior (interventions) and learn from actual experiences.

In "Issues in Police-Community Relations," Eleanor Harlow, with the National Council on Crime and Delinquency, summarizes the literature regarding the nature, programs, and purposes of PCR. She especially points out the consequences police-citizen interactions have for effective policing and for crime control in society. The paper also discusses such issues as the "police subculture," "police prejudice," and "community control of police" as topics related to police-community relations.

Reference

Blau, Peter M. and W. Richard Scott
    1962   Formal Organizations: A Comparative Approach. San Francisco: Chandler Publishing Co.

CHAPTER 1-1

police and public cooperation

DON R. DERNING

Over the past decade national attention has been increasingly drawn to the problem of police and public cooperation. Countless material has been written on the multitude of police-community relations projects that are presently underway throughout the country. Campaigns for the involvement of concerned citizens have been made nationwide. In every major city, the police and the public are opening lines of communication and fostering a dialogue of reform.

To avoid the risk of adding mere rhetoric to this problem with more "how to" information, I would like to explore the subject from the viewpoint of the total need and its development with regard to the general public as well as the police.

Are the programs working? Is there resentment and/or opposition? If so, why? What are the problems and how are they solved? Let's identify these areas and build on them. The cynics have told us why it cannot work—now we indicate why it *must* work.

To fully understand the reasons why police-public cooperation is so essential to a democratic society, one must necessarily look back on its development. Here we will pinpoint those periods in our history that sowed the seeds of resentment and provided the greatest change in police performance. Indeed, there is opposition. And it has developed over many long years, dating as far back as the founding of our nation.

Source: International Association of Chiefs of Police. *The Police Yearbook—1973:* pp. 34–38. Reprinted with the kind permission of the editors of *The Police Yearbook.*

Police-Public Relations

First, let's take a hard and honest look at the evolution of *police-public relations*. Until as late as 1800, ninety percent of America's settlers were from England. The only reference to policing held by early Americans was their knowledge of European police systems as instruments of tyranny and oppression by which emperors and kings maintained their hold on the will of the people. Law enforcement was created out of the only method familiar to the people that was conducive to some kind of civilian control—the old "watch and ward" system of the homeland.

Having vowed never to align themselves with government services even remotely akin to repression, early citizens gave law enforcement little support. Most illustrative of this early opposition is the statement of a leading merchant and highly esteemed politician in Boston in 1815, "If ever there comes a time when Americans have to have in their cities a paid professional police force, that will be the end of freedom and democracy as we know it." But the watch itself precipitated the concept of paid professional police services.

Other national leaders saw the system as a means to preserve and defend freedom and advance our democratic values. Many communities voted to support the effort through subscription. Even then it was recognized that better services nurtured public support.

Police-public cooperation developed slowly and painfully through the following century. Law enforcement struggled through the political interference of the Spoils Era, the lawlessness of the Prohibition Era, and the manpower drains of two world wars.

Two more rungs of the professional ladder were reached during those lean years. Depression recruiting was the first. It brought highly educated dedicated people to the police service. And, civil service was next. Selection and promotion was now based on merit and qualifications. The police had waged a long campaign for civil service and a new esprit de corps permeated the service.

Then, in 1945, the nation's finest returned from the battlefields. Mature, disciplined, highly motivated young veterans entered the police service by the thousands. Many of them occupy administrative and command ranks today. The country, with the war ended, could turn its resources to civil needs. Law enforcement won greater public esteem and was given a larger share of the tax dollar. New facilities and equipment were procured. Industry developed products for a peacetime nation and the police service was able to equip itself with the most sophisticated crime fighting aids available. Many educators turned their efforts to police training and elected officials provided the mandates for more efficient service.

Less than 200 years ago, when our fledgling nation boasted a population of fewer than four million, little more than four percent of the people lived in the towns and cities. By 1970, with a population of over two hundred million, more than seventy percent resided in the urban areas. Urbanization brought with it unique law enforcement problems as well as greater opportunities for improved service.

Ethnic groups of vastly differing mores and cultures, still seeking refuge from oppressive governmental restrictions, came to America and found their way to the main industrial centers to make their living. The proximity of people with often opposing points of view provided law enforcement with its most interesting challenge.

As urbanization continued, greater insight to a burgeoning problem was afforded us by more recent developments. A prolonged war in Southeast Asia and an economic depression focused attention on critical domestic issues. Unemployment, poverty, discrimination, and labor disputes moved the people to protest. The age of confrontation was to serve as the catalyst for far-reaching social changes, but the price we paid was high.

Activist factions, under the guise of social reformers, seized the opportunity to by-pass the democratic process of justice in favor of revolutionary techniques. Protest marches and demonstrations were conducted throughout the country. A president, a senator, and a civil rights leader were assassinated. Massive civil disorders resulted in wholesale destruction, killing, and looting. In the name of civil rights and social reform the streets of our nation were used by dissident groups bent on furthering their own interests. The fact that they violated the civil rights of others did not appear to temper their efforts.

Again, law enforcement became the focal point in preservation of the democratic social values. Any nation worthy of the name "Democracy" cannot condone violence as a means to effect change. The police, by nature of their role in society, found themselves between the people and the objects of their distress. As the uniformed representatives of government, the police became the targets of public frustration. The role of police was questioned by everyone—the police as well as the public. As a peacekeeping force, they were required to be in the forefront at public protests. As the protector of individual rights and freedoms, they were required to enforce the laws with impartiality. Pressure was brought to bear on the need for clear identification of law enforcement responsibilities.

The sociological approach to law enforcement was on the threshold. Oversimplified, it was recognized that law enforcement could not be fissioned off amoeba-like from the general society. The police are the people, and the police powers are vested in them by the people. Law enforcement was recognized as a sorely needed service deserving support.

Community Relations

It again became evident that modern effective services were the only way to earn public support. Money was allocated, plans were made; and law enforcement moved full-swing into police-community relations functions. The following basic principles were established and recommended to the policy community as standard procedure.

Community relations must be based on efforts to gain public understanding through information. Enlightened citizens are basic to good law enforcement. Public information offices became an integral part of major city and state departments.

To earn public confidence, it is necessary to build citizen trust and respect. The psychology of human relations became part of most recruit training curricula.

The public support must be solicited for a respect of the laws, assistance in police matters, and support of improvement measures. Storefront centers, mobile information services, speakers bureaus, and other programs were implemented to gain a greater interaction with the people.

Building on these basics, police-public cooperation reached new heights. The long sought-after "two-way" communications were taking effect, and the police role was being defined.

Over the years we have broadly defined the police mission as the preservation of the peace, the enforcement of the law, the protection of life and property, the prevention of crime, and the apprehension of offenders of the law. This definition leaves extreme tolerances for catch-all services and defies efforts toward true professionalism.

Through interpretation of their role as preservers of the public peace, police officers are charged with the responsibility of intercession if public protest violates the covenants of "public assembly to petition the government for a redress of grievances," regardless of what individual government authority is the source of the protest.

Also, interpretation under the enforcement of the law has come to mean that the police are the responsible agencies for the protection of human rights and freedom. This truism makes irony of the fact that people who forcefully seek redress of civil wrongs invariably oppose the police for their intercession.

Recognizing the fact that the police agency is an important arm of a government constitutionally dedicated to the preservation of human dignity and individual rights, and to the concept of a government of laws, it is then obvious that no other agency is more intimately involved in the safeguarding of these rights and the guaranteeing of the dignity of man. For it is the police who must provide sufficient security of the streets to defend life, liberty, and the pursuit of happiness.

When we walk to work, to a market, to a restaurant, or a bank, it is a policeman who is held accountable for our ability or inability to go without fear.

In broader interpretation of the basic concepts, police became involved with duties that sometimes work at cross purposes with their mission. The breakdown of public attitudes occurs when these tasks can never be recognized, in the broadest definition, to fall within any of the above categories. Film and book censorship, enforcement of overtime parking regulations, and private escort duties are just a few frequently used examples.

Community Social Health

The social health of a community is totally dependent upon the effective services of its government. When police attempt to cure social ills, they become least effective and most frustrated. If education fails to prepare the child to assume adult roles, if welfare fails to provide the initiative to the underprivileged, if courts and corrections can do nothing to rehabilitate, if the economy is not sound enough to provide jobs, then the police can do little to prevent crime.

The removal of root causes cannot be achieved by any single agency. The need for a totally cooperative effort and public support is obvious. These are public services, and the public has the only tool to control them—an intelligent vote.

Less enlightened people will sometimes refer to the nature of law enforcement, at its best, as a distinctly repressive function. Modern thinking regards the law enforcement officer not as an impediment to individual freedom, but as the purest expression of it.

We must reach for the realization that recognizing law and order in a free society is the first defense of individual liberties. The law enforcement officer is not the man who curbs freedom—he guarantees it.

In the report, "The Challenge of Crime in a Free Society," filed by the President's Commission on Law Enforcement and Administration of Justice, the investigators astutely brought the problem into focus. "Each time a citizen fails to report an offense, declines to take common-sense precautions against crime—shirks his duty as a juror—or refuses to hire qualified men because of bias, he contributes to crime. That much is obvious. A further duty of every citizen is to familiarize himself with the problems of crime and the criminal justice system."

In its summary, the Commission stressed the overwhelming need for police-public cooperation by setting forth a seven-point proposal to reduce crime in America:

First, society must seek to prevent crime before it happens by assuring all Americans a stake in the benefits and responsibilities of American life, by strengthening law enforcement, and by reducing criminal opportunities.

Second, society's aim of reducing crime would be better served if the system of criminal justice developed a far broader range of techniques with which to deal with individual offenders.

Third, the system of criminal justice must eliminate existing injustices if it is to achieve its ideals and win the respect and cooperation of all citizens.

Fourth, the system of criminal justice must attract more people and better people—police, prosecutors, judges, defense attorneys, probation and parole officers, and corrections officials with more knowledge, expertise, initiative, and integrity.

Fifth, there must be much more operational and basic research into the problems of crime and criminal administration, by those both within and without the system of criminal justice.

Sixth, the police, courts, and correctional agencies must be given substantially greater amounts of money if they are to improve their ability to control crime.

Seventh, individual citizens, civic and business organizations, religious institutions, and all levels of government must take responsibility for planning and implementing the changes that must be made in the criminal justice system if crime is to be reduced.

Implementation of Reform

The groundwork for cooperation has been laid. The machinery is available for the implementation of reform. Public cooperation holds the promise of faithful, dedicated, professional public service. Professional services hold the promise of increased support for programs, respect for law, and public participation.

We have presented those moments of history that served as turning points of police-public cooperation to indicate the effect of the effort and the problems involved. In closing I would like to reflect on the general description of present programs that are being used throughout the nation.

Possibly the first requisites to good community relations are the very obvious needs for good professional police work and a strong, clear and enforced policy of equal treatment for all members of the community. These are the fundamentals. They represent professional goals of high quality, and when they are achieved, it is much easier to obtain the community cooperation and understanding that must be added if good police work is to result in an effective job of policing.

Good community relations work is based upon communication and interpretation and it develops a sensitivity to conditions that indicate areas of social unrest.

Problems do exist. They exist through ignorance, suspicion, resentment, disrespect, neglect, and fear by police and public alike. Whether or not they are groundless is unimportant. The fact that they exist at all is reason enough to make every effort to dispel them. It can be done—and must be done. But success can only be achieved through a concerted effort of the public and the police through closer and more meaningful participation. No modern police department can operate effectively without the support of the citizens. Neither can it secure the needed support of citizens without going out and working for it in a constructive and meaningful way.

The President's Commission on Law Enforcement and Administration of Justice said, "Private citizens on their own or through their organizations must interest themselves in the problems of crime and criminal justice, seek information, express their views, use their vote wisely—and get involved."

Justice, domestic tranquility, common defense, general welfare, and the blessings of liberty are no less important to us today than when they first introduce the U.S. Constitution. I can think of no better justification for the cause of police-public cooperation.

THE police ANd THE COMMUNITY

WILLIAM P. BROWN

... Any prescription for police action in regard to community disorder must be based upon the balancing and the ordering of a series of value judgments. These deal with the police relationship to the law, to the people we serve considered both as communities and as individuals, and to the process of social conflict within our communities. The complex of action called forth by disorder within the community can only approach consistency and propriety when it is frequently checked back against these fine balancings of value judgments which constitute our basic premises.

In addition to serving as a beacon towards clearer thinking, our stated premises help to ease the understanding of police action by the representatives of those other disciplines which have so much to offer in dealing with critical social issues. We need the insights to our problems that can be supplied by the sociologists, the psychologists, the cultural anthropologists. Unfortunately, in working with us, they face a major problem of seeing police work in terms of the problem definitions and ideas with which they are familiar. To a visitor from another field of study, our premises are more intelligible than our tactics. Premises stand and may be judged by themselves. Tactics always leave the suspicion that they have been adopted on the basis of unstated facts or beliefs unknown to any but the experienced practitioner.

Source: National Conference of Christians and Jews. *The Police and Community Conflict.* 1962: pp. 1–6. Reprinted with the kind permission of the author and of the National Conference of Christians and Jews.

1. *Equal Service to All*—The first and most important of our premises is one we have heard so often that each of us must consciously rescue it from that Limbolike state of the things that are so familiar that we say them or hear them without any longer giving thought to what they mean. Moral and constitutional law alike have affirmed it; no recognized student has even disputed it. Still, most police problems in intergroup relations spring from its violation or the belief or the accusation that it has been violated. This premise, then, is that the police owe all persons in the community equal and effective service, including an equal interpretation of the law.

2. *Police Enforce Only the Law*—The second premise is less familiar and deserves some explanation, for it deals with the police relationship to many of those emotionally charged issues about which group conflicts seem to arise. Conflict among groups is a natural and ordinarily most acceptable part of life—when it is carried out in a legal manner and one consistent with the beliefs of the community. As long as we have legality and acceptability, we get along very well with our differences of opinion. In business or social life, channeled conflict adds zest, pattern and motivation to our lives.

In a rapidly changing society such as ours, it is also natural—though it is usually most unacceptable to many of those involved—that some groups will change the rules of the conflict to give themselves more advantage. Thus—again looking specifically at our Negro-white interrelationship—minority group members have in recent years adopted the economic boycott, the sit-in and other similar tactics. Pro-segregationist forces, for their part, have devoted much ingenuity and effort to delaying tactics that have removed many of the immediate and sweetest fruits of the legal victories the anti-segregationists have won. Invariably, when either group resorts to the tactics which are available to it, there is a cry of "foul" from the other. Each side becomes excessively legalistic—or illegalistic, where its purpose is suited. Economic or political leverage is used whenever possible. The pro-segregationists, since they profess to represent the largest segment (the white 90%) of our society, use social or community pressure to enforce their demands. In turn, the minority group undergirds its position by constantly referring to its more clearly documented legal and moral position and to its support from the intellectual strata of our society.

The police problem is to view this complex and strongly emotional scene and to impose on these frequently conflicting demands an order which can be translated into professionally proper action. In particular, we must develop the ability to pick out the legal and professional determinants of our action from the pressures for action based on the unqualified acceptance of what is demanded by the leaders of either our community or of our intelligentsia. It should be stated that we recognize clearly our obligation to both of these groups. We are not anti-community or anti-intellectual. All we ask is that their demands be taken from the arena of partisanship and made legal and professional guidelines for our conduct. *We enforce the law, not truth or social custom or good intentions.*

3. *Disorder Planning Is Based On a Combination of Conventional Police Mobilization Tactics and an Understanding of the Community—* The violence in our communities stemming from the inability of some to adjust in a lawful manner to new situations can be considered as a malfunction of the process of community life. It is of great importance to the police. It must be thought about and plans for meeting it must be made. It is important to remember, however, that our plans for dealing with this malfunction must be understood as part of all the rest of the police-community relationship. They cannot be considered as something entirely apart, in which all of our previous understandings do not apply. If that were so, the police acting in the emergency would be in the position of a strange force rushed in to deal with a strange situation by the use of mysterious rituals rather than objectively determined methods. The plans we make for dealing with an emergency situation are based on composites of two sets of principles. We utilize first those rules which have been developed for assembling police strength and using it effectively in the time of any emergency, and, secondly, the general rules that apply for all police-community relations work.

4. *Communication and Interpretation are the Basic Processes of Police-Community Relations Work—*Good community relations work is based upon communication and interpretation. The police must strive to establish the possibility of communication with all persons who are interested in a lawfully ordered community. They must do all within their power to increase communication with groups having important police problems, or affecting important police problems, or affected by important police problems. Then the police can learn from the community, and the police executive is given an opportunity to interpret police problems to the community. The tasks of interpretation of information available from the public, or of the police role in the community, merit far more attention than they have been given.

5. *The Prevention of Intergroup Violence Is an Important Goal—* Disorder of the character that is involved when there is serious overt conflict between groups within the community is a scarring process making criminals out of many ordinarily legal persons and leaving bitter memories which are difficult to heal or overcome. It helps no one unless it is by way of lancing a festering situation which has developed to a point where it is not amenable to self-help. In such a case, it is equivalent to major surgery and harms most of those involved as participants. The police owe the community protection from violence regardless of the cost. When violent men rise, they must be crushed with all necessary and proper force. However, to the extent that the community can be saved by preventing violence without sacrificing legality, ethical position, or the proper police function, this benefit should be earnestly sought. In community situations of the type under discussion, a good statement or a wise police executive action can be worth a platoon of men in accomplishing the police tasks.

At the same time, it spares the community the scars which make future progress toward community amity so difficult.

6. *A Major Disorder Is the Culmination of a Building-Up Process*— Major disorder usually is the culmination of an observable building-up process brought on by some strong precipitating factor. Where this developing process is under way, the police executive is seriously at fault if he does not make an earnest attempt to observe and understand it. He is doomed to ineffectiveness if his interpretation is not reasonably correct.

7. *There is a Serious and Complex Area of Police-Community Relations Work*—If the preceding premises have validity, it follows then that there is an area for police work in the community at a considerably more sophisticated level than "making people like us." We must develop sensitivity to conditions which are the indications of potential lawlessness or conflict in our jurisdictions. We must be prepared to point out these signs and to help our authorities and our publics to do something about them. Particularly important, we must keep this broad view of our community in mind in our administration of our departments so that police actions do not in themselves constitute an unnecessary irritant in the development of a community problem.

CHAPTER **1-3**

CHANGING URBAN POLICE: PRACTITIONERS' VIEW

ROBERT M. IGLEBURGER, JOHN E. ANGELL,
AND GARY PENCE

Why Change Police?

The basic purpose of public administration in American society is to fulfill those needs of the community that cannot be met through individual action or private enterprise. The definition of community needs is arrived at through a process referred to as politics. By responding to community needs, the government gains the consent of those who are served. However, this consent is not dependent on providing satisfactory responses for all unfulfilled citizen needs; it is also gained by the government providing an arena for controversy and conflict (Appleby, 1965, p. 334). It is through citizen interaction in this arena that the citizens arrive at the necessary cohesion to require governmental action, and the power of public officials is limited.

While the role of the police is to some extent defined by custom, culture, and law, it is constantly being redefined through the political processes. Therefore, police administrators must be cognizant of their political environments and provide organizations that are capable of making appropriate adjustments in their operations.

Source: U.S. Department of Justice, Law Enforcement Assistance Administration, National Institute of Law Enforcement and Criminal Justice. *Innovation in Law Enforcement.* 1973. pp. 76–114.

Political Responsiveness

Police administrators must participate in political processes because of their responsibility for ensuring police services that satisfy communities' demands for services and security. However, police officials do not have sufficient responsibility nor authority to adequately fulfill the demands of all citizens for police service and security. They share responsibility and authority with a variety of other organizations, governmental agencies, and social institutions.

Unfortunately, there are many police chiefs who display a willingness to accept total responsibility for objectives over which they have little control, such as reducing crime. It would be far more realisitic to admit that the community, other governmental agencies, and a variety of social organizations share this responsibility. Such recognition would enable police administrators to legitimately involve a much broader reservoir of resources in the solution of their problems.

Aside from the preceding question of responsibility and authority, the police organizational hierarchy, which should be designed to receive and respond to community needs, has evolved to the point where the political environment has little impact on it (Tullock, 1965, pp. 137-141). A police department must be capable of accurately receiving popular demands, injecting them with considerations of prudence, perspective, principle, and concern for individual rights, and responding to them. Therefore, the police organization cannot be evaluated solely on the efficiency with which it performs rote functions. It must be assessed by its ability to reconcile diverse community needs into a response that is tempered by concerns for the individual and legitimatized by community support (Appleby, 1965, p. 335). Appropriate change within police organization will not come through piecemeal efforts designed strictly to improve operational efficiency. It will come through organization techniques that provide continuous monitoring of the total environment of law enforcement.

The Community Environment

Over the past two decades, the urban environments within which police organizations exist have changed drastically. The changes in demographic characteristics alone have been profound enough to stagger one's imagination. For example, the racial composition of Dayton has changed from 90 percent to 70 percent white. The average income of citizens has remained constant in a period of sharp inflation. The heterogeneity of our residents has increased.

The once powerful and stable middle class whites have been losing their power to a wide range of other groups. The *carte blanche* that was once given to the police to deal with social deviates has been withdrawn. The once illegitimate street people, radical groups, young people, and social deviates have become organized. These organized groups have been legitimized by such actions as the civil rights movement of the 60's, the increased attention to the demands of youth and minorities, and the reclassification of social behavior such as alcoholism and deviate sexual behavior among consenting adults as non-criminal.

Undoubtedly, the most significant influences that have changed the community environment for the police have been the Supreme Court and the educational system. For the first time in the history of society, a powerful government institution, the United States Supreme Court, actually took giant steps to guarantee both the political equality of men, as well as the subservient nature of government to men.

The educational system began to move in the same direction. Old authoritarian techniques and approaches have been replaced by individual instruction that encourages self-motivation on the part of the student. Basic education has become universal, and continuous adult education has been accepted as a necessity. Schools have actually begun to deal with social information. They are recognizing the need to respond to students who are questioning the concepts of universal righteousness of the "American system."

The changes in community environments have caused police administrators to question themselves as to their clients, goals, organizational arrangements, strategies, and procedures. Police officials who have previously enjoyed the luxury of dealing with a well-defined power group are faced with pressure from groups that only a few years ago could not have commanded recognition from a passing police patrolman.

Consumer Orientation

Given the circumstances that have been described, it is not surprising that many communities are demanding better and different services; what is surprising is the community's reaction to the lack of police responsiveness. Public law enforcement officials have for a number of years monopolized the service of security of persons and property. The monopoly is now being broken. In Dayton, we have experienced competition from the Republic of New Africa, a Black militant organization, which provides limited patrol service. Recently, a former Dayton policeman, who is now operating a private security agency, submitted a proposal to a Neighborhood Priority Board, formed under the auspices of the Model Cities Program, to develop a private, special police force for a white working-class area of our city.

Our experiences in Dayton are not significantly different from those of other cities. The police monopoly is being broken by volunteer citizens' groups and private police who are attempting to provide service on a neighborhood basis. We, the police, have now been placed in a situation where we can no longer "not give a damn." No longer can we count on the protection provided us by our positions as a monopoly. We must compete for citizen support.

The change process has always been crisis oriented in Dayton. Dayton is noted for originating the City Manager form of government. However, it was not originated until after the great flood of 1913 and the threat of the NCR Company to relocate unless city government became more efficient. The destruction of the police monopoly may well generate the spark that ignites the demand for change within the internal structure of police organizations. If this occurs, police administrators may realistically be able to reorganize with the necessary support base to become consumer oriented instead of product oriented. What has been described as an occupational army may through market analysis become an agent for providing service.

Professional police administrators in the United States appear to have difficulty adopting a consumer orientation because of self-imposed collusion of ignorance. However, increasingly, chiefs are attempting to modify their approaches; and their efforts are resulting in their being heralded by community leaders, and at the same time, stifled by the internal structure of the police organization. The process of implementing change is always difficult; within police agencies, it appears to be an impossible dream. The following are a few of the characteristics of the police sub-culture that stifle change.

Blind Chauvinism

One of the areas of concern for progressive police administrators in law enforcement today is the blind chauvinism; i.e., that belief that the solution to the police problem is *esprit de corps* that permeates many police departments. Many of these chauvinistic individuals are more concerned about the length of a man's sideburns than the quality of his work. There appears to be an increasing hue and cry within some of these monolithic structures for more "spit and polish." The purpose of these comments are not to negate the importance of discipline but to place it in its proper perspective. Meaningful discipline and *esprit de corps* are the products of an organizational structure, which provides for the integration of the individual goals with the objectives of the organization. This does not mean the elimination of professional discretion or individuality.

We believe the level of chauvinism within a police department is directly related to the degree of authoritarianism present. Our value system is grounded in conservatism and dictates that crime be suppressed by whatever means necessary. Many police officers believe that the Constitution and civil liberties serve only to thwart their efforts. The work of William Vega indicated that most police officers see crime as the response of the individual, not associated with his environment. This value system of police conservatives enables them to disassociate the acts of individuals from society. Even well-read moderates find this value system difficult to accept.

A study performed by Smith, Locke, and Walker within the New York Police Department indicates that non-college police tend to be more authoritarian than college-educated police. This provides a basis for assuming that the police would be more realistic if they had a broader base of experience. However, Vega has pointed out that even liberals are coopted by police organizations. Liberals within police departments either alter their beliefs to conform, drop out, or go underground. If this is the case, most police departments do not have a significant population of resident liberals. However, there is no more reason for all police officers to be liberal than there is for them all to be conservative; but police departments need employees who are representative of the communities they serve.

Many police officers, who work in urban areas, are removed from the problems that mandate change because they have spent most of their lives in environments and cultures removed from the lifestyles of modern urban citizens. They grew up in rural areas, small towns, or white middle-class neighborhoods. Their parents were blue-collar whites. After joining an urban police agency, they move to middle-class suburban communities where they do not have to confront the problems faced by the urban people they serve. They travel into the city to spend as much of their eight hours as possible isolated from their clients by a car, an office, and bureaucratic rules and status. They socialize mainly with other police; they fight for two-man cars which ensures they will be further re-enforced by a person with values like their own.

A police organization, in order to interact with a community, should have a diverse representation within its membership. If a rule-oriented police organization does not permit any officers to wear long hair or beards, is it not saying that there is something wrong or distasteful about people who do? Will such an organization provide the same quality of service to members of the community who wear long hair and beards?

Management by Abdication

Another symptomatic problem associated area is management by abdication (MBA). This consists of rule-oriented management personnel who attempt to implement change through fiat while simultaneously abdicating responsibility for it. A MBA organization is rule-oriented as opposed to goal-oriented and responsibility for service is difficult to identify because the emphasis is on procedure as opposed to results. The vast majority of police organizations are structured along para-military lines of command and control. This approach requires specialization and the development of functional responsibilities which facilitates management by abdication.

Responsibility for providing police service in specific geographic areas of a city is difficult to identify in highly specialized police departments. Field lieutenants are normally held responsible for eight-hour time periods. Captains are responsible for bureaus such as investigation, operations, or records. Beat patrolmen share responsibility for police service with many specialized technicians. The order maintenance function and crime control functions have become the responsibility of specialized public relations units and crime control teams respectively, in many police departments. The only person within this type of framework who can be held directly responsible for police service is the chief of police. Thus, there is little or no impetus within other areas of the organization for change. This has culminated in a situation in most areas where the chief of police not only makes the decision to change, but quarterbacks the entire process. Change that occurs through this type of process has been compared by McBride to hanging ornaments on a Christmas tree (1971, p. 20). These ornaments are normally removed when the Christmas season is over and change that occurs through this process has a life expectancy directly proportional to that of the chief of police. Productive change on the other hand, results from a spontaneous process which is ignited when the conditions are right for it.

The rule orientation of MBA is one of the primary defects within police management today. The vast majority of police agencies have become secure within the classical organizational structure that has been described. The operation of such an organization is mechanical. The duties of members are described in detail, and there are hard and fast rules along with a hierarchy of superior officers to make sure procedures are carried out according to rules. Such a structure was created to give and maintain status based upon an individual's ability to follow departmental rules and regulations which are in many cases of questionable value and often are not flexible enough to respond to the changing needs of a heterogenous community. This became painfully obvious to us in Dayton when two police officers decided that they could better deal with a disorderly group by removing their firearms and placing them in the trunk of their car. Many individuals within the department reacted to this act with tremendous hostility because of a departmental policy that required police officers to carry their weapons at all times, both on and off duty. This rule has since been changed to give the individual officer the right to decide when he should not carry a weapon. The rule orientation of specialization has not only caused the police not to respond to the changing character of the community, but also in some cases to resist change which threatens the established status quo. If John Gardner (1965, p. 45) is correct in saying the last act of a dying organization is to produce a better and more comprehensive version of the rule book, then surely we are listening to the death gasp of many police organizations today.

Police chiefs are in the position of sitting on top of a giant pyramid. In this position, they are only able to cushion the police response not form it. The real power within the organization is at the operational level. The problem is that this level lacks the responsibility of direction and is not accountable to the community; therefore, it does not have to be responsive to it. The police chief, however, is normally in an appointed position and responsible to his community. The chief is in many cases attempting to direct change that operational personnel see no benefit in implementing. The change is usually goal-oriented as opposed to rule-oriented and therefore, threatening to the existing status quo and social relationships (Davis, 1968, p. 55).

The chief who attempts to bring about change is confronted by the phenomenon of MBA; i.e., rule-oriented management personnel who implement change through fiat while simultaneously abdicating responsibility for it. Change within this setting becomes damned as the child of the Ivy League Boys in Research and Development, who lack credibility and common sense, or of a starry-eyed chief, who has somehow become misdirected.

Why does this situation exist? One reason is related to efforts to insulate police departments from the spoils system (Smith, 1960, pp. 316-317). This attempt to professionalize the police has at times backfired. If we look at James Q. Wilson's paper, "The Police and Their Problems: A Theory," we note that the professional model he describes involves a legalistic approach which strives to eliminate discretion. If this is taken in conjunction with the insulation of the police from the spoils system without any mechanism to realistically replace it, then the lack of police responsiveness to the community should be expected.

Role Confusion

Role confusion is the symptom of another problem area within the police bureaucracy. Police officers at the line level have not been prepared to differentiate in response requirements. They are the product of a rule-oriented structure that provides "cookbook solutions" to problems (Fosdick, 1969, p. 313). Police officers are constantly confronted with demands from the community for varying types of service which they have not been trained to handle. This has resulted in a situation where police officers are threatened by the changing needs of the community. The status of police work is based upon law enforcement; the enforcement of the law has a certain aura of glamour associated with it. To be a public servant is to be less than an enforcer. Yet, police officers are confronted with a paradox since the community demands more service than law enforcement (Webster, 1970). Does a police officer enforce laws or provide service to the community? Since individual police officers have no direct responsibility to the community, and little or no contact with the political process, they are, in effect, free agents.

Police officers respond to the community as enforcers of the law. If there is any conflict in values, they become confused and respond in the manner in which they have been trained. They enforce the law without regard for the consequences. Enforcement of the law, in many cases, such as in Detroit in 1967, may result in disorder. However, the rule-oriented structure allows for no variance in response. Priorities are left to the individual officer and are affected by each officer's bias and values. The result is periodic chaos and an inability

.to understand why. The line-level officers who provide the services receive only the gut-level dissatisfaction of the street people, "The man is a pig." Yet, the "man" did his job. He enforced the law. The individual officer has not been prepared to analyze his job but has been provided with an overabundance of defense mechanisms (Vega, p. 17).

The police bureaucracy has been too effective in insulating people below the chief administrator from the conflicting changes and competing demands of the public. Seldom does a police officer below the chief have to face the demands of legislative officials, pressure groups, and private citizens with which the chief must deal. This type of conflict is normally almost entirely handled by the chief executive because of his position at the apex of the classical hierarchical structure. Given the dynamic nature of modern society, the chief is constantly subject to pressure in this position. When the chief decides that he must modify his organization to respond to his citizens, the members of the organization refuse to support him. Chiefs need not wonder why they are denied employee support; the chief has effectively insulated his subordinates, and they have not had to suffer through the confrontations and conflicts that have caused him to change. *Ex post facto* attempts by the chief to educate his subordinates to the reason for his deciding to change are usually not successful. The lower they are in the bureaucracy, the more insulated employees are from the problems faced by the chief and the less supportive they will be for significant changes that effect their behavior.

Conclusion

Police administrators are responsible for providing a police operation that serves the public needs. On the surface, this responsibility appears to be simple enough; however, the complexities involved in operationalizing it are enormous.

The democratic political process is an appropriate device for providing a police organization with information about public needs, but police organizations have become so removed and insulated from the political processes that the service they provide is at times almost totally unrelated to citizen problems. Even in those situations where the chief of police is sensitive to the problems and needs of his citizens, he alone cannot decipher sufficient information to determine the appropriate priorities for his organization to address. In addition, due to the inherent rigidity of a modern police bureaucracy, the chief's ability to initiate organizational change is severly limited.

If police organizations are to fully realize their objective of addressing community needs, it is essential that police administrators adopt a philosophy supporting a consumer orientation and take steps to ensure that their organizations have sufficient exposure and flexibility to align themselves with the needs of their clientele.

Our experience indicates that an administrator should consider a number of factors in preparing his organization for change. First, he should take steps to neutralize resistance and establish support for change among his subordinates. Among the techniques that can be utilized for reducing resistance are (1) rewards and threats, (2) rationality and indoctrination, (3) cooption and replacement, and (4) camouflage and diversionary tactics.

Second, he should take steps to structure his organization to facilitate consumer-oriented change. In developing a new structure, he should consider emphasizing the following: (1) opening the organization, (2) supporting tolerance, (3) reducing organizational rigidity, (4) improving communications, (5) reducing reliance on formal authority, and (6) establishing a Centralized-Decentralized Organizational Model.

Administrative actions to facilitate the development of dynamic police organizations will create difficult problems regardless of the approach utilized. Outsiders may criticize the organization for its disjointed appearance. However, as John W. Gardner has pointed out, ". . . creative organizations or societies are rarely tidy. Some tolerance for inconsistencies, for profusion of purposes and strategies, and for conflict is the price of freedom and vitality" (1965, p. 70).

Although we believe the methods we have suggested will, in the long run, be most effective, they will not provide a completely smooth transition from a traditional police bureaucracy to a new organizational design. They will most likely cause frustration for police officers involved. Initially, officers will demand that they not be subjected to such threatening techniques; they will insist on stronger rules for personal security; they will plead low morale; and they may be disruptive to the organizational processes in an attempt to emphasize their dissatisfaction with the responsibilities they are asked to assume. However, we believe that the probability that these techniques will pay off in developing a more effective, consumer-oriented police department where police can achieve a higher level of work satisfaction and professionalism, makes it reasonable for administrators to assume the risks involved.

Bibliography

Appleby, Paul H. "Public Administration and Democracy." *Public Administration and Democracy*. Roscoe D. Martin, (Ed.) Syracuse, New York: Syracuse University Press, 1965.

Angell, John E. "An Alternative to Classical Police Organizational Arrangements." *Criminology*, Vol. 9, No. 2 & 3, (Aug.-Nov., 1971), pp. 185-207.

Argyris, Chris. *Organization and Innovation*. Homeward, Illinois: Richard D. Irwin, Inc., 1965.

Baldwin, James. *Nobody Knows My Name*. New York: Dial Press, 1961.

Bennis, Warren G. "A New Role for the Behavioral Sciences: Effecting Organizational Change." *Administrative Science Quarterly* (Sept., 1963).

Bennis, Warren G. *Changing Organizations.* New York: McGraw-Hill Book Co., 1966.

Bennis, Warren G., *et al* (Eds). *The Planning of Change.* New York: Holt, Rinehart and Winston, 1961.

Bordua, David J. *The Police: Six Sociological Essays.* New York: John Wiley and Sons, Inc., 1967.

Chapman, Samual G. *Police Patrol Readings.* Springfield: Charles C. Thomas, Publisher, 1964, pp. 245-274.

Coch, Lester and John R.P. French, Jr. "Overcoming Resistance to Change." *Human Relations,* Vol. 1, No. 4 (1948).

Colin, J.M. "After X and Y Comes Z." *Personnel Journal* (January, 1971).

Coser, Lewis A. *The Functions of Social Conflict.* Toronto, Ontario: Free Press, March, 1968.

Davis, James A. "Authority—Flow Theory and the Impact of Chester Bernard." *California Management Review,* Vol. XIII, No. 1 (Fall, 1970).

Dayton/Montgomery County Pilot Cities Program: *Evaluation of Community-Centered Team Policing.* Dayton: Community Research, Inc., 1971.

Downs, Anthony. *Inside Bureaucracy.* Boston: Little, Brown, 1967.

Elliott, J.F. and Thomas J. Surdino. *Crime Control Team.* Springfield: Charles C. Thomas, 1971.

Etzioni, Amitai. *Modern Organizations.* Englewood Cliffs, New Jersey: Prentice-Hall, Inc., 1964.

Fosdick, Raymond B. *American Police Systems.* Montclair, New Jersey: Patterson Smith Publishing, Rev. 1969.

Gardner, John W. *Self Renewal: The Individual and the Innovative Society.* New York: Harper and Row, 1965.

Gazell, James A. "Authority—Flow Theory and the Impact of Chester Bernard." *California Management Review,* Vol. XIII, No. 1 (Fall, 1970).

Geneen, Harold S. "The Human Element in Communications." *California Management Review* (Winter, 1966).

Golembiewski, Robert T. "The Laboratory Approach to Organization Change: Scheme of a Method." *Public Administration Review* (September, 1967).

Golembiewski, Robert T. *Men, Management, and Morality.* New York: McGraw-Hill, 1965.

Goodwin, Watson. "Resistance to Change." *American Behavioral Scientist,* Vol. 14, No. 5 (May-June, 1971), pp. 745-765.

Greenwood, Noel. "Quiet Revolution Under Way in Police Training, Education." Oakland Police Department Information Bulletin. Reprinted from *Los Angeles Times* (1972).

Judson, Arnold S. *A Manager's Guide to Making Changes.* New York: John Wiley & Sons, Inc., 1966.

Katz, Daniel and Kahn, Robert L. *The Social Psychology of Organizations.* New York: John Wiley & Sons, Inc., 1966.

Katz, Daniel and Kahn, Robert L. *The Social Psychology of Organizations.* New York: John Wiley & Sons, Inc., 1967, pp. 390-452.

Leavitt, Harold J. *Managerial Psychology.* 2nd Ed. Chicago, Illinois: University of Chicago Press, 1964.

Lindblow, Charles E. *The Policy-Making Process.* Englewood Cliffs, New Jersey: Prentice-Hall, Inc., 1968.

March, James G. *Handbook of Organizations.* Rand McNally & Co., 1965.

McNamara, John H. "Uncertainties in Police Work," in *The Police.* New York: John Wiley & Sons, Inc., 1967, edited by David J. Bordue, pp. 203–207.

McBride, Thomas F. Speech given at the Management Institute of the National Association of Attorneys General. Denver, Colorado, November 6, 1971.

National Advisory Commission on Civil Disorders. *Kerner Commission Report.* Washington, D.C.: U.S. Government Printing Office, 1968.

Rogers, David. *The Management of Big Cities.* Beverly Hills, California: Sage Publications, 1971.

Saunders, Charles B. *Upgrading the American Police.* The Brookings Institute, 1970.

Schein, Edgar H. *Organized Psychology.* Englewood Cliffs, New Jersey: Prentice-Hall, Inc., 1965.

Smith, Alexander B., Bernard Locke, and William F. Walker. "Authoritarianism in College and Non-College Oriented Police." *Journal of Criminal Law, Criminology, and Police Science,* Vol. 58, No. 1.

Toffler, Alvin. *Future Shock.* New York: Bantam Books, 1971.

Trojanowicz, Robert C. *A Comparison of Behavior Styles of Policemen and Social Workers.* Unpublished doctoral dissertation, Michigan State University, 1969.

Tullock, Gordon. *Politics of Bureaucracy.* Washington, D.C.: Public Affairs Press, 1965.

Vega, William. "The Liberal Policeman: A Contradiction in Terms?" *Issues in Criminology,* Vol. 4, No. 1.

Webster, John A. "Police Task and Time Study." *Journal of Criminal Law, Criminology, and Police Science* (March, 1970).

Williams, Edgar G. "Changing Systems and Behavior." *Business Horizons* (August, 1969).

Wilson, James Q. "The Police and Their Problems: A Theory." *Public Policy XII.* Carl J. Friedrick and Seymour E. Harris, (Eds.). Graduate School of Public Administration, Harvard University, 1963.

References

1. We undertook this paper as three practitioners who have been heavily involved in attempts to improve urban policing. The material we have developed is based on both personal experiences and our interpretation of the implications of the research findings. Although we are indebted to many people who have reacted to the ideas expressed herein, we are particularly grateful to Mr. Edward A. Lettus, a Research Associate on the Dayton/Montgomery County Pilot Cities staff. Mr. Lettus devoted a tremendous amount of his time to collecting resource material, reacting to our ideas, and editing the various drafts of the paper. We sincerely appreciate his efforts.

2. Information concerning variations on the recommendations contained under this sub-heading can be found in Samual G. Chapman, *Police Patrol Readings* (Springfield: Charles C. Thomas, Publisher, 1964), pp. 245–274; The President's Commisson on Law Enforcement, *Task Force Report: The Police* (Washington, Government Printing Office, 1967), pp. 117-118; J.F. Elliott and Thomas J. Surdino, *Crime Control Team* (Springfield: Charles C. Thomas, 1971); and John E. Angell, "An Alternative to Classical Police Organizational Arrangements," *Criminology* (Vol. 9, No. 2 & 3, Aug.–Nov., 1971), pp. 185-207.

THEORiES of COMMUNiTY

COLIN BELL AND HOWARD NEWBY

In considering the concept of community, the sociologist shares an occupational hazard with the architect and the planner: the more he attempts to define it in his own terms, the more elusively does the essence of it seem to escape him. The concept of community has been the concern of sociologists for more than two hundred years, yet a satisfactory definition of it in sociological terms appears as remote as ever. Most sociologists seem to have weighed in with their own idea of what a community consists of—and in this lies much of the confusion. For sociologists, no more than other individuals, have not always been immune to the emotive overtones that the word community consistently carries with it. Everyone—even sociologists—has wanted to live in a community; feelings have been more equivocal concerning life in collectivities, groups, networks or societies. The subjective feelings that the term community conjures up thus frequently lead to a confusion between what it *is* (empirical description) and what the sociologist feels it *should be* (normative prescription). The reasons for this enduring confusion can be related to the history of sociology itself. What the concept *involves* has not proved too difficult to elaborate; attempts to describe what it *is*, however, have proved impossible without making value judgements.

Source: Community Studies: An Introduction to the Sociology of the Local Community by Colin Bell and Howard Newby pp. 21–53. © George Allen & Unwin Ltd. 1971. Excerpted and reprinted by permission of Praeger Publishers, Inc., New York.

The Theoretical Inheritance

'Community' was thought to be a good thing, its passing was to be deplored, feared and regretted. The events surrounding the supposed causes of its eclipse— the democratic political revolutions of America and France and the industrial revolutions of Britain and, later, the remainder of Western Europe—were to a remarkable extent the starting point of Tocqueville, Comte, Tönnies, Le Play, Marx and Durkheim, some of the most eminent of sociology's founding fathers. What they understood by community makes an appropriate starting place for a discussion of community studies, for in the nineteenth century 'community' occupied a position in the minds of intellectuals similar to the idea of 'contract' in the Age of Reason. The concept of community, however, was not a cold, analytic construct. On the contrary, the ties of the community, real or imagined, came from these thinkers' images of the good life. Community was thus used as a means of invidious comparison with contemporarily exemplified society, yet community, consisting as it did of what the particular writer believed it *ought* to consist of, was capable of encompassing any number of possibly contradictory values which each saw fit to include. This amorphous quality allowed an endless array of social thinkers to unite in their praise of community, no matter how diverse their interpretations of it might be.[1] Overlying this positive evaluation of community, there was frequently a pervading posture of nostalgia—of praising the past to blame the present— and the two themes combined when present 'society' was criticized with reference to past 'community'. The upheavals of industrialization enabled these feelings to be given full rein. Industrial society—and its ecological derivative, the city—was typified by competition and conflict, utility and contractual relations; the community—and its ecological derivative, the village or, at the most, the small town—was the antithesis of these. The impersonality and anonymity of industrial society were highlighted by reference to the close personal ties of the community. The trend appeared to be away from the latter and towards the former: thus there is in writers such as Comte an anguished sense of the breakdown of the old.[2] Comte's sociological interest in community was, as Nisbet has pointed out, born of the same circumstances that produced his conservatism: the breakdown or disorganization of the traditional forms of association. The community, in other words, was viewed as man's *natural* habitat.

Sir Henry Maine was not concerned with the community as such, but his work exercised a great influence upon his contemporaries and successors and, most importantly from our point of view, upon Tönnies. Thus, while we should be wary of plundering the corpus of his work looking for antecedents to our present concerns,[3] Maine's work forms an important prelude to later, more narrowly sociologically inclined, thinkers. What Maine wanted to know was how the institutions of his day had evolved from those of antiquity. On the basis of the early writings of the Hebrews, Greeks and Romans, Maine argued that early society was patriarchal, the oldest male having held absolute supremacy over the extended family. Society as a whole was a conglomeration of familial units. In contrast, Maine noted, the basic unit of modern society was not the family in its extended form but the individual. Using the legal system as evidence, he discovered that primitive law was concerned with family groups as corporate entities defined by kinship. Crime was a corporate act, land was held jointly. When societies expanded, however, locality rather than kinship became the basis of organization. The crux of Maine's argument was that the powers, privileges and duties once resident in the family had shifted to the state. And the nature of men's interrelations, instead of being based on his *status*, became based on individually agreed *contracts*.

Another who used law as an index of social change, was of course, Emile Durkheim. While Comte's overriding emotion was anguish, Durkheim's was concern, concern for the 'moral consolidation' of the society in which he lived. If Durkheim's work was 'a memorial to the ability of a gifted man to utilize the work of others in the pursuit of his own designs',[4] it is as well to be aware of what these designs were. What Durkheim feared was the disintegration of social relations into 'anomie'—a state of 'normlessness' where there was complete social breakdown—but what he perceived in contemporary society was not so much the breakdown of community as the transition from community based on one kind of social relations to community based on another, from mechanical solidarity to organic solidarity.[5] According to Durkheim the increased division of labour in more advanced societies leads to organic solidarity—solidarity based upon the interdependence of specialized parts, on diversity rather than similarity. He used legal indicators to show that as one type of solidarity advances, the other regresses; and it was organic solidarity that was increasing. Durkheim was gratified to conclude that, far from community disintegrating, society was becoming one big community.

If there is a founding father of the theory of community, however, the label perhaps suits Ferdinand Tönnies more than any other individual. Tönnies' book *Gemeinschaft and Gesellschaft* (usually translated as *Community and Society*) was first published in 1887. It has provided a constant source of ideas for those who have dealt with the community ever since.[6] In *Gemeinschaft* ('community') human relationships are intimate, enduring and based on a clear understanding of where each person stands in society. A man's 'worth' is estimated according to *who* he is not *what* he has done—in other words, status is ascriptive, rather than achieved. In a community, roles are specific and consonant with one another: a man does not find his duties in one role conflicting with the duties that devolve upon him from another role. Members of a community are relatively immobile in a physical and a social way: individuals neither travel far from their locality of birth nor do they rise up the social hierarchy. In addition, the culture of the community is relatively homogeneous, for it must be so if roles are not to conflict or human relations to lose their intimacy. The moral custodians of a community, the family and the church, are strong, their code clear and their injunctions well internalized. There will be community sentiments involving close and enduring loyalties to the place and people. So community encourages immobility and makes it difficult for men to achieve status and wealth on the basis of their merits. Community makes for tradition-alistic ways and at the very core of the community concept is the sentimental attachment to the conventions and mores of a beloved place. Community will reinforce and encapsulate a moral code, raising moral tensions and rendering heterodoxy a serious crime, for in a community everyone is known and can be placed in the social structure. This results in a personalizing of issues, events and explanations, because familiar names and characters inevitably become associ-ated with everything that happens. Tönnies continued the nineteenth-century theme that community makes for solidary relations among men, a theme which over the years has laid stress on one factor for its basis—the territorial factor, the place, the locality. When sociologists now talk about community, they almost always mean a place in which people have some, if not complete, solidary rela-tions. Yet community as originally used, though it included the *local* commun-ity, also went beyond it. It encompassed religion, work, family and culture: it referred to social bonds—to use Robert Nisbet's own key term—characterized by emotional cohesion, depth, continuity and fullness.

Opposed to the concept of community was *Gesellschaft* (variously trans-lated as 'society' or 'association') which essentially means everything that com-munity is not. *Gesellschaft* refers to the large scale, impersonal and contractual ties that were seen by the nineteenth century sociologists to be on the increase, at the expense of *Gemeinschaft*. Here is the central idea that runs through so many community studies: social change is conceptualized as a continuum be-tween two polar types: *Gemeinschaft* or community and *Gesellschaft* or society. For Tönnies, there are three central aspects of *Gemeinschaft*: blood, place (land) and mind, with their sociological consequents of kinship, neighbour-hood and friendship. Together, they were the home of all virtue and morality. *Gesellschaft*, however, has a singularity about it; in Tönnies' terms, 'all its activities are restricted to a definite end and a definite means of obtaining it'.[7] This rationality is, of course, usually seen as a key aspect in the development of western capitalism. Indeed it might be claimed that in *Gemeinschaft* would be found what Max Weber calls 'traditional' authority whereas *Gesellschaft* incorpo-rates what he would call 'rational-legal' authority. Yet it should be understood that whereas the loss of community is something that is treated as a conse-quence of capitalism by Marx—and others since then, making it a strong tradi-tion today—for Tönnies capitalism was treated as a consequence of the loss of community. Chicken-and-egg arguments are rarely easily soluble and no attempt at a solution is made here. Nevertheless, it is important to realize that the conferring of causal status on the concept of community is at the very essence of Tönnies' typological use of it.

Tönnies' greatest legacy is this typological usage—a typology usually expressed in terms of a dichotomy. The 'community-society' dichotomy along with 'authority-power', 'status-class', 'sacred-secular', 'alienation-progress', have been represented by Nisbet as the unit ideas of the sociological tradition. They are, as he wrote, 'the rich themes in nineteenth-century thought. Considered as linked antitheses, they form the very warp of the sociological tradition. Quite apart from their conceptual significance in sociology, they may be regarded as epitomizations of the conflict between tradition and modernism, between the old order made moribund by the industrial and democratic revolutions, and the new order, its outlines still unclear and as often the cause of anxiety as of elation and hope.'[8] These ideas were not, of course, new to the nineteenth century— Sorokin, for example, takes the basic idea of community back to Confucius and runs through Ibn Khaldun and St. Thomas Aquinas.[9] They remain, though, the most relevant theoretical inheritance for modern community studies, and must be the starting place for more recent conceptualizations of the concept.

The *Gemeinschaft-Gesellschaft* dichotomy can be incorporated into the structural-functional theories of Talcott Parsons. What Parsons terms 'pattern variables' form the basis of his system for the analysis of social action. They are seen as continua or 'ranges' between polar opposites, each of which expresses a 'dilemma' of choice between two alternatives that every 'actor' faces in every social situation. As Parsons states, the clusters at the end of these continua 'very closely characterize what in much sociological literature have been thought of as polar types of institutional structure, the best known version of which perhaps has been the *Gemeinschaft-Gesellschaft* dichotomy of Tönnies'.[10] These pattern variables are:

1. Affectivity versus affective neutrality: which refers to whether immediate self-gratification or its deferment is expected.
2. Specificity versus diffuseness: which refers to whether the scope of a relationship is narrow, like that between a bureaucrat and his client, or broad and inclusive as between a mother and her child or between spouses.
3. Universalism versus particularism: which refers to whether action is governed by generalized standards (equal opportunity) or in terms of a reference scheme peculiar to the actors in the relationship (e.g. nepotism.)
4. Quality versus performance (also called ascription verses achievement): which refers to whether the characterization of each actor by the others is based on who or what the person is or on what he can do, on whether he is the son of a duke (ascription) or a college graduate (achievement).

Community would seem to involve particularism and ascription and diffuseness and affectivity—as a consequence, for example, of kinship being important and of stability and 'knowing' everyone. On the other hand, the emergent pattern in most industrial societies is that of universalism and achievement and specificity and affective neutrality. There is a clear tendency for these pattern-variables to co-vary between the extremes, although all societies show mixtures of the two sets of characteristics. The relative emphasis clearly differs and the pattern-variables can be used as more precise analytic tools to describe the loss or otherwise of community. It should be noted, however, that Parsons is not talking particularly about local social systems but society in general. The pattern-variables can be applied to all forms of social action, having emerged out of the classic dichotomies of the sociological tradition, and their application to community represents only a small part of Parsons' much grander theoretical scheme.

Definitions of Community

While the foregoing has described how sociological theory has impinged upon the concept of community, we have yet to examine in detail precisely what the term has been believed to denote. The difficulties involved in this somewhat intricate task have already been alluded to. Every sociologist, it seems, has possessed his own notion of what community consists of, frequently reflecting his ideas of what it *should* consist of. Exhortations to 'define your terms' have been taken to heart in this case—sociologists have frequently launched into defining community with a will bordering on gay abandon. Indeed, the analysis of the various definitions was at one time quite a thriving sociological industry. The *piece de resistance* was George A. Hillery Jr's analysis of no fewer than ninety-four definitions in his paper, 'Definitions of Community: Areas of Agreement'.[11] Needless to say, the very thing that was missing was agreement—indeed Hillery's conclusion hardly seemed to advance the analysis much further. In the convoluted verbiage beloved of many American sociologists he concluded, 'There is one element, however, which can be found in all of the concepts, and (if its mention seems obvious) it is specified merely to facilitate a positive delineation of the degree of heterogeneity: all of the definitions deal with people. Beyond this common basis, there is no agreement.'[12] This hardly seems very encouraging.

Hillery's efforts, however, were not entirely wasted, for from his inspection of the ninety-four definitions he was able to discover, he abstracted sixteen concepts. These concepts were linked by twenty-two different combinations, and though one may regard sixteen elements as an unwieldy classification, at least it is an advance in parsimony compared with ninety-four. Table 1-4-1 is an adaptation of Hillery's. We have followed Hillery in his two major distinguishing categories. *Generic* community refers to the use of the word community as a conceptual term. *Rural* communities refer not to the community but to a particular type of community. The prevalence, which Hillery discovered, of con-

The Context of Police-Community Relations

TABLE 1-4-1. A Classification of Selected Definitions of Community
(after Hillery)

Distinguishing Ideas or Elements Mentioned in the Definitions	Number of Definitions
I. Generic Community	
A. Social Interaction	
1. Geographic Area	
A. Self-sufficiency	8
B. Common Life	9
Kinship	2
C. Consciousness of Kind	7
D. Possession of common ends, norms, means	20
E. Collection of institutions	2
F. Locality Groups	5
G. Individuality	2
2. Presence of some common characteristic, other than area	
A. Self-sufficiency	1
B. Common Life	3
C. Consciousness of Kind	5
D. Possession of common ends, norms, means	5
3. Social System	1
4. Individuality	3
5. Totality of Attitudes	1
6. Process	2
B. Ecological Relationships	3
II. Rural Community	
A. Social Interaction	
1. Geographic Area	
A. Self-sufficiency	1
B. Common Life	3
C. Consciousness of Kind	3
D. Possession of common ends, norms, means	3
E. Locality group	5
Total Definitions	94

joining community with a specifically rural environment, can be seen as the continuing presence of the anti-urban trait in sociology referred to earlier. We have followed Hillery in believing, that, while the division of definitions into 'generic community' and 'rural community' is not a logical one, the attempt to delimit the characteristics of community contained in the latter should not be discarded.

Despite Hillery's conclusion that there is an absence of agreement, beyond the fact that community involves people, a considerable amount can now be salvaged from his analysis. A perusal of the table should lead to the conclusion that not all the definitions can be correct, that is to say that community cannot be all of these definitions in their entirety. A community cannot be an area and not be an area, though significantly Hillery found that no author denied that area *could* be an element of community. All but three of the definitions clearly mention the presence of a group of people interacting; those that do not have an ecological orientation. This is one reason for examining the ecological approach more closely later in the chapter. Sixty-nine of the ninety-four definitions agree that community includes social interaction, area and some ties or bonds in common. Seventy, or almost three-quarters, agree on the presence of area and social interaction as necessary elements of community; but more than three-quarters (seventy-three) agreed on the joint inclusion of social interaction and common ties. Thus a majority of definitions include, in increasing importance for each element, the following components of community: area, common ties and social interaction.[13]

If the reader now believes that we are achieving a sight of the trees after having hacked away much dead wood, the progress since Hillery's analysis is a salutary warning against optimism. A consideration of a few definitions that have enjoyed wide circulation since Hillery's analysis will serve to show what we mean. Sussman has produced a particularly fine example of an omnibus definition: 'A community is said to exist when interaction between individuals has the purpose of meeting individual needs and obtaining group goals . . . a limited geographical area is another feature of the community. . . . The features of social interaction, structures for the gratification of physical, social and psychological needs, and limited geographical area are basic to the definition of community.'[14] The utility of this definition is, however, severely hindered by the fact that the specification of individual and group goals is an exceedingly troublesome task.

Kaufman's paper, 'Toward an Interactional Conception of Community'[15] argues—in a manner consistent with the traditional formulations discussed above—that centralization, specialization and the increase of impersonal relationships are hastening the decline of the community. The first two aspects of his formal definition are very similar to those of Sussman—that community is a place (a relatively small one at that), and secondly, that community indicates a configuration as to way of life, both as to how people do things and what they want, that is, their institutions and their collective goals. Kaufman's third notion is a more radical departure and concerns collective action: 'Persons in a community should not only be able to, but frequently do act together in the common concern of life.'[16] There are thus three elements in Kaufman's interactional model of the community: the community participant, the community groups and associations, and finally the phases and processes of community action. In other words, who, with whom, does what, when? This would seem very relevant to the study of, say, local politics, but of less relevance to the analysis of the community as an object or unit of study. Kaufman's difficulties become more apparent later in the paper when he conceptualizes, again very traditionally, community as an independent rather than dependent variable: 'One may visualize the community field as a stage with the particular ethos of the local society determining the players and the plays.'[17] While Kaufman admits that this is 'much more an enumeration of elements . . . than a precise statement of their interrelationships',[18] one feels justified in asking where the community is in all this. Since he refers to the community *field* it is presumably not the 'stage'. Is it then the 'ethos', the 'players', the 'play' or perhaps the most likely candidate, 'local society'? But the use of 'local society' merely begs the question: semantic sleight of hand is not substitute for rigorous definition.

Sutton and Kolaja add some variables to the study of action *in* the community, but do not really elaborate a definition despite the title of their paper, 'The Concept of Community'.[19] Community is defined in the by-now-familiar way as 'a number of families residing in a relatively small area within which they have developed a more or less complete socio-cultural definition imbued with collective identification and by means of which they solve problems arising from the sharing of an area'.[20] The four crucial variables as they see them are:

1. Number of actors
2. Awareness of action
3. Goal of action
4. Recipients of action

They are attempting a convergence between conceptions of community and conceptions of community action. To do this they cross-classify these four variables and develop a sixteen-fold table which, they argue, can be used to classify community action.

It should be apparent by now that it is impossible to give *the* sociological definition of the community. However, we offer one last attempt at defining the concept, the one which, at least to us, seems to have the most to commend it: that of Talcott Parsons. Earlier, when discussing the sociological tradition out of which emerged Parsons' pattern variables, it was pointed out that particularism, ascription, diffuseness and affectivity (and their opposites) are categories of social action with no necessary local reference. Without this territorial reference it is difficult to distinguish social action within, say, a family from that within a village. So Gidean Sjoberg has found it necessary to significantly modify Parsons' definition in *The Social System*[21] and to call a community 'a collectivity of actors sharing in a limited territorial area as the base for carrying out the greatest share of their daily activities.'[22] Parsons originally wrote 'common' not 'limited' so Sjoberg obviously feels that he wants to include some notion of size in his definition, yet does not build into his definition any notion of what the limit to this size should be.

Parsons, in a more recent paper entitled 'The Principal Structures of

Community',[23] avoids begging this question as well as others just as crucial. There has been, as Hillery's discussion showed—and it is more marked than he implied—a dichotomy in community studies between those which focus, to put it crudely, on the people, and those which focus on the territory. Parsons avoids forcing a choice between the two. His tentative definition (which should be treated as such) is as follows: '... that aspect of the structure of social systems which is referable to the territorial location of persons (i.e. human individuals as organisms) and their activities'.[24] There follows an important qualification. 'When I say "referable to" I do not mean determined exclusively or predominantly by, but rather *observable and analysable with reference to location as a focus of attention* (and of course a partial determinant).'[25] As Parsons states, the territorial reference is central, though it is necessary to stress, with him, that we should be concerned with 'persons acting in territorial locations' and, in addition, 'since the reference is to *social* relations, persons acting in relation to other persons in respect to the territorial location of both parties. . . . The *population*, then, is just as much a focus of the study of community as is the territorial location.'[26]

Our motive in discussing these definitional exercises is partially the negative one of demonstrating the non-cumulative nature of so much of the work on community. It is also hoped that it has had the positive function of showing the catholicity of the field despite these terminological arguments. It now appears that something of an impasse has been reached concerning the definition of community—some might even call it exhaustion. This must lead us to examine the theory of community from other points of view. After all, as Hillery has rightly observed 'The significant question concerns the nature of social groups, not whether a ninety-fifth definition of community is possible.'[27] It would now seem more profitable to consider some distinct streams or approaches to community studies rather than to pursue or attempt to resolve the definitional debate. Rather as intelligence is what intelligence tests measure perhaps we can, for the time being at any rate, merely treat community as what community studies analyse. . . .

Community, Locality and Network

A consensus on the theory of community appears as remote as ever, though this is not to say that the area of discourse has not shifted somewhat. The broad lines of debate are now between those who regard the community as a legitimate *object* of sociological inquiry, while at the same time, perhaps, wishing to alter the nomenclature, and those who do not.

Those who regard the community as a legitimate object of sociological enquiry clearly have to resolve the problems of definition and value judgments. There must be a departure from the *Gemeinschaft* conceptualizations of communities where, as John Jackson has written, there is a 'harking back to some pre-existing rural utopia' in which 'the natural condition of man is sedentary',[28] and movement away from which is a deviant activity 'associated with disorganization and a threat to the established harmony of *Gemeinschaft* relationships which are implied by a life lived within a fixed social framework'.[29] Value judgements are one problem, ambiguity is another: König has shown that 'there is a good deal of very obvious ambiguity', even in the German derivation of the word (*Gemeinschaft, Gemeinde, Gemeinderschaft*) and particularly between the 'community as an administrative unit and the community as a social reality'.[30]

One solution to the problems of the definition of community, indeed an avoidance of the term 'community' altogether, has been proposed by Margaret Stacey.[31] If institutions are locality based *and* interrelated there may well be, she argues, a *local social system* that is worthy of sociological attention. She does not want to call this local social system a 'community' for the latter, she feels, is a non-concept. In other words, Stacey claims that the definitional debate about community is something more; it represents a much more serious conceptual disagreement about whether the community is a geographical area, or a sense of belonging, or non-work relations and so on. Instead, sociologists should concentrate on institutions and their interrelations in specific localities. Stacey is not concerned whether a locality is isolated or not. She writes, for example, that 'the consequences for the social relations within a locality of changes introduced from outside have after all produced some interesting studies'.[32] Stacey's approach brings a welcome rigour to the field and she writes that it is possible to talk with some certainty about '(i) the establishment and maintenance of a local social system; (ii) local conditions where no such system can be expected; (iii) some circumstances under which an existing system might be modified or destroyed; (iv) certain interrelations between systems and their parts; (v) the interaction of local and national systems'.[33]

Stacey's concept of a 'local social system' will obviously be empirically varied, for the nature and configuration of the interrelations of social institutions are very diverse. Rarely will there be a completely interrelated social system, with all institutions present: in any given locality it is likely, as she says, that 'there will either be no local social system, or some kind of partial local social system'.[34] Stacey does not intend that the 'complete local social system' should be open to the same sort of objections as the concept of 'community' or, for that matter, 'folk society'. She is arguing that it is theoretically possible to list systematically the social institutions which might be present in a locality with all their interconnections. This can be regarded as a model and against it the empirically observed presence and absence of institutions and connections can be plotted. Another significant aspect of Stacey's argument is her insistence on the inclusion of time as a dimension—'. . . the state of a system at a given moment in time will be considered and the temporal conditions which have led to that state and what may follow will be indicated'.[35]

References

1. For an interesting account of this theme in relation to the British literary and philosophical tradition see W. Peterson, 'The Ideological Origins of Britain's New Towns', *American Institute of Planners Journal*, XXXIV, 1968, pp. 160-70.

2. See R. Nisbet, *The Sociological Tradition*, London, Heinemann, 1966, Chapter 3.

3. See J. Burrows, *Evolution and Society*, London, Cambridge U.P., 1966, for the dangers inherent in the Whiggish interpretation of nineteenth century intellectual history.

4. H. Stuart Hughes, *Consciousness and Society*, New York (and London), MacGibbon and Kee, 1967, p. 280.

5. E. Durkheim, *The Division of Labour in Society*, New York, Free Press, 1964 (London, Collier-Macmillan).

6. See for example, J.C. McKinney and C.P. Loomis, 'The Application of *Gemeinschaft* and *Gesellschaft* as Related to Other Typologies', in the introduction to the American edition of F. Tönnies' *Community and Society*, New York, Harper Torchbook, 1957, pp. 12-29.

7. Tönnies, *op. cit.*, p. 192.

8. Nisbet, *op. cit.*, p. 6.

9. See his introduction to Tönnies, *op cit*.

10. T. Parsons and E. Shils, *Toward a General Theory of Action*, New York (and London), Harper Torchbook, 1952, pp. 207-8.

11. G.A. Hillery Jr, 'Definitions of Community: Areas of Agreement', *Rural Sociology*, 20, 1955.

12. *Ibid.*, p. 117.

13. *Ibid.*, p. 118.

14. Marvin B. Sussman (ed.) *Community Structure and Analysis*, New York, Crowell, 1959, pp. 1-2.

15. Harold F. Kaufman, 'Toward an Interactional Conception of Community', *Social Forces*, 38, 1959.

16. *Ibid.*, p. 9.

17. *Ibid.*, p. 10.

18. *Ibid.*, p. 10.

19. Willis A. Sutton and Jivi Kolaja, 'The Concept of Community,' *Rural Sociology*, 25, 1960.

20. *Ibid.*, p. 197.

21. Talcott Parsons, *The Social System*, London, Tavistock Publications, 1952.

22. Gideon Sjoberg, 'Community' in J. Gould & W.L. Kolb, *Dictionary of Sociology*, London, Tavistock, 1965, p. 115.

23. Talcott Parsons, 'The Principal Structures of Community', in his *Structure and Process in Modern Society*, but originally in Carl J. Friedrich, *Community*, New York, Liberal Arts Press, 1959.

24. *Ibid.* (Friedrich), p. 250.

25. *Ibid.*, p. 250 (our emphasis).

26. *Ibid.*, p. 250 (emphasis in the original).

27. G.A. Hillery, *Communal Organizations*, Chicago, Chicago U.P., 1969, p. 4.

28. J.A. Jackson (ed.), *Migration*, London, Cambridge U.P., 1969, p. 3.

29. *Ibid.*, p. 3.

30. Rene Konig, *The Community*, London, Routledge, 1968., p. 1.

31. Margaret Stacey, 'The Myth of Community Studies', *British Journal of Sociology*, 20, 1969.

32. *Ibid.*, p. 139.

33. *Ibid.*, p. 139.

34. *Ibid.*, p. 141.

35. *Ibid.*, p. 141.

CHAPTER **1-5**

THE definition of NEiqHBORHOOds

ALAN A. ALTSHULER

In both everyday and social science usage, ... the terms "community" and "neighborhood" are quite distinct. The former, as Robert Nisbet has written, refers to ties that "are characterized by a high degree of personal intimacy, emotional depth, moral commitment, social cohesion, and continuity in time."* The most common bases for such ties in contemporary America are family, religion, ethnicity, race (the ethnicity of Afro-Americans), occupation, and income class. The essence of "neighborhood," by contrast, is spatial contiguity.

This has led some critics of the movement for community control to pose the question: Are neighborhoods relevant? To be more precise, they have suggested that contemporary neighborhoods lack *both* the scale to deal with the problems that people care about and the sense of community that might make the exercise of political responsibility within them a source of profound satisfaction to their members.

The demand for participation, in this view, cannot be satisfied by providing for the expression of just any small community interests. The needs are to

Source: From *Community Control* by Alan A. Altshuler, copyright © 1970 by Western Publishing Company, Inc., reprinted by permission of The Bobbs-Merrill Company, Inc. pp. 124–130.
*He goes on: "Community is founded on man conceived in his wholeness rather than in one or another of the roles, taken separately, that he may hold in a social order. ... It achieves its fulfillment in a submergence of individual will that is not possible in unions of mere convenience or rational assent. ... Its archetype, both historically and symbolically, is the family, and in almost every type of genuine community the nomenclature of family is prominent."[1]

cultivate community life along the social dimensions that most matter to people, and to imbue the whole political system with an ethic stressing active consultation and responsiveness. The sorts of organizations they have in mind are churches, labor unions, ethnic and racial associations, professional associations, and so on. Whether participation should involve formal delegations of public authority to such groups is another matter. Most adherents of this position think not. . . .

Groups vary widely, of course, in the substance of their neighborhood desires and the strength of their neighborhood commitments. What is most striking, however, is that poor people and black people (and thus particularly poor black people) have the greatest stake in their particular "turfs." Affluent whites can abandon any particular locale with ease if it becomes uncongenial. This has been, in fact, their most important mode of urban political expression over the past generation. And, despite their mobility, they defend with passion the political independence of their new "neighborhoods." The poor, on the other hand, tend to move within much smaller radii. They find changes of neighborhood both difficult and discomforting. They are also less likely to have cars; and even when they do, the friends and relatives with whom they visit are much more likely to live close by.[2]

Melvin and Carolyn Webber have noted that the population can be laid along a continuum in terms of its perceptions and uses of space. At one extreme, the intellectual elite communicates along networks of specialization over enormous distances. Its channels are the telephone, academic conventions, professional publications, and so on. Although face-to-face contact may be infrequent, the quality of interaction is quite intense. Membership in the professional community is a vital part of each member's identity. Moreover, "it is these spatially dispersed peers who will understand his work and, in evaluation, convey the rewards that matter most to him."[3]

But at the other end of the continuum, the Webbers write, may be found the "working-class locals." The consistent findings of social science studies indicate that these people, "whether residents of central city slums or suburban housing tracts, have retained the 'intense localism' and the limited 'close-knit networks' of social relations that are also found in many peasant societies." The critical distinction between the cosmopolite and the local is not whether he lives in an urban or rural place, but rather his income, education, occupation, and outlook. The forest ranger is likely to be well along toward the cosmopolite end of the spectrum; the central city day laborer will tend to be near the local end. Generally speaking, it can be said that among working class locals, "in striking contrast to middle-class groups, social organization (encompassing both family and friends) is territorially coterminous with the neighborhood place". . . .[4]

The studies to which the Webbers refer deal mainly with whites. At all income levels in American society, however, the social lives of blacks are more spatially concentrated than those of whites. It is even true, despite the popular stereotype, that they move less—at least, between locales. Dire economic necessity has forced a great migration from countryside to city, and from South to North, upon American Negroes in the present century. The most careful survey to date has found, though, that once Negroes find a city in which there is any work at all, they tend to stay put. They are much less prone to move about the country in response merely to *improved* job opportunities than whites.*

There is little reason for surprise, then, either that ghetto residents think neighborhoods *are* relevant, or that a good many intellectual critics consider them obsolete. What is surprising is that so little notice has been taken of the paradox that, among American urban residents, those whose perspectives are most limited spatially are concentrated in the largest jurisdictions—or, to put it another way, that those to whom neighborhood means the most enjoy opportunities for neighborhood self-government the least.

To establish that neighborhoods matter, of course, is quite something else from determining their boundaries. In performing the second task, it would be necessary to reconcile the overlapping perceptions of residents and, even more important, to balance these perceptions against numerous considerations of scale, simplicity, diversity, and capacity to evolve. . . .

References

1. Nisbet, Robert A., The Sociological Tradition. New York: Basic Books. 1966:47–48.

2. Cf. Greer, Scott, "Individual Participation in Mass Society," in Roland Young, ed., Approaches to the Study of Politics, Evanston, Ill.: Northwestern University Press. 1957:329–342; and Melvin Webber and Carolyn C. Webber, "Culture, Territoriality, and the Elastic Mile," in H. Wentworth Elredge, ed., Taming Megalopolis. Garden City, New York: Doubleday. Vol. I. 1967:35–54.

3. Ibid. p. 37.

4. Ibid. pp. 40–44.

5. Lansing, John B. and Eva Mueller. The Geographic Mobility of Labor. Ann Arbor: Survey Research Center, University of Michigan. (undated). Ch. 10. See esp. 270–271.

*To repeat, the measure being applied here is interlocal moves. Negroes do make more intra-local moves than whites, a phenomenon which can be explained statistically by their lower incomes and rates of home ownership. Some of the poorest urban families, who have few white counterparts in modern America, exercise a disproportionate influence on the overall rate by the astonishing frequency—up to several times yearly—of their intralocal moves.

At the time of the 1960 census, 16.8 per cent of American whites were living in a different county from five years earlier, by comparison with only 8.5 per cent of nonwhites.

Among family heads who had experienced occasional or frequent unemployment, the white rate of movement had been nearly twice the Negro rate (23–12 per cent). Among family heads who had been steadily employed during the five-year period, the white rate of movement was seven times the Negro (21–3 per cent).[5]

CHAPTER **1-6**

UNDERSTANDiNG THE COMMUNITY

JAMES B. McKEE

. . . . the whole concept of community is fraught with illusions and is to a very considerable extent a misleading concept. It's misleading largely because it's a very ancient and honorable word that conveys certain ideas that seem to me to be no longer as applicable as they once were. That is, we have images of what we mean by community. The word tends to imply a sense of organization, a sharing of values, a sharing of a common way of life among that population that inhabits a given locality. But all of this in the modern world, in the modern urbanized community, is an over-statement, if not an outright illusion. Community is no longer like that, if it ever was.

But if we leave aside the question what it once was, at least I think we can recognize that the roots of the term are located in the concern of men about the change from a distinctly rural community to an urban one. A rural community largely encompassed the totality of human lives where men were born, raised, and lived in the same community, and shared a common way of life with the same group of people, and that not a very large group.

Community in that sense meant you knew your neighbor, you knew who belonged there. You could readily identify on the street a friend from a stranger. All of this is involved in the notion of community: of people who live together, share a way of life together, have deep understandings about their most basic values and about how they want to live their lives, exist together in a funda-

Source: Institute on Police and Community Relations. Kellogg Center for Continuing Education. Michigan State University. 1965. pp. H 1-12. Reprinted with the kind permission of the editors of the Institute on Police and Community Relations and the author.

mental agreement about what is most significant, about how people should behave.

What I am saying is that none of this applies to the modern community. Yet, we still use the term "community" to identify a town, a city, a locality, a geographical area within which there is some concentration of population; where people live and work. At least some of them work there, for it's no longer necessary, obviously, to work in the same community in which you reside. Indeed, this is one of the significant ways in which community has now changed.

At one time a community encompassed the totality of a human life; it need not do that any longer. It does not, in fact, do that any longer for a large proportion of those who in fact have residence in a given community. There are significant implications in this kind of change for the phenomenon we call community and for the understanding of community. I'm going to pursue a little bit this one thread.

What I am saying is that the community is not the kind of integrated entity that the term itself has long seemed to imply. It's not that at all. This makes it very difficult for us, therefore, to assess the meaning of community as a locality, a place where people reside and work. Thus, our recognition of the simple reality of the urban community of today would be to emphasize, in the language of the sociologist, that it is *segmentalized*, that it is *stratified*, that it is *differentiated* and that it is *un-integrated*. Now, all I am saying there in about four different ways, is that the community is a lot of different pieces that are not well tied together. There are different patterns of life among the distinct groups that are located in the same boundaries of a city and there are several different strata, or social ranks, that have the most minimum, if any, social contact or communication with one another.

One basic idea, of course, of community in the older sense was that it was a single system of communication, that people spoke the same language and understood one another. I am saying here that the lines of differentiation that mark groups off from one another, the lines of stratification that separate several different kinds of social ranking and prestige levels, and the ways of life that go with these, inhibit communication, indeed, mark a community in which there are discontinuities in communication, not a continuous flow that reaches every single person within it.

The most common error in trying to understand community, it seems to me, is to jump to the conclusion, to the illusion, really, that community is integrated around a common set of values that are shared by those who make up a community by virtue of living there. This is not so. The concept of community, once one imputes to it the notion of common values, then also leads, as the next logical idea, to the notion of effective social controls in maintaining standards of behavior. Clearly, standards of behavior accepted within the community are easier to maintain when there is a common body of values that animates all members of the community, a common body of values to which they have all been properly socialized in their youth elsewhere. But most important of all, being young and undergoing the processes of socialization in the community today does not introduce one to any single body of values or any single standard of behavior maintained in that community. In part, the community of old by its greater approximation at least to this ideal sense of what a community was and the exemplification of certain common values by the most significant members of the community, and the influence which their positions gave them within the community, made it possible to exercise a somewhat greater control over those less integrated members, so much so that it was possible for all of us in looking at communities of the past to exaggerate their consensus, and to exaggerate the processes of integration and to admire the effective social controls characteristic of the smaller community of the past.

Indeed, one of the first lessons in sociology that I learned in studying the city was that in the transition from the more rural community of the past to the modern urban community of today, social controls, as they came spontaneously and informally out of a common way of life, broke down, because the newer urban community did not effect one common way of life. For purposes of social control there was a more necessary reliance on formal controls, on law and on the exercise of authority and law enforcement by police.

The conception of the community of the past was . . . one in which one was born, raised, and lived one's life within the same community and largely within the same station of life. It is, if we examine it closely, a conception of a fairly static, relatively unchanging community. That alone, it seems to me, would disqualify it for serious consideration in examining community life today. The contemporary community is not an isolated phenomenon set apart; it is a part of the larger society. It stands, in a sense, in the way of, and therefore gets caught in the wash of the sweeping events of our time. It is not independent of what goes on in the larger society.

The individual today is free, to a very great extent, from local control because he's mobile. We live in a society in which mobility, both vertical and horizontal—moving from one community to another, from one place to another around this large society of ours, as well as moving up and down the social ladder—are common facts of life.

But what is significant about this, in examining community, is that community is not the only significant grouping in the life of an individual. For what is the most important sociological implication of the idea of mobility is that one changes the groups of which one is a member, or in the language of the social psychologist, one changes one's *reference group*, which may be the group of which one is a part or the group one desires to be a part; anyway, the group to which one refers one's self, in taking cues for behavior and styles of conduct in living one's life. Almost every individual changes his membership groups and his reference groups sometimes in his life. And many of us, as a matter of fact, change them any number of times. We also, therefore, change the human beings we are. For, as we change the groups within which we live, the groups in which we play our roles and act toward others and are some kind of person, we change ourselves.

The older notion that you shape the person in the earliest years of life and that's what he is from then on, is no longer tenable as a way of perceiving human beings in this kind of society. Individuals change as the circumstances of their lives change, and we as Americans are a kind of people who have personalities that are relatively adaptable to the circumstances of change. We do not find it too difficult to do this. Mobility, then, is a fact that loosens the natural tendency of a community to exert control over its members, for it is no longer the exclusive reference group that defines acceptable standards of conduct and it no longer defines any *one* standard of conduct, anyway.

Sociologists like to point out that you can rather simply, and crudely, in any given community, distinguish between those whose major orientation is to the local community, whose roots are there and who are less likely to be mobile, and whose life is focused around what goes on in the community, from those who have a larger focus, a larger involvement and a larger interest in what goes on elsewhere. These may be, for professional reasons or whatever else, tied into groups that are not distinctively local groups, as against those whose whole life is wrapped up in what goes on within the community.

Localites and cosmopolites is a kind of sociological phrase coined to convey this distinction. Localites are those who have a primary stake in the community. What happens in the community is significant because it happens to them. The local business men, who are not all the business men but certainly the main street merchants, the men whose property and business is centered in that community, and who will rise and fall with the community, are locally oriented. So are the realtors who buy and sell or serve as the brokers for buyers and sellers of commercial and residential property that constitutes that community. Those leaders who are leaders in local terms, around local issues, and local concerns and whose capacity for leadership is effectively exercised only within the community, have a stake in that community. There are those whose relatively higher social status is based upon the organization of the community. It is local status, high only within the community; a status that would be lost if they moved elsewhere.

Localite never includes all those who in fact are members of the community, for there are some who have no significant stake within it. There are people who have social status that is derived from social groups and collectivities that are not based necessarily in one community, but stretch across communities. We need to recognize that many people are no longer primarily oriented only to community, but that in a great mass society, in a world of bureaucratic association, people are involved in other kinds of networks of human association in which they have status, within which they find significant human association, and within which they find significant experience and attachment to others, as well as significant rewards.

An interest in community is frequently competitive with other interests so that those who are locally oriented are not all one would define as members of the community, but only those whose own rewards in life and whose own status is derived more from the organization of the local community, and who thus have a greater stake in it. These are likely to be less mobile people and they may be less mobile people because they have less capacity, for one reason or another, to be mobile, or because they have less reason to be mobile. That is, they start out advantaged by the community alone. The old families, for example, that have both property and status, have a stake in the community. They have less reason to be mobile and more reason to be strongly rooted and more reason therefore to be active participants and to provide some of the local leadership. But this by no means designates all who live in the community, nor all the talent within the community, nor all the capacity for leadership within the community, for some of the talent and leadership may be exercised in organizations and collectivities that reach beyond the community to wider publics and audiences.

It seems to me that one should never fail to note that in the modern community the minorities, particularly the Negro, the youth, and the poor, are three categories of people who are sometimes localites only because the opportunities to be otherwise are limited, but on the other hand are not integrated in any genuine value-sense into the community. Now these are not three mutually exclusive categories. . . . The minorities, the youth and the poor, as a matter of fact, are somewhat over-lapping categories. There are human beings who are all three of these. There are . . . others who are in at least two of these categories. These are significant categories of people in our modern communities just because they are least touched by the rewards of the status system within the community; just because they have least access to the lines of influence and power within the community; because they live by values that are perhaps most remote from those whose status and stake make them the natural, advantaged leaders of the community; because the discontinuities of communication probably exhibit their greatest break between the stable, established leadership of the community and these segments of it; and because in all three cases they are potentially mobilizable, particularly the minorities and the young. They are mobilizable for lines of action that may threaten those who feel they have the strongest stake in the community as it is. They are mobilizable in terms of values, criticism and discontent, that may reach beyond a particular community to be reflected in the sweeping patterns of dissent and protest that run across the country.

The problem of dealing with its least integrated members is not unique to any community. Rather, while the youth find it difficult to communicate with the leadership of their own community, they do not find it difficult to communicate with other youth across the whole broad strand of America, and to be involved in communication about social movements, ideals, values, forms of protest, lines of action, that bring youngsters in contact with one another from Maine to California, from North to South. They can talk or they can communicate about values, engage in a meaningful discourse with other youth, when they can't talk across the street to city hall. What this suggests is that there are ... individuals who do not share in the most dominant values of a community, and as far as I am concerned, this is the most fundamental lesson in understanding community today.

What does attach even the seemingly least attached person to community? It seems to me the one common denominator that every person who is a member of a community shares, of course, is the simple fact of residence. But that means more than the physical fact that your dwelling is located within the boundaries of some community. If that's all it means, then there is no attachment, because there is no reason for attachment. But what common residence more typically means, I think, for the adult at least, is a cluster of values about family, home, and children, and about an environment for them. It means a common life style that maintains an aura of congeniality enabling people to live in some agreement about what makes for a good life. People search for a satisfying basis for residence within a community in terms of these clusters of values. Even the property values that some people invoke when invasion by minorities occurs within their area is not, of course, simply a dollar and cents matter; it is more than that. It is, however mistaken the line of thought, indicative of the terms and conditions under which residence is a symbol for home and family and the raising of children. And thus, it touches upon very deeply held values. This is why the conflict of race and residence is the tougher of the several conflicts about race that a community has to face.

Let me wind up, then, by raising the question that I have touched upon only in passing. What about leadership in this? The quality of leadership in a community that is as fragmented, as segmentalized, as differentiated as the urban community of today, then becomes a matter of crucial importance. More than that, high social status, long residence in the community, membership in an old family whose grandfather was mayor and whose greatgrandfather staked out the boundaries of the community, is no guarantee of effective leadership. It is no guarantee that large numbers of the people in the community any longer care what your father or your grandfather was. That may look good in the society pages, for society editors are still concerned with these kinds of things. And there may be small circles in which one is more welcome because of these kinds of status claims, but they are no longer a basis for effective leadership. They no longer integrate the community.

What I am saying is that the integration of a community does not naturally arise any longer out of a common way of life, nor does its leadership come naturally out of those who occupy the positions of high status. Rather, community leadership has to be sought after and has to be developed. Effective community leadership, for there is such, seems to reside in those who, whatever their positions are in the community, or whatever their own kind of social background and set of social experiences, are capable of producing some kind of reasonable political consensus. This is why leadership in the contemporary community is fundamentally *political leadership*. That doesn't necessarily mean seeking political office, though the political offices, it seems to me, become increasingly significant as the forms of effective leadership.

If a community is no longer the kind of value-integrated ideal that it was in the past, which may not have been true anyway, what it is today, if it is a community at all, is politically integrated. This is simply the working out by agreement and compromise of some understandings, not intended to last forever, but simply as of now, for an indefinite period, not only about what the community is, but more importantly of where the community is going. For the whole difficulty with the conception of the community of the past, the older integrated notion of the community, was that it was a view from the present looking backward, and the only possible sensible view of the community today, is from the present looking forward. For every community changes and goes somewhere. It may drift into problems, into chaos, or it may somehow organize what resources it has, what interests it has, what values that are there, even its concerns and anxieties and fears, into some kind of relatively stable, political consensus around which it can move.

This implies, as a corollary of that, that community leadership needs to carefully cultivate and develop patterns for effective representation in decision making. One of the most significant sociological lessons from an examination of communities of the past, in American life, is in fact, how undemocratic they were, how unrepresented were significant segments of the community. This is no longer viable, it is no longer possible. The political consensus that really makes a locality into a community today, requires that there by the constant searching for the means and mechanisms and instrumentalities by which there can be effectively represented, not merely symbolically represented, but *effectively* represented, every significant current of opinion and way of life within the community. And that includes now the minorities, and increasingly I think it will require that the poor will be consulted, not merely talked to as they have been in the past. And . . . it may even involve the youth. For these are the kinds of people who have been left out of representation.

Today, it seems to me, the urban community, if it is a community, can only act on the basis of a political consensus achieved in spite of the fragmentations that characterize its internal life and the intense pressures and pulls from a larger society around it. And it can only act on a political consensus that involves effective representation in decision-making by all those who are in the community. For we no longer live in a day in which there can be sizable numbers of human beings in the community who for all practical purposes do not count. We are living through a literal revolution in which I think we can all recognize that no longer in any community can one say of the Negroes—they don't count. Now, they do, and in large part, they count because they insisted on being counted, and every other group in our society including the youth, I think, are going to insist on being counted. Integration is the effective involvement of these people in the achievement of a consensus that enables any community to act in some kind of intelligent fashion in directing its energies toward action on its numerous problems.

pOliCE-COMMUNiTY RElATiONS

BERNARD J. CLARK

In these times of social upheaval much has been said and written about the subject of police-community relations. Usually this subject has been confused with
the term public relations. The police do use public relations but PUBLIC RELA-
TIONS IS NOT POLICE-COMMUNITY RELATIONS. What then is police-
community relations? We must first define some terms in order to avoid any
confusion on this subject.

Definitions

The title itself conveys the most common definition of Police-Community Relations. Here the term is used to refer to the positive interaction between members
of the Police Department and members of the Community. In actuality, Police-
Community Relations may be considered as all forms of interaction or relations
that exist between the Police Department and the Community. This involves
both negative and positive relations. The negative relations are generally those
that are unplanned, break-downs in communication, and obstacles to further
interaction situations. The positive relations are various interaction experiences

Source: Bernard J. Clark. Police-Community Relations. Criminal Justice Monograph,
Vol. 1, No. 5, 1969. Institute of Contemporary Corrections and the Behavioral Sciences.
Sam Houston State University. pp. 1-9. Reprinted with the kind permission of the editors
of Criminal Justice Monographs, Institute of Contemporary Corrections and the Behavioral
Sciences, Sam Houston State University, Huntsville, Texas.

that stimulate further communication and cooperation between the community and police. In speaking of Police-Community Relations, one usually has only the positive planned relations in mind. But both exist and must be considered in any discussion or program centered around the topic of Police-Community Relations.

Public relations, on the other hand, is the art of achieving good will through such techniques as publicity, advertising, promotions and even propaganda.

Publicity is the technique of telling the story of an organization, person or cause. Briefly, Webster tells us that it's advertising of any kind, or information with a news value designed to advance the interests of a person, place, cause, or institution usually appearing in public print. Basically, publicity is news.

Advertising can be treated rather briefly, because if we understand that publicity is news the basic difference between publicity and advertising is that with your advertising you have news but you must purchase space or time on a media in order to get your story told.

Promotion is usually a large scale operation which is well coordinated and has but one purpose in mind, and that is selling a product. It is a commercial venture that includes both publicity and advertising because in any promotional scheme there will be certain on-the-spot news items which can be considered publicity but there will be much more news that the promotion campaign may want to promote that actually will have to fall in the purview of advertising.

During the last few years the term "propaganda" has been used more often in a derogatory vein, connoting deception or distortion. This is unfortunate, when we hear the term "propaganda" as connected with any person or group it certainly leaves much to be desired and there is definitely a fear of the purposes of this person or group. Properly, propaganda is any organization or movement working for the propagation of a particular idea, doctrine, practice, or something of this nature.

History

The unplanned Police-Community Relations have a very long history. In fact, such relations have existed ever since the first organization of law enforcement agencies. Here, the major or greatest number of interactions with the community were quite negative. A person or group had little or no direct contact with the law enforcement officers unless he had broken the law or was suspected of breaking the law. The communication that existed was both unidirectional and authoritative, and marked with extreme antagonism, emotion, conflict, and other forms of negativism. Those who were not directly involved in interaction with police officers generally felt that police officers were a necessary evil to uphold the laws of the land. If anything they were feared, but definitely not loved. The image of police officers that developed was that of someone with a "strong

The Context of Police-Community Relations

back and a weak mind" that through brutal force enforced the law. The remnants of this image or attitude still exist today.

The actual organization of a Police-Community Relations Division by a police agency is a very recent event. The first such division was established in about 1957 by the St. Louis Board of Police Commissioners. Since 1957 Police-Community Relations Divisions have been set up in virtually all large police departments. However, a good many of these divisions have been poorly organized, lack real constructive programs and guidelines for constructive improvement of police-community relations, and are merely "eye wash" to impress city officials and the public in general. Hence, one must consider most Police-Community Relations projects as embryonic and in need of much more development, research, planning, and constructive action. Many have jumped on the band wagon of police-community relations without knowing or preparing to handle the problems and obstacles that must be resolved in order to realize any of the potential benefits. This then seems to be the state of police-community relations at the present time.

Need

At the present time we are faced with wide-ranging social change and population explosions which have produced an enormous amount of strain on the very fabrics of our society. Institutions and groups of people have grown apart through lack of communication, prejudices, discrimination, philosophies, and outright alienation from each other. In the brink of this situation, it becomes almost mandatory that we try to alleviate or resolve these problems by organized and constructive action. Law enforcement agencies of nation, cities, and towns need the support of the citizens they serve in order to provide better law enforcement services and a more harmonious law abiding nation as well as individual communities. In order to do this, the cooperation and assistance of each institution, group, and individual citizen must be stimulated and sustained. Police-Community Relations can provide a major step in this direction. It has the potential for creating and strengthening bonds of communication and participation between the police department and community so that they both are supported in fulfilling their responsibilities in law enforcement and honorable citizenship.

Functions and Goals

The major goal of all Police-Community Relations programs is to establish a better relationship and understanding between police officers and the citizens. Thus, there would ultimately be greater harmony and cooperation between the police and all people of the community. In order to achieve this goal, several functions have been proposed to be included in a Police-Community Relations Division. Some of these are as follows:

1. Develop programs to bring about a better understanding and improved cooperation with the community. Spearhead programs which would be designed to gain greater public support and confidence with a goal of reducing crime and delinquency.

2. Actively engage in various community relations projects and programs with civic and fraternal organizations, as well as the schools, in developing and presenting programs which contain material to stimulate greater respect for the law.

3. Coordinate activities of the Police Department in the area of Public Relations: speakers, tours, and development of special programs such as law enforcement week, and national police week.

4. Develop a positive and true image of the police function in maintenance of law and order, preservation of peace, and protection of the public.

5. Develop programs for presentation in police recruit and in-service training classes. These programs would be centered around the individual police officer's role in the area of police-community relations.

6. Provide a direct liaison between the police and minority group organizations in the handling of grievances and winning support for the police responsibilities.

7. Promote programs geared to assist the ordinary citizen and the rank-and-file policeman in getting along. This would entail as a vital part the support of the uniformed officer in the actions required of him in his line of duty.

8. Coordinate activities with community agencies and grassroots groups to assist their leaders in methods, systems, and referral contacts to resolve problems dealing with needed police service.

Acceptance of Police-Community Relations by Police Officers

The first, and maybe the most important and hardest, challenge of establishing a Police-Community Relations Division is to sell their program to other members of the police department. All personnel from the staff on down to the rank-and-file must support the program both verbally and in action. One officer who does not present the image that is trying to be conveyed to the general public by the police-community relations officers can raise havoc with the whole program. In fact, he can destroy in minutes the work of several men over many months or years.

The Context of Police-Community Relations

There seem to be at least two significant reasons why it is often very difficult to sell all police personnel on the importance of police-community relations. First, there exists the feeling that police-community relations should not be one of the functions or roles of a police officer. Second, the potential threat it seems to have for the maintenance of the *status quo*. The administration (power structure) are prone to see a police-community relations division as a threat to their status positions as well as a change in their responsibilities. Both the informal and formal arrangements that have been operating are affected by the change introduced with the bringing in of a police-community relations division.

Misconceptions or Bad Connotations of Police-Community Relations Programs

It is often felt that Police-Community Relations programs are geared to put the police officer on the spot by soliciting complaints from the public on how they were treated by individual officers. Such programs as complaint questionnaires or meetings of the citizens particularly for the purpose of allowing them to make complaints definitely tend to support the above adverse assumption. However, police-community relations programs should be aimed at supporting and enhancing the image of police officers instead of tearing it down. Complaints and problems should only be a small part of these programs. Even here, the complaints and problems should come from both the officers and citizens in a constructive attempt for them to work together in order that they may be resolved or alleviated. The stress must be on a mutual give and take in the common objective of making the situation better by all concerned taking an active and constructive part.

Many view police-community relations as merely "eye wash" to appease the public. In fact, it is often referred to as the "soft soap," "soft touch," or other like names connected with being servants to any whims of the citizens. In this light, police-community relations is seen to destroy the authoritarian function of the police department and make it a slave to the citizens, particularly minority groups.

Some police-community relations divisions have actually fallen into the above trap and have become nothing more than an "eye wash" operation. However, this does not have to be the case. Police-community relations programs can point out to the community the role of both the police department and each individual citizen in keeping the law and seeing that others also keep the law. Citizens can be made to understand the authority role of the police officer and how his role is required for the safety and protection of all the community. At the same time citizens can see how they have a responsibility to themselves and the community in helping police officers enforce the law.

An Adverse Consequence or
Possible Danger Inherent in Police-
Community Relations

There is the possibility that certain individual citizens or groups will try to take advantage of the police-community relations programs to further their own interest. In so doing they fail to consider the bad consequences their actions might have on the majority of people living in the community. Two examples come immediately to mind. First, people who have it in for the whole authority system of society may vent their feelings, hostilities, and anxieties on the police department. Here, the police department becomes a convenient scapegoat. Second, special interest groups, such as certain minorities, may attempt to use the police department as a lever to gain them more recognition, favors, and other partial treatment to gain their individual goals at the expense of the rest of society. Some individuals may claim police brutality in order to escape just punishment for unlawful acts.

Possible Benefits of Police-
Community Relations

The benefits that may come from a properly developed and planned police-community relations division are numerous. Some of the most evident and important benefits to both the community and police department are as follows:

1. A greater harmony between the police and all people of the community.
2. A decrease in the rate of crime and delinquency.
3. A better control of crime and delinquency through the apprehension, punishment, and rehabilitation of a larger number of law violators.
4. A re-establishment of communication lines into the community so that both community and police problems can be worked on and resolved.
5. Increased working relationships with citizen and official groups.
6. Strengthening of the recruit and in-service training programs to cover community relations subjects and programs in depth.
7. Prevention of situations of high tension between the police and community residents, and to help deal with such situations when they occur.
8. A more professional and influential police department.
9. A greater understanding and cooperation between the police department and citizens of the community.
10. A much better police image in the community.
11. Higher salaries for all personnel in the police department.

The Context of Police-Community Relations

Summary

Although Police-Community Relations is quite a recent phenomenon, it has shown real promise in making a much stronger working relationship between the police department and citizens of the community. At least this seems to have been the case for Police-Community Relations Programs that have been well planned, organized, directed, and put into operation.

However, many times police-community relations divisions have sponsored "watered down or eye wash" programs that have been merely to appease the public and have had little or no significant benefits to either the public or the police department. In fact, these type programs have soured both the citizens and police department personnel on even the mention of police-community relations.

In conclusion, the many important obstacles and problems connected with police-community relations are very evident. These must be acknowledged, taken into account, and effectively dealt with in order to realize the potential benefits from police-community relations programs. However, the benefits that can come to both the community and the police department far outweigh the several problems and obstacles. The united cooperation and participation of the police department personnel and all citizens of the community can make a better place to live for everyone.

COMMUNİTY RELATİONS

EGON BITTNER

One of the most vigorously advocated new developments in the field of police-craft is known under the heading of "Community Relations." The endeavors thus designated deserve consideration at two relatively distinct levels of analysis. First, in terms of their proximal causes and objectives and, second, as possibly part of an incipient shift in the overall orientation of all systems of remedial social control functioning in modern society.

Like most other recent accretions to police work, community relations activities take the form of a special assignment. Accordingly, departments have created Community Relations Units or appointed Community Relations Officers, whose task it is to achieve and maintain an ongoing exchange of views between the police and all segments of society, *especially* those groups whose aggrievement and disadvantage expresses itself in the waves of demonstrations of discontent that have been sweeping our cities in this decade.[1] Though one could probably not show that every effort in this direction has been mounted only after some specific incident of civil strife, there can be no doubt that the undertaking as a whole has been *reactive* in the sense that it followed external pressure rather than the spontaneous appreciation of the need. There is no strong argument against the police to be built on this observation. After all, they were not the only ones to learn the hard way, nor were they the last ones. But the emergency nature of the timing gave rise to serious difficulties.

Source: Egon Bittner. *The Functions of the Police in Modern Society*. Rockville, Maryland: National Institute of Mental Health, Center for Studies of Crime and Delinquency. 1970. pp. 114–118.

The Context of Police-Community Relations

In the first place, the response to outside conditions came to be viewed by many policemen as a coerced concession to rebellion. These men, who view themselves as custodians of the official order, consider it deplorable to enter any kind of negotiations with parties that dared to challenge this order. Second, because of the haste in which community relations work was undertaken the units were carelessly staffed and they suffered from a great deal of personnel turnover. This strengthened the argument of those who felt that the whole thing was unworkable in the first place. Finally, even though the units received broadly formulated mandates, it has not been made clear what sort of activities they should engage in.[2] Under the combined pressure of these difficulties, and under the pressure to do something, the work of the units tended to follow one or the other of the following two models.

PR Models

The simpler of the two options consists of implementing a public relations program along lines of least resistance. To transcend the limitations of past public relations efforts which consisted mainly of furnishing speakers on invitation, the Community Relations Units proceeded to organize committees of citizens in various parts of cities, which were supposed to function as market places for the exchange of ideas. Organizationally, the resulting set-up is not unlike the PTA in being closely attuned to the needs of the existing system. But it actually never came to function even as well as the PTA. The shortcoming of the approach has been stated in these terms: "The formalized program is impressive on paper but in action we found a serious communication blockage. It is difficult to clearly determine the reasons for this blockage but certainly the defensive attitude of the police is a contributing factor and has inhibited the productivity of the district committees. Additionally, selection of committee members is based on those whom the police consider 'responsible' and our discussion of this issue with top police commanders brought forth a feeling that those people were responsible if they 'agreed' with police thinking. This line of thought is a major stumbling block toward community involvement in the program."[3] It must, of course, not be assumed that responsible citizens in the above sense are wholly unrepresentative of community sentiments, but in view of the fact that the program was primarily oriented to those groups with whom relations were strained, the outcome scarcely qualifies as a success. It merely displays the availability of already existing support and it leaves all existing misunderstandings and animosities intact. Indeed, alienated groups tend to view such activities as further evidence of the refusal of the police to hear their grievances and as an underhanded ploy that forces them further into estrangement from the "establishment."

PCR Model

The more ambitious alternative is for Community Relations Units to reach to the grassroots of discontent. While this does lead to the establishment of genuinely trusting relations between some policemen and some leaders of alienated groups, it results, where it succeeds, in the isolation of the effort within the police department. Officers who manage to establish viable and reciprocally understanding ties with people living in ghettos, skid rows, and tenderloin districts are often viewed by their colleagues as having joined "the opposition,"[4] or, somewhat more sanely, as being engaged in an activity that has nothing to do with police work and should be left to social workers. Thus, while the first approach fails because it leaves out those groups to which the program is primarily directed, the second fails because it leaves out the police department.

Program Evaluation

Neither of the two programs should be judged a total failure, however, and there is at least a chance that the second may learn to cope with internal resistance as it learns to overcome external opposition. In a situation where success is hard to come by, every small gain counts. But realism requires the recognition that the gap community relations work was intended to bridge still exists. At best, a few lines of communication have been strung across it. Whether they will avail when they are truly needed is highly uncertain. Surely the effort must be strengthened as far as possible under conditions of abated stress, and in this respect the recommendations of the President's Commission on Law Enforcement and Administration of Justice are highly meritorious. In this it is of utmost importance that the perimeter of police interest be as all encompassing as possible. Some groups may remain permanently beyond reach, but as the endeavor contains no room for hurt feelings or indignation, there can be no end to trying. In particular, and this is far more serious risk to the enterprise than is allowed, those men in the Community Relations Units who are strongly impressed by the grievances against their institution must not yield to the temptation to give up on the police.

But police community relations work can be conceived as having an import that goes beyond its function of, so to speak, helping to "keep the lid on." Leaving the public-relations-type programs entirely out of consideration, let us first take note that the activities do not constitute a social service in the ordinary sense. Though it often takes the form of finding jobs for persons with police records who cannot obtain employment otherwise, or of organizing recreational facilities for youth who might otherwise turn to delinquency, there are merely instrumentalities to reach an ulterior objective. That is, on the surface it is always some individual or group of individuals whose descent into misery or transgression is intercepted. The real targets of the interventions are, however, networks of social relations. More than changing persons, it is the changing of alignments among persons, and between parts of society, that is the aim of community relations work. This involves a profound reorientation in the direction of police interest.

According to inherited conceptions of remedial control, risks to the social order are always found in individuals and the preferred way of handling the problems they create is to do something for them or against them. The police are not unique in focusing on individuals; the whole spectrum of preventive and remedial control in our society is principally person-oriented. Every problem always turns to something being the matter with someone in particular. Thus, physicians and psychiatrists combat diseases in patients, and lawyers and social workers aid clients, and policemen deal with delinquents and derelicts. But recently a new and not yet well formulated interest has come to the fore—of which we take police community relations work to be a part—which directs its interests less to the sick, the incompetent, and the deviant as individuals, and more to conditions of existence, to the social fabric, and to cultural change. Though this interest draws support from scholarly sources, mainly social science research, and is in this sense well founded, it has been, thus far, an uncertain quest.[5]

Because the critique of the social order is a matter of political concern and because professionals seek to remain aloof of politics, they have not found any fully acceptable ways of dealing with what they discern to be the ills of society. Nor are there any easy solutions of this dilemma in sight. The main direct result of the new interest has been that the person who creates difficulties, or who is failing, is perceived as presenting a far more complex problem than when he was considered as an isolated case. Thus, for example, from the vantage points of this new interest, a diabetic patient is no longer viewed as merely a case of a diseased pancreas, but someone with inherited dietary habits, occupying a role in a network of reciprocal obligations, encumbered by certain culturally set prejudices about health and illness, and commanding limited resources for his care, all of which becomes a part of the picture and plays a role in setting a course of remedies. In short, the changes were not earthshaking and have been largely confined to making care more careful. This is, by and large, what is meant by social medicine, social psychiatry, and is what Judge Allen appears to have in mind when he calls for the "socialization" of the administration of criminal justice.[6]

Opportunities to Learn

In sum, the interest in situations, in circumstances, in background, in relatedness, or broadly speaking, in the sociocultural—as opposed to concern for individual and isolated cases—has not led to radical changes in professional practice; instead, it functioned mainly as a general educative influence.

It does not seem too far fetched to suppose that police community relations work might be the vehicle for such broadening educational experiences. The men assigned to the units could retain the specific role assigned to them in the administrative scheme of things. In addition to this, however, all recruits could have a protracted period of supervised practice in the field at an early point in their training. This experience contains opportunities for learning three lessons that cannot be taught adequately in formal courses of instruction. The first concerns the dynamics of community organization. The second has to do with deviance as a cultural rather than an individual phenomenon.[7] The third pertains to the effects of policy on the lives of the people to whom it applies.

Of these the last is by far the most important because it affords the policeman the opportunity to look at the effects of his own activity. In the professionalization of the police it is, of course, of decisive significance that the practitioner gain a firm understanding of the product of his interventions. In the past policemen have disavowed such concerns under the pretense that they merely enforce the law and that it is not their business to decide whether this is good or bad in the long run. But we know that this is a misconception; that they, in fact, have an enormous degree of freedom in setting peace-keeping and law-enforcement policies. Thus they cannot be allowed to evade the question raised long ago by social scientists about the extent to which defining someone officially as a deviant has the effect of solidifying his deviant identity and of contributing to the proliferation of deviance in society.[8] Unfortunately such questions are deeply embedded in long standing ideological conflict. But avoiding them for this reason is also an evasive tactic. For if knowledge and clarity is the hallmark of the professional, then obscurantism cannot be permitted any defense at all.

References

1. The desire of the police to open consultative contacts with ethnic minorities and lower class groups is part of a larger drive in this direction. Mayor A.J. Cervantes of St. Louis explained it in these terms: "We have found out that ghetto neighborhoods cannot be operated on from the outside alone. The people within them should have a voice, and our experience has shown that it is often a voice that speaks with good sense, since the practical aspects of the needs of the ghetto people are so much clearer to the people there than they are to anyone else." As quoted in the *Report of the National Advisory Commission on Civil Disorders*, New York: Bantam Books, 1968, p. 287.

2. See, President's Commission on Law Enforcement and Administration of Justice, *Task Force Report: The Police*, Washington, D.C.: U.S. Government Printing Office, 1967, pp. 149–163.

3. *A National Survey of Police and Community Relations,* a report prepared by the National Center on Police and Community Relations, School of Police Administration and Public Safety, Michigan State University, East Lansing, Michigan, for the President's Commission on Law Enforcement and Administration of Justice, Washington, D.C.: U.S. Government Printing Office, 1967, at p. 72.

4. In one department a unit of this nature is referred to by some officers as the "Commie Unit."

5. The formulation of the new interest is most advanced in psychiatry where a specialty known as Social Psychiatry has developed; its drift is described in Egon Bittner, "The Structure of Psychiatric Influence, *Mental Hygiene,* 5 (1968) 423–430.

6. F. A. Allen, "The Borderland of the Criminal Law: Problems of 'Socializing' Criminal Justice," *Social Service Review,* 32 (1958) 107–119.

7. The study of deviance as a cultural phenomenon is perhaps best exemplified in the papers collected in H.S. Becker (ed.), *The Other Side,* New York: The Free Press, 1964. It is rather obvious that policemen doing community relations work are in a uniquely advantageous position to engage in such studies.

8. E.M. Lemert, *Social Pathology,* New York: McGraw-Hill, 1951, see also, R.D. Schwartz and J.H. Skolnick, "Two Studies of Legal Stigma," *Social Problems,* 10 (1962) 134–142.

CHAPTER **1-9**

issues in police-community relations

ELEANOR HARLOW

Attitudes toward Police

A number of recent studies[1] of public attitudes toward police reveal that a majority of citizens have a high opinion of police work. This finding would appear to indicate that there is no significant problem in the area of police-community relations, which would no doubt be true if hostility toward the police were evenly distributed throughout the population.[2] However, according to a survey conducted by the National Opinion Research Center, nonwhites, especially Negroes, hold significantly more negative opinions of police performance: 23 per cent of all white people thought that police were doing an "excellent" job of enforcing the law, as compared with only 15 per cent of nonwhites; 7 per cent of whites felt the police were doing a "poor" job, contrasted with 16 per cent of nonwhites.[3] There is considerable disparity in the attitudes of black and white Americans with regard to police effectiveness, police discourtesy and misconduct, police honesty, and the need for police protection; and similar differences in attitudes have been found among other ethnic minority groups and the poor.[4]

The development of the civil rights movement has significantly affected police work, especially in the area of police-community relations. The movement has raised the group consciousness of minorities and increased their aware-

Source: Eleanor Harlow. *Problems in Police-Community Relations: A Review of the Literature.* Information Review on Crime and Delinquency. Vol. 1, No. 5, 1969. Reprinted with permission of the National Council on Crime and Delinquency.

ness of their rights under law, thus lowering their tolerance of indignities inflicted by police and greatly intensifying the demand for equal law enforcement. In recent years the emphasis of the civil rights movement on nonviolent integration has been displaced by feelings of hatred and frustration resulting from the belief that white society will never end discrimination voluntarily. This presents the police, the most visible representative of white society and the established power structure, with new situations and problems which they have not been adequately prepared to handle.

The two major complaints of minority group members against law enforcement are inadequate protection in ghetto areas and discriminatory practices such as brutality and disrespectful treatment.[5] There is little doubt that police misconduct does occur; more, certainly, than is recorded. The President's Commission on Law Enforcement and Administration of Justice reports that it has "evidence from its own studies and from police officials themselves, that in some cities a significant percentage of policemen assigned to high-crime areas do treat citizens with disrespect and sometimes abuse them physically."[6]

Still, there is considerable disagreement between the police and some members of the public as to whether police brutality is a common practice in this country. Even the definition of brutality is debated; the police maintain that only unnecessary physical force can be considered brutal, while many citizens include such aspects as verbal and psychological abuse and harassment. If brutality is broadly defined to include the latter, as indeed appears appropriate, there can be no doubt that it exists in a large number of police organizations today.[7] Even if limited to physical abuse, police brutality toward citizens appears to be far from rare.[8]

However, some of the friction which exists between the police and the community with regard to police malpractice is actually the result of misunderstanding or misinterpretation. Where there is anonymity of individual officers, there is generalization and stereotyping by citizens; where there is racial hatred and distrust, there is misinterpretation of police actions; and where there is a lack of communication with and confidence in the police, there is also a tendency on the part of citizens to believe the worst. Thus, the actions of those police who do behave unprofessionally reflect not only upon the entire department but on police in general, and whenever questionable tactics are employed against minority group members anywhere, hostility to police everywhere is increased.

One important fact to consider is that whether or not police brutality exists, if significant numbers of people believe that it does, it then becomes a serious and very real problem. For example, a widespread belief that police are unjust or brutal results in loss of respect for and cooperation with any police officer. When people do not accept police authority as legitimate and challenge their authority at every point of contact, the police feel the need to assert personal authority by force in order to "handle the situation" in the absence of respect for the badge and uniform. Thus the belief that police are brutal often becomes a self-fulfilling expectation.

Although the focal point of the conflict between law enforcement and the community is often the relationship between the Negro or other ethnic minorities and the police, there is a highly vocal minority of whites who are hostile to police and dissatisfied with their police departments. Whites from the lower socio-economic groups, "liberals," and especially youths have the same general complaints against the police as the minority groups.[9]

Recent studies indicate that adolescents, not only from the ghetto areas but also from the middle class, tend to be extremely hostile toward police.[10] On the other hand, the police attitude toward juveniles in some areas has been characterized as "typically and constantly aggressively hostile."[11] It is possible that, since police attitudes tend toward preservation of the status quo, youth today are perceived as a serious threat, if only in terms of dress and behavior. Since a large percentage of offenses in the United States are committed by youths, this mutual lack of respect and understanding is a major problem. Many police departments recognize the importance of improving relationships with youths and in some places police originate and operate recreational activities such as boys' clubs, baseball teams, and summer camps, or organize Junior Police or Safe Driving Clubs.[12] Police juvenile units have been established and staffed with specialists to work with juveniles. But, judging from the hostility and lack of understanding between youths and the policeman on the beat, much remains to be done.

The growing opposition between the police and some segments of the public would seem to imply that new methods of law enforcement are necessary. In the past, the main source of hostility and noncooperation came from those persons who were actively engaged in crime and the police role was more explicit. Police generally could count on the assistance, or at least passivity, of the law-abiding population. Today, however, civil disobedience, active resistance, and harassment on the part of otherwise noncriminal citizens complicates enforcement of the law.

> The fact that the police can no longer take for granted that noncriminal citizens are also nonhostile citizens may be the most important problem which even the technically proficient department must face.[13]

Police "Subculture"

The current forces of change in society, including urbanization, racial integration, automation, secularization, and redistribution of power, are presenting unprecedented problems for the police, for which they are not responsible and with which they are not prepared to deal. Generally, their response has been to align themselves against those groups which favor change and to attempt to control their activities repressively.

> As the complexity of our urban society increases, the black and white absolutes in which the police have traditionally dealt are becoming totally inadequate. Because the greatest part of police work is now concerned with non-criminal matters, the police are confronted with a bewildering array of new problems for which their stereotyped views are hardly a match. Thus ill equipped to solve problems, the police have developed a vindictiveness toward those elements of society they feel are responsible for their plight.[14]

As a result, police isolation in many areas has become acute. The absence of communication and support from the community has resulted in a police "subculture" within which police interact in a closely knit and largely self-regulated group.

> The policeman's sense of alienation from society results in the development of a distinctive "subculture" or "code" among police officers by which they can live, thus providing a basis for self-respect independent to some degree of civilian attitudes.[15]

Some of this in-group feeling may be an understandable response to public apathy and noncooperation, role ambiguity and conflict, and contradictory demands and restrictions. In his study of the police in eight communities, James Q. Wilson found that patrolmen and administrators alike were critical of the community for not having clear and agreed-upon law enforcement objectives; resentful of criticism the police receive when, by default, they must handle awkward situations which the community itself has created; angry at the "leniency" of the courts and the "sensationalism" of the press; and distressed at the attention awarded groups which urge others to disobey the law and which resist legitimate authority with charges of "police brutality."[16] Faced with this situation, the police may have some justification for their defensiveness and clannishness, but the result is that they have turned inward and, as pointed out by Turner, have become in effect a closed society which is jealous of its prerogatives, resentful of criticism and "outside meddling," and anchored to tradition.[17]

The tendency of police to defend the status quo and to decry the "moral decay" of society and the "disrespect for law and order" sets them against the forces of social change and alienates those groups which favor such change.

> Their somewhat Victorian view of life places them on a collision course with a sizable segment of the public who view the "system" which the police represent as an anachronism in our modern urban society.[18]

Police overstep their proper role in society when they attempt to prevent political or social change and they lose much public support by placing themselves in this untenable position.

> Just as police are not responsible for programs to change social mores, neither are they justified in taking steps to prevent such change. Police authority derives only from the law and not from social mores. Police are required to enforce the law but are not authorized to enforce social mores.[19]

Police Prejudice

Police attitudes and values significantly influence their relations with the community. Persons attracted to police work and those most "successful" on the job tend to be more conservative or reactionary, and the "police subculture" as well as the structure itself reinforce these attitudes.

> The inherent conservatism of the police is hardened by their feeling of being unjustly maligned and deprecated. . . . Since their severest critics seem to be partisans of the left, the police reflexively polarize to the right.[20]

These prejudices, if uncontrolled, will be manifested in their enforcement of the law. Since police cannot enforce all laws all of the time but must give priority to those offenses they believe most gravely affect the community, selection often will be strongly influenced by their own value system. One view of this is expressed by William W. Turner, a former FBI agent, in his book, *The Police Establishment:*

> These right-wing prejudices on the part of the police show up most pointedly in the hounding of leftists, liberals, review-board proponents, civil rights demonstrators, anti-Vietnam war protestors, campus radicals, and just about anyone who is not a brass-band patriot.[21]

Recently, this kind of prejudice has been most apparent in the police response to mass demonstrations and "protest marches." Mass demonstrations of a political or social nature are a relatively new phenomenon, at least in the form they are now taking. Today, a demonstration involving thousands of people is the common response of citizens with grievances. Police, who in the past have been accustomed to receiving respect and compliance from the average noncriminal citizen, are faced with what appears to them as widespread disrespect for the law and a personal threat both to their beliefs and to their own status and authority. Finding the expected obedience lacking, the police may attempt to extract the respect of the public by aggressive methods.[22]

Except for those instances where tight control by police superiors or the political administration has been operative, the handling of mass demonstrations by police has been generally inadequate and often has been the prime element in aggravating police-community tensions. Unable to successfully separate personal philosophy from job performance, "even the more scrupulous police have a tendency to apply dual standards to 'average' citizens and to nonconformists, members of minority groups and persons of unorthodox political and religious beliefs."[23] This selective enforcement of the law, especially when consistently favoring one group over another, has its consequences in loss of respect for police and the law even by persons who are not directly affected.

Prejudicial application of the law by police has resulted in a polarization of community attitudes along emotionally charged lines which only intensifies the political and social polarization already taking place in this country. Thus, if you are "for" ending the war in Vietnam, you must be "against" police and thus against "law and order"; if you march for civil rights, you are expected to be "against" police and "for" social anarchy; a bumper sticker reading "Support your local police" is assumed to imply "rightist" tendencies. By taking sides in political and social issues, the police have become a "hot" issue themselves and politicians all too frequently take advantage of such irrational thinking. All of this adds to community tensions and prevents the discovery of realistic solutions to law enforcement problems.

Because of strong support from reactionary elements of society, police have tended to return the favor by adopting and supporting conservative attitudes while excluding or opposing more liberal groups.[24] What does not seem to be acknowledged is that police need the cooperation of all segments of society. "The alternative may be a police force which, however competent, functions as an army of occupation."[25]

The "Police Problem": What Are the Issues?

Much attention is given, in the literature and in the press and other media, to the question of police "prejudice," discriminatory application of the law, and the "improper" use of police discretion. It is proposed that undesirable police candidates be weeded out by means of psychological testing; that civilian review boards be set up to judge police behavior and punish malpractice; that political control over the policing function be increased; that police "discretion" be minimized by establishing detailed standards of police procedure; or that police be "professionalized" in terms of education and training, better weapons, improved communications, and specialization by function. The police emphasize that, while they *are* educating, specializing, professionalizing, standardizing, and supervising, nothing seems to please the public or make their job any easier. In sum, there is little agreement within the community and between the police and community as to the proper role of law enforcement or the best means of carrying it out.

Discretion

The second major issue in the debate over police practices in the community is the use of personal discretion by police officers in matters of law enforcement and maintenance of order.[26] Officially the police are supposed to have almost no discretion. James Wilson writes that, although by law in many places and in theory everywhere police are supposed to arrest everyone they see committing an offense, discretion is inevitable, partly because police cannot do everything, partly because many laws require interpretation before they can be applied, and partly because public opinion would not tolerate full enforcement of all laws all the time.[27]

With regard to setting down specific instructions for police practices, Wilson points out that it is seldom possible to specify in advance the circumstances under which a patrolman should intervene or the way in which he should handle a given situation. With respect to the preventive patrol function, the patrolman can be given instructions about *how* to intervene even if not about *whether* to intervene, but with regard to maintaining order, guidance on how to intervene is especially lacking. What not to do can be clearly specified but what the officer should do cannot because so much depends on the particular time, place, event, and personality. Rules may be prescribed for order maintenance situations but they will of necessity be either ambiguous (open to various interpretations and failing to specify the circumstances under which they are operative) or equivocal (combining inconsistent or competing values). Faced with such policies, the patrolman is likely to perceive standards and rules as unrealistic and irrelevant. Wilson found that the patrolman most frequently expresses the view that "you can't go by what the book says."[28]

If the police feel that they cannot "go by the book," and therefore that they must rely on their own judgment to meet an immediate situation, then the basis for much of the conflict between police and the community becomes obvious. First, the public believes in the legal fiction that the police are supposed to be the impartial instrument of the law and that, if the law is to be applied equally, they must remain personally uninvolved in their job of bringing to justice those persons who violate any part of the legislated criminal code. Their response to the police problem is to demand more controls over police "misbehavior" or "malpractice" as if the police had deliberately chosen to use their own discretion when in fact they could have followed the letter of the law. In reality, while no doubt clear-cut violation of the law by police does occur, in many cases personal discretion is unavoidable and the problem becomes not one of eliminating discretion (an impossible goal) but of improving the ability of those men exercising it to do so in accord with community norms and values.

Wilson emphasizes the difference between two functions of the police, that of enforcing the law and that of maintaining order, and explains that the patrolman's role is defined more by his responsibility for the latter. Police procedures in handling cases of homicide or assault require little or no discretion as the law is quite specific with regard to enforcement issues. The problems arise with regard to preventing or controlling "disorder." Statutes defining "disorderly conduct" or "disturbing the peace" are examples of laws which are not only ambiguous but, as Wilson points out, necessarily so.[29] What is considered disorderly behavior varies widely with the community, and whether the policeman intervenes in a given situation depends, in the absence of a complaint by a citizen, on his own determination of what "society" believes to be disorderly or "disturbing." Wilson found that the policeman believes that most people share his disapproval of public impropriety and agree with his judgment that a person who publicly ignores community mores is more likely to break community laws than one who does not ignore them.

Thus lacking specific rules and guidelines, the police feel they must go on what cues they have to determine what behavior shall be considered unseemly, who is to blame for conduct that is agreed to be wrong, and which persons are most likely to cause further trouble. Wilson writes that "the patrolman believes with considerable justification that teenagers, Negroes, and lower-income persons commit a disproportionate share of all reported crimes"; that being in those population categories at all makes one, statistically, more suspect than other persons; and that to be in those categories and to behave unconventionally is to make oneself a prime suspect. The police believe that they would be neglecting their duty if they did not treat such persons with suspicion, routinely question them on the street, and detain them for longer questioning if a crime has occurred in the area.[30]

The use of discretion by police, then, depends not so much (as the public tends to believe) on the whim of the individual officer as it does on the nature of the policing task. As Wilson explains, it depends on whether the situation is primarily one of law enforcement or one of order maintenance and whether the police response is police-invoked or citizen-invoked.[31] This means that any attempt to alter the way in which police use their discretion must consider the extent to which officers can or cannot be induced to act in accordance with rules set down in advance. The extent to which discretion can be limited may depend not on the personal qualities or skills of the officers but on the organizational and legal definition of the policeman's task.[32]

Community Control of Police

Before the community can modify the way in which police functions are carried out, it must understand to what extent the "style" of policing is subject to its decision-making processes. Wilson observes that, although deliberate community choices may have a great effect on police personnel, budgets, salaries, and organization, they rarely have more than a limited and direct effect on police behavior.

> How the police, especially the patrolmen, handle the routine situations that bring them most frequently into contact with the public can be determined by explicit political decisions only to the extent that such behavior can be determined by the explicit decisions of the police administrator, and the administrator's ability to control the discretion of his subordinates is in many cases quite limited by the nature of the situation and the legal constraints that govern police behavior.[33]

This fact is particularly important, in the present context, with regard to one major source of community conflict: civilian review of police practices or police handling of citizen grievances. It is generally assumed by partisans of both sides that the establishing of a civilian review board will seriously affect (positively or negatively) police operations and the entire style of policing. However, it appears reasonable that, although the existence of a review board controlled by civilians probably would affect police-community relations (for better or for worse, depending on the politically engendered passions involved), there might be little or no effect on underlying policies of the police department. In support of this view, Wilson maintains that "though the [civilian review board] issue is passionately debated, it is not clear that, however it is resolved, it will have much effect on the substantive police policies that are in effect—partly because some are not 'policies' at all but styles created by general organizational arrangements and departmental attitudes and partly because grievance procedures deal with specific complaints about unique circumstances, not with general practices of the officers."[34]

Even if political control of police by the community were possible, problems in police-community relations would exist, especially in areas where the community is least homogeneous. Both the nature of our society and that of the police function within it lead to conflict between the police and at least some members of society.

> Order maintenance means managing conflict, and conflict implies disagreement over what should be done, how, and to whom. Conflict is found in all social strata and thus in all strata there will be resentment, often justified, against particular police interventions (or their absence)....[35]

In those places in which disagreement and conflicting norms and values are most evident (metropolitan areas) or where attitudes and behaviors differ most from those of the middle-class legal code (lower-class, minority group ghettos) or moral order (intellectual or "hippie" communities), managing conflict and "disorder" will be most problematic and police-community relations most volatile.

At this juncture the bases for "the police problem" become apparent. Policing in a democratic society is essentially a job of managing conflict, especially for the patrolman, who spends a great part of his time handling order-maintenance situations. Conflict is inherent in this type of social order and is greatest in a time of transition when norms and values are changing, when the bases for power are shifting, and when social groups are splitting, coalescing on different grounds, and polarizing in a struggle for power. The police, whose individual members are drawn from one of these social groups, are given the responsibility (and the authority) to "maintain order and prevent disorder" in terms of vaguely defined (legally and socially) law. Because what the police should do and how they should do it cannot be standardized for every situation, they are required to decide for themselves, often instantly and in a hostile environment, not merely what is "legal" or illegal, but what is right and wrong, what is "order" and when does order become "disorder," what is an "antisocial" act within a given context, and what behavior can be considered "disturbing" to society. These are issues which social scientists and lawyers might be hard put to answer and over which different groups and individuals certainly would disagree. The police cry that no matter what they do they are criticized is valid and probably necessaily so. In a situation of competing and conflicting values and norms, someone is going to feel that police interference was unnecessary, morally wrong, inadequate, illegal, discriminatory, badly undertaken, or unjust.

Police-Community Relations Programs

One popular solution to the problem of conflict mediation, which has been widely proposed and is being tried in many places, is the police-community relations unit operating within the department to establish and operate community relations programs of various kinds. The community relations program is most frequently proposed as a solution to police-minority group relations.

The emphasis is understandable since the most striking deterioration in police relations with the community has occurred in nonwhite ghetto areas, and the issues of law enforcement and the role of the police in society have become intricately tied to the issues of race and racial conflict in this country. It appears that minority group attitudes toward police and police mishandling of situations in ghetto areas often have sparked the riots which have caused much destruction in many American cities. In April 1967, the President's Crime Commission virtually predicted the July riots in Detroit and Newark. In a warning largely ignored by the police and city authorities, the Commission identified a dozen cities which were potentially dangerous because "police relations with minority groups had sunk to explosively low levels. . . . The trouble stemmed in large measure from real and imagined grievances that led minorities to view the police as enemies. . . . Unless the police confronted frankly and effectively the legitimate grievances of the minorities, trouble was in the offing."[36]

Many police departments do recognize the importance of good community relations even if only to ensure support for their operations and simplify the job of law enforcement. However, because of this emphasis much of the police effort to improve relations with the community has shortsightedly emphasized the "public relations" function, essentially the upgrading of the police image by "propaganda" and advertising techniques.[37] While the police image does indeed need upgrading, this activity, combined with occasional pacifying statements to problem groups, is inadequate for anything but the most temporary conciliation.

> A community-relations program is not a *public*-relations program to "sell the police image" to the people. It is not a set of expedients whose purpose is to tranquilize for a time an angry neighborhood. . . . It is a long-range, full scale effort to acquaint the police and the community with each other's problems and to stimulate action aimed at solving those problems.[38]

Also, police-community relations is not merely police-minority group relations. Although, as the President's Commission has pointed out, community relations "is a matter of greatest importance in any community that has a substantial minority population,"[39] such programs must be more broadly based.

> Police-community relations programs should not be thought of as being solely aimed at relieving racial tensions. They should be much broader in scope than that. They can reasonably be expected to help channel the developing attitudes of the community's young people, regardless of race, into more constructive views of the police function.[40]

There are many groups within a community, and though police may be tempted to establish relations only with those who appear to need it most, they are obligated to serve all groups impartially. One way is to provide a forum for representatives of these groups and subgroups for regular discussion of mutual problems.[41]

> The [President's] Commission recommends: Police departments in all large communities should have community-relations machinery consisting of a headquarters unit that plans and supervises the department's community-relations programs.[42]

The Context of Police-Community Relations

However, there is no specific formula which can be applied in all communities. Although there are some national trends, problems in and solutions to police-community relations are often unique at the local level, depending on the particular political, social, and economic conditions as well as on the nature of the police department and its operations in that area. No two programs can be identical but certain patterns can be found.

Conclusion

Although a number of police departments have made admirable efforts to improve their relationships with the public they serve, the police generally have not recognized the full importance of maintaining good relations with the community. The more common response to the problems of contemporary law enforcement has been negative. Instead of updating their approach, reorganizing the system, and adapting to new conditions, the police have frequently been resentful of constructive criticism, blaming increasing difficulties on the "meddling" of the courts, the "moral decay" of society, and the "anarchist" tendencies of dissident groups. Their approach to community relations has been unimaginative and, except for a few notable examples, has consisted mainly of token gestures to youth and minorities or communication only with those groups which already support them.

Refusing to accommodate changes which are taking place, the police have become increasingly alienated from significant segments of society; the result is a loss of citizen cooperation, without which enforcement tends to repression and sometimes violence.

Although meaningful police-community relations programs will help to alleviate problems facing law enforcement through mutual understanding and cooperation, ultimately the entire police system will have to be reorganized and restructured and a new conception of the role and functions of police formulated if law enforcement in the United States is to be more than a malfunctioning anachronism.

Although society must keep an open mind to accept and support improvements on the part of the police and must understand that policing a democratic society is an extremely difficult job, "one imperative is clear: it is police who must get in step with society, not vice versa."[43]

References

1. National Opinion Research Center, *A National Sample Survey Approach to the Study of the Victims of Crime and Attitudes Toward Law En-*

forcement and Justice (Chicago: unpublished, 1966); Gallup Poll, *Tabulation Request Survey*, AIPO no. 709, prepared for the President's Commission on Law Enforcement and Administration of Justice, 1966; Bureau of Social Science Research, *Salient Findings on Crime and Attitudes toward Law Enforcement in the District of Columbia*, a preliminary technical report submitted to the U.S. Department of Justice, Office of Law Enforcement Assistance, 1966; Joseph D. Lohman and Gordon E. Misner, *The Police and the Community*, Field Surveys IV, vol. 2, report submitted to the President's Commission on Law Enforcement and Administration of Justice (Washington, D.C.: U.S. Government Printing Office, 1966); *A National Survey of Police and Community Relations*, Field Survey V, report submitted to the President's Commission on Law Enforcement and Administration of Justice (Washington, D.C.: U.S. Government Printing Office, 1967).

2. President's Commission on Law Enforcement and Administration of Justice, *Task Force Report: The Police* (Washington, D.C.: U.S. Government Printing Office, 1967), p. 146.

3. President's Commission on Law Enforcement and Administration of Justice, *The Challenge of Crime in a Free Society* (Washington, D.C.: U.S. Government Printing Office, 1967), p. 99.

4. *Op. cit. supra* note 2, pp. 146–48.

5. *A National Survey of Police and Community Relations*, report prepared for the President's Commission on Law Enforcement and Administration of Justice (Washington, D.C.: U.S. Government Printing Office, 1967), p. 14.

6. *Op. cit. supra* note 3, p. 115. Also, see *Police Power and Civil Rights: The Case for an Independent Police Review Board* (New York: American Civil Liberties Union, no date), pp. 6–13.

7. *Op. cit. supra* note 5, p. 154. For examples of police brutality and discussion of issues, also see Ed. Gray, *The Big Blue Line* (New York: Coward-McCann, 1967).

8. Direct observation of police practices in encounters with citizens in three large U.S. cities revealed that use of unnecessary physical force is not uncommon. Albert J. Reiss, "Police Brutality: Answers to Key Questions," *Transaction*, July 1968, pp. 10–20

9. *Op. cit. supra* note 5, p. 12.

10. George Edwards, *The Police on the Urban Frontier* (New York: Institute of Human Relations, 1968), pp. 82–83.

11. Lohman and Misner, *op. cit. supra* note 1, p. 153.

12. George W. O'Connor and Nelson A. Watson, *Juvenile Delinquency and Youth Crime: The Police Role* (Washington, D.C.: International Association of Chiefs of Police, 1964).

13. James Q. Wilson, "Police Morale, Reform, and Citizen Respect: The Chicago Case," *The Police: Six Sociological Essays*, David J. Bordua, ed. (New York: John Wiley, 1967), p. 158.

14. William W. Turner, *The Police Establishment* (New York: G.P. Putnam's Sons, 1968), pp. 20–21.

15. *Op. cit. supra* note 13, p. 138.

16. James Q. Wilson, *Varieties of Police Behavior: The Management of Law and Order in Eight Communities* (Cambridge, Mass.: Harvard University Press, 1968), p. 78.

17. William W. Turner, *The Police Establishment* (New York: G.P. Putnam's Sons, 1968), pp. 20–21.

18. *Op. cit. supra* note 5, p. 24.

19. Nelson A. Watson, *Police-Community Relations* (Washington, D.C.: International Association of Chiefs of Police, 1966), pp. 35–36.

20. *Op. cit. supra* note 17, p. 269.

21. *Id.*, p. 271.

22. Gerhard J. Falk, "The Public's Prejudice Against the Police," *American Bar Association Journal*, August 1964, pp. 754–57.

23. *Op. cit. supra* note 17, p. 14.

24. *Id.*, p. 18.

25. *Op. cit. supra* note 10, p. 85.

26. For an in-depth analysis of police discretion and the role of police and the law with respect to the decision to arrest, see Wayne R. LaFave, *Arrest: The Decision to Take a Suspect into Custody* (New York: Little, Brown, 1965).

27. *Op. cit. supra* note 16, p. 7.

28. *Id.*, p. 66.

29. *Id.*, p. 21.

30. *Id.*, p. 40.

31. *Id.*, p. 85.

32. *Id.*, p. 11.

33. *Id.*, p. 227.

34. *Id.*, p. 229.

35. *Id.*, p. 296.

36. *Op. cit. supra* note 17, p. 305.

37. Charles E. Moore, "PR—Public Relations, Public Responsibility," *Police Chief*, March 1967, pp. 12–27.

38. *Op. cit. supra* note 3, p. 100.

39. *Id.*, pp. 100–01.

40. *Op. cit. supra* note 19, p. 19.

41. James J. Allman, "Establishing a Police-Community Relations Office within a Police Department," *Police and the Changing Community: Selected Readings*, Nelson A. Watson, ed. (Washington, D.C.: International Association of Chiefs of Police, 1965), p. 104.

42. *Op. cit. supra* note 3, p. 100.

43. *Op. cit. supra* note 17, p. 27.

PART II

THE POLICE ROLE iN CONTEMPORARY SOCiETY

Introduction

Individual policemen and law enforcement agencies are both praised for their services and condemned for their insensitivity to citizen and community needs. Regardless of kind or quality of criticism, however, almost everyone agrees that we need policing and that the level of performance which is needed to keep and maintain safe communities demands improvement. The National Advisory Commission on Criminal Justice Standards and Goals, in *Police*, puts it this way:

> The police in the United States are not separate from the people. They draw their authority from the will and consent of the people, and they recruit their officers from them. The police are the instrument of the people to achieve and maintain order; their efforts are founded on principles of public service and ultimate responsibility to the public (1973:9).

While many police departments enunciate the role an individual officer is expected to play in terms of routine tasks, there is no precise agreement among law enforcement practitioners or theoreticians on how these activities should be prioritized. That is, there may be common agreement that a police department is responsible for keeping the peace, maintaining order, providing social services, and apprehending criminal suspects. But there is less consensus on which of these activities, among others, is the most important and/or how best to implement operational procedures for each of these tasks.

In the last half century, law enforcement has strived to professionalize itself. There is considerable dispute, however, as to whether or not such pro-

The Police Role in Contemporary Society

fessionalization can ever be a reality. Some argue that without a specific body of knowledge to be learned, without commonly accepted standards and ethics of practice, and without some form of meaningful self-policing, law enforcement can never achieve the professional levels of medicine and law. Nonetheless, the police themselves are seeking to upgrade through higher education, by being less secretive about operational decision-making, and by developing greater tolerance of public involvement in disciplinary procedures for those within the ranks.

Simultaneous with the above developments has been that of increasing use of technological advances. This means that the police have become more efficient and more effective in routine operations. They have been able to shorten routine response time on citizen-initiated calls as a result of improved communication systems. They utilize more scientific aids in routine investigations. Further, increased education has widened their personal horizons so that they have become less the social pariahs that they once were thought to be. Clearance rates have not necessarily increased, but, at least, the police are beginning to examine their own procedures and processes with a view toward improving crime control measures.

Many writers who used to look only at individual police behaviors now analyze the police in systemic terms, especially the flow of work among and between the various operational units. Additionally, these writers are exploring the relationships the police have with other criminal justice agencies and comment on the role of the police as just one among numerous agencies needed in society to deal with the problem of crime. This is occurring, perhaps, because the police are more open about their activities, but is also due to increasing concern and willingness to cooperate by individuals and groups within society.

Discretion in daily policing can never be eliminated (LaFave, 1965; Skolnick, 1966; Davis, 1969), for an officer is constantly called upon to use his own judgment, frequently without any opportunity to confer with colleagues or superiors. But it is this discretionary behavior which has produced so much of the animosity that exists between citizens and police as they confront one another in daily interactions. When not exercised appropriately, the policeman is accused of brutality or discrimination. When utilized discreetly and compassionately, the policeman can become a hero. If he is allowed unlimited discretion, the problem can never be resolved. On the other hand, if properly trained and otherwise controlled and held accountable for his behavior, it is likely, as some maintain, that citizen-police interactions can improve markedly and in a positive direction.

The first selection in this section offers the reader an opportunity to view police-community relations as a regular function of police work. In "Historical Perspectives on the Police Community Service Function," author Jack Whitehouse examines the policeman's role and defines such terms as "community relations" and "community service," pointing out their similarities and differences. He illustrates other police functions, such as in health and welfare matters, and the general assistance provided to citizens and groups in communities. He also suggests history indicates that police have always provided peacekeeping as well as community service functions, that this is not a newly developed dual role.

Continuing with this historical perspective, sociologist Lawrence Sherman, in "The Sociology and the Social Reform of the American Police: 1950-1973," reviews the relationship between the police role and efforts to bring about reform in American policing. He identifies 10 major conclusions in the sociological literature on police. They include such issues as the isolation of the police from the community, discretion, authoritarianism of the law enforcers, and police subcultures.

From the Federal Bureau of Investigation's Uniform Crime Reports, *Crime in the United States—1974,* we have extracted a selection which describes the numbers and kinds of law enforcement personnel who worked in the field that year, including civilians. With such numbers giving us a perspective, we next present Professor Herman Goldstein's "Toward a Redefinition of the Police Function." In this paper, the author discusses three broad generalizations that have been drawn regarding the police function. He cites these as the noncriminal aspects of police activity, the prevention of crime and the outbreak of violence, and the discretionary behavior of individual policemen. He then discusses these issues in terms of further research that is required and how change possibly can be effectuated in order to cast police in a more helpful, supportive, and positive role in the communities they serve.

In a study of the New York City Police Department, Project Director George McManus and his associates examined what policemen did on the job and what their performances actually looked like. We have extracted from *Police Training and Performance Study* a section entitled "What Does a Policeman Do?" The selection reviews a number of studies regarding police role and activities and the actual amount of time spent for each function. It also reviews some traits and attributes which are thought to be important for the individual policeman to possess insofar as successful performance on the job is concerned. Additionally, some attention is given to the views of the police role by policemen themselves as well as those of the community.

The Advisory Commission on Intergovernmental Relations issued a report called *State-Local Relations in the Criminal Justice System,* from which we have extracted a selection, "The Local Police Function." Here, police services are analyzed in terms of the differences between local and state law enforcement agencies, with particular emphasis on the former. An analysis of field, staff, and auxiliary services is presented. Further, the relationships between police and other criminal justice agencies concerning police functions are described. The Commission points out that policing "is the frontal part of the criminal justice system" and what such agencies as the courts and corrections do with offenders is determined, in large measure, by the operations of the police. There is also a commentary on the meaning and effect of police discretion on peacekeeping and law enforcement activities.

In the final reading, "Changing the Rhetoric of 'Professionalism,'" Professor Franklin Ashburn attempts to define the meaning of profession, especially as the concept is being used in police circles. He suggests that there is no consensus on what a profession really is nor what it can—or should—do for law enforcement. He comments that since there is no real agreement on the proper role and function of the policeman, it will be difficult to reach agreement on how best to professionalize the police. Furthermore, he lists a number of obstacles to professionalism, including the commitment by many to "traditional methods of operation," "rites of passage," and the apparent lack of accountability of the discretionary behavior of the policeman on patrol. He also points out that there are so many misconceptions and expectations about the police role by the public, especially with regard to their "crime fighting skills," that a true profession in law enforcement may be impossible to obtain in the near future, if at any time.

References

Davis, Kenneth C.
    1969   Discretionary Justice: A Preliminary Inquiry. Baton Rouge, Louisiana: Louisiana State University Press.
LaFave, Wayne R.
    1965   Arrest: The Decision to Take a Suspect into Custody. Boston: Little, Brown.
National Advisory Commission on Criminal Justice Standards and Goals.
    1973   Police. Washington, D.C.: U.S. Government Printing Office.
Skolnick, Jerome H.
    1966   Justice without Trial: Law Enforcement in Democratic Society. New York: Wiley.

CHAPTER **2-1**

historical perspectives on the police community service function

JACK E. WHITEHOUSE

A great deal of controversy exists today over the municipal policeman's role. Many of society's public and private agencies, including the police, are taking a more humanistic view of their functions. A number of police officers have examined this trend with misgivings. Other police officers view a humanistic service approach to their duties as being in keeping with contemporary cultural trends.

Today many policemen of the traditionalist school believe it is their role to handle only the criminal element. Therefore, according to their thinking, some other agency in society must be responsible for the feebleminded, the nonconforming, and others rejected by society. Those from this group will say, "Our job is to protect life and property and keep the peace. We do this by investigating crime, making arrests, and assisting in the prosecution of wrong-doers." Others in the police service recognize that traditional police methods have been something less than a total success. These officers recognize that traditional police methods, such as aggressive patrol and thorough investigations, are decidedly a part of the picture, but that they do not constitute the entire answer to police problems. These officers recognize that the way to achieve optimum police success is through optimum cooperation between the police and the public.

Public cooperation comes when the police and the public are able to

Source: Jack E. Whitehouse. "Historical Perspectives on the Police Community Service Function." Reprinted by permission of the *Journal of Police Science and Administration,* Copyright © 1973 by Northwestern University School of Law, Volume I, Number 1.

enjoy positive contacts with each other. These positive contacts do not occur when the policeman is issuing traffic citations or making arrests. They occur when the citizen cries out for help to the police and is immediately helped and aided by knowledgable, sympathetic officers.

The traditionalists in law enforcement seem to believe that helping and aiding people in distress is something new. These officers look longingly at the "good old days" when policemen were allegedly "thief-catchers" and did not concern themselves with social problems. Traditionalist policemen seem to live with the fear that today's policemen are being turned into social workers and will be leaving the law enforcement function behind. This is patently a myth not borne out by the facts. American policemen in past centuries were at least as service oriented as today's police officer, if not more so.

Definition of Terms

Community Relations. This term has been defined as being, "the management function which evaluates public attitudes, identifies the policies and procedures of an individual or an organization with the public interest, and executes a program of action to earn public understanding and acceptance."

Community Service. Community service programs are geared to help alleviate individual and community social problems of a noncriminal nature. In other words, the basic function here is in the helping of individual citizens by individual police officers. This help is given most often in one to one, face to face situations. If the needs of the individual cannot be met by utilizing existent police resources, the person is directed to a social service agency that can help.

The basic difference between community relations and community service programs is that community relations programs are directed to entire communities or specific groups within the community. Public and community relations refer to programs very often devoted to enhancing the police image. The money spent on these programs is a study in bribing and buying self-imagery. These traditional programs are frequently devoted to the ideal of "what's in it for us" rather than "what can we do for you." In other words, these programs are geared to the needs of the police instead of the needs of the people.

Early History

Oxford historian Charles Reith tells us that every society throughout history has had some form of law enforcement. Reith points out that at least 1,200 years ago the law enforcement officers of that era had a peacekeeping community service role as well as a law enforcement function. At that time, the Arab world consisted of Egypt, Palestine, Syria, Mesopotamia, Assyria, and Babylonia. Arab police helped to conduct the postal service, inspected weights and measures, supervised commercial transactions to prevent fraud and exorbitant prices of goods, insured that goods offered for sale were of the advertised quality, prevented the playing of musical instruments in public places, found suitable husbands for widows, protected slaves from the imposition of tasks which they were not strong enough to undertake, and saw to it that beasts of burden were not maltreated by being underfed or overworked.[1]

In 1634, one Joshua Pratt was chosen to be constable for Plymouth, Massachusetts. He had a variety of duties which consisted of sealer of weights and measures, surveyor of land, jailer, and announcer of marriages approved by civil authorities.[2]

The duties of the English constable between 1835 and 1840 included a number of community service duties: maintenance and control of sanitation, relief of destitution, issue and control of licenses of every kind, fire fighting, regulation and inspection of weights and measures, and mail delivery in outlying areas.[3]

Nineteenth Century Boston and New York

In their histories of police in the 1880's, Lane in Boston and Costello in New York offer us a number of examples which seem to have been typical of American municipal police agencies for that era. It appears that, if anything, the police were more deeply involved in the community service aspects of their jobs a hundred years ago than today. For example, in 1824, the city of Boston passed an ordinance which provided that:

> ... the department of internal police be placed under the superintendence of the City Marshal ... and to this department shall belong the care of the common sewers, and the care of the vaults, *and whatever else affects the health, security, and comfort of the city,* from cause or means arising or existing within the limits thereof.[4]

Miscellaneous Police Duties

Police officers of the last century performed many public services which now seem strange. Today's police officer will, however, recognize a number of duties which are still performed with striking regularity, such as handling family disturbances and finding lost children.

Policemen in the middle 1800s in Boston were always instructed, *"to remove obstructions from the streets and sidewalks, to put out fires, test doors, and turn off running water".* It was also the patrolman's duty to serve as the eyes and ears of other city departments and note broken street lamps, smells, and the like.[5]

The Police Role in Contemporary Society

In 1853, 506 drunken Boston citizens were taken home; the police handled disturbances—many and perhaps most of which were family quarrels in private homes on 539 occasions, 32 stray horses were given shelter; 7 children were found; and 29 physicians were called.[6] In the 1870s part of the duties of the New York policemen was to remove obstructions from public streets, guard the public health, and *"assist, advise, and protect immigrants, strangers, and travelers in public streets."*[7]

Other duties of the Boston police consisted of handling:

> misdemeanors and irregularities affecting the safety, the peace, and convenience and comfort of the community. In this branch may be included the violation of the license laws, the infraction of the several ordinances, regulating the streets, trucks, carts, carriages and horses, dogs, exhibitions, and public shows . . . trespasses and offenses on the common and malls . . . the sale and stands of wood and bark . . . woodsawers . . . unauthorized fireworks . . . danger from lighted pipes and cigars . . . games and plays . . . paving of streets and footwalks . . . dirt and rubbish . . . erecting of buildings . . . repairs of steps and cellar doors . . . projections on steps, signs, balconies, and awnings . . . merchandise, snow, and ice on sidewalks, . . . coursing on sleds on the highways . . . swimming in exposed places . . . and various other subjects.[8]

Health

In 1834 in Boston the police removed 1,500 loads of dirt, apparently emptied 3,120 privies, and daily visited *"every house in Boston"* to check on cholera. The city physician and some volunteers made daily visits to police stations because the cells and floors served as temporary hospital facilities for the dead and dying.[9]

In the 1880s policemen were required to keep a list of physicians who were registered in the precinct in order to refer them to those needing medical assistance. Policemen were detailed to call upon doctors and conduct them to the residences of the patients. The physician was paid from public funds and the precinct captain was required to endorse the payment order.[10]

During this same time, police officers inspected all tenement and lodging houses to determine sanitary conditions. The police also inspected steam boilers and tested and licensed steam boiler operators. This service was perfromed by the police due to the large number of boiler explosions.[11]

Welfare

Boston distributed an earlier form of relief and the police, in this case, administered this charity fund provided by the municipality. Policemen also set up a charity of their own, distributed coal to the poor, and, *"in the 1850's, the police began to act as agents for the overseers of the poor, investigating and recommending action on several hundred cases a year.*"[12] In 1864, patrolmen were directed to assist applicants for shelter and relief by directing them to the proper agency.[13]

One facet of early police work that seems most strange to modern police officers was the police practice of furnishing lodgings for the poor in police stations. In 1853, in a three-month period, 1,048 persons received lodging for the night at the Boston Police Station.[14] New York City had similar experiences. In nine years (from 1861-69), 880,161 persons were furnished lodgings by police of that city. It is interesting to note that during this nine-year period, the police arrested almost precisely the same number of people for which they provided mere lodging (898,489).[15]

Early Twentieth Century

At the beginning of this century, a number of departments in the United States made it a police responsibility to report conditions of individual distress. The commissioner of police in New York City noted that:

> "Policemen on the beat probably come more intimately into contact with the life of the people than any other class of men, and their wide opportunities for observation can be harnessed into various forms of *constructive social work.*"[16]. . . .

Fosdick in his classic book, *American Police Systems* noted the following:

> In many cities such as Indianapolis, Newark, and Seattle, it is the practice to detail policemen to assist probation officers attached to juvenile courts . . . this work involves the constant association of the (police) welfare or juvenile officers with representatives of other organizations . . . such as truant officers, the Children's Society, etc. This is a point of great importance. *Police work cannot be isolated from other welfare agencies of the community concerned with social problems.* It cannot be divorced from all the organizing influences . . . working for better conditions in city life . . . *The new policing demands a type of officer interested and trained in social service.*[17]

Assisting Young People

The New York City Police Department initiated a number of community service activities designed to help the youth of the community. In January, 1917, carefully chosen patrolmen were assigned to 10 precincts with the single duty of looking after young people who seemed to be going wrong. Commissioner

Woods observed that huge gains to the city could be obtained in this manner. He said: "That is what these *welfare officers* are working for." The system was so successful that it had been investigated and some action had been taken in each case. "These cases often involved . . . destitute home conditions which could be corrected by enlisting the aid of some private welfare association."[18]

The police were instrumental in establishing new city playgrounds, and play streets were located where traffic was excluded between certain hours so that children could play. In conjunction with private agencies, a number of backyard playgrounds were opened in high-crime areas. In order to strengthen this program, uniformed policemen were assigned to talk to children in public schools so as to establish a better relationship.[19]

In 1916, 40,000 New York City children were entertained at Christmastime in police stations. Lists of needy children were made up by precinct captains. This information was furnished by the patrolman on the beat and the children were those who would not otherwise have had a Christmas. Each child received articles of clothing, toys, candy, and fruit. Each station house had a large Christmas tree and, instead of prisoners, the cells contained gifts for the children. The police captain in each precinct acted as Santa Claus and the children were frequently brought in shifts in order to take care of all of them. This plan of having Christmas parties for children was adopted in New York in 1915, and other cities soon copied the idea.[20]

In 1917, the New York Police Department established the system of Junior Police. Approximately six thousand boys between the ages of 11 and 16 had groups in 32 different precincts. The boys were uniformed, drilled, and given classes in safety and first aid, traffic safety, and law and order. They held games and athletic meets, all under the control and management of the police. Commissioner Woods felt that attitudes were changed for the better toward the police and there was a marked decrease in juvenile delinquency.[21]

The Police and Unemployment

The winter of 1914-15 was particularly severe and unemployment was rampant. To help the needy, a small fund was raised among the police themselves. The captain of every precinct had a supply of books of tickets with monetary amounts on them. The police made arrangements with restaurants, groceries, and fuel dealers to honor these tickets and to send a bill to the police station every week. Throughout the city a policeman took any person in need to the station house where:

> . . . the captain or lieutenant in charge would provide *at once* for his immediate needs and would then put him in touch with some private association or church where help would be continued as long as necessary. 'We believed it was the duty of the police,' said Commissioner

Woods, 'to protect society by preventing as much as possible of the crime that might be committed by these unfortunate people in their distress.' During the three years in which this plan was in operation in New York, 3,262 families and individuals were thus assisted.[22]

During this time period, the police considered themselves to be an employment agency for the large number of people out of work. Frequently, the police created jobs where none existed, such as keeping streets and sidewalks clean by picking up waste paper and other litter. From 1914-17, over three thousand people were employed by the police in one capacity or another.[23]

About the time of World War I, the New York City Police Department was very active in finding employment for ex-convicts. The Police Commissioner spoke to the inmates of Sing Sing Prison and promised them that the New York Police Force would not hound ex-convicts. Further, the Sing Sing inmates were told that if they wanted to earn an honest living and lead an honest life, the Police Department would not only give them a chance but would assist them in finding jobs.

In placing these men in positions, the police made every effort to find jobs that were suitable and from which they could earn enough money to support themselves and their families. The police in New York were primarily interested in preventing crime and they believed that helping ex-convicts find jobs was directly related to this end.[24]

The Police As Rehabilitation
Case Workers

Prior to 1920, the police were extensively used as parole and probation officers. In New York, 84 police sergeants were assigned to act as parole officers looking after men released from jails, penitentiaries, and workhouses. Almost fifteen hundred men and boys were assigned to the care of these officers. These police/parole officers were instructed to help their charges get work, make contact with them at least once a week, demonstrate to the parolee that the officer was his friend, and demonstrate that the parole officer and the department stood ready to assist him do what was right. The St. Louis and Los Angeles Police Departments also maintained parole and probation bureaus within their agencies which were staffed by sworn officers.[25]

Conclusion

The police of yesterday performed a variety of health, welfare, and other social service functions. These duties were considered commonplace and essential. There is no indication that there was a problem with what today's social scientists call "role conflict". They did not have the advantage of sociologists talking to them about incompatibility of roles, role conflict, or other trauma which might result in neurosis for the officer. Some modern police officers having had these advantages seem to believe that it is beneath their dignity to perform help-type activities. One cannot help but yearn for the days when policemen did not know they could not do a certain thing and simply went ahead and did it.

Yesterday's policemen had no conflict over being termed 'social workers.' They simply went about their business and distributed charity and relief to the poor, investigated and recommended action on charity cases, directed people to the proper agency to receive shelter and relief, furnished lodging for the poor, visited homes to check on communicable diseases, saw their police stations used as temporary hospitals, and escorted intoxicated people home.

After reading accounts of 19th century police practices, one can only wonder what all the shouting is about today. Some present-day policemen seem to be under the impression that their community service functions are a newly acquired activity. They speak longingly of the two-fisted policeman who ruled his beat with an iron hand and performed no "sissified" social worker functions. This mythical character probably never existed. Yesterday's policeman was probably more of a street social worker than today's modern officer.

It would appear that police traditionalists have not read their police history closely enough. The police officer's dual function of performing law enforcement duties and peacekeeping community services has apparently been present as long as there have been municipal police departments.

References

1. Charles Reith, *The Blind Eye of History* 235-6 (1952).

2. Herbert Baxter Adams, *Norman Constables in America* (1883).

3. Charles Reith, *A New Study of Police History* 231 (1956).

4. Roger Lane, *Policing the City, Boston: 1822-1885* 17 (1967). (Emphasis added.)

5. See footnote 4, p. 109.

6. See footnote 4, p. 97.

7. A.E. Costello, *Our Police Protectors* 294 (privately published by the author, 1885).

8. See footnote 4, p. 19.

9. See footnote 4, p. 114.

10. See footnote 7, pp. 300-1.

11. See footnote 7, pp. 461-2.

12. See footnote 4, p. 114.

13. See footnote 4, p. 135.

14. See footnote 4, p. 97.

15. See footnote 7, pp. 233-4.

16. Raymond B. Fosdick, *American Police Systems* 375-6 (1920). (Emphasis added.)

17. See footnote 16, p. 371. (Emphasis added.)

18. See footnote 16, p. 371.

19. See footnote 16, p. 369.

20. See footnote 16, p. 320.

21. See footnote 16, p. 369.

22. See footnote 16, pp. 374-5.

23. See footnote 16, pp. 375-6.

24. See footnote 16, pp. 365-7.

25. See footnote 16, p. 377.

CHAPTER **2-2**

THE SOCIOLOGY AND THE SOCIAL REFORM OF THE AMERICAN POLICE: 1950-1973

LAWRENCE W. SHERMAN

The sociology of the American police, like the sociology of many institutions, has been closely linked to its social reform. The histories of each can be, and have been, discussed separately.[1] But since developments in one have resulted from developments in the other, it is more meaningful to discuss them together, even if the discussion must be brief.

To define our terms, the "sociology of the police" means research done by academics (not necessarily sociologists), with the central purpose of advancing knowledge rather than changing social policy. Thus, many national commission reports are excluded (though academic research sponsored by the commissions is included). "Social reform of the police" means all those events, proposals, and programs (except academic research) which tried to, or did, effect change in the American police. In this broad conception, social reformers of the police include newspaper editors, participants in race riots, and police administrators. Indeed the social reform of the American police after 1950 differs from most previous reform in that there were social reformers *inside* police departments as well as outside.

While discussion of police sociology can be fairly specific, discussion of police reform requires outrageous generalizations. As of 1965, there were 40,000 law enforcement agencies in the U.S.: 50 federal, 200 state, and 39,750

Source: Lawrence W. Sherman. "The Sociology and the Social Reform of the American Police: 1950-1973." Reprinted by permission of the *Journal of Police Science and Administration,* Copyright © 1974 by Northwestern University of School of Law, Volume II, Number 3.

county, city, town and village agencies.[2] A five-man Alabama sheriff's department and New York's 30,000-man force are hardly comparable, yet they are
both "the police". Though we shall restrict this discussion to municipal police
departments of 200 or more officers, there are such great regional and community differences in the extent and kinds of police reform that such trends as
"professionalization" can only be identified with great qualification. As the
ABA Police Standards note:

> Given the common lag between proposals for change and their implemen-
> tation, the police field is in the rather awkward situation today of having
> some police agencies aspiring to effect changes that are being substantially
> modified or abandoned by those agencies that have already adopted
> them.[3]

Thus, keeping the problem of lag in mind, trends in police reform will
refer to the vanguard of national opinion: in the press, in police professional
publications, and among the most innovative police administrators.

Chronology

1950-1959

The year 1950 was an important one for both police sociology and social
reform. William Westley, a University of Chicago graduate student, was in Gary,
Indiana beginning the first in-depth analysis of an American police organization.
And in Berkeley, Professor O.W. Wilson was publishing the first edition of
Police Administration, which was to become the source of much police change
as the bible of "professionalism." Based on the scientific management principles
of Frederick Winslow Taylor,[4] Wilson's book stressed efficiency, hierarchy,
and bureaucratic regularity as the key to police reform. Yet, at the same time,
Westley was finding that a complex informal organization governed such things
as illegal police violence.[5] Police sociology and social reform were clearly not
talking to each other.

Westley's study went unpublished for 20 years, while Wilson's became
required reading for most police promotion exams. And while academics ignored
the police for the rest of the decade (except for the massive ABA arrest study
in three Midwestern states, done in 1955-56 and not fully published until
1965),[6] the Wilson-inspired trend in police reform was to abolish footbeats and
motorize patrols, close local station houses, and centralize both radio dispatching and command decision-making. Los Angeles, Cincinnati and Oakland were
leaders in this trend, while Boston, Chicago and other cities had little reform
at all.

1960-1966

Pressures for reform, however, soon hit many old style police departments. Between 1960 and 1963, Chicago, Boston, Denver, Syracuse, Buffalo, New York, Indianapolis, Burlington, and other cities, experienced police scandals of corruption and burglary, all of which received nationwide publicity.[7] A typical, though not universal result of a scandal was the appointment of a reform police chief to do things "by the book," and the only book then available was O.W. Wilson's. The newly vitalized International Association of Chiefs of Police sent field survey teams to many scandalized departments, recommending reforms along the, by now, familiar lines of classic organization theory.

Meanwhile, academics ignored the scandals and busied themselves with the juvenile delinquency control projects of the Ford Foundation and the Kennedy Administration. These projects inevitably led to the police as a research topic, and two hypotheses were developed: first, that police apprehension of juveniles may stimulate more crime than such actions control, and second, that criminal apprehension is a selective process dependent primarily on situational factors in the police-juvenile encounter.[8] While the first hypothesis (labelling theory) has not been tested much further with regard to the police, the second hypothesis was called into question with Banton's emphasis on community factors (in his 1962 Scottish-American comparative research)[9] and Skolnick's emphasis on organizational factors (in his 1963 case study of the Oakland Police)[10] in determining the outcomes of police encounters.

More research on that second issue—police encounters—was stimulated by events in police reform. In the summers of 1964 and 1965, New York and Los Angeles, respectively, experienced major racial disorders. The police (or police brutalities) were alleged to have precipitated the riots. And in 1965, President Johnson established a national commission to examine crime and crime control, in response to massive reported crime increases. Thus, it is not surprising that in 1965 two major comparative studies on the urban police began: the Harvard study of eight medium-sized communities led by J.Q. Wilson,[11] and the University of Michigan study of three big cities led by Reiss (done for the U.S. Crime Commission).[12] Both these studies continued into 1966, the busiest year ever for police research. Bayley and Mendelsohn did a study of Denver, focusing on police relations with minority groups.[13] Bordua was editing six scholarly essays on the police,[14] Skolnick's book was published,[15] and Niederhoffer's case study of the New York Police was in preparation.[16]

Police reform activity, however, was as intense as police research. The Supreme Court had, allegedly, "handcuffed" the police by defining more precisely the rights of citizens regarding arrest, detention, search, and interrogation. A reform mayor in New York had created a civilian-dominated board for reviewing citizen complaints against the police and lost it through a referendum skillfully manipulated by a highly politicized Patrolmen's Benevolent Association. The national attention given to the New York civilian review battle sparked similar controversies in other cities, and police brutality became a national issue.

1967–1969

By 1967, enough police sociology had been published, and enough national concern about the police had been generated for the sociology and the social reform of the police to converge. While there were some policemen who felt that the revelations of police deviance in the work of Skolnick and Reiss were unethical violations of trust, more important were the thoughtful police reactions to the criticism of professionalism in the academic studies, particularly the Michigan study.[17] In the backdrop of the worst race riots yet (Detroit and Newark 1967), the Crime Commission,[18] and a year later the Riot Commission,[19] echoed the attack on professionalism: it had sacrificed the humanity and community relations skill of the old-style beat-cop.

In 1968, the riots after the assassination of Dr. Martin Luther King and during the Chicago Democratic convention kept the police in the center of controversy. In response, there emerged a new program for police reform: community control. Best articulated by Waskow (an academic social reformer),[20] the community control idea was to abolish the large law enforcement bureaucracies which dispensed "consensus law" in highly varied local communities, and establish locally recruited and governed peace-keeping units in their stead. But again, police sociology spoke to social reform. The 1968 publication of J.Q. Wilson's *Varieties of Police Behavior*,[21] while clarifying the differences in patrol styles between police agencies and some political reasons for the differences, concluded that community control was not a workable idea. Instead, Wilson suggested that administrative decentralization of power within existing police agencies could increase police responsiveness to the desires of local communities.[22]

Although community control was never a viable possibility, J.Q. Wilson's administrative decentralization provided an alternative means of reform that addressed the same issue as community control: community responsiveness. Combined with the Crime Commission's recommendation for team policing (which would operationally unite various police specialities—patrol, investigation, traffic—in a small local area)[23] and the growth of "human relations" organization theory in police thinking,[24] administrative decentralization became the social reform program for departments that had tried and failed with O.W. Wilson's bureaucratic centralization. Less "progressive" departments, of course, had just discovered *Police Administration* and were abandoning their old-style administrative decentralization.

The 1968 Omnibus Crime Control and Safe Streets Act established the Federal Law Enforcement Assistance Administration (LEAA) to give $1 billion per year in aid to local criminal justice systems. Much money was spent on scholarship aid to send policemen to college, and police science programs grew rapidly in state-operated colleges and junior colleges. Required reading often included the recent police sociology, so its link to police reform became even stronger. LEAA funds also enabled police departments to experiment with new ideas in training and organization, ideas that had been influenced at least somewhat by the sociological literature.

1970-1973

By 1970, the LEAA projects were starting to get off the ground, and the Ford Foundation established a $30 million Police Foundation to concentrate on police improvement on a more limited scale than LEAA's massive mandate. Both funding units began with a comprehensive strategy of making many reforms at once in a police department, rather than creating piecemeal demonstration projects. The implications of such a strategy for organizational change are not yet clear, though the strategy's controversial nature became obvious immediately. While the evaluations conducted for LEAA projects were too goal-specific to tell much about organizational change, the Police Foundation's social science consultants in Dallas, Cincinnati, and Kansas City will pay particular attention to that issue as those projects evolve.

The Police Foundation projects, perhaps more than any other social reforms of the police, have made particular use of the police sociological literature. Bittner's observation that the police receive less respect *inside* their station house than out[25] was one of several sources of the increased involvement of lower levels of police departments, especially patrolmen, in planning Police Foundation experiments. Reiss' analysis of patrol as a *reactive*, rather than *proactive* form of organization[26] ("dial-a-cop") led to an increased awareness of what the police actually do, and to Foundation-sponsored experiments in developing proactive styles of policing.[27]

But, as police sociology and social reform have converged, sociology has become as applied as social reform is now theoretical. Very little "pure" research is now being done to answer purely sociological questions about policing as an occupation, as a complex organization, as a social control mechanism, or as a law-making mechanism. The sociological focus on the police, like that on most service organizations, in our neo-welfare state, is that of a social problem, and to the extent that sociologists hope to *correct* the police, it may hinder their ability to *understand* the police sociologically. But before considering this issue further, we should summarize sociology's substantive contribution to police reform and the questions police reformers are now asking of applied sociologists (see Table 2-2-1).

TABLE 2-2-1. Chronology of Major Events

(In the interests of brevity, important events on both sides have been omitted.)

	Sociology
1950	Westley in Gary.
1955-56	ABA Midwest Arrest Study.
1960-65	Juvenile Delinquency Studies.
1962	Banton comparative study.
1963	Skolnick Oakland Study.
1965-66	Wilson and Reiss Comparative Studies; Bordua's 6 essays, *Justice Without Trial* appears; Bayley and Mendelsohn in Denver.
1967	*Behind the Shield* appears.
1968	*Varieties of Police Behavior* appears.
1970	*Functions of Police* appears.
1971	*Police and the Public* appears.
1972	Police Foundation organizational change research begins.

	Social Reform
1950	*Police Administration* published.
1955-56	Wilsonian professionalism spreads to progressive departments.
1960-63	Major police scandals.
1964-65	N.Y. and L.A. race riots
1966	*Miranda v Arizona* N.Y.C. Civilian Review Board Fight.
1967	Worst urban race riots; U.S. Crime Commission report appears.
1968	U.S. Riot Commission report; King and Chicago Convention riots.
1969	LEAA established; Chevigny's *Police Power* appears.
1970	U.S. Violence Commission report appears; Police Foundation established.
1971	Police college programs and minority recruitment grows; Knapp Commission hearings begin.
1972	Police Foundation and LEAA "major cities" programs under way.

Sociological Conclusions and Police Response

With extreme simplification and omission of many important points, we can identify 10 major conclusions of recent police sociology (roughly in chronological order) and the response of police administrators to them:

1. *The police occupation is isolated from the general community, with great internal solidarity and secrecy.* (Westley, Niederhoffer, others). When not interpreting this as a criticism, police administrators have made their departments more "open" in a public relations sense, with station house receptions, citizen ride-alongs, etc.

2. *The patrolman, due to his extraordinary discretion, is the most powerful criminal justice official.* (LaFave, J.Q. Wilson). Some police administrators have tried to control police discretion through a proliferation of rules, while others have sought to train officers to use discretion more wisely.

3. *The effect of police action on many lawbreakers, particularly young ones, is to amplify the seriousness and frequency of their deviance.* (Piliavin and Briar, others). This conclusion was largely dismissed as liberal nonsense, but is now being followed in such new programs as "alternatives to arrest" and diversion of offenders from criminal justice to welfare programs.

4. *Varieties of police behavior depend upon specific situational, organizational, and community factors.* (A synthesis of Reiss, Skolnick, J.Q. Wilson and Banton.) This comparative analysis has been put to little use by locally oriented police reformers.

5. *Police recruits are neither more "authoritarian" nor more deviant in any other respect than people of similar socio-economic backgrounds who do not become policemen, but they may become so through occupational socialization.* (Niederhoffer, Bayley and Mendelsohn). This observation was originally used to rebut police critics, and has recently become the basis of peer-group pressure programs to reduce police violence in the Oakland and Kansas City police departments.

6. *The vast majority of police manhours are expended in activity having little to do with law enforcement, but much to do with social service and peace-keeping.* (Reiss, Wilson). While common knowledge to policemen, this conclusion demolished an organizational myth and brought discussion of what the police do into the open. One result has been a movement to divide patrol functions into two separate forces, one for social service and one for crime,[28] notably in Miami.

7. *Police organization is primarily reactive to citizen requests for service.* (Reiss). This conclusion has been much discussed in relation to patrol, but its full implications for detectives and the overall police strategy towards crime have yet to be realized by most police reformers. Indeed, a proactive police role in a democratic society could provoke a very intense controversy, as it already has in such issues as wiretapping and "stop and frisk".

8. *Police subcultures often contain general values and practices which deviate widely from legal and organizational rules.* (Skolnick, Reiss, and Wilson.) This point has also been made by non-police social reformers, who demand stricter external accountability for the police. The police internal response has been a general increase in the existence and activities of internal investigation units.

9. *Policemen work within a nondemocratic organizational context which is antithetical to the democratic values they are supposed to protect in society.* (Chwast,[29] Reiss, Bittner). While there has been no outright move to abandon the paramilitary structure of police organization, like in the liberalized "New Army" there have been many efforts to increase

supervisors' sensitivity to human relations within police organizations. (The English police call this "man-management"). Team policing and participative management by objectives are two examples.

10. *Community control won't work, but administrative decentralization and de-bureaucratization can increase responsiveness to community desires.* (Wilson, Reiss). In addition to numerous team policing experiments,[30] major decentralization programs are presently under way in New York, Dallas, and Los Angeles.

Social Reform Concerns and Police Questions

Our chronology observed that the convergence of police sociology and social reform did not occur until the mid-1960s. Yet the focal concerns for police social reform have been in continual change, both before and after its convergence with sociology. From 1950-1960 the focal concern was inefficiency; from 1960-65 corruption; 1965-75 racial discrimination; and from 1970 on organizational change and, again, corruption (though more so in the East than elsewhere). The aforementioned 10 major sociological conclusions were largely developed within the focus on police racial discrimination. While many of the conclusions are applicable to the new focal concerns, they are not sufficient, and more police sociology—both pure and applied—will be sought by police reformers.

Specifically, police reformers may well ask of sociologists:

—How can the police control crime better?
—How can police-community relations be improved?
—How can police corruption be minimized?
—How can police organizations be changed to answer each of the above questions?

Sociology as Intelligence for Social Change

The question sociologists must now ask themselves is whether they *can*, and whether they *should*, try to answer the police reformers' questions. The blind faith that science can solve any problem, based on such physical science successes as the space program, may not be justified in the realm of human problems. While sociologists may be better equipped than anyone else to deal with the police reformers' questions, they would do both themselves and society a disservice by pretending that all the answers can be found. The fact is that they *cannot* be found, at least not in the same sense that answers to physical science questions have been found.[31]

Moreover, a conception of the sociologist's task for police reform as purely pragmatic—the discovery of the most "effective" solutions—denies the fundamental role of values in social change. One view of social action is that it is essentially, and not just incidentally, a discussion of values.[32] And for that discussion, sociologists are no better equipped than anyone else.[33]

Nonetheless, social science does perform "willingly or not, an intelligence function in the political process", as Black points out. And for sociologists to ignore the police reformers' questions would be, to my values, as wrong as answering them in a purely pragmatic way. There need be no dilemma so long as sociologists carefully distinguish fact and value, policy and science. Even though values may unknowingly influence scientific statements, this need not erase their distinction from value statements; scientific statements can be tested, value statements cannot.[34]

Thus, if a sociologist personally agrees with the values implied by the police reformers' questions, he can attempt to deal with them—to the limited extent of social science's ability—in a fashion that points out what is fact, what is value. And as a participant in a political process, there is no reason why he should not make the case for his own values.[35]

Directions for Pure and Applied Research

The ability of sociologists to deal with the scientific aspects of the police reformers' questions depends not only on their applied research, but also on the pure research that supports it. We have noted that major "pure" research on the American police (that which attempts to understand it as a social institution) has virtually stopped. The present sociology of the police is almost entirely "applied". It seeks to evaluate the effectiveness of alternative courses of action in reaching certain goals. But as Black has argued, applied sociology in the realm of law has rather little to apply.

Such criticism is not as serious as it seems when one considers the value of applied science in developing pure science. The view that the quality of applied science depends solely upon the quality of pure science[36] ignores the mutually beneficial nature of the two. Applied police sociology, blundering along in its ignorance, may provide important questions and data for a general theory of policing.

Even so, the present dearth of pure research on the police is cause for concern. If pure and applied research are to benefit from each other, both should be ongoing activities. Further, there is no intellectual reason why the same sociologists cannot engage in both activities (though there may be practical difficulties).

Since the applied police sociologists necessarily study one place at one brief period in history, the pure police sociologists should concentrate on comparative and historical methods. They should examine the stability or

The Sociology and the Social Reform of the American Police: 1950-1973

change over time, and in different cultural settings, of such phenomena as pro-active/reactive methods, recruitment patterns and salaries relative to the general population, the centralization of police control, police relationships to criminal organization and organized crime, patterns of leadership succession, the use of discretion in arrests, corruption, brutality, and so on. The list of topics is endless, and the selection of each will, no doubt, be guided by the values of the researcher. But to the extent that pure research can formulate any general theories of policing, applied sociology will have that much more to apply. To the extent that pure research can improve the research methods of social science—e.g. Reiss' systematic observation design for analyzing police encounters[37]—applied sociologists will have better tools for their work.

Applied police sociologists, for their part, must depart from the previous emphasis on patrol in order to deal with the police reformers' questions. Police tactics and crime should not just be an issue of alternative (uniformed or plain-clothes, saturation or mobile) patrol tactics, but of criminal investigation organization as well. Community relations must be viewed in the entire range of police activity—C.I.D., traffic, vice narcotics, as well as patrol. Corruption should not just be a question of recruitment or training, but of organizational controls in general and internal investigation procedures in particular. And the concern for organizational change must take the broadest view possible, including the effects of corruption controls on morale, the way in which new community relations are viewed by line officers, the effects of experiments on internal job status and promotion possibilities, and the interrelated effects of simultaneous changes in different aspects of the organization. A broad view should also include the mapping of the informal network throughout the organization. This may seem esoteric, but its importance to organizational change was demonstrated by both O.W. Wilson in Chicago and Patrick Murphy in New York.

In sum, the recommendation here is that pure research should develop more specific foci for its general theories, and that applied research should adopt a broader view of the local problems it studies. If this paper has a moral, then it is that research for the sake of knowledge and research for the sake of action should complement, not contradict, each other. More specifically, the evidence presented here suggests that the common distinction between sociology *of* and *for* the police is false; in the long run, they both have the same functions.

References

1. Maureen Cain critically assesses recent Anglo-American police sociology in *Society and the Policeman's Role* (London, 1973), pp. 13-25. Recent American police reform is discussed in the American Bar Association's *Stan-

dards Relating to the Urban Police Function (New York: Institute of Judicial Administration, 1972), pp. 27–30.

2. U.S. President's Commission on Law Enforcement and the Administration of Justice Task Force Report: The Police (Washington, D.C. U.S. G.P.O., 1967), p. 7.

3. American Bar Association Standards, footnote 1, p. 29.

4. Taylor, F.W., *Scientific Management* (1947).

5. Westley, W.A., *Violence and the Police* (1970).

6. LaFave, W., *Arrest* (1965).

7. Smith, R.L., *The Tarnished Badge* (1965).

8. See, in particular, Piliavin, I., and Briar, S., "Police Encounters with Juveniles," *Amer. J. Sociology*, Vol. 70, p. 206–214 (1965).

9. Banton, M., *The Policeman in the Community* (London, 1964).

10. Skolnick, J., *Justice Without Trial* (1966).

11. Wilson, J.Q., *Varieties of Police Behavior* (1968).

12. Black, D.J. and Reiss, A.J., Jr., "Patterns of Behavior in Police and Citizen Transactions," U.S. President's Commission on Law Enforcement, etc., *Studies in Crime and Law Enforcement in Major Metropolitan Areas*, Vol. 2, Field Surveys III (Washington, D.C.: U.S.G.P.O., 1967).

13. Bayley, D., and Mendelsohn, H., *Minorities and the Police* (1968).

14. Bordua, D.J., (Ed.), *The Police* (1967).

15. Skolnick, footnote 10.

16. Niederhoffer, A., *Behind the Shield* (1967).

17. Furstenburg, M., Paper to the American Political Science Association, September, 1972 Convention.

18. Footnote 2.

19. National Advisory Commission on Civil Disorders, *Report* (U.S. G.P.O., 1967).

20. Waskow, A.J., "Community Control of the Police," *Transaction*, December, 1969.

21. Footnote 11.

22. For an interesting and sensible compromise between community control and administrative decentralization, see Danzig, "An Alternative, Decentralized System of Criminal Justice," a paper presented to the Association of the Bar of the City of New York, September, 1970.

23. Footnote 2, p. 53.

24. A particularly popular book for police management courses has been McGregor, D., *The Human Side of Enterprise* (1960).

25. Bittner, E., *The Functions of the Police in Modern Society* (Bethesda: N.I.M.H., 1970).

26. Reiss, A.J., Jr., *The Police and the Public* (1971).

27. See *Experiments in Police Improvement* (Washington, D.C.: The Police Foundation, 1972), p. 30.

28. See Furstenburg, footnote 17, for a critical assessment of the separation of functions ideas.

29. Chwast, J., "Value Conflicts in Law Enforcement," *Crime and Delinquency*, Vol. 11, p. 151 (1965).

30. Sherman, L.W., et al, *Team Policing* (Washington, D.C.: The Police Foundation, 1973).

31. See Knight, F., "Fact Value in Social Science," *Freedom and Reform* (1947).

32. Footnote 31.

33. See Donald Black's provocative essay, "The Boundaries of Legal Sociology," *Yale Law Journal*, Vol. 81, No. 6, (June 1972).

34. Footnote 33.

35. For example, F.H. McClintock notes that even if science found capital punishment to control crime more "effectively," his value of human life would be the basis of his argument against it.

36. Black, footnote 33.

37. Reiss, footnote 26. See also his "Systematic Observation of Natural Social Phenomena," in H.L. Costner, (Ed.) *Sociological Methodology* (1971).

Law Enforcement Employee data

FEDERAL BUREAU OF INVESTIGATION

This . . . section (deals) with . . . Law Enforcement Employee Data which shows average police employee strength by geographic division and population group. This data is sub-divided by sex of employees (and) percentage of civilian employees. . . .

Employee Rates

The average number of law enforcement employees per 1,000 inhabitants (including civilian employees) was 2.5, which has remained constant since 1971. Male employees represented 88.9 percent of total police employee strength.

Many cities in the United States continue to operate with a police employee ratio of less than the national average of 2.5 per 1,000. Fifty percent of all law enforcement agencies in cities had police ratios ranging from 1.4 to 2.5 police employees per 1,000 inhabitants.

Nationally, large cities with 250,000 or more inhabitants as a group had an average ratio of 3.5 employees per 1,000 inhabitants.

The average ratio of police employees to population in the suburban areas was 2.1 per 1,000 inhabitants; an increase from the 1.9 rate in 1972. One-half of the suburban police departments had from 1.3 to 2.4 employees per 1,000 inhabitants. The average rate of full-time employees in sheriff's de-

Source: Crime in the United States–1974. Uniform Crime Reports. FBI.

partments was 1.6 per 1,000 inhabitants; however, in three-fourths of the departments the rate was 1.3 or less.

Police departments in the Middle Atlantic and South Atlantic States continued to have the highest average rate with 3.0 employees per 1,000 inhabitants. Cities in the West South Central and West North Central States had the lowest average ratio with 2.0.

Civilian Employees

The percentage of total law enforcement personnel represented by civilian employees is tabulated by population group. On the average during 1974, 15.3 percent of all city police personnel were civilian employees; up from 14.6 percent in 1973. Of all civilian employees, 61 percent were female and 39 percent were male personnel. Law enforcement administrators are continuing to utilize greater numbers of civilian employees, thereby relieving sworn personnel for active police duties.

Sworn Personnel

Law enforcement employee rates based on sworn personnel only (excluding civilian employees) show that the average for all cities was 2.1 in 1974 compared to the 1973 rate of 2.1 per 1,000 inhabitants. The city rates, nationally, range from 0.1 to 9.6 per 1,000 inhabitants. In city agencies, males represented 98 percent of all sworn personnel, while males in suburban agencies constituted 97 percent and in county sheriff and police departments 94 percent. The average ratio of sworn employees in sheriff's departments was 1.3 per 1,000 inhabitants and the rate range for the 2,503 reporting county agencies was 0.1-11.2 per 1,000 inhabitants. Caution should be exercised, however, in using rates for comparative purposes since there is a wide variation in the responsibilities of various law enforcement agencies throughout the country. Just as the conditions which affect the amount and type of crime that occurs vary from place to place, so do the requirements for types of police service based upon the conditions which exist in a given community. For example, the increased need for police service in a community which has a highly mobile or seasonal population, differs from a community which has a relatively stable or fixed population. In addition, a small community situated between two large cities may require a greater number of law enforcement personnel to handle crime conditions based solely on its geographic location.

The functions of the sheriffs also vary widely in different sections of the country. In certain areas the sheriffs' responsibilities are limited almost exclusively to civil functions and/or the administration of the county jail facilities. The sheriffs' departments used in computing rates, however, are all engaged in law enforcement activity and are responsible for all phases of policing in their jurisdiction.

It is pointed out that the figures set forth . . . represent national averages. They should be used as a guide or indicator and not considered as recommended or desirable police strengths. Adequate manpower for a specific place can only be determined after a careful study and analysis of the various factors which contribute to the requirement for police service in that community.

Editor's Note: According to the 1974 Uniform Crime Reports, by the FBI, there were 338,895 employees in law enforcement in the United States in 6,771 cities, representing a population of 136,064,000. Of these, 84.7 percent, or 287,044, were sworn personnel and 15.3 percent, or 51,850, were civilian employees. 3,761 suburban law enforcement agencies, representing a population of 60,318,000, employed a total of 124,992 persons. Sheriffs, representing 2,503 agencies and a population of 51,649,000, employed 82,972 civilian and sworn personnel in 1974.

TOWARd A REdEfINITION OF THE POLICE fUNCTION

HERMAN GOLDSTEIN

Some Generalizations Regarding the Police Task

As one . . . explore(s) the police function, one quickly finds that the principal and most valuable source of information is the police officer—the officer having years of experience at the operating level and, to a somewhat lesser extent, the officer who has carried some administrative responsibilities. But a combination of factors constrains these men from conveying their wealth of understanding into the public forum. Much of what he sees and does, the average officer feels, is defined by the nature of the public's interest in the police as being of minor consequence. More inhibiting, however, is the fact that the officer is a member of a semimilitary organization that places a value on secrecy and that discourages free expression by subordinates.

Frequent contact with the experienced officer and five years of administrative responsibility in a police agency have led me to conclude that there are several generalizations that can be drawn regarding the police function that are helpful in any further analyses that might take place.

1. *Solving crimes and apprehending criminals constitute but a small percentage of the total activity of a police force.*

Source: Administration of Criminal Justice. Report No. 7. Southern Regional Education Board and Institute of Government, University of North Carolina. 1967: 1-20. Reprinted with the kind permission of the Southern Regional Education Board.

A St. Louis County police officer was recently quoted in an article in *The National Observer* as stating: "I thought of police work as a life full of adventure and daily heroic deeds. It turned out to be mostly settling family fights, answering complaint calls about loud parties, dogs running loose, and that sort of thing." This characterization of police work coincides with the impression received by many individuals who have taken the opportunity to accompany a police officer on a night's tour of duty—even in an area of a large city having a high crime rate. Persons taking advantage of such an opportunity almost invariably report that the officer considered the night unusually "slow" and apologized for the lack of "action." But the consistency of the reported experiences suggests that what the observer saw is probably more typical of the manner in which the officer spends his time than he is prepared to recognize.

Police activity unrelated to the solving of crimes and the apprehension of criminals falls into four major categories: (a) the provision of social services; (b) the suppression of nuisances; (c) the control of motor vehicle traffic; and (d) the provision of a wide range of miscellaneous emergency-type services.

2. *Police have relatively little potential for preventing crime and outbreaks of violence.*

From the very beginnings of the police service in England, emphasis was placed upon the role of the police in preventing crime. Indeed, Sir Charles Rowan, the first commissioner of the Metropolitan Police, in speaking of prevention, said: "To this great end every effort of the police is to be directed. The security of person and property, the preservation of the public tranquility and all the other objects of a Police Establishment will thus be better effected than by the detection and punishment of the offender after he has succeeded in committing the crime. . . ." The degree to which Rowan and others were dedicated to this "principle of prevention" is reflected in the apparent opposition that they voiced to the appointment of the first individuals who were to devote all of their efforts to detection—the prototype of our modern-day detective.

In the intervening years, prevention as a principle of policing, in the sense in which it was first developed, has come to have little influence on the organization, staffing, and operations of our police forces. Modern police agencies are primarily geared to catching criminals. Prevention, as the term is used today, has come to characterize some of the activities in which the police are engaged, such as their patrol efforts, their work with juveniles, and their efforts to educate the public on conditions in one's home, car, or business that accommodate burglars and thieves. Within the total context of the police function, these activities, aimed at preventing crime, must compete with the more dominant concern for solving crime and apprehending criminals. In practical terms, this means competition for police manpower and for the budget dollar. The end result is that the preventive function tends to receive attention only when personnel are not otherwise occupied.

Toward a Redefinition of the Police Function

Despite the relatively small percentage of total police resources that go directly into preventive programs, police administrators in this country have continued to characterize prevention as one of their primary responsibilities—if not their most important one. Such a contention is an appealing one, for it has a positive ring to it, drawing public attention away from the somewhat negative image of the police as being exclusively oriented toward the catching and punishment of wrongdoers. The position has created a double-edged sword for the police, however, since it has encouraged the public to hold the police responsible for that crime which does occur. The number of reported crimes in a community, for example, are often taken as an indication of police efficiency. An upward trend in the crime rate is viewed as indicative of a failure in police operations. And, in similar fashion, the occurrence of an especially vicious crime is often followed by a public indictment of the police for having failed to prevent it.

All of these claims, on the part of both the police and the public, tend to ignore what is obvious to those who have been involved in the provision of police services: the capacity of the police to prevent crime is, indeed, very limited.

The primary method that the police must depend on for preventing crime implements the very elementary concept that a person contemplating a criminal act will not commit it if he can be convinced that he will be identified or apprehended in the process. As a result, most police efforts have been directed at making their presence felt to the maximum degree—as reflected in their use of conspicuously painted cars and their increased use of motorized patrol which, in contrast with foot patrol, has the potential for creating an impression of police omnipresence. There have been no serious efforts to measure the effectiveness of patrol as a crime-prevention method. It is clear, however, that whatever impact it has is limited to certain types of crimes that occur on the streets. A patrolling police officer, for example, is not likely to deter crimes of passion or to interfere with the carefully planned offenses of the professional criminal—most of which occur within private premises.

A dramatic and much heralded experiment conducted some years ago in New York City proved the obvious—that the saturation of an area with police officers will reduce crime. It did not examine the influence upon the crime rate outside the saturated area, nor did the experiment include any effort to determine whether the residents of the area were well prepared to tolerate such an intense degree of surveillance on a continuing basis and whether the taxpayers of the community at large were prepared to underwrite the cost of the required manpower. Police patrolling, as a preventive technique, is inherently limited in its effectiveness by all of these considerations.

An underlying assumption of patrol activities is that the offender fears the consequences of apprehension. The effectiveness of patrol, therefore, as a crime-prevention technique, is largely influenced by the reputation which the criminal justice system of a jurisdiction establishes as to its handling of given types of offenders and especially as to the sentence imposed upon an offender found to be guilty.

Another factor, often ignored, is that there is no firm legal basis for police work aimed at preventing crime. Most police authority over an individual usually begins when a police officer has reasonable grounds to believe that the individual committed a crime. Police cannot, for example, simply in the interest of preventing crime, search cars, explore private premises, or detain an individual.

All of these considerations force recognition of the limited capacity of the police to perform in a preventive role and—more basically—force a renewed awareness that, while the police may reduce the opportunity for the commission of a crime, their efforts do not begin to affect the deep-rooted causes of crime. Obvious as this realization may be, somewhat the same error that has been made in looking to the police for the prevention of crime is now being repeated with regard to the police role in preventing the outbreak of racial violence. It is true that the police can do much to lessen the likelihood of violence by assuring that their practices in the policing of the minority community are fair and proper and by promoting a dialogue that facilitates the filing of complaints. But even with the best programs in this area, the police, alone, cannot prevent riots. If civil disorder is to be avoided, communities must deal with the prejudices and bigotry that give rise to discrimination in employment, housing, and education.

Police efforts to prevent crime and to prevent outbreaks of violence, if they are to be meaningful, must be more realistically defined. Continuation of the existing approach that places demands and expectations upon the police that are impossible of achievement is disruptive of any serious efforts to improve the police service.

3. *Individual officers are required to exercise broad discretion in the fulfillment of their police responsibilities.*

The police are commonly viewed as a ministerial agency having no discretion in the exercise of their authority. While this view is occasionally reinforced by a court decision, there is a growing body of literature that cites the degree to which the police are, in fact, required to exercise discretion—such as in deciding which laws to enforce, in selecting from among available techniques for investigating crime, in deciding whom to arrest, and in determining how to process a criminal offender. Broad and often-times ambiguous statutes defining their powers and the limited resources made available to them are the major factors among several that require the police to assume a discretionary role.

In practical terms, the necessity for exercising discretion is reflected, for example, in the need for a police administrator to decide how much of his resources are to be devoted to traffic enforcement, as distinct from criminal investigations; in the decision of a police officer to arrest a disorderly group or order the members to "move on"; and in the determination of a juvenile officer to release a child to his parents rather than take him before the juvenile court. However the police officer acts, his decision is likely to have a major impact on the individual involved. Americans tend to be sensitive to any exercise of police authority—even if it does not result in an arrest and prosecution.

Most such decisions, in the absence of adequate legislative guidelines or administrative policies, are left to the discretion of individual officers. Confronted each day by frequently recurring situations, they either develop their own informal criteria for disposing of matters coming to their attention—depending heavily upon their imagination and resourcefulness— or they employ informal criteria which have, over a period of years, developed within the agency of which they are a part. The individual officer succeeds, to an amazing degree, in muddling his way through: disputes are resolved; dangerous persons are disarmed; people not in control of their capacities are protected; and many individuals are spared what, under some circumstances, would appear to be undue harshness of the criminal process. The results, however, are sometimes less satisfactory—primarily because the criteria that are employed emerge largely in response to a variety of pressures to which the police are exposed and which are, therefore, not carefully developed. For example, the high volume of work which an officer must handle dictates a desire to take shortcuts in the processing of minor incidents. The personal conveniences of the officer— in making a court appearance, in completing reports, or in working beyond a scheduled tour of duty—become important determinants of how a case is handled. The high value attached to solving crime becomes a dominant consideration—often to the exclusion of other, more important values. And such indefensible criteria as the status or characteristics of the complainant, the victim, or the offender are often found to be among the most seriously weighted factors, since an officer, left to function on his own, understandably tends to respond to a given situation on the basis of his personal norms regarding individual or group conduct. The criticism commonly directed against police agencies regarding the exercise of police authority most frequently relates to discretionary actions rather than the clearly illegal use of police powers.

The Need for Research and
Public Discussion

My purpose in making these three broad generalizations regarding the nature of police work (i.e., the noncriminal aspects of much of police activity, the limited role of the police in preventing crime, and the fact that the police are required to exercise discretion) is threefold: (1) to call attention to the significant difference between the actual functioning of the police and the widely-held notions regarding the character of police operations; (2) to illustrate some of the major problems and issues that are raised by actual police functioning; and (3) to point up the need for addressing these problems and, more broadly, for clarifying our thinking regarding the police role in our society as a prerequisite to undertaking specific programs intended to strengthen and improve our law enforcement agencies.

Directions for Change

If I were at this time, without the benefit of research and public discussion, called upon to suggest the major paths for development of the police field in the years ahead, I would settle upon two major objectives.

The first would be the *development within the police field of a stronger and more basic commitment to the values that must attach to the police function under democratic government.* In a society that places so high a value on freedom and individual rights, we must insist that police officers, who are authorized to interfere with these rights, not only understand them, but that they and the agencies of which they are a part have a basic commitment to championing them above all other considerations as they are called upon to exercise their authority. This means, at the operating level, that, however isolated is the contact between an officer and an alleged offender, the officer would, on his own volition, be dominated in his choice of action by a desire to exercise proper concern for the rights of the offender. The police of this country must come to be viewed, foremost, as the guarantors of constitutionally granted rights and, only secondarily, as the catchers of criminals. Among the benefits that would flow from such an orientation would be a greater willingness to give to the police the authority and discretion which are needed if their effectiveness in the prevention and solution of crime is to be increased.

My second objective would be the *development within the police field of a desire to meet more effectively the variety of social problems of a noncriminal nature that come to police attention.* It is apparent that many social problems, such as family discord, mental illness, or inadequate housing, will continue to come to the surface in a way which brings them, initially, to police attention. Police intervention at so critical a moment can have the effect of aggravating an already difficult situation, or it can constitute the first step, in collaboration with other community resources, toward solving the underlying problems. It can have a direct effect upon the incidence of crime by preventing an assault from occurring, or it can have a more long-range effect by strengthening the stability of the family unit. It follows that the devotion of more attention by police administrators to such problems has the potential for increasing substantially both the efficiency and effectiveness of the police response. Greater police involvement in this area also has the potential for diluting the harshness that often characterizes the police as enforcers of the law—casting the police in a more helpful, supportive, and positive role in the community.

CHAPTER **2-5**

WHAT does a policeman do?

GEORGE P. MCMANUS

In addition to making a determination as to what the duties of the police are, an attempt has been made in this report to determine what the policeman thinks his role should be. A high degree of correlation may not be essential in this area but certainly an attempt should be made to explain any substantial differences between the former and the latter. Community expectations will also be noted and analyzed. Does the community expect from the police a different role than the analysis of the police task has indicated? Does the community expect a different role of the policeman than the policeman himself expects?[1] Once again, it may not be necessary to demonstrate exact relationships but marked differences should be explained.

If the duties described by the police training curriculums, the policeman, and the community correspond, relating community concepts to the police curriculum will be relatively simple. If, however, inconsistencies are uncovered it will become possible to identify them and determine the magnitude of the inconsistency.

A New Jersey Police Training Commission report of January 1969 listed 32 specific police activities.[2] This police activity scale comprised the following:

Control traffic
Stop and question
Issue traffic tickets

Source: George P. McManus, Project Director. *Police Training and Performance Study.* U.S. Department of Justice, Law Enforcement Assistance Administration, National Institute of Law Enforcement and Criminal Justice. 1970.

Interview victims and witnesses
First aid
Search crime scenes
Inspect places
Arrest
Good relations in community
Testify
Give directions
Search and question prisoners
Escort parades
Preserve evidence
Mentally disturbed persons
Give information
Family disputes
Guard visitors, property
Rescue lost persons
Help people who have lost keys
Advise, warn, or arrest youngsters
Control crowds
Assist motorists
Drunks and alcoholics
School crossings
Make written reports
Pick up stray dogs
Check business licenses
Refer citizens' complaints
Public nuisances
Election day
Recover property

Although the purpose of the above study was to rank activities by the community's attitude toward their importance (and will be referred to again in that context), it provides a useful starting point in the listing of police activities.

In outlining the job description for patrolmen, Allen Z. Gammage identifies 16 activities and describes the training needs under each of the 16 categories as follows:[3]

1. Patrols Assigned Beat or Post
   Care and operation of departmental equipment
   Care and operation of departmental vehicles
   City and county ordinances
   Penal code
   Departmental rules and regulations
   General and special orders
   Discipline and deportment
   Principles of beat patrol and observations

Human relations
Public relations
Geography of the city, district, and beat
Techniques of arrest, search, and seizure
Law of arrest, search, and seizure
Military drill
Gymnasium and calisthenics
Defensive driving

2. Advises, Directs, and Gives Information to the General Public
Geography of the city, district, and beat
Departmental procedures in handling lost children
Location and use of emergency health and medical facilities
Human relations
Public relations

3. Responds To and Handles Emergency Calls
Geography of the city, district, and beat
Care and operation of departmental equipment and vehicles
City and county ordinances
Penal code
Law of arrest, search, and seizure
First aid
Life saving
Departmental procedure in handling catastrophes, disasters, and fires
Departmental procedure in handling juveniles and lost children
Departmental procedures in handling sick, injured, and insane persons
Self defense
Firearms
Vehicle code
City and county traffic ordinances
Traffic accident procedure
Gymnasium and calisthenics

4. Enforces State Laws, City and County Ordinances
City and country ordinances
Law of arrest, search, and seizure
Law of evidence
Criminal procedure
Philosophy of law enforcement
Civil rights (guarantees)
Self defense
Firearms
Juvenile law
Traffic law

5. Makes Arrests and Searches
Penal code
City and county ordinances

Civil rights

Techniques of arrest, search, and seizure

Departmental procedure in the transportation of prisoners

Departmental procedure in stopping suspicious vehicles

Departmental rules and regulations

Law of arrest, search, and seizure

Law of evidence

Self-defense

Firearms

Gymnasium and calisthenics

6. Investigates Citizens Complaints and Makes Preliminary Investigations of Major Crimes

Penal code

City and county ordinances

Laws of evidence, arrest, search, and seizure

Civil rights

Departmental procedure relating to civil complaints, domestic complaints, mental illness, dog bite cases, ambulance reports, trespass complaints, prowler complaints, drunk and drunk driving complaints, and the like

Conduct preliminary investigations of auto thefts, burglaries, robberies, assaults, rapes, and other sex cases

Crime scene protection and investigation

Collection and preservation of physical evidence

Crime laboratory services

Scientific investigation techniques

Departmental records and forms

Report writing

Conduct field interrogations

Conduct general interrogations and interviews

7. Interrogates and Interviews Victims, Complaints, Witnesses, and Suspects

Civil rights

Departmental procedure in taking statements, admissions, and confessions

Field notetaking

Departmental records and forms

Report writing

Departmental rules and regulations

Penal code

Techniques of interviewing and interrogation

8. Makes Necessary Reports and Records

Organization and functions of the police records division

Departmental rules and regulations

Departmental reports, records, and forms

Basic records procedures

Field notetaking and principles of report writing

9. Safeguarding Property
Organization and function of the police property section
Departmental procedure in handling lost, stolen, and recovered property
Departmental procedure in handling of impounded vehicles
Departmental procedure in handling prisoner's property
Police duties at catastrophes, disasters, and fires
Departmental procedure in protecting property at scenes of crimes, public gatherings, and recreational facilities

10. Collects, Preserves, and Safeguards Evidence
Patrolman's duties at crime scenes
Collection and preservation of physical evidence
Basic principles in scientific investigations
Laws of evidence, arrest, search, and seizure
Principles of criminal identification
Principles of criminal investigation

11. Testifies in Court
Organization of State and local courts
Organization and functions of the coroner's office
Departmental rules and regulations
Criminal procedure
Jurisdiction and venue
Law of evidence
Court demeanor and testimony

12. Regulates and Controls Traffic
General traffic procedure
Philosophy of traffic law enforcement
Departmental procedure in handling traffic violators and traffic summonses
Traffic accident investigation
Traffic direction and control
Traffic engineering
Traffic safety education
Scientific techniques for drunk driving control
Traffic law

13. Cooperates with Other Police Units and Allied Agencies
Federal law enforcement agencies and principal areas of cooperation
Local law enforcement agencies and principal areas of cooperation
State law enforcement agencies and principal areas of cooperation
Organization and administration of the city government, police department, and of local allied agencies

14. Operates and Cares for Departmental and Personal Equipment
Care and operation of departmental equipment, vehicles, emergency equipment, and weapons

Departmental rules and regulations

Traffic laws

Organization and functions of the police property section

Departmental procedure in purchasing equipment

15. Performs Miscellaneous Duties and Provides Services

Handling of bombs and explosives

Police procedures in emergencies and disasters, procedures in handling strikes, mobs, racial disturbances, and the like

Election duties

Licensing bicycles and taxicabs

Specialized duties including the work of jailor, warrant clerk, information clerk, complaint clerk

16. Maintains a Professional Attitude

History of law enforcement

Philosophy of law enforcement

Career opportunities in law enforcement

Law enforcement as a profession

Police ethics

Civil rights

Departmental rules and regulations

Civil service rules and regulations

Discipline and deportment

Introduction to professional police associations

Introduction to professional police publications

Introduction to police education programs

Human relations

Public relations

Although at first glance it appears that there is unnecessary duplication in the above training recommendations, close scrutiny reveals that the duplication serves a real purpose. For example, knowledge of the geography of the beat, district, and city is required not only of category 1 (patrol), but also of categories 2 (advises, directs, and gives information to the general public), and 3 (response to and handling of emergency calls). Further, care of equipment and vehicles is required not only in category 14 but also in categories 1 and 3.

Twentieth Precinct Project

The 20th precinct, on New York's West Side is a moderately active precinct which experiences a variety of police problems associated with neighborhoods ranging from the high-income area of Central Park West to ghetto areas. As a representative precinct the 20th has been periodically assigned the status of a laboratory where various experiments have been undertaken. One of the experiments involved a study of what a policeman does, frequency of occurrence of incidents, total time spent in each activity, and average time spent per incident.

Forty-five incidents or police duties were isolated. Total time spent on each activity, frequency of occurrence, and average time spent per incident, is shown for each type of incident in Tables 2-5-1 and 2-5-2.

As would be expected, homicides accounted for the largest average time spent per incident (290.6 minutes), followed by narcotics investigations and auto accidents with serious injury or death. It is apparent that ordering incidents by average time spent per incident provides a possible ranking of tasks in order of complexity of task. This should provide an indication of complexity of the training task with at least a clue as to necessary training time. Strangely, the "other" category appears as No. 1 in frequency of occurrence and as No. 2 in total hours devoted to the incident. However, it ranks 38th in average time per incident. This indicates that although the category was frequently recorded, relatively little time (28.8 minutes) was expended per incident. The "other" category was used as a catchall for services which did not fit exactly into one of the other 44 categories. It is probably safe to assume that if a police officer doubted just how to classify an event he dropped it into the "other" category. Some examples of the "other" potpourri follow:

Utility trouble. Electricity, telephone.
Persons locked out of, or in, apartments, cars.
Call for help. Often involving a report of a woman screaming; however, the responding officers were unable to locate trouble.
Meet city marshal. Police stand by at eviction scenes to prevent trouble between the tenant and landlord from developing into violence.
Stuck elevator.
Notifications of arrest, injury, or death.
Meet complainant. Sometimes results from a jumbled call where the officers are not certain of the nature of the call.
Licensed premises check.
Smoke conditions from chimneys and smoke stacks in violation of air pollution regulations.
Meet another unit.
Auto alarms sounding.
Stuck auto horn.
Stray or injured animal.
Runaway horse, and so on.

Another 6-month study in the 20th precinct disclosed that 85 percent of a patrolman's time is spent on preventive patrol while the remaining 15 percent is devoted to answering calls for services.[4] Of the time devoted to calls for services, 30 percent is associated with crime while 70 percent is noncriminal in nature. Of the "criminal" category, crimes against property consumed the most time while, in the "noncriminal" category, aid to sick and injured consumed the most time.[5] The data also reflected that during 1964 and 1965 about 1,300 man-hours were required to guard the President of the United States during his

TABLE 2-5-1. Incidents in the 20th precinct, New York City Police Department, ranked in order of total time spent per incident, 1967–68

Incident type	Number of incidents	Total time (in minutes)	Average time (in minutes)
1. Sick	4,552	202,143	44.4
2. Other	5,629	162,310	28.8
3. Other misdemeanors	1,190	106,034	89.1
4. Dispute	3,582	106,016	29.6
5. Burglary	2,518	104,881	41.7
6. Unfounded	5,132	102,881	20.7
7. Dead on arrival	402	60,126	149.8
8. Injured	1,170	46,063	41.1
9. Intoxicated person	1,555	41,830	25.9
10. Disorderly groups	1,693	37,780	22.3
11. Robbery	512	33,476	65.4
12. Auto accident	547	32,943	60.2
13. Alarm of fire	1,013	30,483	30.0
14. Felonious assault	309	26,982	87.3
15. Auto accident–injury	286	25,334	88.6
16. Larceny from auto	514	17,579	34.2
17. Malicious mischief	435	16,261	37.4
18. Utility trouble	378	14,502	38.4
19. Narcotics	59	13,582	230.2
20. Auto larceny	104	12,556	120.7
21. Grand larceny	235	11,598	49.4
22. Other felonies	64	9,559	149.4
23. Motor vehicle recovered	73	7,221	98.8
24. Traffic violation	270	7,201	27.1
25. Vehicles mechanical trouble	201	7,201	35.8
26. Accidental alarm	264	6,873	26.0
27. Grand larceny–pocketbook snatch	130	6,366	48.9
28. Auto safety check	126	4,175	33.1
29. Prowler	121	3,549	29.3
30. Dangerous condition	81	3,510	43.0
31. Found persons	46	2,802	60.9
32. Auto accident–serious injury or death	13	2,587	199.0
33. Arrest–serving summons	81	2,480	30.6
34. False alarm of fire	86	1,865	21.7
35. Property recovered	35	1,848	52.8
36. Homicide	6	1,744	290.6
37. Rape	29	1,622	55.9
38. Weapons	9	1,298	144.2
39. Missing persons	24	1,096	45.7
40. Prostitution	7	1,090	155.7
41. Attempted suicide	13	1,056	81.2
42. Gambling	7	813	116.1
43. Traffic court warrants	40	713	17.8
44. Suicide	6	607	101.2
45. ABC violation	5	160	32.0

TABLE 2-5-2. Incidents in the 20th precinct, New York City Police Department, ranked in order of frequency of occurrence, 1967–68

Incident type	Number of incidents	Total time (in minutes)	Average time (in minutes)
1. Other	5,629	162,310	28.8
2. Unfounded	5,132	102,881	20.0
3. Sick	4,552	202,143	44.4
4. Dispute	3,582	106,016	29.6
5. Burglary	2,518	104,881	41.7
6. Disorderly groups	1,693	37,780	22.3
7. Intoxicated person	1,555	41,830	25.9
8. Other misdemeanors	1,190	106,034	89.1
9. Injured	1,170	46,063	41.1
10. Alarm of fire	1,013	30,483	30.0
11. Auto accident	547	32,943	60.2
12. Larceny from auto	514	17,579	34.2
13. Robbery	512	33,476	65.4
14. Malicious mischief	435	16,261	37.4
15. Dead on arrival	402	60,216	149.8
16. Utility trouble	378	14,502	38.4
17. Felonious assault	309	26,982	87.3
18. Auto accident injury	286	25,334	88.6
19. Traffic violation	270	7,201	27.1
20. Accidental alarm	264	6,873	26.0
21. Grand larceny	235	11,598	49.4
22. Vehicle mechanical trouble	201	7,201	35.8
23. Grand larceny—pocketbook snatch	130	6,366	48.9
24. Auto safety check	126	4,175	33.1
25. Prowler	121	3,549	29.3
26. Auto larceny	104	12,556	120.7
27. False alarm of fire	86	1,865	21.7
28. Arrest—serving summons	81	2,480	30.6
29. Dangerous condition	81	3,510	43.0
30. Motor vehicle recovered	73	7,211	98.8
31. Other felonies	64	9,559	149.4
32. Narcotics	59	13,582	230.2
33. Found person	46	2,802	60.9
34. Traffic warrants	40	713	17.8
35. Property recovered	35	1,848	52.8
36. Rape	29	1,622	55.9
37. Missing persons	24	1,096	45.7
38. Auto accident—serious injury or death	13	2,587	199.0
39. Attempted suicide	13	1,056	81.2
40. Weapons	9	1,298	144.2
41. Prostitution	7	1,090	155.7
42. Gambling	7	813	116.1
43. Homicide	6	1,744	290.6
44. Suicide	6	607	101.2
45. ABC violation	5	160	32.0

visits; and that 58 men are required year round to guard foreign missions and consulates mainly located in other precincts.

In his 1969 study of a South Bronx precinct, Capt. John F. Skelly analyzed the job of the patrolman and wrote:

> * * * the foot patrolman rarely makes notations about the legitimate but minor jobs that he performs—i.e., the visits to business premises, the door and glass checks, the advice and directions given to citizens in distress, the information given to other members of the department or the members of other agencies, the settling of minor disputes on his post, the official reports that he prepares, etc.—unless he is worried about the presence of a shoo-fly.

Skelly divided the tasks of the patrolman (foot patrol and motorized patrol were examined separately) into the following ten categories:

Patrol and observation.—Tasks included building checks, preventive patrol, foot patrol by motorized patrolmen, and special area patrol. They are best described as "routine" patrol to which foot patrolmen devoted 55 percent and car crews over 35 percent of their time. Beat men on the late tour (midnight to 8 a.m.) did little else.

Public service.—(This task covered time spent on escorts, aid to sick and injured, referrals and notifications, school and church crossings, aid to stranded motorists, and aid to distressed residents and pedestrians.

Patrol investigations.—Components of this task included action taken in burglaries and burglar alarms, licensed clubs, assault and robbery, stolen cars, suspicious cars and persons, gambling operations, youth crimes and cases, and conferences with detectives.

Disputes.—Disputes included family fights, landlord-tenant arguments, taxicab fare disagreements, and disorderly groups.

Aid to other agencies.—This service included assistance given to employees of municipal agencies and other law enforcement groups.

Miscellaneous field services.—Services included transport members of the force, assist members of the force, pick up and deliver material, carry the mail, transport supervisors to and from the precinct, division, and borough commands, and guard crime scenes.

Enforcement action.—Enforcement included making arrests, and issuing summonses and warnings.

Reporting.—The preparation of reports and forms, memorandum book entries, and telephone reports to the station house comprised the bulk of reporting.

Community relations.—This item was included under category 2, "Public Service."

Other activity.—This category was a catchall for miscellaneous activities such as car maintenance, unit training, coffee breaks, and meal periods.

Table 2-5-3 presents a time-study made of these tasks. Foot patrol and motorized patrol are treated separately and are listed by hours expended on the task and by the percentage of total time consumed by each task. This study involved only 18 patrolmen, three sergeants, and one lieutenant. The work of the officers was tabulated by 15-minute intervals for 3 weeks and was supplemented by personal interviews. Due to the brevity of the study no attempt is made to evaluate its representative character. Hopefully, the study adds knowledge in an area where valid information is scarce.

A 1963 study of the functions of the foot patrolman in the 30th precinct revealed a series of anachronistic duties and rules and procedures related to these duties.[6] In performing his duties in the well-known broad general categories of preventing crime, arresting offenders, enforcing laws, preserving the peace, and protecting life and property, the foot patrolman carries out the following duties:

School crossing duty.—3 to 5 hours per day, even though the department employed 1,250 civilian school crossing guards who were paid $1.90 per hour in 1963.

Bank services.—Banks are guarded for 1 hour before opening to opening. This practice was initiated in 1955 after robbers entered a bank with employees who were reporting for work. The plan fails to account for the remainder of the day when the bank remains unguarded by police. Nor does it consider businesses other than banks which, it would seem, should be entitled to equal protection.

Messenger services.—The foot patrolman is used for a variety of messenger services, including mail delivery, and transportation of fingerprint cards from

TABLE 2-5-3. Job assignments for patrolmen in 1 precinct New York City, 1969

Job category	Foot patrol		Motorized patrol	
	Hours	Percent	Hours	Percent
Patrol and observation	42	53	342	36
Public service	14	17	166	17
Investigations	3	4	118	12
Disputes	1	1	34	4
Assist other agencies	0	0	28	3
Miscellaneous services	0	0	90	9
Enforcement	1	1	32	3
Reporting	2	2	34	4
Community relations	4	5	10	1
Other	13	16	106	11
Total	80	100	960	100

Source: John F. Skelly, master's thesis, 1969.

the precinct to the identification center. Transportation for the latter is by public conveyance.

Details for public gatherings.—The foot patrolman is utilized for extra details such as parades, strikes, political meetings, public assemblies, sporting events, state visits, and a multitude of other events which require specialized police coverage.

Caretaker for dead human bodies.—Foot patrolmen must guard dead human bodies in cases that require the attention of the medical examiner. Even under nonsuspicious circumstances, where competent family members are present, the patrolman must remain with the body until it is removed to the morgue or released to a mortician. The time involved in this duty can range from 2 to 8 or more hours.

Caretaker of the mentally disturbed.—Foot patrolmen guard mentally disturbed persons from the time they come to their attention to the time they are either admitted or refused admittance to the psychiatric ward. In many cases where the subject exhibits violent tendencies this is a legitimate duty. In many other instances where the subject is nonviolent, senile, or disoriented other police services suffer while the police officer remains with the patient.

Property protection.—The foot patrolman guards recovered stolen vehicles until a tow truck arrives, ostensibly to prevent the vehicle from being restolen. It would appear that other preventive measures could be adopted which would free the patrolman to return to his general patrol duties.

A psychological study carried out for the Chicago Police Department isolated 20 behavioral requirements in a job analysis for patrolmen that was admittedly not all inclusive.[7] However, the study was thought "* * * to contain many of the attributes which are crucial to the successful performance of the patrolman's job." These essential requirements are—

The ability to react instantly after long periods of monotony.
The ability to exhibit initiative, to use judgment and imagination in problem solving, in other words to exhibit "street sense."
The ability to know the patrol area, to know the normal routine events as well as the unusual behavior patterns of its residents.
The ability to make the right decision quickly.
The ability to demonstrate mature judgment.
The ability to judge out-of-the-ordinary situations.
Good psychomotor skills, e.g., ability to drive a vehicle, fire a weapon, and handle himself physically.
The ability to communicate, orally and in writing.
The ability to act "effectively in extremely divergent interpersonal situations." In other words, the ability to deal with people ranging from criminal to noncriminal.
The ability to endure physical and verbal abuse.

Exhibit a professional and self-confident manner.

The ability to restore equilibrium to social groups; that is, the ability to restore order from disorder.

The ability to skillfully question participants of, as well as witnesses to, a crime or incident.

The ability to take charge of situations, particularly emergency situations such as a crime or accident.

The ability to work under loose supervision.

The ability to tolerate stress in its many forms.

The ability to exhibit courage.

The ability to remain objective.

The ability to maintain a balanced perspective even though being constantly exposed to the worst in human behavior.

The ability to maintain the highest personal integrity.

These 20 personal characteristics pose some interesting questions for the police trainer and the academician. Can a trainee be instructed in such a way as to be made competent in all of these abilities? Certainly it is possible to train a patrolman in the physical geography of his beat and district although it would appear mainly to be a case of self-education conducted in the field. However, how is one trained to exhibit mature judgment? An individual can be taught communication skills and questioning skills but how is one taught personal courage or a balanced perspective? This is not to imply that these skills or attributes cannot be taught but only that they are much more abstract than the usually defined police role. Assistance from professionals will be required to formulate curriculums and teach in many of these abstract areas.

Generally speaking, the police training curriculum has been skills oriented. It is, perhaps, time to give attention to intangibles such as problem solving, use of discretion, use of authority and learning the proper role of police in society.

In his study of the role of the patrolman James Q. Wilson stated that his, "* * * role is defined more by his responsibility for maintaining order than by his responsibility for enforcing the law."[8] A patrolman does more than simply prevent crime and apprehend criminals. He recovers stolen property, directs traffic, provides emergency medical aid, gets cats out of trees, checks on the homes of families on vacation, and helps little old ladies who have locked themselves out of their apartments.

A sample of citizens' complaint calls to the Syracuse Police Department during the week of June 3 through 9, 1966 (based on a 20-percent sample of a week's calls) illustrates this point as shown in Table 2-5-4.

Approximately 20 percent of these calls required the officer to get information, about one-third of the calls were for service, and only about one-tenth pertained to law enforcement as such.

The Police Role in Contemporary Society

TABLE 2-5-4. Citizens' complaint calls, Syracuse, N.Y., Police Department, June 3-9, 1966

Type of call	Number	Percent
Information gathering	69	22.1
Book and check	2	–
Get a report	67	–
Service	117	37.5
Accidents, illness, and ambulance calls	42	–
Animals	8	–
Assist a person	1	–
Drunk person	8	–
Escort vehicle	3	–
Fire, powerline or tree down	26	–
Lost or found person or property	23	–
Property damage	6	–
Order maintenance	94	30.1
Gang disturbance	50	–
Family trouble	23	–
Assault, fight	9	
Investigation	8	–
Neighbor trouble	4	–
Law enforcement	32	10.3
Burglary in progress	9	–
Check a car	5	–
Open door, window	8	–
Prowler	6	–
Make an arrest	4	–
Totals	312	100.0

Source: James Q. Wilson, "Varieties of Police Behavior," Harvard University Press, 1968.

Characteristics Common to Police Duties

Whether the police function is divided into 32, 16, 45, or x number of specific duties, an analysis of these duties will reveal that most involve a whole series of common incidents. This fact has an important bearing on police training as it relates to police work.

A patrolman learns of an incident requiring his services in one of two ways. He either witnesses the incident or he is called to the incident. Patrolmen, detectives, plainclothesmen, and supervisors all face exactly the same problem in responding to calls, to get there as fast and safely as possible. Here then is a phase of training that applies to all policemen no matter what role he is performing at the time. Policemen who drive or operate vehicles (cars, scooters, trucks, motorcycles, and even helicopters) must be trained in their use. The foot patrolman must be trained in his approach to a specific action. As an

example, he must be told not to run up six flights of stairs to quell a disturbance. The winded patrolman will be ineffective in cases where additional
physical demands are encountered.

What other elements do most of the patrolman's duties have in common?
How can training be applied to these similar duties?

Once the patrolman arrives at the scene of the incident, be it a homicide
or a traffic collision, he must—

Protect the scene;
Detain participants and witnesses;
Search for and recover evidence;
Take required reports;
Possibly effect an arrest;
Aid injured; and
Clear the scene.

From what would the scene be protected? People, including other officers—so training in how to deal with people is indicated. Detention of participants and witnesses also requires the ability to deal with people. Witnesses often
must be persuaded of their value as witnesses. Interviewing requires listening.
There are techniques which can be learned which will increase a person's effectiveness as a listener. The successful search and recovery of evidence not only
requires training in criminalistics but also in the rules of evidence. The preparation of required reports requires abilities that can be improved by training;
abilities such as penmanship, spelling, composition. Ability to deal with people
also is required in the taking of reports since much of what an officer reports is
what he has been told by witnesses and participants. Effecting the arrest, again,
requires the ability to deal with people. Aiding injured requires first-aid training
and also requires some understanding of psychology. Finally, clearing the scene
involves leaving the area so that the people using it will be inconvenienced as
little as possible. Almost every duty, job, role of the policeman involves interaction with other people. The need for training in human interaction cannot
be stressed enough.

Attitudinal Research

The Community View of the Police Role

A 1968 Vera Institute study of the New York City Police Department revealed
that none of the 14 police-community relations activities studied received a
great amount of acceptance. Neither did they receive outright rejection by
the community. Interestingly, a majority of patrolmen who work in areas which

utilize the community council program believe that the program is fairly well accepted by the public, with organized sports activities for youth receiving the most acceptance.[9]

The fact that the police are more optimistic about their community relations programs than the study indicates that they should be, is probably explained by the natural lack of objectivity that one has of one's own efforts. However, an improvement in communications between the police and the community would probably remedy the difficulty. The correlation between police and community attitudes in this field must necessarily be high. Anything else would indicate that the police are giving to the community something that the community does not want. New York City Police are aware of the importance of the community relations problem within their city and they wish to do something about it.

A recent public opinion survey in Hamilton Township, Mercer County, N.J., asked two relevant questions. What do people believe the police should do and what do people consider important in police service? According to the survey, police functions ranked in the following order of importance:[10]

Advise, warn, or arrest youngsters
Preserve evidence
Stop and question
Arrest
Good community relations
Crowd control
Search crime scenes
Interview victims and witnesses
Issue traffic tickets
Search and question prisoners
Make written reports
Testify
Inspect places
First aid
Give information
Mentally disturbed persons
Drunks and alcoholics
Rescue lost persons
Recover property
Control traffic
Assist motorists
Give directions
Guard visitors, property
Refer citizen's complaints
Public nuisances
Election day
Escort parades

School crossings
Check business licenses
Help people who lost keys
Family disputes
Pick up stray dogs

Naturally, any generalization based on the above listing outside of Hamilton Township, should be made with care. However, this effort should be considered as a start toward a more complete compilation of community attitudes toward police, and, supplemented by studies of communities throughout the Nation, a pattern of community expectations should emerge which will aid the police trainer in developing meaningful and useful police training curriculums.

The Policeman's View of His Role

The Vera Institute of Justice study in New York City indicates that patrolmen feel that leniency on the part of the courts has damaged their effectiveness. The *Mapp* decision and the *Miranda* decision are particularly resented. "Half the patrolmen also say the Civilian Complaint Review Board has impaired the efficient performance of their duties a great deal."[11]

The stop and frisk law and the Patrolmen's Benevolent Association are regarded favorably by the policeman. However, he has little confidence in established grievance systems.

By and large patrolmen are dissatisfied with the amount of backing they receive from the department. They feel they lack the authority to do their job as the community would have them do it.[12] The patrolman sees a general trend toward permissiveness in society which results in leniency in the administration of justice. He sees this attitude as the opposite to the aggressive action he believes will do a better job of prevention of serious crimes. In general, patrolmen believe that the public wants more aggressive law enforcement and they believe police-community relations would improve if more police protection could be provided, particularly by foot patrols.

Patrolmen feel that the end result of a police-community relations program is to develop better public understanding of the police role in the maintenance of law and order. It would seem, however, just as important for the police to develop a better understanding of the community and its attitudes toward the police role in the maintenance of law and order.

In black and Puerto Rican areas the opinion of patrolmen is divided on whether or not the public wants greater minority representation among the patrolmen assigned to the minority areas.

Although a majority of patrolmen feel that people in their area have at least "a fair amount" of respect for the police, 43 percent of police polled felt that people in their area have little or no respect for the police. Many patrolmen think that the police vocation receives less public respect than other public service occupations. Of nine occupations listed, 46 percent of the police polled felt that none were less respected than the police. The vast majority of patrolmen feel that the public does not understand the job of the police. This lack of understanding leads the public to place unrealistic demands upon the police.

Police believe that the public is critical of the slowness of police action; the public wants less attention paid to minor violations; the public favors legalized gambling but does not favor legalized marijuana or homosexuality; the public is satisfied with police aid to sick and injured; the public wants more policemen assigned to their communities; and the public's chief criticism of the police concerns the alleged police failure to prevent serious crime.

Nearly half of the policemen interviewed believe that the public thinks that policemen should be of the same racial and ethnic background as the public they serve. However, the majority believe that the public is satisfied with the proportions of blacks and Puerto Ricans now on the force. The majority also believe that the public is satisfied with the way citizen complaints against the police are now handled. Additionally, no public criticism of the actions of off-duty policemen is seen. The police believe they are unjustly blamed by the public for the failures of other city departments. These criticisms are concentrated primarily in low social-income areas.

Policemen cite a variety of reasons for public hostility toward the police. Among the cited reasons are—

The public feeling that it can get away with being hostile toward police;
General hostility toward authority of any kind;
A tendency to blame police for many of society's problems;
Past unhappy experiences with police;
The communication of unhappy experiences that others have had with the police;
Outside agitators;
People who take their troubles out on police;
The results of drinking;
The results of drugs or narcotics;
Police inability to reduce crime; and
Police inability to solve a greater percentage of crimes.

Approximately one-half of the patrolmen interviewed believe that the public understands their problems; few patrolmen, however, believe that the public is enthusiastic about police-community relations programs, youth sports activities excepted.

Three out of four patrolmen believe that the public has reason to commend the police for the job they are doing and furthermore most patrolmen feel little or no reason for public criticism. Strangely, however, most patrolmen feel they would receive little or no help from the public if their lives were in danger.

Patrolmen see less permissiveness toward lawbreakers as the most helpful step toward improved police-community relations. Table 2-5-5 is a compilation of police answers to the question: "In view of the attitudes you have described and your own experience as a policeman, how helpful to you think each of the ideas listed below would be in improving relations between the police and the people in your area?"

Not only do patrolmen believe that court leniency has reduced their job effectiveness, they also believe it has caused a deterioration in their relationships with the community. The compilation in Table 2-5-6 signifies the police atti-

TABLE 2-5-5.

	Total patrolmen (percent)[1]			
	Very helpful	Fairly helpful	Not too helpful	Not at all helpful
Less leniency on the part of the courts	82	5	2	8
Educating the public on the role of the police	60	24	8	5
Stricter enforcement of the law by the police	60	20	12	5
Longer assignments in one area so the police can get to know the people better	49	25	13	10
Assigning more police to the area	34	29	20	13
Having policemen of the same racial and ethnic background as the people in their area	23	25	27	22
Community relations programs	21	49	19	8
Giving police more training in human relations and psychology	16	36	28	17
More police involvement in housing and sanitation problems	4	7	30	56
Use of name plates identifying the police	2	3	16	76

Source: Vera Institute of Justice.
[1]Percent expressing no opinion is not shown.

TABLE 2-5-6.

	Total patrolmen (percent)[1]			
	A great deal	A fair amount	Very little	Not at all
A tendency toward leniency on the part of the courts	84	8	2	2
The Mapp decision which forbids the use of illegally obtained evidence; i.e., evidence secured during an illegal search or seized under illegal circumstances	52	24	13	6
The Civilian Complaint Review Board	52	21	15	8
The Miranda decision which requires police to advise those in custody of their right to remain silent and to have an attorney	41	25	18	11

Source: Vera Institute of Justice.
[1] Percent expressing no opinion is not shown.

tude to the question: "In your opinion, to what extent, if any, does each of the following impair the efficient performance of your duties?"

The stop and frisk law and the PBA were seen, by patrolmen, as being more helpful than department grievance procedures. To the question "How helpful do you think each of the following is in reducing the pressures of your work?" the police replied as is shown in Table 2-5-7.

In his classic 1951 study of department X, William Westley described the police perception of how the public regards the police as follows:

> The policeman divides the public into five general categories, according to the way he thinks they feel about him, the way in which he must approach them in order to obtain respect, their political power, and their reference to his aims. The groups then form a rough continuum ranging from the child who is thought to like the police, to react to kindness, to have political power, and to have reference to the aims of the police only in his status as a future citizen, through the better class of people, the slum dwellers and the Negroes, to the criminal who is thought to hate the police, to have no political power, to whom force is

TABLE 2-5-7.

	Total patrolmen (percent)[1]			
	Very helpful	Fairly helpful	Not too helpful	Not at all helpful
The stop and frisk law	42	28	16	8
Representation by your line organization (PBA)	41	29	17	7
The informal means afforded of discussing your problems with your supervisors and commanding officer	24	31	21	17
The formal departmental grievance machinery	19	20	30	25

Source: Vera Institute of Justice.
[1]Percent expressing no opinion is not shown.

the only intelligible language, and who is useful to the police as he is apprehended and convicted.[13]

Further, William Westley found that the police regard "respect for the police" as so important they are willing to exert their power to preserve it, even if the use of this power itself approaches the unlawful. In fact, the "maintenance of respect for the police" is characterized as one of the two "major occupational norms of the police."

Seventy-four patrolmen in department X were asked by Westley to define incidents where they would feel justified in "roughing a man up." Thirty-nine percent felt that this procedure would be proper in cases of disrespect for the police. This "* * * supports the thesis that the maintenance of respect for the police is a major orientation of the police."

The symbol, to the patrolman of department X, of disrespect to the police is the "wise guy." A method of handling this individual is described in the following response:

* * * for example when you stop a fellow for routine questioning. Say a wise guy, and he starts talking back to you and telling you you are no good and that sort of thing. You know you can take a man in on a disorderly conduct charge but you can practically never make it stick. So what you do in a case like that is to egg the guy on until he makes a

remark where you can justifiably slap him and then if he fights back you can call it resisting arrest.

William Westley points out that the policeman feels the need to punish this individual. Although the officer knows he cannot legally do a thing to the man, he determines a way to punish him and still keep himself out of trouble.

Although the police in department X seemed sensitive to public opinion concerning the use of force, they exhibited lack of sensitivity in their method of achieving respect. Their attitude was one of demanding respect. Respect would be taught to those who failed to exhibit proper respect.

Violence was also condoned when the police were sure of the guilt of the suspect, particularly if the alleged crime was a sex crime. This attitude can be summed up as follows: "The offender had used violence and it was violence that he deserved in return." The policeman is a cynic living in a hostile world, according to this study of department X. To protect himself, the policeman lives in a secret world of police solidarity. He feels degraded and inferior (70 percent of department X members interviewed stated they would not want their sons to become policemen), looks for the selfish motive, feels rejected, and consequently intensifies his need for self-assertion, which becomes articulate as a need for maintaining respect for the police.

Another study, however, develops information from a different perspective which tends to counterbalance Westley's excessively "force oriented" police. New York City patrolmen tested in a recent study did not strongly concur that disrespect shown to the police is justification, by itself, for the use of force.[14] Table 2-5-8 shows the responses in this area; a recapitulation of answers to the question, "Most officers agree that some force is necessary and justified when a citizen insults and curses a police officer."

The fact that a policeman's attitude toward his role can change over time—can vary with his experience and background—is illustrated by Arthur Niederhoffer's study of police cynicism.[15] The police recruit will be less cynical than the experienced patrolman. The new recruit will be less cynical than the more seasoned recruit. Superior officers will be less cynical than patrolmen (cynicism being a defense against frustration). Patrolmen with a college education will be more cynical than those without. Patrolmen with preferred details will be less cynical than those without. Foot patrolmen will be more cynical than those who are assigned to other duties. Patrolmen who receive awards will be less cynical than those who do not. Jewish patrolmen will be more cynical than non-Jewish patrolmen (the assumption being that the Jewish tradition stresses success in the professions). Members of the youth division will be less cynical than members of the vice division. Finally, middle-class patrolmen will be less cynical than patrolmen coming from the working class.

The degree of cynicism that a patrolman feels toward his work will increase in proportion to his length of service up to about 5 years. From 5 to 10

TABLE 2-5-8.

Year in academy and time tested		Strongly agree (percent)	Agree (percent)	Uncertain (percent)	Disagree (percent)	Strongly disagree (percent)	Total
1961:	End of training	5	33	28	28	6	100.0
	2 years in field	4	44	10	39	3	100.0
1962:	Start of training	2	25	15	50	8	100.0
	End of training	3	23	18	49	7	100.0
1963:	1 year in field	1	34	16	45	4	100.0
	3d month of training	2	30	15	46	7	100.0
	4th month of training	4	31	19	43	3	100.0

Source: John H. McNamara in "The Police: Six Sociological Essays," ed. by David J. Bordua (New York: John Wiley & Sons, 1967).

years it will level off and, finally, at 17 or 18 years (approaching retirement) cynicism will be reduced. Arthur Niederhoffer defines the preliminary stages of cynicism, at the recruit level, as "pseudocynicism." His second stage, "romantic cynicism," reached in the first 5 years, is particularly damaging because the most idealistic members of the force are most susceptible to this cynicism. The third stage, "aggressive cynicism," occurs near the 10-year point and is marked by resentment and hostility. Finally, in the last few years of his career, "resigned cynicism" replaces the former, more blatant type. This detachment may be passive and apathetic or express itself as a form of mellow, if mild, good will. It accepts and comes to terms with the flaws of the system.

Another study analyzes the trait images that are defined by police recruits (in three stages of training), Police Academy instructors, detective candidates, and superior officers. Forty desirable personality traits were selected. These traits were those expressed by 60 randomly selected New York City Police Department sergeants. The traits were expressed as "those personal qualities constituting a 'good' policeman."[16]

Before the actual beginning of training, recruits selected the following traits ranked in order of importance:

1. Alertness
2. Honesty
3. Job knowledge
4. Common sense
5. Intelligence
6. Dedication
7. Appearance
8. Well trained

At the end of their formal academy training the recruits were tested again and the traits were ranked as follows:

1. Alertness
2. Honesty
3. Courage
4. Common sense
5. Intelligence
6. Appearance
7. Well trained

Finally, at the end of the 9-month probationary period, 5 months of which had been devoted to field experience, the test was again administered. Two important changes took place: Job knowledge was added to the list; and courage was dropped, indicating, perhaps, that a period of field training had emphasized the importance of occupational information. Concomitantly, exposure to the danger involved in actual job performance had, evidently, reduced its perceived importance, thus relegating courage to a position of lesser selection frequency.

The study made in connection with this present research project examines the change that takes place in the occupational image of the same group over a lengthy period of some 10 years of practical experience. As in most longitudinal studies, the effect of social change over the intervening period must be separated from the effect of occupational experience, the variable under evaluation. This is particularly true of a study which purports to measure the police image. The past decade, with its civil rights upheaval has seen major changes in the role of the police officer. His tact, discretion, and human relations expertise have supplanted his law enforcement functions to the extent that scholarly civilian students of police science now describe him as primarily a "peace keeper" rather than a "law enforcer." It would be reasonable to expect that, with this variation in public perception, the current police applicant would view his anticipated occupational role much as does the public of which he is a member and, to a lesser extent, in terms of his anticipated police career. Similarly, but to a lesser extent, it would be expected that the occupational image of the experienced police officer, since he has interacted with the public over the period of social change, would be affected by the role the public has created for him.

Thus, two major questions are raised in the present study: Does a lengthy period of police experience alter the early opinions of an individual about the personal qualities required for effective job performance? If so, to what extent is the change attributable to an altered public image of the function rather than occupational experience? The answer to the first question is sought by analyzing responses to the checklist administered now, for the fourth time, to 10-year veterans and observing variations between their present responses and those on the three administrations during their earlier police careers. The second question relating to the effect of social factors is answered by testing a current recruit group at time of entrance to the academy. To the extent that differences in the veterans' present choices vary in concordance with those of the current neophytes, the change may be attributable to a general public change in attitude. Changes in veterans' responses in a fashion discordant with those of the new group may be attributed to occupational experience.

Survey Methodology

Several refinements in the statistical methodology were employed in the present study. The sensitivity of the scale was enhanced by awarding differential values to the various ranks selected in the summary scoring. The previous method had simply scored the trait a value of one if selected and a zero if not selected. The rank value differentiation, too, created a myriad of fine discriminations in the statistical expectancies for each choice. Therefore, the chi square formula, which depends upon the difference between expected and observed frequencies,[17] was discarded and a model utilizing the normal distribution was substituted. This method simply compared the differences between the arithmetic mean selection frequency of each trait, after allowing for appropriate rank values. Thus, the trait selected as first choice received a value of 40, second choice 39, and so on to the 10th choice, which received a value of 31.

After summing and averaging the scores, those traits which had been selected with significant frequency; i.e., greater than chance probability, were identified and discussed. The differences between administrations were determined by a statistical formula known as the "t" test which, similarly, indicates those which changed to a degree greater than chance.

One difference in the recruit subject population should be noted. In the earlier study there were 40 who had taken all three previous tests. During the intervening decade, nine had left the department for various reasons; thus, only 31 remained available for testing on this, the fourth administration. In order that the observed change might reflect a precise measure of difference between identical individuals, the choices of the nine missing subjects were eliminated from all four administrations. Thus, two changes in methodology are incorporated into the present study, which might alter the previous results as well as affect the present findings; namely, the differential values for rank order of choice and the exclusion of nine subjects' responses previously included.

Results of Survey

The first comparison in the tabulation of survey results concerns the answer to the second question; namely, the effect of the social changes during the past decade on the choices of present day police recruits. An entering class of 246 recruits was tested, that of July 1, 1968. Table 2-5-9 lists the 10 traits most frequently selected by this group and, for comparison, the 10 most popular choices of the 1959 group at the time of their entrance into the department. The data are calculated by the revised methodology previously described and the numerical values awarded the traits represent the arithmetic mean average attained out of a maximum of 40.

The traits selected at entrance by the two groups, appointed 10 years apart, show a remarkable similarity, almost identical. True, the rank order shows a trifling variation, but none of the changes in rank have statistical significance.[18] If reliability and responsibility are regarded as similar in definition, they may have been interchanged without altering the overall intent of the subjects. "Courage," too, was omitted from the 1959 recruits' selections, having averaged only 21.29; however, the difference here, as in the above case, was also below the 5-percent level, the t score being 1.52.[19] The values of these traits

TABLE 2-5-9. 10 traits most frequently chosen by recruits of 1959 and July 1968

1959		July 1968	
Trait	Average	Trait	Average
Alertness	30.32	Alertness	32.24
Job knowledge	30.19	Job knowledge	29.19
Honesty	27.73	Honesty	27.07
Common sense	27.44	Well trained	26.54
Dedication	26.87	Dedication	26.08
Intelligence	26.10	Common sense	25.53
Respect superiors	25.45	Intelligence	24.33
Well trained	24.63	Responsibility	24.18
Appearance	24.29	Courage	24.14
Reliability	22.52	Appearance	22.99

are not given in Table 2-5-9 for the group which did not accord them prefer-ence. "Responsibility" averaged 21.29 in the 1959 group. This differed from the 1968 value at the 1.54 level. "Reliability" with the 1968 group averaged 22.83 and the significance of the difference was only 0.178. Therefore, even without according the traits similar definition, neither difference reached the 1.96 value required for the 5-percent confidence level.

One difference is significant, however. "Respect for Superiors," which re-ceived a value of 25.45 with the earlier group, was accorded an average of only 21.28 by the 1968 recruits. This difference was significant at the 5-percent level, the t score being 2.38. This may reflect a general trend among present day youth to regard persons in authority with a tinge of contempt, or, perhaps, the phi-losophy of a generation ago which may have accorded automatic respect to age and authority. The test for the effect of social change, then, showed a mini-mal influence on the occupational image of entering policemen, it being limited to the current problem of youth with authority figures. A later test, not re-ported here, following 8 months' field experience, resulted in a significant in-crease in "respect for superiors" ($t = 2.54$), the average choice being 23.43, a value which would have included the trait in the select 10. They learned.

The primary objective of this study is, of course, to answer the first question posed; namely, does a relatively lengthy 10-year period of occupational experience serve to change the opinion of policemen about their ideal occupa-tional image as expressed by trait preferences? As indicated previously, the experimental group of recruits appointed in 1959, their number now reduced to 31, were tested at the time of entering the occupation; again, at the termina-tion of their 4 months of training at the academy, and a third time, after 9 months tenure, following their first 5 months of field experience. The change observed was considerably smaller than previous experimental evidence on the effects of the intake of additional occupational information would have led us to expect. One possible explanation of the relative durability of the occupational stereotype may be found in the notion that the lifetime careers, such as doctor, lawyer, policeman, nurse, and the like, frequently form the basis of children's games. As such, they become so familiar to individuals at an early age that their occupational image becomes stereotyped and may persist even under a forced reappraisal such as the trait checklist, and in spite of some actual job experience. Obviously, a year of police experience, including both early training and field work, failed to alter the early impressions of the police recruits under study to any appreciable extent. The effects of 10 years' experience, however, are delineated in Table 2-5-10.

The differences between the three different tests given the 1959 class are not identical with the results reported earlier in this chapter owing to changes in statistical methodology and the difference in the content of the group. Only one significant change occurred between the first two administrations of the test. "Dedication" was reduced in value from 26.9 to 21.6 and does not even appear among the highest 10 traits on the results of the past administration. This difference is significant at the 5-percent level (t = 1.99). Other changes were decreases in "respect for superiors" (t = 1.66) and "job knowledge" (t = 1.84). Both of the latter changes, although substantial, did not reach the 5-percent level of statistical significance. An increase was noted in the choice of "courtesy," but, as in the case of the previous two traits, it did not reach the required level of significance.

No trait changed significantly between tests two and three, the period of field service. "Cooperation" (t = 1.66) and "physical strength" (t = 1.80), neither of which appear among the top 10, showed substantial decreases, but since neither had received a high degree of acceptance on either test, the significance of the change must be conjectural.

The differences, of course, which are of primary concern are those which appear on the fourth test after 10 years police experience. A striking change took place in the popularity of "alertness." After having maintained a consistent first place on all previous tests and having been chosen at a statistically significant level in all three cases, "alertness" was relegated to fifth choice by the veterans and not even accorded acceptance at the 5-percent level. Similarly important is the emergence of "emotional maturity" to a position of prominence. The trait, which had averaged only 18.5 on the administration following early field experience, was accorded a value of 24.2 by the veteran patrolmen, not quite enough to reach a statistically significant level, but, being chosen seventh, it was within the highest 10 choices. "Dedication," which had failed to reach visible popularity in the two tests subsequent to entrance, reappeared strongly in third place, its 28.3 average being significant at the 10-percent level. The change between test 3 and test 4 (t = 1.73) approached significance.

TABLE 2-5-10. 10 most frequently selected traits (recruits appointed October 1959)

Test 1 (at appointment)		Test 2 (after academic training)		Test 3 (5 months in field)		Test 4 (after 10 years' experience)	
Trait	Average	Trait	Average	Trait	Average	Trait	Average
Alertness	30.32	Alertness	32.76	Alertness	31.86	Honesty	31.95
Job knowledge	30.19	Intelligence	29.82	Common sense	30.69	Common sense	31.02
Honesty	27.73	Honesty	27.44	Honesty	28.50	Dedication	28.29
Common sense	27.44	Well trained	27.24	Intelligence	27.23	Job knowledge	27.71
Dedication	26.87	Common sense	26.98	Job knowledge	27.19	Alertness	25.69
Intelligence	26.10	Courtesy	25.19	Well trained	26.37	Integrity	24.36
Respect superiors	25.45	Job knowledge	25.15	Appearance	25.00	Emotional maturity	24.26
Well trained	24.63	Appearance	25.00	Courage	24.17	Well trained	24.16
Appearance	24.30	Courage	24.65	Courtesy	24.15	Intelligence	24.08
Reliability	22.52	Efficiency	23.02	Reliability	23.71	Initiative	23.48

Two changes occurred in traits which did not reach a significant popularity level on any pervious test, "even temp~red" (t = 1.96) and "compassion" (t = 2.50). The latter changes are important because their increase in choice frequency is significant and they are in the direction which would be expected in the light of changing times.

"Integrity" was included in the top 10, but fell slightly short of the required significance level. The importance of the emergence of "integrity" as a choice is underlined by the selection of "honesty" for first place and at the 1-percent level of choice, and by the return to favor of "dedication," a quality which had been relatively neglected since the preappointment test. It is worth mentioning, however, that "dedication" was also selected by the recruits in 1968.

A trend toward more humanitarian traits is observable in the changes bebetween test 3 and test 4 and this trend is clearly evident in Table 2-5-11.

It is apparent that the decreases occurred in traits which reflect the police officer's image predominantly as that of a law enforcement officer. These are the action oriented variables, the so-called "practical" qualities. The "alert," "well-trained," "courageous," "reliable" police officer who presents a natty appearance is a thing of secondary importance to the veteran police officer of today. On the contrary, the present-day officer, experiencing as he does, a daily confrontation with pathetic situations of a nonlaw enforcement nature, is more an "agent of social control" than the "frontier marshal." As such, he perceives himself as embodying the qualities of "emotional maturity," "integrity," "honesty," and "dedication." The movement toward "even temper" may reflect his need for restraint in the face of the insult and abuse which have been his lot of recent years. The trend toward "compassion," too, is compatible with the officers' awareness, now, of their role with the sick, the injured, and the emotionally disturbed people with whom they are so often thrown in contact.

TABLE 2-5-11. Variations in choice frequency between test 3 and test 4

Increase	Decrease
Honesty	Appearance.
Dedication	Alertness.[1]
Integrity	Intelligence.
Emotional maturity[1]	Well trained.
Compassion[1] [2]	Reliability.
Even tempered[1] [2]	Courage.[2]

[1] Significant difference.
[2] Not selected within 1st 10 on either test.

References

1. Ralph Lee Smith, "The Tarnished Badge," (New York: Thomas Y. Crowell Co., 1965), p. 93, and Paul Chevigny, "Police Power," (New York: Pantheon Books, 1969), p. 134. Chevigny states: "* * * the police reflect, with surprising sensitivity, the attitudes of the larger society."

2. Ralph Green, Geraldine Schaeffer, and James O. Finckenauer, "Law Enforcement Training Project—Survey of Community Expectations of Police Service: A Pilot Study—First Report." (The New Jersey Police Training Commission, January 1969), pp. 16-17.

3. Allen Z. Gammage, "Police Training in the United States," (Springfield: Charles C. Thomas, publisher, 1963), pp. 157-162.

4. John F. Skelly, "Portrait of a Precinct" (Master's thesis, John Jay College of Criminal Justice, the City University of New York, January 1969), p. 115.

5. Sorrel Wildhorn, "Research on New York City's Police Problems" (report by the Rand Corp., November 1, 1968), p. 7.

6. Alfred E. Doran, "The Foot Patrol Concept in the New York City Police Department." (Master's thesis, Bernard M. Baruch School of Business and Public Administration, the City University of New York, June 1963), ch. III.

7. Melany E. Baehr, John E. Furcon, and Ernest C. Froemel, "Psychological Assessment of Patrolman Qualifications in Relation to Field Performance," (Washington: Superintendent of Documents, November 5, 1968), pp. 7-11.

8. James Q. Wilson, Varieties of Police Behavior (Cambridge, Mass.: Harvard University Press, 1968), p. 16.

9. "Police-Community Relations—A Survey Among New York City Patrolmen"—A study for the New York City Police Department and Vera Institute of Justice. (Report of Opinion Research Corp., Princeton, N.J., August 1968), p. vi.

10. Ralph Green, op. cit., pp. 16-17.

11. "Police-Community Relations," op. cit., p. vii.

12. However, for a different viewpoint cf. Skelly, p. 123.

13. William Westley, "The Police: A Sociological Study of Law, Custom and Morality" (doctoral dissertation, Department of Sociology, the University of Chicago, 1951), pp. 175-179.

14. John H. McNamara, "The Police: Six Sociological Essays," ed. by David J. Bordua (New York: John Wiley & Sons, 1967), p. 213.

15. Arthur Niederhoffer, "Behind The Shield" (Garden City: Doubleday & Co., Inc., 1967).

16. William Wetteroth, "Variations in Trait Images of Occupational Choice Among Police Recruits Before and After Basic Training Experience," (master's thesis, Psychology Department, Brooklyn College, 1964), "The Center for Law Enforcement Research Information," Washington, D.C.: International Association of Chiefs of Police, (vol. 1, No. 3, autumn, 1965), p. 29.

17. The chi square rationale is explained in considerable detail in most texts on statistical methodology. The reader is referred to Edwards, Allen L., "Experimental Design in Psychological Research," New York, Rinehart & Co., 1950.

18. The term, "Statistical Significance" refers to a difference of sufficient magnitude to rule out, for the most part, the probability that it could have occurred by chance.

19. An explanation of 't' scores and their values will be found in Griffin, John I., "Statistics: Methods and Applications," New York: Holt, Rinehart, and Winston, 1962.

CHAPTER **2-6**

THE LOCAL pOLICE fuNCTION

ADVISORY COMMISSION ON INTERGOVERN-
MENTAL RELATIONS

The Tradition and Scope of
The Local Police Function

The police function has traditionally been a local one. Original police systems, both in America and England, were based on resistance to a national police force and reliance on local community responsibility for apprehending law-breakers. Community groups of "hundreds"[1] were accorded responsibility for the control of criminal activity. These groups eventually came to be supervised by constables and sheriffs. Professional police, however, were unheard of until the nineteenth century.

The "hundreds" system of law enforcement with its reliance on voluntary participation began to deteriorate as people found various ways to evade their police responsibilities. Constables became paid officers as did members of the "night-watch" in American communities. Voluntary participation gradually tapered off.[2]

The concentration of the function in the hands of paid law enforcement officials, however, did not guarantee improved police work. The police function was still highly decentralized. In many communities, the function was organized along ward lines with no unified control over daytime and nighttime protection. This confused state of administration rendered local police ineffective in han-

Source: ACIR. *State-Local Relations in the Criminal Justice System.* A Commission Report 1971, pp. 72–75.

dling the mass violence and organized crime that plagued some American cities in the early and middle nineteenth century.[3]

As public toleration of such crime and violence decreased, citizen support mounted for organized police departments. New York City organized a unified department in 1844, Chicago in 1851, New Orleans and Cincinnati in 1852, and Boston and Philadelphia in 1854. By the turn of the twentieth century, all major cities had organized forces.

In America's rural areas, there were fewer organized police departments. The police function was still handled under the elective sheriff-constable system. Although having readily documented inefficiencies, this system was a matter of local preference.[4]

There has been a natural division of labor between State and local governments with regard to the police function. State governments drew up criminal codes which determined the basic structure of the police function whereas local governments were entrusted with the responsibility of enforcing the code. Given the more limited range of criminal mobility in earlier times, crime control undoubtedly was more a purely local problem than it is now.

The police function remained localized for political reasons as well. Law enforcement officials—sheriffs and constables—were traditionally elected officials. They and their deputies often served as part-time political lieutenants, providing considerable political pressure for keeping the police function as it was—local. For all these historical reasons the police function has remained largely local in nature, even though there has been increased State involvement in the more specialized facets of police work.

Elements of the Local Police Function

Both State and local police departments normally provide a "package of activities" in police work. These activities fall into three main categories: (1) *field services or line operations,* which include general patrol, traffic supervision, criminal investigation, juvenile work, and criminal intelligence activities; (2) *staff services,* which include police recruitment and training, internal control, planning and research, and public information activities; and (3) *auxiliary services,* which include such operations as records and communications activities, jail management, and crime laboratory services or "criminalistics." A police department is said to be self-sufficient if it performs all these activities.

The size of a police department, the extent and type of criminal activities it must deal with, and whether it is in a central city, suburb, or rural area all affect the department's ability to perform the various facets of its police work. To illustrate, a small police force must often combine its investigative and intelligence activities in one division or forego such activities altogether.[5] A larger police department, on the other hand, may have separate divisions for investigative and intelligence operations and be able to employ various types of skilled personnel, such as evidence technicians.[6] Police work is also affected by location. A community bisected by large arterial roads will have a greater traffic responsibility than another community which is more "off the beaten path." Finally, the amount and type of crime a police force must deal with will affect its police work. Communities having racial disturbances more frequently will have sophisticated community relations programs than racially homogeneous communities.[7]

Field Services

Local police departments usually perform several distinct types of line operations or field services. These include general patrol, traffic supervision, criminal investigation, juvenile delinquency control, and undercover criminal intelligence work. The size of the police department usually determines whether various line operations have a distinct identity within the municipal police department. Smaller departments, usually those under 25 full-time personnel, often do not have separate divisions for various line operations. These departments, moreover, may over-assign personnel to particular line operations, neglecting the personnel needs of other line functions.[8] In general, larger departments perform their line operations in a more specialized fashion. Thus, annual reports of the International City Management Association indicate that larger police departments more often are able to delegate traffic supervision to civilian personnel,[9] employ a greater number of specialized vehicles in their police work,[10] and provide more in-service training to their policemen in handling mass violence.[11]

The scope of field services which police departments perform also may differ among localities. General patrol in a resort community may consist of protecting unoccupied property and discouraging vagrancy. General patrol in a large city is more dynamic, involving the prevention of such serious crimes as robbery, assault, or grand larceny. Traffic control in a smaller locality may consist of a local "speed trap," while a larger department may have mobile traffic control units as well as a separate force to direct rush-hour traffic.

In like manner, criminal investigation may not have a separate status in smaller departments. Sophisticated criminal investigation can demand a full-time officer who is trained in the basic principles of criminal detection and who has working relationships with the local prosecutor. Specialization in criminal investigation may also be necessary to determine the *modus operandi* of certain types of crime. Therefore, investigation may be a separate line function in a police department, though this is not an altogether healthy development in the local police function as it can create an artificial division between the patrol and investigative function.[12]

Juvenile work and criminal intelligence operations are only provided by larger police departments in any systematic fashion. With the greater availability of resources and specially trained personnel, larger police forces can accord the above line operations separate status. Smaller communities lack the funds and personnel for juvenile work,[13] and often obtain criminal intelligence from either large city, State, or Federal agencies.

Staff Services

Staff services include such activities as police recruitment and training, internal controls and inspection, planning and research, public information, and community relations activities. These operations support the field services of the municipal police department. Again, the scope of these services often depends on the size of the police department. Smaller departments generally do not have the money or manpower to invest in these services nor are such services always essential to such departments (e.g., internal control might be handled by the police chief in smaller departments).

While most departments have recruitment and training programs, it was estimated that 18 per cent of all municipal police forces in 1968 had no established program of recruit training.[14] In communities of under 25,000 population this proportion rose to 25 per cent. Furthermore, in 1968 only 31 per cent of all communities under 50,000 population had training facilities for police recruits while only 20 per cent of all communities under 50,000 population had a full-time training officer for police recruitment.[15]

In like fashion, smaller departments often have only ad hoc internal control or planning and research capability. Larger police departments will have separate internal control divisions and may have planning and research activities which can provide a police department with alternative programs for combating crime.[16] Another staff service is in the area of community relations. Here again data indicates that larger departments are more apt to implement full-scale community relations programs.[17]

Auxiliary Services

A police department provides another set of specialized services which further aid its line operations. These auxiliary services include record-keeping and communication, jail management and criminal laboratory services.

Almost all departments have at least rudimentary record-keeping capacity. Over 5,700 police agencies maintain liaison with the FBI in annual reporting on criminal offenses and arrests. These reporting jurisdictions accounted for 88 per cent of the country's total population in 1967. Thus, while there have been continuing proposals for a more sophisticated system of crime reporting,[18] most of the local police systems do have a basic record-keeping capability which could be worked into a national crime reporting system.

Jail management is another auxiliary function of municipal and county police. Local jails are used for such purposes as (1) short-term confinement of criminals and misdemeanants serving sentences of less than one year, (2) preventive detention of persons awaiting trial, and (3) "lock ups" for minor offenders, mainly public drunkards. There are over 3,000 county jails,[19] and the last reliable estimate put the total number of local jails at around 10,000.[20] Most local jails are small. Of more than 600 local jails inspected by Federal officials in 1966, it was estimated that more than 40 per cent were constructed before 1921.[21]

The jail function has been a traditional task of the local police though police administrators often have expressed the desire to move it to the correctional system. Many police administrators state that only minimal detention facilities should be maintained by the police and, that they should not be required to perform short-term correctional work.

Police departments also perform criminal laboratory services which aid in the evidence-gathering activities inherent in the police function. Laboratory services, however, are more centralized than most other police functions. Quite often many local departments receive their laboratory services from State or Federal sources, though some of the larger local departments have renowned criminalistic laboratories.[22]

The Objectives of the "Police Function"

Police forces also vary in the emphasis they place on the different elements of the police mission, because of differences in community attitudes on the extent and nature of the "police function." These attitudes condition the style in which police work is performed in a locality.[23]

James Q. Wilson has pointed out two basic concepts of what police work should entail.[24] The first holds that police should *maintain order* within the community. In this role, police act to prevent situations which may induce criminal actions. Resolving family quarrels, preventing juvenile disputes, softening interracial crises are the policeman's functions under this concept. Rather than only enforce the law, the policeman insures the law is not violated. The second concept stresses the *law enforcement* duties of the policeman, that the prime duty of the officer is to apprehend the criminal and begin to process him through the criminal justice system. This concept emphasizes the legalistic style of police work.

Some contend that these two basic functions should not be the responsibility of a single policeman. Rather, there might be specialized personnel to deal solely with peace-keeping activities, while other police officers would assume the law-enforcement function.[25] This division of labor would reduce the ambiguity of the policeman's role and place his law-enforcement responsibilities in clearer perspective.

Others note the complexity of a policeman's task makes him a ". . . craftsman rather than a legal actor, . . . a skilled worker rather than . . . a civil servant obliged to subscribe to the rule of law."[26] Being such a skilled worker, the policeman may perceive attempts to professionalize or bureaucratize his duties as a failure of public and governmental confidence in his ability to perform his responsibilities, however complex they may be.[27] In light of the intricate nature of police work, attempts should be made to respect the discretionary powers of the individual policeman. To that end, an "all-purpose" rather than specialized policeman is called for.

The debate about the "essential" nature of police work may never be satisfactorily resolved. Yet, this debate remains a pivotal element affecting the quality of local police protection. Where there is community agreement with or understanding of the demands of modern police work, there is greater likelihood of a more proficient police force.

Police Relations with Courts, Prosecution and Corrections

The police are but one element of the criminal justice system. Major decisions affecting the system can be made by any of its several main components and can affect the performance of the other divisions. Thus, a lenient parole policy by a correctional system may increase or lessen police work due to recidivism or the lack of it among parolees. Prosecutors may set demanding standards for police arrest and collection of evidence and thereby increase the general patrol and investigative demands of local police work.

Alternatively, the police department may affect the activities of other parts of the criminal justice system. Aggressive arrest policies may increase the workloads of both prosecutors and judicial personnel. On the other hand, "station-house adjudication" may lighten the work-load of criminal prosecutors, yet increase court work if criminal charges are brought against the police for such practices.

The main interrelationships between the police and other elements of the criminal justice system may be summarized as:

Police-Prosecution: The police affect prosecutor workloads by their arrest policies. The investigative arm of the police department aids the prosecutor in collecting evidence in criminal prosecution and police officers frequently furnish testimony in criminal cases.

The prosecutor affects the police when he sets standards for the collection of evidence or indicates the criteria whereby he will bring arrest cases to court. Prosecutors may interpret the applicability of judicial decisions to ongoing police work. They also may affect police arrest policies since they use bargaining procedures with criminal defendants in order to prosecute successfully a wide variety of criminal cases.[28]

Police-Court: Police also affect judicial workloads by their arrest policies.

Moreover, the skill of police work in various situations (i.e. handling mass violence) affects the frequency with which judges have to make rulings about the propriety of police activities.

Judicial-police relationships condition police attitudes about arrest and prosecution policies. Setting standards in such matters as admissibility of evidence, bail policy, and sentencing are factors which influence the law enforcement activities of police. Since the judge is often held to be the chief administrator of the criminal justice system, he often exerts administrative control which affects the work of police, prosecution, and corrections agencies. Furthermore, judicial rulings not only condition the way in which orthodox police practices operate, but they also bear on the acceptability of more unusual police practices (i.e. electronic surveillance, harassment of known criminals, etc.).[29]

Police-Corrections: Police-corrections relationships are relatively indirect. The police may operate short-term detention facilities, but they do not attempt to provide for treatment or rehabilitation of the individual offender. However, police affect correctional practices insofar as they offer support or opposition to correctional programs that affect recidivism.

Correctional-police relationships center around police assistance in monitoring the activities of probationers or parolees. Correctional agencies also have working arrangements with police departments in the transportation of prisoners from police to correctional facilities.

The police function is the frontal part of the criminal justice system. Its operation often determines the extent and scope of involvement of an individual with the criminal justice system. Much of the police function turns on the discretionary authority of the police. They may arrest or not arrest. They may arrest and practice "station-house adjudication," or they may formally book a criminal offender. In short, the police often have a wide range of discretion in which to perform their peace-keeping and law-enforcement responsibilities.

The police function is made difficult in modern society due to the wide discretion which must be used when enforcement is exercised. The discretionary role of the police is affected by community attitudes and the actions of the other elements of the criminal justice system. Also, police attitudes towards their power often determine whether police will devote more attention to peace-keeping or to law-enforcement activities. In short, the police function is the most visible as well as most volatile part of the criminal justice system. Yet, its operation is conditioned strongly by external factors which account for the wide variety of police practices in the United States.

References

1. "Hundreds" were groups of local families, 100 in number, which were the base of the voluntary local police force. The President's Commission on Law

Enforcement and the Administration of Justice, Task Force Report: *The Police* (Washington: U.S. Government Printing Office, 1967), p. 3.

2. Bridenbaugh, Carl, *Cities in Revolt* (New York: Capricorn Books, 1964), pp. 107-110.

3. Brown, Richard Maxwell, "Historical Patterns of Violence in America," in National Commission on Causes and Prevention of Violence, *Violence in America: Historical and Comparative Perspectives* (Washington: U.S. Government Printing Office, 1969), pp. 40-41.

4. Smith, Bruce, *Rural Crime Control* (New York: Institute of Public Administration, 1933).

5. Investigative activities are related to the solution of a specific criminal act. Intelligence activities are broader in scope, often taking the form of general surveillance of known criminals. These facets of police work may be separate functions in the largest police department.

6. International City Management Association, *Municipal Police Administration,* (Washington: ICMA, 1969), p. 136.

7. Public Administration Service, *Police Services in Saint Louis County* (Chicago: Public Administration Service, 1967).

8. *Ibid.* p. 37.

9. International City Management Association, *Municipal Year Book - 1963* (Washington: ICMA, 1963), p. 416.

10. ———, *Municipal Year Book - 1964* (Washington: ICMA, 1964), p. 412.

11. ———, *Municipal Year Book - 1966* (Washington: ICMA, 1966), p. 468.

12. Thus, the Massachusetts State Planning Agency proposed that ". . . experimentation begin to abolish the traditional split in the police function and to attempt new divisions of the police function, such as the testing of the concept of *team policing,* which would place the patrol force and investigative personnel under common supervision." See Massachusetts Committee on Law Enforcement and the Administration of Criminal Justice, "A Summary of the Comprehensive Criminal Justice Plan for Crime Prevention and Control" (Boston: 1969), p. 14.

13. International City Management Association. *Municipal Police Administration.* (Washington: ICMA, 1969), pp. 152-153.

14. ———, *Municipal Yearbook - 1968* (Washington: ICMA, 1968), pp. 339-350.

15. *Ibid,* pp. 342-343.

16. The "police-lawyer" is one example of an innovative police practice which has come about as police must deal with new legal dimensions of their work.

17. International City Management Association, "Recent Trends in Police-Community Relations," *Urban Data Service,* March 1970, Vol. 2, No. 3.

18. U.S. Bureau of the Census, *Report on the National Need for Criminal Justice Statistics* (Washington: U.S. Bureau of the Census, 1968).

19. Joint Economic Committee, *State and Local Public Facility Needs and Financing.* Vol. I (Washington: U.S. Government Printing Office, 1968), p. 653.

20. Casey, Roy, "Catchall Jails," *The Annals,* May 1954, Vol. 293, p. 28.

21. Joint Economic Committee, *op. cit.,* p. 653.

22. The President's Commission on Law Enforcement and the Administration of Justice, *op. cit.,* pp. 90–92.

23. James Q. Wilson, *Varieties of Police Behavior: The Management of Law and Order in Eight Communities* (Cambridge: Harvard University Press, 1968).

24. James Q. Wilson, "Dilemmas of Police Administration," *Public Administration Review,* September-October 1968, Vol. XXVIII, No. 5, pp. 407–416.

25. President's Commission on Law Enforcement and The Administration of Justice, *op. cit.,* Chapter 5.

26. Jerome H. Skolnick, *Justice Without Trial: Law Enforcement in a Democratic Society* (New York: John Wiley, 1967), p. 231.

27. James Q. Wilson, *Varieties of Police Behavior: The Management of Law and Order in Eight Communities* (Cambridge: Harvard University Press, 1968), p. 283.

28. See James D. Mills, *The Prosecutor* (New York: Farrar, Straus, & Giroux, 1969).

29. The President's Commission on Law Enforcement and the Administration of Justice, *op. cit.,* p. 31.

CHANGING THE RHETORIC of "professionalism"

FRANKLIN G. ASHBURN

The Meaning of "Profession"

One thing that appears to be lacking in police circles is a clear concept of just what a "profession" really is, particularly as it pertains to law enforcement. It is suggested here that a "profession" is service-oriented and has certain identifiable characteristics, among which are: (1) it contains a body of knowledge which is formally presented to candidates by members of the "profession"; (2) it requires successful completion of examination and licensing procedures by the candidate; (3) it contains a code of ethics to which all members subscribe; (4) it allows for sanctions to be imposed by the peer group if a member violates group norms. Such sanctions may well include dismissal from practice in the "profession"; and (5) it is suggested that members perform research to advance the "state of the art" and disseminate the results of such inquiry to the "profession".

Obstacles to Professionalism of Police

While this definition of "professionalism", or one similar to it may be accepted in theory by some progressive law enforcement agencies, it is not practiced, to

Source: Franklin G. Ashburn. "Changing the Rhetoric of 'Professionalism.'" U.S. Department of Justice, Law Enforcement Assistance Administration, National Institute of Law Enforcement and Criminal Justice. *Innovation in Law Enforcement.* 1973. pp. 1–11.

the author's knowledge, in any police department today. Certain attitudes, traditional methods of operation, and "rites of passage" tend to block sustained efforts to reach the level of maturity implied in such a definition.

What the policeman does on the street—what he does on the job—defines his role. That role, according to James Q. Wilson, is ". . . unlike any other occupation . . . one in which subprofessionals working alone, exercise wide discretion in matters of utmost importance in an environment that is apprehensive and sometimes hostile," (Wilson, 1970, pp. 29-30). Such a job description suggests that today's policeman is not selected and trained as a professional, but as some sort of semi-skilled para-professional. Ahern offers two alternative solutions to this disparity. "One is to narrow the police role to the point where it can be performed by a semi-skilled laborer. The other is to professionalize the police to the point where they can handle their jobs as they are presently constituted" (Ahern, 1972, p. 178).

. . . the first problem encountered in changing the rhetoric of "professionalism" to a meaningful working definition, therefore, lies with the police themselves—in their attitudes toward themselves, toward the job, and toward the people they must serve. The first innovation must be a *changed attitude* among law enforcement practitioners.

The second major problem area in changing the rhetoric of "professionalism" lies in the public's misconceptions and expectations of the police. Many segments of our society view with alarm the concept of "police professionalism." "Professional" law enforcement somehow conjures up an image of a potential police state in a democratic society. Much of this is based upon the myth that the police are primarily "crime fighters," that they are an "army" fighting "criminals." Nothing could be further from the truth than this misconception that the police "fight crime." A more realistic appraisal is that the police *respond* to crime, after the fact, and *record* the incident as historical data. Occasionally, the police apprehend a person who has committed a crime. This person is then arrested, but for the most part, the police are ill prepared to prevent an act of criminal behavior; and, because they are *responders* to citizens calls for service, the arrest constitutes an exception to the normal police function.

This leads to a crucial question of professional police service which, simply stated is: What do the police actually do? This question aroused the interest and curiosity of the author when he served as Director of the Planning and Research Division of the Baltimore Police Department. Consequently, a survey of over 700,000 calls for police service in Baltimore during the year 1970 was conducted with the results shown in Table 2-7-1.

This data tends to support an unverified assumption on the part of many law enforcement practitioners that the police do much more than "fight crime" or chase "criminals." If the "other calls" and "unfounded calls" are grouped into a single category, it is seen that approximately 70 percent of all calls for service were, at least, initially non-crime related.

The Police Role in Contemporary Society

TABLE 2-7-1.

Type of Call	Per Cent of Total Calls
Index Crimes	10.7%
Other Crimes	8.4%
Other Calls including sick persons, dog bites, sanitation complaints and the like	63.0%
Accidents involving vehicles and/or pedestrians	5.0%
Duplicate Calls (more than one person calling to report same incident)	6.8%
Unfounded Calls (like a false alarm of fire, an officer had to respond)	6.1%
Total	100.0%

It is suggested that the function of the police today and indeed, the expectation of the community itself, is one of assuming the responsibilities of other agencies which cannot respond to citizens needs on a 24-hour-everyday basis. Thus, with the "order maintenance function" as suggested by Wilson (1970) and performing the services of other agencies in their absence, one must conclude that the police have little time remaining to perform their traditional law enforcement duties. Such activities tend to detract from the crime prevention and deterrent function and force the police to act in a capacity and at a level which is less "professional" in the true sense of the word.

This perceived public image of the police as "errand boys" and "crime fighters" represents the second problem area in police "professionalism."

The final problem area of "professionalism" to be discussed here is a *functional* rather than a *rhetorical* one. It concerns the decision-making and discretionary aspects of law enforcement practice.

As indicated previously, police work is a unique and specialized kind of occupation. This uniqueness is highlighted by the fact that police must work within a bureaucratic framework of rules and regulations promulgated by a centralized authority. Yet, in actual practice, the police officer *on the job* must act alone, making decisions and discretionary judgments which affect the lives of other people. In many instances, the officer's judgment and discretion in the line of duty may be in conflict with the rules of the bureaucracy. Even though his decision may not be final in *each* case, however, in *all* cases, the police officer is held accountable for his actions.

As Reiss points out:

A command organization threatens professional status because it expects men to follow orders regardless of their judgment. The professional ideal holds that orders are antithetical to the exercise of discretion. . . All bureaucracies, then, pose problems for the exercise of discretion (Reiss, 1971, p. 124).

Therefore, in actual practice, the police officer is being asked to act in a "professional" capacity in *all* of his direct actions with the public. At the same time, his autonomy as a "professional" is challenged by bureaucratic review and sanction.

Until such time as the needed changes in law enforcement agency and society take place, the police officer will continue to work as a "semi-skilled laborer" and not as a client-centered, service-oriented "professional."

Conclusion

Attention is now directed to those considerations needed to effect change in any law enforcement agency. Accordingly, it is suggested that:

1. Law enforcement agencies develop a posture of more "open" interaction with the communities they serve. In order to accomplish this, the police must seek to redefine their relationships toward the people they serve. A keenly sensitive awareness of the conflicting needs of various segments of society is essential to this effort. The police in the role of "mediator" or "referee" would even be conceivable in some instances of social interaction.

2. Intelligent recruitment and training toward the development of the "total police officer" should be initiated. Such a police officer should be trained not only to handle problems of "order maintenance," but problems of so-called white collar and organized crime as well. Today's police officer has no training in this area at all. The result is that Federal "task forces" must be called in to handle such cases.

3. Minimum performance standards should be established for all police officers. With some local orientation, an officer properly trained in the fundamental requirements should be able to transfer to other geographical locations and jurisdictions. Lateral entry, particularly in specialized areas using civilian personnel in nonenforcement areas of police work, should become a part of this effort.

4. Law enforcement agencies should develop a capacity for referral to other departments, agencies, or services for those cases which do not pertain directly to law enforcement. Such procedures should result in more concentrated efforts toward providing better police service to the community.

5. Law enforcement needs to develop better methods of evaluating its present activities and disseminating this information to others in the profession. A national clearing house for such information should be established at the Federal level to accomplish this task. Such an effort would

serve to prevent duplication of effort nationwide, wasting of scarce funds, and unwise police management decisions. It would serve to provide continuity in the "state of the art" of law enforcement nationwide, thereby allowing even the smallest department to benefit from the mistakes and accomplishments of others.

Resolving these dilemmas surrounding the "rhetoric of professionalism" may well be the law enforcement challenge of the seventies. Without their resolution, no change will take place.

Bibliography

Ahern, James F. *Police In Trouble*. New York: Hawthorn Publishers, 1972.
Reiss, Albert J., Jr. *The Police and the Public*. New Haven: Yale University Press, 1971.
Wilson, James Q. *Varieties of Police Behavior: The Management of Law and Order in Eight Communities*. New York: Atheneum Publishers, 1970.

PART III.

poLice-community iNTERACTioN

Introduction

One of the most common descriptions of police duties is encompassed by the concept of social control. Most people consider police chiefly as officials who place significant restrictions on their behavior. And police themselves emphasize their authority to impose limitations upon citizens' activities as the major aspect of their functions. Most people—and particularly those adhering to the "law and order" philosophy—do indeed consider the police task of regulating human behavior as critical for the survival and the well-being of the state. Unfortunately, as Holden (1970:240) states, "the behaviors defined as criminal are more likely than not the behaviors of the poorer and politically less skillful members of the polity."

Thus, many consider the decisions of legislatures and of the judiciary which create, interpret, and shape criminal law as an important type of political activity. The practices of the police in actually enforcing these decisions are seen as reflecting an even more fundamental form of political activity, this time at the street level. Since the laws cannot envision and encompass the myriad circumstances in which they might be invoked, the task of actually determining the nature of human behavior is left to the police officer who is on the scene.

The enormous power and the sweeping discretion police possess and exercise are obvious. The potential for misuse, abuse, and injustice is patent. The growing public demands for the control and suppression of "crime in the streets" may be easily misinterpreted to mean an unlimited license granted police to stop, frisk, harass, or arrest those labeled by society at large as "undesirables" because of some characteristic, be it color, race, ethnic background,

177

economic status, place of residence, peculiar habits, etc. Most people do indeed draw a line with varying degrees of sharpness and clarity between those who supposedly are "criminal" and those who are "law abiding." Oftentimes "criminal" is equivalent to unfamiliar, strange, threatening, insulting, or simply different.

As a consequence, the stage is set for the complicated and at times dramatic set of interactions locking police and different groups of citizens in tense struggles. In fact, because of the dichotomy mentioned above, contacts between police and the public are not uniformly distributed throughout society. The types of offenses that ordinarily elicit police intervention are those that are most prevalent among the lower classes. Inasmuch as the law reflects the distribution of political influence and clout in society, this pattern of intervention clearly illustrates the success of higher-status people in protecting themselves and their own trespasses not only from the restraints imposed by the criminal law but also from unpleasant and upsetting encounters with police, who, after all, belong to those lower classes many want to be protected from.

Ironically, what many persons clamoring for "law and order" (that is, for the enforcement of their own definitions of public order) do not perceive, is that the same police forces whom they would like to unleash upon their less fortunate or less conforming fellow citizens, could very easily turn against them, should for any reason the political balance of power change.

Carrying out this special mandate in American society has led police to develop their own occupational ideology and to behave accordingly. There is in fact a deep chasm between the official policies of a police department and the police academy training on the one hand, and the "locker room" advice on the other. As Arthur Niederhoffer wrote:

> In the case of the young policeman the choice between professionalism and pragmatism is apt to depend largely on the circumstances of the case. It is, for example, no great feat for a policeman working in an upper class neighborhood to protect the rights of his white clientele. It is much more difficult in a lower-class community. In a slum area the professional ethic loses most of the time; the civil rights of lower-class individuals do not count as much as the necessity to accomplish a staggering amount of police work as expeditiously as possible. Shifting from idealism to pragmatism, the newcomer to a lower-class precinct house enters a new reference group whose members are a little contemptuous of all the Academy represents (1967:54).

The new policeman soon understands not only that every law on the books cannot be enforced but that in fact many laws are to be enforced with ample discretion according to that immortal rule, "who, when, where, how, and when." Two elements are particularly important in the occupational ideology learned by police—danger and authority. They have a great impact on the actual exercise of law enforcement. Jerome Skolnick describes how these two elements influence the policeman's working personality:

> The element of danger seems to make the policeman especially attentive to signs indicating a potential for violence and lawbreaking. As a result, the policeman is generally a "suspicious" person. Furthermore, the character of the policeman's work makes him less desirable as a friend, since norms of friendship implicate others in his work. Accordingly, the element of danger isolates the policeman socially from that segment of the citizenry which he regards as symbolically dangerous and also from the conventional citizenry with whom he identifies.
>
> . . . The element of authority reinforces the element of danger in isolating the policeman. Typically, the policeman is required to enforce laws representing puritanical morality, such as those prohibiting drunkenness, and also laws regulating the flow of public activity, such as traffic laws. In these situations, the policeman directs the citizenry, whose typical response denies recognition of his authority, and stresses his obligation to danger. The kind of man who responds well to danger, however, does not normally subscribe to codes of puritanical morality. As a result, the policeman is unusually liable to charges of hypocrisy. That the whole civilian world is an audience for the policeman further promotes police isolation and, in consequence, solidarity. Finally, danger undermines the judicious use of authority (1966:44).

Such occupational values provide a strong rationale for using harsh and even illegal methods. Thus, violence, brutality, and illegality are often resorted to by police to accomplish their goal. The "law abiding" citizens applaud and even encourage such tactics, regarding them as efficient law enforcement, as long as they are directed to those minorities—whatever they are at any given time—whom they define as the "criminal" element. Since public trust in the police stems from the public's perception of the legitimacy of law enforcement activities, it is no wonder then that large numbers of the American people do not have this fundamental confidence in the police (Feagin, 1971:101–118).

In the first selection, the complex and confusing relationship and reciprocal influence which exist between any given community and the police is discussed by Albert Morris. He analyzes what effects the community has on police policy and performance, how community expectations affect police-community relations, and how communities can affect the "style" of police work and the level of crime control.

Campbell and Schuman focus on the problem of racial hostility among policemen as measured by its pervasiveness and by the quality of violence it can generate. Their work, "Police in the Ghetto," was sponsored by the Kerner Commission and is based on a survey of respondents in 15 large northern cities.

Police-Community Interaction

In particular, they document the often heard contention that blacks and whites view their police departments in quite a different light, particularly as to the frequency with which the police use harassment and abuse.

Sociologists and psychologists involved in role theory find the police role question particularly interesting. A good example of the possibilities in the application of role theory to the police is Martin Miller's "Systematic Model of Police Morale." He discusses the importance of the congruence of perception and role enactment in behavioral processes and offers a composite portrayal of the inter-relationships of several social systems as an explanatory key to police-community relations.

Stan Cross and Edward Renner approach the subject from the standpoint of interaction analysis. While most cu rent work, as they say, has focused on the personalities of the actors involved and on the belief that if one could change attitudes, behavior would improve, they stress behavior as a problem in itself. They state that the best way to change behavior is to work directly on it. They also indicate what steps might be taken, in "An Interaction Analysis of Police-Black Relations."

The actual behavior of police while on duty and its impact on the community, on other branches of the criminal justice system, on the public's perceptions, and on levels of satisfaction are discussed by Nathan Goldman as they apply to juvenile offenders, by Paul Smith and Richard Hawkins in relation to victims of crime, and by Peter Bloch and associates in reference to the use of policewomen on patrol.

References

Feagin, Joe R.
    1971   "Home Defense and the Police: Black and White Perspectives."
                In Harlan Hahn (ed.), Police in Urban Society. Beverly Hills, Ca.:
                Sage Publications: 101-118.
Holden, M., Jr.
    1970   "Politics, Public Order and Pluralism." In J.R. Klonoski and
                R.I. Mendelsohn (eds.), The Politics of Local Justice. Boston:
                Little, Brown: 238-255.
Niederhoffer, Arthur
    1967   Behind the Shield: The Police in Urban Society. Garden City,
                N.Y.: Doubleday.
Skolnick, Jerome H.
    1966   Justice Without Trial: Law Enforcement in Democratic Society.
                New York: John Wiley.

CHAPTER **3-1**

WHAT is THE ROLE of
THE COMMUNITY iN THE
development of police systems?

ALBERT MORRIS

What Effect Does The Community Have
On Police Policy and Performance?

Social scientists are sometimes charged with absolving the criminal offender of all responsibility for the evil of his ways by explaining his behavior as due to the unfortunate and miserable conditions of his early life and upbringing. While social scientists would not accept this as an accurate or adequate statement of their position it has in it some element of truth. To the extent that it is true, the effects of environmental circumstances upon social scientists and policemen also explains why they behave as they do. And if indeed such a procedure relieves offenders of responsibility for their misbehavior it will also relieve social scientists and policemen of any blame for their failures—not to mention any credit they might take for their ability to behave lawfully and usefully. In any event the community is certainly a factor in shaping the kind, the quality and the effectiveness of its police department.

With varying degrees of intensity the community conditions that have the greatest influence on police work within it are:

Population size, density, and age distribution.
Population characteristics including homogeneity-heterogeneity in terms

of educational level, income, ethnic-cultural similarities and differences.

Degree of population stability or change in terms of duration and continuity of residence and in and out migrations.

The economic base and orientation of its people and the primary functions of the community for its residents.

The predominant values and attitudes expressed in community behavior
by the community as a whole or its major sub-groups.

In general it may be assumed that the smaller and more homogenous and
stable the community is the more likely it is that its police will reflect the values
of that community and its attitudes and behavior towards residents and outsiders of different ethnic, economic or other categories. The smaller the community the more likely it is that police relations with its members will be on a
personal, even a kinship basis, and that police behavior not consistent with
community expectations will result in pressures upon the policeman, and also his
family, that will to a greater or lesser degree make life as a policeman miserable
or impossible for him. The police will therefore act vigorously against behavior
that the community rejects and tolerate what the community permits. In such
communities the chief deterrent of behavior unacceptable to the community is
the power of community sentiment itself. The taking of graft to permit the
existence of forbidden activities is limited by the smaller market for unlawful
goods and services in less populous communities and by the difficulties of con-
cealment of such unlawful acts. To the extent that unlawful activities are tolerated by community sentiment there is no basis on which the police can collect
illicit payment since their protection of unlawful behavior is unnecessary.

Conversely the larger and more heterogeneous the community the more
likely are the police to seek support and to adopt policies suggested by or congenial to whatever political, economic, civic or other groups appear to have
power. They may tread more cautiously among conflicting groups when no one
has a clear-cut or durable preeminence of power. However, under such circumstances the police may be able to render special services to different groups and
so create informal obligations that may bring support when it is needed. In the
larger and more heterogeneous communities to the extent that there is no clear
and strong community sentiment expressed through civic, religious, economic,
ethnic, or political groups with reference to specific types of unlawful behavior,
police enforcement of the law—whether it be with reference to auto parking, jay
walking, prohibition of the sale of liquor, bookmaking, auto theft or any of the
types of socially visible law-breaking that the uniformed police are best equipped
to deal with—will be difficult and ineffective.

In the few communities—more probably with populations under 25,000
than over—where a majority of the people are members of families that have
lived there for a generation or more, the likelihood that the police will recognize

183

What is the Role of the Community in the Development of Police Systems?

and follow a reasonably clear-cut, though informally expressed, community code will be greater than in areas where there is a rapid turnover of residents.

In an upper middle class suburban community whose members are primarily white-collar executives and professional people with college or university educations such crimes as are committed by adults will more largely be the less visible violations of codes regulating business and professional practices that do not lend themselves to control by the uniformed local police. Youthful offenders in such communities who may get involved in vandalism, drunkenness, auto theft, narcotics use and sex offenses are more likely to be dealt with by family referral to psychiatrists, professional counselors, by school transfer, or other informal procedures without formal action by the police and the courts which are generally pleased that they do not have to accept responsibility for dispositions. On the other hand, individuals, who drive through such communities or who come into them temporarily for recreational or other purposes, especially if they have the high visibility of youth and blackness, may quickly attract at least casual police surveillance and may be dealt with more quickly and formally for law-breaking than would residents of the community.

To the extent that the business enterprises of a community or some section of a major city depend for their profits upon a seasonal or vacation clientele that seeks temporary release from the behavioral restrictions binding upon them when they are at home, the police may be enjoined by the community or power groups within it from enforcing laws that would discourage patronage. Such an easy moral climate produced by people who give priority to profits derived from people who seek commonly unlawful forms of recreation, when they are away from home, invites the take-over and corruption of legitimate business enterprises and the police by organized criminal groups that need legitimate fronts for financing and income tax purposes.

It would appear that large segments of the American population do not consider gambling, prostitution, sex exhibitionism, or the use of some narcotics to be wrong; or else, they wish occasional opportunities for such behavior but do not accept them as a desirable part of normal life in their communities of permanent residence.

Probably all societies make provision for the temporary licensing of behavior that is usually forbidden. This raises a question as to whether such unlawful activities should be legalized in specific cities or states, as has been done at one time and place or another, and whether citizens are sufficiently concerned about them as to study the probable consequences of the alternatives we have. In any event the effectiveness of the police and the image they have of themselves is affected by the type of community response that emerges to the demand for forbidden fruit. To the extent that community behavior encourages, and indeed requires police acquiescence in persistent law violation in some communities, the attractiveness of police work as a career may be reduced and the difficulty of getting professionally oriented recruits into police work magnified.

How Do Community Expectations Affect
Police-Community Relations?

The unawareness of many communities that they are expecting their police to perform incompatible, and therefore impossible, tasks has been to create community attitudes towards the police which tend to make them defensive. Coupled with constant reminders of human failings—even where least expected—and a vocational imperative to be suspicious, this finds expression in a tendency of the police to isolate themselves from the general community and to form their own in-group alliances with others in police work from whom they derive emotional and ideological support. The resulting police "sub-culture" is protected and nourished by a degree of secrecy and by its isolation from the main channels of communication in the community.

Although both communities and police departments differ in the extent of their isolation from one another, social scientists, and others who have had occasion to try, to study police departments, would agree essentially with Skolnick that:

> . . . if the police are ever to develop a conception of legal as opposed to managerial professionalism, two conditions must be met: First, the police must accustom themselves to the seemingly paradoxical yet fundamental idea of the rule of law, namely, that the observance of legal restraints may indeed make their task more difficult. That's how it is in a free society.
>
> Second, the civic community must support compliance with the rule of law by rewarding police for observing constitutional guarantees, instead of looking to the police as merely an institution responsible for controlling criminality. In practice, regrettably, the reverse has been true. . .[1]
>
> Indeed, if any one finding can be said to characterize all of the recent studies of police, it is this fact of social isolation, not only from black people in the ghetto, but also from the white citizenry as well. This isolation is accompanied by a police culture which, in general, tends to be characterized by a high degree of suspiciousness of outsiders. In my own contacts with police, I have found them to be at their most understanding and at their most flexible in private conversation when I was part of their working team. By contrast, in public situations, I have found police to be almost incredibly inflexible and defensive. . .[2]

How Do Communities Affect The
"Style" Of Police Work?

In an able field research study of police work and administration James Wilson identifies three different operative styles each of which characterize the administrative policy and strategy of one or more of the eight departments studied.[3] In

185

What is the Role of the Community in the Development of Police Systems?

the type of department referred to as having a "watchman style" there is less concern with law enforcement than with maintaining order. Under a "watchman" policy certain forms of law violation are tolerated and the police use considerable discretion as to when police action should be taken depending on the persons, the place and the circumstances. The police are activated more largely by complaints than by their own initiative.

Departments characterized as having a "legalistic style" permit less discretion to police officers and do not place emphasis upon differences in the significance and consequences of behavior under different circumstances. Instead the police are expected to enforce the law without reference to time, place or person. Such a department makes a larger proportion of arrests and does not wait upon complaints to take action.

In departments characterized by a "service style" the police are active in response to law violations and to complaints but they more often deal with situations informally rather than legalistically warning traffic violators rather than taking them to court, unless the offenses are serious, and bringing parents in to talk about the unlawful activities of their children when they feel that will accomplish more than an arrest. They attempt to understand what the community wants and may proceed vigorously against behavior which the community indicates it will not tolerate—especially on the part of outsiders—but may deal with local and minor violators quietly and without recourse to formal legalistic procedures.

These differences in "police style" are reflected in both the proportion of time devoted to common police tasks and the way these tasks are performed. However, the relation between crime rates and police activity is not easy to ascertain; there is always the question as to whether the rate for a particular offense appears high because the police are enforcing the law vigorously or whether the police are unusually active with reference to a particular offense because it has a high commitment frequency. Probably, as Wilson suggests, the rate at which traffic tickets are issued—in contrast to the rates of arrest for murder, for example—is due chiefly to police policy rather than to the characteristics of the community. Some police administrators expect each man, or division, to write a specified minimum number of tickets per week or per hour. In two cities both of which purchased a radar speed indicator and assigned officers solely to use it, the rate of traffic citations doubled in one year.[4]

How Does the Community Affect Crime Control?

High rates of assault, robbery, burglary, and rape—or the belief that they are high—will more universally arouse a community than will the extent of such unlawful activities as gambling, prostitution, and the use of narcotics. In the larger and more heterogeneous cities, in recreation and convention cities, in cities employing males in unskilled or routine manual tasks there will tend to be greater public tolerance of illegal gambling, prostitution, and narcotics use than in suburban residential areas which may expect those residents who seek opportunities for such behavior to find them outside the local community. If the police do not exercise the sort of control over prostitution, gambling and narcotics use that a community expects, the problem may burgeon into a public discussion leading to demands by church, parent, or other civic groups, and the whole issue may become political, leading to formal investigations and to changes in police administration and police policies.

Another community factor of much influence on police work is unresolved conflict between the traditional concept of the police as a local service unit and the realities of modern crime. The demand for such "welfare" services as the regulation of parking and traffic flow, transportation of the injured, sick, and elderly to and from hospitals, emergency assistance to motorists, the temporary detention of "drunks," searching for lost children, counseling parents, and so on, comes chiefly from residents of the community. The need for these services and the sort of aid required is immediate and obvious. It is also a type of help the local police are qualified and equipped to give. Moreover it is the sort of work the police like to do because it is recognized by the community as useful and the community appreciates it. Not uncommonly in residential communities local newspapers publish letters written by grateful individuals commending individual policemen who have assisted them in some emergency.

Serious crimes committed in a community—especially the more common offenses of theft by breaking and entering or robbery that are thought of by the public as "real crimes"—are not so likely to be committed by local residents in middle class communities nor is the identification and apprehension of such offenders a task that can usually be accomplished with directness and certainty. Currently, for the country as a whole, about one out of five (19.4%) known offenses of breaking, entering and larceny are cleared by arrest; and the proportion for robbery is a bit over one in four (27.4%).[5] These offenses, moreover, are not violations of local ordinances such as pertain to parking but are crimes defined by the laws of the state—or in some instances the United States—and they are prosecuted in state courts and punishable by the state after prosecution and conviction in its name.

So there exists the anomaly of nearly 40,000 individual city, borough, town, village and county police forces, each with its own separate policy making and supervisory administration, each with its own budget and its own normally inadequate resources, limited in its jurisdiction to its own geographical boundaries but trying to enforce state laws against crimes being committed by offenders who are not limited by any jurisdictional boundaries but who move freely from one community to another.

Many of the offenses that are susceptible to control by uniformed metro-

187

What is the Role of the Community in the Development of Police Systems?

politan type police departments require that police have equipment and specialized training that none but the handful of major municipal police departments have. In dealing with the ramifications of organized crime in the areas of gambling, prostitution, loan-sharking, fraudulent bankruptcies, racketeering, narcotics importation and distribution, the related and supportive activities of murder, mayhem, bribery, and corruption, and the infiltration of labor unions, legitimate business enterprises, and state and municipal public agencies, all but a handful of the major municipal police departments are helpless.

Another aspect of local police control is referred to by the Honorable George Edwards, Judge of the U.S. Court of Appeals for the Sixth Circuit who was also the Police Commissioner in Detroit in 1962-63:

> . . . Decentralized, local control of police also accounts, in large measure, for the objectionable police and court practices that have figured so large in the civil rights debates of the 1960's. Among them: investigative arrests, detention without prompt judicial hearing, improper methods of police interrogation, and denial of the citizen's right to refuse to testify against himself, or to confront and cross-examine his accuser. As we have seen, these topics have been progressively clarified by constitutional decisions of the United States Supreme Court and by lower Federal and state courts. But it is a long way from the Supreme Court, and its increasing concern for securing constitutional liberties, to the police officer on the city street, whose main concern is order. That is one big reason why national civil rights policy has been so slow in being translated into practice. . .[6]

The continuance of police inadequacy with reference to crime control—not welfare assistance—is self-compounding in part because the atomization of police into local departments prevents the establishment of career opportunities in police work that would attract recruits who have the potential and the interest to develop police work into a recognized profession. In 25 out of the 50 states there is probably not a single city that has a police force large enough to provide the sort of promotional and operating opportunities that would attract a college graduate who might become interested in a career in police work or indeed to interest any capable, career-oriented young man who is ambitious to grow in his chosen field as far as his abilities may permit.

What Are The Arguments in Favor Of Locally Administered Police Forces?

Arguments for and against locally administered police forces have gone on in the United States and in England since before uniformed municipal police forces were established. In most other countries, different in their political structure from the United States, national control of police is assumed to be the obviously desirable arrangement and the fragmental situation that is characteristic of the United States is often viewed as an incomprehensible curiosity.

Presently the discussion generally turns on the assumption that only locally administered police forces can understand local needs. The close-knit rural or suburban residential community distrusts the impersonality of a police department not subject to local direction nor responsive to local interests. This seems to be the historically established and well-nurtured fear of vesting power over men's lives in some remote and potentially autocratic authority. It is perhaps inevitable that it also appears at times to bespeak a degree of contentment with special prerogatives and immunities on the part of locally influential people. However, those in local positions of authority are also likely to be more quickly responsive to the sentiments of their communities and more fully aware of the consequences of their actions. Whether this results in constructive and imaginative police responses to local needs or whether it assures the continuance of outmoded, oppressive, and discriminatory action against ethnic minorities, "foreigners" or others will necessarily vary with the communities and the general area involved.

How Do These Assumptions Apply To Major Cities?

Especially in the larger and more heterogeneous cities the "locally" administered city police may actually be viewed by ghetto residents as a remote and impersonal agency of the larger community from which slum dwellers are isolated both physically and by their different needs, resources, and behavior patterns. Among the poor and powerless, whether they are black or white—but perhaps especially when they are black—such unprofessional, inconsiderate, and illegal practices as may occur raise the spectre of a "foreign tyranny" that is difficult to overcome even though it be in their own city. Residents of such areas might well wish they could have a truly local neighborhood police.

The President's Commission on Law Enforcement and Administration of Justice, agreeing that many allegations of police misconduct are unwarranted and that it is not possible for the police to enforce the law without incurring the hostility and resentment which is inherent in police work, nevertheless, notes also that its surveys reveal practices that cannot be justified.[7] Their consequences in community antagonism are indicated by the comments of two men in Harlem cited by the President's Commission from Kenneth Clark's, "Black Ghetto":

> . . . A bunch of us could be playing some music, or dancing which
> we have as an outlet for ourselves. We can't dance in the house, we don't

What is the Role of the Community in the Development of Police Systems?

have clubs or things like that, so we're out on the sidewalk, right on the sidewalk; we might feel like doing dancing, or one might want to play something on his horn. Right away here comes a cop. 'You're disturbing the peace!' No one has said anything, you understand; no one has made a complaint. Everyone is enjoying themselves. But here comes one cop, and he'll want to chase everyone. And gets mad. I mean, he gets mad! We aren't mad. He comes into the neighborhood, aggravated and mad. . .

Last night for instance, the officer stopped some fellas on 125th Street. . . (T)he officer said, "All right, everybody get off the street or inside." Now, it's very hot. We don't have air-conditioned apartments in most of these houses up here, so where are we going if we get off the streets? We can't go back in the house because we almost suffocate. So we sit down on the curb, or stand on the sidewalk, or on the steps, things like that, till the wee hours of the morning, especially in the summer when it's too hot to go up. Now where were we going? But he came with his night-stick and wants to beat people on the head, and wanted to—he arrested one fellow. The other fellow said, "Well, I'll move, but you don't have to talk to me like a dog."[8]

The President's Commission notes more generally that:

 . . . Minor crime statutes are frequently misused. They are employed as a means of clearing undesirables or unsightly persons from the street or driving them out of town, aiding the police in detaining a suspected person during an investigation of a more serious crime, and regulating street activity in slum neighborhoods. Often, under pressure from the community, the police will "declare a war on bums, prostitutes, homosexuals, and narcotic traffickers" by making wholesale arrests for vagrancy, disorderly conduct, drunkenness, or loitering. Justice William O. Douglas found that in Tucson, between 1958 and 1960, the poor were discouraged to come to the city for employment by the policy of picking "up any vags spotted within the city limits." In 1966, a District of Columbia judge found that "the typical accused under [the vagrancy] law is a miserable derelict whose principle offense is poverty and affinity for cheap wine, or an individual, male or female, suspected of engaging in prostitution or homosexuality." The court concluded that the "basic design" of the vagrancy law is "preventive conviction imposed upon those who because of their background and behavior are more likely than the general public to commit crimes and . . . the statute contemplates such convictions even though no overt criminal act has been committed or can be proved." Recent studies of the use of public drunkenness statutes in two cities found that they were often employed to arrest skid row types who were not drunk but were aesthetically displeasing. Until 1965, one department was arresting women under an ordinance which made it a crime for a "woman of notorious character" to walk or ride up "the streets of this city."

This practice is even more harmful to a person than an unwarranted field interrogation, since the suspect is not merely stopped, but he is arrested and confined, at least until he can make bail. While such arrests may serve some investigative value to the police, there is grave question as to their propriety.

The American Bar Foundation, in its study of 1956–57, found that the "Police assume that these (vagrancy) statutes are intended primarily as aids to investigations." For example, if the police desire to undertake an in-custody investigation of a person, and investigative arrests are not used, they often arrest a person for violating a vagrancy-type statute. In one observation made during the American Bar Foundation study, a man was seen near a pawn shop with a jacket on his arm. When questioned, he said that he was unemployed because he had just come to the city to find work and that he had no identification because his wallet had been stolen; he also gave other evasive answers. The officers arrested him for vagrancy because they suspected him of burglary but lacked evidence. Similarly, a man suspected of homicide was arrested for vagrancy so that a prolonged investigation could be made while he served his sentence. Other statutes were found to be used for the same purpose. A man suspected of carrying narcotics, whom the officers did not have evidence to arrest, was arrested for a minor traffic violation which would ordinarily result in a warning and his car was searched.

Arrests for failure to move on, loitering, blocking the sidewalk, or public drinking are predominantly made in slum neighborhoods. One reason is that more officers are stationed in these neighborhoods because of the greater amount of serious crime. As a result, residents sometimes charge "over policing" at the same time they seek more protection from crimes such as robbery and burglary. Minor crime statutes, however, are also more used in poor areas because it is harder to keep order there. As a precinct captain in Washington, D.C., stated: "We do tend to enforce the drunk laws more rigidly on 14th Street than in, say, Crestwood, a better part of the precinct. If we overlooked things on 14th Street, we would have a more serious problem."

The source of these difficulties in enforcement of minor crime statutes reaches beyond the police. The community often demands that the police rid the city of undesirable persons, harass persons engaged in vice activities, and keep the unsightly off the streets, even though the police do not have the legal means of doing so. Hence, until the public recognizes the dilemma facing the police in regulating such behavior, the police will continue to be placed in an untenable position.[9]

References

1. J. Skolnick, *The Police and the Urban Ghetto* (Chicago, American Bar Association, 1968), p. 12.

2. Ibid., p. 22.

What is the Role of the Community in the Development of Police Systems?

3. J. Wilson, *Varieties of Police Behavior,* (Cambridge, Harvard Univ. Press, 1968).

4. J. Wilson, *Op. Cit.* p. 96.

5. Uniform Crime Reports, *Crime in the United States 1968* (Washington, D.C.: U.S. Department of Justice, 1969) p. 100.

6. G. Edwards, *The Police on the Urban Frontier* (New York: Human Relations Press, 1968) p. 36.

7. President's Commission on Law Enforcement and Administration of Justice, *Task Force Report: The Police* (Washington, D.C.: U.S. Government Printing Office, 1967) p. 178.

8. President's Commission on Law Enforcement and Administration of Justice, *Op. Cit.* p. 187.

9. President's Commission on Law Enforcement and Administration of Justice, *Op. Cit.* p. 187.

CHAPTER **3-2**

police in the ghetto

ANGUS CAMPBELL AND HOWARD SCHUMAN

The Policeman's Job

The task of a policeman, to paraphrase the Report of the National Advisory Commission on Civil Disorder, is to protect persons and property in a manner that embodies the predominant moral values of the community he is serving. This role is one of the most difficult in the society. Furthermore, the conscientious policeman in the predominantly Negro areas of our central cities faces perhaps the greatest difficulties of all. At present the total efforts of the police departments neither effectively control crime in the ghetto nor achieve legitimacy in the eyes of many residents of the community. The policemen interviewed clearly reflected this situation. Seventy-three percent said they worked in neighborhoods where the crime rate was higher than average for the city. Almost forty-five percent listed their neighborhoods among the highest in the city in its crime rate. At the same time a majority of the respondents felt that a lack of support from the public, from the courts, from other officials and agencies were among the major problems in doing their job in the neighborhood to which they were assigned.

The police interviewed were asked to name the two or three major problems they faced. Forty-eight percent of the responses (Table 1) dealt with the lack of external support for the policeman. Answers to other questions confirm

Source: Supplemental Studies for the National Advisory Commission on Civil Disorder, The National Advisory Commission on Civil Disorders, pp. 104–114; 42–43. Published by the United States Government Printing Office, 1968.

TABLE 1. What Policemen See as the Major Problems Facing Them in Doing Their Job in Negro Neighborhoods [Q 1–Police] [100 percent = 622]

	Percentage of all responses given[1]
Lack of external support–public, courts, officials, and other agencies	48
Internal departmental problems in doing the job–facilities, supervision, policies	21
Crime, violence, riots, etc.	16
Racial problems–hostility, agitation	9
Living conditions of residents–unemployment, housing, schools, government services, etc.	6

[1] Each of the 437 respondents could give several answers, the first three of which were coded and used in this analysis. Individuals gave an average of 1.4 answers.

this assessment. Forty-two percent of the policemen considered non-cooperation from residents a very serious problem; and sixty-four percent thought lack of support from the laws and courts was very serious (Table 17). Likewise, almost fifty-nine percent of the policemen thought that most of the residents in the precinct where they worked either regarded policemen as enemies or were indifferent towards them (Table 5). As both Table 5 and 17 illustrate, Negro policemen are less likely to perceive the ghetto as hostile and non-supportive.

Police work in these neighborhoods was viewed by the majority both as harder (sixty-one percent) and more hazardous (sixty-two percent) than elsewhere in the same city (Table 2). However great the difficulties and hazards of the job, the police did not express a comparable overall dissatisfaction with the job of a policeman. Seventy-three percent seemed at least somewhat satisfied with being a policeman, and only twenty-six percent preferred another assignment somewhere else in the city. There was no striking difference between Negroes and whites in these assessments.

The respondents were asked if they were very satisfied, somewhat satisfied, somewhat dissatisfied, or very dissatisfied with eight aspects of their work. The largest number complained about poor pay and lack of respect from citizens (Table 3). The policemen's assessment of the eight job aspects might best be summarized as indicating that these men are the most dissatisfied with the external rewards, only moderately dissatisfied with the immediate conditions under which they usually work, and quite satisfied with their colleagues. Such a pattern is consistent with the observation of James Q. Wilson[2] that, when there is little public respect for policemen, they tend to develop subcultural identification or "codes" in order to achieve self respect independent of civilian attitudes.

TABLE 2. Comparative Ratings of Assignments in Ghetto Precincts and Overall Satisfaction [Q 2-3 Police]

	Percent
A. Harder or easier than other assignments?	
Harder	61
About the same	30
Easier	6
Don't know and no answer	3
B. Is work safer or more hazardous than in other assignments?	
Safer	6
No difference	36
More hazardous	62
Don't know and no answer	2
C. Would you prefer working here or some other assignment?	
Prefer present assignment	47
Prefer another assignment	26
Does not matter	26
Don't know and no answer	1
D. How satisfied are you with police work?	
Very satisfied	36
Somewhat satisfied	36
Somewhat dissatisfied	21
Very dissatisfied	6
Don't know and no answer	1

Internal Resources

As Table 1 shows, the second most frequent spontaneous complaint voiced by the policemen was of the lack of internal support for their work: manpower, facilities, supervision, etc. Twenty-one percent of the police citations of major problems were of this type. Within this category of problems, the most frequently mentioned single item was manpower. Ten percent of the policemen listed this as one of three major problems facing them.[3]

Even though the policemen felt disliked by so many citizens, and operated with inadequate facilities and support, very few mentioned low morale as a problem they faced. Only three respondents volunteered a comment about pay or morale as major problems they faced in doing their jobs. A few more, six percent (Table 2), reported that they were "very dissatisfied" with a policeman's job. Apparently, high morale has been maintained, at least among most of the respondents, in spite of many perceived difficulties and negative sanctions.

Another aspect of the policeman's resources is the training given him to cope with the problems he faces daily. While our information does not enable us to assess the effectiveness of comprehensiveness of police training for these difficult assignments, we can report that eighty-five percent of our respondents

TABLE 3. The Policeman's Satisfactions and Dissatisfactions with His Job
[Q 33—Police]

| | Dissatisfied | | Satisfied | | | | No |
	Very	Some- what	Very	Some- what	Don't know	100	an- swer
	Per- cent	Per- cent	Per- cent	Per- cent	Per- cent		
The respect you get from citizens	22	32	10	33	1	(434)	3
Pay	28	26	9	36	0	(435)	2
Physical danger you often face	17	32	11	28	11	(431)	6
Resources and facili- ties for your job	22	27	19	31	0	(436)	1
Working conditions	13	34	11	42	0	(436)	1
Flexibility in doing your job	15	22	24	38	1	(435)	2
Other policemen with whom you work	2	12	52	33	1	(436)	1
Your supervisor	3	10	51	33	1	(432)	5

have had special training in riot control and prevention, and seventy-eight percent have had some training in human relations, psychology, counseling, etc.
Very few policemen reported lack of training as a major problem they faced in
doing their job (only seven respondents spontaneously referred to this).

When we consider some of the findings shown later on in this chapter,
our respondents' feelings of satisfaction with their training can easily be brought
into question.

External Relations of Police Departments

Ghetto critics of the police often charge them with being essentially "occupation" forces rather than "community protectors:" agents of external, often
alien, norms and interests rather than agents of social control for the community in which they are assigned. Undoubtedly much of this charge rests on exag-
geration of actions and attitudes of both sides; however, it is important that we
search for indications of such large scale group conflict as opposed to isolated
individual defiance of legal norms. In addition, we shall examine how the police
tend to explain or justify actions that are deemed by many to be provocatively
and punitatively directed against a large class of people—those with black skins
and little money.

From their own reporting (Table 3), fifty-four percent of the policemen queried were dissatisfied with the respect they receive from citizens. In fact (Table 4), thirty percent suggested that the average citizen in their patrol precincts held the police in some degree of contempt. The police were asked several questions about whether residents considered the police as enemies, assuming this to be a good indication of the degree to which the policemen feel like aliens in the community. Nineteen percent suggested that most people in the precinct in general look on the police as enemies (Table 5). While thirty-seven percent reported the people they protect as regarding police on their side, the largest portion (forty percent) perceived the residents as indifferent.

When asked about the attitudes of Negroes, a higher proportion of policemen (twenty percent) felt they were viewed as enemies. Indeed, the policemen's perceptions of hostility were primarily reserved for the Negroes. Only one percent of the respondents thought most whites considered them enemies, and seventy two percent thought whites considered them on their side.

The policemen apparently feel much more a part of the "white community" than of the "Negro community" at least in regard to their official activities within their patrol precinct. What hostility is perceived by the police seems not to be a manifestation of racial antagonism against individual policemen. Negro policemen report the same pattern of perceived hostility that the whites report, although a consistently smaller percentage of the Negro police regard any one group of people (except whites) as antagonists (Table 5).

Perhaps more important to observe than the relatively low respect and cooperation between police and Negroes in general is the marked distance between police and the young generation. At a time in which juvenile crime is rapidly on the increase and complaints are loudly voiced about the lawlessness of ghetto youth, the police seem to be least in touch with the people. While it is beyond the scope of this report to analyze whether the generation and perhaps racial gaps between police and Negro youth are more an antecedent or consequent of a reported increase in antisocial and criminal behavior among that group, we can

TABLE 4. Respect Accorded to Police by Average Resident of Precinct
[Q 5—Police]

	Percent
"How much respect does the average resident of this precinct have for the police?"	
A great deal of respect	12
Some respect	44
Neither respect nor contempt	11
Some contempt	20
A great deal of contempt	10
Don't know and no answer	3

TABLE 5. The Policeman's View of Whether the Residents Consider Police as Enemies, Friends or are Indifferent [Q 6–Police]

	As on their side	*As enemies*	*Indif- ferent*	*Don't know*	*100 percent*	*No answer*
				Regard police –		
	Percent	Percent	Percent	Percent		
Residents in general	37	19	40	3	(432)	5
Most old persons in the neighborhood	94	1	5	0	(437)	–
Most storekeepers	83	0	14	0	(436)	1
Most teachers	83	1	13	2	(435)	2
Most whites	72	1	25	2	(437)	–
Most Negroes	34	29	35	2	(434)	3
Most young adults	16	39	44	1	(437)	–
Most adolescents	16	51	32	1	(436)	1

The policeman's view of whether or not the residents consider the police as enemies, by race of respondent

[Percentage responding that most regard police as enemies]

	White[1] *(N = 335)*	*Negro*[1] *(N = 101)*
The residents in general	21	11
Most old persons in the neighborhood	1	0
Most storekeepers	0	0
Most teachers	2	0
Most whites	1	2
Most Negroes	30	22
Most young adults	43	27
Most adolescents	52	46

[1] One respondent was neither white nor Negro, or was miscoded.

quite clearly see that police think themselves disliked more by the young than by any other segment of the population. Fifty-one percent of the policemen believe that most adolescents view them as enemies, and thirty-nine percent think most young adults share that hostility. In contrast, the elderly, the storekeepers, and the teachers are perceived as friends or at least friendly.

What lies behind this perception of hostility? The National Advisory Commission on Civil Disorders' report[4] cited several surveys of the opinions of Negroes and whites about such things as police brutality and police respect, indicating that in the last two or three years a sizeable fraction of urban Negroes

Police-Community Interaction

believe that there has been police brutality, while considerably fewer whites believe that police use unnecessary force. Although a survey of the opinion of residents would be the most appropriate measure of their view of police actions, we had to rely upon the police themselves as informants, asking how frequently they had heard certain complaints from the citizens. Six types of actions were listed and the respondents asked how frequently they had heard them—often, sometimes, seldom, or never—as complaints about the police.

As we can see from Table 6, policemen think that residents frequently see them as brutal, annoying and inconsiderate. They sometimes hear complaints about corruption and general hostility, but seldom are charged with being too lenient. In fact only sixteen percent of the policemen "often" hear complaints that they are not tough enough, while thirty-one percent never hear these charges. In the view of the policemen themselves the residents complain frequently about the actions of the police but there is no widespread demand for a crackdown on "crime."

What truth is there to many of these complaints? What actions and attitudes of policemen might stimulate such complaints? A closer examination of the common practices of the police might indicate possible situations and types of police-resident contact that would be most likely to generate hostile feelings. Six types of activity were listed, and each respondent was asked to tell whether he was frequently, sometimes, seldom or never called upon to do each. (Table 7)

Although we cannot compare these types of activity with ones considered more supportive by those possibly affected by the actions, some conclusions are reasonable. It is clear that police quite frequently intervene in domestic quarrels

TABLE 6. Complaints Policemen Hear About Their Actions [Q 26—Police]
[In percent]

	Often or sometimes	Seldom or never	Don't know
Policemen are physically brutal to people on the streets	75	25	0
They give too many tickets and do not help the residents	64	35	1
They do not understand the problems of the residents	64	36	0
They are corrupt and take bribes from those with money	52	48	1
Policemen are generally hostile to the residents	52	48	0
Policemen do not adequately prevent crime because they are not tough enough	42	57	1

and break up loitering groups. This often places them in delicate situations where they interfere with groups of people who may consider their own behaviour normal and legitimate, and at the least not a proper subject of forceful interference. The tension that may be created by indelicate actions in these circumstances is hardly helped by the frequent practice of placing the least skilled policemen in the higher crime areas.

The other activities that policemen report frequently engaging in seldom can be expected to endear them to the residents. About a third are frequently stopping people to question or frisk them, implying thereby that the person stopped is suspected of some crime or potential crime. Almost a fourth report frequently searching without a warrant, further indicating to a great number of residents that they do not merit the justification of due cause to a court.[5] More than a third frequently interrogate suspected drug users. Since the use of the less habituating drugs is considered less onerous by ghetto norms than by white middle class standards, such interrogation is easily interpreted as the imposition of alien and unjustified standards of conduct upon a powerless people. The police, then, are constantly interfering with many of the day-to-day activities of a significant portion of the residents of the neighborhood. It is quite understandable how this imposition—whether justified or not—could generate a considerable level of hostility.

Some degree of hostility can be expected to be generated by the regular surveillance activity of the police. Those who were innocent of any intended or actual wrong-doing are likely to dislike being stopped and frisked. Indeed, the probability of a person who is stopped and frisked by the police being innocent is much larger than the probability of being caught in some illegal activity. The President's Commission on Law Enforcement and the Administration of Justice reported that, in some high crime areas only ten percent of those stopped and frisked were found to be carrying a gun, and another ten percent were found to be carrying knives. The policemen in our sample claim a higher success rate, as

TABLE 7. What Policemen are Called Upon To Do [Q 9—Police]

	Fre-quently	Never	100 percent	No answer
	Percent	Percent		
Intervene in domestic quarrels	94	0		(2)
Breakup loitering groups	63	1		(2)
Interrogate suspected drug users	35	6		(4)
Stop and frisk suspicious people	34	11		(2)
Search on suspicion but without a warrant	24	16		(4)
Search with a warrant	20	7		(4)

the evidence in Table 8 indicates. The median number of persons found to be "carrying something that might lead to a crime" when stopped and frisked is 5.1, according to our policemen. Furthermore, the police also claim that a median of 3.5 individuals were found to be wanted criminals or to have committed some illegal act.

We think it would be safe to assume that the policemen are claiming more positive results from the stop and frisk procedure than is actually the case. In any event, the majority of persons stopped are innocent of any wrong doing. If the rate of stopping and frisking in the Negro community is very high, then it would not take long for the police to antagonize a large number of residents.[6] Interestingly, there were no differences between Negro and white policemen in the reported median frequency with which suspicions were verified in frisks.

The general tenor with which the policemen reported their dealings with people in the neighborhood seemed to be a hardened Hobbesian pessimism in only a fraction of the respondents. In dealing with suspects only ten percent suggested that the policemen should "deal aggressively and authoritatively from the start so that the suspect knows who is in control," while eighty-nine percent agreed that they should "deal firmly from the start, but be polite until a hostile move is made by the suspect." Similarly, only eight percent felt that most people they deal with on the job respond primarily to power and force. A full forty percent thought that people respond in the end primarily to reason and respect, with few responding only to power and force. The rest (fifty-two percent) thought there were some of both kinds of people. In total, sixty percent felt that some sizable proportion of people responded only to power and force, providing some justification for its frequent use.

The typical interaction between policemen and suspect, when people are questioned and frisked, is not congenial. Only nine percent of the policemen report that people they stop are usually fully cooperative (Table 9). More than eighty percent admit that the usual reaction is at least a dislike of being frisked. Forty-one percent of the policemen report that they usually have to use threats or force to get the suspect to respond adequately. Eleven percent find that their suspects usually physically resist their efforts to question and frisk. Such responses from suspects would be expected from hardened criminals. But in a situation on which a majority of those stopped are neither carrying weapons nor are criminals, and in which thirty-four percent of the policemen frequently stop and frisk people, it is clear that considerable hostility is generated among many others than those directly engaged in criminal behavior. Table 9 illustrates that hostility is generated in stopping and frisking by police of both races. However, citizens are perceived as slightly more cooperative by Negro policemen.

Some critics have suggested that it is easy for a policeman to get away with brutal treatment of Negroes. But, whether or not police actions are more aggressive in the Negro ghetto than elsewhere, the police seem to worry more about the restraints placed upon them there. When asked whether they worried about

TABLE 8. Proportion of Positive Finds in Stopping and Frisking [Q 10–Police]

Out of every 10 persons stopped		Carrying something that might lead to crime (e.g. gun, knife)	Actually turned out to be criminals you are looking for
None	percent	3	5
One	do	13	22
Two	do	10	13
Three	do	10	10
Four	do	7	10
Five	do	12	16
Six	do	8	3
Seven	do	12	6
Eight	do	11	7
Nine	do	10	5
Ten	do	3	3
100 percent equals		(366)	(344)
Median number[1]		5.1	3.5
Number responding otherwise			
Desk job		18	17
Illegal to frisk		24	26
Don't know, no answer		29	50

[1] Calculated assuming that responses "five," for example, are evenly distributed between 4.5 and 5.5.

getting into trouble because of their mistakes or because of citizens' complaints, a sizable proportion (thirty-nine percent) expressed more anxiety about such constraint in their Negro precincts than in other sections of the city. Most saw no difference. Only six percent indicated that they need be less cautious in the Negro precinct to which they currently were assigned. Interestingly, this pattern holds for Negroes as well as whites (see Table 10). The complaints that bring the threat of discipline apparently do not arise primarily from racial antagonisms alone. As suggested earlier, the conflict stems more from the overall nature of the police relationship to the Negro community.

The relationship between police and the Negro residents is partially characterized as extensive "anti-crime" activity by the police and many outraged complaints, sometimes leading to collective expressions, by the residents. The desire by city and police leadership for some measure of caution is understandable. The policemen on the beat, defining the precincts as high crime areas, frequently frisk people, break up loitering groups, and intervene in domestic quarrels. The residents complain about many of these activities and resent the manner in which they are carried out. Complaints of police brutality are frequently heard by the police themselves. Seventy-five percent said they "often"

Police-Community Interaction

TABLE 9. Response of Suspects When They are Stopped and Frisked
[Q 12—Police]

Response		Race of policemen		
		White	Negro	All police
Cooperative	percent	10	8	9
Cooperative, but don't like being frisked	do	36	48	39
Respond finally under threats and pressure	do	30	29	30
Physically resist	do	13	5	11
Don't know, don't frisk, no answer	do	11	10	11
100 percent equals		(335)	(101)	(437)

TABLE 10. How Much Policemen Worry About Mistakes and Complaints
[Q 15—Police]

Worry about mistakes, complaints from public		White	Negro	All
Worry more here than elsewhere in city	percent	40	35	39
Worry more in most other precincts	do	5	11	6
Makes no difference	do	53	52	54
Don't know, no answer	do	2	2	1
100 percent equals		(335)	(101)	(437)

or "sometimes" heard them (Table 6). Few policemen (four percent), however, listed complaints of police brutality as major problems in doing their jobs.

Both Negro and white policemen often hear these complaints from citizens, but only the Negroes consider black-skinned people to be ill-treated by police, public officials, and the general public. Table 11 indicates that a majority of Negro police felt that Negroes are treated worse than others by police and public officials; only five percent of the white police believed this. Similarly, as shown in Table 12, sixty-two percent of the white policemen felt that Negroes are treated equally or better than any other part of the population, while only eight percent of the Negroes agreed. The pervasive feeling among white policemen that Negroes are treated equally, or even better, than whites may indicate that many feel that the Negro community has more power and privilege than it deserves, including the power to wield some restraint upon police.

TABLE 11. Police Attitudes Towards Treatment of Negroes by Police and
Public Officials [Q 6—CORE]

Treatment of Negroes	Race of police	As well off	Less well off	Better off	Don't know, no answer	100 percent
		Percent	Percent	Percent	Percent	
Treatment by police	White	78	5	17	1	(335)
	Negro	36	57	6	1	(101)
Treatment by public officials	White	59	5	34	2	(335)
	Negro	39	54	5	2	(101)

TABLE 12. Policeman's View of How Negroes are Treated in His City
[Q 5—CORE] [Percentage of respondents agreeing with statement]

	White	Negro	Total
Treated better than any other part of the population	20	2	16
Treated equally	42	6	33
Treated as other people of the same income	26	24	26
Treated worse than other people of the same income	8	38	14
Treated worse than any other part of the population	2	26	7
Don't know or no answer	2	5	3

Note: 100 percent equals: white—335; Negro—101; total—437.

In summary, the complaints from ghetto residents are not considered
major obstacles by most police. If a policeman feels more anxiety about these
complaints in some precincts than in others, he is likely to perceive more pressure in Negro areas. Furthermore, as the preceding considerations suggest, and
as later discussions will indicate, it is clear that the white policeman finds less
justice in these constraints than does the Negro.

Attitudes Towards The Community

What do the policemen think of the people in the neighborhoods where they
patrol? Some earlier studies have indicated that a large fraction of white policemen working in Negro neighborhoods exhibit prejudice toward Negroes. Albert

Reiss reported to the National Advisory Commission on Civil Disorders that three out of four of the white policemen in predominantly Negro neighborhoods in one city studied exhibited some prejudicial attitudes.[7] As noted earlier, not many of the police, especially white, were sympathetic to Negro causes: fifty-nine percent claimed that the Negroes were moving "much too fast" or "too fast" in gaining what they feel to be equality. Seventy-three percent of the whites and twelve percent of the Negroes felt this way. Forty-nine percent of the whites expressed some chagrin about Negroes socializing with whites, and fifty-six percent were at least "slightly disturbed" with Negroes moving into white residential areas. Very few, including the Negro policemen, expressed any active support of Negro causes. Five percent of all the respondents had been active in a civil rights group during the previous two years (four percent of the whites and seven percent of the Negroes).

The images an individual holds of traits and attitudes of a group have often been used as an index of prejudice. At least, the policeman's stereotypes of the residents with whom he is working can be expected to influence the manner in which he deals with them. In assessing six characteristics, police were quite mixed.(Table 13.) On each characteristic a sizable fraction thought highly of the residents, but a large fraction held low opinions. Comparing positive to negative assessments, both Negro and white policemen rated the residents best on "honesty." Negroes thought somewhat better of the residents than did whites, on the average.

Police Ascription of Responsibility
For The Community Problems

Many factors influence the collective behavior of a community, particularly the characteristics of the people themselves, the relationship they have with organizers and representatives of many outside agencies, their relationship to various government agencies—welfare, police, educational system, etc., and the economic exchange relationships they have with those who control economic resources. The National Advisory Commission on Civil Disorders, in assessing the basic causes of rioting, stressed the centuries of neglect and discrimination on the part of the white community toward their Negro neighbors. The Commission concluded that agitators and militants were not basically responsible for the outbreaks of violence; even less responsible was the general nature of the Negro community. Rather, the lack of adequate private and governmental response to the problems of unemployment, housing, deficient education, and most basically, the pervasive discrimination against Negroes in American life were seen as the root causes of the disturbances.

The policeman, who is the most visible agent of the society in maintaining law and order, sees the causes of rioting and civil disturbances quite differ-

TABLE 13. Attitudes Toward Residents of the Precinct [Q 8—Police] [In percent]

Attribute (stated positively)	Very positive assessment		Very negative assessment		Partially true		Don't know, no answer		Total
	White	Negro	White	Negro	White	Negro	White	Negro	
They are often friendly to outsiders	22	40	32	21	42	37	4	3	100 / 101
They look after their health very well	22	28	28	16	42	52	8	4	100 / 100
They are industrious people	16	26	28	12	53	60	2	2	99 / 100
They care very much for law and order	33	48	22	14	44	38	2	1	101 / 101
They are respectable, religious people	19	28	18	3	59	67	4	2	100 / 100
They are honest people	32	50	10	4	56	46	1	0	99 / 100
Average on six items	24	37	23	12	49	50			100

Note: N(White) = 335; N(Negro) = 101.

ently. It is reasonable to expect that his viewpoint will reflect the enforcement actions and strategy which he daily uses in an attempt to minimize violence and disorder. The viewpoint he expresses appears to be one of short-run criminal control, rather than one of long-term eradication of the causes of discontent. While individual policemen differed considerably in their ascription of responsibility for the problems they face, most tended to see disorders as a result essentially of a lawless, negligent, belligerent, and criminal uprising of some elements of the Negro community.

All respondents were asked what they considered the major causes of the 1967 civil disturbances. Fifty-six percent of the reasons given (Table 14, categories one, forty-four percent; three, eight percent; and seven, four percent) ascribed the causes to the lawlessness, anger, disorder and agitation in the Negro community. The remaining forty-four percent of the reasons given ascribed at least some responsibility to the total society and by implication to the white community.

But, if we probe deeper, the policeman's emphasis becomes clearer. For example, the profile of responses for policemen who reported their city having a major civil disturbance in Summer, 1967, was somewhat different than that for policemen reporting no serious disturbance that Summer. Where there had been a serious disturbance, forty nine percent of the reasons given cited agitation and criminal elements—basic Negro lawlessness—while twenty-two percent of the causes ascribed some responsibility to the failure of the system and the white community. In cities where policemen reported no serious disturbance that summer the frequency of reasons listed was reversed. Thirty-five percent of the responses blamed the criminal and lawless elements, while thirty-eight percent blamed the system in part.

Whether this difference is due primarily to the impact of the riots and subsequent rationalizations for police actions or whether it existed prior to the riots and might have, in part, been responsible for whether or not there was a riot cannot be known from our limited information in those interviews. However, in our judgment such a difference in police assignment of causes is primarily a result of having recently experienced a riot. Those cities in which policemen emphasized social-economic causes seemed just as likely to have had a riot in 1968 as did the other cities.

Quite significant racial differences appear, as Table 15 illustrates. Twice as many whites basically blame the Negro community as blame the socioeconomic system. The reverse is true for the Negro policemen. In addition, approximately three times as many Negroes as whites place the emphasis upon lack of interracial communication.

When police were more directly questioned about the causes of riots, they strongly supported the agitation, criminal element explanations as opposed to police brutality or white neglect (Table 16). Seventy-eight percent and sixty-nine percent, respectively, saw militant agitation and criminal elements as either

TABLE 14. Reasons Given for Civil Disturbances [Q 15 and 18–CORE]
[In percent]

Reasons	Reporting riot in 1967 in city (N = 289)	Reporting no serious disturbance in city in 1967 (N = 141)	All police responding (N = 430)
(1) Causes attributed to faults of the Negro community–disrespect for law, crime agitation, unrest, broken families, etc.	49	33	44
(2) Causes attributed to failure system to meet problems–unemployment, housing, poverty, welfare, schools, indifference, leadership	22	38	27
(3) Negro anger, frustration, and unfulfilled aspirations	7	8	8
(4) General white and official discrimination and provocation	7	5	6
(5) Contagion–media, rumors, etc.	5	4	5
(6) Lack of interracial communication	3	8	5
(7) Lack of adequate enforcement and control by authorities	3	5	4
(8) Specific person or event	4	0	2
Total responses, 100 percent equals	(542)	(274)	(816)

TABLE 15. Reasons Given for Civil Disturbances [Q15 and 18–CORE]

	(Total for all police)[1]		
	White (N = 329)	Negro (N = 100)	Both (N = 429)
Causes attributed to faults of Negro community–disrespect for law, agitation, crime, unrest broken families, etc.	50	24	44
Causes attributed to failure of system to meet problems–unemployment, poverty, bad housing, poor schools, poor leadership from city, etc.	21	44	27
Lack of interracial communication	3	9	5
All other reasons	25	23	25

[1] Seven of the 437 interviewers did not give answers to these questions; the eighth was neither white nor Negro.

Note: 100 percent equals: White 609; Negro 206; both 815.

TABLE 16. How Negro and White Policemen Differ in Attributing Causes to the Riots [Q 67–72–CORE] [Percent agreeing that cause listed is main reason or largely true]

	White (N = 335)	Negro (N = 101)	All police (N = 437)
Local authorities not paying sufficient attention to complaints	24	52	30
Result of criminal element in Negro ghetto	74	52	69
Result of militant agitation	84	55	78
Deliberate political actions	28	23	27
Police brutality	4	25	9
Negroes basically violent and disrespectful	33	11	28

the main reason or a major reason for the recent civil disturbances. Only nine percent and thirty percent, respectively, subscribed to the police brutality and unresponsiveness explanations. Table 16 also shows that Negro police subscribe much less than whites to the militant and criminal explanations, and much more than whites to the police brutality and unresponsiveness explanations.

While very few of the policemen considered inadequate laws or lenient courts as direct causes of riots (two percent volunteered this explanation), they quite strongly resented the restraint placed upon them by the courts and the laws. In a question asking for their major problems as policemen, fifteen percent volunteered complaints about courts and judges being too lenient. This was second only to the forty percent who gave "lack of public support" as one of the major problems they face in doing their jobs. In another question (Table 17) more of the policemen considered laws and courts to hamper their jobs than any of the other three problems.

Table 17 illustrates again how the races differ. Laws and courts were most frequently perceived as an obstacle by whites, but only third most frequently by Negroes. In contrast, Negroes felt most hampered by inadequate resources for themselves, and by the inadequate resources of other agencies in the city. The white police were least concerned about the supportive functions of the other agencies in dealing with community problems.

The policeman is under conflicting pressures and expectations. As Reiss[8] and Bordua point out, enforcement of the laws is separated from the outcome of an arrest. The policeman is under professional and public pressure to catch criminals and to keep public order, but the final conviction and sentencing of an offender is out of his hands, as are judgments of police brutality. It is therefore expected that the average policeman should resent occasional court rejection of his decisions, and frequent court scrutiny of his actions. Likewise, we might add to this conflicting expectation another—that enforcement is separated from pre-

TABLE 17. Seriousness of Four Problems in the Policeman's Job [Q 16—Police] [Percent of policemen who consider problem "Very serious" and "Not at all serious"] (N[White] = 335; N[Negro] = 101)

	Very serious			Not serious		
Problem	White	Negro	Total	White	Negro	Total
Noncooperation of residents	44	32	42	10	18	12
Laws and court decisions hamper investigations and convictions	68	50	64	5	17	8
Inadequate resources: Men, cars, facilities, etc.	61	60	61	12	10	11
Other agencies lack adequate resources	40	57	44	13	6	12

vention. Prevention of many of the situations a policeman handles rests in hands other than his own—city officials, poverty workers, employers, teachers, et al. He has at his disposal only the resources of persuasion and force. With this he must handle the results of the inadequacies of all other segments of the system.

The policeman's perception of other people who work on social problems in his neighborhood is varied. We asked whether the efforts of four types of agencies, organizations or individuals made his job easier or more difficult (Table 18). Consistent with their assessment of the causes of riots, the policemen rated the more militant organizations as most deleterious to law enforcement. For every one policeman who considered the civil rights and poverty organizations helpful in the long run, eight thought they were deleterious. On the other hand those workers most directly associated with the same work as the police consider themselves doing—the gang workers—are considered beneficial to the policeman's work by five policemen for every one who thinks them harmful. Policemen are much more evenly split on the benefit of poverty and welfare workers, though the poverty workers are perceived slightly more helpful. A large fraction of the respondents considered poverty and welfare workers as irrelevant to the policeman's job of law enforcement.

The Negro policemen have a greater appreciation for the functions of the various organizations (Table 18). The percentage of Negro police who consider all of the four types of agencies to be beneficial is approximately twice that of white police. Consistently fewer Negroes than whites consider the agencies deleterious. In all cases, however, the Negro and white policemen agree in the way most think about each type of organization. A larger fraction of both races think that civil rights groups make life more difficult, while the others make it easier.

TABLE 18. How the Work of Other Agencies Affects the Policeman's Job [Q 14–Police] (N[White = 335; N[Negro] = 101) [In percent]

Agency	Easier			More Difficult			No Difference			Don't Know			Total		
	White	Negro	Total	White	Negro	Total	White	Negro	Total	White	Negro	Total	White	Negro	Total
Gang workers	46	71	52	13	5	11	31	18	28	10	6	9	100	100	100
Poverty program workers (Headstart, VISTA, CAA, etc.)	36	61	42	23	4	19	34	31	33	6	4	6	100	100	99
Welfare workers	29	36	30	20	13	18	46	46	46	5	6	6	100	101	100
SNCC, CORE, NAACP, and Povery Rights groups[1]	6	16	8	75	39	68	10	22	13	8	22	12	99	99	100

[1] Five percent of the whites and sixteen percent of the Negroes indicated that NAACP makes their job easier, while other groups make it more difficult.

Police Participation In The Community

The policeman's task consists primarily of the immediate enforcement of rules of law and order, and hence he is concerned with establishing a criminal-non-criminal dichotomy in his encounters with citizens. McNamara[10] observed in his study of New York police that such dichotomous stereotypes can often interfere with the policeman's ability to skillfully handle a variety of situations and different types of people in a sensitive manner. This ability partly requires an understanding of the community in which the policeman works. Such an understanding, in turn, would seem to require extensive and frequent informal and non-hostile communication with all major segments of the population with which the policeman is dealing. Not only would this communication increase the policeman's information about the neighborhood and the activities of its residents—thus minimizing mistakes and increasing surveillance of possible criminals—but such communication would tend to increase the policeman's perception and understanding of the resident's problems and concerns and activities, enabling him to avoid insensitivity in treatment of subjects. In short, in seeking the community cooperation and effectively creating a legal order, the policeman could perform best—if this argument is valid—if he is personally familiar with the adult and youth leaders, the community agency volunteers, the possible troublemakers, et al.

Our respondents, however, seem strikingly isolated from the neighborhoods in which they patrol. As noted earlier fifty-one percent of the police thought adolescents, and thirty-nine percent thought young adults, regarded police as enemies. In contrast, ninety-four percent of the police perceived storekeepers as regarding police as friends. Whether isolation has caused the hostility or hostility the isolation is beyond our scope to determine. However, it is clear that police communicate very little with the youth and a lot with the merchants. Thirty-one percent of the police do not know a single important teenage or youth leader in the neighborhood well enough to speak to him when they see him (Table 19). Fifty-nine percent know five or fewer this well. On the other hand over fifty-five percent of the policemen report that they know more than twenty-five shop owners, managers, and clerks well enough to speak with them whenever they see them. Where the most communication is occurring between the police and citizens in the neighborhood is reasonably clear. Such a pattern illustrates the grounds on which policemen are often perceived as a force of occupation, stationed in the ghetto to protect the property of the white merchant.

Table 19 shows the policeman's priorities in the community. He makes it his business to be aware of the "continual troublemakers" and the merchants. But the community adult and youth leadership, as well as people working on eradicating the social and economic conditions that contribute to crime, are apparently considered largely irrelevant to the policeman's work of law enforce-

Police-Community Interaction

TABLE 19. Extent of Personal Acquaintance with People in the Precinct [Q 23—Police] Question: ". . . In your precinct, for example, about how many people among (name group) do you know well enough to speak with whenever you see them?" (N = 437)

Group	None	Five or fewer	Six or more	Don't know	100 per-cent	No answer
	Percent	Percent	Percent	Percent		
Shop owners, managers, clerks	3	9	89	1	(435)	2
Residents in general	5	12	86	1	(433)	4
Continual trouble makers	6	14	84	2	(436)	1
Important adult leaders	15	49	54	2	(436)	1
People from various government and private agencies who work in the neighborhoods, eg. welfare, religious, utilities	19	49	49	1	(436)	1
Organizers of unlawful activities like crime syndicates, numbers rackets, drug pushers	31	57	40	3	(434)	3
Important teenage and youth leaders	31	59	38	2	(433)	4

Note: (Answers were recorded in seven categories, which were collapsed to form the third category above. The second response category listed above is cumulative, including the first category.)

ment. One would not usually expect the average patrolman to know very many organizers of crime well enough to exchange greeting on occasional meetings. But he knows as many of these as he does of teenage and youth leaders. Yet the policeman regards juveniles as presenting a particularly pressing problem. We should note that comparison and conclusions from the information on Table 19 must be made with caution, since there are quite different numbers of people in the neighborhood in each category considered. Thus, there are probably many more merchants than important youth leaders in any precinct. Secondly, we must note that thirteen percent of the respondents (about equal percentages for Negro and white), have desk jobs. While this would not necessarily mean that they would not be acquainted with anyone in the community, it would be expected to reduce the number of residents with whom they frequently communicate. However, what we are particularly emphasizing is the large percentage of

TABLE 20. Extent of no Personal Acquaintance with People in the Patrol Neighborhood [Q 23–Police] [Percentage of respondents admitting knowing none well enough to casually speak with]

	White (N = 335)	Negro (N = 101)
Shop owners, managers, clerks, etc.	3	1
Residents in general	5	4
Continual troublemakers	5	6
Important adult leaders	18	7
People from various government and private agencies	22	12
Organizers of crime, et al.	31	30
Important teenage and youth leaders	35	18

policemen who know just a very small number, or even none, of the teenage and youth leaders and the people from other agencies.

Table 20 compares by race of respondent his contact with people in the neighborhood. With one exception (continual troublemakers) the white police are more isolated—as measured by the percent who have no acquaintance at all—than the Negro police.

One of the reasons that Negro policemen have more contact with the neighborhood in which they patrol, and have a greater sympathetic understanding of its problems, is that they are much more likely to informally participate in the community than are their white colleagues. Table 21 lists four measures of community participation. The general level of participation is rather low. Eighty-three percent of the respondents do not live where they work; and seventy-six percent do not have relatives in the neighborhood. Only twelve percent have friends there they see "a lot" off duty. On these three measures the Negro policemen understandably rate considerably higher. But for both races, the number who have friends in the neighborhood whom they see "a lot" is smaller than the percentage of policemen who live in that neighborhood.

Even if a policeman does not live in the neighborhood, he can engender community cooperation by attending meetings of various organizations. While thirty percent reported attending meetings at least occasionally only seven percent attend "often." But policemen in general, as would be expected of lower-middle-class occupational groups, are not frequent participants in groups and organized activity outside the job. Sixteen percent do not belong to any organization, and fifty-six percent belong either to one or none. Their informal contact with their own residential community, aside from the neighborhood in which they work, is not very high.

Another set of questions has frequently been raised about the police department's relationship to the community. These deal with training in human

TABLE 21. Neighborhood Participation by Policemen [Q 29-32—Police]
[Percentage who responded affirmatively]

	White (N = 335)	Negro (N = 101)	Total (N = 437)
Live in same area as work	11	37	17
Any relatives live where you work	13	56	24
See friends from neighborhood socially "a lot"	6	30	12
Attend meetings in neighborhood "often" or "sometimes"	16	37	21

relations for the individual officers, and with departmental policies that may be interpreted as discriminatory. Seventy-eight percent of the sample reported some training in human relations, psychology, counseling, law, etc. We have no way to assess the nature, extent, and effectiveness of this training.

The outward symbol of integration is a mixed patrol. Eight-four percent of those who are on patrol report that they have patrolled with an officer of the opposite color. However, only thirty-six percent of those on a beat report travelling interracially more than "once in a while." The more subtle form discrimination might take is in hiring and promotion. Recently, of course, most cities have been encouraging Negroes to join the force, particularly placing them in the Negro community. When asked how likely it would be that a man of another race would take one's place if he were to change his present job, seventy-one percent reported that it would be either "very likely," or "somewhat likely." Only six percent said it would be not at all likely. While this gives no indication of promotion and assignment practices—since most of the respondents were patrolmen (eighty-three percent)—it does signify that very little effective discrimination in hiring or in general assignment to a Negro neighborhood is perceived by those presently employed. . . . The nature of the police relationship to the community is of critical importance in maintaining order and in protecting persons and property. We have found that in the predominantly Negro areas of several large cities, many of the police perceive the residents as basically hostile, especially the youth and adolescents. A lack of public support—from citizens, from courts, and from laws—is the policeman's major complaint. But some of the public criticism can be traced to the activities in which he engages day by day, and perhaps to the tone in which he enforces the "law" in the Negro neighborhoods. Most frequently he is "called upon" to intervene in domestic quarrels and break up loitering groups. He stops and frisks two or three times as many people as are carrying dangerous weapons or are actual criminals, and almost half of these don't wish to cooperate with the policeman's efforts. Most police, however, report that a sizeable proportion of people they deal with respond to reason and respect in the end.

The broader relationship between the officers and the community with which they deal is one of low participation, and often unfavorable attitudes toward the residents, especially among the white policemen. Those segments of the population which the police perceive as most hostile, they are least in touch with on a day-to-day basis. Thirty-one percent admit not knowing a single important youth leader well enough to casually greet him when they see each other. Few police participate in community organizations or have friends they regularly see in the neighborhood. Seventeen percent actually live in the neighborhood in which they work.

There are no obvious signs of discrimination by race in most of these police departments, at least by report of the interviews. However, many differences appear between races in the way individuals view community problems. White policemen see riots as stemming primarily from agitation and criminal elements in the ghetto, seeing their job as one of short term criminal control. Negro policemen, however, tend to see disturbances as caused by more underlying social and economic conditions. The white policemen typically feel that Negroes are treated as well or better than anyone else. Quite to the contrary, the Negro policeman sees his people as mistreated and not moving too fast to achieve equality. Few policemen of either race, however, have recently participated in any civil rights groups. Most of the overall difference between the Negro and white respondents can most likely be attributed to their race, and related community ties and associations. However, the fact that fifty percent of the Negro policemen interviewed had at least some college education, while only thirty-two percent of the whites had some college, might contribute somewhat to the broader and more sympathetic outlook and analysis of the Negro policeman.

Generally speaking, the policemen are dissatisfied with the external rewards for their job, about half-way satisfied with the immediate conditions under which they work, and very happy with their colleagues. Such in-group solidarity, while maintaining morale in the department, might well tend to remove them even further from an already unsupportive, and even threatening world in which they work. Such isolation most likely exacerbates the already marked hostility that exists in many areas between the "residents" and the "enforcers."

The Community Experience

In view of the importance of the police in the complicated social problems of the cities, our survey invested a considerable segment of the questionnaire in exploring the experiences of our Negro and white respondents with the police of their community. Our data make it clear that this is an area of urban life which looks quite different to white and Negro citizens.

We began this series with a question dealing with what we thought would be the most common complaint that might be offered concerning the police: they do not come quickly when they are called. We asked our respondents first whether they thought this happened to people in their neighborhood, then whether it had ever happened to them personally, and finally whether it had happened to anyone they knew. As Table 22 demonstrates, Negroes are far more likely than whites to feel that people in their neighborhood do not receive prompt police service, one in four of them report they have experienced poor service themselves (compared to about three-fifths as many whites) and they are twice as likely as whites to say they know people to whom this has happened.

TABLE 22. "Now I want to talk about some complaints people have made about the (Central City) police. First, some people say the police don't come quickly when you call them for help. Do you think this happens to people in this neighborhood?" [In percent]

	Negro			White		
	Men	Women	Total	Men	Women	Total
Yes	51	52	51	29	24	27
No	36	31	34	58	62	60
Don't know	13	17	15	13	14	13
	100	100	100	100	100	100

"Has it ever happened to you?" [In percent]

	Negro			White		
	Men	Women	Total	Men	Women	Total
Yes	24	26	25	16	13	15
No	39	42	40	25	24	24
Don't know	1	0	1	1	1	1
Don't think it happens in their neighborhood	36	31	34	58	62	60
	100	100	100	100	100	100

"Has it happened to anyone you know?" [In percent]

	Negro			White		
	Men	Women	Total	Men	Women	Total
Yes	31	35	33	18	15	17
No	27	30	28	20	20	20
Don't know	6	4	5	4	3	3
Don't think it happens in their neighborhood	36	31	34	58	62	60
	100	100	100	100	100	100

The second question dealt with the incidence of the show of disrespect or use of insulting language by the police. The racial differences in response to this inquiry are even more pronounced (Table 23). While relatively few white people felt this sort of thing happened in their neighborhood and even fewer reported it had happened to them or to people they know, substantial numbers of Negroes, especially men, thought it happened in their neighborhoods and many of these reported that they had experienced such treatment themselves.

The third question asked if the police "frisk or search people without a good reason" and the same pattern of racial differences emerges (Table 24). This

TABLE 23. "Some people say the police don't show respect for people and use insulting language. Do you think this happens to people in this neighborhood?" [In percent]

	Negro			White		
	Men	Women	Total	Men	Women	Total
Yes	43	33	38	17	14	16
No	38	41	39	75	75	75
Don't know	19	26	23	8	11	9
	100	100	100	100	100	100

"Has it ever happened to you?" [In percent]

	Negro			White		
	Men	Women	Total	Men	Women	Total
Yes	20	10	15	9	5	7
No	40	49	45	15	19	17
Don't know	2	0	1	1	1	1
Don't think it happens in their neighborhood	38	41	39	75	75	75
	100	100	100	100	100	100

"Has it happened to anyone you know?" [In percent]

	Negro			White		
	Men	Women	Total	Men	Women	Total
Yes	28	23	26	12	9	11
No	29	34	32	11	13	12
Don't know	5	2	3	2	3	2
Don't think it happens in their neighborhood	38	41	39	75	75	75
	100	100	100	100	100	100

Police-Community Interaction

is not an experience which occurs to many white people and they do not think it happens in their neighborhoods. Three times as many Negroes do believe it happens in their neighborhoods and report that it has happened to them personally.

Finally, we asked a direct question about "police brutality"—do the police rough up people unnecessarily when they are arresting them or afterwards? Over a third of the Negro respondents reported this happened in their neighborhoods, while 10 percent of the whites so reported (Table 25). Much smaller numbers of both races reported that they had experienced unnecessary roughness themselves but Negroes were four times more likely to report such treat-

TABLE 24. "Some people say the police frisk or search people without good reason. Do you think this happens to people in this neighborhood?" [In percent]

	Negro			White		
	Men	Women	Total	Men	Women	Total
Yes	42	30	36	12	9	11
No	41	40	41	78	75	76
Don't know	17	30	23	10	16	13
	100	100	100	100	100	100

"Has it ever happened to you?" [In percent]

	Negro			White		
	Men	Women	Total	Men	Women	Total
Yes	22	3	13	6	1	4
No	36	55	45	16	24	20
Don't know	1	2	1	0	0	0
Don't think it happens in their neighborhood	41	40	41	78	75	76
	100	100	100	100	100	100

"Has it happened to anyone you know?" [In percent]

	Negro			White		
	Men	Women	Total	Men	Women	Total
Yes	28	20	24	8	6	7
No	28	36	32	12	17	14
Don't know	3	4	3	2	2	2
Don't think it happens in their neighborhood	41	40	41	78	75	75
	100	100	100	100	100	100

ment. Far more Negroes than whites report knowing someone who had been roughed up by the police. The great discrepancy which we find between the numbers of Negroes who say they were themselves unnecessarily frisked or roughed up and the numbers who testify that they know someone to whom this has happened reflects the manner in which reports of such incidents travel through the Negro community.

Reports of unfavorable experiences with the police are clearly more numerous among the younger members of both racial groups than among their elders. ... Younger people are more likely to think police offenses occur in their

TABLE 25. "Some people say the police rought up people unnecessarily when they are arresting them or afterwards. Do you think this happens to people in this neighborhood?"

	Negro			White		
	Men	Women	Total	Men	Women	Total
Yes	37	32	35	10	9	10
No	42	41	41	80	76	78
Don't know	21	27	24	10	15	12
	100	100	100	100	100	100

"Has it ever happened to you?" [In percent]

	Negro			White		
	Men	Women	Total	Men	Women	Total
Yes	7	1	4	2	0	1
No	50	56	53	18	23	20
Don't know	1	2	2	0	1	1
Don't think it happens in their neighborhood	42	41	41	80	76	78
	100	100	100	100	100	100

"Has it happened to anyone you know?" [In percent]

	Negro			White		
	Men	Women	Total	Men	Women	Total
Yes	27	20	24	7	6	7
No	28	35	32	11	15	13
Don't know	3	4	3	2	3	2
Don't think it happens in their neighborhood	42	41	41	80	76	78
	100	100	100	100	100	100

neighborhoods, to report that offenses have been committed against them personally, and to know other people against whom they have been committed. . . . [A] brasive relations with the police are not only a racial problem in these northern cities, they are also a problem of youth. Negro young people are much more likely to complain of police offenses than the older generations of their race, especially of those police actions which involve bodily contact. However, the same age trend, about equally pronounced, is found in the white population. These findings are consistent, of course, with police records of the age characteristics of arrestees of both races.

References

1. Further reports from this study will contain interviews with police in all cities, save Boston and Milwaukee. In both those cities, police officials ordered their men not to cooperate with our interviewers.

2. "Police Morale, Reform, and Citizen Respect: The Chicago Case," David J. Bordua, Ed., *The Police: Six Sociological Essays* (New York, Wiley, 1967), p. 138.

3. When asked in another context whether the control of crime and the enforcement of the law is hampered by shortage of men, cars, facilities, etc., eighty-nine percent considered this to be a problem; sixty-one percent thought it "very serious."

4. Chapter 11, Section I.

5. From the way in which the question was worded we are uncertain whether respondents referred to searching premises, searching persons, or both.

6. It may also be the case that those policemen who do a great deal of stopping and frisking may have lower overall "take rates," even though they may apprehend more criminals in total. Hence a policy which would increase the amount of stopping and frisking bears the risk of antagonizing very large proportion of the non-criminal even though it would significantly increase the number of criminals or alleged criminals who are apprehended.

7. Chapter 11, Section 1.

8. Environment and Organization: A Perspective on the Police", in David Bordua, op. cit.

9. John H. McNamara, "Uncertainties in Police Work: The Relevance of Police Recruits' Background and Training," David Bordua, *op. cit.*

SYSTEMATIC MOdEL of police

MORALE: A PERSONALITY ANd

SOCIAL STRUCTURE ANALYSIS

MARTIN G. MILLER

Theoretical views of the police and public adversary relationship are of minimal heuristic research value. None of the theorists clearly define terms or present a consistent theory based on environmental, organizational, and personality variables. The systemic model presented here attempts to rectify this deficiency with the interactional approach needed to understand the effects of police and citizen relationships on police morale. The model is based on an open systems approach that considers organizational interval development and environmental adaptation (Katz and Kahn, *The Social Psychology of Organizations*) and incorporates a role and self-identity theory in understanding the police organization (James Q. Wilson, *The Police and Their Problems*). It is intended to serve as a basis for investigating such crucial police and community relations issue as poor morale, police isolation, the respect syndrome of police, and so on. It should be noted that the model is a highly simplified theory of real-life situations and is presently in its early developmental stage. Its verification and modification is contingent on future research.

The theoretical model addresses itself to these questions:

1. How does the community contribute to the problem of poor police morale?
2. Is there a causal link between police isolation and alienation *and* community perceptions of police?

The model centers on the following terms and their definitions:

1. *Social system:* an ordered arrangement of social roles, patterned through allocative and integrative processes, and having boundaries relative to an environment.

2. *Personality system:* an ordered arrangement of self-identities, patterned through allocative and integrative processes, that is characteristic of a particular individual.

3. *Cultural values:* consensually validated standards for evaluating social acts that are characteristic of a particular social system. In other words, conceptions of desirable states of affairs.

4. *Social role:* a set of expectations defining what is appropriate behavior in a particular position in a system of social relationships.

5. *Self-identity:* a set of need-dispositions or tendencies toward behavior expressed in the form of an image of self in a particular position in a system of social relationships.

6. *Norm:* a consensually validated behavioral prescription or proscription.

7. *Isomorphism:* a condition in which the content of a role expectation, a need-disposition, and a cultural value are identical.

8. *Congruence:* a condition in which the content of a role expectation, a need-disposition, or a cultural value are appropriate to the content of one or more of the others.

9. *Social structure:* form and distribution of, and relationships among, units within a social system.

10. *Degree of structural differentiation;* the number of units within a social system.

11. *Degree of structuring:* the extent to which the functioning of a social system is normatively regulated.

12. *Self-esteem maintenance system* (to be referred to as SMS): the hierarchical ordering of cultural values and social roles within a *personality* system. The ones on top are most important to self-esteem, the ones on the bottom least. It is a process of maintaining favorable images of self.

13. *Status assignment system* (to be referred to as SAS): the process of status ordering and giving within a *social* system. The hierarchical ordering of cultural values and social roles by the participants of a social system. The ones on top possess the most status (prestige) in the system, the ones on the bottom least. This reflects the central value system of the social system.

The key to understanding the effects of social structure on personality is the analysis of the structure of the social system's SAS and a personality system's SMS. This calls for a determination of isomorphism and congruency between the systems. What processes produce isomorphism and congruency or no isomorphism and congruency?

The theory is based on the following assumptions:

1. People try to maintain favorable self-identities.
2. Any kind of favorable image of self needs social support and confirmation (as Cooley and Mead have stated).
3. We are part of many social systems, therefore many SASs feed into our SMSs.
4. In contemporary unstructured society, people are socialized within highly structurally differentiated social systems: thus, they possess many self-identities.
5. In contemporary unstructured society, high structural differentiation has led to people possessing a complexity of values and roles.
6. The degree to which there is isomorphism and congruency between our SASs and our SMSs is the degree to which we possess favorable self-identities.

A hypothesis of our theoretical model is that isomorphism and congruence do not exist between the SMS of the *policeman* (personality system)—particularly the low-ranked patrolman—and the SAS of the *police department* (social system) and the SAS of the *community* (social system). Talcott Parsons defines a community as a social system in which people share an area, and this shared area is the base of operations for their daily activities. The hypothesis stated above is supported by Preiss and Ehrlich's finding (*An Examination of Role Theory*) that in the state police organization studied, there was a low order of consensus on role areas of policemen among officers' audience groups.

Table 1 presents a hypothetical example of SMS and SAS hierarchical ordering that shows divergences between the systems with respect to the policeman's role and status. It is evident that little congruency or isomorphism exists between the SMS and the SASs. As a result, there develops status discrepancy, i.e., "a lack of consistency between property, occupation, education on the one hand and prestige on the other" (J.C. Davis, *Human Nature in Politics*). Fig. 1 is a graphic scheme of the interrelationships of these systems.

When the SMS is not identical to (isomorphic) the SASs, then the subjects (in this case, police officers) suffer from:

1. *Alienation:* a rejection of the legitimacy of status assignment systems (*isolation* in Seeman's terms, "On the Meaning of Alienation") and self-estrangement, an awareness of the discrepancy between one's ideal self and one's actual self image.
2. *Psychological stress:* (stress used in a broad sense of anxiety, inability to function normally, fright, etc.) A. Pepitone has written a most pertinent article, "Self, Social Environment, and Stress," relating to our concern for the reaction of stress to the unequal SMS and SASs. He states that the amount of stress experienced is dependent on losing status. Pepitone presents several laboratory experiments showing that stress reactions are correlated with threat of loss of personal esteem. If a person does not achieve status, he evaluates himself negatively. Such a person, in a situa-

Police-Community Interaction

TABLE 1. Systemic Model of Police Morale: An Example

Self-esteem Maintenance System (SMS) of Patrolman Hierarchies

	Cultural Values	*Role Concepts: Community*	*Role Concepts: Police Department*
High	Respect	Policeman	Patrolman
	Wealth	Doctor	Detective
	Power	Grocer	Juvenile Officer
Low	Honesty	Banker	PCR Officer

Status Assignment System (SAS) of Police Social System (Department) Hierarchies

	Cultural Values	*Role Concepts: Community*	*Role Concepts: Police Department*
High	Respect	Policeman	Detective
	Power	Doctor	Juvenile Officer
	Honesty	Banker	PCR Officer
Low	Wealth	Grocer	Patrolman

Status Assignment System (SAS) of Community Social System Hierarchies

	Cultural Values	*Role Concepts: Community*	*Role Concepts: Police Department*
High	Honesty	Doctor	PCR Officer
	Wealth	Banker	Juvenile Officer
	Power	Grocer	Detective
Low	Respect	Policeman	Patrolman

– – – – – = Important divergences in ordering that indicate lack of isomorphism between systems.

tion where status is won or lost, defends himself from further loss at any cost. Another significant point is that organizations having a pattern of vertical structural differentiation shaped as a triangle, i.e., few positions on top, many on the bottom (as in the case of police departments), cause stress due to lack of mobility opportunity.

The problems of alienation and psychological stress resulting from status discrepancy may be lessened to the extent that ways can be found to form isomorphism and congruency among the SMS of the policeman's personality system and the SASs of the police department and community social systems.

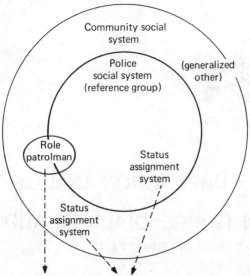

FIGURE 1. Interrelationships of systems

CHAPTER **3-4**

AN iNTERACTiON ANAlysis
of policE-blAck RElATiONS

STAN CROSS AND EDWARD RENNER

Many policemen feel their lives are in danger when they enter the black community, and many segments of the black community regard policemen as a repressive force. The hostility has become open and emotions are high. The accumulation of fire power by both groups can be used to support the charge and countercharge of armed insurrection and genocide. The self-defensive measures taken by police are understandable, as is the sense of repression felt by an increasingly wider segment of the black community. In turn, both reactions contribute to the felt danger and result in defensive reactions, thereby creating a vicious circle which generates a momentum of its own.

The problem of police-black interaction has many sides and aspects, and many solutions have been proposed. They have ranged from more policemen and the addition of modern weapons and communication equipment, through storefront offices and human relations components within the police force, to joint police-community training programs. Yet, some types of programs are in apparent conflict with others, as when the visible addition of fire power is concurrent with a human relations effort to project a new image of the policeman. Other proposals, such as those for civilian review boards, seem to produce new conflicts and deepen distrust.

Source: Stan Cross and Edward Renner. An Interaction Analysis of Police-Black Relations. Reprinted by permission of the *Journal of Police Science and Administration*, Copyright ©1974 by Northwestern University School of Law, Volume II, Number 1.

Prerequisites For Solution

It is understandable that past efforts have not always been helpful, because there is not *a specific problem* for which a solution is needed. Instead, there are numerous problems which require different levels of analysis. A useful prerequisite, which currently is lacking, is an overview which can give a sense of coherence to these problems. Thus, an initial step is to isolate the aspects of the problem which belong together and can be approached at the same level of analysis. This would yield clear implications for the practical steps to be taken, and the limitations to be expected.

Our goal in this analysis is to provide a basis for conceptually organizing that aspect of the problem which is best seen at one particular level of analysis: specifically, the person-to-person process which characterizes a high percentage of police-black interactions. The material will be organized in a way which isolates the sources of interactional difficulty. It is important, however, not to overgeneralize the usefulness of such an interaction analysis, because it only deals with one small part of a total context. This context goes well beyond a police department and its daily practices.

The roots of the problem are sustained by social, political and economic forces which lie beyond police functions. For example, the situation of poverty limits private space and requires the poor to make greater use of public space. This results in greater exposure to police contact and arrest, even for behavior identical with that of the non-poor.[1] With less money for bail, any resulting police-citizen interaction is qualitatively different for the poor than for the rich; detainment is likely to be longer and more frustrating.

The socially defined role of the policeman toward the black community is a role dictated by the white community. When the socially defined purposes of the police are basically in conflict with those of ghetto residents, a cooperative venture cannot be made. Although the problem of conflicting social roles is clearly important, an interaction approach cannot resolve these difficulties. Nor does an interaction approach deal with variations arising from the unique personalities of individual policemen and citizens. The intervention efforts to produce change through improvement of the adjustment and maturity of policemen, blacks, or both, represent a psychological approach based on a psychotherapy model.

To confront either the social role problem or the personalities of the participants requires a different level of analysis and different methods from those to be presented here. The former issue is located largely outside police departments in political and social institutions, and the latter in personnel selection and agencies for community mental health. Both are important problems, but not ones that logically should precede or follow the framework outlined here. Each needs to be assessed in its own context. We suggest that an interactional level of analysis is a particularly useful beginning because it has immediate implications which may in the long run indirectly influence the less accessible social roles and individual personalities.

The acknowledgement of a larger context does not eliminate the scientific and practical necessity of focusing on more restricted conceptualizations. It is just as naive to conclude that one should wait for complex and interrelated social and economic structures to change as it is to assume that the proposed analysis will solve the problem of police-black interaction. At this point, it is both realistic and profitable to concentrate on subareas of the problem which are theoretically and empirically manageable. It is our belief that through such limited but clearly formulated ventures, a better perspective of the total context can be achieved. Also, awareness, involvement and above all public commitment toward a solution can develop. All of these are necessary prerequisites for an eventual solution.

An Interaction Analysis

Although our analysis will be at a group level, this does not imply that all blacks (or policemen) are interchangeable, except in the limited sense that our level of analysis ignores variation arising from individual personalities. It is recognized that neither blacks nor police constitute a homogeneous group. However, the degree of differentiation which is useful within each group is an empirical matter, to be determined from an actual analysis of the interaction process. It should be noted that the degree of differentiation will vary with the types of encounters between the police and blacks. Thus, useful differentiations must always be seen as specific to the particular analysis and not necessarily typical of either blacks or the police.

Components of Interaction Affecting Behavior

Given that members of two reference groups (e.g., a black and a policeman) are engaged in an interaction, they may either share or not share a particular role definition for that situation (e.g., the policeman is an authority to be shown respect). The role, whatever it is, may be clear or not clear to the individual. When a role is clear the person understands what is expected of him to fulfill his part of the role, and he has the behavioral skills to meet those expectations. For either the policeman or the black a role may be clear or not clear. In addition, the two parties may share or not share the evaluation they make of the role. Both may agree that it is good or bad, or they may disagree, with one of the parties positively valuing and the other negatively valuing the particular role in question. These possibilities are shown in Table 1, which also permits us to define explicitly the component of interaction on which we have based our approach.

When an individual does not possess the necessary skills for interaction or when the guidelines for behavior are inadequate, the individual will be unsure of how to behave, he will not know what to expect from the other person, and he will have great difficulty interpreting the behavior that occurs. If a person is to feel safe in an interpersonal encounter he must have confidence in his skills to understand and anticipate accurately the behavior of the other. The experience of *threat* occurs when there is no role to be assumed or where one or both parties do not have the skills for interaction with the other.

When an individual encounters someone whose expectation for that situation is different from his own there is a *role definition conflict.* Each party is seeking to have the other abandon his own definition of the situation and accept the alternative being offered. It is a contest. Contests often demand that there be a winner and a loser.

Although the police have certain expectations, it is not always easy for the black citizen to meet these expectations even though he may wish to do so. An offender who is looked upon as a deviant by the police, such as a gang member, has definitions of behavior set by his own group that differ from those of the police. "When the individual senses that others are unsuitably involved, it will always be relative to the standards of his group that he will sense the others have behaved improperly."[2] Thus, the police and citizen definitions of appropriate behavior for self, other, or both, can be in direct conflict.

Likewise, conflict can arise when the two reference groups place a different evaluation on a particular role definition. An interpersonal role definition about respect for authority which is positively valued by the police is likely to be negatively valued by the members of the street gang. The result is a *role evaluative conflict.*

Many policemen find themselves on the alert for the slightest sign of disrespect. One author has shown that the policeman is often prepared to coerce respect and will use force if he feels his position is being challanged.[3] Likewise, the attitudes and emotions of the black citizen may be similar when confronted with a policeman. Intervention by police is often seen as an infringement on the blacks' rights and as oppression by the white population. Consequently, many blacks are on the alert for the slightest sign of disrespect that might be displayed by the policeman.

For both the policeman and the black, the emotions of belittlement, or fear of self-danger, are powerful forces which may disrupt effectively neutral behavior and make the situation potentially volatile. Aggression may occur when one party is threatened or when one party by virtue of his power or authority uses whatever force is necessary to attempt to make his definition or evaluation prevail.

By way of contrast, the role of the policeman in the white middle and upper class community frequently comes close to what the community desires. The police are seen as protecting life and property, not as oppressing the population. Thus, the interaction of a policeman with middle and upper class white citizens often is based on a mutually acceptable role relationship. Although it is true that the policeman's role and his consequent actions may not be fully understood by the white citizen, whites are less likely to lack skills necessary for the interaction because both share similar language patterns and basic reference groups. Consequently the experience of threat is seldom a disrupting factor.

It should be clear from Table 1 that a *mutual role relationship* can exist only when both parties have shared definitions and evaluations of a clearly defined role. Stable and satisfying interpersonal interactions are characterized by mutual role relationships. However, many interactions between police and blacks are moving toward the opposite extreme, that of threat, role definition conflict, and role evaluation conflict.

Tolerated Variation

When considering breakdowns in interactional encounters, the concept of toleration is useful. If a particular role definition is rejected as inappropriate for the situation or if it is negatively evaluated, the situation is unstable and the person is unlikely to tolerate it willingly. He may be expected to exert some effort to modify the interaction toward a new definition which he positively values. However, a particular definition or evaluation may be tolerated behaviorally (actual role behavior) although rejected psychologically (ideal role behavior), either because the person is not in a powerful enough position or the difference is not important enough to challenge the definition or the evaluation.

A discrepancy between actual and ideal role expectations gives the concept of toleration its meaning. One may think of the *range of tolerated variation* as the discrepancy between actual and ideal behavior which will be accepted. As the size of the difference increases, toleration is less likely to occur, all other things equal. In the case of police-black interaction all other things are not to remain equal. As the willingness to accept a conflicting role definition or evaluation (i.e., tolerance) decreases, the potential for aggression (active rejection) increases for both groups. A show of strength through guns or large numbers may be used as a solution. In this case, an attempt is made to strengthen one's position through power and thereby force compliance. This solution raises the threshold at which the other person is likely to move from tolerance to active rejection. However, such a "solution" is self-defeating in the long run because it fails to deal with the source of the problem while deepening conflict, a potential source of further aggression.

When an individual is pushed past his threshold of active rejection, the

TABLE 1. The Components of Interaction Affecting Behavior at an Interactional Level of Analysis

The Evaluation of a Role by the Two Reference Groups	An Interpersonal Definition of a Role			
	Shared		Not Shared	
	Clear	Not Clear	Clear	Not Clear
Shared (positive or negative	Mutual role relationship	Threat	Role definition conflice	Threat and role definition conflict
Not Shared (one positive, one negative)	Evaluative conflict	Threat and evaluative conflict	Role definition conflict and evaluative conflict	Threat, role definition conflict, and evaluative conflict

breakdown of interaction is likely. This is due to a disruption of the normal process of accommodation characteristic of most encounters. If either the policeman or the black citizen fails to perform his complementary role transaction, there is a greater potential for indignant behavior to develop on one or both sides. "An environment, then, in terms of the ceremonial component of activity, is a place where it is easy or difficult to play the ritual game of having a self."[4] The environment of police-black interaction, which is rife with threat and conflict, is such that it is difficult to play the ritual game of having a self. Goffman refers to affronts which have gone too far as passing critical points.[5] In our terminology, the affront has taken the individual across the threshold from tolerance to active rejection. The discrepancy between his real and ideal role expectations has become large enough to overcome pressure for compliance. If the affront falls outside the range of tolerated variation the potential for aggression increases. The policeman, in this type of situation, is faced with an offender who refuses to abide by the policeman's definition or evaluation of the role relationship. Often it does not appear possible for the policeman to tone down evaluational and definitional conflict long enough to escape the interaction and prevent unacceptable damage to his image of self.

Similar critical points exist in which the policeman's behavior crosses, in a provocative sense, the threshold of active rejection for the black citizen, such as prodding with a nightstick, twisting the handcuffs, or calling him "boy." Such acts may be serious enough for the black citizen to respond, crossing in turn the threshold of active rejection of the policeman. The victim of the first crime is himself made a criminal. The circle can continue until it is too expensive for one party to actively reject. Then the difference must be tolerated, but with strong negative feelings.

When thresholds of active rejection are surpassed and interactions break down into disputes, both parties suffer in the long run. Irrespective of who "wins," each side reinforces its antagonistic conception of the other, intensifying evaluative and role definition conflict and increasing the likelihood of similar occurrences in the future. With each confrontation it becomes more and more difficult to establish mutually acceptable role relationships.

A Conceptual Approach to Specific Interactions

To this point, our presentation has been abstract and general. The account also provides, as we shall attempt to demonstrate, a very practical tool for conceptualizing the specific sources of tension which characterize minority-police interaction.

Any typical day-to-day encounter can be conceptualized in terms of two sets of expectations by the police and by blacks for that particular encounter. These expectations concern what the self and the other should ideally do (ideal role behavior) and what is likely to be done (actual role behavior).

The difference between the actual expectations of blacks and the police indicates the degree of behavioral clarity in the situation and the degree of threat involved. The difference between the ideal role prescriptions given by the blacks and by the police indicates the degree of convergence at an ideal level and the potential for a mutual role relationship. The difference between the actual behavior of the police and ideal expectations of blacks shows the stress the black is under to reject the interaction, or what we earlier called the range of tolerated variation. Likewise, the difference between the actual behavior of the blacks and the ideal expectations of the police reflect the stress the policeman is under to tolerate or reject the interaction. Finally, the degree to which either the policeman's or the black's actual behavior deviates from his own ideal reflects the potential loss or maintenance of self-esteem.

The policeman's reliance on the use of authority to control interactional encounters may pose a threat towards the black citizen's self-image. When a policeman tells a black to "shut up" with a strong voice of authority, his actual and ideal behaviors are identical and police self-esteem is high; he has behaved as he thinks a policeman should. If the black, in that situation, had actually expected the policeman to "show a big man image" then neither party at this point would have experienced threat because the expectations of one matched the reality of the other's behavior. For the black, however, if the ideal was for an explanation by the policeman in a pleasant tone of voice, then the two parties are in conflict because their definition and evaluation at the ideal level are in disagreement. The black is under pressure to reject the terms of the relationship because the actual behavior of the policeman is different from the ideal held by the black for the policeman. Other factors will determine if this deviation is outside the range of tolerated variation, such as how important the particular act is to his self-conception and the perceived pressure (price) of noncompliance.

With the increase in black awareness, blacks are becoming less willing to accept as appropriate the role thrust on them; in short, their ideal expectations are changing and the gap is widening between the blacks and police. Many blacks now feel that an actual response which is closer to the ideal and which will preserve self-esteem must be made in response to the policeman's order to "shut up." Such a response protects the self-esteem of the black, but may be threatening to the policeman who had expected compliance. A likely outcome is for the policeman to raise the price for noncompliance through the use of force or arrest. Such compliance can be achieved, but only with greater loss of self-esteem and resentment by the black because his previous threshold for active rejection had already been crossed and the new threshold demands even more of self be given up.

We have illustrated how the descriptive concepts of the interaction process (from Table 1) and how the concept of toleration may be operationalized for any particular interaction situation. Any interaction process can be empirically analyzed by exploring with both parties the behaviors which actually occur and those which should ideally occur in given situations. In principle, many of these interactions could be brought into common purpose because it is in the self-interest of both parties to identify and establish mutual role relationships to the extent that the larger context permits. But current interaction patterns are moving the two groups farther apart because the day-to-day, situation-by-situation, encounters are not understood.

Descriptive studies have emphasized that both groups are moving farther apart because of incomplete cognitive differentiation. The failure to differentiate the black community into different segments, or treating the entire community or all police functions as if they were homogeneous, interferes with the establishment of adequate role relationships. The result is threat, conflicting role definitions and evaluative conflict between the police and the black community. The lack of differentiation can be seen as setting limits on the range and type of behavioral variation which is tolerated in interpersonal roles.

Regardless of whether police are characterizing the honest black citizen in the ghetto as a symbolic assailant, are relying on stereotypes in determining delinquency, or are simply allowing the people of the ghetto to work things out for themselves, they are defining a role for themselves which is not shared and which is negatively evaluated by the black community.

Minority groups also develop an incomplete picture of the policeman. Over and over again, they hear stories of physical violence and they relate police brutality with all policemen. There is then a situation in which both sides expect the worst, and as a consequence often succeed in producing it. As a consequence, each police-black encounter becomes a potentially explosive one.

There are, of course, many other causes of the divergence from mutual roles. These causes can be identified on both theoretical and rational grounds. But, issues surrounding lack of differentiation are central. Mutual role relationships can never develop until both parties have made sufficient distinctions to allow nonthreatening and realistic interpersonal communication between two people. Such a capacity requires differentiation which is at least as complex and detailed as the important beliefs and emotions of the people themselves and of the situations which bring them together. For these reasons, an empirical focus on the actual behavioral transactions is necessary in order to analyze the interaction process in its basic situational components.

The distinguishing feature of a formal interaction analysis as opposed to a descriptive analysis lies in the potential for systematic characterization, and quantification, of the salient dimensions. Also, the structure of the formal process provides a pansituational conceptual scheme which permits greater generality and provides a basis for comparative analysis.

Implication Of An Interaction Analysis

There are also theoretical implications of a formal interaction analysis which should be noted. Our approach is based on a level of analysis of police-black interaction which is somewhat different than much of the work done to date. Most current work has focused on the personalities of the people, and has been based on the faith that if one could change attitudes, the behavior of both groups would somehow improve.

The present analysis is based on the alternative assumption that the lack of role complementary *behavior* is a problem itself, and that the best way to change behavior is to work directly on the behavior. From an interaction perspective, it is the unpredictability of the interaction which creates the fears and emotions of attitudes, more than attitudes which have produced unpredictable behavior. This *behavioral assumption* has been neglected, although it should be a useful approach in terms of existing knowledge of how to help change the actual situation.

Although such a behavioral approach has been neglected for police-community relations training, there is ample precedent from other areas. The approach is related to the critical incident technique in which behavioral accounts of real incidents as reported by the participants are used for personnel selection, training, and proficiency measures.[6] The procedure has been used successfully in military and industrial training programs. More recently, similar procedures have been used to provide undersocialized delinquents with the critical behavioral skills necessary to deal effectively with problem situations and college freshmen to deal with the abrupt demand for the new interpersonal skills required to adjust to a college campus.

An additional important aspect of our level of analysis is the isolation and the definition of roles which can be developed and which are mutually acceptable to police and blacks. In part these would be clarifications of old roles, but in part such an interaction analysis would isolate and specify possible new roles for policemen to fill within the black community. In this sense, the behavioral approach could be innovative by providing functions that can properly be defined as police work and which will serve to improve relations with the black community as well.

Effective law enforcement and police functions ultimately rest upon public support and citizen participation. Crime prevention, job satisfaction for the policeman and community support require that a mutually acceptable relationship exist between the policeman and the community. Our approach provides a conceptual basis for moving toward this idea. Through an interactional analysis, understanding can be established which would help both police and blacks behave in a way which fulfills the expectations of the other. Such communication at a behavioral level should open the way for further mutual accommodation at the level of social roles and at the level of factors which support individual emotional reactions and attitudes.

A model such as we have outlined delimits what is a coherent level of analysis. It indicates what steps may be taken to improve interactions and equally important what aspects are outside the realm of the approach. Significantly, it permits an empirical approach, subject to evaluation and refinement, which can specify the degree of differentiation necessary to adequately conceptualize the reference groups of blacks or police.

References

1. Stinchcombe, "Institutions of Privacy in the Determination of Police Administration Practice," *American Journal of Sociology,* Vol. 69, p. 150–160 (1963).

2. Goffman, *Interactional Ritual,* p. 124 (1967).

3. McNamara, "Uncertainties in Police Work," *The Police: Six Sociological Essays* (1967).

4. Footnote 2.

5. Footnote 2.

6. Flanagan, "The Critical Incident Technique," *Psychological Bulletin,* Vol. 51, p. 327–358 (1954).

CHAPTER 3-5

diffERENTiAl sElECTioN of juvENilE offENdERs by poliCE

NATHAN GOLDMAN

Research Design

This research was undertaken to test the general hypothesis that there is a differential selection of juvenile offenders for court appearance of such a nature that in the juvenile court there is found a biased sample of the population of juvenile offenders known to the police. This broad hypothesis, based on previous experience, on the research literature, and on observations made during a preliminary study in Chicago, might be tested by a consideration of the differences between a population of juvenile offenders known to the police, and those referred by the same police to a juvenile court. In the following study, the extent to which two such groups differ in types of offenses, racial characteristics, sex composition, and age distribution, will be investigated. Statistical evidence will be adduced to test the hypothesis that only a portion of the juvenile offenders known to the police are referred to the juvenile court. Data will be presented to show how this sample of delinquents referred to the juvenile court varies from community to community. Finally, having indicated the validity of this general hypothesis, the nature of this selection process will be examined by means of information obtained from the police in personal interviews.

    The procedure of this study thus falls into two parts. First, quantitative or statistical information is presented with regard to the composition of the

Source: Nathan Goldman. *The Differential Selection of Juvenile Offenders for Court Appearance.* National Research and Information Center, NCDD 1963, pp. 25-30, 125-33. Reprinted with permission of the National Council on Crime and Delinquency.

juvenile court sample of the population of delinquents known to the police, as obtained from police records. For this purpose statistical data obtained from police records in several municipalities are analyzed. These data are considered from the point of view of the disposition of each case by the police, with respect to the several variables mentioned above, age, race, sex, and nature of the offense. Inter-community comparisons as well as intra-community analysis of the data are attempted.

The second part of the research consists in the analysis of a series of interviews with police officers in a number of communities in Allegheny County outside the city of Pittsburgh, and in several police districts of Pittsburgh. These interviews were aimed at obtaining statements with regard to the policeman's attitude toward those various factors on which the court and non-court populations of juvenile offenders were found to differ. These interviews may be considered as a qualification of the statistical data presented in the previous section.

It was difficult to find many communities in Allegheny County where police records on juveniles were kept and to which access was allowed. Of five such communities which were found out of twenty-two visited, the records of only four could be used. The other data were discarded because it was found that records had been kept only on those cases which the police chief thought might be needed in the future for referral to the juvenile court. Needless to say, such records can be of little use for research purposes.

The municipalities from which police data were available fortunately represented areas of different socio-economic structure. However, one must guard against considering these "typical" of similar communities in the county. The fact that adequate records were kept and made available by the police chief for research purposes would in itself indicate a superior degree of social interest. The selection of such a police chief and subordinate may well be a reflection of community attitudes toward social problems. To preserve the confidential nature of these data, code names will be used to designate the four communities and population figures will be given in round numbers. However, for a better understanding of the problem, some minimal description of the communities involved was deemed necessary. It is hoped that the identify of these municipalities will thus not be made public.

The Juvenile Court Law of Pennsylvania designates as a child any minor under the age of eighteen years. A juvenile delinquent child is defined as:

1. A child who has violated any law of the Commonwealth or ordinance of any city, borough or township.

2. A child who, by reason of being wayward or habitually disobedient, is uncontrolled by his or her parent, guardian, or custodian or legal representative.

3. A child who is habitually truant from school or home.

4. A child who habitually so deports himself or herself as to injure or endanger the morals or health of himself, herself or others.

The juvenile courts in Pennsylvania have full and exclusive jurisdiction in all proceedings affecting delinquent children, except in cases of a capital offense.

Area of Study

Through a cooperative arrangement between the Western State Psychiatric Institute and Clinic, and the Juvenile Court of Allegheny County, the writer was afforded the opportunity to conduct [his] research in the Pittsburgh area. All the communities falling within the scope of this research are served by the Juvenile Court of Allegheny County.

From a sociological point of view Allegheny County allows for the observation of various types of municipalities. Around Pittsburgh we find a wide range of community structures—industrial, commercial and residential—each fairly homogeneous and autonomous. Also, in these minor civil divisions of Allegheny County, there is quite a variation in size, ethnic composition, political structure, and what might be called the dominant personality pattern of the community. The city of Pittsburgh also has its distinct community types, but nowhere are they so clearly defined as in the different minor civil divisions of Allegheny County.

With regard to police organization, some differences also appear. A policeman in the city of Pittsburgh does not necessarily reside in the district where he works. The police in the small municipalities around Pittsburgh, however, not only are residents of the community, but usually were born and raised there. Such a situation makes for a personal as opposed to an official contact between the police and the public. In Pittsburgh, as in most large cities of mixed population, the contact is more impersonal and is largely carried out on a secondary rather than on a primary level. There would seem to be a much greater tendency for the individual policeman to leave decisions up to the more impersonal forces of the system or to let the court, in the case of juveniles, make the decision.

Our sample contains four distinct and rather typical communities: a small mill town, an industrial center, a trade center, and an upper-class residential area. Since these represent only four of about 125 municipalities in the county, it cannot be claimed that the obtained data are representative for the county as a whole. However, since our sample contains four distinct and probably typical kinds of community, we assume that we are viewing some sort of cross-section of county life.

The land use in Allegheny County is largely for industrial purposes. It had in 1950 a population density of 3.02 persons per acre, with a spread from a low of 0.1 to a maximum of 55 persons per acre. Of the population 12.71 per cent were foreign born and 6.38 per cent Negro. The major foreign-born groups in the county came from Italy and from the British Isles. The median monthly rental in Allegheny County was $28.57. Clerical, sales, and kindred workers made up the largest occupational group—23.1 per cent of the total persons employed. Operatives and kindred workers came next, followed by laborers, and then by craftsmen and foremen. The median number of school years completed by persons twenty-five years of age and over was 8.3 years; 5.5 per cent had completed four years or more of college. Comparative social data for the four communities included in this study may be found in Table 1.

Steel City is a large industrial community with a population around 55,000. It has a relatively high density of population and relatively high percentages of laborers, Negroes, and foreign born. Trade City is a residential and commercial area with a population of about 30,000. It has a low percentage of foreign born and of Negroes. The median rental in Trade City is higher than that for Allegheny County as a whole. The major occupational groups are clerical,

TABLE 1. Social Characteristics of Areas Studied*

	Allegheny County	Steel City	Trade City	Manor Heights	Mill Town
Population (1940 census)	1,411,539**	55,000	29,900	20,000	12,700
Population, age 10–17	–	8,117	3,387	2,631	2,070
Land use	–	Industrial	Residential and commercial	Residential	Industrial
Population density (per gross acre)	3.02	25.6	23.1	6.0	18.9
Percentage foreign born (white)	12.71	15.77	7.03	4.84	13.77
Percentage Negro	6.38	3.95	1.58	0.45	3.28
Nationality groups	Italy Br. Isles Poland	Hungary Czech. Br. Isles	Br. Isles Germany Italy	Br. Isles Germany	Italy Poland Austria Br. Isles
Median rental	$28.57	$28.56	$42.06	$81.88	$27.87
Occupations	Clerical-sales operatives	Laborers operatives clerical	Clerical craftsmen foremen	Clerical proprietor managers officials	Laborers clerical operatives
Median school grade completed	8.3	10.7	12.6	14.8	10.5
Percentage completed college	5.5	3.4	10	21.5	3.5

*From Social Facts About Pittsburgh and Allegheny County (Pittsburgh: Federation of Social Agencies, 1945)

**52.4 per cent living outside Pittsburgh.

craftsmen, and foremen. The third community, Mill Town, is the smallest of the four with a population of about 12,700 in 1940. Mill Town is an industrial community with a population density below that of Steel City and Trade City. It has a high percentage of foreign born. Its Negro population is between that of Steel City and Trade City. The major occupational groups are laborers, clerical workers, and operatives. The median rental in Mill Town is below that of Allegheny County. Manor Heights is a well-to-do residential area with a median rental about three times that of Allegheny County. Its 1940 population was about 20,000. It has the lowest population density, about one-fourth that of Steel City and one-third that of Pittsburgh. It has only a small proportion of foreign born, and less than 0.5 per cent Negroes. The largest occupational categories are clerical workers, proprietors, managers and officials, and professional workers. The proportion of college graduates in Manor Heights is six times that of Steel City and of Mill Town and twice that of Trade City.

Conclusions and Discussion

The following set of conclusions is based on an analysis of the police records of the four communities, Steel City, Trade City, Mill Town, and Manor Heights, and on a series of interviews with police in the city of Pittsburgh and in twenty-two minor municipalities around Pittsburgh. The problem of this research was to test the general hypothesis of the differential selection, by police, of juvenile offenders for court referral and to investigate this process of selection. These conclusions are presented with the reservation that, since they are based on four individual communities and a sample of policemen in a relatively circumscribed industrial and commercial area, generalizations to other communities may not be justified.

Conclusions

I. There is a wide variation in rates of arrest in different communities.
   A. Arrests per 1,000 population aged ten to seventeen ranged from 12.4 to 49.7, with an average rate of 32.6 per thousand.
   B. The gross variations in arrest rates may be accounted for principally by variations in arrests for minor offenses.
      1. In some communities citizens are more apt to complain about minor offenses such as trespassing, mischief, and disorderly conduct which are disregarded in other communities.
II. Not all children apprehended in law violation are recorded in the juvenile court.
   A. Among those apprehended by citizens, few are reported to the police.

    B.   Among those apprehended by the police, not all are inscribed on police records.

        1.   It is estimated that about half of the children who come to the attention of the police for law violation are taken to the police station.

    C.   Among those officially registered on police records, only a small proportion, 35.4 per cent, are referred to the juvenile court for official action.

III.   There are wide variations in rates of court appearance of juveniles in various communities.

    A.   Court appearances per 1,000 population aged ten to seventeen varied from community to community.

        1.   Rates ranged from 4.1 to 17.1 with an average of 9.9 per thousand.

    B.   The proportion of arrests referred to the juvenile court varied between communities.

        1.   Rates ranged from 8.6 per cent to 71.2 per cent with an average of 35.4 per cent.

IV.   There is a differential handling by police of arrests, based on the seriousness of the offense.

    A.   The proportion of arrests for serious offenses varies from community to community.

        1.   Such offenses range from 6.1 per cent to 37.1 per cent of arrests with an average of 20.3 per cent.

    B.   Arrests for serious offenses are more frequently referred to court than are arrests for minor offenses.

        1.   Between 71.4 per cent and 100 per cent with an average of 80.2 per cent of serious offenses were reported to the court.

        2.   Between 2.3 per cent and 71 per cent with an average of 24.1 per cent of arrests for minor offenses were referred to court.

    C.   Differences in the court referral rates are largely a result of the differential handling of minor offenses.

V.   There are differentials in court referral rates of Negro and white children arrested for law violation.

    A.   Arrests of Negro children are more frequently referred to court than arrests of white children.

        1.   33.6 per cent of the arrests of white children and 64.8 per cent of the arrests of Negro children were referred for juvenile court action.

        2.   Although arrests of Negro children were 5.7 per cent of the total juvenile arrests, these cases constituted 10.5 per cent of the total court referrals.

    B.   The rate of referral of Negro juvenile offenders to court varies from community to community.

        1.   51.2 per cent to 84.6 per cent of the Negro children arrested in three communities were referred to court.

C. The differences in rates of referral of arrests of Negro children are largely a result of the more frequent referral of minor offenses of Negro children.
   1. 79.3 per cent of arrests of white children and 87.5 per cent of arrests of Negro children for serious offenses were referred to court.
   2. 22.6 per cent of the arrests of white children and 53.2 per cent of the arrests of Negro children for minor offenses were so referred.

VI. Conclusions regarding the differential disposition of arrests of boys and of girls are not justified because of the small number of female arrests.
   A. It is suggested, however, that girls brought to the attention of the police are more liable to court referral than are boys.
      1. Slightly more than half, 54.2 per cent of the girls arrested, and 35.1 per cent of the boys were referred to court. The differences between these rates, however, are *not statistically significant.*
   B. There appears to be considerable variation in the court referral of girls in different communities.
      1. These referral rates varied from zero to 75 per cent.

VII. The rate of court referrals of arrested children increases with the age of the child.
   A. Offenders below age ten are less frequently referred to court than are older children.
      1. 20.9 per cent of the children below age ten are referred to court.
   B. Children between ages ten and fifteen were more frequently referred to court than were younger children and less frequently so referred than older children.
      1. 30 per cent of children aged ten to fifteen were referred to court after arrest by police.
   C. Offenders between the ages of fifteen and eighteen were more frequently reported to court than were younger children.
      1. 45.4 per cent of these arrests were referred to court.
   D. The increase in the rate of court referral with age is fairly consistent in different communities.
      1. In one of the four communities studied there was a decrease in the rate of referral of offenders aged fifteen to eighteen. This appeared to be a special result of police attitude toward court "leniency."

VIII. There are distinguishable patterns of handling cases of juvenile offenders in different communities. These patterns are as follows:
   A. A low arrest rate coupled with a high court referral rate. Very little differentiation in handling cases. Offense, sex, and race seem of little influence in disposition, with age the only discernible differentiating factor (Trade City).
   B. A high arrest rate, coupled with a high arrest rate for minor of-

fenses. A very low court referral rate, based on seriousness of offense, sex, and age of the offender (Manor Heights).

C. A moderately high arrest rate with a relatively moderately high court referral rate for all offenses. Differential reporting based on race and age (Steel City).

D. A moderately high arrest rate with a low court referral rate. Referral varies with seriousness of the offense, sex, race, and age of the child (Mill Town).

IX. These patterns are a function of the relations between the police and the community.

A. In general, police will attempt to reflect what they consider to be the attitudes of the public toward delinquency.

1. The concern of the public with respect to minor offenses such as shoplifting, trespassing, mischief, disorderly conduct, etc., will determine the police arrests of such offenses.

2. The desires of the public with regard to official court handling of delinquency problems, as opposed to informal handling of offenses within the community will affect court referral rates.

B. Where there exists an objective, impersonal relation between the police and the public, court referral rates will be high and there will be little discrimination with respect to seriousness of offense, race, and sex of the offender.

C. Where there exists a personal face-to-face relation between the police and the public, there will be more discrimination with respect to court referral of an arrested juvenile.

1. Rates of court referral will be low:
   a. More cases will be carried on an unofficial level.

2. Disposition will be significantly determined by the seriousness of the offense.
   a. Minor offenses, even though they make up the bulk of the arrests, will be reported only rarely.

3. Sex and race of the offender will vary as factors in the referral process.

X. The differential selection of offenders for court by police is determined by the attitudes of the policeman toward the offender, his family, the offense, the juvenile court, his own role as a policeman, and the community attitudes toward delinquency.

A. *The policeman's attitudes toward the juvenile court.* This may be based on actual experience with the court or on ignorance of court policies. The policeman who feels the court unfair to the police or too lenient with offenders may fail to report cases to the court since, in his opinion, nothing will be gained by such official referral.

B. *The impact of special individual experiences in the court, or with different racial groups, or with parents of offenders, or with specific offenses, on an individual policeman.* This may condition his future reporting of certain types of offense or classes of offenders.

C. *Apprehension about criticism by the court.* Cases which the policeman might prefer, for various reasons, not to report for official action may be reported because of fear that the offense might subsequently come to the attention of the court and result in embarrassment to the police officer.

D. *Publicity given to certain offenses either in the neighborhood or elsewhere may cause the police to feel that these are too "hot" to handle unofficially and must be referred to the court.* In the discussion of police interviews it was indicated how this factor might operate to bring into court an offense of even a very insignificant nature.

E. *The necessity for maintaining respect for police authority in the community.* A juvenile who publicly causes damage to the dignity to the police, or who is defiant, refusing the "help" offered by the police, will be considered as needing court supervision, no matter how trivial the offense.

F. *Various practical problems of policing.* The fact that no witness fees are paid policemen in juvenile court was mentioned by a small number as affecting the policy of some police officers with respect to court referral of juveniles. The distance to the court and the detention home and the availability of police personnel for the trip were likewise indicated as occasionally affecting the decision of the policeman.

G. *Pressure by political groups or other special interest groups.* Such pressure may determine the line of action a policeman will follow in a given case. He considers it necessary to accede to such pressures in order to retain his job.

H. *The policeman's attitude toward specific offenses.* The reporting or non-reporting of a juvenile offender may depend on the policeman's own childhood experiences or on attitudes toward specific offenses developed during his police career.

I. *The police officer's impression of the family situation, the degree of family interest in and control of the offender, and the reaction of the parents to the problem of the child's offense.* A child coming from a home where supervision is judged to be lacking, or where the parents—especially the mother—are alcoholic, or one whose parents assume an aggressive or "uncooperative" attitude toward the police officer, is considered in need of supervision by the juvenile court.

J. *The attitude and personality of the boy.* An offender who is well mannered, neat in appearance, and "listens" to the policeman will be considered a good risk for unofficial adjustment in the community. Defiance of the police will usually result in immediate court referral. Athletes and altar boys will rarely be referred to court for their offenses. The minor offenses of feeble-minded or atypical children will usually be overlooked by the police. Maliciousness in a child is considered by the police to indicate need for official court supervision.

K. *The Negro child offender is considered less tractable and needing more authoritarian supervision than a white child.* He is generally considered inherently more criminal than a white offender. Exceptions to this general attitude were found in the upper-class residential area and also among white policemen in the crowded Negro slum area of Pittsburgh. The statistical data, except for the small mill town, do not corroborate these discriminatory attitudes expressed by the police.

L. *The degree of criminal sophistication shown in the offense.* The use of burglar tools, criminal jargon, a gun, or strong-arm methods, or signs of planning or premeditation, are generally taken by the police to indicate a need for immediate court referral.

M. *Juvenile offenders apprehended in a group will generally be treated on an all-or-none basis.* The group must be released or reported as a whole. Some police may attempt to single out individuals in the gang for court referral. Such action, however, exposes the policeman to the censure of the court for failing to report the others involved in the offense.

Discussion

It must be borne in mind that in this study the several variables were artificially isolated. In relaity, no one of the factors which have been shown to operate in the determination of which offenders are officially reported to the court by the police can be found to exist alone. There is an interrelationship between the variables which cannot be expressed in statistical terms. Some of the factors discussed above may automatically exclude consideration of other factors. At times the task of the policeman may be akin to that of solving a problem containing a number of variables. At other times, *one* of the considerations mentioned above —such as political pressure—may force the decision of the police officer in a given direction.

The concept of juvenile delinquency is to some extent determined by the policeman in selectively reporting juvenile offenders to the court. Institutionalized delinquents, and offenders in a juvenile court had been, for the most part, apprehended and officially reported by the police.

This research has shown that the police base their reporting partly on the act of the offender, but also on the policeman's idiosyncratic interpretation of this act, and the degree of pressure applied by the community on the police. The collective pressures mentioned above, the attitudes of the community toward the offense, toward the offender and toward his family, affect the decision of the policeman in his reporting of juvenile offenses. In addition, the policeman's own private attitudes, his special experiences, his concern for status and prestige in the community may be important factors in determining which particular juvenile offender will be referred to the court. Once reported to the court, the child then becomes available for official scrutiny and study. The availability of a juvenile offender for official recording and for research studies on delinquency thus depends ultimately on the responsiveness of the police officer to a series of collective social pressures and personal attitudes. The policeman's interpretation of these pressures serves to select or determine the composition of the sample of those juvenile offenders who will become officially recognized from among all those known to him.

Selection of a sample of the population of offenders on the basis of collective pressures and private attitudes cannot help but result in a marked and unpredictable bias. It is on this biased sample that most of the juvenile delinquency research has been conducted. Generalizations based on such a sample can have only limited validity. For a more adequate understanding of the social and psychological processes involved in juvenile delinquent behavior it is necessary to observe juvenile offenders in the community in their earliest contacts with the police, before they have been selected by differential treatment. There can be no complete study of the etiological factors in juvenile delinquent conduct unless the unpredictable variable of the policeman is removed from the process. An adequate study of juvenile delinquency must begin at a point before the one at which the police officer begins to operate. To provide more valid generalizations, juvenile delinquency must be studied in the community where it occurs, where a relatively unselected sample of juvenile offenders may be observed.

The decision regarding the disposition of a given instance of juvenile law violation, by the policeman, may have some very significant effects on the future conduct of the child. The consequences of any act will significantly affect the behavior of the actor in similar situations in the future. The interaction, or exchange of gestures, between the policeman and the child apprehended in law violation may serve to increase or to decrease the probability of future excursions into delinquency. Thus the behavior of the police toward the child may be a significant determinant of the child's continued participation in delinquent conduct.

An important corollary of these observations is that the police must be provided training in the problems of handling children who come to their attention for law violation. They must be aided in understanding the possible effects of their attempts to "help" the apprehended violator by giving him "another chance," or the possible effects of discrimination with respect to the race of the child. Since he will be, by virtue of his job, in a position where he has to make decisions crucial to the child's welfare, and of great significance for the child's future conduct, it is important that he be supplied with the proper sensitivities and perceptions for making the best decisions for the child and for the community.

CHAPTER **3-6**

VICTIMIZATION, TYPES Of CITIZEN-POLICE CONTACTS, ANd ATTITUDES TOWARD THE POLICE

PAUL E. SMITH AND RICHARD O. HAWKINS

One of the ironies of police-community relations is that the high visibility via the mass media of public reaction against police has created the impression that public attitudes are predominantly negative. Evidence from field surveys suggests the opposite—that attitudes are predominantly positive and supportive of police (Gourley, 1954; Cleaver, *et al.*, 1966; Preiss and Ehrlich, 1966; Ennis, 1967; McGaghy, *et al.*, 1968; Bayley and Mendelsohn, 1969; Smith, 1969). In a similar vein, police often view citizens as holding more hostile attitudes toward the police than is in fact the case (McNamara, 1967: 221; Wilson, 1968: 28; Bayley and Mendelsohn, 1969). This shared misunderstanding can have self-fulfilling consequences. Police expect a hostile citizen reception and hence take a more authoritarian attitude in order to assure that actions will be seen as legitimate and authority will not be questioned (Westley, 1953; Skolnick, 1966: 62; Werthman and Piliavin, 1967). The public, expecting the worst from the police, may alter their perceptions so that criticisms of police behavior are more likely. This shared misunderstanding produces more conflict between citizen and police. Instances of police brutality are covered by the media, and the cycle continues.

This is not to suggest that segments of the public do not hold strong negative views about police, nor would we argue that a flood of social science information will automatically dispel the shared misunderstanding. These facts are cited to suggest that public attitudes toward police are important both to the

Reprinted by permission from *Law and Society Review*, Vol. 8, no. 1, Fall 1973, pp. 135–152.

police specifically, and to the quality of law enforcement which accrues to the community in general. In this study we will outline a number of reasons why some citizens hold negative "attitudes toward the police" (ATP). We shall try to assess the role of the police themselves in creating these negative attitudes as well as examine extra-police factors which produce negative views. After examining evidence on a number of hypotheses, we shall present the policy implications of our findings for the problems of community-police relations.

Previous studies of attitudes toward the police suggest a large number of determinants: minority group membership (Biderman, *et al.*, 1967; Ennis, 1967; Bayley and Mendelsohn, 1969; Hahn, 1971; Jacob, 1971), age (Preiss and Ehrlich, 1966; Gourley, 1954), fear of police (Block, 1971), occupational contacts with police, *e.g.*, truck and taxi drivers (Gourley, 1954), anxiety about crime (Biderman, *et al.*, 1967), aggressive patrols, *e.g.*, stop and frisk actions (Bordua and Tifft, 1971) and other variables. This study will attempt to assess the impact of variables in two general areas. The first is not directly related to the police, but involves perceived threat of criminal victimization and past experience as a victim. The second area involves various types of contacts with the police. Contacts are subdivided into: (a) contacts or observations of police on duty, (b) contacts where respondents were the object of law enforcement, and (c) contacts not related to police roles, per se.

Background

The study was designed as a community survey of criminal victimization and attitudes toward the police (*see* Appendix on Research Procedures for details). Consequently we sought a representative sample of citizens within Seattle. Because the proportion of minority groups in Seattle is quite low compared to many other American cities its size, our N for minority groups is smaller than we would like for analysis purposes. Ninety-one percent of our sample was Caucasian, five percent Black, three percent Oriental, and one percent American Indian or Mexican American. These proportions are consistent with the Seattle census data for 1970.

Our dependent variable, attitudes toward the police, was designed to assess respondents' views of the fairness of the police as a group, *i.e.*, attitudes about discrimination, selective law enforcement, and general feelings about police impartiality. Five items[1] were used to indicate opinions on police fairness, and Likert-type response categories[2] were coded 1-5 in a pro- to anti-police direction. Scores were summed for all five items and four categories of "favorableness" toward the police were created: Most Favorable (5-9), More Favorable (10-14), Less Favorable (15-19), and Least Favorable (20-25).

Data from our Seattle survey indicate that the majority of citizens held positive views of the police. Seventy-two percent of the respondents were in the "Most Favorable" or More Favorable" categories. This finding of majority favorableness parallels survey results in Denver (Bayley and Mendelsohn, 1969), in Milwaukee (Jacob, 1971) and a NORC national survey (Ennis, 1967). A majority (55%) of respondents reported being criminally victimized within the last 12 months. Less than half of these incidents were reported to the police by the victims (*see* Hawkins, 1973). The type and extent of citizen contact with the police will be detailed below.

Prior to a discussion of specific hypotheses, a review of the influence of background characteristics of our sample on attitudes toward the police is in order. The variables of education, income, occupation and sex of the respondent did not significantly affect attitudes toward police (ATP). In addition to occupation, we asked respondents if their work involved rule or norm enforcement. We felt respondents who were charged with norm enforcement, *e.g.*, teachers, foremen, store managers, etc. would be more positive toward other norm enforcers, specifically the police. This was not the case; occupational rule enforcement did not influence ATP. The only background variables that appeared to significantly affect ATP were age and race.

As expected, race was strongly related to attitudes about police fairness. Table 1 shows that the majority of non-whites hold negative ATP, while the large majority of whites hold positive views.[3]

This negative sentiment did not stem from greater vitimization. In contrast to other victimization surveys (Biderman, *et al.*, 1967; Ennis, 1967; Reiss, 1967), race was not related to victimization within the past year. Also the proportions of past arrests reported by respondents were not particularly divergent for the two groups; 20% of the non-whites said they had been arrested in the past compared to 14% of the white respondents. The high level of negative feelings about the police among minority groups was not significantly influenced by either arrest or victimization experiences.

In accord with research cited earlier, our data show that younger respondents held more negative attitudes toward the police (Gamma = -.21, z = 3.41).[4] The young were more likely to have had police contact because they had higher victimation rates and a higher proportion admitted a past arrest than did middle and older age groupings.

Age and race can be seen as indicators of specific socialization and reference group influences. Negative ATP is often seen as a subcultural phenomenon in minority group neighborhoods (Jacobs, 1971). The young may be more anti-police because of the influence of the youth culture, as well as more specific experiences with the police. When age and race are simultaneously related to ATP, we can make some inferences about the reference group effects.

Table 2 indicates that white youths are more negative toward police than their elders, but age does not differentiate non-white attitudes about police fairness. Thus there appears to be a subcultural anti-police view among non-whites of all ages. The police officer in the ghetto faces a fairly uniform hos-

Police-Community Interaction

TABLE 1. Percentage Distribution of Attitudes Toward the Police by Race**

| ATP | Race | | |
(Favorableness)	White	Non-White	Total
Most	7.8	2.4	7.5
More	65.7	43.5	64.3
Less	23.7	28.2	24.0
Least	2.9	25.9	4.3
Total	100.0	100.0	100.0
N***	1322	85	1407

Gamma = .54*   z = 4.63
*significant (p < .05)
**Orientals included in "white" category
***Total N varies across tables due to non-response.

TABLE NOTE:
Gamma is a proportional-reduction-in-error measure of association for ordinal level data which ranges from +1.00 to –1.00 (see Costner, 1965). The Z score for each gamma was computed by the following formula:

$$Z = Gamma \sqrt{\frac{Concordance + Discordance}{N\,(1\text{-}Gamma^2)}}$$

(See Goodman and Kruskal, 1963). Gammas with Z scores at or above 1.96 are statistically significant at the .05 level, two-tailed test. Z scores at or above 2.57 are significant statistically at the .01 level, two-tailed test.

tility, while the officer in white neighborhoods may experience the greatest resentment by the young. Notice that the levels of ATP for the young are not the same across ethnic groups. The majority of white youth holds positive ATP (61%), while non-white youth hold negative views (56%). While more direct tests of racial and youth subcultural influences are required, our indirect evidence suggests ethnic membership has a larger impact on attitudes toward police than age. If the youth culture were a major determinant of ATP, we would expect few differences in attitudes across ethnic groups among the young.

Hypotheses and Findings

Anticipation of being a victim of a criminal act may influence attitudes about the police. People who fear that they are likely targets for criminals may feel the police are doing an inadequate job of protecting their homes or persons, and, therefore, hold more negative ATP. Our first hypothesis suggests:

Victimization, Types of Citizen-Contacts, and Attitudes Toward the Police

TABLE 2. Percentage Distribution of Attitudes Toward the Police by Age, Controlling for Race*

ATP (Favorableness)	Race							
	White				Non-White			
	Age					Age		
	16–34	35–54	55–89	Total	16–34	35–54	55–89	Total
Most	8.3	9.3	5.6	7.8	4.2	.0	.0	2.4
More	52.9	69.0	73.9	65.7	39.6	48.1	50.0	43.5
Less	32.6	20.3	19.1	23.7	33.3	22.2	20.0	28.2
Least	6.1	1.5	1.4	2.9	22.9	29.6	30.0	25.9
Total	100.0	100.0	100.0	100.0	100.0	100.0	100.0	100.0
N	408	464	444	1316	48	27	10	85
Percent Column Total of Table Total	31.0	35.3	33.7	100.0	56.5	31.8	11.8	100.0

Gamma = –.19*   Gamma = .03**
    z = 2.95   z = .10
*significant (p < .05)
**not significant (p = .05)
***Orientals included in "white" category

　　1. The greater the threat of victimization, the more negative the view of the police.

Respondents were asked to estimate the probability (in percent) that they would become a victim in the next year. Table 3 shows that anticipation of property victimization did not have the hypothesized affect on ATP.

When perceived threat of crimes against the person was compared to attitudes about the police, the relationship was still not significant (Gamma = .10, z = 1.46). These original relationships did not change when we controlled for background characteristics of age, education, income, race and sex.

Although fear of victimization did not influence views about the police, perhaps actual experience as a victim might create negative feelings. Citizens who have been recently victimized may feel the police let them down, that police inefficiency or neglect contributed to the victimization.[5] Thus we propose:

　　2. Recent victims of criminal acts will hold more negative attitudes toward police than non-victims.

TABLE 3. Percentage Distribution of Attitudes Toward the Police by Perceived Threat of Crime Against Property

ATP (Favorableness)	Threat/Property				
	00–20%	25–45%	50–70%	75–100%	Total
Most	6.1	7.2	7.6	10.9	7.6
More	63.9	67.6	63.0	61.4	64.1
Less	25.1	21.8	25.0	24.3	24.1
Least	5.0	3.4	4.3	3.5	4.2
Total	100.0	100.0	100.0	100.0	100.0
N	363	321	460	202	1346

Gamma = −.04*   z = .59
*not significant (p = .05)

Respondents were asked if they had been victimized in the past 12 months. About half the respondents reported at least one victimization incident during this time, with the vast majority being crimes against property (83%). There was no difference in attitudes about police fairness among victims and non-victims (Gamma = −.03, z = 0.47). Since crimes against the person are generally seen as more serious than property offenses, we controlled for type of victimization. Victims of crimes against the person were more likely to hold negative ATP than property victims, but the relationship was not significant (Gamma = .14, z = 1.04). While the more serious victimization experience did produce a change of attitudes in the predicted direction, it did not have a significant impact on attitudes about police. Control of background characteristics did not alter the original relationships.[6]

A second set of hypotheses evolved around the question of police-citizen contacts. These specific contacts may influence ATP more than general experiences with crime. First, we examined contacts or observations of police on duty. One setting for these contacts is the service and assistance rendered when victimization is reported to the police.

3. *Individuals not satisfied with police action following reported victimization will have more negative ATP than individuals who are satisfied with police action.*

Respondents who reported to the police victimization incidents occurring in the last year were asked to give an evaluation of police performance on that occasion. Table 4 suggests that our third hypothesis was supported.

Dissatisfaction with police handing of victimization incidents was reflected in more negative ATP. It may be the case that individuals holding negative ATP

Victimization, Types of Citizen-Contacts, and Attitudes Toward the Police

TABLE 4. Percentage Distribution of Attitudes Toward the Police by Degree of Satisfaction With Police Action

ATP (Favorableness)	Degree of Satisfaction				
	Very Satisfied	Satisfied	Dis-satisfied	Very Dis-satisfied	Total
Most	10.7	8.5	3.8	2.0	7.4
More	71.8	66.9	55.8	66.0	66.6
Less	14.6	21.2	30.8	24.0	21.1
Least	2.9	3.4	9.6	8.0	5.0
Total	100.0	100.0	100.0	100.0	100.0
N	103	118	52	50	323

Gamma = .27*   z = 2.17
*significant (p < .05)

would be less likely to report victimization to the police in the first place. To test for this possibility, we compared reporting and non-reporting victims and found that they did not differ significantly in their views of police fairness. (Gamma = .12, z = 1.17). A related study using these same data found that attitudes about police efficiency of operations and about police personnel did not differ for reporting and non-reporting victims (Hawkins, 1970: 122-126). Block (1970), in a national survey, also found that prior attitudes about the police did not affect decisions to initiate sanctions, *i.e.*, report victimization to the police. We conclude that unsatisfactory experience with police investigating victimization does have an affect on ATP, making these attitudes more negative.

A second form of contact with police on duty is the witnessing of police action. We hypothesize that:

4. *Observations of what the public considers wrongdoing or misconduct by police will negatively affect attitudes toward the police.*

To test this hypothesis, respondents were asked if they had ever seen a police officer do something considered improper or illegal. Table 5 shows that observing police officers "do wrong" did produce more negative feelings about the police.

This relationship remained strong when age, sex, race, income and education were controlled. Twenty-seven percent of the sample said they had witnessed improper police behavior. When asked to delineate the incidents of wrongdoing, the following types were most frequently mentioned: traffic violations (37%), witnessed police brutality (15%), drinking or drunk on duty (12%), criminal offenses such as gambling, bribes, etc. (9%) and rudeness or

TABLE 5. Percentage Distribution of Attitudes Toward the Police by Contacts With the Police—Seen a Policeman Doing Something Wrong

ATP	Seen Wrong		
(Favorableness)	No	Yes	Total
Most	8.3	5.0	7.4
More	69.6	50.5	64.5
Less	19.8	34.7	23.9
Least	2.2	9.7	4.3
Total	100.0	100.0	100.0
N	1024	380	1404

Gamma = .42*   z = 5.89
*significant (p < .05)

verbal abuse by officer (8%). Traffic violations frequently mentioned were such things as illegal turns, speeding, and running stops. Many of these actions may have been in the line of duty, but what is important from a police image viewpoint is that citizens saw them as violations. Although much of the police wrongdoing was relatively minor, it did have a significant impact on attitudes toward the police.

A second type of contact between the police and the community occurs when the police are actually enforcing the law. Although relatively little police time is actually spent in law enforcement (Cumming, et al., 1965), those who are the objects of this enforcement activity may be influenced by the experience. Generally we would expect that:

> 5. Individuals who have been the object of police enforcement activities will hold more negative ATP than individuals who have not been the object of law enforcement.

Two indicators of enforcement experiences were used to test this hypothesis: receipt of a traffic ticket in the last 12 months, and past arrests. There was no relationship between receiving a traffic ticket and negative ATP (Gamma = .07, z = 0.69). The relationship was not affected by background characteristics, with the exception of income. Receiving a ticket was strongly related to negative ATP for those with low incomes, i.e., less than $3000 per year (Gamma = .49, z = 2.20). Traffic tickets were perhaps more salient to low income respondents because resulting fines were relatively more costly.

Respondents reporting being arrested were predictably more negative in their attitudes about police fairness.

Table 6 shows that fourteen percent of the respondents in our sampling reported an arrest experience. About half of those arrested[7] were young—under

TABLE 6. Percentage Distribution of Attitudes Toward the Police by
Arrest Ever

ATP	Arrest Ever		
(Favorableness)	No	Yes	Total
Most	7.3	8.4	7.5
More	66.7	50.0	64.3
Less	22.2	34.7	24.0
Least	3.8	6.9	4.3
Total	100.0	100.0	100.0
N	1205	202	1407

Gamma = .24*   z = 2.46
*significant (p < .05)

35—which is consistent with actual arrest patterns (Knudten, 1970: 732-733). As noted earlier, this age group is the most critical of police. When the effects of age are statistically controlled, the arrest-ATP relationship remains strong for the younger group, but is reduced for middle and older age categories. This may be due to the relatively recent occurrence of arrests for youth, compared to older groups. Those reporting arrests in middle and older categories probably refer to arrests in the more distant past. Hence the conditional relationship of age may be in part an artifact of arrest recency. More recent arrests, being more salient, produced more negative attitudes toward police. However, the reference group impact of age, plus the greater "vulnerability" to arrests in younger age groupings (Reiss, 1967), perhaps contributes to these negative attitudes. When race was controlled, another interesting change occurred. Arrest was related to ATP for whites arrested, but not for non-whites who reported arrest. As noted above, non-whites have a larger reservoir of negative ATP. Apparently experiencing arrest does not increase resentment for this group. This is revealed by looking at race and ATP when arrest history is controlled.

Notice in Table 7 that non-white attitudes remain the same regardless of arrest experience, while whites experiencing arrest do have more negative attitudes about police fairness than whites not reporting this kind of police contact.

Finally we examined the impact of citizen-police contacts in non-official settings. It was felt that friendly contacts, and personal acquaintanceship with police officers may mediate negative ATP.

> 6. Individuals who know individual police officers are less likely to hold negative ATP than individuals who are not acquainted with a member of the police force.

Two indicators of police-citizen acquaintanceship were used. First, re-

Police-Community Interaction

TABLE 7. Percentage Distribution of Attitudes Toward the Police by Race,*** Controlling for Arrest Ever

ATP (Favor- ableness)	Arrest Ever					
	No			Yes		
	White	Race Non-White	Total	White	Race Non-White	Total
Most	7.6	3.0	7.3	9.3	.0	8.4
More	68.0	43.9	66.7	50.8	42.1	50.0
Less	21.8	28.8	22.2	35.5	26.3	34.7
Least	2.6	24.2	3.8	4.4	31.6	6.9
Total	100.0	100.0	100.0	100.0	100.0	100.0
N	1139	66	1205	183	19	202
Percent Column Total of Table Total	94.5	5.5	100.0	90.6	9.4	100.0

Gamma = .55*   Gamma = .47**
    z = 4.13   z = 1.82
*significant (p < .05)
**not significant (p = .05)
***Orientals included in "white" category

spondents were asked if they knew any policeman well enough to call him by name or to say hello if they saw him on the street. The data show that respondents knowing police officers at this level of familiarity were no different in ATP than respondents who did not know individual officers (Gamma = -.03, z = 0.33). A second more intimate level of contact was assessed by answers to the question: Do you have a close friend or relative who is a policeman or other kind of law-enforcement officer? Again no significant affect on ATP was found (Gamma = .05, z = 0.72). Consequently, knowing individual officers does not seem to influence attitudes about the police in general.

If the police are viewed as a minority group, this finding is more easily understood. Police are a minority group in a number of ways. First, they have a high degree of solidarity growing out of a common external threat and danger. Police tend to be socially isolated, partly by choice, but also by exclusion by others in society. Police families associate more with other police families, partly because of the difficulty of acceptance by outsiders (Skolnick, 1966: 49-62). Police are also highly visible in their daily rounds—distinctive uniforms, marked cars, etc.—which is another characteristic of minority groups (Goldstein, 1971: 316). Apparently citizens stereotype police much as they do other minority groups. Consequently, knowledge of specific individuals may not alter the stereotyped view held about the group in general. The "good cop" known through personal acquaintanceship may be seen as the exception rather than the rule.[8] The citizen who knows individual police officers may separate the man from the role, and while accepting the man, may still hold negative views about the police in general.

Conclusion

Our findings have policy implications for police-community relations programs which seek to improve attitudes toward the police. One of the problems with current police efforts to improve community relations is that police departments have set up special units within the organization to act as public relations agents in the general community.

> This arrangement tends to mean that police-community relations are handled by this unit and not on the street by officers. It also means that police policies that directly contradict, make necessary, and aggravate the work of these special units or programs are not challenged. Further, it means that the patrolman on the street feels "they do the police-community relations; we do police work" (Bordua and Tifft, 1971: 156).

This means that police officers often oppose their own department's community-relations efforts. The failure of the San Francisco Police Community Relations Unit, due mainly to police opposition, is a case in point (Skolnick, 1970: 228-234). Our data suggest that impressions made by police on the beat do have significant impact on citizen attitudes about the police. Before suggesting what might be done to improve police-community relations, we will suggest a number of extant *fallacies* about improving the police image which many current programs seem to unquestioningly accept as true.[9] We shall also assess the validity of the implicit assumption that "good" police-community relations will indirectly increase citizen reporting of criminal victimization.

> *Fallacy* 1. *If victimization is reduced, community attitudes toward the police will improve.*

Evidence presented above shows that experience as a victim did not influence attitudes about the police. Biderman, *et al.* (1967: 141) also found no relationship between recent victimization history and attitudes held toward police by residents of Washington, D.C. Block (1970: 12), using a national sample, found that experience as a victim did not affect citizen support for the police.

Corollary 1.1. *If police improve their public image, citizens will be more likely to report victimization to the police.*

A previous analysis of these data found that decisions to report victimization were not influenced by attitudes about the effectiveness of police, nor by attitudes held about police personnel (Hawkins, 1973). Consequently, the conjecture that "current attempts at improving police-community relations conceivably could produce sharp 'paper increases' in some classes of crimes . . ." (Biderman and Reiss, 1967: 7) because of increased reporting is not supported.

Fallacy 2. *Fear of crime produces negative attitudes toward police, and therefore, programs designed to reduce citizen anxiety about crime may improve the image of the police.*

Law Enforcement Day programs sponsored by local police in many communities are an example of attempts to reassure citizens that everything is being done to prevent crime and improve community safety (Angell, *et al.,* 1967: 41). Our data show that threat of criminal victimization, either property or personal, does not influence ATP. Similarly, Block (1971: 95) found no relationship between fear of attack and support for the police. An exception is the study of four high crime precincts in Washington, D.C. which found that a general crime anxiety index was related to ATP (Biderman, *et al.,* 1967: 121, 140). Thus, if attitudes about the police are influenced by fear of crime, it seems to be primarily true of high-crime ghetto neighborhoods.

Corollary 2.1. *Fear of crime reduces the probability that citizens will report victimization to the police.*

Our data do not support this assumption. Respondents threatened by property victimization were more likely to report victimization than those feeling less threatened; those threatened by crimes against the person were also more likely to report victimization experiences to police (*cf.* Hawkins, 1973).

Fallacy 3. *Since the police contacts with ordinary citizens for traffic violations create hostility and resentment, programs must be developed to foster police-citizen interaction in non-enforcement settings.*

Our concern here is with the validity of the assertion that traffic tickets produce negative attitudes towards police. Skolnick (1966: 55) suggests that police believe this to be the case:

When considering how authority influences rejection, the policeman typically singles out his responsibility for enforcement of traffic violations.

Resentment, even hostility, is generated in those receiving citations, in part because such contact is often the only one citizens have with police, and in part because municipal administrations and courts have been known to utilize police authority primarily to meet budgetary requirements, rather than those of public order.

Our evidence suggests that receipt of traffic citations does not produce negative attitudes toward the police, except among the poor. While receiving a ticket may produce momentary hostility and resentment, there seem to be no long-term effects.

Fallacy 4. *Programs designed to create personal, friendly contacts between police and citizens should reduce negative ATP.*

Community meetings and "Say Hi" programs for elementary students are examples of attempts by police to improve their image (Angell, *et al.*, 1967: 43). Our data suggest that close personal relationships with police do not significantly affect attitudes about police. Knowing individual officers does not influence general attitudes about the police. Ironically, the establishment of programs designed to structure more intimate police-citizen relationships reinforces the minority group conception of enforcement agents, *e.g.*, "cops *must* be authoritarian; they have to *work* at being friendly."

Fallacy 5. *Programs to ameliorate the attitudes of young minority group members will improve the police image held by these minority groups.*

We found that minority groups held low images of the police regardless of age. Jacob (1971) also found a subcultural element to minority sentiments about police in a Black ghetto of Milwaukee. While it may be true that minority youth create more problems for police than older age groups, focusing only at this level will probably not produce changes in attitudes of older residents in the short run.

Implications

Both the police and the community must be concerned with solving the problems of police-citizen relations. In one study, when police were asked to enumerate the problems they faced, the most frequent response was "relations with the public" (Skolnick, 1966: 50). Ninety-eight percent of the police officers in a Denver study reported that they have experienced verbal or physical abuse from citizens (Bayley and Mendelsohn, 1969: 46). A negative and hostile public makes the enforcers' job extremely difficult. Hahn (1971: 191) found that those holding low opinions of the police were less willing to call the police for assistance or to report crimes. Police rely on community cooperation both to attain information on crimes and to appear as complainants in court. A hostile citizenry also increases the probability that police will use physical or verbal abuse. Westley (1953) found the most frequently mentioned situation in which police felt force to be legitimate was when there was disrespect for the police. Finally, negative community attitudes about police work make this occupation generally less appealing, especially to college graduates who have other employment opportunities.

Our findings suggest a number of things which might reduce negative attitudes toward the police. First, police must take greater care in their on-duty behavior. Minor traffic violations on the part of policemen helped to produce negative feelings among the public. Departmental directives to obey traffic rules and to use lights and perhaps sirens when "violating" these laws in the line of duty could be easily implemented. Other wrongdoing, such as police brutality, is more difficult to reduce. Indeed much of this brutality is both the result of negative attitudes held by citizens and the cause of increasing antagonism. Much of the problem may be due, however, to a failure of police officers to remember that they are highly visible at all times and their actions are constantly monitored and evaluated by the public.

A second source of negative ATP in Seattle was police handling of victimization incidents. In most cases, it was simply a failure to inform the victim of what was being done, or to show courtesy and understanding in regard to the incident under investigation. Reporting victims were asked what the police did in each incident. One-third of the respondents classified police action as negative: that is, 16% of reporting victims said the police did nothing, 6% said police never informed them of the outcome of the investigation, and 3% said the police did not respond to the call or were very uncooperative in their investigation. Another one-third classified police action as "routine" while the remaining third viewed police action as positive. Bordua and Tifft (1971: 169-171) studied citizen reaction to police investigation and found more negative ATP when police did not demonstrate a concern for the victim or when incidents were handled in a superficial manner.

These data suggest that police need to be more cognizant of the feelings and state of mind of the victim. Police must be able to reduce the momentary resentment caused by victimization, and they must recognize they serve a "cooling-out" function in many cases (cf. Blumberg, 1967). Just as the con man must be skilled in "cooling out the mark" to prevent harmful repercussions, so must police "cool out the victim" as part of their service function in order to maintain a positive image.

A third determinant of negative ATP was experience during arrest. While it would be absurd to suggest the police stop making arrests to improve their image, some procedural changes might be in order. While we have no evidence on reactions to police patrols, Bordua and Tifft (1971) found that aggressive patrols, *e.g.*, stop and frisk, did produce greater hostility and resentment toward police. Police have also been criticized for enforcing "crimes without victims" which leave them open to charges of hypocrisy (Schur, 1965; Skolnick, 1966). While changes in aggressive patrol tactics and changes in substantive law to reduce the problems of over-criminalization would probably improve the image of the police, it is doubtful that police will be in favor of such changes. Changes in the first two areas, however, are relatively easy to make and the potential for improvement of the police image seems worth the cost.

In sum, our data indicate that the police are much to blame for poor police-community relations, but in ways more easily rectified than previously realized. Determinants of negative views of the police suggest that each individual officer must be included in the changes. Without these changes, the special units and the more general community-oriented public relations approach will continue to have limited, if any, success. These data also suggest that the recommended changes in police behavior will not greatly improve the police image in non-white groups. The high level of minority resentment was not greatly influenced by types of police-citizen contacts. Improvement of the police image for these groups will require more drastic and sweeping structural changes within society as well as within the organization of the police.

References

1. The following five items were used to indicate opinions on police fairness:

    (1) People who know the ropes and have money to afford good lawyers don't really have anything to worry about from the police.

    (2) Generally speaking, all people are treated the same by the police regardless of race or color.

    (3) Negroes tend to get harder treatment from the police than most other people get.

    (4) Policemen try to give teenagers an even break in most cases.

    (5) The way you are treated by the police depends pretty much on who you are and who you know.

These items are similar to those used in studies done for the President's Commission on Law Enforcement and Administration of Justice (Biderman, *et al.*, 1967 and Ennis, 1967).

2. Respondents were asked if they strongly agreed, agreed, disagreed, or strongly disagreed with each item. An undecided choice was not offered, but interviewers were instructed to code uncertainty or neutrality on the part of respondents as "undecided."

3. The non-white groups included here were Blacks, Mexican-Americans and American Indians. Orientals were included in the white category because,

although numerically a minority, the Oriental population of Seattle is not restricted to ghetto areas; this group has higher income and educational levels than other minorities, they are more easily assimilated into white society, and they are less likely to experience over-surveillance and selective law enforcement than other minorities in Seattle. A study of police discretion in Seattle found that police were more likely to give Oriental juveniles the benefit of the doubt than white or black youth (Chambliss, 1969: 101).

4. Age was trichotomized into age categories of 16-34, 35-54, and 55 and over. Not all studies have found age to be significantly related to police attitudes (e.g., McCaghy, et al., 1968, and Bayley and Mendelsohn, 1969).

5. This sentiment has been institutionalized in legislation which makes the State liable for damages to private property destroyed during civil disorders; the underlying principle is that the State has failed to provide adequate protection and the citizenry has the right to recover losses (Sherrard, 1968: 87-93).

6. When race was controlled, victimization experience did not affect attitudes toward the police. This finding is not consistent with Biderman's results in Washington, D.C. He found recent reporting Black victims held lower attitudes toward the police than Blacks in general (Biderman, et al., 1967: 142). Unfortunately, comparisons between the Seattle and Washington D.C. surveys are difficult due to sampling variation and racial composition. Biderman selected four high crime precincts within Washington, while our sample represents the entire city of Seattle. Also the majority of Washington, D.C. residents are Black, while Seattle had a Black population of about five percent at the time of the survey.

7. Respondents were asked to report whether they had been arrested in the past year, and if they had ever been arrested. As expected, there were very few respondents who experienced an arrest in the past year. To insure a large enough N to permit statistical analysis, we used the "arrest ever" information. The use of an un-anchored time period complicates the recall problem. Since middle and older age groupings had a greater temporal "distance" to recall, they may have under-reported past arrests. For a discussion of the recall problems for un-anchored time periods; see Biderman, et al., 1967: 39-41, 58-60.

8. This point was suggested by a former colleague of Hawkins, Mike Hodson.

9. For a description of current police-community relations programs, see Angell, et al., 1967.

Appendix on Research Procedures

This study is based on data collected by a survey of households in Seattle, Washington, in the summer of 1968. A modified interval sampling plan was devised which produced 2,212 addresses from the Polk's Seattle City Directory (1967) address section in order to produce a representative sample of citizens living within the Seattle city limits. Letters describing the study and stating that an interviewer would call were sent to these addresses. Interviewers were randomly assigned to request either the male or female head of the household to insure a representative number of each sex. Black interviewers were used in predominantly Black sections of the city. Interviewing efforts produced 1,890 contacts which resulted in 1,411 completed interviews. 312 addresses did not produce interviews for the following reasons: 123 were "inaccessible"—no one home after five or more interviewer attempts; 175 addresses were either vacant or the address had been changed since the city directory survey was completed; 14 were non-residential addresses inadvertently included. Details of the sampling procedure are presented in Smith, 1969.

The refusal rate was about 25% (489 cases out of 1890 contacts). The refusal rate was high for two reasons. First, the interview was rather long and interviewers had to request about one hour of the respondent's time; although respondents were promised a summary of the findings in return for cooperation, many said they did not have the time. Second, interviewing commenced two days before Robert F. Kennedy's assassination, and this produced increased rates of refusals, *e.g.*, professional polling agencies reported refusal rates as high as 40% in the week following the events in California (*see* Auchinclass, 1968: 23–27).

To check for the possible bias of non-response, a one-page questionnaire was mailed to all "refusals" and "inaccessibles" to get background information as well as data on self-reported victimization and contacts with the police. Our concern with non-response was that it might be positively correlated with our independent variables: victimization experience or contacts with the police. Over 40% of the follow-up questionnaires were returned. Results indicated that victimization was lower in the non-response group than in the interview sample. Taking into account the greater recall potential of interviews over question-naires, we concluded that non-response was not systematically related to victim-ization. Police contacts did not vary between questionnaire and interview respondents. In terms of background characteristics, there was very little differ-ence between the non-respondents and the initial sample. Comparison of the demographic characteristics of these two groups with census data for Seattle indicates that our sample is quite representative of the population from which it was drawn. The data presented here are from the original interviewed sample.

Bibliography

Angell, John E., *et al.*, (1967) A National Survey of Police Community Rela-tions. Washington, D.C.: U.S. Government Printing Office.

Auchinclass, Kenneth (1968) "The polls and the pols and the public," News-week 72: 23–27 (July 8).

Bayley, David H., and Harold Mendelsohn (1969) Minorities and the Police, New York: The Free Press.

Biderman, Albert D. and Albert J. Reiss, Jr. (1967) "On exploring the 'dark figure' of crime," 374 Annals 1.

—— Louise A. Johnson, J. McIntyre and A. W. Weir (1967) Report on a Pilot

Study in the District of Columbia on Victimization and Attitudes toward Law Enforcement. Washington, D.C.: U.S. Government Printing Office.

Block, Richard L. (1970) "Police action, support for the police and support for civil liberties." Paper delivered at the American Sociological Association Meetings (September).

—— (1971) "Fear of crime and fear of the police," 19 Social Problems 91.

Blumberg, Abraham S. (1967) "The practice of law as confidence game: organizational cooptation of a profession," 1 Law and Society Review 15.

Bordua, David J. and Larry L. Tifft (1971) "Citizen interviews organizational feedback, and police-community relations decisions," 6 Law and Society Review 155.

Chambliss, William J. (1969) Crime and the Legal Process. New York: McGraw-Hill Book Company.

Cleaver, Patrick T., A.D. Mylonas and Walter Reckless (1966) "Gradients in attitudes toward law, courts, and police," 2 Sociological Focus 29.

Costner, Herbert L. (1965) "Criteria for measures of association," 30 American Sociological Review 341.

Cumming, Elaine, Ian Cumming and Laura Edell (1965) "Policeman as philosopher, guide and friend," 12 Social Problems 276.

Ennis, Philip (1967) Criminal Victimization in the United States. Washington, D.C.: U.S. Government Printing Office.

Goldstein, Jeffrey (1971) "Crisis in blue: the police as a minority group," in Edward Sagarin (ed.) The Other Minorities. Waltham, Massachusetts: Ginn and Company.

Goodman, Leo and William H. Kruskal (1963) "Measures of association for cross classifications: III. Approximate sampling theory," 58 Journal of American Statistical Association 310.

Gourley, G. Douglas (1954) "Police public relations," 291 Annals 135.

Hahn, Harlan (1971) "Ghetto assessment of police protection and authority," 6 Law and Society Review 183.

Hawkins, Richard (1970) Determinants of Sanctioning Initiations for Criminal Victimization. Unpublished Ph.D. Dissertation, Sociology, University of Washington.

—— (1973) "Who called the cops?: decisions to report criminal victimization," 7 Law and Society Review 427.

Jacob, Herbert (1971) "Black and white perceptions of justice in the city," 6 Law and Society Review 69.

Knudten, Richard D. (1970) Crime in a Complex Society. Homewood, Illinois: Dorsey Press.

McCaghy, Charles H., Irving L. Allen and H. David Colfax (1968) "Public attitudes toward city police in a middle-sized northern city," 6 Criminologica 14.

McNamara, John H. (1967) "Uncertainties in police work: the relevance of police recruits' background and training," in D.J. Bordua (ed.) The Police: Six Sociological Essays. New York: John Wiley and Sons.

Polk, R.L. (1967) Polk's Seattle City Directory. Seattle: R.L. Polk and Company

Preiss, Jack J. and Howard J. Ehrlich (1966) An Examination of Role Theory: The Case of the State Police. Lincoln: University of Nebraska Press.

Reiss, Albert J., Jr. (1967) Studies in Crime and Law Enforcement in Major Metropolitan Areas (2 volumes). Washington, D.C.: U.S. Government Printing Office.

Schur, Edwin M. (1967) Crimes Without Victims. Englewood Cliffs: Prentice-Hall.

Sherrand, Thomas J. (1968) "The ghetto disorders: a recommendation of post-riot remedies," 21 University of Florida Law Review 84.

Skolnick, Jerome H. (1966) Justice Without Trial. New York: John Wiley and Sons.

—— (1970) "The police and the urban ghetto," in A. Niederhoffer and A.S. Blumberg (eds.) The Ambivalent Force: Perspectives on the Police. Waltham, Mass.: Ginn and Company.

Smith, Paul E. (1969) Attitudes toward Norm Enforcers: The Case of the Police. Unpublished Ph.D. Dissertation, Sociology, University of Washington.

Werthman, Carl and Irving Piliavin (1967) "Gang members and the Police," in D.J. Bordua (ed.) The Police: Six Sociological Essays. New York: John Wiley and Sons.

Westley, William A. (1953) "Violence and the police," 59 American Journal of Sociology 34.

Wilson, James Q. (1968) Varieties of Police Behavior. Cambridge, Massachusetts: Harvard University Press.

CHAPTER **3-7**

policewomen on patrol and citizens' satisfaction

PETER BLOCH, DEBORAH ANDERSON,
AND PAMELA GERVAIS

The interpretation of attitude surveys is difficult. The women's performance may influence attitudes toward women's capabilities. However, the attitudes of supervisors, fellow officers and community residents can influence their assessments of the women's capabilities. In addition, attitudes or expectations may affect the women's performance.

In order to roughly determine the interaction between attitudes and performance, attitudes which existed before women were assigned to patrol were obtained for patrol officers (pre-test of the Patrol Survey) and community residents (Community Survey). In addition, attitude measures were taken in the comparison districts, to which only a few women were assigned. These results may be compared to attitudes expressed by policemen in the experimental districts after the women were on patrol.

Community Attitudes

Chilton Research Services completed 420 telephone interviews with a representative sample of citizens, selected to represent all age, sex and racial groups living in the experimental and comparison districts. In this survey, there were no marked differences between residents of experimental and comparison districts.

Reprinted by permission from the Police Foundation and the editors of *Policewomen on Patrol, First Report*, Vol. I (1973), pp. 28–32.

Citizens tended to approve of having policewomen doing the same thing as policemen, that is, patrolling the streets and responding to police calls. Their average opinion, given five scaled choices, was between "somewhat approve" and "neutral." Twenty-three percent were "neutral," 23 percent "somewhat approved," 23 percent "strongly approved" and the rest either "somewhat disapproved" or "strongly disapproved."

Citizens also had a slight tendency to agree that women should have the same opportunity as men to be police officers. Twenty-four percent "agreed" and 35 percent "strongly agreed."

The average citizen felt that "the attempt to get equal rights for women is going . . . about right." Forty-two percent said the attempt was going "about right" and another 29 percent were about equally divided between "a little too far" and "not quite far enough."

A policewoman and a policeman working as a team are believed by the average citizen to have a slight advantage of an all-male team in handling a fight between a man and a woman. Forty-three percent said the male-female team would do "about the same" and 22 percent said "somewhat better."

On the other hand, policewomen and policemen working together were believed, by the citizen, to have a slight advantage in two situations, "handling a street corner flight" and a "riot." In both of these situations, about 35 percent felt the presence of a woman would make "no difference," about 20 percent felt it would make things "somewhat more likely to get out of hand."

Citizens rate policewomen and policemen as equally competent in handling a serious auto accident involving injured people and in investigating crime scenes.

The average opinion of citizens is that, if half the police officers were women, the number of criminals caught and the crime rate would not be affected.

Citizens felt policewomen would show slightly more respect for citizens and would receive slightly more respect from citizens. The average opinion on both of these questions was between "about the same" and "somewhat more respectful."

Citizen Opinions About Policewomen

When a policewoman was present at an incident, the citizen was asked to make an additional rating of the woman. Thirty-eight percent of the citizens said the women did a "very good" job and 25 percent said they did a "good" job.

When asked whether their contact with a policewoman had altered their attitude toward policewomen, 51 percent of the respondents said it caused no change in attitude and 39 percent said it caused them to have a "somewhat more favorable" or "much more favorable" attitude.

Police-Community Interaction

When citizens were asked whether they would prefer an all-male or a male-female police team if they called the police in the future, the majority said that sex made no difference. However, respondents who had experience with female officers were a little more likely to prefer a male-female team.

Community Reactions To Police

In an anonymous paper-and-pencil survey of 202 patrol officers ("Patrol Survey"), including 57 women, officers were asked several questions about the reactions they received from the public. Male officers[1] consistently and strikingly indicated a less favorable public response than did females. (See Table 3-7-1.) Males felt the public was less cooperative when they were trying to obtain crime information than did females. Males also reported receiving about 50 percent more insults, close to three times as many threats or attempts at injury and less than half the number of compliments than females reported during the month prior to the time of the survey. Black males reported more compliments, fewer insults and more public cooperation in obtaining crime information than white males.

The [Police] Department survey conducted [in Washington, D.C.] by Chief Wilson indicates that the new women and comparison men received the same number of "written or oral commendations" from the public. The new women, however, received 63 "complaints," versus only one for the comparison men. A spot check of the three indivduals who received the most complaints in District 1 revealed that none of the complaints were written or filed in per-

TABLE 3-7-1. Community Cooperation Questions

	Males		Females	Black Males		White Males
Public cooperation in obtaining crime information[1] (scaled score)	3.5	*	5.1	3.9	*	3.1
Number of insults in the last month	9.2	*	6.0	7.3	*	10.6
Number of attempts or threats of injury in the last month	1.3	*	.5	1.0		1.6
Number of compliments in the last month	4.8	*	11.9	6.3	*	3.8

[1]Question is scored on an 8-point scale. Zero is "very uncooperative," 4 is "neutral," 8 is "very cooperative."
*Differences between the two groups are significant at the .05 level.

sonnel records. All complaints apparently were received verbally by the sergeant in charge of the individual's squad. That squad sergeant was given the responsibility for completing the "complaint" and "ratings" sections of the Chief's survey.

Judging from all surveys taken, the women are being received as well as or better than the men and the frequency of complaints does not reflect average citizen reactions.

References

1. On the average, male officers were more experienced than female. To ascertain whether differences were attributable to an officer's sex or to his seniority, regression equations (using seniority in both a linear and logarithmic form) were used. All reported sex differences were significant in equations which also used seniority as a variable. Seniority never was significant on the community cooperation questions.

PART IV

TENSIONS ANd CONflicTS

Introduction

Although police perform an indispensable service, a love-hate relationship may be said to exist between them and the people they supposedly serve. "We Serve and Protect" is the motto of the Chicago police force, yet blacks and other minorities question whether the Chicago police, or any big city police force for that matter, serves and protects them.

In recent years accounts of the relations between the police and ghetto dwellers have often been described in the language of warfare. In the slums of any city the angry, hostile, and resentful residents reportedly see and describe the police as an "army of occupation." As Niederhoffer states:

> For the urban poor, the police are those who arrest you. In almost any slum, there is a vast conspiracy against law and order. If someone approaches asking for a person, no one there will have heard of him, even if he lives next door. The outsider is a "cop", . . . and in the ghetto, most dramatically he is the "Man" (1967:139).

In the slums the situation is often highly volatile. Any incident may touch off violent conflicts and riots. Unfortunately, the precipitating factor in many urban riots has been the arbitrary conduct of the police in dealing with the urban poor. The Harlem Riot Commission summarized the situation as follows:

> The police in Harlem show too little regard for human rights and constantly violate their fundamental rights as citizens. . . . The insecurity of the individual in Harlem against police aggression is one of the most potent

causes for the existing hostility to authority. It is clearly the responsibility of the police to prove themselves the guardians of the rights and safety of the community rather than its enemies and oppressors (Skolnick, (1969:184).

The Report of the National Commission on Civil Disorders (1968:158) reported that blacks firmly believed that police brutality and harassment occurred with alarming frequency in ghetto neighborhoods. This led the Commission to conclude that this belief was unquestionably one of the major reasons for inner city residents' intense resentment against the police. It is of course undeniable that a certain amount of stereotyping is involved in black perceptions of police over the brutality issue. Still, it is a fact that minorities believe that police brutality exists and that it is widespread. As Coffey states:

> Police brutality, harassment, dispersal of social gatherings and stopping blacks on foot and in cars without cause are significant items of contention to blacks since they seem to strip them of the one thing they have left—dignity (1971:12).

Biderman found black males very critical of police on the issue of police brutality (1967:137). Part of the problem can be found in the following:

> Police action and attitudes do the most damage when law officers touch a man's relationships to his womenfolk and his children. . . . He must not be humiliated in front of his wife or the women he loves or his children. He must not be devalued in the presence of his neighbors and the community. . . . (Minority) males have been subjected to insult and humiliation again and again . . . by the white police. . . . One such expression of attitude and action cancels out all the work of police community relations efforts (Black, 1968:31).

Not surprisingly, therefore, the ghetto community believes that police do not want to listen or understand minority culture or people. They look on the police as impersonal, hardened, and as restraining open hostility with a cloak of coldness. A policeman is perceived likely to discriminate against minorities and to abuse the people should the occasion arise. His only tactic is force. People in the ghetto believe police think that everyone who is black, brown, or yellow is the same; that minorities, because of color and/or heritage, are likely to break the law, threaten the maintenance of peace, and endanger life and property (Lohman and Misner, 1966:II, 163–64; Somerville, 1968:39).

Ironically, the police provide more essential services to lower-class residents than most other governmental service organizations (Mendelsohn, 1970:-748). Libermann, in *Police as a Community Mental Health Resource*, found that 50 percent of the mentally ill patients and their families in Baltimore utilized the police as a community resource as other resources were not as readily available (Johnson and Gregory, 1971:95). This finding gives some indication of the importance of police assistance in times of sickness, injury, and trouble. It is indeed a fact that police responsibilities in the slums and the ghettos of America's cities are greater than elsewhere primarily because other institutions are simply not there or have little impact if they are present. Schools are often old, inferior, and decaying; religion is irrelevant—ghetto dwellers lost faith when they lost hope; career aspirations are not evident and family foundations have frequently broken down. The police find themselves in an institutional vacuum and must fill it.

If one keeps the foregoing in mind, it is no wonder that minorities look upon their residential setting as a "zoo" and the police—whom they fear and mistrust, but with whom they must live—as the "zookeepers" (Rustin, 1968:-350; Cross, 1964:406). The police are perceived as an occupying force whose behavior is provocative and offensive, "particularly when the policeman's actions and the suspect's protests are visible and the reasons for an arrest are not" (Lang and Lang, 1968:123).

Police racism is not the only reason behind the strained relationships between inner city residents and law enforcement. The ghetto dweller believes, with good reasons in some instances, that the police play a part in ghetto crime, corruption, and drug traffic, by protecting illicit activities for a bribe. Thus, they are seen as "symbols of the pathology smothering the ghetto" (Clark, 1968:289).

It should not come as a surprise to the informed reader that the disorders and riots of the 1960s were symptoms of frustration and bitter despair. The urban poor had been striving to divest themselves of their second-class citizenship. Efforts at integration failing, they attempted to seek out and maintain their own identity as well as group identification, pride, and self-respect through the "Black is beautiful" and "Black power" philosophies. Snubbed by a hypocritical society, "the black community accepts its alienation as a virtue, and in turn rejects the legal channels of protest. Black power is converted to force" (Niederhoffer, 1967:194-95).

When riots and disorders occur, police have frequently been the spark in the initiation of such experiences. But;

> The police are not merely a "spark" factor. To some blacks, police have come to symbolize white power, white racism and white repression. And, the fact is that many police do reflect and express these attitudes. The atmosphere of hostility and cynicism is reinforced by a widespread belief among blacks in the existence of police brutality and a "double standard" of justice protection—one for blacks and the other for whites (Coffey, et al., 1971:2).

Recurrently, in American history, the plight of the American poor—mostly the ghetto Americans—has been dramatized by riots and other civil disturbances.

In the late 1960s, for a brief time, the Black Panthers held center-stage, focusing the attention of the American people on the reality of what it means to be black and poor. They also pointedly called the nation's attention to the fact that black people have few rights that police respect. While many today optimistically feel that the "hot summers" are gone forever, deep tensions remain. At this moment, when recession has cut deeply into the inner city, when inflation has seriously eroded the economic gains of recent years, when youth gangs and drug traffic have become more firmly entrenched in the ghetto, some more realistic observers have expressed fear about the potential for unrest and turmoil. Recent disturbances may presage a new round of urban insurrections, although it is more likely that they merely demonstrate that the killing of a black person by a white one in the ghetto will elicit a violent response. Ghetto dwellers are keenly aware that the forces arrayed against them should they take to the streets again would be far more imposing than they were in the 1960s. In the years since the great riots, urban and state police forces have improved their riot-control techniques. Furthermore, in the slums there is little left to destroy.

But the hopelessness and misery of the ghetto communities—be they black, white, brown, or yellow—invite individual, almost suicidal, acts of violence, and clearly suggest that the deep rooted causes of unrest and hostility are still at work in America's cities.

While racial minorities see themselves as the major target of police brutality and neglect, it would be unrealistic to assume that whites or more established people—regardless of race—are immune and exempt from "scrapes" with police, or that they always receive prompt and concerned service from them. As an example, while ghetto residents in Washington D.C. were complaining that police were not active enough in investigating the murders of several young women because, it was said, the victims were "only" black, equally enraged middle-class whites were raising a storm of protest in Texas when it was discovered that police had not investigated at all the reported disappearance of several young males who had meanwhile been murdered and buried in shallow sites by a homosexual.

It should also not be forgotten that there are many people of different race and social status—prostitutes, homosexuals, drug users, members of counter-cultures, consumer and political activists, union organizers etc.—who have learned to distrust and fear the police and see them not as the upholders of the law but mainly as the enforcers of the intolerance, hypocrisy, and venality of our society.

Tensions between the community and the police are surfacing even at a higher, broader level: that of cities' finances. Police, increasingly organized in militant unions and willing to strike, are demanding costly pay and pension agreements from cities caught in a financial vise. In 1975 in New York, the police did not hesitate to engage, among others, in tactics aimed at scaring off would be tourists and conventioneers at the national and international level. In the measure that they succeeded, they not only further damaged the already poor financial situation of the city, but also jeopardized the income of countless businesses which depend on tourism for survival. Such instances of holding an entire city "hostage" by not providing needed police protection, while demanding that taxpayers accept additional long-term financial burdens, may add serious strains to already precarious police-community relations.

Quite possibly we can and should better understand the present if we were to look back at the past. This is especially true in the case of police, where tradition plays such an important role in determining policy and behavior. James Richardson, in the first selection, offers an excellent historical overview of the tensions that have always accompanied police-community relations. For instance, there are labor union members still alive who remember very well how police broke picket lines and clubbed striking workers to the ground.

"Police and Justice in San Diego" examines within a concrete setting the dynamics, the frustration, and the stress that pervade police work as a consequence of citizens' constitutional rights and of recent important court decisions.

Daniel Walker and his research associates vividly describe and analyze one of the better known "police riots" in recent times, that which took place in Chicago in 1968 during the Democratic Party convention. This report, written for the President's Commission on the Causes and Prevention of Violence, represents 53 days of investigation of the battle between civilians and the Chicago police and shows that, ironically, those charged with maintaining "law and order" actually caused a major disturbance.

Police corruption is one of the major reasons for the distrust and suspicion which minorities, youth, the non-conformists, display toward police. According to recent surveys, many inner city residents believe that police are indeed "not tough enough" on the "real" criminals. The Knapp Commission made the headlines while hearing testimony outlining corrupt practices of New York City police. An excerpt from those hearings gives a glimpse of the extent of that corruption and of the damage that ultimately it inflicts upon effective law enforcement.

Wayne Cotton reports on a study which shows an essentially negative appraisal of the police in El Barrio, New York's Puerto Rican neighborhood. Cotton probes into the reasons for his findings and discusses at length their implications.

In a similar vein, Robert Crosby and David Snyder, in "Distrust of the Police and Crime Reporting," summarize the results of a survey conducted in America's black neighborhoods to evaluate the attitudes of blacks about the crime problem in the cities. In particular, Crosby and Snyder focus on findings which reflect on the respondents' feelings toward police and on the impact that such feelings have on police-community relations.

Paul Takagi reports on a study of police officers killed in the line of duty and of civilians killed by police, in an article entitled "A Garrison State in

Tensions and Conflicts

TABLE IV-1. Washington D.C. Metropolitan Police Department: Number of Sworn Members by Rank and Race, 1975

	Race			
Rank	*Black*	*White*	*Other*	*Total*
Chief	0	1	0	1
Assistant Chiefs	2	2	0	4
Deputy Chiefs	0	8	0	8
Inspectors	4	24	0	28
Captains	3	48	0	51
Lieutenants	31	162	0	193
Sergeants	142	471	5	618
Officers	1,753	1,943	33	3,729
Total Sworn Members	1,935	2,659	38	4,632

'Democratic' Society." The study was undertaken in 1971 in reaction to news reports based on FBI statistics indicating that police officers were being "assassinated" at an alarming rate. Takagi attempts to balance such reports by studying the other side of the coin, police homicides of citizens. Quite correctly, his theoretical framework views police duties as an extension of public authority, that is, as essentially political in nature. The implications for democracy of a police force constantly increasing in numbers and sophistication are also carefully examined.

The FBI official report on law enforcement officers killed in 1974 follows.

Finally, James Campbell and his associates, in "The Police in Conflict," focus on a different type of tension affecting the police: their conflict with other criminal justice agencies and among themselves. While many people like to think that criminal justice is a "system," this notion has been severely challenged from both theoretical and practical points of view (Cohn, 1974). Such discussion is not entirely as academic as it might seem since this issue has wide-ranging implications for practical operations and future programming. For instance, it may very well be that society has been unable to understand and control crime simply because criminal justice is not a system but instead a collection of assorted and disjointed services.

But police are not only in conflict with courts and corrections. They are in conflict among themselves as well. In recent years, police departments at the city, county, and state levels, have had to grudgingly admit minority applicants in increasing numbers either as a countermeasure to rioting or as the outcome of a successful legal challenge on the part of civil rights groups. While ethnic tensions have always been present in large, urban police departments, the influx of black, brown, or yellow officers has created, at times, wide schisms and deep hostility. In several departments, minority police officers have felt the need to form their own professional associations to fight harassment, discrimination, segregated patrolling, unsuitable dress code requirements and the like.

Thus, the tensions existing in the streets surfaced inside the police stations. Even in those cities where the police department has reportedly been following an "enlightened" policy toward racial minorites, serious and potentially explosive problems exist. For instance, when the Washington D.C. City Council conducted hearings on June 12, 1975 on departmental employment practices, the data of Table IV-1 emerged. Thus, of the top 285 jobs (lieutenant and above) whites hold 245 or 86 percent. There is a black female lieutenant and no Spanish-Americans among those jobs. If one keeps in mind that Washington D.C. is at least 75 percent black and that it has a sizable female and Spanish-speaking population, one can realize why human rights remain as the main struggle of our times, even inside the police departments.

References

Biderman, Albert, Louise A. Johnson, Jennie McIntyre, and Adrianne Weir
    1967   Report on a Pilot Study in the District of Columbia on Victimization and Attitudes toward Law Enforcement. Washington D.C.: U.S. Government Printing Office.

Black, Algernon
    1968   The People and the Police. New York: McGraw-Hill.

Clark, Kenneth B.
    1968   "The Wonder Is There Have Been So Few Riots." Pp. 287–295 in S. Endleman (ed.), Violence in the Streets. Chicago: Quadrangle Books.

Coffey, Alan, Edward Eldefonso, and Walter Hartinger
    1971   Police-Community Relations. Englewood Cliffs: Prentice-Hall.

Cohn, Alvin W.
    1974   "Training in the Criminal Justice Nonsystem." Federal Probation 38 (June) 2:32–37.

Cross, Granville
    1964   "The Negro, Prejudice, and the Police." Journal of Criminal Law, Criminology, and Police Science 55 (September) 405–411.

Johnson, Deborah and Robert J. Gregory
    1971   "Police-Community Relations in the United States: A Review of Recent Literature and Projects." Journal of Criminal Law, Criminology, and Police Science 62 (March) 94–103.

Lang, Kurt and Gladys E. Lang
    1968   "Racial Disturbances as Collective Protest." Pp. 121–130 in Louis A. Masotti and Don R. Bowen (eds.), Riots and Rebellion: Civil Violence in the Urban Community. Beverly Hills, California: Sage Publications.

Lohman, Joseph and Gordon E. Misner

1966   The Police and the Community: The Dynamics of their Relationship in a Changing Society. Washington D.C.: U.S. Government Printing Office.

National Advisory Commission on Civil Disorders
1968   Report. Washington D.C.: U.S. Government Printing Office.

Niederhoffer, Arthur
1967   Behind the Shield: The Police in Urban Society. Garden City, N.Y.: Doubleday.

Rustin, Bayard
1968   "Some Lessons from Watts." Pp. 347–356 in Shalom Endleman (ed.), Violence in the Streets. Chicago: Quadrangle Books.

Skolnick, Jerome
1969   The Politics of Protest: Violent Aspects of Protest and Confrontation. Washington, D.C.: U.S. Government Printing Office.

Somerville, Bill
1968   "Double Standards in Law Enforcement with Regard to Minority Status." Issues in Criminology 4 (Fall) 35–43.

CHAPTER **4-1**

CONflict ANd diffeRENCES
OVER police peRfoRMANce:
AN histoRical oveRview

JAMES F. RICHARDSON

Police-community relations have always been problematic in America's big cities. From their inception, American police forces have operated to shield the elite from the masses, to impose middle-class standards upon the poor, or at least to confine unacceptable behavior to the slums and red-light districts. If police were not as zealous in these tasks as some of the elite demanded, they received considerable criticism from "reform" groups. If police did act energetically to control the masses, they were regarded as tyrants and traitors by people they lived and worked among. Departments could never satisfy all of the elements of their diverse constituency; police performance that pleased one segment of the diverse urban population had to displease another.[1]

During the 1930s and 1940s, however, these conflicts and differences over police performance were not very severe. William F. Whyte's study of Boston's North End, *Street Corner Society*, showed an almost ritualistic pattern of relationships between the police, numbers bettors and bookies, and the "better elements." When moralistic pressure rose to a certain peak, an "untouchable" came into the neighborhood as the precinct commander and closed operations. After the heat died down, he was transferred to another post and business as usual resumed.

Neither side expected complete victory. The moralists did not expect that all gambling would be eliminated, while the numbers runners and bankers realized they would have to accept periodic arrests and occasional reform waves when business would be difficult and unprofitable. Policemen, customers, and numbers operators formed part of the same social world, while the moralists were outsiders. Yet officers knew they could not ignore the formal demands of the law entirely, and they had to maintain some sort of communication with those who wanted to alter their traditional practices.[2]

The most dramatic conflicts between police and civilians before World War II came in labor disputes. American society, with its emphasis on individualism and the primacy of property rights, proved the most resistant of any major industrial nation to the establishment of collective bargaining and union recognition. Employers often tried to maintain operations in the face of strikes, which made for violence on the picket line between strikers and strikebreakers. To such employers the police function of protecting life and property meant getting strikebreakers past picket lines no matter what means had to be employed, while strikers wanted the police to arrest "goons," to keep strikebreakers from coming into town, or at the very least to be neutral toward the dispute.[3]

Obviously it would be difficult to generalize about police performance in the thousands of labor disputes in cities large and small over a long span of time, but a few observations are in order. First, police despised strikes as potentially disorderly situations which increased their workload and exposed them to abuse and danger. Furthermore, contested strikes exposed the vulnerability of the police. Their function was to maintain the peace and good order of the community against the minority which refused to abide by the rules of the game. But what happened when the community split, when there was no agreement on the rules of the game, when desperate men prepared to fight for more money, or better working conditions, or union recognition, and equally determined men insisted that they alone had the right to make these decisions?

In grappling with the dilemmas posed by the community polarization, the police tended to follow the lines of power and influence. In general, departments had no use for strikes and strikers, but the key variable in their performance seems to have been the community's attitude toward a particular dispute. If the authorities favored the workers or were at least neutral, the police remained neutral. If, on the other hand, political leaders and newspapers viewed the strikers as unAmerican radicals or a threat to a town's prosperity by making industry reluctant to locate there, then the police acted as agents of employers in their strikebreaking activities. The New York police clubbed many immigrant workers in the garment industry who tried to set up picket lines. The department long perceived anarchists, socialists, and Communists to be the fomenters of labor discord and responded accordingly.

Under John Purroy Mitchel, mayor of New York from 1914 to 1917, the police adopted a more neutral stance; but it was not until the mayoralty administrations of Fiorello La Guardia between 1933 and 1945 that neutrality became confirmed policy.[4]

Conflict and Differences Over Police Performance: An Historical Overview

The Chicago police provide one of the most notorious examples of anti-labor bias. In the words of a noted labor historian, "The Chicago police had a long, notable, and dishonorable record of breaking strikes with force on behalf of employers in defiance of civil liberties." Harold Ickes, who served as Secretary of the Interior under Franklin Roosevelt, had a long and unhappy experience with the Chicago police during his career as an attorney and civic leader in the city. He wrote in July, 1937:

> I don't know whether any city has a worse police force than Chicago but I doubt it. I have known something about it for a good many years and I have had two or three clashes with it over invasions of obvious civil rights. . . . The Augean stables emanated delicate perfume compared with some of the odors that have been redolent in this Department in the past. From the time of the Haymarket riots [1886] in Chicago, police always justified brutal invasion of civil rights by calling those whom it manhandled "anarchists."

Ickes' letter was called forth by the behavior of the Chicago police on Memorial Day in 1937, when they charged, clubbed, and shot a group of peaceful strikers and their families outside the Republic Steel plant in south Chicago. Ten civilians died, most of them shot in the back as they tried to escape from the rampaging bluecoats.[5] It would be interesting to know how many of the survivors and descendants of that Memorial Day approved of the actions of the Chicago police department during the Democratic convention of 1968, when the targets were youthful, primarily middle-class dissidents.

In the great steel strike of 1919, police performance varied widely in different communities. In western Pennsylvania steel towns, where the companies virtually owned the community, the police, aided by mounted state police and militiamen, ran union organizers out of town and prevented any public gathering of more than three people without a permit, which would not be granted anyone in favor of the strike. In Cleveland, on the other hand, Mayor Harry L. Davis had the police turn back strikebreakers coming into the city. Until stopped by a court injunction, the police treated any potential strikebreaker as a suspicious person and presented the classic alternative of get out of town or go to jail.[6]

The police were not and are not solely a general public service, oblivious to questions of power and prestige; they often act as an instrument to protect the interests of the dominant groups in the community. In day-to-day life this principle is not particularly visible; people can believe the motto of the Cleveland police that "Our Men Serve All Men." In the crisis situation of a contested strike, serving all men was impossible. The police, like it or not, had to take sides and their action or inaction had important implications for the outcome of a strike.

In the years since World War II the police role has declined in labor disputes as federal law dictates the conduct of contestants and most companies have decided that the risks of continued operation in the face of strikes outweigh any possible benefits. This is not to say that labor relations might not again become a pressure point upon the police; that possibility is always present. For the recent past and foreseeable future, however, the most important conflicts facing the police are those involving clashing life-styles between alienated youth and more settled members of the community, and the tremendous problems surrounding the declining economic base and the changing racial composition of central cities.

In the last twenty or twenty-five years police-community relations have worsened considerably under the impact of massive social and economic changes.[7] The problems associated with racial distinctions and discrimination and poverty have become so concentrated in our cities that "urban problems" has become a shorthand designation of national social ills. Larger and larger percentages of the populations of older core cities are made up of the poor, the trapped, and the deprived as individuals and businesses with any choice seek suburban and exurban locations.[8]

Traditionally, cities have grown and developed at major breaks in transportation. The classic nineteenth-century city was a port, whether on the seacoast, the Great Lakes, or one of the great rivers, with extensive railroad connections. Businesses and individuals wanted to be as close to the major transportation and communication facilities as possible, and central city land appreciated in value constantly as the urban areas developed, thus putting a premium on intense use, crowding if you will.[9]

In contrast, current technology favors dispersion within metropolitan or megalopolitan areas rather than concentration in core cities. Industry finds the single-story, continuous-flow plant by far the most efficient; deliveries and shipments are often by trucks, which are most effective away from the congestion of the central city and near an interstate highway connection; and the labor force drives to work, which necessitates large land areas for parking lots. Increasingly only those businesses with large capital investments which they do not wish to write off or with specialized needs which require proximity to outside firms and specialists remain in the central city.[10] In addition, the combination of the automobile and various kinds of government subsidies, such as those for federally insured home mortgages and highway building, has permitted the rapid development of the suburban residential districts which have attracted good taxpayers from the core city. Cities such as New York, Newark, Cleveland, and San Francisco find themselves in a fiscal crisis as their revenue providers, taxpaying businesses and individuals, move outside the political boundaries and therefore the taxing power of the city, while the cost of providing municipal services keeps rising.[11]

Blacks have been escaping the hopeless poverty and discrimination of the rural South by moving to the cities, both southern and northern, since the 1890s. The movement increased considerably during the two world wars. Since 1940 the movement has reached mammoth proportions and shows little sign of diminishing. One hundred years ago, race was primarily a "problem" of the rural South; now the exclusion and deprivation that is the lot of the black lower class in the United States is our most serious urban problem. Technological changes in agriculture have made many southern blacks economically super-fluous and therefore in danger of starvation as the activities that used to provide subsistence, if nothing more, no longer exist or are performed more cheaply and efficiently by machines.[12]

Unfortunately, the same trend has occurred in the urban economy as unskilled and semiskilled factory jobs have declined in number and those that do exist are increasingly found outside central cities. Thus blacks are trapped in the central city because of poverty and suburban housing discrimination at the same time that entry-level jobs are declining or moving out. Traditionally, people have learned of entry-level jobs either by applying at the plant gate or learning from a friend or relative that a firm is hiring. When the plant is twenty miles away such word-of-mouth information is hard to obtain. Even if one learns of a job, there is still the problem of transportation. Public transportation is usually not available, so a car must be financed and run on a beginner's wages. The combination of these trends has resulted in a serious unemployment and under-employment pattern among inner-city blacks. Unskilled women, both black and white, especially have a difficult time in locating and arranging transportation to decent jobs.[13]

Cities are thus caught in a vicious downward spiral of a declining economic and tax base and a continued immigration of unskilled, uneducated, and dis-criminated-against people who impose heavy burdens on services like welfare, schools, police and fire protection, and the courts and correctional system.

Many white middle- and stable working-class people see the contemporary urban crisis in simplistic terms. Blacks won't work; "they" have no morals; all they do is drink and fornicate, desert their wives, and neglect their children. This used to be a good neighborhood before "they" moved in. Few citizens are aware of, or at least most do not think very systematically about, the complex interrelation between economic and technological change, the long-standing exclusion and deprivation blacks have faced in this country, and the resultant cultural and behavioral patterns. As Lee Rainwater has brilliantly demonstrated in his *Behind Ghetto Walls,* lower-class blacks have adopted various strategies for survival and getting some gratification out of life under the conditions of extreme deprivation forced on them by the white majority. Negroes were slaves for their first two hundred years in America; then slavery was followed by a freedom which left them economically defenseless and subjected and segregated in every aspect of social life.

In the South and the North alike, the police used both their formal and informal powers to maintain the subjugation of the Negro population. In Chicago and other cities, the protected vice area where the police left the brothels and the prostitutes alone was located in the black belt. Thus parents who wanted to shield their children from commercial and exploitative sex could not do so. The numbers racket flourished and flourishes openly in the black ghettos, and children by the age of four know what the game is all about. The major share of the enormous profits has gone to whites rather than blacks, from the policemen on "the pad" who are bribed to let the business operate to the top bankers and controllers who moved in after the repeal of prohibition closed off that avenue of illicit enterprise. Those Negroes with ambitions for respectability and a moral atmosphere in which to raise their children found their efforts thwarted by the combination of housing discrimination and police tolerance of illicit activity in their neighborhoods. If they complained, the indifference or hostility they received confirmed their powerlessness.[14]

Often the police seemed more interested in confining blacks and black crime to the ghetto than in protecting residents of the area. In New York until recent decades, some policemen supported saloonkeepers who refused to serve black customers, no matter what the public accommodations law said.[15] In many cities, especially in the South but to some extent in the North as well, the police took the view that if a black man kills a white, that's murder; if a white man kills a black, that's justifiable homicide; and if a black man kills a black, that's one less nigger. In short the police permitted or ignored criminal behavior as long as only blacks were involved. Most complaints against the police derive from their indifference to crime and disorder in the ghetto, not disrespect and brutality, although there are plenty of complaints on that score as well. Blacks who perceive their environment as chaotic and violent resent the police for not protecting them better. The Civil Rights Commission found in 1966 that in Cleveland the police took four times as long to answer calls in black neighborhoods as they did comparable calls from white areas.[16] The New York department traditionally used Harlem as a dumping ground for its incompetents and those who had incurred official wrath for some reason.[17] In most cities slum precincts like slum schools get the rejects of the system. The men who are the least well educated, the least likely to be sensitive to minority cultures and frustrations, and the most prone to take a "tough" approach to police work and contacts with civilians patrol those areas which pose the most sensitive, dangerous, and complex police problems. Lower-class whites also face police harassment and insensitivity. In some ways they are worse off than the blacks because they have few organizations and spokesmen to make their case to the media and to other agencies.[18]

The ecological fact is that criminals prey most often on those nearest and most accessible to them, so the biggest sufferers from black criminals are other blacks who live in their neighborhoods. As indicated in the previous chapter, there may not be very much the police can do about crime and criminality, but they can indicate a greater degree of concern and sympathy and at least give ghetto residents a feeling that somebody cares and that something is being done. And police indifference toward crime and vandalism does encourage more people to engage in such behavior.[19]

The social conditions that lead to crime are beyond police control; they cannot do anything about low incomes and broken families. They can only try to keep the personal and social damage to a minimum. The spread of addiction to drugs, especially heroin, presents particularly vexing problems. Heroin addiction is endemic among black and Spanish-speaking youths in decayed urban neighborhoods; in the late 1960s addiction spread tremendously among servicemen in Vietnam and made substantial inroads among middle-class youth. Heroin addicts face the dilemma of not being able to hold a steady job while needing money, lots of it, to support their habits. Prostitution and theft are obvious sources, and many police officers see almost a one-to-one relationship between rising rates of addiction and increased burglary and robbery.

Narcotics control and the other crimes it generates is a frustrating business. If heroin becomes scarce, the price goes up and addicts must commit even more crimes to satisfy their needs. Addicts have mutilated themselves to secure hospital admission and therefore access to some drugs in time of famine. Police announcement of a seizure of a large cache of heroin may be a source of congratulation for the officers who achieve it, but it brings about headaches for their colleagues. In addition some policemen have succumbed to the large amounts of money involved and entered into corrupt relations with narcotics dealers. With the best will in the world, narcotics enforcement is still difficult, extremely time-consuming, and frustrating. Enforcing the law involves sticky constitutional questions, and there is the serious problem of what happens after arrest. No jurisdiction has enough treatment facilities for addicts, and there is a distressingly high rate of relapse when apparently cured people go back to the same environment in which they became addicted in the first place.

Narcotics and related criminal problems form one of the most dramatic instances of the truism that policemen are charged with picking up the pieces of the failure of the social order in general. Seemingly, society does not know how to prevent addiction in the first place or how to cure it afterwards. Heroin provides an escape from the despair and hopelessness of the ghetto environment or from the boredom and purposelessness that afflict large numbers of youth. No one has yet done much to solve these basic social problems and the related increases in criminal behavior.[20] Understandably, however, citizens demand some form of action against the greater possibility of being burglarized, robbed, or assaulted, and so the police are under great pressure to do something, even if there are no very clear ideas as to what actions would be both effective and consistent with the principles of a free society.

When the police do saturate a high-crime area and engage in aggressive preventive control in an effort to control crime, they greatly increase tension and hostility, especially in view of the technological and residential changes of the last quarter century. The foot patrolmen had much more of an opportunity to keep in touch with the values of the community and the more positive aspects of human behavior than the man in the radio car. The radio car patrolman interacts with civilians most often in an adversary situation. He lacks the other contacts that kept the relation between police and people from being simply that of combatants. The radio car man sees civilians only at their worst, when they are trying to escape the negative consequences of actions like speeding or when they are in trouble, drunk, defeated, or degraded. He must make his judgments on the basis of visible signs such as color, age, dress, and attitude rather than on his intimate knowledge of the people on his post.[21]

In high-crime areas, which now are those populated by blacks and the Spanish speaking, a large number of field interrogations and a high arrest rate are the evidence a patrolman offers to his superiors to show that he is on the job, that he is efficient. However, in so doing, he can further alienate the people among whom he works. Stops and searches in the ghetto, especially if accompanied by racial epithets or disrespectful language or attitudes, further impress upon the residents their powerlessness and their outcast position. The hostility young lower-class males exhibit toward the police means that they will fail the attitude test, which makes arrests more likely. A policeman is more prone to make an arrest in a discretionary situation if a juvenile expresses contempt and hostility toward police authority than if he is apologetic and respectful. In this vicious circle, police practices and ghetto responses reinforce each other in such a way as to intensify the hatred and contempt policemen and black youth feel toward each other.[22]

Physical brutality and the third-degree practices of beating confessions out of suspects are not so common now as they were at the time of the Wickersham Commission investigation in the late 1920s and early 1930s. What does remain is what one author calls "institutionalized malpractice," various procedures which violate the law or the constitutional rights or the human dignity of civilians. One form of malpractice is to make an arrest to cover an infringement of civil rights. Apparently such arrests are rare, but no matter how few there is no justification for them. If a policeman oversteps his authority and a civilian protests, the policemen then might make an arrest for resisting an officer or some other charge. The arrest then justifies legally any police activity, even to the point of using force to overcome unlawful resistance.[23]

More serious in the long run than any verbal or physical abuse a civilian might suffer is the arrest record itself, which will haunt the individual for the rest of his life. Blacks and other minority groups are much more likely to be arrested and the arrest is much more serious for them than for many whites in view of their difficulties in finding jobs. In many inner-city neighborhoods, relatively few boys reach their twenty-first birthday without some sort of a record, and employment applications often ask, Have you ever been arrested?

Note: not, Have you ever been convicted? but simply arrested. A yes answer often closes any possibility of getting the job; so the police decision to make an arrest itself imposes severe penalties upon the individual, whether the arrest was warranted or not. An arrest in a discretionary situation may have a lifetime impact upon a boy whose major offense was that he was not sufficiently respectful and deferential toward the police.

Juveniles themselves are very much aware that for the same action one boy may get simply a chewing out while another winds up serving a year in jail; they also know that it is the policeman who makes the key decision of whether to invoke the process of the criminal law at all or to deal with the situation informally. In making these decisions, policemen rely on such visible attributes of status and attitude as color, age, dress, and demeanor as well as the nature of the offense itself and the reputation of the boy and his family.[24] This awesome discretionary authority of the police, their power to impose *Justice Without Trial*, as Jerome Skolnick entitled his important book on the police, has always been present, but never before has it seemed so questionable and indeed illegitimate to so many citizens. Many ghetto residents view arrests as a technique of control and repression, not as a valid exercise of law-enforcement powers.[25]

As a result of the increased isolation of policemen from civilians because of the spread of the radio car and the demographic changes in cities, policemen may be more contemptuous than ever of civilians, "assholes," who are animals at worst and at best do not have the officer's capacity for quick decisions and effective action. The policeman sees people as victims of drink and drugs, or acting out the impulses to greed, lust, and perversion, or trying to bluster or wheedle their way out from the consequences of their actions. Many policemen come to believe that no matter how respectable the facade, most men and women are still animals underneath and that it does not take much for the veneer to be stripped away and the reality underneath to show through. The patrolman's view of the world and the people in it, his tendency to socialize with his fellow officers, and the instinctive resentment that many civilians have toward policemen, on or off duty, sets him dangerously apart from the rest of urban society.[26]

The process of separation is even more pronounced as a result of the white migration, including policemen, to the periphery of metropolitan areas. Few officers actually live in the ghetto or the inner city; their incomes and their color enable most of them to escape its congestion, filth, and crime. The man who commutes from a suburb to an inner-city neighborhood may not always be sensitive to the nuances of the community, its complexities, its decent people who are forced to live side by side with pimps and muggers, and its frustrations. He sees himself as a man doing an important, a dangerous, and an unappreciated job, putting life and limb on the line every time he goes on the street, and for people who hate him.

James Baldwin noted the cop's dilemma in the ghetto. No matter what his original intentions, the man in blue found that "the only way to police a ghetto is to be oppressive." Policemen represent "the force of the white world, and that world's real intentions are, simply, for that world's criminal profit and ease, to keep the black man corralled up here, in his place." Clubs and guns remind the residents of the costs of resistance. The citizens of Harlem retaliate by unremitting hatred of the policeman. "He moves through Harlem, therefore, like an occupying soldier in a bitterly hostile country; which is precisely what, and where he is, and is the reason he walks in twos and threes." No matter how unimaginative a man on a ghetto post might be, he has to realize the inhuman conditions under which most of its residents must live, and to be uneasy.[27]

> He can retreat from his uneasiness only in one direction: into a callousness which very shortly becomes second nature. He becomes more callous, the population becomes more hostile, and the situation becomes more tense, and the police force is increased. One day, to everyone's astonishment, someone drops a match in the powder keg and everything blows up. Before the dust has settled or the blood congealed, editorials, speeches, and civil-rights commissions are loud in the land, demanding to know what happened. What happened is that Negroes want to be treated like men.

Baldwin's eloquent words, published in 1961, foreshadowed the actions of Harlem in 1964, of Watts in 1965, of Detroit and Newark in 1967, and of a number of cities, especially Washington, D.C. in 1968. Many of the ghetto upheavals of these years were precipitated by a police-civilian incident. In Harlem it was the fatal shooting of a black teen-ager by an off-duty white police lieutenant, and in Newark allegations of brutal police treatment of a black cab driver and of police charging a group of civilians who had gathered outside the station house.[28] The riots provide the most spectacular manifestation of the breakdown of police-minority groups relations; there are also substantial problems involved in day-to-day contacts.

The motto on New Orleans patrol cars reads "to protect and to serve"; that on Cleveland's emphasizes the department's commitment to all citizens. But, as Baldwin points out, many ghetto residents do not agree with this conception of the police role. To them the police are oppressors, hired Hessians of the dorminant whites whose function it is to keep the lid on, to remind the minority poor of their powerlessness, to milk the community with their demands for payoffs from the numbers' operators and prostitutes, and to keep established white areas safe from contamination.

The police, recruited from those social groups most hostile and fearful of blacks, the white working and lower-middle classes, may have their prejudices intensified by the nature of their work, although attitude studies show policemen in all-white precincts just as hostile to blacks as their colleagues who patrol the ghetto. The police subculture perceives and transmits to its white members images of strong antipathy between policemen and blacks no matter what conditions are in a particular city. Black policemen are more influenced in their views of these matters by the climate of the community in which they work.[29] As sociologist William Westley pointed out many years ago, policemen are trained to demand respect and deference from lower-class civilians. They cannot count on the moral authority of their uniforms—indeed as Baldwin indicates the reverse is true—so they must impress on the civilians they deal with that they are ready to use force to achieve this goal. In the department Westley studied, the most important reason advanced by policemen for the use of force was to induce respect. The policeman must "take charge"; if he backs down to a civilian, he makes the work of his fellow officers that much more difficult and dangerous.[30]

The results have been counterproductive; police hostility and belligerency breed increased community resentment and violent resistance to police action. This in turn heightens the policeman's sense of fear and danger and makes him more likely either to avoid a troublesome situation, and thus not provide protection for a potential or actual victim in a criminal or disorderly incident, or to take aggressive action at the first sign of disrespect or potential resistance.

The state of police-community relations assumes such vital importance not only because of the legal monopoly the police have on the use of force and their ability to deprive a person of liberty and mark him for life by making an arrest, but also because lower-class people often use the police as a general social service agency. The police are one of the few agencies available on a round-the-clock basis, seven days a week. The only other services similarly available are the emergency agencies, such as the fire department, the emergency rooms of hospitals, and the crisis maintenance crews of the utilities. These agencies have highly specialized functions; they come into play with the occurrence of specific situations, a fire, a bad automobile accident, or a breakdown of a gas or water line. But the police have a very broad mandate; preserving the peace and keeping order may involve them in a wide variety of situations, often highly emotional and personal in nature. Moreover, lower-class people call on the police in circumstances where middle-class people consult some other agency. A middle-class marriage going on the rocks leads to the services of a clergyman, a marriage counselor, or divorce attorney; a lower-class family dispute can get physical and have the neighbors calling the cops. People in trouble or disturbed at two o'clcok in the morning know that the police will have someone on the other end of the line. If it is impossible to sleep because of a noisy party next door, or the possibly paranoid fear of prowlers, the police are the one agency that might reasonably be expected to do something about it.[31]

Since the police are so often called upon for peace-keeping and general-service functions, their attitude toward this aspect of their work is critically important. If the police conceive of their role primarily as law enforcement, they will terminate noncriminally related contacts abruptly as a waste of time and manpower, as not real police work. If they are hostile toward the people they serve, they will render any service grudgingly and condescendingly and in such manner as to remind ghetto dwellers of their powerlessness and oppressed condition. The combination of indifference toward peacekeeping functions and hostility to minority members often breeds animosity between the police and civilians even in noncriminal situations. Policemen who realize the importance of their non-law-enforcement functions do a great service both to the people they serve, who often have no other recourse than to call them, and to the state of police-community relations. Policemen who provide support for people in trouble and who do so in a civil manner make a significant contribution to urban life.[32]

According to George Berkley, police in western Europe do emphasize their general service functions, all of the varied things police do that are not really law enforcement. In many instances European officers think of themselves as akin to social workers.[33] Most American policemen would sneer at such a job description. Despite the fact that more calls to the police relate to disputes and disturbances than crimes per se, and even though most policemen spend most of their time on matters other than law enforcement, the popular image of the police is that of crime-fighters. As previously noted, the more professional the department, the more likely this is to be the case. Even in departments lacking the professional orientation of a William Parker, the "good collar" or the "good pinch" paves the way for recognition and advancement.[34]

The dream of almost every rookie patrolman is to get out of "the bag" (the uniform) and into the detective bureau. (Police slang differs widely from one city to another, an indication of the isolation of individual departments and the absence of lateral movement within police work. "Bag" is a New York expression.) The detective by definition is involved in the discovery and apprehension of criminals; the patrolman deals with the whole range of police activities, most of which deal with noncriminal matters. Yet surprisingly, most criminal arrests are made by the patrol force, not the detectives. To move from patrol to the detective bureau usually requires either a good connection or a good pinch. If the good pinch involves a gun battle, so much the better. The good pinch not only brings individual recognition and prestige, it also justifies the department to the public and takes the pressure off. The public demands action on major crimes, especially homicide where children or respectable adults are the victims. A speedy arrest in such a case reassures the citizens that the police department is doing its job.[35]

Police-training manuals and programs reinforce the law-enforcement conception of "real police work" as opposed to the service and peace-keeping tasks which occupy the majority of police time and manpower. College programs refer to "law-enforcement technology," while police academies spend considerable time upon evidence in criminal cases, from its gathering and collecting to the legal and judicial determinations of its admissibility in court. In many training programs, handling the domestic dispute—one of the most frequent police calls and one of the trickiest to handle—receives less than one hour of classroom time.[36]

The importance of specialized training in this area has recently been demonstrated. In 1967 New York established a pilot program, a Family Crisis Intervention Unit which began in a single precinct. Men with specialized training in psychology handle these calls, with an eye to restoring domestic tranquility without making an arrest or escalating actual or potential violence by their presence.

The value of the project can be seen in comparing the experience of the experimental precinct with a matched control precinct where domestic disputes were handled in the traditional manner. In twenty-two months the experimental precinct where the Family Crisis Intervention Unit was established had three times as many interventions as the control precinct; many of these were repeated interventions in the same family. People in trouble obviously came to be more willing to call on the police for help when they learned that the men involved were sympathetic and skilled. In the control precinct there was a higher rate of assault and homicide generally and specifically within families. The Family Crisis Intervention Unit lowered the level of violence by aiding people before their tensions and disputes reached the violent state. There were no homicides in any family where the unit had intervened. And since a significant proportion of all assaults and homicides occur within family groups, the possibilities for a general reduction in violence are substantial. Traditionally the domestic dispute has accounted for a high proportion of police injuries; men and women enraged at each other frequently turn on the policeman when he arrives. But no officer in the Family Crisis Intervention Unit was unjured while on the job during these twenty-two months.[37]

Men assigned to this unit must believe that this is "real police work" and that their status is not compromised among their fellows and the public as a whole. For this to happen, the department as a whole and the public at large must come to see that keeping the peace and easing tensions is not only legitimate police activity, but perhaps the most important and most realizable occupational goal the police can establish.

It might be impossible to get the newspapers and television to deemphasize their coverage of the sensational, whether it be exposés of police corruption, medals for police heroics, or concentrated attention on major crimes involving respectable people. Police departments themselves, however, in their training programs and their reward systems, should give more emphasis to their peacekeeping and general-service roles. Humane and effective handling of domestic disputes should not be limited to a few men in experimental precincts. If a man does an effective job in restoring order in troublesome situations without making an arrest or using force, he should be recognized and rewarded just as much as the man who makes a good pinch. In practice patrolmen deal with disputes and disturbances by "cooling out" the participants and without making any arrests.[38] But that fact is not emphasized in the popular media. Both superior officers and civilian commentators should encourage policemen to be conciliators rather than to seek confrontations in "field interrogations" and the like. Textbooks and curricula for college and in-service training programs for future and existing policemen should recognize the nature and the importance of their general place in urban society. Achieving a reorientation of the police role both among civilians and within departments will not be easy at a time of public and political concern about crime in the streets.[39]

Moreover, as James Baldwin suggests, as long as blacks are systematically excluded and deprived, the police will be hated as the most visible symbol of that oppression no matter how they perform. The police suffer from the sins of society as a whole; almost as much as the residents of the ghetto, they are "niggers" who bear the brunt of social hypocrisy. Society has created the ghetto and then condemned the residents for the negative results and charged the police with picking up the pieces. As long as this pattern continues, it may be impossible for departments to improve community relations no matter what they do. Remaking the police image of their social role may bring only marginal or incidental gains, but that is at least better than nothing.[40] And who knows, it might be just possible to reverse the negative vicious circle now prevailing in which hostility feeds upon hostility by a more positive one in which police attention and concentration upon their general-service role might increase public respect and cooperation with the police in their law-enforcement role.

Civilian cooperation is vital to effective police work, no matter how defined. Citizen initiative was taken for granted in the days before the establishment of organized police. A police officer in the eighteenth or early nineteenth century acted only after being hired by a citizen. An organized police, designed as "preventive," had the legal authority to intervene in private affairs without being called upon to do so. But the legal power and the workaday reality are not the same thing. The vast majority of police intervention is "reactive," entering a situation after being called upon to do so by citizens, rather than "proactive," in which the policeman enters on his own initiative. This formulation is well developed by Albert J. Reiss, Jr. in his book, *The Police and the Public*.[41]

Reiss and his research associates rode in the back of patrol cars observing police-citizen encounters. Only rarely did cars on patrol come upon a crime or disturbance in progress. In almost all cases, someone had to call the communications center, which then dispatched a car to deal with the situation. If no one decides to call, the police will not find out about it. For the most part, civilians will call only when they see some personal advantage; they are not likely to ask the police to intervene out of a sense of public obligation. If citizens are assured of police civility and a willingness to provide whatever service is required, it seems probable that they will call more frequently and cooperate more fully when the police arrive.

Civilians are much more likely to resent "proactive" interventions such as stopping a motorist for speeding or those other cases when a policeman decides to intervene in a citizen's affairs on his own initiative. Policemen know this and so avoid such encounters whenever possible. A departmental emphasis on "aggressive preventive patrol" thus runs counter to citizen beliefs about when policemen may validly intervene in people's lives and the desires of patrolmen themselves. The police receive the most cooperation from civilians, and are therefore most effective, when there is a climate of civility between police and their constituency that encourages people to ask them to intervene and to accept that intervention as legitimate.[42]

Paradoxically, better police performance will probably make an individual department look bad. If police efficiency is judged by the clearance rate, the ratio between the number of crimes cleared by arrest compared to the number of crimes known to the police, the more people are encouraged to call and report the worse the clearance rate, and therefore the department's image, will be. Perhaps departments should be judged more by the willingness of people to call on them. The President's Commission found in a study of high-crime precincts that at least four times as many crimes occurred as were reported to the police because civilians would not call if they did not see any advantage for themselves or if they were likely to be treated uncivilly.[43] If a department responds effectively and civilly to calls for service, whether in criminal or non-criminal matters, there will be a much greater number of crimes known to the police. Such a rise should be considered as a hopeful rather than a distressing statistic, provided that departments have enough resources to handle the complaints.

The general-service, peace-keeping, and law-enforcement functions of the police, may be conceptually separable, but in practice there is considerable overlap. How well the police perform in one area may determine whether citizens decide to mobilize them in another. If policemen do a good job "cooling" disputes, they will probably get more criminal calls. Secondly, when a policeman is dispatched, he is never sure of the kind of situation he is entering. A tenant at odds with his landlord may think himself the victim of a crime, when there is only a civil dispute in law. How does anyone know when a peace-keeping problem may become a criminal situation? Is an argument in danger of becoming an assault? Will the parties in a domestic dispute turn on the policeman? One of the hazards of police work is that a man is likely to get hurt when he least expects it. A seemingly ordinary situation may explode into violence with little or no warning. Joseph Wambaugh's novel *The New Centurions* makes this point very effectively. Wambaugh is a veteran Los Angeles police officer. When the policeman intervenes, he is never sure whether it will be as service officer, peace-keeper, or law-enforcer, and sometimes he will have to change roles during an encounter. Albert Reiss has demonstrated that the prospects for injury to a police officer are much greater when he intervenes on his own authority than when he is asked to by a citizen. Probably there is also greater danger when he intervenes at the behest of a third party, as in the case of many domestic disputes.[44]

For these reasons there is justification for some skepticism about proposals to remove general-service functions from the police. Those observers who are concerned about the crime rate often propose that all non-law-enforcement functions be given to some other agency to free the police to concentrate on criminal matters. Why should patrolmen give out dog licences or provide ambulance service, as they do in a number of cities? Almost everyone would agree, I think, that there are some functions which could easily be transferred to other departments. The men who have a soft berth in passing out dog licenses would disagree as would those who have developed an amazing amount of interior work to be done to escape the rigors of the streets. But if the police did not provide round-the-clock availability for noncriminal matters, some other agency would have to be established which did. It would need the same sort of automobile and communications equipment that the police now have. On balance, then, it makes sense to continue to maintain police departments as general-service agencies with the emphasis on peace-keeping and law-enforcement.

Another possibility would be to separate policemen into those who would concentrate on law enforcement and those who would perform various other functions. This separation already exists with the division between the detective and the patrol branches, but some observers wish to go further. The President's Commisson on Law Enforcement and the Administration of Justice recommended three levels of entry into police departments. The first level would be that of community-service officer, a position open to young men between the ages of 17 and 21 who would perform many of the general-service functions of the police. Their law-enforcement powers would be limited and they would not carry arms. The second level would be that of police officer, open to community-service officers or men who joined the department after some further education. The police officer would direct traffic, deal with disturbances, and handle other routine patrol matters. The highest entry level, also open to men from the other units who had proven themselves, would be that of police agent. Agents would require at least two years of college before appointment, with the ultimate goal of a bachelor's degree for all agents. The agent would perform the most sensitive and demanding departmental tasks, whether working with juveniles or investigating major crimes.

The proposal would serve to encourage both men with higher education and slum youth to enter police work. Varying entry levels would mean that not all police officers had to begin as patrolmen, thus making the initial stages of a police career more attractive to ambitious and well-educated men. On the other hand, recruitment of minority youth, not necessarily high school graduates and even those with minor arrest records, would help bridge the gap between police and community in inner-city neighborhoods. This proposed organizational change is intended to broaden the range of police recruiting above working- and lower-middle-class men to college grads and below to street youth. The commission further recommended that blacks and Spanish-speaking men be recruited at all levels and not simply as community-service officers. Furthermore, movement from one level to another should be encouraged with age and further education.

Police agents, police officers, and community-service officers could be organized into neighborhood teams to provide police service within a limited area, thus decentralizing police operations to some extent and, hopefully, overcoming some of the separation between police and community so common in many cities. The police agent, the most highly educated and skilled member of the team, would replace existing detectives as well as supervise the work of officers and community-service officers.[45]

On the negative side there exists the possibility that this proposal will slight peace-keeping and general service in favor of crime deterrence and detection. The commission did recognize that police service functions are important, even to the point of recommending that officers participate in general community planning because of their knowledge of conditions which hamper human development. For example, policemen would know about substandard housing and street conditions or other hazards to the people of an area. But for the most part, the commission, in keeping with its charge to concentrate on crime and law enforcement and its membership of professionals in the field, gave top priority to crime-fighting in its hierarchy of police duties. There may also be some danger that officers and community-service officers would be treated as, and have the self-image of, second-class citizens. Departments would have to be careful to avoid the same kind of fragmentation and jealousy among the different classifications proposed that now prevails between patrol and detective forces. Sociologist Rodney Stark proposes that all men and women doing investigative work be separated from the police department entirely and put under the district attorney's control.

In the final analysis, the most important step departments can take to reverse the current trend of escalating hostility between themselves and minority groups is to end the double standard of police performance which cuts across class and ethnic lines. Middle-class whites usually perceive the police as protectors, except in their role as speed-limit enforcers, whereas members of lower-class groups, especially black and Spanish-speaking, see officers as corrupt, disrespectful, and brutal. In a poll taken for the President's Commission by the National Opinion Research Center, 63 percent of whites felt the police are "almost all honest"; only 30 percent of the nonwhites answered yes to this. Even more startling is that 10 percent of the nonwhites thought the police to be "almost all corrupt." While 15 percent of the nonwhites thought the police did an "excellent" job, 16 percent believed they did a "poor" job. The comparable figures for whites were 23 percent for "excellent" and 7 percent for "poor." In the years since this poll was taken, the image of the police among minority groups deteriorated even further.[46]

To decrease minority distrust and open more lines of contact between police and people will not be easy, as is demonstrated by the history of community-relations programs and proposals for civilian review boards to investigate citizen complaints against policemen. Most departments either do not have community-relations units at all or use them as public-relations gimmicks. In 1964 only 37 of 165 cities had community-relations units within their police departments. In too many instances these units were separated from the rest of police operations, staffed by light-duty men, or regarded as a dead end from which ambitious officers wished to escape. According to the Vorenburg Commission, an effective program required a large number of men, perhaps 1 percent of all sworn officers, with a full-time member in each precinct under the command of a senior officer who reported directly to the chief administrator. The unit had to be open to community feelings and to have a voice in appointments, assignments, and promotions. Under no circumstances should it be used to gather intelligence.[47]

Line officers of various ranks simply do not believe in community relations. As cops become increasingly defensive, any criticism stemming from citizens' groups, politicians, or speakers at community-relations meetings is bitterly resented. Policemen want to avoid or prevent situations where criticisms might be made. To some line officers, community relations means Commie relations, providing a forum for radicals and loudmouths and in general consorting with the enemy. San Francisco had one of the nation's most effective programs until 1967, when the district captains, backed by extensive rank-and-file support, succeeded in stripping it of any power. Its commander, Lieutenant Dante Andreotti, who had organized the unit in 1962, left the San Francisco Police Department for more congenial employment in the Department of Justice. Subsequent to the demise of the community-relations program, the San Francisco force has shown increased evidence of police militance and hostility to any external control.[48]

Civilian review boards, actual and potential, have had an even more difficult time. Existing review boards lack disciplinary authority; in most cases they can make recommendations to the commissioner or chief, who can either support or reject the recommendations. They do provide an avenue of complaint outside the department itself, so that civilians who feel that they have been abused or otherwise been the victim of malpractice can have the assurance that their complaints will receive a careful hearing. However, most boards lack independent investigative capabilities. People who might be intimidated by other officers would not hesitate to bring their complaints before a civilian body which would be free from the group pressure of the police to protect each other if at all possible.

It is for these reasons that policemen fiercely resist the establishment of such boards and work toward their abolition where they do exist. They certainly do not want civilians second-guessing them. To department members civilians can never judge complex matters of police judgment. Insulated, fearful, and hostile, the police would like to eliminate all civilian influence in their work. They resent intellectuals, labor leaders, and minority group members who might staff such boards and argue that the existence of such review handcuffs them and makes them afraid to take proper action. In their view only men with police experience can judge the validity of a given action.[49] Policemen feel secure only if they are being judged by their own. As men of action who are called upon to make rapid decisions which may have vital consequences, policemen do not want to admit the possibility that they might have made a mistake. This would impair their self-confidence and make decisions more difficult in the future.[50]

Philadelphia provides an interesting case study of the various forces for and against independent review. The Philadelphia civilian review board was established in 1958 after a particularly outrageous case of police mistreatment of a black civilian. The board functioned effectively for a number of years, following procedures designed to give maximum fairness both to complainant and officer. The police, however, never accepted the moral authority of the board and fought constantly against its continued existence. When a sympathetic mayor, James Tate, came into office, the department succeeded in eliminating the board.[51] In New York City in 1966, the Patrolmen's Benevolent Association forced the civilian review board, established under Mayor John Lindsay, to a referendum, in which the board was abolished by a vote of two to one.[52] Many middle- and stable working-class residents obviously saw no reason for the board. To them it looked like a plot hatched by blacks, radicals, and upper-class do-gooders to destroy police effectiveness and endanger law and order. They were more concerned about criminals than about police misconduct because the police usually treated them civilly, if not respectfully; and they had increased reason for concern about being victimized by criminals. People in such circumstances could not see why others hated the men in uniform; many of them were probably not aware of the extent to which police behavior varied toward different social and racial groups.

William A. Westley has offered the most convincing explanation for the differences in police behavior toward various social groups in his book *Violence and the Police,* published in 1970 but based on a 1951 doctoral dissertation. Westley studied the department in Gary, Indiana, an industrial city of about 140,000 people, with a large black and recent immigrant population and a substantial number of transient, unattached males. Policemen in Gary were recruited from large working-class families where there was little aspiration for higher mobility. The most important motive for becoming an officer was the security and good pension that the job offered. When a young man became a patrolman he found that he had done more than just take a job; he entered into a new social milieu, almost a way of life. The irregular hours, the separation from the community, the pattern of discipline, and the lure of the pension kept men highly conscious of their occupational and social role.[53]

As an occupational and social group, the police came to define their goals primarily as the maintenance of their position and their self-respect, not the enforcement of the law or keeping the peace. The men Westley studied felt themselves to be a small and isolated group in the midst of a hostile public. Most civilians either patronized or despised them and posed constant threats to their security and self-esteem. To counter these threats, the police adopted the norms of secrecy and violence. Anyone who violated the norm of secrecy was a "stoolie" and suffered the silent treatment. This was a powerful sanction as it deprived the man of necessary information. Secrecy demanded that a man never inform on a brother officer, even if it meant commiting perjury. Outsiders were not to be told department business; anything that might bring discredit upon an individual or the department had to be suppressed. In a later study of Philadelphia policemen, Leonard Savitz found that older patrolmen who had little prospect for promotion most strongly supported this norm of secrecy, whereas detectives were most ready to inform on fellow officers. Detectives also placed a higher premium on making a good pinch than in aiding an officer in distress. In general, detectives were most prone to place their individual interests ahead of police solidarity.[54]

The second major norm sanctioned the use of violence where it was not permitted by law. For example, policemen justified the use of force against sex offenders. The public put great pressure on the department to deal with such offenders, often in situations where the victims refused to testify or where women brought charges against men to further other ends. The police found these cases to be confusing and troublesome, and one accepted way to deal with a peeping tom or exposer was to administer a good beating. The man involved was hardly likely to protest because public knowledge of his actions would bring worse injury than the beating. Aggressive drunks caused numerous breaches of the peace and posed threats to the policeman's self-esteem, his person, or the cleanliness of his uniform. The club could settle these matters before they became serious. In Gary most of the drunks were black, and the prejudiced white policemen thought blacks inherently inferior anyway and criminal to boot, thereby stengthening the norm of the use of force in such cases.

The most common reason given for the use of force was to induce respect for the police. The maxim "You gotta make them respect you" was drilled into the rookies and became, along with the maintenance of secrecy, their most important occupational guideline. In dealing with some elements of the population, children and higher-class men and women, policemen believed that the best way to induce respect was to be respectful themselves. They often resented the patronizing attitude of the "better elements," but they respected their political power and their access to communications media.

With slum dwellers, and especially black slum dwellers, the pattern was far different. Here officers felt themselves to be in an alien and hostile world, as indicated previously in the quotation from James Baldwin. The police did not question the social patterns that created the ghetto; indeed departments have always functioned to protect and advance the interests of the dominant groups in the community. What they did insist on was respect from the slum dwellers who they knew despised them. The use of rough treatment, up to and including force, was an accepted way to achieve this respect. In Gary, policemen did not talk to blacks; they shouted at them in the hope that this would curb lying. Policemen considered blacks to be inherently inferior and prone toward crime. Verbal or physical attacks upon the policemen's self-esteem could easily trigger violent responses. The maintenance of respect and self-esteem took precedence over the enforcement of the law.[55]

So twenty years ago, policemen and civilians faced each other in hostile confrontation; in the intervening time the polarization has obviously become much more pronounced as a result of the social changes outlined earlier in this chapter. The situation became even more serious with the emergence of large-scale rioting among ghetto residents and dissident students and hangers-on around universities in the second half of the 1960s.

References

1. This theme is fully developed in James F. Richardson, *The New York Police: Colonial Times to 1901*. New York: Oxford University Press, 1970.

2. Willaim F. Whyte, *Street Corner Society*. Chicago: University of Chicago Press, 1955, pp. 123–139.

3. Richardson, *op. cit.*, pp. 195–201.

4. Melvyn Dubofsky, *When Workers Organize: New York City in the Progressive Era*. Amherst, Mass.: University of Massachusetts Press, 1968, pp. 63, 92–97.

5. Irving Bernstein, *Turbulent Years: A History of the American Worker, 1933-1941*. Boston: Houghton-Mifflin, 1970, pp. 485–490.

6. David Brody, *Steelworkers in America: The Nonunion Era*. New York: Harper Torchbooks, 1969, pp. 250–253.

7. For a review of the recent literature, see Deborah Johnson and Robert J. Gregory, "Police-Community Relations in the United States: A Review of Recent Literature and Projects," *The Journal of Criminal Law, Criminology, and Police Science* 62 (March 1971), 94–103.

8. For a good journalistic survey of the plight of cities, see Jeanne Lowe, *Cities in a Race with Time*. New York: Random House, 1967.

9. David Ward, *Cities and Immigrants, A Geography of Change in Nineteenth Century America*. New York: Oxford University Press, 1971, is excellent on the inner-city concentration of employment before 1900.

10. On recent employment patterns, see John F. Kain, "The Distribution and Movement of Jobs and Industry," in John Q. Wilson (ed.), *The Metropolitan Enigma*. Garden City, New York: Anchor Books, 1970.

11. Kenneth T. Jackson, "Metropolitan Government versus Political

Autonomy: Politics on the Crabgrass Frontier," in Kenneth T. Jackson and Stanley K. Schultz (eds.), *Cities in American History*. New York: Alfred Knopf, 1972. pp. 452-457.

12. Frances Fox Piven and Richard A. Cloward, *Regulating the Poor: The Functions of Public Welfare*. New York: Pantheon Books, 1971, pp. 200-217.

13. Arnold R. Weber, "Labor Market Perspectives of the New City," in Benjamin Chinitz (ed.), *City and Suburb: The Economics of Metropolitan Growth*. Englewood Cliffs, N.J.: Prentice Hall, 1964, pp. 66-81.

14. Allen Spear, *Black Chicago*. Chicago: University of Chicago Press, 1967, pp. 24-26.

15. Cornelius W. Willemse, *Behind the Green Lights*. New York: Alfred Knopf, 1931, pp. 84-86.

16. National Advisory Commission on Civil Disorders, *Report*. New York: E.P. Dutton, 1968, p. 309.

17. Arthur Niederhoffer, *Behind the Shield: The Police in Urban Society*. Garden City: Anchor Books, 1969, pp. 138-39.

18. Albert J. Reiss, Jr., *The Police and the Public*. New Haven: Yale University Press, 1971, pp. 147-151.

19. President's Commission on Law Enforcement and the Administration of Justice. *The Challenge of Crime in a Free Society*. New York: Avon Books, 1968, pp. 96-97.

20. *Ibid.*, pp. 212-224.

21. President's Commisson on Law Enforcement and the Administration of Justice, *Task Force Report: The Police*. Washington, D.C.: U.S. Government Printing Office, 1967, pp. 181-190.

22. Irving Piliavin and Scott Briar, "Police Encounters with Juveniles," *American Journal of Sociology*, 70 (September 1964), pp. 206-214.

23. Paul Chevigny, *Police Power: Police Abuses in New York City*. New York: Pantheon Books, 1969, pp. 137-144.

24. See Piliavin and Briar, *supra*, note 22.

25. Jerome Skolnick, *Justice Without Trial*. New York: John Wiley, 1966.

26. Joseph Wambaugh, *The New Centurions*. Boston: Little, Brown and Company, 1970.

27. James Baldwin, *Nobody Knows My Name: More Notes of a Native Son*. New York: Dial Press, 1961, pp. 65-67.

28. *The Challenge of Crime*, p. 206.

29. Eugene W. Grove and Peter H. Rossi, "Police Perceptions of a Hostile Ghetto: Realism or Projection," in Harlan Hahn (ed.), *Police in Urban Society*. Beverly Hills: Sage, 1971.

30. William A. Westley, *Violence and the Police*. Cambridge, Mass.: M.I.T. Press, 1970, pp. 121-128.

31. Elaine Cumming et al., "Policeman as a Philosopher, Guide, and Friend," *Social Problems*, 12 (Winter 1965), pp. 278-286.

32. Herman Goldstein, "Police Response to Urban Crisis," in Jameson

Doing (ed.), "The Police in a Democratic Society: A Symposium," *Public Administration Review* 28 (September–October 1968), pp. 417–423.

33. George E. Berkley, *The Democratic Policeman*. Boston: Beacon Press, 1969.

34. Westley, *op. cit.,* pp. 139–140.

35. *Ibid.* Also, Niederhoffer, *op. cit.,* pp. 82–84.

36. Raymond I. Parnas, "The Police Response to Domestic Disturbances," *Wisconsin Law Review* 1967 (Fall) pp. 914–960.

37. Morton Bard, "Family Intervention Police Teams as a Community Mental Health Resource," *The Journal of Criminal Law, Criminology and Police Science* 60 (June 1969) pp. 247–250.

38. Reiss, *op. cit.,* p. 76.

39. Some Universities's programs in law enforcement put greater emphasis on law enforcement than peace-keeping, although including a substantial amount of "human relations" material.

40. James Q. Wilson, "Dilemmas of Police Administration," in Jameson Doig (ed.), *op. cit.,* pp. 407–417.

41. Reiss, *op cit.,* pp. 88–105, 115–116.

42. *Ibid.,* pp. 57–65.

43. *Challenge of Crime,* pp. 97–100.

44. Wambaugh, *op. cit.,* pp. 118–120, 235–237, 374–375.

45. Task Force Report, pp. 122–124.

46. *Challenge of Crime,* pp. 255–257.

47. Task Force Report, pp. 150–151.

48. Rodney Stark, *Police Riots.* Belmont, Cal.: Wadsworth, 1972, pp. 204–205.

49. William W. Turner, *The Police Establishment.* New York: Putnam, 1968, pp. 209–210.

50. Westley, *op. cit.,* p. 81.

51. Turner, *op. cit.,* pp. 207–208.

52. Chevigny, *op. cit.,* pp. 105–106.

53. Westley, *op. cit.,* pp. 27–28, 44–45, 205–210.

54. *Ibid.,* pp. 110–118.

55. *Ibid.,* pp. 72–73, 96–99, 121–122, 121–152. In particular pp. xii–xvii where Westley provides a useful summary of some of the major changes in police-community relations in the twenty years since his study was done.

police aNd justice iN saN dieqo

JOSEPH D. LOHMAN AND GORDON E. MISNER

A. The Police and Due Process

The "Administration of Criminal Justice" is a term which seeks to describe a complicated *process* designed by our society to engage and deal with the problems of crime and delinquency and its threat to the larger community. This term describes a *process* and some of the implications of this term become apparent when one considers the large number of formal agencies which exist to deal with different aspects of the problems of crime and delinquency. The police, the prosecutor, the courts, and other agencies are formally organized to operate within at least a portion of the process of justice. In addition, large numbers of unofficial agencies or community organizations are also organized to give assistance and to have a role in the *process.*

Justice, therefore, is not easily achieved. Each of the agencies—official or unofficial—which takes part in the process of administering criminal justice may have either a functional or dysfunctional effect upon the entire system. The task of one agency may be assisted or hampered by the policies and procedures which are followed by another agency. The actions of any one of these agencies may have unintended consequences for the planned programs and goals of another agency, or of the process as a whole.

In the United States, it is assumed that the courts will occupy a dominant

Source: The Police and the Community, A Report prepared for the President's Commission on Law Enforcement and Administration of Justice, Vol. I, pp. 132-140. Published by the United States Government Printing Office, October, 1966.

position in the administration of criminal justice. It is the courts, in particular the appellate courts, which interpret the meaning and scope of such principles as due process of law, the presumption of innocence, the reasonableness of searches and seizures, etc. Few of our citizens, however, come into any contact at *any* time during their lives with the functioning of our appellate courts. If citizens are to have dealings with any of the agencies of justice, then this contact for most of them will come about as the result of their dealing directly with lower, magistrate-level courts, or with the police.

Justice, for the most part, can be measured by the actual contact which the average citizen has with the police or lower courts. The enunciations of the highest courts notwithstanding, the content of justice, the real meaning of justice, is determined by the types of relationships the individual can consistently expect to receive when he deals with these two lower-level agencies. If the average citizen—one without personal power or influence—can reasonably expect to receive fair and sympathetic treatment from the police and from the lower courts, then justice to him is both fair and sympathetic. It is for these reasons, therefore, that the operating policies and procedures of the police are of crucial importance. Contacts with the police, more than any other matter, determine citizen evaluation of the administration of criminal justice, as a whole. Justice, in fact, consists of those rights which the average citizen enjoys "out on the streets."

The role of the police in the administration of criminal justice can be divided, basically, into six parts. They are as follows:

1. The prevention of crime.
2. The detection of crimes which have been committed.
3. Identification of the person or persons responsible for crimes.
4. Apprehension of the person or persons responsible.
5. Detention of the person for processing by the judiciary; and
6. Presentation of the evidence to the prosecutor.

Throughout the performance of these functions, any attempt to deprive a person of any of the rights guaranteed him by law represents a violation of due process.

Police violation of due process may take the form either of technical legal violations or they may, in fact, be more subtle violations of the "spirit" of due process. Technical legal violation of due process may take a variety of forms. The police may falsify the evidence which they present, or they may be guilty of illegal arrests or detention. On the other hand, the police may have used an excessive amount of force in apprehending or detaining the person accused of the crime; or they may have performed unreasonable or illegal searches or seizures. In addition, they may have used physical or psychological coercion in extracting a confession or admission, or they may have inflicted all sorts of other punishments upon the person which are prohibited by law. Police violations of due process, therefore, may take many forms. Consequently, a careful examination of the practices employed by the San Diego Police Department was made in an effort to determine possible violations of due process. If violations were found, procedures were established by the research team which would enable a distinction to be made between random or accidental individual violations and those which took the form of a traditional and systematic organizational violation of due process. The rationale for this orientation by the research team was that it is just as important to uncover propensities toward the violation of due process as it is to uncover the actual violations. A report of our findings in this regard is submitted.

It is noteworthy that nowhere in the findings of this study were allegations of the falsification of evidence or the forcible extraction of admissions and confessions advanced by any person interviewed; nor were they otherwise suggested by observation and investigation. It can be assumed, however, that the high judicial standards which prevail today would make the exercise of these unconstitutional acts meaningless in the accomplishment of the police purpose. Accordingly it is not expected that any law enforcement agency would subscribe to technical practices which may have been more common in earlier times.

Allegations of unreasonable search have been implied by accounts of persons concerning officers making their field interrogations, particularly of juvenile subjects. Similarly, this kind of violation of due process, if substantiated, would be related to that of illegal detention, and, possibly, actual arrest not in conformity with the law. In addition, complaints of the use of excessive force, carrying the inference of an exactment of a kind of punishment outside the authority of law enforcement officers, were examined. All of these charges of due process violation were subjected to careful scrutiny.

First, it must be noted that the San Diego police officer is well indoctrinated in the principles of law and in their application to modern police practice. The manual of instruction placed in the hands of each officer lays great stress on the rights of the police and the restrictions placed upon them in accomplishing their mission.The test includes elaborate coverage of both federal and state court decisions which define the proper exercise of the duties imposed upon the police agency. A recent device for familiarizing all members of the Department with the evolving law on human rights is a three-hour classroom presentation on the subject. This training is prescribed for all police personnel.

Next, the matter of field interrogation presents itself. This is a field patrol procedure entailing the stopping and questioning of persons on the streets and in public places with the purpose either of disclosing criminal activities or of making a record of information to be employed in a later investigation of crime. Approximately 200,000 field interrogations are made annually. The majority of these apparently are directed towards juveniles. The manual of training for recruits devotes much space to the purpose and manner of making the field interrogation. Legal justification stemming from case law is presented in exacting form. While the Department makes a uniform denial that specific quotas are imposed upon the policeman to make field interrogations, it is apparent that the Patrol Division officers are required to submit a "fair" volume of reports on their activity in this regard. Departmental supervisors determine what is an appropriate number of field interrogations.

California law does not require that information be given to a police officer by a citizen *except* under very limited circumstances. Section 647 of the Penal Code, for example, prescribes that information as to identity and presence must be given only when one:

> ... loiters or wanders upon the street or from place to place without apparent business ... if the surrounding circumstances are such to indicate to a reasonable man that public safety demands such identification.

Evaluation of whether the San Diego Police Department abuses its authority in field interrogations is individualized. Certainly, there is much resentment over the practice.

While the resentment against the field interrogation embraced by certain persons may be high, there is no evidence that the widespread practice represents a violation of due process. That the field interrogation can be subject to abuse, that it can be employed to hurt one's dignity, that it may be at the core of a deficient (aspect of) relationship between the citizenry and the police must be recognized. However, it can be labeled as being either unconstitutional or otherwise illegal—*only* if it is used excessively or as a tool of harassment.

Unlawful arrest by the San Diego Police Department does not appear to be a major concern of citizens. There are few complaints charging false arrest, and no allegation has been made of such illegal action in the interview of any official involved in the administration of justice. Therefore it can be concluded that the action of the San Diego police officer in making arrests is usually in accord with the law.

Finally, there is the matter of undue force. One aspect of this is the policy of handcuffing all adult prisoners and many older juveniles. This policy was constantly mentioned by members of the Police Department, itself. It was also a matter of strong complaint by many citizens. The procedure is to handcuff persons' wrists behind their backs when transported from the scene of arrest to jail. The protection of the arresting officer—in most cases alone at the wheel of his vehicle—is repeatedly given by superior officers as the reason for this restraint. Since Sections 835 and 835a of the California Penal Code authorize the use of "reasonable" force and restraint, it would appear that the practice of handcuffing everyone represents no illegality or other violation of due process. The Department provides further precautions inasmuch as all patrol care are equipped with heavy wire screens between the front and back seats in order that no physical assaults may be made by prisoners. Also, every officer is out-fitted with a helmet, which he must wear at all times. The negative implications of a practical nature will be commented upon elsewhere.

Excessive physical force is the subject of widespread charges and some-times concrete complaints. In a sample of eighty [80] complaints made by citizens against members of the Patrol Division in the first six months of 1966, there were sixteen which charged some degree of physically abusive behavior. In addition, the commonly accepted use of the "sleeper hold" and the tempo-rary use of pressure on the vessels of the neck to deprive the brain of its blood supply might be considered as measures possibly implying a use of force in excess of that permitted by law.

Nevertheless, there is little substantial evidence of actual physical brutality by San Diego policemen. Department administrators are emphatic in their pronunciations that it will not be tolerated. Policemen deny its exercise. Repre-sentatives of other agencies engaged in the administration of justice, and mem-bers of the bar, discount rumors of its use. Even the most vociferous critics of the police attest to the absence of any regular exercise of physical abuse of persons by the police. Examination of the few actual complaints of physical brutality presented for our consideration offered little to substantiate the charges.

It can be said that technical-legal violations of due process by the San Diego Police Department are isolated. When they exist, they are individual acts and cannot be fairly interpreted as representing the consequence of a pattern of organizational attitude and practice. It is not part of the administrative style of the San Diego Police Department to encourage technical-legal violations of due process.

Due process, however, has another face, i.e., the "spirit" of due process, the spirit of fair play. In order to gain an insight into this aspect of due process, it is advisable to examine the role which the San Diego Police Department has set for itself and for its members. In this way, one can delineate the dominant concept of due process which characterizes members of the Department. It is necessary to determine if there is only a grudging acceptance of the "rules of the game," or if, in fact, the members of the Police Department use certain restrictions as a necessary and vital part of democratic policing. Begrudging adherence to the letter of due process may have a different social effect than willing, wholehearted acceptance. Much of the latter is dependent, of course, upon the top leadership of the Department. These high-ranking officers set the administrative and organizational tone and style with which the police mission is accomplished.

Comments by police officers upon the judicial process came to the atten-tion of researchers in a variety of ways. Interview schedules, of course, were designed to elicit the attitudes and comments of policemen about the process. Data which were accumulated on this point did not come, however, solely in response to specific questions by researchers on the point. Much of the data was volunteered or initiated spontaneously by officers prior to any specific question by interviewers. Comments were also accumulated during parts of random observations, in patrol cars, in headquarters, on the streets, etc. In addition, comments were accumulated as a result of panel method sessions which were held with members of the Police Department.

Of all the data, the striking characteristic is its uniformity. From the data accumulated in this research one could easily make the observation that policemen in San Diego represent almost a monolithic structure when they express an opinion about due process, the judicial process, the administration of justice, etc. There certainly must be exceptions to this typical attitude within the Police Department; but the research staff simply did not come into contact with them! Typical of responses which the staff encountered is this direct quotation which poses the question as a moral issue:

> I fail to see the moral rightness in allowing a killer to walk free because of technicality. I feel that in some ways this country has gone overboard in protecting the rights of the individual and lowering the rights of the general public as a whole.

Resentment over recent appellate court decisions is posed not only in moral terms, but also in political terms.

> ... if the courts want to release dangerous rapists and murderers because of technical problems related to arrest procedures that is the problem of the country and not really a problem of the police because the people are going to suffer as a result.

Our data demonstrate that officers throughout the San Diego Police Department, from the highest to the lowest ranks, are intensely concerned about the effect which recent appellate courts decisions (state and federal) have had upon their ability to do their work. High-ranking officers express particular concern over the effect they suppose these decisions will have on the task of apprehension. Officers on all levels point to these decisions as being a major factor in police morale.

Credit can be given Departmental leadership for having created an internal working environment which sustains high morale, a condition which prevails despite the supposed deleterious effect of court decisions. Patrolmen also point to recent court decisions as having an effect upon morale, and those able and willing to make projections predict that police morale will be even lower five years from now precisely because the court will impose "further restrictions" on police agents.

It is obvious from the various data collected that the police officer in

San Diego is comparatively well trained in the technical aspects of criminal law, procedure, and related portions of constitutional law. These matters are stressed throughout the Department in a variety of ways. They are covered extensively in both recruit and in-service training programs; legal matters are regular subjects of staff conferences, Department training memos, and in roll-call training. Data leaves little doubt that the police in San Diego are well-prepared in these areas of technical-legal knowledge. However, little emphasis is ever given to the theoretical framework upon which the laws are based.

On the other hand, it seems equally clear that little is done in the way of instilling knowledge and values of "American Institutions." Insufficient attention is apparently given to the matter of pointing out the social and democratic importance of due process, the presumption of innocence, and other legal theories which are basic components of a democracy. In no place does the data demonstrate that attention is given to such matters as the powerlessness of most persons when they are confronted by the legal resources of government. In no place does the data reveal that the "perspective" of the accused is dealt with in any form in Departmental training, supervision or leadership. Rather than this perspective, emphasis throughout the Department is upon techniques and methods of improving efficiency in such matters as investigation, apprehension, patrol procedures, etc.

This observation may seem to be petty or of minor significance to police officials. To the research staff, however, this matter may be of crucial importance and central to at least a portion of the police-community relations problem. Just as a teacher who ridicules the academic process or who is antiintellectual may have a dysfunctional effect upon the educational process for children, so too, a policeman who is "anti-process" may have a dysfunctional effect upon persons he encounters in his official capacity.

Ranking officers in San Diego, for example, are indignant when the Department is accused of "harassment." This is a charge which is often leveled at the Department by minority group persons. The Department denies the charge and takes the posture that such practices are specifically guarded against by close supervision. This enunciation of policy is, however, at variance with statements (and justifications) made by personnel on the operational level. Many officers stated in private conversations, for example, that motorcyclists are controlled by rigid vehicle "inspection" practices. These inspections are justified socially on the ground that they keep "undesirables" from congregating in the city and creating disturbances.

Other officers admit the practice of concentrating Departmental resources in sections of the city where "trouble-makers" are known to congregate. Although the deployment and procedures used are admittedly "harassing," they are rationalized on the ground that they are preventive in result. According to some police, they do keep the problems, which inevitably occur, from occurring, and this is the presumed social goal of police action. Furthermore, these practices are seen as being particularly effective in controlling juveniles, at least, harassment bordering upon "verbal brutality" is rationalized by some officers. To quote one officer who justified the practice:

> ... Sometimes it is necessary to embarrass, let us say, one teenager in front of his friends. If, for example, he can be verbally put down, no matter how this was done, the rest of his friends will sometimes then follow his example, once he has been put in his place. This is a tactic used by the Police Department, it is necessary, and it is comprised of things that a person would not normally say, but he feels that it was necessary to resort to.

The policeman in San Diego, therefore, is dedicated to doing things which experience tends to demonstrate have an effect upon his work-load and overall mission. He tends to resent those practices, complaints, or rules which restrict his application of "proven" methods. In San Diego, according to his folkways, the effectiveness of field interrogations, a show of force, selective enforcement, etc., has been "proven" to his satisfaction. To him, these methods work and he resents persons from the "outside" who question these methods.

It may be that the policeman is impressed more by utilitarianism than by the theoretical or symbolic implication of certain matters. He sees his job and his role in a particular way. He seems much less concerned about the theoretical function he may serve in the administration of criminal justice than he is by the ever-present danger that awaits him and the general society.

B. Differential Standards of Enforcement

It is not surprising that the minority community feels that the degree of law enforcement to which it is subjected differs from that exercised in parts of the city predominantly occupied by Caucasians.

Persons interviewed make conflicting allegations of too much and too little enforcement in minority group neighborhoods. For example, emphasis was placed by many on gross toleration of vice in the parks of Logan Heights. Heavy concentrations of rowdy youngsters, glue sniffing, gambling, and drinking—these were practices described as persisting in the Negro community while these same practices were being suppressed in the white neighborhoods.

On the other hand, there is a feeling in some quarters that the police do not respond to calls for assistance made by Negroes. At the same time, the police are presumed to go out of their way in enforcing the law against members of the minorities.

A widespread allegation made by both whites and Negroes is that the San Diego Police Department does discriminate against juveniles of all races. According to this belief, the juvenile is the chief target in traffic enforcement, and he is the most frequent subject of the field interrogation. The screening at the Mexican border check station also is directed at the juvenile. The heavy policing of high school sporting and social events is designed to cope with his supposed propensity to violate the law.

The expressed feeling that there is differential treatment of the young person is too common to be ignored. Like the Negro, the juvenile is highly visible and is easily singled out for enforcement attention. However, the incidence of crime and traffic violation committed by him, coupled with the youthful propensity of becoming involved in disturbances, makes a higher degree of enforcement directed at him easily explainable. The adult community readily accepts the screening to which the juvenile is subjected at the Tijuana border. Adults view the device as one designed for the juvenile's protection.

It is not the purpose of this study to pass on the merits of the police technique employed in juvenile enforcement. It may be questioned, however, whether the enforcement policy is sufficiently understood, in view of the undercurrent of thought which holds the young person to be the object of discriminatory police practice. Perhaps the Department is deficient in enunciating the significance of its enforcement policy as it relates to the young subject.

While the Department disclaims any official policy of double standards in law enforcement it, nevertheless, is manifested by many individual policemen. Thus, the minority community has gained the impression that the Department condones discrimination. Also, the increased incidence of vice activity and the added difficulty in suppressing it may have led to the assumption that it is condoned. The relatively high incidence of crime in the minority community are Departmental reasons for stepped up police activity which may be mistakenly considered discriminatory.

Concerning any lack of zeal in handling the request for police assistance made by the Negro, neither the study of complaints against police personnel, nor the personal observations of the researchers bears out this contention. There is no indication that the San Diego Police Department renders less service to the Negro complainant than in cases where it deals with the Caucasian. That an individual officer may exercise differential treatment of a race in occasional or several contacts must, however, be recognized.

CHAPTER **4-3**

THE CHICAGO POLICE
RIOT OF 1968

DANIEL WALKER AND THE CHICAGO STUDY TEAM

By about 5 p.m. Wednesday the U.S. Attorney's report says about 2000 persons, "mostly normally dressed," had already assembled at the [Conrad] Hilton [Hotel]. Many of these were demonstrators who had tired of waiting out the negotiations and had broken off from the marchers and made their way to the hotel. It appears that police already were having some difficulty keeping order at that location. Says the U.S. Attorney's report: "A large crowd had assembled behind the police line along the east wall of the Hilton. This crowd was heavily infiltrated with 'Yippie' types and was spitting and screaming obscene insults at the police."

A policeman on duty in front of the hotel later said that it seemed to him that the obscene abuses shouted by "women hippies" outnumbered those called out by male demonstrators "four to one." A common epithet shouted by the females, he said, was "Fuck you, pig." Others included references to policemen as "cock suckers" and "mother fuckers."

A short time later a reporter noticed a lot of debris being hurled from one of the upper floors of the Hilton. He climed into a police squad car parked in the area and with the aid of police binoculars saw that rolls of toilet paper were coming from the 15th floor, a location he pinpointed by counting down from the top of the building. He then went to the 15th floor and found that the sec-

Source: Rights in Conflict. A Report submitted to the National Commission on the Causes and Prevention of Violence, pp. 235–285. Published by the United States Government Printing Office, 1969.

311

tion the paper was coming from was rented by Senator McCarthy campaigners. He was not admitted to the suite.

If Dellinger's marchers in Grant Park now moved to the Hilton area, an additional 5000 demonstrators would be added to the number the police there would have to control......

The Crossing

At about 6 or 6:30 p.m., one of the march leaders announced by loudspeaker that the demonstrators would not be allowed to march to the Amphitheatre. He told the crowd to disperse and to re-group in front of the Conrad Hilton Hotel in Grant Park.....

Police in the area were in a far from cheerful mood. A neatly dressed sociology student from Minnesota says he stepped off the sidewalk onto the grass and two policemen pulled their billy clubs back as though ready to swing. One of them said, "You'd better get your fucking ass off that grass or I'll put a beautiful goddam crease in your fucking queer head." The student overheard another policeman say to a "hippie-looking girl of 14 or 15, 'You better get your fucking dirty cunt out of here.'" The growing feeling of entrapment was intensified and some witnesses noticed that police were letting people into the park but not out. The marshal referred to the situation as a "trap."

As the crowd moved north, an Assistant U.S. Attorney saw one demonstrator with long sideburns and hippie garb pause to break up a large piece of concrete, wrapping the pieces in a striped T-shirt.

Before the march formally disbanded, an early contingent of demonstrators, numbering about 30 to 50, arrived at the spot where Congress Plaza bridges the Illinois Central tracks at approximately the same time as a squad of 40 National Guardsmen. The Guard hurriedly spread out about three feet apart across Congress with rifles at the ready, gas masks on, bayonets fixed.

Now as the bulk of the disappointed marchers sought a way out of the park, the crowd began to build up in front of the Guard. "I saw one woman driving a new red late-model car approach the bridge," a news correspondent says: "Two demonstrators, apparently badly gassed, jumped into the back seat and hoped to get through the Guard lines. Guardsmen refused to permit the car through, going so far as to threaten to bayonet her tires and the hood of her car if she did not turn around. One Guardsman fired tear gas point blank beside the car.".....

The crowd's basic strategy, a medic recalled, was "to mass a sizeable group at one end of the line," as if preparing to charge. Then, when Guardsmen shifted to protect that area, a comparatively small group of demonstrators would push through the weak end of the line. Once the small group had penetrated the line, the medic says, members would "come up behind the Guardsmen and taunt them, as well as push and shove them from the rear." A Guard official said later that his men were attacked with oven cleaner and containers filled with exrement. . . . . .

As the crowd swelled, it surged periodically towards the Guard line, sometimes yelling, "Freedom, freedom." On one of these surges a Guardsman hurled two tear gas canisters. Some of the tear gas was fired directly into the faces of demonstrators. "We came across a guy really badly gassed," a college coed says. "We were choking, but we could still see. But this guy we saw was standing ere helpless with mucous-type stuff on his face, obviously in pain."

An Assistant U.S. Attorney says he saw "hundreds of people running, crying, coughing, vomiting, screaming." Some women ran blindly to Buckingham Fountain and leaped into the water to bathe their faces. The Guard medic quoted earlier says he was again assaulted by demonstrators when he went into the crowd to treat a man felled by "a particularly heavy dose of tear gas."

"In Grant Park, the gassed crowd was angered . . . more aggressive," says the history professor. Shortly after the gassing, says the Guard medic quoted earlier, "two forces of police arrived. They immediately waded into the crowd with clubs swinging indiscriminately, driving them off the bridge and away from the area." Once more, the Guardsman said, he was assaulted by demonstrators— this time when he tried "to treat an individual who received a severe head injury from the police."

Surging north from Congress Plaza to a footbridge leading from the park, the crowd encountered more Guardsmen. More tear gas was dispensed. Surging north from the site of the gassings, the crowd found the Jackson Boulevard bridge unguarded. Word was quickly passed back by loudspeaker, "Two blocks north, there's an open bridge; no gas." As dusk was settling, hundreds poured from the park into Michigan Avenue.

The Crowd on Michigan Avenue

At 7:14 p.m., as the first groups of demonstrators crossed the bridge toward Michigan Avenue, they noticed that the mule train of the Poor People's Campaign was just entering the intersection of Michigan and Jackson, headed south. The wagons were painted, "Jobs & Food for All."

The train was accompanied by 24 policemen on foot, five on three-wheelers, and four in two squadrols. A police official was in front with the caravan's leaders. The sight of the train seemed to galvanize the disorganized Grant Park crowd and those streaming over the bridge broke into cheers and shouts. "Peace now!" bellowed the demonstrators. "Dump the Hump!" This unexpected enthusiastic horde in turn stimulated the mule train marchers. Drivers of the wagons stood and waved to the crowd, shouting: "Join us! Join us!" To a young man watching from the 23rd floor of the Hilton Hotel, "the caravan seemed like a magnet to demonstrators leaving the park."

The Balbo-Michigan Crowd Builds Up

When the crowd's first rank reached the intersection of Balbo and Michigan, the northeast corner of the Hilton, it was close to approximately 2000 to 3000 demonstrators and spectators. The police were armed with riot helmets, batons, mace, an aerosol tear gas can and their service revolvers (which they always carry). Behind the police lines, parked in front of the Hilton, was a fire department high pressure pumper truck hooked up to a hydrant. Pairs of uniformed firemen were also in the vicinity. The growing crowds, according to the U.S. Attorney's report, were a blend of "young and old, hippies, Yippies, straights, newsmen and cameramen," even two mobile TV units. . . . . .

From within the crowd were rising the usual shouts from some of the demonstrators: "Hell no, we won't go!" . . . "Fuck these Nazis!" . . . "Fuck you, L.B.J.!" . . . "No more war!" . . . "Pigs, pigs, pigs." . . . "The streets belong to the people!" "Let's go to the Amphitheatre!" "Move on, Move on!" . . . "You can't stop us." . . . "From the hotel," recalls a student, "people who sympathized were throwing confetti and pieces of paper out of the windows and they were blinking their room lights." . . . . .

Isolated Incidents

Occasionally during the early evening, groups of demonstrators would flank the police lines or find a soft spot and punch through, heading off on their own for the Amphitheatre. On the periphery of the Hilton and on thoroughfares and side streets further southwest, a series of brief but sometimes violent encounters occurred.

For example, says the manager of a private club on Michigan Avenue, "a large band of long-haired demonstrators . . . tore down the American flag" overhanging the entrance to the club "and took it into Michigan Avenue attempting to tear it."

At about 7 p.m. from the window of a motel room in the 1100 block of South Michigan, a senator's driver noticed a group of demonstrators walking south, chanting: "Hell no, we won't go!" and "Fuck the draft." They were hurling insults at passing pedestrians and when one answered back, the witness says, "five demonstrators charged out of Michigan Avenue onto the sidewalk, knocked the pedestrian down, formed a circle around his fallen body, locked their arms together and commenced kicking him in a vicious manner. When they had finished kicking their victim, they unlocked their arms and immediately melted back into the crowd. . . ." . . . . .

Back at the Conrad Hilton

Vice President Humphrey was now inside the Conrad Hilton Hotel and the police commanders were afraid that the crowd might either attempt to storm the hotel or march south on Michigan Avenue, ultimately to the Amphitheatre. The Secret Service had received an anonymous phone call that the Amphitheatre was to be blown up. A line of police was established at 8th and Michigan at the south end of the hotel and the squads of police stationed at the hotel doors began restricting access to those who could display room keys. Some hotel guests, including delegates and Senator McCarthy's wife, were turned away.

By 7:30 p.m. a rumor was passing around that the Blackstone Rangers and the East Side Disciples, two of Chicago's most troublesome street gangs, were on their way to the scene. (This was later proven to be untrue; neither of these South Side gangs was present in any numbers in either Lincoln Park or Grant Park.) At this point, a Negro male was led through the police line by a police officer. He spoke to the police officer, a city official and a deputy superintendent of police. He told them that he was in charge of the mule train and that his people wanted no part of this mob. He said he had 80 people with him, that they included old people and children, and he wanted to get them out of the mob. The police officer later stated the group wanted to go past the Hilton, circle it, and return to the front of the hotel where Reverend Ralph Abernathy could address the crowd. . . . . .

In a few minutes, Reverend Ralph Abernathy appeared and, according to the police officer's statement, "said he wanted to be taken out of the area as he feared for the safety of his group." The police officer directed that the train be moved south on Michigan to 11th Street and then, through a series of turns through the Loop, to the West Side. . . . .

A policeman on Michigan later said that at about this time a "female hippie" came up to him, pulled up her skirt and said, "You haven't had a piece in a long time." A policeman standing in front of the Hilton remembers seeing a blonde female who was dressed in a short red minidress make lewd, sexual motions in front of a police line. Whenever this happened, he says, the policemen moved back to prevent any incident. The crowd, however, egged her on, the patrolman says. He thought that "she and the crowd wanted an arrest to create a riot." Earlier in the same general area a male youth had stripped bare and walked around carrying his clothes on a stick. . . . . .

The intersection at Balbo and Michigan was in total chaos at this point. The street was filled with people. Darkness had fallen but the scene was lit by both police and television lights. As the mule train left, part of the group tried to follow the wagons through the police line and were stopped. According to the deputy superintendent of police, there was much pushing back and forth between the policemen and the demonstrators.

Continual announcements were made at this time over a police amplifier for the crowd to "clear the street and go up on the sidewalk or into the park area for their demonstrations." The broadcast said, "Please gather in the park on the east side of the street. You may have your peaceful demonstration and speechmaking there." The demonstrators were also advised that if they did not heed these orders they would face arrest. The response from many in the crowd, according to a police observer, was to scream and shout obscenities. A Chicago attorney who was watching the scene recalls that when the announcements were broadcast, "No one moved." The deputy superintendent then made another announcement: "Will any non-demonstrators, anyone who is not a part of this group, any newsmen, please leave the group." Despite the crowd noise, the loudspeaker announcements were "loud and plainly heard," according to an officer. . . . . .

While this was happening on Michigan Avenue, a separate police line had begun to move east toward the crowd from the block of Balbo that lies between Michigan and Wabash along the north side of the Hilton.

Just as the police in front of the Hilton were confronted with some sitdowns on the south side of the intersection of Balbo and Michigan, the police unit coming into the intersection on Balbo met the sitting demonstrators. What happened then is subject to dispute between the police and some other witnesses.

The Balbo police unit commander asserts that he informed the sit-downs and surrounding demonstrators that if they did not leave, they would be arrested. He repeated the order and was met with a chant of "Hell no, we won't go." Quickly a police van swung into the intersection immediately behind the police line, the officers opened the door at the rear of the wagon. The deputy chief "ordered the arrest process to start."

"Immediately upon giving this order," the deputy chief later informed his superiors, "we were pelted with rocks, bottles, cans filled with unknown liquids and other debris, which forced the officers to defend themselves from injury. . . . My communications officer was slugged from behind by one of these persons, receiving injuries to his right eye and cheekbone." . . . . .

The many films and video tapes of this time period present a picture which does not correspond completely with the police view. First, the films do not show a mob moving west on Balbo; they show the street as rather clean of the demonstrators and bystanders, although the sidewalks themselves on both sides of the street are crowded. Second, they show the police walking east on Balbo, stopping in formation, awaiting the arrival of the van and starting to make arrests on order. A total of 25 seconds elapses between their coming to a halt and the first arrests.

Also, a St. Louis reporter who was watching from inside the Haymarket lounge agrees that the police began making arrests "in formation," apparently as "the result of an order to clear the intersection." Then, the reporter adds, "from this apparently controlled beginning the police began beating people indiscriminately. They grabbed and beat anyone they could get hold of." . . . . .

"The crowd tried to reverse gears," the reporter says. "People began falling over each other. I was in the first rank between police and the crowd and was caught in the first surge. I went down as I tried to retreat. I covered my head, tried to protect my glasses which had fallen partially off, and hoped that I would not be clubbed. I tried to dig into the humanity that had fallen with me. You could hear shouting and screaming. As soon as I could, I scrambled to my feet and tried to move away from the police. I saw a youth running by me also trying to flee. A policeman clubbed him as he passed, but he kept running.

"The cops were saying, 'Move! I said, move, god dammit! Move, you bastards!'" A representative of the ACLU who was positioned among the demonstrators says the police "were cussing a lot" and were shouting, "Kill, kill, kill, kill, kill!" A reporter for the *Chicago Daily News* said after the melee that he, too, heard this cry. A demonstrator remembers the police swinging their clubs and screaming, "Get the hell out of here." . . . "Get the fuck out of here." . . . "Move your fucking ass!" . . . . .

The crowd frantically eddied in a halfmoon shape in an effort to escape the officers coming in from the west. A UPI reporter who was on the southern edge of the crowd on Michigan Avenue, said that the advancing police "began pushing the crowd south." A cherry bomb burst overhead. The demonstrators strained against the deputy superintendent of police's line south of the Balbo-Michigan intersection. "When I reached that line," says the UPI reporter, "I heard a voice from behind it say, 'Push them back, move them back!' I was then prodded and shoved with nightsticks back in a northerly direction, toward the still advancing line of police."

"Police were marching this way and that," a correspondent from a St. Louis paper says. "They obviously had instructions to clear the street, but apparently contradicting one another in directions the crowd was supposed to be sent."

The deputy superintendent of police recalls that he ordered his men to "hold your line there" . . . "stand fast" . . . "Lieutenant, hold your men steady there!" These orders, he said, were not obeyed by all. He said that police disregarded his order to return to police lines—the beginning of what he says was the only instance in which he personally saw police discipline collapse. He estimates that ten to 15 officers moved off on individual forays against demonstrators. . . . . .

Thus, at 7:57 p.m., with two groups of club-wielding police converging simultaneously and independently, the battle was joined. The portions of the throng out of the immediate area of conflict largely stayed put and took up the chant. "The whole world is watching," but the intersection fragmented into a collage of violence.

Re-creating the precise chronology of the next few moments is impossible. But there is no question that a violent street battle ensued.

People ran for cover and were struck by police as they passed. Clubs were swung indiscriminately......

"I saw squadrons of policemen coming from everywhere," a secretary said. "The crowd around me suddenly began to run. Some of us, including myself, were pushed back onto the sidewalk and then all the way up against ... the Blackstone Hotel along Michigan Avenue. I thought the crowd had panicked......

"Fearing that I would be crushed against the wall of the building ... I somehow managed to work my way ... to the edge of the street ... and saw police everywhere.

"As I looked up I was hit for the first time on the head from behind by what must have been a billy club. I was then knocked down and while on my hands and knees, I was hit around the shoulders. I got up again, stumbling and was hit again. As I was falling, I heard words to the effect of 'move, move' and the horrible sound of cracking billy clubs.

"After my second fall, I remember being kicked in the back, and I looked up and noticed that many policemen around me had no badges on. The police kept hitting me on the head."

Eventually she made her way to an alley behind the Blackstone and finally "bleeding badly from my head wound," was driven by a friend to a hospital emergency room. Her treatment included the placing of 12 stitches......

A lawyer says that he was in a group of demonstrators in the park just south of Balbo when he heard a police officer shout, "Let's get 'em!" Three policemen ran up, "singled out one girl and as she was running away from them, beat her on the back of the head. As she fell to the ground, she was struck by the nightsticks of these officers." A male friend of hers then came up yelling at the police. The witness said, "He was arrested. The girl was left in the area lying on the ground."......

A *Milwaukee Journal* reporter says in his statement, "when the police managed to break up groups of protesters they pursued individuals and beat them with clubs. Some police pursued individual demonstrators as far as a block ... and beat them. ... In many cases it appeared to me that when police had finished beating the protesters they were pursuing, they then attacked, indiscriminately, any civilian who happened to be standing nearby. Many of these were not involved in the demonstrations."

In balance, there is no doubt that police discipline broke during the melee. The deputy superintendent of police states that—although this was the only time he saw discipline collapse—when he ordered his men to stand fast, some did not respond and began to sally through the crowd, clubbing people they came upon. An inspector-observer from the Los Angeles Police Department, stated that during this week, "The restraint of the police both as individual members and as an organization, was beyond reason." However, he said that on this occasion:

> There is no question but that many officers acted without restraint and exerted force beyond that necessary under the circumstances. The leadership at the point of conflict did little to prevent such conduct and the direct control of officers by first-line supervisors was virtually non-existent.

The deputy superintendent of police has been described by several observers as being very upset by individual policemen who beat demonstrators. He pulled his men off the demonstrators, shouting "Stop, damn it, stop. For Christ's sake, stop it."

"It seemed to me," an observer says, "that only a saint could have swallowed the vile remarks to the officers. However, they went to extremes in clubbing the Yippies. I saw them move into the park, swatting away with clubs at girls and boys lying in the grass. More than once I witnessed two officers pulling at the arms of a Yippie until the arms almost left their sockets, then, as the officers put the Yippie in a police van, a third jabbed a riot stick into the groin of the youth being arrested. It was eveident that the Yippie was not resisting arrest." . . . . .

"In one incident, a young man, who apparently had been maced, staggered across Michigan . . . helped by a companion. The man collapsed. . . . Medical people from the volunteer medical organization rushed out to help him. A police officer (a sergeant, I think) came rushing forward, followed by the two other nightstick-brandishing policemen and yelled, 'Get him out of here; this ain't a hospital.' The medical people fled, half dragging and half carrying the young man with them. . . ." . . . . .

During the course of arrests, one girl lost her skirt. Although there have been unverified reports of police ripping the clothes from female demonstrators, this is the only incident on news film of any woman being disrobed in the course of arrest.

While violence was exploding in the street, the crowd wedged, behind the police sawhorses along the northeast edge of the Hilton, was experiencing a terror all its own. Early in the evening, this group had consisted in large part of curious bystanders. But following the police surges into the demonstrators clogging the intersection, protesters had crowded the ranks behind the horses in their flight from the police.

From force of numbers, this sidewalk crowd of 150 to 200 persons was pushing down toward the Hilton's front entrance. Policemen whose orders were to keep the entrance clear were pushing with sawhorses. Other police and fleeing demonstrators were pushed from the north in the effort to clear the intersection.

Thus, the crowd was wedged against the hotel, with the hotel itself on the west, sawhorses on the southeast and police on the northeast.

Films show that one policeman elbowed his way where he could rescue a girl of about ten years of age from the vise-like press of the crowd. He cradled her in his arms and carried her to a point of relative safety 20 feet away. The crowd itself "passed up" an elderly woman to a low ledge.

"I was crowded in with the group of screaming, frightened people," an onlooker states, "We jammed against each other, trying to press into the brick wall of the hotel. As we stood there breathing hard . . . a policeman calmly walked the length of the barricade with a can of chemical spray [evidently mace] in his hand. Unbelievably, he was spraying at us." Photos reveal several policemen using mace against the crowd. . . . . . "Some of the police then turned and attacked the crowd," a Chicago reporter says. A young cook caught in the crowd relates that:

"The police began picking people off. They would pull individuals to the ground and begin beating them. A medic wearing a white coat and an armband with a red cross was grabbed, beaten and knocked to the ground. His whole face was covered with blood." . . . . .

As a result, a part of the crowd was trapped in front of the Conrad Hilton and pressed hard against a big plate glass window of the Haymarket Lounge. A reporter who was sitting inside said, "Frightened men and women banged . . . against the window. A captain of the fire department inside told us to get back from the window, that it might get knocked in. As I backed away a few feet I could see a smudge of blood on the glass outside."

With a sickening crack, the window shattered, and screaming men and women tumbled through, some cut badly by jagged glass. The police came after them. "A patrolman ran up to where I was sitting," said a man with a cut leg. "I protested that I was injured and could not walk, attempting to show him my leg. He screamed that he would show me I could walk. He grabbed me by the shoulder and literally hurled me through the door of the bar into the lobby. . . .

"I stumbled out into what seemed to be a main lobby. The young lady I was with and I were both immediately set upon by what I can only presume were plainclothes police. . . . We were cursed by these individuals and thrown through another door into an outer lobby." Eventually a McCarthy aide took him to the 15th floor.

In the heat of all this, probably few were aware of the Haymarket's advertising slogan: "A place where good guys take good girls to dine in the lusty, rollicking atmosphere of fabulous Old Chicago. . . ." . . . . . There is little doubt that during this whole period, beginning at 7:57 p.m. and lasting for nearly 20 minutes, the preponderance of violence came from the police. It was not entirely a one-way battle, however.

Firecrackers were thrown at police. Trash baskets were set on fire and rolled and thrown at them. In one case, a gun was taken from a policeman by a demonstrator.

"Some hippies," said a patrolman in his statement, "were hit by other hippies who were throwing rocks at the police." Films reveal that when police were chasing demonstrators into Grant Park, one young man upended a sawhorse and heaved it at advancing officers. At one point the deputy superintendent of police was knocked down by a thrown sawhorse. At least one police three-wheeler was tipped over. One of the demonstrators says that "people in the park were prying up cobblestones and breaking them. One person piled up cobblestones in his arms and headed toward the police." Witnesses reported that people were throwing "anything they could lay their hands on. From the windows of the Hilton and Blackstone hotels, toilet paper, wet towels, even ash trays came raining down." A police lieutenant stated that he saw policemen bombarded with "rocks, cherry bombs, jars of vasoline, jars of mayonnaise and pieces of wood torn from the yellow barricades falling in the street." He, too, noticed debris falling from the hotel windows. . . . . .

A number of police officers were injured, either by flying missiles or in personal attacks. One, for example, was helping a fellow officer "pick up a hippie when another hippie gave [me] a heavy kick, aiming for my groin." The blow struck the officer partly on the leg and partly in the testicles. He went down, and the "hippie" who kicked him escaped.

In another instance, a Chicago police reporter said in his statement, "a police officer reached down and grabbed a person who dove forward and bit the officer on the leg. . . . Three or four fellow policemen came to his aid. They had to club the demonstrator to make him break his clamp on the officer's leg." In another case, the witness saw a demonstrator "with a big mop of hair hit a police officer with an old British Army type metal helmet." The reporter said he also heard "hissing sounds from the demonstrators as they were spraying the police." Later he found empty lacquer spray and hair spray cans on the street. Also he heard policemen cry out, "They're kicking us with knives in their shoes." Later, he said, he found that demonstrators "had actually inserted razor blades in their shoes." . . . . .

Wild in the Streets

By 8:15 p.m., the intersection was in police control. One group of police proceeded east on Balbo, clearing the street and splitting the crowd into two. Because National Guard lines still barred passage over the Balbo Street bridge, most of the demonstrators fled into Grant Park. A Guardsman estimates that 5,000 remained in the park across from the Hilton. Some clubbing by police occurred; a demonstrator says he saw a brick hurled at police; but few arrests were made.

Now, with police lines beginning to reform, the deputy superintendent directed the police units to advance north on Michigan. He says announcements were again made to clear the area and warnings given that those refusing to do so would be arrested. To this, according to a patrolman who was present, "The hippie group yelled 'fuck you' in unison."

Police units formed up. National Guard intelligence officers on the site called for Guard assistance. At 8:30 the Secret Service reported trucks full of Guard troops from Soldier Field moving north on Michigan Avenue to the Conrad Hilton and additional units arrived about 20 minutes later. The troops included the same units that had seen action earlier in the day after the bandshell rally and had later been moved to 22nd Street.

By 8:55 p.m., the Guard had taken up positions in a U-shaped formation, blocking Balbo at Michigan and paralleling the Hilton and Grant Park—a position that was kept until 4 a.m. Thursday. Although bayonets were affixed when the troops first hit the street, they were quickly removed. Explains a Guardsman who was there: "The bayonets had gotten in our way when we were on the Congress Street bridge." At one point, a demonstrator tried to "take the muzzle off" one of the Guardsmen's rifle. "All the time the demonstrators were trying to talk to us. They said 'join us' or 'fuck the draft.' We were told not to talk to anyone in the crowd." One Guard unit followed behind the police as a backup group.

With the police and Guard at its rear, the crowd fractured in several directions as it moved away from Balbo and Michigan. Near Michigan and Monroe another casualty center had been set up in the headquarters of the Church Federation of Greater Chicago. This, plus the melding of the crowds northbound on Michigan and east-bound on Monroe, brought about 1,000 persons to the west side of Michigan between Adams and Monroe, facing the Art Institute. There were few demonstrators on the east side of Michigan.

At 9:25 p.m., the police commander ordered a sweep of Michigan Avenue south from Monroe. At about this same time the police still had lines on both the west and east sides of Michigan in front of the Hilton and additional National Guard troops had arrived at 8th Street.

At 9:57 p.m., the demonstrators still on Michigan Avenue, prodded along by the southward sweep of the police, began marching back to Grant Park, chanting "Back to the park." By 10:10 p.m., an estimated 800 to 1,000 demonstrators had gathered in front of the Hilton.

By then, two city street sweeping trucks had rumbled up and down the street in front of the hotel, cleaning up the residue of violence—shoes, bottles, rocks, tear gas handkerchiefs. A police captain said the debris included: "Bases and pieces of broken bottles, a piece of board (1″ X 4″ X 14″), an 18-inch length of metal pipe, a 24-inch stick with a protruding sharpened nail, a 12-inch length of 1/2-inch diameter pipe, pieces of building bricks, an 18-inch stick with a razor blade protruding . . . several plastic balls somewhat smaller than tennis balls containing approximately 15 to 20 sharpened nails driven into the ball from various angles." When the delegates returned to the Hilton, they saw none of the litter of the battle.

As the crowd had dispersed from the Hilton the big war of Michigan and Balbo was, of course, over. But for those in the streets, as the rivulets of the crowd forked through the areas north of the hotel, there were still battles to be fought. Police violence and police baiting were some time in abating. Indeed, some of the most vicious incidents occurred in this "post-war" period. . . . . .

The U.S. Attorney states that as the crowd moved north on Michigan Avenue, "they pelted the police with missiles of all sorts, rocks, bottles, firecrackers. When a policeman was struck, the crowd would cheer. The policemen in the line were dodging and jumping to avoid being hit." A police sergeant told the FBI that even a telephone was hurled from the crowd at the police. . . . . .

In the first block north of the Hilton, recalls a man who was standing outside a Michigan Avenue restaurant, demonstrators "menaced limousines, calling the occupants 'scum,' telling them they didn't belong in Chicago and to go home."

As the police skirmish line moved north, and drew nearer to the squad cars, the lieutenant said, he saw several persons shoving paper through the cars' broken windows—in his opinion, a prelude to setting the cars on fire. A theology student who was in the crowd states that "a demonstrator took a fire extinguisher and sprayed inside the car. Then he put paper on the ground under the gas tank. . . . People shouted at him to stop." To break up the crowd, the lieutenant said, he squirted tear gas from an aerosol container and forced the demonstrators back. . . . . .

"Two or three policemen, one with a white shirt, advanced on the crowd," one witness said, "The white-shirted one squirted mace in arcs back and forth before him."

A cameraman for the *Chicago Daily News* photographed a woman cowering after she had been sprayed with mace. A *News* representative states that the officer administering the mace, whom the photographers identified as a police lieutenant, then turned and directed the spray at the cameraman. The cameraman shot a photograph of this. The police lieutenant states that he does not remember this incident.

A priest who was in the crowd says he saw a "boy, about 14 or 15 white, standing on top of an automobile yelling something which was unidentifiable. Suddenly a policeman forced him down from the car and beat him to the ground by striking him three or four times with a nightstick. Other police joined in . . . and they eventually shoved him to a police van."

A well-dressed woman saw this incident and spoke angrily to a nearby police captain. As she spoke, another policeman came up from behind her and sprayed something in her face with an aerosol can. He then clubbed her to the ground. He and two other policemen then dragged her along the ground to the same paddy wagon and threw her in.

"At the corner of Congress Plaza and Michigan," states a doctor, "was gathered a group of people, numbering between 30 and 40. They were trapped against a railing by several policemen on motorcycles. The police charged the people on motorcycles and struck about a dozen of them, knocking several of them down. About 20 standing there jumped over the railing. On the other side of the railing was a three-to-four-foot drop. None of the people who were struck by the motorcycles appeared to be seriously injured. However, several of them were limping as if they had been run over on their feet."

A UPI reporter witnessed these attacks, too. He relates in his statement that one officer, "with a smile on his face and a fanatical look in his eyes, was standing on the three-wheel cycle, shouting. 'Wahoo, wahoo,' and trying to run down people on the sidewalk." The reporter says he was chased 30 feet by the cycle.

A few seconds later he "turned around and saw a policeman with a raised billy stick." As he swung around, the police stick grazed his head and struck his shoulders. As he was on his knees, he says someone stepped on his back.

A Negro policeman helped him to his feet, the reporter says. The policeman told him, "You know, man I didn't do this. One of the white cops did it." Then, the reporter quotes the officer as saying, "You know what? After this is all over, I'm quitting the force."

An instant later, the shouting officer on the motorcycle swung by again, and the reporter dove into a doorway for safety.

Near this same intersection, a Democratic delegate from Oklahoma was surrounded in front of his hotel by about ten persons, two of them with long hair and beards. He states that they encircled him for several minutes and subjected him to verbal abuse because they felt he "represented the establishment" and was "somewhat responsible for the alleged police brutality." The delegate stood mute and was eventually rescued by a policeman.

At Van Buren, a college girl states, "demonstrators were throwing things at passing police cars, and I saw one policeman hit in the face with a rock. A small paddy wagon drove up with only one policeman in it, and the crowd began rocking the wagon. The cop fell out and was surrounded by the crowd, but no effort was made to hurt him."

At Jackson, says the graduate student quoted earlier, "People got into the street on their knees and prayed, including several ministers who were dressed in clerical garb. These people, eight or ten of them, were arrested. This started a new wave of dissent among the demonstrators, who got angry. Many went forward to be arrested voluntarily; others were taken forcibly and some were beaten. . . . Objects were being thrown directly at police, including cans, bottles and paper."

"I was in the street," a witness who was near the intersection states, "when a fire in a trash basket appeared. . . . In a few minutes, two fire engines passed south through the crowd, turned west on Van Buren and stopped. They were followed by two police wagons which stopped in the middle of the block. As I walked north past the smaller of the two wagons, it began to rock." (The wagon also was being pelted by missiles, the U.S. Attorney states, and "PIGS" was painted on its sides.)

"I retreated onto the east sidewalk," the witness continued. "Two policemen jumped out of the smaller wagon and one was knocked down by a few demonstrators, while other demonstrators tried to get these demonstrators away. The two policemen got back to the wagon, the crowd having drawn well back around them." The U.S. Attorney's report states that one of the policemen was "stomped" by a small group of the mob.

A young woman who was there and who had attended the bandshell rally earlier in the afternoon states that the crowd rocked the wagon for some time, while its officers stayed inside. "Then," she says, "the driver came out wildly swinging his club and shouting. About ten people jumped on him. He was kicked pretty severely and was downed. When he got up he was missing his club and his hat."

A police commander says that at about this moment he received "an urgent radio message" from an officer inside the van. He radioed that "demonstrators were standing on the hood of his wagon . . . and were preparing to smash the windshield with a baseball bat," the commander recalled. The officer also told him that the demonstrators were attempting to overturn the squadrol and that the driver "was hanging on the door in a state of shock." The commander told the officer that assistance was on the way.

"I heard a '10-1' call on either my radio or one of the other hand sets being carried by other men with me," the U.S. Attorney states, "and then heard, 'Car 100-sweep!' [Car 100 was assigned to the police commander.] With a roar of motors, squads, vans and three-wheelers came from east, west and north into the block north of Jackson."

"Almost immediately a CTA bus filled with police came over the Jackson Drive bridge and the police formed a line in the middle of the street," says a witness. "I heard shouts that the police had rifles and that they had cocked and pumped them. Demonstrators began to run." . . . . .

"I ran north of Jackson . . . just as police were clearing the intersection and forming a line across Michigan," says the witness quoted above. "The police who had formed a line facing east in the middle of Michigan charged, yelling and clubbing into the crowd, running at individuals and groups who did not run before them." . . . . .

"As the fray intensified around the intersection of Michigan and Jackson, a big group ran west on Jackson, with a group of blue-shirted policemen in pursuit, beating at them with clubs," says the U.S. Attorney's report. Some of the crowd ran up the alleys; some north on Wabash; and some west on Jackson to State with the police in pursuit." . . . . .

An Assistant U.S. Attorney later reported that "the demonstrators were running as fast as they could but were unable to get out of the way because of the crowds in front of them. I observed the police striking numerous individuals, perhaps 20 or 30. I saw three fall down and then be overrun by the police. I observed two demonstrators who had multiple cuts on their heads. We assisted one who was in shock into a passer-by's car.

"A TV mobile truck appeared . . . and the police became noticeably more restrained, holding their clubs at waist level rather than in the air," a witness relates. "As the truck disappeared . . . the head-clubbing tactics were resumed." . . . . .

One demonstrator states that he ran off Michigan Avenue on to Jackson. He says he and his wife ran down Jackson and were admitted, hesitantly, into a restaurant. They seated themselves at a table by the window facing onto Jackson and, while sitting at the table, observed a group of people running down Jackson with policemen following them and striking generally at the crowd with their batons. At one instance, he saw a policeman strike a priest in the head with a baton.

At the intersection of Jackson and Wabash, said a student whose wife was beaten in the race from Michigan, "the police came from all four directions and attacked the crowd. Demonstrators were beaten and run to the paddy wagons. I saw a black policeman go berserk. He charged blindly at the group of demonstrators and made two circles through the crowd, swinging wildly at anything." . . . . .

An Assistant U.S. Attorney watching the action on various side streets reported, "I observed police officers clearing people westward . . . using their clubs to strike people on the back of the head and body on several occasions. Once a policeman ran alongside a young girl. He held her by the shoulder of her jacket and struck at her a few times as they were both running down the sidewalk." . . . . .

A traffic policeman on duty on Michigan Avenue says that the demonstrators who had continued north often surrounded cars and buses attempting to move south along Michigan Avenue. Many males, in the crowd, he says, exposed their penises to passers-by and other members of the crowd. They would run up to cars clogged by the crowd and show their private parts to the passengers."

To men, the officer says, they shouted such questions as, "How would you like me to fuck your wife?" and "How would you like to fuck a man?" Many of the demonstrators also rocked the automobiles in an effort to tip them over. A policeman states that bags of feces and urine were dropped on the police from the building. . . . . .

As the crowd moved south again on Michigan, a traffic policeman, who was in the vicinity of Adams Street, recalls, "They first took control of the lions in front of the Art Institute. They climbed them and shouted things like, "Let's fuck" and "Fuck, fuck, fuck!" . . . . . At this same intersection, an officer rescued two Loop secretaries from being molested by demonstrators. He asked them. "What are you doing here?" They replied, "We wanted to see what the hippies were like." His response: "How do you like what you saw?"

Old Town: The Mixture as Before

While all that was going on in and around Grant Park, Lincoln Park on Wednesday was quiet and uncrowded; but there was sporadic violence in Old Town again that night. Two University of Minnesota students who wandered through the park in the morning say they heard small groups of demonstrators saying things like "Fuck the pigs," and "Kill them all," but by this time that was not unusual. They also heard a black man addressing a group of demonstrators. He outlined plans for the afternoon, and discussed techniques for forming skirmish lines, disarming police officers, and self defense.

Also during the morning Abbie Hoffman was arrested at the Lincoln Hotel Coffee Shop, 1800 North Clark, and charged with resisting arrest and disorderly conduct. According to Hoffman's wife, Anita, she and her husband and a friend were eating breakfast when three policemen entered the coffee shop and told Hoffman they had received three complaints about an obscene word written on Hoffman's forehead. The word was "Fuck." Hoffman says he printed the word on his forehead to keep cameramen from taking his picture. . . . . .

Most of the violence against police, from all reports, was the work of gang-type youths called "greasers." They dismantled police barricades to lure squad cars down Stockton Drive, where one observer says "punks engaged in some of the most savage attacks on police that had been seen." Ministers and hippies in the area were directing traffic around the barricades and keeping people from wandering into the danger area. Two ministers in particular were trying to "keep the cool." . . . . .

Back at the Hilton

By 10:30 p.m., most of the action was centered once more in Grant Park across from the Hilton, where several hundred demonstrators and an estimated 1,500 spectators gathered to listen to what one observer describes as "unexciting speeches." There was the usual singing and shouting. Twice during the evening police and Hilton security officers went into the hotel and went to quarters occupied by McCarthy personnel—once to protest the ripping of sheets to bandage persons who had been injured and a second time to try to locate persons said to be lobbing ashtrays out of the windows. But compared to the earlier hours of the evening, the rest of the night was quiet.

In Grant Park, the sullen crowd sat facing the hotel. Someone with a transistor radio was listening to the roll call vote of states on the nomination and broadcasting the count to the rest of the throng over a bullhorn. There were loud cheers for Ted Kennedy, McCarthy, McGovern and Phillips ("He's a black man," said the youth with the bullhorn.) Boos and cries of "Dump the Hump" arose whenever Humphrey received votes. "When Illinois was called," says the trained observer, "no one could hear totals because of booing and the chant, 'To Hell with Daley.'"

During this time the police line was subject to considerable verbal abuse from within the crowd and a witness says that both black and white agitators at the edge of the crowd tried to kick policemen with razor blades embedded in their shoes. Periodically several policemen would make forays into the crowd, punishing demonstrators they thought were involved.

At about "Louisiana," as the roll call vote moved with quickening pace toward the climax of Humphrey's nomination, the crowd grew restless, recalls a trained observer. About this same time, according to the Log, the police skirmish line began pushing the demonstrators farther east into the park. A report of an officer being struck by a nail ball was received by police. Film taken at about this time shows an officer being hit by a thrown missile, later identified as a chunk of concrete with a steel reinforcement rod in it. The blow knocked him down and, as he fell, the crowd cheered and yelled "More!" The chant, "Kill the pigs," filled the air.

"At 'Oklahoma,'" recalls an observer, "the Yippie on the bullhorn said, 'Marshals ready. Don't move. Stay seated.'"

The front lines rose [facing the police] and locked arms, and the others stayed seated. Humphrey was over the top with Pennsylvania, and someone in the Hilton rang a cow bell at the demonstrators. Boos went up, as did tension. A bus load of police arrived. Others standing in front of the Hilton crossed Michigan and lined up behind those in front of the demonstrators.

The chant of "Sit down, sit down" went out. An American flag was raised on a pole upside down. Wandering began among demonstrators and the chant continued.

Shortly before midnight, while Benjamin Ortiz was speaking, National Guard troops of the 2/129 Inf. came west on Balbo to Michigan to replace the police in front of the Hilton. "For the first time," says an observer, "machine guns mounted on trucks were pulled up directly in front of the demonstrators, just behind the police lines. The machine guns, and the Guard's mesh-covered jeeps with barbed wire fronts made the demonstrators angry and nervous. Bayonets were readied. In films of this period the word 'pig' can be seen written on the street.

"Ortiz continued, 'Dig this man, just 'cause you see some different pigs coming here, don't get excited. We're going to sleep here, sing here, sex here, live here!'"

As the police moved off, one of the first Guard maneuvers was to clear demonstrators from Michigan's east sidewalk. This was done to allow pedestrian traffic. The crowd reacted somewhat hostilely to the maneuver, but by and large, the demonstrators seemed to view the Guard as helpless men who had been caught up in the events and did not treat them as badly as they had the police. Having secured the sidewalk, the guards shortly retired to the east curb of Michigan Avenue. A line of "marshals" sat down at the edge of the grass at the feet of the guards. Access to the hotel was restored and people began to move from the hotel to the park and vice versa. By now, there were an estimated 4,000 persons assembled across from the Hilton. Most of the crowd sat down in a mass and became more orderly, singing "America" and "God Bless America." McCarthy supporters joined the crowd and were welcomed.

By 12:20 a.m. Thursday, the crowd had declined to 1,500 and was considered under control. By 12:33 a.m., the police department had retired from the streets and the Guard took over the responsibility of holding Michigan from Balbo to 8th Street. At 12:47 a.m., another contingent of Guard troops arrived at the Hilton. Delegates were returning and were being booed unless they could be identified as McCarthy or McGovern supporters. Those delegates were cheered and asked to join the group.

The crowd grew in number. By 1:07 a.m., the Secret Service estimated 2,000 persons in the park across from the hotel. Ten minutes later the crowd had grown by another 500. Those in the park were "listening to speeches—orderly" according to the log.

CHAPTER 4-4

police corruption
in new york city
THE KNAPP COMMISSION

Testimony of Waverly B. Logan
Former Policeman

The witness is Waverly B. Logan, a former New York City policeman. Mr. Logan
testified that he was appointed to the Police Department in June, 1968, and
served his two and a half years on the force at the Police Academy, with the
tactical patrol force, in the 80th Precinct, in the 73d Precinct and with the pre-
ventative enforcement patrol. For the last year he has been a cab driver.

The questions were asked by Michael F. Armstrong, chief counsel of the
Kanpp Commission.

Q. During that period of time, did you come in contact with any activities involving the taking by police officers of benefits in exchange for services
or anything else of that sort?

A. When I was in T.P.F.* I was sort of young, taken right from the academy, and there's very little corruption I experienced in the T.P.F. unit. They
know about corruption in the precinct from talking with them. They tell—all
the guys in T.P.F. tell me about contracts, when the T.P.F. unit comes in that
they would give out summonses and break contracts and that's why they wasn't
liked. . . . They wasn't liked by the precinct because they would break contracts.

Q. So that in T.P.F. there was no corrupt activities as far as you were concerned?

Source: Public hearings of the Knapp Commission in New York City as reported by
The New York Times, October 20, 27, 30, December 15 and 29, 1971.
    *Tactical Patrol Force, an elite police unit.

A. There was no corrupt activities as far as money was concerned.

Q. I see. They occasionally get free meals and soft drinks and things like that?

A. Free meals they would occasionally give. If you was walking the foot post, the guy on the foot post, if he ever had that foot post before, he would tell you what places to go to eat, who would give you half prices, who would give it to you on the arm.

Q. What would (a policeman in the 73d Precinct do) if he were assigned to a foot post?

A. If he was assigned to a foot post and if it was on a 12 o'clock to 8 o'clock, he would come in the station house and go down to the basement and drink coffee. Or if he knew a place to coop, a girlfriend's house, he would go up to his girlfriend's house in the precinct. If he lived close enough, he would even go home.

Q. And leave a telephone number where he could be reached.

A. Yes. You would always leave your telephone number at the switchboard, so that the switchboard operator can always get in touch with you if there was a front break or something on your post and you need a man to send, they would always need a foot man.

Q. Do you recall incidents happening when burglaries were reported, your being introduced to a particular kind of behavior in connection with burglary?

A. Usually when a burglary occurred in the precinct, more than one car, if a car responds, regardless of whose sector they are in, as many cars as possible respond for backup. So this particular burglary was on Pitkin Avenue around Saratoga, in a men's clothing store. So I responded to this burglary. Me and my partner went into the back of the building where a door was open. We went in.

There was about six or seven radio cars out in front. A lot of cops was inside. Everybody was stuffing clothes down their pants, in their shirt, up their sleeve. Everybody looking fat because they were stuffing so much clothes in their pants. And my partner was telling me that the owners usually take it out on their income tax. Usually declare—say more was stolen than was actually taken or they would take it out on their insurance.

So he say this way you just getting a little back. He said, "Go ahead and take some, it's all right if you do."

So I took a shirt. And I was kind of afraid. I don't think I even wore the shirt.

Q. How long were you on the PEP squad?*

A. Eleven months.

Q. What was the attitude of the men when the squad was formed?

A. The men felt that they was in a new Police Department. They was in a Police Department all by itself. It was going to be a good squad, have good

*Preventive Enforcement Patrol, a special squad of black and Puerto Rican policemen operating in the ghetto areas of New York City.

bosses. That there was no holds barred. That they see violations of the law, they was going to make an arrest. Everybody was anxious to work. Wanted to really do a good job, like being born again.

Q. And how long do you think this attitude lasted?

A. A month, maybe two.

Q. And then do you recall hearing about a particular incident?

A. Yes, I did.

Q. Tell us what that incident was.

A. Two patrolmen that was in my unit was patrolling in the 32d Precinct. They came across one of those policy spots. They had a bell alarm on the door. So they rung the bell. The guy opened the door. He went inside and they arrested the policy bank. Took him to the 32d Precinct. Booked him, I understand 32d Precinct said that they knew where it was all the time and they were just waiting to get it.

Then we left there and went back to the squad room. And the squad room seemed like our sergeant was very excited about it because we had made a felony police arrest while in uniform.

And he called up one of the assistant chief inspectors right away at his home, tell him that we had just made a policy collar in uniform, and he felt it was great. And when he got off the phone he said. "The chief inspector said, 'We wasn't up in Harlem to make policy arrests.'"

Q. Do you recall an incident involving a raid on a large crap game in December of 1969?

A. Two patrolmen and myself was on foot patrol on Lenox Avenue when we saw two plainclothesmen cops. They was assigned to the 32d Precinct to watch out for taxi stickups. They was fairly new. One of them, as I recall, they had been to the academy with me. They told us about a big crap game on 139th Street in a basement. There was a big contract for that 32d Precinct and that they couldn't hit it.

They weren't allowed to make an arrest on it. So we told them that we don't have contracts and we will go and take that game. So they gave us the address and we went up there. As a matter of fact, we walked up there. It was quite a few blocks. Went down in the basement. Kicked the door open there. Took the game. Had everybody up the side of the wall, about 30 guys. Then we called on the radio for the sergeant. One was a radio patrol and one of them was the sergeant's car, with the sergeant in it.

The sergeant stayed outside. He called me out in the hallway then and asked me what did I have? So I told him what had happened. And I told him that our boss was on the way and he should be here shortly. And when my boss came one of the older patrolmen was there, from the 32nd. He seemed to know my sergeant and he seemed to shake his hand and called the sergeant by his first name, his arms around him, they had been friends for years.

So I observed this same patrolman, he took one of the guys that was in the dice game. He said he knew him for a long time. He walked him all the way down this long hallway to the front. And he had his arms around him and he came. And then he let him go.

So when he came back he told me as a friend of mine, he'd been giving me narcotics arrests.

I said "I'm no fool."

So he didn't say no more. So a little while later this—we were still waiting for the patrol wagon to respond to take all these prisoners. It happened two or three more times. It kept happening.

Then they started letting guys go because he was on the Sanitation Department. Letting guys go because he was working this place, that place. And it got down to but we didn't have but 12 prisoners.

Q. Twelve out of originally 30 or 40?

A. Thirty people, 30 or more. So we put them in the wagon and everybody was in there. The other prisoners was in there. They saw what had happened, they was trying to force $10 in my hand, saying: "I'll give you $10. Let me go, let me go."

* * * * *

Testimony of Captain Daniel McGowan

The witness is Captain Daniel McGowan of the Police Department. He testified that he had been a member of the city's police force for 23 years and had served as a patrolman, sergeant and lieutenant before becoming a captain in 1966.

Unless otherwise indicated, the questions were posed by Michael F. Armstrong, chief counsel to the commission.

Q. With respect to the feeling of cooperation within the Police Department, it is in the area of rooting out corruption, do you find in your work that it is easy to get information from police officers with respect to corruption?

A. No, it's very difficult. The police do not volunteer this information generally.

CHAIRMAN KNAPP: Do they go further than that and refuse to give it?

THE WITNESS: Well, I don't know of any specific instances where you could pin somebody down that they refused to give it. I think the attitude is not get involved unless you have to.

Q. Can you give us some idea of what your understanding and experience has been as to the feeling of police officers and why they feel this way?

A. Well, the mentality of the policeman is an insular one. They are surrounded by a hostile city. He has to be defensive. There are many forces that would like to destroy the department and its effectiveness. And so they are subject to insularity.

This is one of the big problems that we face.

Q. And they develop a sense of loyalty to each other; is that the idea?

A. That's correct, yes.

Q. Does this sense of loyalty, in your view, carry over to the point where it makes it difficult to uncover someone who is genuinely corrupt?

A. Well, I think policemen have been aware of some horrible examples of other police officers who have come forward, with all good intentions, to uncover a corrupted situation.

I remember in Denver, I think 1961, the Police Department was relatively free of corruption. It developed a burglary ring amongst some of the patrolmen there, and another patrolman became aware of it, reported his findings to the chief, and the chief sent him to a psychiatrist for examination.

When the psychiatrist sent him back to the chief, saying he was perfectly sane and telling the truth, the chief reluctantly acted on the accusation. There were indictments and a substantial portion of the department was found to be involved.

But the chief had to leave, had to resign, and the officer who uncovered it had to resign and leave the city.

So this is a problem—that policemen know that if they expose corruption, that they are taking a substantial risk of alienating themselves from their fellow officers.

Q. And you say this attitude exists in the New York City Police Department, within your experience.

A. Yes, it's been well documented.

CHAIRMAN KNAPP: Captain McGowan, is there a term called "standup cop"?

THE WITNESS: Yes.

CHAIRMAN KNAPP: What does it mean?

THE WITNESS: Well, it means he wouldn't inform on his fellow officers.

CHAIRMAN KNAPP: Does it mean particularly that he will lie if necessary to protect his fellow officers from corrupt charges?

THE WITNESS: If necessary, yes.

Q. How about the supervisors? How about their role with respect to this attitude in the department?

A. Well, they were all patrolmen themselves at one time, and they have the same police attitude toward it. It is still defensive.

Q. Have you found that the supervisors are reluctant to—I don't mean this as a general thing, but that there is a tendency among supervisors to protect themselves by not exposing corruption under them which might reflect upon them?

A. Yes, as in the instance of the Denver police chief, the fact that he moved strongly and did act upon the information once he was convinced that it was true, and he was removed, he had to resign.

And I think there was a general reluctance on all of us not to show our weaknesses, that we have not been able to control our subordinates. And it is very unrealistic to expect that the subordinate is going to show up his own ineptitude.

Q. Are there sometime credibility gaps between the superior officers and the men working under them, where the superior officer, himself, may have a bad reputation in the corruption area?

A. Yes, I think if he had a bad reputation and it is known and he's issuing stock orders that corruption will cease and desist, then everybody will say, "Well, he's saying it for the record but he doesn't really mean it."

Q. Do you have in mind specific instances within the department where this kind of a situation apparently exists?

A. Oh, I think, you know, over the 23 years that has happened, where the Police Commissioner or the inspector will issue these orders, and the captain will say, "Oh, I've seen this thing before," and adopt a cynical attitude towards it.

Q. And at a lower supervisory level, right up to today, there are supervisors who are in this position, where their men feel that they, themselves, are involved and, therefore don't take seriously what they say about corruption?

A. I suppose there are some few, I don't know. I can't give you any specific examples, but I'm sure there are some few examples.

Q. Now, there are superior officers involved in actively trying to combat corruption within their own commands; is that right?

A. Yes. Yes.

Q. What are the difficulties that they run into when they try to make an effort in this direction?

A. Well, one of the difficulties is, they have too great a span of control; there are not enough subordinate superiors to assist them in the supervision of their men.

Then again, the unrealistic goals that are set for them, the enforcement goals. This is particularly true in, I think, plainclothes, gambling enforcement and narcotics enforcement, that they are saddled with a tremendous amount of paper work, a volume of paper work that is constantly increasing.

And that, in addition to taking away from their primary responsibilities by being assigned to other duties temporarily because of some duty or strike duty or U.N. situations—they spend so little time sometimes in their offices that when they get back to them they are just signing papers and have little opportunity to fulfill their primary responsibility—supervision.

Q. In your view, what has been the department's response to the problem of corruption, historically? How they have gone about it and how, in your view, has this been effective or ineffective?

A. Well, this has been mostly from the case method; that is, responding to specific complaints and allegations rather than going out and trying to uncover the basic problems and trying to correct them at that level.

Q. Do you think that this approach has been successful?

A. Quite obviously the Knapp Commission wouldn't be in existence if it were.

Q. In your view, in the past, in other words, the reaction of the department to the corruption problem has been a defense one, just handling the cases that are brought in by way of allegation; is that right?

A. Yes, for several reasons. One is the sheer volume. The volume is a tremendous amount and I think, you know, somewhere along the line decisions were made—well, you know, if we really go all out for this, are we going to unalterably destroy the efficiency and the morale of the department?

I take the opposite view. I think that you have to—in order to get good efficiency and good morale, you have to root out the widespread corruption problem.

Q. Do you have a view about the so-called rotten-apple theory as it applies to corruption, Captain McGowan?

A. Well, the Knapp Commission hearings, I think . . . have shown the range if not the depth of police corruption. I would say that we should point out the vast difference between gratuities and corruption itself; one as different as between morals and ethics. But it's all there for us to see. And we can quibble about the amount of personnel involved, it's 5 per cent or 50 per cent, but it's unacceptable levels.

And I think the few rotten apples in the barrel is a rationalization, a dilution, so many of us do not want to face up to the fact that we can be associated with an organization that has so many aberrant members.

Q. How about the attitude of the public?

A. I think this is the single most important thing. If the public is aroused, if they want a better Police Department, if they want a more honest Police Department, they will have it. And if they don't concern themselves with this matter, then we won't have it.

* * * * *

Testimony of Detective Frank Serpico

The witness is Detective Frank Serpico. He testified that he joined the Police Department on Sept. 11, 1959, and has been assigned to the 81st Precinct in Brooklyn, the Bureau of Criminal Identification, the 90th Precinct in Brooklyn for plainclothes duty, the Seventh Division in the Bronx, Patrol Borough Manhattan North and the Narcotics Division in Brooklyn.

CHAIRMAN KNAPP: Please go ahead.

A. Through my appearances here today I hope that police officers in the future will not experience the same frustration and anxiety that I was subjected to for the past five years at the hands of my superiors because of my attempt to report corruption.

I was made to feel that I had burdened them with an unwanted task. The problem is that the atmosphere does not yet exist in which an honest police officer can act without fear of ridicule or reprisal from fellow officers.

We create an atmosphere in which the dishonest officer appears the honest one and not the other way around. I hope that this investigation and any future ones will deal with corruption at all levels within the department and not limit themselves to cases involving individual patrolmen.

Police corruption cannot exist unless it is at least tolerated at higher levels in the department. Therefore, the most important result that can come from these hearings is a conviction by police officers, even more than the public, that the department will change.

I also believe that it is most important for superior officers in the Police Department to develop an attitude of respect for the average patrolman. Every patrolman is an officer and should be treated as such by his superiors.

Importance of Attitude

A policeman's attitude about himself reflects in large measure the attitude of his superiors toward him. If they feel his job is important and his stature, so will he.

It is just as important for policemen to change their attitudes toward the public. A policeman's first obligation is to be responsible to the needs of the community he serves.

The department must realize that an effective continuing relationship between the police and the public is more important than an impressive arrest record.

The system of rewards within the Police Department should be based on a policeman's over-all performance with the public rather than on his ability to meet arrest quotas. Merely uncovering widespread patterns of corruption will not resolve the problem.

Basic changes in attitude and approach are vital. In order to insure this, an independent permanent public investigative body dealing with police corruption, like this commission, is essential.

* * * * *

Testimony of Detective Sergeant David Durk

The following statement is excerpted from testimony before the Knapp Commission by David Durk, a police officer.

I'm here because I'm a policeman, and it is just very hard to say it, but these have been a lonely five years for Frank Serpico, Paul DeLees and me. I've had a lot of time to think about what being a cop means to me, and maybe you can understand better some of the things I've said.

At the very beginning, the most important fact to understand is that I had and have no special knowledge of police corruption. We knew nothing

... that wasn't known to every man and officer in (the police) divisions. We knew nothing about the police traffic in narcotics that wasn't known and testified to here by Paul Curran of the State Investigations Commission. We knew these things because we were involved in law enforcement in New York City, and anyone else who says he didn't know had to be blind, either by choice or by incompetence.

The facts have been exposed. This commission, to its enormous credit, has exposed them in a period of six months.

We simply cannot believe, as we do not believe today, that those with authority and responsibility in the area, whether the District Attorneys, the police commanders or those in power in City Hall, couldn't also have exposed them in six months, or at least in six years; that is, if they wanted to do it.

> We were met with suspicion and hostility,
> inattention and laziness.

I am not saying that all those who ignored the corruption were themselves corrupt. Whether or not they were is almost immaterial in any case. The fact is that the corruption was ignored.... The fact is that almost wherever we turned in the Police Department, wherever we turned in the city administration, and almost wherever we went in the rest of the city, we were met not with cooperation, not with appreciation, not with an eagerness to seek out the truth, but with suspicion and hostility and laziness and inattention, and with our fear that at any moment our efforts might be betrayed.

To me, being a cop means believing in the rule of law. It means believing in a system of government that makes fair and just rules and then enforces them.

Being a cop also means serving, helping others. If it is not too corny, a cop is to help an old lady walk the streets safely, to help a 12-year-old reach her next birthday without being gang-raped, to help a storekeeper make a living without keeping a shotgun under his cash register, to help a boy grow up without having needles in his arms.

To me it is not a job, but a way of life.

Some people say that the cops live in the midst of inhumanity, amidst all the violence and cheating, violence and hate, and I guess to some extent it is true. But being a cop means also to be engaged with life. It means that our concern for others is not abstract, that we don't just write letters to The Times or give $10 once a year. We hit the street every day of our lives.

In this sense police corruption is not about money at all, because there is no amount of money that you can pay a cop to risk his life 365 days a year. Being a cop is a vocation or it is nothing at all, and that's what I saw being destroyed by the corruption of the New York City Police Department, destroyed for me and for thousands of others like me.

We wanted to believe in the rule of law. We wanted to believe in a system of responsibility. But those in high places everywhere, in the Department, in the DA's office, in City Hall, were determined not to enforce the law, they turned their heads away when law and justice were being sold on every street corner.

We wanted to serve others, but the Department was a home for the drug dealers and thieves. The force that was supposed to be protecting people was selling poison to their children, and there could be no life, no real life for me or anyone else on that force when, every day, we had to face the facts of our own terrible corruption.

I saw that happening to men all around me; men who could have been good officers, men of decent impulse, men of ideals, but men who were without decent leadership, men who were told in a hundred ways every day, go along, forget about the law, don't make waves and shut up.

They did go along. They did learn the unwritten code of the Department. They went along and they lost something very precious. They were a long way toward not being men anymore. And all the time I saw the other victims, too, especially the children—children of 14 and 15 and 16, wasted by heroin, turn into street corner thugs and whores, willing to rape their own mother for the price of a fix.

That was the price of going along, the real price of police corruption—not free meals, but broken homes in dying neighborhoods, and a whole generation of people being lost.

They went along and they lost something
very precious.

That's what I joined the Department to stop. So that is why I went to The New York Times, because attention had to be paid. And in a last desperate hope that if the facts were known, someone must respond. Now it is up to you. I speak to you now as nothing more and nothing less than a cop.

We need you to fix responsibility for the rottenness that was allowed to fester. It must be fixed both inside and outside the Department. Inside the Department, responsibility has to be fixed against those top commanders who allowed the situation to develop.

Responsibility has to be fixed because no patrolman can believe he should care about corruption if his superiors can get away without caring. Also because commanders, themselves, have to be told again and again, and not only by the Police Commissioner, that the entire state of the Department is up to them, and most of all, responsibility has to be fixed because it is the first step toward recovering our simple but necessary conviction that right will be rewarded and wrong-doing punished.

Responsibility must also be fixed outside the Police Department, against all the men and agencies that have helped bring us to our present pass, against all those who could have helped expose the corruption but never did.

Like it or not, the policeman is convinced that he lives and works in the middle of a corrupt society, that everybody is getting theirs and why shouldn't he, and that if somebody cared about corruption, something would have been done about it a long time ago.

So your report has to tell us about the District Attorneys and the courts and the Bar, and the Mayor and the Governor and what they have done, and what they have failed to do, and how great a measure of responsibility they also bear. Otherwise, if you suggest or allow others to suggest that the responsibility belongs only to the police, then for the patrolmen on the beat and in the radio cars, this commission will be just another part of the swindle.

> The policeman is convinced he lives in a
> corrupt society.

You have to speak to the conscience of this city, speak for all of those without a voice, all those who are not here to be heard today, although they know the price of police corruption more intimately than anyone here.

The people of the ghetto and all the other victims, those broken in mind and spirit and hope, perhaps more than any other people in this city, they depend upon the police and the law to defend not just their pocket-books but their very lives and the lives and welfare of their children.

Tow-truck operators can write off bribes on their income tax. The expense-account executive can afford a prostitute. But nobody can repay a mother for the pain of seeing her children hooked on heroin.

Of course, all corruption is bad, but we cannot fall into the trap of pretending that all corruption is equally bad. There is a difference between selling free meals and selling narcotics. If we are unable to make that distinction, then we are saying to the police that the life of a child in the South Bronx has the same moral value as a cup of coffee, and this could not be true for this society or for the police force. You must show us the difference.

Finally, you must speak for the policemen of this city, for the best that is in them, for what most of them want to be, for what most of them will be, if we try.

Once I arrested a landlord's agent who offered to bribe me if I would not lock up a tenant who was bothering other tenants in the building. I put the cuffs on him. A crowd of people actually were around and actually said, "Viva policia!"

Of course, it was not just me or even the police that they were cheering. They were cheering because they had glimpsed in that one arrest the possibility of a system of justice that could work to protect them, too. They were cheering because if that agent could get arrested, maybe they had rights, that they were citizens and maybe one day life would really be different for their children. For me, that moment was what police work is all about.

It took five years of Frank Serpico's life and five years of mine to help bring this commission about. It has taken the lives and dedication of thousands of other to preserve as much of a police force as we have. It has taken many months of effort by all of you to help show this city the truth.

What I ask of you now is to help make us clean again, to help give us some leadership to look to the force, to walk at ease with their fellow citizens and perhaps one day on a warm summer night, hear again the shout. "Viva policia!"

PERCEPTIONS of POlICE PRACTICES iN NEW YORK's "El bARRiO"

WAYNE L. COTTON

An increasing crime rate and a recurrence of civil disorder are two major problems which affect all elements of our society and all of our major institutions. At an operational level these problems most directly involve the members of ghetto communities (comprising a number of different minority groups in our society) and the police. These minority communities are involved so deeply because it is here that increasing crime takes its major tool, and that social and racial tensions, pressures for social change, and civil disorders are largely concentrated. Since the police are the instrument of control and enforcement in the society, they are the most directly involved in these processes on a day-to-day basis.

For a variety of reasons, methods of policing such communities have, in the majority of cases, proved inadequate. These methods have not protected the residents from the climbing crime rate nor have they given them a sense of security either in their homes or in the streets. There is little doubt that the abrasive nature of police-community contacts in the ghetto areas is at least partially responsible for the inadequacy of police protection, and that an improvement in the attitudes on both sides is a necessary step in any overall improvement of the situation. The problem is especially critical because of the feeling among ghetto residents that police treatment of them is much worse than of other segments of the general public, and that they in particular are often singled for police brutality and harassment. Christopher Rand (1958:58) states that an

Source: Paper presented at the 2nd Interamerican Congress of Criminology, Caracas, Venezuela, 1972. Reprinted by permission of the author. © 1972, Wayne L. Cotton.

especial amount of hostility is felt by New York Puerto Ricans toward the police, often as a result of police tactics.

There have been a number of studies, most of which have come to the same conclusion: that ghetto residents do not like the police, and that the police return the compliment in their attitudes and actions. Citizens complain that the police are neglectful of their duties, unfair, and too preoccupied with minor crimes to be efficient in solving major ones. The latter belief is attested to by Kadish (1967) concerning the entrapment policies of many police departments in enforcing laws against "vice." Even though there are increasing numbers of minority group members in urban police departments, they are often viewed by ghetto residents at best as misled and at worst as servile "lackeys of the establishment."

A study, conducted by Toro Calder, Cedeno and Reckless (1968) in Puerto Rico, found negative attitudes toward the police. Although this study was formulated to obtain attitudes of prisoners, guards and police as well as of laborers, it proved useful in indicating the wide-spread negative feeling that is directed toward police and law enforcement.[1]

But while most research has indicated a strong dislike for police, it has often not gone further and examined in more detail some of the root causes of such negativism. For example, are the police themselves seen as the culprits, or unfair laws which they impose? Could the feelings against the police be changed by different police procedures? Do ghetto residents want no police around at all, or do they simply want *better* police? Has antagonism gone so far now that even improving police service would be to little avail in changing attitudes in the community? Such questions apply especially to the younger members of the community because they are usually the most articulate in expressing their views, and because they will shortly be the leaders and spokesmen of these communities.

There have been studies, on the other hand, that have indicated a much more positive appraisal of the police in some ghetto areas, or more positive than would be imagined from the unfavorable publicity that police-community relations have recently received in such communities. The President's Commission on Law Enforcement and Administration of Justice (1967), for example, found a generally high regard for the police among all groups studied including black men, who felt that the police do not get enough credit or support for the community.

A Baltimore study for the Office of Economic Opportunity (Wallach and Carter, 1971) suggests that the residents of the black ghetto have an essentially positive orientation toward the police, albeit with considerable ambivalence, and would welcome more rather than less interaction with the police officers who patrol their communities. However, they would like such interaction to be more personal and reciprocal than at present, and would expect the police to modify some of their present behavior patterns.

The present study shows an essentially negative appraisal of the police in *El Barrio*. This may perhaps be summed up (much as Rand, cited above, has observed) by the attitude that the police pick on Puerto Ricans more than on other groups in the city. In fact the responses to a direct question to that effect elicited the belief among the sample population that police treat Puerto Ricans worse or even much worse than any other group, by a margin of more than two to one. In any case, it is obvious that the police suffer much criticism, which often becomes a "damned if they do, and damned if they don't" type of situation. And there are suggestions that the most negative attitudes of all toward the police are held, not by minorities, but by upper middle-class whites. Nevertheless, whatever the truth of that assertion may be, one returns to the central problem of the role of the police in regard to the ghetto communities.

One of the most important factors in this regard is the type of community in which the police have to operate; i.e., does the community represent a life-style that is similar to that of most police who work there, or does it differ radically from it? In this respect, Banton (1964:180) indicates that there are reasons to believe that many police prefer to work in lower-class neighborhoods since the middle-class areas provide less of a challenge (and perhaps less chance for promotion), and are in many cases "boring beats." On the other hand, it cannot be denied that ghetto areas are likely to be more dangerous for the police, and the inhabitants less cooperative than in middle-class precincts.

How far such a difference in values and outlook between police and a community affects law enforcement is a debatable but important point. In an article in the New York Post of May 13, 1972, the question of assigning an all-black force to Harlem was discussed; evidence indicated that a considerable percentage of the community would welcome such a move. David Riley (1969), in discussing community control of police, seems to think that such control may be the only workable solution short of violence.

Wayne LaFave (1965) demonstrated the dilemma of police justification in taking account of the local mores in deciding whether the process of enforcement should be invoked against a member of the particular community. LaFave indicates that, in his observation, there are many variations in enforcement from place to place, attributable in part to differing public attitudes in various locales.

William F. Whyte (1965) brings up the point of public relations and police behavior as a major problem in enforcement, and the image of the police and the law itself. If often becomes a question of class or ethnic values to which the policeman does not subscribe. The public need and demand for protection of a professional nature is also a most important variable in the whole process of enforcement; if the community sees the policeman as an interloper, he can hardly do an efficient job, and such feelings on the part of the public can cancel positive aspects of the legitimate demand for protection. Establishment of efficient law enforcement depends on a desire and a demand on the part of community residents for that type of service. Nothing less will do (Banton, 1964:1).

It would seem that one way to solve the conflict in values between police and community would be to assign more patrolmen of the same racial and ethnic background to ghetto neighborhoods, and indeed this procedure has been demanded by various militant groups. Most police departments do not subscribe to the view that this would be desirable or help very much in law enforcement, and many citizens interpret it as just another form of racism in reverse. The respondents for the present study did not support this approach either, as only some 30% felt that assigning more Puerto Rican policemen to their community would notably improve the quality of law enforcement. The general comment was that, in any case, such police would still be representing the "system," although it was admitted that an ability to speak Spanish would be a distinct advantage.

The police, on the other hand, have another viewpoint on the problem of enforcement. According to Skolnick (1966), they are very cognizant of the problem of community relations, although they seem to emphasize different factors than does the general public. For example, the police felt that lack of respect, lack of cooperation, and lack of understanding of themselves were the greatest difficulties, while the public in ghetto communities placed racism and lack of understanding of different values as most important. Police usually did not mention racism in the first rank of problems, and this omission may be interpreted variously as: indifference to the feelings of minorities, avoidance of the issue, or a simple refusal to discuss what is considered a delicate matter.

In order to examine some of the attitudes from the community side of the question of law enforcement and police behavior, the present research examines the attitude of residents of one ghetto community in New York City, East Harlem or "El Barrio." While there are considerable numbers of other minority groups—mainly blacks, but with some Italians and a few others—the area is largely populated by Puerto Ricans. Whereas in many areas of the country it is primarily the blacks who see the police as oppressors and as victimizers of their group so far as brutality, corruption, and other related social ills are concerned, in New York the Puerto Ricans see themselves in that position or, in the opinion of some, in an even worse position.

The population of respondents used in the present study was composed of young Puerto Rican males between the ages of 18 and 30. A considerable number of these were migrants from Puerto Rico, with the expected language and cultural difficulties, but the majority were born and reared in New York, able to cope with conditions in the city, and often very articulate. Those respondents were interviewed by bilingual interviewers using a questionnaire designed to test some of the attitudes toward police and their activities in law enforcement. The final sample consisted of 230 respondents.

The area of El Barrio is one of the most congested parts of the city, with almost no home ownership and very high absentee ownership of buildings and businesses. Housing ranges from the very worst kind of outmoded tenement with just bare essentials, and sometimes not even those, to a large number of public housing projects, which while providing much better physical facilities, are often overcrowded and in many cases heavily crime-ridden. Narcotics use and sale is an ever-present problem to the residents of this area. In other words, it is a typical inner-city ghetto area, with all the accompanying problems.

For purposes of making comparisons, the respondents were divided into three categories according to level of acculturation. That is, those who were born and reared in New York, speak English fluently, and have considerable social contacts with non-Puerto Ricans, among other variables, are considered as highly acculturated. Those who are fairly recent migrants, speak little English, and restrict their lives mostly or entirely to other Puerto Ricans, are considered poorly acculturated. The third category of the moderately acculturated consists of those respondents who are at neither extreme and who have a somewhat marginal existence between the two worlds. It was expected that these three groups would have significantly differing perceptions of the police and so it turned out, but not wholly as anticipated.

In asking questions in this area, several different factors were probed. These include: the law itself and its fairness, general police image, police efficiency, and police method of operation. It is obvious that all of these do not have to be either positive or negative. For example, one might feel that the police are efficient, but deplore the method used to obtain that efficiency. Or, the law might be seen as basically fair, but the way in which the police carry it out looked on as unfair.

The results indicate that very few of the respondents, only about one in five, feel that the law is usually fair. This would indicate that in El Barrio there is much dissatisfaction with the law itself, as well as with its method of enforcement. In addition, about half of the respondents thought that the police did not enforce the laws strictly enough, but the reasons for this were not so much support of the law itself as the belief that police do not take action against the really serious violators, or play favorites, or get involved with payoffs and bribes. The consensus appears to be that by strictly enforcing the laws, the police would make themselves more honest as well.

In considering the overall police image, the negative opinions become even more obvious. A good indicator of attitude would be an appraisal of the honesty of the police. In the present sample only about one-third of the respondents believe that the police usually are honest, and more than one in five feels that they are almost never honest. An even stronger indictment is shown by the fact that 35% feel that police are just as bad as the criminals.

In like manner, police efficiency is doubted to a large extent, as shown by the belief that police do not do a good or efficient job, with almost half (45%) saying that their performance is poor or very bad. None believe that the police perform very well, which contrasts markedly with official proclamations of how the police show restraint and skillfully perform in the face of vast difficulties, especially in dealing with trouble in ghetto areas. The residents of El

Barrio simply do not think this is so. Nor do they believe that the police are especially efficient in apprehending criminals, since 55% indicate that they think the police do not usually arrest those who commit serious crimes. About the same proportion believes that the police waste a great deal of time on petty criminals and minor violations. The negative opinions of efficiency are not so widespread as of the police image. This may indicate that the people are willing to tolerate some inefficiency rather than run the risk of overzealousness on the part of the police, which could be considered more of a danger to the average citizen.

Police methods of operation are also looked on with a great deal of negativism. Like the overall image, this aspect of police work seems to arouse more emotion than efficiency per se. The overwhelming majority believe that police are brutal from time to time, and almost one third (30%) think that brutality occurs often. About the same proportion feels that police respect the rights of suspects rarely or never, and a large majority (80%) feels that police are not sufficiently careful before arresting innocent persons.

In spite of all this negativism, two interesting findings emerge. These are that somewhat over 50% of all respondents agree that having more police on the job would be desirable, and just about the same number think that the police should be paid higher salaries for dangerous work. While this may appear contradictory to all that has just been stated, it is not necessarily so, because there is much evidence that the respondents feel that higher salaries and greater police coverage would increase their professionalization and make them more cognizant of the community's problems. They definitely want police protection, and do not feel that they are getting it.

Further observations can be made regarding the three levels of acculturation into which the respondents were divided. With few exceptions, both the poorly acculturated and the highly acculturated had similar views, while those more marginal had differing views, and these latter were more often positive in their appraisal of the police than the other two categories of respondents. It had been thought that the least acculturated individuals would give the poorest ratings to the police and the most acculturated persons would rate them higher.

Summary

The overall picture that emerges from these findings is that the police have a very bad image in Spanish Harlem. These respondents feel that the police do not like them and treat them very badly; they also believe their methods of operation to be questionable at best and brutal at worst, and their efficiency open to much improvement. In spite of these attitudes, a small majority feels that things would be better if there were more police, and that the police ought to receive higher salaries. It would seem obvious that the residents of El Barrio do not entirely reject the concept of the police as a social force, and would probably welcome better police services. They do, however, seriously object to the police as presently constituted and do not have much faith in either their methods or their efficiency. But to say, as some have done, that the police must go, or that no matter what changes are made, the ghetto will never accept the police in any way, is not borne out by the attitudes expressed here.

The level of acculturation of these respondents is related very definitely to the favor or disfavor with which they view the police, with those who are relatively little acculturated indicating the most negative opinions. However, while it had been expected that the most acculturated respondents would show the most positive attitudes, such was not the case. Rather it is those in a more marginal status, the partially acculturated, who indicate greater approval and support for the police and the law. In many ways, the poorly and well acculturated individuals are closer to each other in their attitudes than either is to the partially acculturated.

It appears somewhat difficult at first sight to explain the reasons for this finding. It might be expected that with increased socialization toward the general American culture, individuals would come to accept the police as representatives of the law and give them greater support. While this does occur, it does not manifest itself to anywhere near the degree expected. One possible explanation relates to the marginal status of the partially acculturated Puerto Rican. A possible analogy might be found in the situation of social classes in the general society. According to many polls, news reporting, and sociological analysis, the middle-class American, and especially the lower middle-class individual, is most insecure about his status, both economically and socially. The "law-and-order" philosophy gets its strongest support from that segment of the population. While this, like most analogies, leaves much to be desired, it is quite possible that the only partially acculturated member of society—in this case the Puerto Rican—feels most keenly his marginal status, and is somewhat confused about the place he occupies both in relation to his own ethnic group, and the larger society. In a sense, the better acculturated Puerto Rican has "made it" within the larger society, and is somewhat more secure in his self-image, while the least acculturated person is still trying to cope with just existing and is likely to feel the full brunt of discrimination by the society at large, even his own people perhaps, and most especially by the police. In other words, the moderately acculturated person is trying very hard to be accepted and to find a place in the total culture, and may become somewhat ritualistic in his views of social institutions and their representatives.

The main reason, perhaps, why the most highly acculturated respondents may have such negative opinions of the police could reside with their better education and a greater awareness of just what ghetto law enforcement entails. While they may not personally feel the brunt of discrimination and bad police practice to the extent that their less acculturated brothers do, it may rankle them even more because of their awareness. They are able to analyze what is happening, and to develop very intense feelings of resentment and hostility toward those who are making it difficult for "their people." These same individuals may also feel somewhat guilty about their better fortunes than many others in El Barrio, and react with stronger attitudes.

One implication that this study brings out is that increasingly these young, better educated members of the ghetto communities are going to have to be dealt with. This evidence supports the opinions voiced by youth leaders and social workers familiar with ghetto problems. Their attitudes are going to be increasingly the ones that count, and any plans for future police-community relations will have to take them into account. A practical consideration derived from the reality of these trends would seem to indicate a policy of trying to bolster and reinforce the realization of identity of ethnic groups and to make it a useful force in strengthening law enforcement in the whole society. What many leaders—and interestingly, the most acculturated among them—in the Puerto Rican community are calling for is a recognition of and respect for their Hispanic culture and identities, and this is being stressed in ways never attempted by earlier immigrant groups.

Other possible areas for research in this area could include studies of police attitudes toward Puerto Ricans, similar to those done by Skolnick and LaFave. It might be useful to know if the police make distinctions, and if so, what kind of distinctions, according to their perceived level of acculturation of individuals with whom they have to deal. The matter of police discretion in making arrests in Puerto Rican ghettos could also prove informative. In addition, further information concerning the young, better educated Puerto Ricans, who are often in the vanguard of the more aggressive assertions of "Puerto Rican Power," would prove useful in formulating the types of reforms necessary or practical in law enforcement.

Note

1. I am indebted to the authors of this research, especially Dr. Reckless, for permission to use a number of the questions used by them in the present study, and for insights into the problems of phrasing such questions to elicit more valid responses.

References

Banton, M.
    1964   The Policeman in the Community. New York: Basic Books.

Kadish, S. H.
    1967   The crisis of overcriminalization. Annals of the American Academy of Political and Social Science, 374: 157–70.
LaFave, Wayne
    1965   Arrest: The Decision to Take a Subject into Custody. Boston: Little, Brown.
New York Post
    1972   Should Harlem Be an All-Black Beat? May 13.
President's Commission on Law Enforcement and the Administration of Justice
    1967   Public attitudes toward crime and law enforcement. In Task Force Report: Crime and Its Impact, an Assessment. Washington, D.C.: Government Printing Office.
Rand, Christopher
    1958   The Puerto Ricans. New York: Oxford University Press.
Riley, David P.
    1969   Should communities control their police? Civil Rights Digest, 2(Fall): 26–35.
Skolnick, Jerome H.
    1966   Justice Without Trial. New York: Wiley.
Toro Calder, Jaime, Cerefina Cedeno, and Walter C. Reckless
    1968   A comparative study of Puerto Rican attitudes toward the legal system dealing with crime. Journal of Criminal Law, Criminology and Police Science, 59: 536–41.
Wallach, Irving, and Colette C. Carter
    1971   Perceptions of the police in a black community. In Study for Office of Economic Opportunity. McLean, Va.: Rand Analysis Corp.
Whyte, William F.
    1965   Street Corner Society. Chicago: University of Chicago Press.

distRust of the police and cRimE REpoRtiNq

ROBERT CROSBY AND DAVID SNYDER

Introduction

The problems of crime are in the forefront of national interest.[1] The rate of crime is continuing to increase in the cities of the United States. Every day, people read in the newspapers about acts of violence, theft, rapes, and other serious offenses committed against the person. Consequently, a fear of crime throughout the urban centers of the nation has eroded the basic quality of life among many Americans. In addition, more people are victimized by crime than is shown in crime statistics; many crimes are not reported; and relations between the community and police are often strained.

It is impossible to determine the nature and extent of the problems crime causes by merely reviewing the latest crime statistics. Contact must be established and maintained with the victims of crime.[2] Resource Management Corporation (RMC) and Roy Littlejohn Associates, in an effort to bridge the gap between crime statistics and society's opinions towards crime, evaluated the attitudes of black Americans about the crime problem in the cities. Several questions were asked on victimization, propensity to report cime, and satisfaction with police protection. This document summarizes the responses to these and other questions and interprets certain key points.

Admittedly, this is not a research paper that purports to draw conclusions of unequivocal significance; it is meant instead to be a convenient summary of

Research Document RD-026, Resource Management Corporation, Bethesda, Maryland. Reprinted by permission.

the survey results, along with some cautious interpretive comments. Those who have an interest and a desire to find out the extent and effects of crime in urban black America are urged to study these results and develop their own conclusions.

Overview of the Findings

The black community generally believes that crime occurs more often than reported by officials, indicating the existence of an information gap in the black urban centers throughout the nation. The survey showed that one out of every three respondents believed that crime occurs more often than reported by official figures. Feelings of distrust of the police may be a contributing cause of this gap.

Nearly one out of five urban blacks (19 percent) has been victimized by crime at some point in his life. The Uniform Crime Reports of 1968 found that approximately 1 percent of the general population is victimized by crime in one year; the average crime rate for individuals over the past 30 years is approximately 0.6 percent per year. It is interesting to note that using a standard probability formula, the victimization percent over time using UCR data is 22 percent, a figure comparable with our findings.[3]

Seventeen percent of those who had been victimized by crime indicated they had not reported it to the police. This contrasts with a survey of 10,000 households conducted in 1965 and 1966 for the President's Commission on Law Enforcement and Administration of Justice, which indicated that approximately 50 percent of all crimes committed in the general population had not been reported or had not entered the statistical system.[4] Thus, either the black urbanite reports crime more readily than the general population or there are serious deficiencies in the present statistical system for gathering crime statistics.

One out of three blacks who reported a crime indicated that police response had not met their expectations, while 41 percent of the crime victims themselves were not satisfied with the police response. For those victims who had not reported the crime, a surprisingly high percentage could or would not give a reason for not reporting the offense. The most prevalent reason for not reporting among those willing to say was the belief that nothing could be done.

The *Report of the National Advisory Commission on Civil Disorders* (March 1968) cited "deep hostility between police and ghetto communities as a primary cause of disorders surveyed by the Commission. . . . Abrasive relationships between police and Negroes and other minority groups have been a major source of grievance, tension, and, ultimately, disorder." Although our statistics do not reflect this hostility, they do picture a black urbanite who distrusts the police and is not satisfied with the services police provide. Table 15-1 presents a general summary of our findings. The following sections discuss these findings in detail.

TABLE 15-1. Summary of Findings

Information Gap	33 percent feel crime occurs more often than reported.
Victimization	19 percent had been victims of crime.
Reporting Crime	17 percent had not reported crime to police.
Expectation	31 percent felt police response was less than what they would expect.
Satisfaction with Police	41 percent felt police response was unsatisfactory.
Failure to Report Crime	61 percent of victims not reporting crime could or would not give a reason.

Information Gap

Overall, one of every three respondents believed that crime occurs more often than what is reported by officials. More blacks between 15 and 34 years old indicated crime occurs more often than reported (as opposed to the over 34 age group), reflecting either a distrustful attitude of the young or more exposure to crime. By sex, 37 percent of the males as opposed to 30 percent of females believed more crime occurred than was reported. Forty-two percent of the college-educated blacks felt that more crime occurred than was reported, as compared with only 31 percent of the noncollege-educated. Forty percent of the white-collar professional workers and blue-collar foremen, as compared with about 30 percent of the laborers, clerical, and nonprofessional occupations, believed that crime statistics understated reality, which verified that a distinction could be made by occupation. This distinction became clear when correlating these answers to household income. As income increases, people felt that crime occurs more often than reported. Figure 15-1 highlights this point; this trend has been tested and found statistically significant.

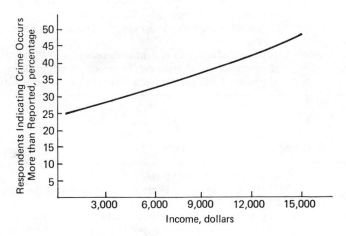

FIGURE 15-1.

Tensions and Conflicts

TABLE 15-2. Crime Occurs More Often Than Reported by Officials

Overall	33 percent of all respondents
Age	35 percent of those younger than 34; 31 percent of those older than 34
Sex	37 percent of males; 30 percent of females
Education	42 percent of college-educated; 31 percent of noncollege-educated
Profession	40 percent of professionals; 30 percent of nonprofessionals
Income	50 percent of high-income group, decreasing with decreasing income

Victimization

Approximately 19 percent of the respondents had been victims of crime. Of these, more blacks under 35 had been victims than those over 35. Approximately one and one-half times more males are victimized than females. The victimization survey conducted by the President's Crime Commission indicated that the ratio between male and female victimization approaches 3.0 in the general population; i.e., three times as many males are victimized as females. In the white community, the white woman is victimized significantly less than the man, according to the Commission. In the black community, on the other hand, the female is a victim almost as often as the male.

The college graduates are victimized almost twice as often as noncollege graduates. As expected, a similar difference in victimization is found when occupation is considered. A higher percentage of professional workers are victimized. The percentage of an income group that is victimized appears to in-

TABLE 15-3. Victims of Crime

Overall	19 percent of all respondents
Age	22 percent of the under-35 age group; 17 percent of the over-35 group
Sex	24 percent of males; 15 percent of females
Education	30 percent of college graduates; 17 percent of nongraduates
Income	33 percent of high-income group, decreasing with decreasing income

TABLE 15-4. Crime Not Reported to Police

Overall	17 percent of all respondents
Age	25 percent of the 15-to-24 age group; 14 percent of the older group
Sex	20 percent of males; 10 percent of females
Occupation	25 percent of the laborers; 14 percent of other occupations
Income	20 percent of low-income group; 14 percent of high-income group

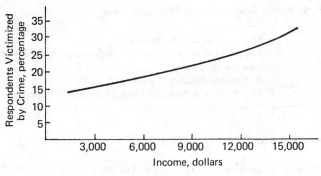

FIGURE 15-2.

crease with the higher income categories, as shown in Figure 15-2. This trend has also been tested to be statistically significant.

Reporting Crime

Seventeen percent of the victimized respondents had not reported the crime. Most of the 65-and-over victims reported crimes to the police, while one out of every four victims in the 15-to-24 age group had not reported the crime, which indicates that young blacks do not feel as compelled to report crimes as their elders.

Male victims refused to report crime considerably more often than the females. Level of education did not seem to be a deciding factor on a person's propensity to report crime to police. However, the victims engaged in labor occupations indicated a relatively high failure-to-report percentage; more than one of every four in these categories had not reported the crime. A higher percentage of respondents in the low-income groups (less than $6,000 annual income) had not reported the crime as compared with the higher income groups (more than $6,000 annually), indicating that income probably has an effect on a person's propensity to report crime.

Table 15-4 presents these data.

Expectation of Police Response

Of all crime victims who reported to police, 31 percent received less police response than they expected. Almost two out of every five respondents in the youngest (15 to 24) and the oldest (over 55) age groups received less response than anticipated. More males than females indicated that police response had not met their expectations. A large portion of the college graduates, who may be more critical due to their educational attainment, indicated that police response to the reported crimes was less than expected. Occupation and income were not determining factors on this percentage.

TABLE 15-5. Police Response Less Than Expected

Overall	31 percent of all respondents
Age	36 percent of the youngest and oldest age groups; 26 percent of the middle age group
Sex	36 percent of males; 26 percent of females
Education	43 percent of college graduates; 29 percent of nongraduates

Satisfaction with Police

A high degree of respondents who had a direct experience with the police felt that police response was unsatisfactory. Almost one out of every two respondents less than 35 years old were not satisfied with the police response, indicating that this age group is either not receiving adequate service or is highly critical of the police. Forty-five percent of the males as opposed to 37 percent of the females said that police response was unsatisfactory. Nearly 52 percent of the college graduates were not satisfied with police response, indicating that the college-educated may be more demanding of police. The highest degree of dissatisfaction was experienced with the black people engaged in a professional or technical occupation, with 53 percent of this group indicating unsatisfactory police response. No trend could be established with income.

Table 15-6 presents the results of this phase of the survey.

These statistics are alarming. The policeman's main function is to enforce the law and maintain order in the community he serves. How well he is performing this job is usually assessed by crime statistics. However, the opinions of people that are served must also be considered. Four of ten people in the black community are not satisfied with the response of the police. This is an extremely high degree of dissatisfaction and may be an important cause in the breakdown of relations and communications between police and the community.

Failure to Report Crime

Of those who did not report the crime, a very high percentage did not give a reason why they had not reported it to police. Almost 61 percent of the respondents could or would not state a reason. At this time we cannot directly assess the cause for such a high percentage of respondents not being able to state a reason, but RMC plans to investigate this further in a forthcoming survey. For those who gave a reason, a majority indicated that they did not think anything could be done, supporting the finding of the President's Crime Commission. Only 3 percent of the respondents to this question cited a reason relating to the effectiveness or relationship with the police, such as police are uninterested, police brutality, or no results from police. Due to the small base in the *Black*

TABLE 15-6. Police Response Unsatisfactory

Overall	41 percent of all respondents
Age	46 percent of age group less than 35; 38 percent of group older than 35
Sex	45 percent of males; 37 percent of females
Education	52 percent of college-educated; 39 percent of noncollege-educated
Occupation	53 percent of professional and technical; 39 percent of other occupations

TABLE 15-7. Reasons for Not Reporting Crime

Overall	61 percent could give no reason.
Most Frequent	They gave personal reasons not relating to police.
Police	Only 3 percent indicated a reason related to police.

Buyer Survey, no analysis could be made of the age, sex, education, occupation, or income factors.

References

1. The research results presented here are based on the summer 1969 *Black Buyer* Survey, a continuing study of the urban Negro heads of households, conducted by Resource Management Corporation in cooperation with Roy Littlejohn and Associates.

2. In 1967, the President's Crime Commission conducted the first national survey of crime victimization.

3. $V = (1 - r)^n$ where r is the percentage of the average yearly crime rate, n is the average age of respondents to our survey (42 years old), and V is the victimization percentage over time.

4. President's Commission on Law Enforcement and Administration of Justice, *The Challenge of Crime in a Free Society* (Washington, 1967).

A GARRISON STATE IN "DEMOCRATIC" SOCIETY*

PAUL TAKAGI

I.

This paper reports on a study of police officers killed in the line of duty and civilians killed by the police. The study was originated in 1971 in reaction to news reporting on the several mass media outlets at the local and national levels, which focused on FBI statistics indicating police officers were being "assassinated" at an alarming rate. A police reporter for an educational television station alarmed viewers with a report that 125 law enforcement officers had been killed in 1971, an increase of almost two and one-half times over 1963 when only 55 police officers were killed in all of that year. Police killings of citizens, however, were reported as isolated events. Although the death of civilians at the hands of police occurred from time to time, no news analyst attempted to show this as a national phenomenon.

Sorel (1950) said people use words in selective ways to create alarm. When a police officer kills a citizen, the official language is "deadly force," suggesting to the audience that the use of force was legitimate. But when a police officer is killed, it is characterized as "violence," and therefore, illegit-

Source: Crime and Social Justice. 1(Spring-Summer)1974: 27–33. Reprinted by permission of *Crime and Social Justice* and the author.

*The study was originally conducted by Philip Buell and Paul Takagi in the Summer of 1971, entitled "Code 984: Death by Police Intervention." The present version was considerably revised for this publication. I wish to express my appreciation to Herman Schwendinger, Virginia Engquist Grabiner, June Kress, and Tony Platt for their comments and criticisms.

imate. In this way, news, reporting the killing of police officers in 1971, conjured the idea that the apparent increase in the killing of police officers was unprecedented. It was seen as an attack caused in part by the rising political militancy among revolutionary groups, and by the increasing race consciousness among people of color venting their frustrations by attacking a visible symbol of authority. This interpretation was entertained by officials at the highest levels. President Nixon, in April of 1971, called upon police officials; and as subsequent events revealed, other representatives from para-military organizations also met to deal with the "problem."

The approach by officials was to consider the problem one of defense, and to search for the best technical means and policies to protect their view of a "democratic" society. It was viewed as a military problem, and the fortification of the police under increased LEAA funding and direction became a national policy (Goulden, 1970).

One hundred and twenty-five police officers died while on duty during 1971; the actual rate of death, however, did not increase because of the greater number of police officers who were on duty during the same year. Even if the number of police personnel has increased two and one-half times since 1963, the rate of death among police officers should not change. This is not said in an attempt to minimize the statistics that concern the officials. One could argue that the rate of police deaths should decrease. The point is to look at all the statistics, including previous studies that actually show the killing of police officers occurs at a relatively stable rate (Bristow, 1963; Robin, 1963; and Cardarelli, 1968).

The source of data is the FBI's own reports, which show an increase in the number of police officers killed, from 55 in 1963 to 125 in 1971, along with an increase of over 50 percent in the numbers of full-time authorized police personnel. The data presented in Chart 1 show that the rate of such homicides, while fluctuating from year to year, does not result in a trend either up or down over the period. The rate did peak nationally in 1967 with 29.9 deaths per 100,000 law enforcement officers. This includes all ranks from patrolmen to higher officials and federal agents. Since patrolmen bear the greatest risk of being killed in the line of duty, they may feel that FBI reports should be more detailed to accurately reflect the hazards they face.

Reports to the FBI on the numbers of police officers on duty and the numbers killed may not give a complete picture, since the agency has been only gradually achieving uniform reporting. Indeed, the number of reporting agencies increased since 1963. California, however, has had fairly complete and uniform reporting throughout the period, and the death rates among California police are available for the whole decade since 1960. They, too, show a peak in 1967, a year in which 12 officers were killed. That did not set a trend, however, as the rate decreased in the next two years.

For the 86 officers who were killed in California from 1960 through

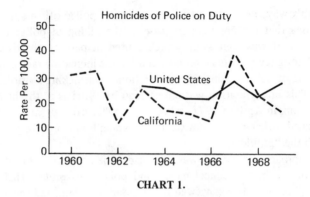

CHART 1.

1970, the police apprehended 117 suspects of whom 55 percent were white, 25 percent Black, and 19 percent Mexican-American. (This is the same percentage distribution of ethnic/racial groups in California's prison population.) At the time of this writing, 65 of the 117 suspects were convicted of either murder or manslaughter, and 7 cases were still pending in court. W.H. Hutchins, Assistant Chief of the California Bureau of Criminal Statistics, noted in a paper delivered to the California Homicide Investigators' Conference on March 5, 1971 that the great majority of homicidal deaths among police officers occurred in situations where robberies were in progress or where robbers were fleeing arrest. But, noted Hutchins, "the ambushing of officers, which has been relatively rare in the past, accounted for 25 percent of peace officers killed in 1970" (Hutchins, 1971).

Mr. Hutchins is not entirely correct when he reports that the majority of police officers killed were in situations involving armed robberies. An earlier report by his Bureau of Criminal Statistics indicates: ". . . 63 percent of these officers died while conducting routine investigations, responding to disturbance calls and taking people into custody . . ." (Beattie, 1968:5). A special study on the deaths of 39 California police officers (1960 through 1966) shows 35 of the 39 died of gunshot wounds, in some instances by their own guns (ibid.: 11-14).

> Klass, Richard J., 25-year-old patrolman, Daly City Police Department, killed May 6, 1966. Shot with his own gun by an escapee with whom he was struggling.
> LeFebvre, Richard R., 23-year-old patrolman, Long Beach Police Department, killed August 15, 1965 at 8:00 PM. Died at the scene of a riot when a shotgun in the hands of a brother officer discharged during a struggle.
> Ludlow, Donald E., a 26-year-old deputy sheriff, Los Angeles County, killed August 13, 1965 at 9:00 PM. Shot to death when brother officers' gun went off during struggle at riot scene.

Ross, Charles M., 31-year-old patrolman, Richmond Police Department, killed February 9, 1964 at 1:00 AM. Shot with his own gun while struggling with two drunks.

The four cases above were classified as homicides. To distinguish accidental death from homicide appears to require considerable judgment among those compiling crime statistics, and it is important to understand that these judgment classifications are included in the annual FBI reports on homicides of police officers.

It was noted earlier that the killing of police officers peaked in 1967 with 29.9 deaths per 100,000 law enforcement officers. Does this mean that law enforcement work is one of extreme peril? Robin (1963) argues otherwise:

> ... there is reason to maintain that the popular conception of the dangerous nature of police work has been exaggerated. Each occupation has its own hazards. The main difference between police work and other occupations is that in the former there is a calculated risk ... while other occupational hazards are accidental and injuries usually self-inflicting (ibid.: 230).

Robin adjusts the death rate among police officers to include the accidental deaths (mostly from vehicular accidents), and compares the death rate among the major occupational groups. It is apparent that the occupational risks in law enforcement are less dangerous than those in the several major industries. Mining with 93.6 deaths per 100,000 employees is almost three times riskier than law enforcement, while construction work is two and one-half times more dangerous, and agriculture and transportation show considerably higher rates of death than does law enforcement. Robin correctly concludes that the data do

TABLE 1. Occupational Fatalities per 100,000 Employees 1955

Occupation	Fatality Rate per 100,000
Mining	93.58
Construction Industry	75.81
Agriculture	54.97
Transportation	44.08
Law Enforcement	32.76
Public Utilities	14.98
Finance, Gov., Service	14.18
Manufacturing	12.08
Trade	10.25

Table adapted from Robin (ibid.: Table 6).

not support the general belief that law enforcement work is a highly dangerous enterprise.

II.

The other side of the coin is police homicides of citizens. This aspect of police-citizen interaction has received little attention except in the work of Robin (ibid.) and Knoohuizen, et al. (1972). For example, the prestigious President's *Task Force Report* on the police (1967) devotes not one line to this issue.

What is generally not known by the public, and either unknown or certainly not publicized by the police and other officials, is the alarming increase in the rate of deaths of male citizens caused by, in the official terminology, "legal intervention of police." These are the cases recorded on the death certificates as "justifiable homicide" by police intervention. After disappearing onto computer tapes, these reappear as statistics in the annually published official volumes of "Vital Statistics in the United States." Here they can be found under "Cause of Death, Code Number 984," where they have attracted very little attention.

The deaths of male civilians ages ten years and over caused by police intervention gradually increased in rate, especially from 1962 to 1968, the latest year in which nationwide statistics were available at the time of this writing (see Chart 2). More dramatic is the trend in civilian deaths caused by California police, where the rate increased two and one-half times between 1962 and 1969. This increase cannot be attributed simply to an increase in the proportion of young adults in the population, among whom a larger share of these deaths occur, because each annual rate is age-adjusted to the age-profile of the population in 1960. There is an increase in the rate of homicides by police, regardless of the changes in that age profile.

Why should such a trend go unnoticed? The crime rate has, of course, increased at the same time, and this, it might be argued, indicates that more males put themselves in situations where they risk a police bullet. This is the

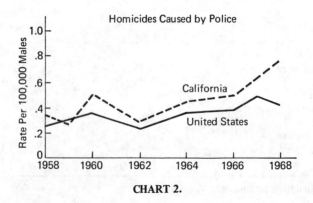

CHART 2.

argument that the victim alone is responsible. But that is too simple an explanation: an increase in such dangerous situations has not led to an increased jeopardy of police lives, for, as we have seen, their homicide rate did not increase over the same period.

The charts show police to be victims of homicides at an annual rate of about 25 per hundred thousand police, while citizens are victims of killings at the hands of police at a rate of 0.5 per 100,000 males ages ten and over, on the national level, and a rate of about 0.8 in California. This huge difference of 30 to 50-fold cannot be taken literally, because the civilian rate is based upon all males over age 9 even though most of them don't have the slightest chance of confronting a policeman in a desperate situation of anyone's making. There simply is no other population base to use in computing that rate. The point, however, is inescapable: the rate of death did not change for law enforcement officers during a period when it changed critically for male citizens.

III.

Black men have been killed by police at a rate some nine to ten times higher than white men. From that same obscure, but published source in our nation's capital, come the disheartening statistics. Between 1960 and 1968, police killed 1,188 Black males and 1,253 white males in a population in which about ten percent are Black. The rates of homicides due to police intervention increased over the years for both whites and Blacks, but remained consistently at least nine times higher for Blacks for the past 18 years (see Chart 3).

That proportionately more Blacks are killed by police, will come as no surprise to most people, certainly to no police officials. The remarkably big difference should be surprising, however. After all, the Black crime rate, even if we rely upon measurement by the arrest rate, is higher for Blacks than for whites. But that does not explain the killing of Black men. In 1964, arrests of Black males were 28 percent of total arrests, as reported by 3,940 agencies to

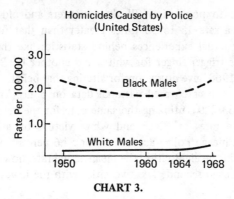

Homicides Caused by Police
(United States)

CHART 3.

the FBI, while Black deaths were 51 percent of the total number killed by police. In 1968 the Statistics were essentially the same.

It might be argued that Blacks have a higher arrest rate for the seven major crimes: homicide, rape, robbery, aggravated assault, burglary, theft, and auto theft; and that arrests for these crimes will correlate better with deaths by legal intervention of police. In 1968, Black males accounted for 36 percent of arrests for the major crimes; four years earlier, in 1964, Black arrests were less than 30 percent during a year when they suffered 51 percent of the deaths from police guns. Besides, it is not certain that the major crimes are a more accurate index of how frequently Blacks and whites commit crimes. Further, the threshold of suspicion is lower when a policeman encounters a Black man, thus the arrest rate is biased against Blacks. No matter how it is viewed, the death rate of Blacks is far out of proportion to the situations that might justify it.

Black people don't need these statistics to tell them what has been happening. The news gets around the neighborhood when someone is killed by the police. It is part of a history. But white people, especially policy-makers, don't live in those neighborhoods, and it is important that *they* explore the statistics further.

Take the age groups where "desperate" criminals are much less likely to be found, the very young and the very old. Male homicides by police during 1964–1968 were:

TABLE 2.

	Number of Deaths		Rate Per Million/Yearly	
	White	Black	White	Black
Ages 10–14	5	11	0.12	1.75
Ages 65+	5	14	0.14	4.76

In proportion to population, Black youngsters and old men have been killed by police at a rate 15 to 30 times greater than that for whites of the same age. It is the actual experiences behind statistics like these that suggest that police have one trigger finger for whites and another for Blacks. The latest statistics, those for 1968, give no reason for altering that belief.

Whereas our analysis covered national data on police killings of private citizens, Robin (1963:229), utilizing the same data for the years 1950 through 1960, examined the rates of Black and white victims by selected cities. In absolute numbers, Chicago police accounted for 54.6 percent of the 350 police slayings of citizens in the eight cities; the mean actual rate, however, was highest for Miami, with Chicago second. The two cities with the lowest police "justifi-

TABLE 3. Rates of Black and White Decedents, by City

City	Black per 1,000,000	White	Black:White Ratio
Akron	16.1	2.7	5.8 to 1
Chicago	16.1	2.1	7.4 to 1
Kansas City, Mo.	17.0	2.2	7.5 to 1
Miami	24.4	2.7	8.8 to 1
Buffalo	7.1	.5	12.2 to 1
Philadelphia	5.4	.2	21.9 to 1
Boston	3.2	.1	25.2 to 1
Milwaukee	13.5	.4	29.5 to 1

able homicide" rate, Boston and Milwaukee, killed Blacks in proportion to whites at a ratio of 25 to 29 times higher.

A more detailed analysis of police killing of private citizens was conducted by Robin for the city of Philadelphia. He reports:

Thirty of the 32 cases (28 were Black victims) were disposed of by the medical examiner, who at the inquest exonerated the officers involved in the killings on the grounds that death was due to justifiable homicide. In the two remaining cases the officers were held for the grand jury, indicted, tried by a jury, and found not guilty (ibid.:226).

Black citizens have long argued that the police are committing genocide on Black people, and there is increasing evidence that these killings are indeed murder, and that real justice is rarely if ever carried out in this process. Knoohuizen, et al. (1972) conducted a study of Chicago police killing of citizens, and provided further credence to the claim that police are murdering Black citizens. In their report, Knoohuizen and associates examined the incidents as reported by the police, the reports of the coroner's office, and testimony or statements by credible eyewitnesses. In Table 15 they summarized their findings from which we extracted three cases.

Case 1. The victim was Linda Anderson. Police action resulting in her death was ruled justifiable homicide because, according to police reports, she was killed accidentally during attempt to gain entrance to her apartment by shooting the lock off the door. The partner of the officer, and independent witnesses, corroborated the police officer's version. An independent investigation revealed that the officer used a shotgun standing four feet from the door, did not warn the occupant of impending shot, and missed the lock completely.

Case 2. The victim was Raymond Jones. Police action was ruled excusable because police officers did not strike the deceased and were only using the amount of force necessary to bring the suspect under arrest. Seven of 9 officers involved in the incident testified and confirmed each other's story. The report of the Coroner's pathologist, however, revealed that Mr. Jones was age 31 and in good health. He was also unarmed. The use of excessive force was implied when 9 police officers cannot subdue a suspect without causing his death.

Case 3. The victim was Charles Cox. The police report did not offer a justification or an excuse claiming the victim died from drug overdose rather than use of police force. Further reports from the police indicate blood analysis revealed some drugs in the victim's body. One of the arresting officers and one of the officers in charge of the lock-up both testified that the victim appeared all right when in their charge. A pathologist testified on the basis of his examination of the body that Cox died of blows to the head.

Knoohuizen and associates conclude from their analysis that in 28 of the 76 cases in which civilians were killed at the hands of the Chicago police, there was substantial evidence of police misconduct; and in 10 of the 76 cases, there was substantial evidence of criminal liability for manslaughter or murder (ibid.: 61).

Despite grand jury findings in those instances where police officers are held criminally liable, the courts have been reluctant to proceed with prosecution. All too often, such matters are thrown out of court or juries return the verdict of not guilty. For example, Superior Court Judge Ross G. Tharp of San Diego County dismissed involuntary manslaughter charges against a California Highway patrolman indicted in the fatal shootings of an unarmed 16-year-old boy. According to police reports, Roland R. Thomas was shot by Officer Nelander following a high speed chase in an allegedly stolen car. The car ran off the road, and Thomas appeared to reach toward his pocket at which point the officer fired his gun. In dismissing the case, Judge Tharp observed: "I think the officer deserves a commendation for doing his duty rather than standing trial."

The only recent cases in which police officers were held accountable for killing civilians were shown on a recent TV program (Owen Marshall, ABC, Saturday, March 2, 1974), in addition to the highly publicized case in Texas were a 12-year-old Mexican-American youngster was shot while under custody in a police car. The circumstances in the latter case were so gross that a dismissal was out of the question. The court, however, sentenced the officer to a prison term of 5 years in a state where sentences of 1,000 years for lesser crimes are not uncommon.

IV.

Authorities have been trying to combat what they view to be a rash of attacks on police, to the neglect of all the data that bear on the problem—a problem in which other lives are involved. The problem has existed all along; at least since 1950, and there is reason to believe for decades before that, Black people have been killed by the police at a tragically disproportionate rate, beyond the bounds of anything that would justify it.

Open warfare between the police and the citizenry might be one of the outcomes. Two recent attacks upon police station houses, one by a bomb and the other by shotgun wielding assailants resulting in the death of two police officers, are indicative. In the latter killing, the gunman thrust a shotgun through the speaking hole of a bullet proof glass shield separating the desk sergeant from the public. Portions of the police station house were protected by cyclone fencing. The wall of isolation surrounding the police is not only social and psychological, but physical, and the breaking down of these walls was considered by the National Crime Commission to be the single most important priority. Yet the federal government in appropriating billions of dollars for the Law Enforcement Assistance Administration program earmarked the funds primarily for the fortification of the police, thereby contributing to their isolation.

Currently, the concept of citizen participation is being stressed by the LEAA. The support the police get from some citizens' groups actually increases the isolation of police from minority communities. In Oakland, California, such a group, called Citizens for Law and Order, has a program of needling judges for their "soft" handling of criminal cases, firing broadsides at the press, television and radio, and appearing before local governmental bodies to promote support for the police and more "discipline" in schools. Programs like these are based on the belief that increasing the penalty for crime, increasing the powers of the police, and invoking police coercion of the citizenry will result in law and order.

Other citizens' groups have encouraged the introduction of reforms. People have worked on a variety of schemes such as Civilian Review Boards, psychological testing and screening of police candidates, human relations training, police community relations, racially integrated patrol units, and efforts to increase the hiring of Black and other minority officers. To the extent that they work to improve only the "image" of police, they fail because the problems go much deeper. And to a major extent, they fail because policemen, most of them willingly and others unknowingly, are used as the front line to maintain the social injustices inherent in other institutions and branches of government.

Perhaps the only immediate solution at this time is to disarm the police. Observers have noted that provinces in Australia where the police are unarmed have a much lower rate of attacks upon the police, compared to neighboring provinces where the police are armed, and the corollary observation, a lower rate of police misconduct.

Disarming the police in the United States will undoubtedly lower the rate of police killings of civilians; it does not, however, get at the causes of police misconduct, particularly toward black people. The findings that Blacks are killed by the police at a disproportionate ratio in cities like Milwaukee and

Boston, and the attitudes of officials like San Diego County's Superior Court Judge Tharp, require a more fundamental understanding of the meaning of policing in contemporary America.

V.

In distinguishing social justice from distributive justice, the former would not have been obtained, if, for example, Officer Lelander had been tried and convicted for the killing of a 16-year-old alleged auto thief; that would have been distributive justice, because it would have symbolized the fact that the police would not have received special treatment from the courts. Instead, the question that must be asked is why the police officer resorted to deadly force involving an alleged theft. To put it differently, why was the value of an automobile placed above the value of a human life? Judge Tharp's comments in dismissing the case provide a partial answer: "For doing his duty," the duty being to enforce the laws having to do with the property rights of an automobile owner. The critical issue here is that the auto theft laws and for that matter most of the laws in American society essentially legitimize a productive system where human labor is systematically expropriated. Examine for a moment the social significance of an automobile: it involves an array of corporate systems that expropriate the labor of people that go into manufacturing its parts, the labor for its assembly, the labor involved in extricating and processing the fuel that propels it, the labor of constructing the roads on which it runs, etc. The fiction of ownership exacts further capital by banking institutions that mortgage the commodity, and automobile insurance required by laws that extorts additional capital. The built-in obsolescence, or more precisely, the depreciation of the commodity, occurs when the muscle, the sweat, and human potential have been completely capitalized. These are the elements embodied in an automobile. It is no longer merely a commodity value, but represents a social value.

The automobile is a commodity created by varied types of wage labor. And as noted by men with ideas as far apart as those of Adam Smith and Karl Marx, the wealth of nations originate in the efforts of labor. But Marx added that wealth based on production of these commodities is accrued through the expropriation of labor power; and thus, the concept of private property based on this form of wealth is in essence the theft of the value-creating power of labor. The criminal laws, the system of coercion and punishment, exist to promote and to protect the consequences of a system based on this form of property.

The rights of liberty, equality, and security are not elements to be exchanged for the right of property acquired by the exploitation of wage labor; nor should they be expressed in relative terms, that is, greater or less than property rights. One person's life and liberty is the same as the next person's. But in a society that equates private property with human rights, they become inevitably reduced to standards and consequences that value some lives less than others. The system of coercion and punishment is intimately connected with the inequitable distribution of wealth, and provides the legitimation under the perverted notion that "ours is a government of laws" even to kill in order to maintain social priorities based on private property. This is the meaning of policing in American society.

Why are Black people killed by the police at a rate nine to ten times higher than whites? We can describe the manifestations of racism but cannot adequately explain it. At one level, we agree with the observation that the existence of racism is highly profitable. The Black urban ghettos, created by America's industries, provided the cheap labor power for the accumulation of some of America's greatest industrial wealth at the turn of the 20th century, and again during World War II. These urban ghettos still provide a highly exploited source of labor. In addition, the ghettos themselves have become a place for exploitation by slum landlords, merchants selling inferior quality goods at higher prices, a justification for higher premium rates on insurance, and the victimizing of people under the credit purchase system. To maintain this situation, the regulatory agencies, including the police, have ignored the codes governing housing, food, health, and usury conditions.

In cities across the country, the infamous ghettos are now deemed to be prime real estate, and the state under the powers of eminent domain claim for finance capitalism the areas for high rise buildings, condominiums, trade complexes, and entertainment centers ostensibly for the "people." Under what has been called urban redevelopment, the police are present to quiet individual and especially organized protest and dissent, and the full powers of the state are employed to evict, to dispossess, and to humiliate.

At another level, the concentration of capital has produced on the one hand, a demand for a *disciplined* labor force and, in order to rationalize its control, to rely increasingly upon administrative laws; on the other hand, it has created a *surplus* labor force that is increasingly controlled by our criminal laws. The use of punishment to control surplus labor is not new, having its roots in early 16th century Europe (Rusche and Kirchheimer, 1968).

Historically, people of color came to the United States not as freepersons, but as slaves, indentured servants, and as contract laborers. They were initially welcomed under these conditions. As these particular systems of exploitation gradually disappeared and the people entered the competitive labor market, a variety of devices were employed to continue oppressing them, including imprisonment. In the present period described by some as the post-industrial era, increasing numbers of people, and especially Black people, find themselves in the ranks of the unemployed, which establishment economists, fixing upon the 5 percent unemployment figure, dismiss as a regular feature of our political economy. Sweezy (1971) disagrees, arguing that the "post-industrial" unemployment figures are the same as that in the Great Depression when one includes

defense and defense related employment data. When arrest and prison commitment data on Black people are viewed from this perspective, especially the
sudden increase in prison commitments from a stable rate of ten percent up to
and during the early period of World War II to almost double that after the war,
there is some basis to suspect that the police killing of Black citizens is punishment to control a surplus labor population.

The labor surplus analysis, however, does not explain the sudden increase
in police killing of civilians beginning around 1962. Did the Civil Rights movement in housing, education, and employment, and more specifically, the militancy of a Malcolm X, and the liberation movements in Third World nations
around the world, re-define the role of the police? Did finance imperialism in
the form of multi-national corporations beginning about this time create an
un-noticed social dislocation? Why do the police kill civilians at a much higher
rate in some cities compared to others, and why do they kill Blacks at a dis-
proportionately higher ratio in cities like Boston and Milwaukee? Why do
California police, presumed to be highly professional, kill civilians at a rate 60
percent higher than the nation as a whole? We are not able to answer these
questions.

We must, however, pause for a moment, and consider what is happening
to us. We know that authorized police personnel in states like California has
been increasing at the rate of 5 to 6 percent compared to an annual population
increase of less than two and one-half percent. In 1960 there were 22,783
police officers; in 1972 there were 51,909. If the rate of increase continues,
California will have at the turn of the 21st century an estimated 180,000 police
officers, an equivalent of 10 military divisions. Is it not true that the growth in
the instruments of coercion and punishment is the inevitable consequence of
the wealth of a nation that is based upon theft?

America is moving more and more rapidly towards a garrison state, and
soon we will not find solace by repeating to ourselves: "Ours is a democratic
society."

Footnotes

The ideas in this section are not original. They come from Fourier, Godwin, Proud-
hon, Marx, Kropotkin, and others.

References

Beattie, Ronald H.
    1968   "California Peace Officers Killed 1960–66." Bureau of Criminal
            Statistics, Department of Justice, State of California (Septem-
            ber).

Bristow, Allen P.
    1963   "Police Officer Shootings: A Tactical Evaluation." The Journal
               of Criminal Law, Criminology, and Police Science 54.
Cardarelli, Albert P.
    1968   "An Analysis of Police Killed by Criminal Action: 1961–1963."
               The Journal of Criminal Law, Criminology, and Police Science
               59.
Goulden, Joseph
    1970   "The Cops Hit the Jackpot." The Nation (November).
Hutchins, W.H.
    1971   "Criminal Homicides of California Peace Officers, 1960–1970."
               A report delivered before the California Homicide Investigators'
               Conference, Los Angeles, March 5.
Knoohuizen, Ralph, Richard P. Fahey, and Deborah J. Palmer
    1972   The Police and Their Use of Fatal Force in Chicago. Chicago
               Law Enforcement Study Group.
President's Commission on Law Enforcement and Administration of Justice
    1967   Task Force Report: The Police. Washington, D.C.: U.S. Govern-
               ment Printing Office.
Robin, Gerald D.
    1963   "Justifiable Homicide by Police Officers." The Journal of Crimi-
               nal Law, Criminology, and Police Science 54.
Rusche, Georg and Otto Kirchheimer
    1968   Punishment and Social Structure. New York: Russell and
               Russell.
Sorel, G.
    1950   Reflections on Violence. Glencoe, Illinois: Free Press.
Sweezy, Paul M., Harry Magdoff and Leo Huberman
    1971   "Economic Stagnation and Stagnation of Economics." Monthly
               Review 22 (April).

CHAPTER **4-8**

Law enforcement officers killed summary for the years 1973 and 1974

Law Enforcement Officers Killed

In 1973, a total of 127 local, county, and state law enforcement officers were killed due to felonious criminal action in the United States. During the ten-year period 1964-1973, 858 officers were killed. Specifically, there were 57 officers killed in 1964; 53 in 1965; 57 in 1966; 76 in 1967; 64 in 1968; 86 in 1969; 100 in 1970; 126 in 1971; 112 in 1972; and 127 in 1973. A greater number of law enforcement officers were killed in 1973 than in any year since 1961, when the FBI began the comprehensive analysis of this data.

The number of law enforcement officers of Puerto Rico feloniously killed has not been tabulated with those in the United States for the ten-year period. An overview of these killings is presented for the three-year period of 1971-1973. Nine officers were killed due to criminal action in Puerto Rico in this time period. Specifically, three officers were killed in 1971; two in 1972; and four in 1973. The killing of eight officers was effected through the use of firearms, and a knife was used to kill one officer. The most frequent types of activity under which these officers were slain were disturbance call situations and civil disorders.

Circumstances Surrounding Deaths

Examination of circumstances under which police officers were slain during the period 1964-1973 continues to disclose that more officers were killed

Source: Uniform Crime Reports, 1973 and 1974. Washington, D.C.: U.S. Government Printing Office, 1974, 1975, with additional data from 1964 through 1973, as reported by the FBI.

attempting arrests than in any other matter. There remains an urgent need for officers to be more alert in connection with all their assignments, regardless of how routine these assignments may seem or have been in the past. No arrest situation can be considered routine and it is thus essential that officers be extremely alert with all individuals they contact. During 1973, 19 officers were killed while attempting arrest for crimes other than robbery or burglary. Twenty-seven officers were slain by persons they encountered during the commission of a robbery, or during pursuit of robbery suspects. In connection with the crime of burglary, eight officers were killed at the scene of burglaries or while pursuing burglary suspects.

During the period 1969-1973, 56 officers were slain in ambush situations. Thirty-one of these officers were entrapped and slain through premeditated action. Twenty-five of the officers were killed in unprovoked attacks which did not involve any apparent element of entrapment.

In 1973, three officers were slain by mentally deranged persons. During the period 1964-1973, a total of 38 officers were killed by mentally deranged persons.

Twenty-five officers were slain while making traffic stops in 1973. Nine officers were killed while investigating suspicious persons or circumstances and 29 were slain responding to "disturbance calls" involving such things as family quarrels, man with gun, etc. Six officers were slain while transporting or otherwise engaged in custody of prisoners and one officer was killed while handling a civil disorder.

In 1973, 47 of the slain officers utilized their service firearms when confronted by their assailants. Thirty-four of these officers fired their service firearms while attempting to protect themselves. Fifty-six percent (or 71) of the officers were within five feet of their assailants when slain. Twenty-five officers were six to ten feet from the offenders when they were killed. In summary, 96 of the 127 officers slain were within ten feet of their assailants when they were killed.

In 1973, 60 officers were slain in the Southern States, 30 in the Western States, 20 in the North Central States, and 17 in the Northeastern States. Figure 4-8-1 shows the number of law enforcement officers killed by region for each of the two five-year periods, 1964-1968 and 1969-1973. Table 4-8-1 shows the officers feloniously killed by geographic division and population grouping in 1973.

Weapons Used

One hundred twenty of the police killings in 1973 were perpetrated through the use of firearms. Eighty-six of these deaths were committed through the use of handguns, 21 with rifles, and shotguns were used to kill 13 of the officers. Seventeen percent (or 21) of the officers slain had their own weapons used against them by the assailants. Two policemen met death as a result of

TABLE 4-8-1. Number of Law Enforcement Officers Feloniously Killed in 1973 (By geographic division and population groups)

Geographic division	Total	Group I over 250,000	Group II 100,000 to 250,000	Group III 50,000 to 100,000	Group IV 25,000 to 50,000	Group V 10,000 to 25,000	Group VI under 10,000	County, State Police and Highway Patrol
Total	127	46	7	3	5	10	13	43
New England	3	1			1			
Middle Atlantic	14	7	1	1	1	2	1	2
East North Central	15	9	1		2	1	1	1
West North Central	5	1						3
South Atlantic	26	7	1			2	4	12
East South Central	11	5				1	2	2
West South Central	23	10	1		1		2	10
Mountain	12		1	2		1	2	6
Pacific	18	6	2			3		7

Law Enforcement Officers Killed Summary for the Years 1973 and 1974

assaults with knives, while two officers were killed through the use of blunt instruments. Three officers were feloniously killed through the use of automobiles while attempting to arrest their assailants.

During the period 1964–1973, firearms were used by felons to commit 95 percent of the police killings. Seventy-one percent of the weapons used were handguns. Specifically, of the 858 law enforcement officers slain by criminal action during this period, 613 were killed through the use of handguns, 104 with rifles, 101 with shotguns, eleven with knives, three with bombs, nine with personal weapons such as hands, fists, and feet, and 17 by other means such as clubs, automobiles, etc. A total of 120 officers, or 14 percent, were slain with their own firearms.

Table 4-8-2 shows the type of weapons used to kill law enforcement officers from 1964 through 1973.

Profile of Victim Officers (see Table 4-8-3)

During the period 1964–1968, 87 percent of the officers were white, 10 percent were Negro, and 3 percent were of other races. The median year of service was five and one-half. Twelve percent of the victim officers had one year or less service. Forty-one percent had less than five years of service, 29 percent had five to ten years of service, and 30 percent had more than ten years service as law enforcement officers.

During the period 1969–1973, 87 percent of the victims were white, 12

TABLE 4-8-2. Law Enforcement Officers Killed, 1964–1973 (By type of weapon]

Type of weapons	1964–1973		1964–1968		1969–1973	
	Total Number	Percent	Number	Percent	Number	Percent
Handgun	613	71.4	219	71.3	394	71.5
Shotgun	101	11.8	37	12.1	64	11.6
Rifle	104	12.1	37	12.1	67	12.2
Total firearms	818	95.3	293	95.4	525	95.3
Knife	11	1.3	2	.7	9	1.6
Bomb	3	.3			3	.5
Personal weapons	9	1.0	6	2.0	3	.5
Other (clubs, etc.)	17	2.0	6	2.0	11	2.0
Total	858	100.0	307	100.0	551	100.0

Due to rounding, percentages may not add to total.

TABLE 4–8–3. Profile of Victim Officers

Law enforcement officers	1964–73	1964–68	1969–73
Percent white	87	87	87
Percent Negro	11	10	12
Percent other race	2	3	1
Median years of service	5	5½	4½
Percent with 1 year or less service	13	12	13
Percent with less than 5 years service	45	41	48
Percent with 5 to 10 years of service	27	29	26
Percent over 10 years of service	28	30	26

percent were Negro, and 1 percent were of other races. The median year of service was four and one-half. Thirteen percent of the victims had one year or less of service, 48 percent had less than five years of service, 26 percent had five to ten years of service, and 26 percent over ten years of service.

For the entire ten-year period, 1964-1973, 87 percent of the officers were white, 11 percent Negro, and 2 percent of other races. The median year for the entire period was five. Thirteen percent had one year or less service, 45 percent had less than five years of service, 27 percent had five to ten years, and 28 percent had over ten years of service.

Types of Assignment

Officers who are assigned patrol duties within law enforcement organizations have the most hazardous type of assignment. During the course of his duties the patrol officer is frequently in contact with suspicious individuals. Each of these situations constitutes a threat to the officer's personal safety. The patrol officer is readily identifiable because of his uniform and/or patrol vehicle. He cannot hide his presence or official capacity, and frequently must determine quickly and accurately if a person is involved in a criminal act. If that person constitutes a danger to his, the officer's, personal safety, he must afford himself reasonable protection. The patrol officer must also react to situations as they occur without the benefit of detailed information or planning, and thus, he places himself in a variety of dangerous situations. The patrol officer risks attack through frequent encounters with criminal offenders at or near crime scenes. These perils are substantiated by the fact that officers assigned to patrol duty are the most frequent targets of the police killer. Officers assigned in other capacities are confronted with equally tense and dangerous types of situations while performing their duties, but not with the same frequency.

During 1973, 91 patrol officers were slain. Eighty-eight of these officers were assigned to patrol vehicles while three were foot patrolmen. Twenty-five officers were detectives or officers on special assignments. During 1973, in the highest tradition of the law enforcement profession, eleven officers, while in an off-duty status, were taking appropriate police action concerning crimes committed in their presence when they were slain. Six of the off-duty officers were slain by persons they encountered during the commission of a robbery, or while in pursuit of robbery suspects. During the period 1964-1973, 68 percent (or 587) of the 858 officers slain by felons were assigned to patrol duties. In 1973, 50 of the on-duty officers were alone and unassisted when killed. During the period 1964-1973, 35 percent (or 299) of the officers were alone and unassisted when they gave their lives for the communities they were sworn to protect. Information is set forth in Tables 4-8-4 and 4-8-5 and Figure 4-8-2 concerning types of assignment and circumstances involved in connection with the killings of officers during the periods 1964-1968 and 1969-1973.

Time of Police Killings (*see Figure 4-8-3*)

The month of January proved to be the most dangerous for law enforcement officers during 1973. During this month 19 officers were feloniously slain.

    In 1973, Sunday was the most dangerous day of the week for law enforcement officers. During the period 1964-1973, 140 officers were killed on Friday, 128 on Saturday, 127 on Sunday, 124 on Wednesday, 122 on Monday, 114 on Thursday, and 103 on Tuesday.

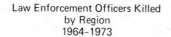

Law Enforcement Officers Killed
by Region
1964-1973

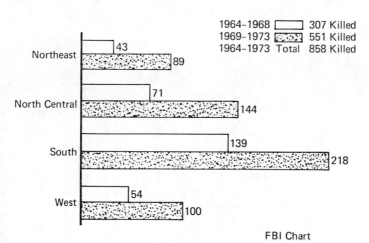

1964-1968 [ ] 307 Killed
1969-1973 [≈≈≈] 551 Killed
1964-1973 Total 858 Killed

Northeast — 43 / 89
North Central — 71 / 144
South — 139 / 218
West — 54 / 100

FBI Chart

FIGURE 4-8-1.

TABLE 4-8-4. Law Enforcement Officers Killed—Percentage of Victim Officers Assisted, 1964–1973

Type of activity	Years	Type of assignment of victim					
		1-man vehicle	Percent assisted	Foot patrol	Percent assisted	Detective or special assignment	Percent assisted
Grand total	1964–1973	321	29.9	42	38.1	190	74.7
Five-year period	1964–1968	119	31.9	18	22.2	66	72.7
Five-year period	1969–1973	202	28.7	24	50.0	124	75.8
Responding to "Disturbance" calls (family quarrels, man with gun, etc.)	1964–1968	17	52.9	1		12	83.3
	1969–1973	27	48.1	6	33.3	9	88.9
Burglaries in progress or pursuing burglary suspects	1964–1968	13	15.4	1		3	66.7
	1969–1973	19	26.3	1	100.0	7	85.7
Robberies in progress or pursuing robbery suspects	1964–1968	20	45.0	2		6	33.3
	1969–1973	34	41.2	4	50.0	21	57.1
Attempting other arrests (excludes robbery and burglary arrests)	1964–1968	38	28.9	6	33.3	24	79.2
	1969–1973	32	34.4	2		49	81.6
Civil disorders (mass disobedience, riot)	1964–1968			2	50.0	3	100.0
	1969–1973					5	100.0
Handling, transporting, custody of prisoners	1964–1968	7	14.3			5	100.0
	1969–1973	5	40.0			11	72.7
Investigating suspicious persons and circumstances	1964–1968	9	13.3	2	50.0	5	60.0
	1969–1973	15				6	83.3

Law Enforcement Officers Killed Summary for the Years 1973 and 1974

	Period						
Ambush (entrapment and pre-meditation)	1964–1968	2					
	1969–1973	3	66.7	3	66.7	6	66.7
Ambush (unprovoked attack)	1964–1968	3	66.7	1		3	
	1969–1973	7	28.6	8	62.5	7	42.9
Mentally deranged	1964–1968	6	66.7	3		7	85.7
	1969–1973	5	60.0			1	100.0
Traffic pursuits and stops	1964–1968	4					
	1969–1973	55	10.9				

TABLE 4-8-5. Law Enforcement Officers Killed—Type of Assignment of Victim Officers, 1964–1973

Type of law enforcement officer activity	Years	Total officers killed	Type of assignment				
			2-man vehicle	1-man vehicle	Foot patrol	Detective, special assignment	Off duty
Grand total	1964–1973	858	224	321	42	190	81
Total five-year period	1964–1968	307	83	119	18	66	21
Total five-year period	1969–1973	551	141	202	24	124	60
Responding to "Disturbance" calls (family quarrels, man with gun, etc.)	1964–1968	52	19	17	1	12	3
	1969–1973	73	27	27	6	9	4
Burglaries in progress or pursuing burglary suspects	1964–1968	22	5	13	1	3	
	1969–1973	39	8	19	1	7	4
Robberies in progress or pursuing robbery suspects	1964–1968	48	15	20	2	6	5
	1969–1973	118	25	34	4	21	34
Attempting other arrests (excludes robbery and burglary arrests)	1964–1968	96	22	38	6	24	6
	1969–1973	113	23	32	2	49	7
Civil disorders (mass disobedience, riot)	1964–1968	6	1			3	
	1969–1973	5			2	5	
Handling, transporting, custody of prisoners	1964–1968	17	4	7		5	1
	1969–1973	21	5	5		11	
Investigating suspicious persons and circumstances	1964–1968	25	7	9	2	5	2
	1969–1973	35	8	15		6	6

Law Enforcement Officers Killed Summary for the Years 1973 and 1974

Ambush (entrapment and premeditation)	1964–1968	8	5	2		6	1
	1969–1973	31	18	3	3		1
Ambush (unprovoked attack)	1964–1968	5	3	3	1	3	1
	1969–1973	25	2	7	8	7	4
Mentally deranged	1964–1968	20	6	6	3	7	2
	1969–1973	18	3	5		7	
Traffic pursuits and stops	1964–1968	8	3	4		1	
	1969–1973	73	18	55			

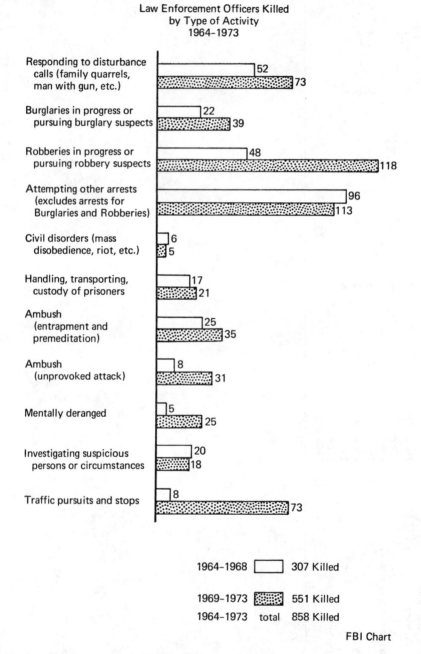

Law Enforcement Officers Killed
by Type of Activity
1964–1973

FIGURE 4-8-2.

Law Enforcement Officers Killed Summary for the Years 1973 and 1974

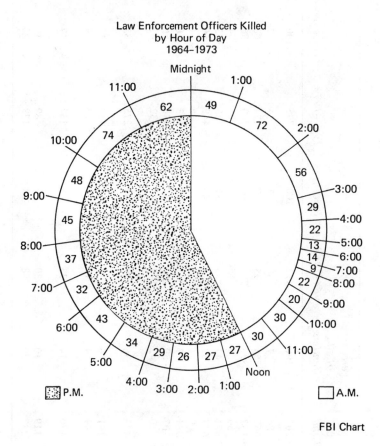

Law Enforcement Officers Killed
by Hour of Day
1964–1973

FBI Chart

FIGURE 4-8-3.

During the period 1969-1973, Sunday was the most dangerous day with 92 officers slain followed by Friday with 90, Monday 79, Saturday 78, Wednesday 75, Thursday 73, and Tuesday 64.

During the period 1964-1973, 68 percent of all killings of law enforcement officers occurred between 4:00 p.m. and 4:00 a.m. The most dangerous times were between 10:00 p.m. and 11:00 p.m. when 74 officers were slain, and from 1:00 a.m. to 2:00 a.m. when 72 officers were killed.

Criminal Offenders

Law enforcement agencies cleared 121 of the 127 police killings that occurred in calendar year 1973. (See Table 4-8-6 and Figure 4-8-4.) One hundred ninety-two offenders were identified in connection with these crimes. Thirty-

TABLE 4-8-6. Profile of Offender

Offenders	Total	Percent of all offenders	1964–1968	Percent	1969–1973	Percent
Total	1,207	100	412	100	795	100
Under age 18	84	7	30	7	54	7
From 20 to 30 years of age	669	55	195	47	474	60
Male	1,157	96	397	96	760	96
Female	50	4	15	4	35	4
White	571	47	233	57	338	43
Negro	627	52	178	43	449	56
Other race	9	1	1		8	1
Prior criminal arrest	934	77	311	75	623	78
Convicted on prior criminal charge	707	59	259	63	448	56
Prior arrest for crime of violence	510	42	178	43	332	42
Convicted on criminal charges— granted leniency	432	36	157	38	275	35
On parole or probation at time of killing	191	16	73	18	118	15
Arrested on prior murder charge	44	4	11	3	33	4
Prior arrest on narcotic drug law violation	170	14	33	8	137	17
Prior arrest for assaulting policeman or resisting arrest	119	10	30	7	89	11
Prior arrest for weapons violation	237	20	58	14	179	23

Law Enforcement Officers Killed Summary for the Years 1973 and 1974

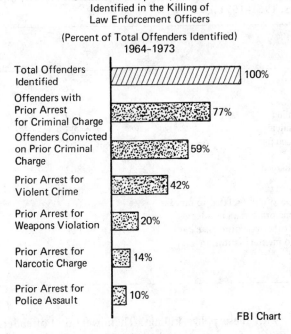

Criminal History of 1,207 Persons
Identified in the Killing of
Law Enforcement Officers

(Percent of Total Offenders Identified)
1964–1973

FBI Chart

FIGURE 4-8-4.

nine percent of the offenders were white, 60 percent Negro, and 1 percent other races.

During the period 1964–1973, 858 officers were slain; 1,207 offenders were identified, clearing 96 percent of these killings. Seventy-seven percent of the offenders had prior arrests for criminal charges, with 59 percent of the offenders having been convicted of those charges. Forty-two percent had prior arrests for violent types of crime such as murder, rape, armed robbery, aggravated assault, etc. Sixty-one percent of those who had previously been convicted on criminal charges were granted parole or probation. Sixteen percent of the offenders were on parole or probation when they were involved with the killing of an officer. Fourteen percent of the offenders had a prior arrest for a narcotics charge and 10 percent had prior arrests for police assault.

Ninety-six percent were male and 4 percent female. During this ten-year period, 47 percent of the offenders were white, 52 percent were Negro, and 1 percent other races.

In the period 1961–1971, 1,025 known persons were involved in connection with the killing of 759 law enforcement officers. (See Table 4-8-7.) One hundred twenty-nine subjects, or 13 percent, were killed at the scene of the crime or soon thereafter, 25 committed suicide, and nine subjects are presently fugitives. A total of 862 individuals, or 84 percent, were arrested and charged

Tensions and Conflicts

TABLE 4-8-7. Disposition of Offenders Involved in Murders of Law Enforcement Officers, 1961-1971

	Total	Percent distribution
Known offenders	1,025	100
Fugitives	9	1
Justifiably killed	129	13
Committed suicide	25	2
Arrested and charged	862	84
Arrested and charged	862	100
Guilty of murder	560	65
Guilty of lesser offense related to murder	71	8
Guilty of crime other than murder	45	5
Acquitted or otherwise dismissed	111	13
Committed to mental institution	42	5
Case pending	23	3
Died in custody	10	1

in connection with these police killings. There were 560 offenders, or 65 percent, found guilty of murder. Available court disposition data regarding the offense related to the officers' deaths disclose that 96 were sentenced to death, 284 were sentenced to life imprisonment, 176 received prison terms ranging from two to 999 years, and four offenders received probation. Seventy-one offenders were found guilty of lesser offenses such as manslaughter, assault, etc. Forty-five offenders were found guilty of other crimes, such as robbery, burglary, etc., committed when the police murders occurred. One hundred eleven individuals, or 13 percent, were found not guilty. Further, 42 offenders were committed to mental institutions and ten offenders died while awaiting trial.

In 1973, 28 offenders were killed at the scene of the crime or soon thereafter, and three offenders committed suicide. For the period 1964-1973, 158 assailants were killed at the crime site or within a short time after the police killing was committed; 28 committed suicide shortly after the killing, and six died from other causes.

During the period 1964-1973, the offenders ranged in age from 13 years to 82. The median age of these offenders was 24 years. Fifty-five percent were between the ages of 20 and 30. Seven percent (or 84) were under the age of 18, and 20 was the most common age of the police killers. In 1973, the 192 offenders identified with police killings had a median age of 23. Fifty-eight percent of these persons were between the ages of 20 and 30. Fifteen of the persons committing these fatal attacks were under the age of 18. The most common age of the police killer was 22 in 1973.

Geographic Locations

The 127 law enforcement officers slain during 1973 were from 100 different law enforcement agencies in 31 states and the District of Columbia. Among the agencies, New York City ranked highest with five officers slain in 1973. Four of these were New York City Police Department officers, while one was a New York City Transit Authority policeman. The New Orleans, Louisiana, Police Department followed with four officers killed.

Among the states, California ranked highest with 17 officers killed while performing their duties as law enforcement officers. The State of Texas followed closely with 15 officers killed. The States of Georgia and New York followed with eight officers killed in each state.

Federal Law Enforcement Officers
Feloniously Killed

In 1972 and 1973 five Federal law enforcement officers were killed in the line of duty. Two of these officers were killed in 1972 and three in 1973. Two of the five victim officers were Agents of the Drug Enforcement Administration (formerly the Bureau of Narcotics and Dangerous Drugs), one was an Agent of the Federal Bureau of Investigation, one was a Park Ranger of the National Park Service, and one was a United States Marshal. Four of these officers were killed through the use of handguns and one with a knife.

Accidental Deaths

Three hundred eighty-eight law enforcement officers have reportedly died as a result of accidents occurring in the line of duty during the nine-year period, 1964–1972. In 1973, 40 additional officers died, bringing the total number of such deaths from 1964 through 1973 to 428. These officers are not included in the preceding information concerning law enforcement officers who were killed as a result of felonious criminal action. The leading cause of accidental deaths in the law enforcement profession is automobile accidents, which have claimed the lives of 196 officers. Sixty-eight officers have been killed in accidents involving motorcycles. Fifty-six officers died as a result of accidents while they were directing traffic or while they were at the scene of a previous accident. The other deaths occurred when firearms were accidentally discharged, helicopter and plane crashes, falls, etc. These latter types of accidents claimed the lives of 16 officers in 1973.

Assaults on Law Enforcement Officers

The following information is based on a detailed monthly collection of data in the Uniform Crime Reporting Program regarding the problem of assaults on local, county, and state law enforcement officers in this Nation. The large number of reported assaults on sworn officers is in part due to a prevalent attitude of disrespect for law enforcement in certain elements of our society.

The uniformed officer is the target of persons with real or imagined grievances against the "system." He also is, in many instances, the first person to render aid to mentally deranged individuals, to calm disturbances and quarrels, to offer protection to those threatened, or rescue those in peril. The officer is the active representative of a society whose members too often forget their individual responsibilities to their fellow human beings. In this role, he suffers a variety of unsolicited and undeserved abuse.

During 1973, 32,535 assaults on police were reported by 4,072 agencies covering an estimated population of 108,532,000. There were, in 1973, an estimated 62,300 assaults on police in the Nation. The rate of assaults on police for the Nation was 15 assaults per 100 officers for the year.

Activity of Police Officers at the
Time of Assault

An examination of the activities of law enforcement officers at the time of the assaults discloses that the greater number of assaults, 26 percent, were in responding to disturbance calls. The second highest incidence activity, 23 percent of the assaults, was "attempting arrests" other than burglary or robbery. Any officer who has answered disturbance calls remembers the situation when he became a substitute target in a husband and wife quarrel or an arbitrator in a customer-proprietor argument. The high incidence of assaults in these common and often repeated police activities should serve as an impetus for greater alertness to all police personnel. The officer must avoid becoming complacent in his pursuit of any type of police activity. The police administrator or command officer should consider procedures to afford the responding officer the fullest possible support in all activities no matter how menial or routine they might seem.

Weapons Used in Assaults on
Police Officers

Nationwide, personal weapons such as hands, fists, feet, etc., were used in 80 percent of the assaults on officers in 1973. Cities with population between 50,000 and 100,000 had the highest incidence of assaults with personal weapons accounting for 89 percent. The greatest percentage of assaults with firearms,

10 percent, occurred in cities with over 250,000 population. These large cities also showed the highest percentage of assaults with knife, 4 percent. By geographic division, the highest incidence of assaults with personal weapons occurred in the Pacific States with 86 percent.

Type of Assignment

Of those officers assaulted in 1973, the type of assignment of the officer assaulted was 42 percent in two-man vehicles, 37 percent in one-man vehicles, 7 percent on detective or special assignment, and 14 percent in other assignments. In the highest assault incidence activity of police responding to disturbance calls, 47 percent of the victims were in two-man vehicles, 43 percent in one-man vehicles, 3 percent in detective or special assignment, and 7 percent in other assignments. The vehicle patrol officer is the victim of assault in 79 percent of the total assaults on police.

Injuries to Law Enforcement Officers

Assaults on officers resulted in 40 cases of serious personal injury to every 100 officers assaulted. The rates showed assault with injury to 8 officers per 100 in the Mountain division as contrasted with 4.2 per 100 in the East South Central division. The national rate of injuries to law enforcement officers was 6 per 100 officers. Cities of 100,000 to 250,000 inhabitants had the greatest rate of assault with injury with 8 per 100 and cities under 10,000 inhabitants had the lowest rate with 3.6 per 100.

Time of Assault

Assaults on officers by time and population group are set forth in Table 4-8-8. Approximately one-half of the assaults on officers occurred during the hours from 8:00 p.m. to 2:00 a.m. The period with greatest incidence was from 10:00 p.m. to midnight. Nearly one-fifth of the assaults, 18 percent, were recorded for this two-hour period. Cities and counties recorded the largest number of assaults against officers in this time period, with the exception of the cities with under 10,000 inhabitants. Cities in this population group showed the greatest assault incidence from 8:00 p.m. to 10:00 p.m.

Clearances in Assaults on Police

Nationwide in 1973, 91 percent of police assaults were cleared by arrest. In cities 100,000 to 250,000, this clearance percentage was highest of any population group with 94 percent being cleared. Assaults of police in disturbance matters were cleared at the rate of 97 percent in cities 100,000 to 250,000.

TABLE 4-8-8. Assaults on Law Enforcement Officers, 1973

		Time of assaults by population group											
Population Group	Total	12–2a.m.	2a.m.–4a.m.	4a.m.–6a.m.	6a.m.–8a.m.	8a.m.–10a.m.	10a.m.–12	12–2p.m.	2p.m.–4p.m.	4p.m.–6p.m.	6p.m.–8p.m.	8p.m.–10p.m.	10p.m.–12
Total													
4,072 agencies: 1973 estimated population: 108,532,000.													
Total assaults	32,535	5,220	3,505	1,247	527	761	1,139	1,516	1,966	2,548	3,330	4,945	5,831
Percent distribution[1]	100.0	16.0	10.8	3.8	1.6	2.3	3.5	4.7	6.0	7.8	10.2	15.2	17.9
Group I													
42 agencies over 250,000; total population 33,507,000:													
Total assaults	17,041	2,560	1,789	630	288	379	679	875	1,131	1,458	1,822	2,490	2,940
Percent distribution	100.0	15.0	10.5	3.7	1.7	2.2	4.0	5.1	6.6	8.6	10.7	14.6	17.3
Group II													
62 agencies, 100,000 to 250,000; total population 9,205,600:													
Total assaults	3,205	526	359	127	64	83	109	144	167	253	336	468	569
Percent distribution	100.0	16.4	11.2	4.0	2.0	2.6	3.4	4.5	5.2	7.9	10.5	14.6	17.8
Group III													
156 agencies, 50,000 to 100,000; total population 10,749,000:													
Total assaults	2,663	483	313	116	45	49	66	93	142	191	246	410	509
Percent distribution	100.0	18.1	11.8	4.4	1.7	1.8	2.5	3.5	5.3	7.2	9.2	15.4	19.1

	Total												
Group IV													
298 agencies, 25,000 to 50,000; total population 10,413,000:													
Total assaults	2,741	516	300	98	34	55	84	107	150	180	246	423	548
Percent distribution	100.0	18.8	10.9	3.6	1.2	2.0	3.1	3.9	5.5	6.6	9.0	15.4	20.0
Group V													
707 agencies, 10,000 to 25,000; total population 11,200,000:													
Total assaults	2,261	409	274	72	31	45	71	79	113	157	205	370	435
Percent distribution	100.0	18.1	12.1	3.2	1.4	2.0	3.1	3.5	5.0	6.9	9.1	16.4	19.2
Group VI													
1,895 agencies under 10,000; total population 8,088,000:													
Total assaults	1,644	315	172	55	17	52	35	60	72	88	162	316	300
Percent distribution	100.0	19.2	10.5	3.3	1.0	3.2	2.1	3.6	4.4	5.4	9.9	19.2	18.2
Counties													
912 agencies; total population 25,371,000:													
Total assaults	2,980	411	298	149	48	98	95	158	191	221	313	468	530
Percent distribution	100.0	13.8	10.0	5.0	1.6	3.3	3.2	5.3	6.4	7.4	10.5	15.7	17.8

[1] Because of rounding, percentages may not add to total.

By police activity, the highest clearance rate for all agencies was 92.8 percent which occurred in assaults on officers who were attempting arrests other than for burglary or robbery. Ambush attacks accounted for the lowest clearance rate with 50 percent.

Overview for the year 1974

A total of 132 local, county, state and Federal law enforcement officers were feloniously killed in the United States and Puerto Rico in the calendar year 1974. (See Tables 4-8-9 and 4-8-10.) In comparison, 134 local, county, state and Federal law enforcement officers were killed in 1973. (See Figures 4-8-5 and 4-8-6.)

One hundred twenty-eight of these killings were perpetrated through the use of firearms. Ninety-five were committed with handguns, twelve with rifles, and 21 with shotguns. Eleven, or eight percent, of the officers were slain with their own firearms. (See Table 4-8-11.)

Fifty-four of the victim officers utilized their service firearms while in contact with their assailants, and 34 of these officers discharged their firearms. Twenty-two of the victim officers had their service firearm stolen by the offenders.

Twenty-three offenders were justifiably killed; four of these offenders were killed by victim officers. Nine offenders were wounded by victim officers. Eight offenders committed suicide. (See Table 4-8-12.)

TABLE 4-8-9. Categories of Highest Frequency of Officers Killed—1974

City: *Chicago (6)*
State: *Illinois (11), Michigan (11)*
Geographic Region: *South (57)*
Geographic Division: *South Atlantic (35)*
Hour of Day: *1-2 am (15)*
Day of Week: *Saturday (25)*
Month: *July (16)*
Type of Police Activity: *Disturbance Calls (29)*
　　　　　　　　　　　　Other Arrests (except robbery and burglary) (28)
　　　　　　　　　　　　Robberies in Progress (25)
Type of Assignment: *1-man Vehicle, Alone (37)*
　　　　　　　　　　2-man Vehicle (33)
Locations of Fatal Wounds in Deaths by Firearm: *Head (54)*
　　　　　　　　　　　　　　　　　　　　　　Upper Torso (65)
　　　　　　　　　　　　　　　　　　　　　　Below Waist (9)
Distance Between Victim Officer and Offender: *1-10 Feet (99)*

TABLE 4-8-10. Profile of Victim Officers Uniform Crime Reports—1974

Profile Data	Officer
Percent white	89
Percent Negro	11
Percent other race	–
Percent male	99
Percent female	1
Percent under age 25	12
Percent 25 through 30	31
Percent 31 through 40	35
Percent 41 and over	22
Median years of law enforcement service	5
Percent 1 year or less service	17
Percent less than 5 years service	45
Percent 5 through 10 years service	33
Percent over 10 years service	22
Average height	5'11"
Percent in uniform	68

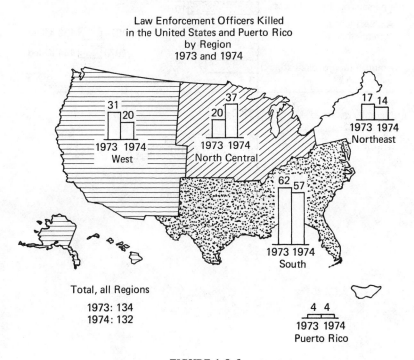

Law Enforcement Officers Killed
in the United States and Puerto Rico
by Region
1973 and 1974

FIGURE 4-8-5.

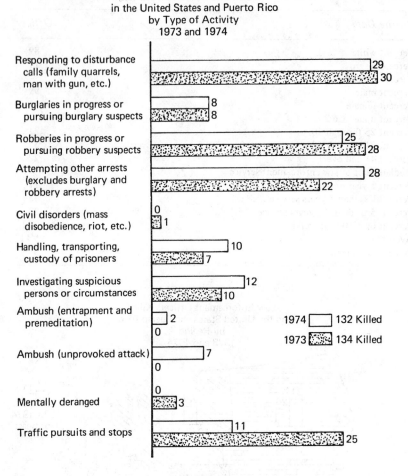

Law Enforcement Officers Killed
in the United States and Puerto Rico
by Type of Activity
1973 and 1974

FIGURE 4-8-6.

Law Enforcement Officers Killed Summary for the Years 1973 and 1974

TABLE 4-8-11. Law Enforcement Officers Killed in the United States and Puerto Rico by Type of Weapon Uniform Crime Reports

	1970	1971	1972	1973	1974	Total
Handgun	73	97	77	93	95	435
Rifle	8	16	16	21	12	73
Shotgun	12	11	18	13	21	75
Total Firearms	93	124	111	127	128	583
Knife or Cutting Instrument	3	2	3	2	1	11
Bombs	2	1				3
Personal Weapons	1	2				3
Other (clubs, etc.)	1	1	1	5	3	11
Grand Total	100	129	116	134	132	611

Ninety-five percent of the officers killed during the period 1970–1974 were killed with firearms. Seventy-one percent of the weapons used were handguns.

Data for Federal law enforcement officers feloniously killed is not included for 1970 and 1971.

TABLE 4-8-12. Profile of Offenders Uniform Crime Reports—1974

	Total	Percent of Total
Total known offenders	167	
Under age 18	10	6
From 20 to 30 years of age	83	50
Male	162	97
Female	5	3
White	87	52
Negro	79	47
Other race	1	1
Prior criminal arrest	125	75
Convicted on prior criminal charge	92	55
Prior arrest for crime of violence	68	41
Convicted on criminal charges-granted leniency	58	35
On parole or probation at time of killing	32	19
Arrested on prior murder charge	10	6
Prior arrest on narcotic drug law violation	29	17
Prior arrest for assaulting policeman or resisting arrest	9	5
Prior arrest for weapons violation	44	26

THE POLICE iN CONFLICT

JAMES S. CAMPBELL, JOSEPH R. SAHID, AND
DAVID P. STANG

Police Conflicts With Other Criminal
Justice Agencies

The police establishment is only one of the agencies constituting the criminal justice system. By the very nature of the criminal justice system, the police are required to cooperate with the other agencies, including the prosecutors, the courts, the jails and correctional institutions. In many locations, however, there is neither formal nor informal machinery for cross-professional dialogue between the police and the representatives of the other agencies involved in criminal justice administration or policy-making, so that minor irritations and misunderstandings often cumulate into major bureaucratic conflicts. The failure to involve the courts, prosecutors, and corrections officials in the training of police, the failure to involve police in the orientation of newly-chosen judges and prosecutors and in the training curricula for newly appointed probation and parole officers, and the even more general failure to consult police in the planning stages of executive and legislative decision-making in areas which may directly or indirectly affect their responsibilities or operations—all further compound this already difficult situation.

In recent years the courts in particular have become more and more the target of severe police criticism. Police problems involving the courts arise at

Source: Law and Order Reconsidered, A Staff Report to the National Commission on the Causes and Prevention of Violence, pp. 288–295. Published by the United States Government Printing Office, 1969.

three levels: (1) Procedural requirements which result in the loss of many hundreds of thousands of police man-hours annually because of inefficient or uncooperative court administration and resistance to changes in traditional practices (*e.g.*, central booking, computerized dockets, the impanelling of additional grand juries, and such apparently simple courtesies as moving cases involving police witnesses to the top of the calendar or the taking of police testimony in pre-trial proceedings);[2] (2) allegedly improper dispositions of cases both at preliminary hearings and arraignments and after trial (*e.g.*, dismissal of charges and release of persons arrested for serious crimes, speedy setting of low bail or release on personal recognizance of offenders police believe dangerous and likely to commit additional crimes or granting probation to dangerous and persistent offenders where probation supervision is inadequate); and (3) constitutional limitations on police tactics and procedures both in general law enforcement and specifically in the area of criminal investigation (*e.g.*, the decisions of the Supreme Court which have forced the police to be more careful in the conduct of searches and seizures, and in warning suspects of their constitutional rights against compulsory self-incrimination).

The question of court-imposed constitutional limitations on police practices is especially sensitive. Whether these restrictions on traditional police practices have actually reduced police effectiveness is a matter of some controversy even among police and prosecutors; but a sifnificant consensus among police officers of all ranks in every part of the country interprets these decisions as favoring the criminal and as deliberately and perversely hampering, indeed punishing, the police.

One police spokesman has stated:

> It would appear that the primary purpose of the police establishment has been overlooked in the tendency of our courts and the other officers of the judicial process to free the most heinous of criminals because of legalistic errors by law enforcement officers. . . . To allow criminals to go free because of legalistic error turns our judicial process into a game and makes mockery of our supposedly sophisticated society. . . . From the police standpoint, one of the very real dangers is that decisions from the courts are breeding indecision and uncertainty in the individual police officer. The inevitable result is that the policeman's duty has become so diffused that it is difficult for him to carry out his responsibilities.[3]

Another observer stated even more dramatically that, "The Courts must not terrorize peace officers by putting them in fear of violating the law themselves."[4] Views of this kind are set forth repeatedly in articles and comments in such respected police professional periodicals as *The Police Chief, Law and Order* and *Police*.[5]

Police in general also have little confidence in the ability of jails and prisons to reform or rehabilitate convicted offenders. This is not surprising, of course, for this view is shared, if perhaps for different reasons, by the great majority of American criminologists and even by residents of our so-called "correctional system." This lack of confidence in institutional rehabilitation programs underlies the strong police opposition to the parole system and the somewhat less aggressive opposition to work release, school release, and prisoner furlough programs, open institutions, and halfway houses. There is a rather generalized feeling among large segments of the police that potentially danger- ous offenders are released far too often on low bail, or their own recognizance or following conviction far too soon by parole boards; that these paroled offend- ers are frequently inadequately supervised by unqualified parole officers with excessive case-load responsibilities; and that they commit new and serious crimes thus adding additional burdens of investigation and apprehension to already overburdened police agencies.

Police in some jurisdictions have encountered difficulties in their relation- ships with the executive and legislative branches of government. These difficul- ties range from the irritation of requests for special treatment for favored traffic offenders and detail of police personnel to jobs as chauffeur and doorman in the Mayor's office to outside interference in internal personnel matters such as assignments and promotions and in general policy matters such as enforce- ment strategies and operational tactics.

Legislatures too have been criticized by police for failure to appropriate sufficient funds to provide adequate law enforcement for repeated investigations and inquiries which contribute to a negative police image; for penal law and criminal procedure changes which reduce penalties, make parole easier, or impose new restrictions on police efforts; and for failure to protect the police from changes in their working conditions which police feel deleterious to their welfare.[6]

Police Role Conflicts

As we stated earlier, perhaps the most important source of police frustration, and the most severe limitation under which they operate, is the conflicting roles and demands involved in the order maintenance, community service, and crime- fighting responsibilities of the police. Here both the individual police officer and the police community as a whole find not only inconsistent public expecta- tions and public reactions, but also inner conflict growing out of the interaction of the policeman's values, customs, and traditions with his intimate experience with the criminal element of the population. The policeman lives on the grind- ing edge of social conflict, without a well-defined, well-understood notion of what he is supposed to be doing there.

Police involvement in order maintenance situations such as family dis- putes, tavern brawls, disorderly teenagers loitering in the streets, quarrels between neighbors, and the like inevitably produces role conflict. One party is likely to feel harassed, outraged or neglected. The police officer quite frequently has no clear legal standard to apply—or one that, if applied, would produce an obviously unjust result.[7] The victim is often as blameworthy as the perpetrator, often the parties really want him only to "do something" that will "settle things" rather than make an arrest. Should an arrest be demanded, he is in many jurisdictions foreclosed from complying since the misdemeanor complained of was not committed in his presence, and the vociferously complaining victim or witness is unwilling to sign a complaint.[8] Thus, he must devise a solution based almost entirely on his own discretion and judgement.[9]

Oftentimes the policeman is forced to arrest persons for violations of laws he does not believe are fair. But more often, he sees the fear and the pain and the damage that crime causes, and he feels that criminals are getting away with too much. This frustration mounts each time he arrives at the scene of a recently-reported crime to discover the offender has escaped. He finds justification for his contempt for the "criminal element" when he reads of public approval of night-stick justice techniques.[10]

Police in the United States are for the most part white, upwardly mobile lower middle-class, conservative in ideology and resistant to change. In most areas of the country, even where segregation has been legally eliminated for long periods, they are likely to have grown up without any significant contact with minority and lower socioeconomic class life styles—and certainly with little or no experience of the realities of ghetto life. They tend to share the attitudes, biases and prejudices of the larger community, among which is likely to be a fear and distrust of Negroes and other minority groups.

Appointed to the police force and brought into day-to-day contact with what is to him an alien way of life, the young police officer experiences what behavioral scientists refer to as "cultural shock." His latent negative attitudes are reinforced by the aggressive and militant hostility which greets him even when he is attempting to perform, to the best of his ability, a community service or order maintenance function, or is attempting to apprehend a criminal whose victim has been a member of the minority community.

Negative responses to minorities and to non-conforming groups such as "hippies," campus militants, antiwar demonstrators, and the new breed of "revolutionaries," are also reinforced by the socialization process which transforms the new recruit into a member of the police community. Not only during the formal training process but in the everyday contacts with his fellow officers and his participation with them in both on-duty activity and off-duty socializing tend to mutually reinforce the police ideology, the closed-ranks defensiveness, which separates "we" who are on the side of law, order, morality and right from "they" who are immoral, criminal, delinquent, idle, lazy, dirty, shiftless or different.

Efforts to bridge the gap between the police and some segments of the community have proved only minimally successful.[11] The realities of police confrontation with these "undesirable elements," whether on occasions of episodic violence or, more importantly, when a police officer is killed or seriously injured as a result of minority group militance, tend to offset the gains made by efforts directed toward improving police attitudes and police-community relationships.

Police Ineffectiveness

The cumulative result of the many limitations and frustrations described above is an evident inability of the police, as presently organized, manned, financed, equipped and led, to meet effectively all of the demands and expectations placed on them by the public. These inadequacies are evidenced in their inability to prevent crime, their declining record in solving crimes known to them; their sluggish response to and indifferent investigation of all but major crimes or those involving important persons, businesses, or institutions.[12] Particularly evident is an inability to deal effectively with crime in minority-populated ghettoes—for reasons which involve minority group attitudes and noncooperation as importantly as police attitudes, facilities and efficiency.

Various analyses of police confrontations, with minority and protest groups have identified 'over-response,' inadequate crowd control training, poor planning, failures in supervision and leadership, as well as the residual hostility of the police to the minorities and nonconformists involved, their suspicion of dissent, and their disagreement with the demonstrators on the substantive issues as causative factors.[13] Nor have these analyses neglected to underline difficult conditions to which the police have been subjected: the provocations, verbal and physical, to which they were subjected by participants in demonstrations;[14] and at least in some instances the distorted or at least unbalanced coverage by news media.[15] That at least some participants in many of these conflict episodes wanted to provoke a police over-response may be true—but that individual police officers, and sometimes apparently whole police units, cooperated enthusiastically with their plans is equally obvious.[16]

That the police and major elements of the public are becoming more polarized is well established.[17] This polarization is intensified by police frustrations growing out of what they perceive as the public's unreasonable expectations of them and even more unreasonable limitations imposed on them, the growing militancy of minority and dissident groups, their strategy of confrontation, and the vicious cycle of police overresponse. These factors often are aggravated by new and highly publicized charges of police brutality and derogatory attitudes toward minority groups, which attract new sympathizers from previously moderate or non-activist segments of the population and often tend to encourage reactive ghetto counter-violence.

Police Politicization

Recently, the police have begun to realize that acting exclusively as individuals in attempting to deal with their role, conflicts, frustrations and limitations has failed to pay dividends. Thus, as is the case with other newly self-aware special interest groups in our society, the police have begun to enter active politics on a much larger scale.

Police participation in the political process in America has traditionally been limited and local: limited to securing favorable legislation as to pensions, working conditions and pay rates,[18] with occasional lobbying for or against proposals to abolish the death penalty, legalize gambling, or raise the age of juvenile court jurisdiction—and local in the sense that it invariably involved approaches by the locally organized police to municipal authorities or at most to the state legislator representing the district. Occasionally charges would be made of more active police involvement in local campaigns, but there was a consensus even among the police that they, like the military, should abstain from active, overt participation in politics. Various police departments incorporated in their police regulations stringent rules prohibiting political activity other than voting.

In the past decade, largely as a result of efforts to raise police pay scales to a parity with those of skilled workmen, more militant police associations—some trade-union affiliated, others in loose state and national affiliations—escalated their pressure tactics so that job action, "blue-flu," and even threatened police strikes became common-place in police-municipality salary disputes.[19]

The major impetus to police politicization, however, was without doubt the attempt to impose a civilian review apparatus to adjudicate complaints against police officers by aggrieved citizens and attempts of citizen groups to restrict police use of firearms.[20] The proposals for civilian review boards were fought in the communications media, in the courts, in the legislature, and finally in a popular referendum in New York City in which the police won a resounding victory after a campaign which did much to further polarize the dissident minorities.[21] The victory[22] convinced many in the police community of the desirability of abandoning the internecine battles which had divided them and reduced their political effectiveness in the past.

The future of expanded police participation in politics is not entirely clear at present. Certainly there has been important police support for conservative, even radical right, candidates in recent national and local elections, and there are signs that police officials are finding increasing opportunities as successful political candidates.

But the police have not had an unbroken record of political successes. In the 1969 legislative session in Albany, a bill abolishing the fifty-eight year old three-platoon system passed by a near unanimous vote, despite strong opposition by the united police pressure groups. Whether activities such as aroused police officers seeking the removal of a judge in Detroit, or an equally aggressive organization (the Law Enforcement group in New York City) seeking to monitor the conduct of judges and their case dispositions, will be widely and successfully imitated cannot be predicted at this time.[23]

What is clear, however, is that a politicized police force united and well financed and perhaps closely allied to conservative political and social forces in the community poses a problem for those interested in preserving internal democracy and insuring domestic tranquility. As the only lawfully armed force within the community, and possessed by the nature of their duties and responsibilities of unique authority and powers over their fellow citizens (including access to derogatory information, potential for discriminatory enforcement of the laws against their opponents, licensing and inspection functions), the united incursion of the police into active politics must be regarded with some trepidation.

More and more, the police community perceives itself as a minority group, disadvantaged and discriminated against, surrounded by, servicing, and protecting a public, which is at best apathetic or unaware of the frustrations and limitations imposed on the police; and at worst, unsympathetic or hostile. The dynamics of this self-perception, assuming a continuation or possible escalation of the external aggravants (verbal and physical abuse of the police; more stringent judicial and legislative restrictions; budgetary difficulties), involve reinforced defensive group solidarity, intensified feelings of alienation and polarization, and a magnified and increasingly aggressive militancy in reaction and response to those individuals, groups and institutions (social and governmental) perceived as inimical—an action-reaction pattern which, unfortunately, will inevitably be replicated within the aggrieved and dissident communities.

References

1. See, generally, O.W. Wilson, *Municipal Police Administration* (1961); Bruce J. Terris, "The Role of the Police," 374 *Annals* 58–69 (1967); and James Q. Wilson, *Varieties of Police Behavior* (1968).

2. See chapter 21, *Law and Order Reconsidered.*

3. Quinn Tamm, "Police Must Be More Free," in *Violence in the Streets,* Shalom Endelman (ed.) (Chicago: Quadrangle Books, 1968).

4. *Id.*

5. See chapter 20, *Law and Order Reconsidered.*

6. E.g., the almost unanimous approval of the so-called "Fourth Platoon" Bill by the New York State legislature in the face of strong opposition by police organizations is a recent example of the complaints falling within the latter category.

7. Schwartz and Goldstein, Police Guidance Manuals (1968) at nos. 4,

7, and 9. See also our discussion of over-criminalization in chapter 23, *Law and Order Reconsidered.*

    8. *Id.*

    9. See Wilson, Varieties of Police Behavior, at 83-139.

    10. 56 percent of the American public expressed approval of the Chicago police handling of unruly demonstrators at the Democratic National Convention in 1968. (*New York Times,* Sept. 18, 1968, at 25).

    11. Such efforts include human relations courses, police-community councils, recruitment of minority group policemen, advanced educational opportunities, and civilian complaint mechanisms.

    12. John Giudici, "Police Response to Crimes of Violence," a paper submitted to this Task Force, at 1-14.

    13. See *Report of the National Advisory Commisson on Civil Disorders* (Washington, D.C.: U.S. Government Printing Office, 1968) and Chevigny, at 161-179.

    14. See, e.g., *Rights in Conflict,* a special report to this Commission by Daniel Walker, Director of the Chicago Study Team.

    15. Giudici, at 7-8.

    16. See *Rights in Conflict, supra* note 14.

    17. See, e.g., *The Politics of Protest*—this Commission's Task Force Report—and *Shoot-Out in Cleveland* and *Miami Report,* two investigative reports submitted to the Commission.

    18. Wilson, *Varieties of Police Behavior,* at 248.

    19. See P. Chevigny, *Police Power: Police Abuses in New York City* (New York: Pantheon Books, 1969), at 51-83.

    20. *Id.* See also Chapman and Crockett, *Gun Fight Dilemma: Police Firearms Policy* (1963).

    21. *Id.*

    22. "The Administration of Complaints by Civilians Against the Police," 77 *Harv. L. Rev.* 499, Jan. 1964. See also Thomas R. Brooks, "'No!' Sayth the P.B.A., *New York Times Magazine,* Oct. 16, 1966, at 37; Ralph G. Murdy, "Civilian Review Boards in Review," and Aryeh Neier, "Civilian Review Boards— Another View," *Criminal Law Bulletin* vol. 21, No. 8(1966) at 3 and 10; Kenneth Gross and Alan Reitman, *Police Power and Citizens' Rights* (New York: American Civil Liberties Union, 1966); "Civilian Complaints Against the Police," 22 *Bar Bulletin* 228 (New York County Lawyers Association) (1964).

    23. See ch. 7 of *The Politics of Protest.*

impROviNq policE-
COMMUNiTy RElATiONS

Introduction

Following the racial disorders in the 1960s, police and government officials ac-
celerated the institution of "police-community relations" programs. The few
existing programs were expanded; new programs were rapidly adopted. The civil
disorders had presented a serious threat for police. It had become clear that the
capabilities of even the best equipped and best staffed departments would be
heavily challenged by future possible recurrences of the disturbances. It had also
become obvious that brute force was both an undesirable and unsuccessful tactic. As Kreps and Weller state:

> While the departments we studied made efforts to organize, equip, and
> train themselves for actual civil disturbance response, they clearly pre-
> ferred not to make those responses at all. Also, police personnel them-
> selves were intimately involved in many of the incidents which triggered
> the initial outbreak of civil disturbances. The difficulty of these problems
> and the uncertainty involved with these threats made noncoercive ap-
> proaches to the problem seem attractive. These factors, the facilitation of
> federal funding, and the catalyst of public pressure combined to promote
> the rapid spread of police-community relations programs (starting in 1965)
> (1973:405).

Rapid growth occurred in all areas associated with police-community relations.
In a 1967 survey of 75 large departments, about 37 percent had formal community relations subunits (National Center on Police Community Relations, 1967).

Improving Police-Community Relations

A larger 1970 survey showed proportional increases in formal community relations programs and specialized subunits. For example, there were formal programs in 100 percent of cities over 500,000, 96 percent of cities between 250,000 and 500,000, 72 percent of cities between 100,000 and 250,000, and 63 percent of cities between 50,000 and 100,000. Of the cities with formal programs, 71 percent had specialzied community relations subunits (Advisory Commission on Intergovernmental Relations, 1971). While these programs clearly emphasized race relations, there was considerable variation in organizational location, size, objectives, and effectiveness. Some units came into existence only after a major racial conflict. Others were clearly the result of diffusion of ideas independent of actual civil disturbance experience. Expansion was particularly apparent in departments from larger cities.

There are several approaches to police-community relations now in use. One is a police-community relations bureau attached to the local police department. Another is the community-wide citizens' groups, sometimes in combination with police officials, the civilian review boards, or the citizens' advisory committees. A few jurisdictions have adopted the Scandinavian ombudsman model, although this idea has not been well received in the United States. Another approach to police-community relations involves large programs of education—or indoctrination—of community members. These programs are based on the notion that knowledge and information through "dialogue" will reconcile differences and conflicts. The President's Commission on Law Enforcement and the Administration of Justice writes on the subject:

> Citizens who distrust the police will not easily be converted by information programs they consider to come from a tainted source. However, even for these groups, long-term education based upon honest and free dialogue between the police and the public can have an effect. Indeed, this is one of the basic goals of the citizen advisory committees. On the other hand, citizens who are neutral or supportive can benefit from increased understanding of the complicated problems and tasks of the police. Informational programs can also generate support for more personnel, salary increases, sufficient equipment, and other resources to improve the effi-cency of police work. It can help the cooperative citizen to avoid becoming a victim of crime and show him how to work more effectively with the police. And, to the extent that the police department is genuinely working at improved community relations, dissemination of this information to the press and other media does have a positive effect on community relations (1967:159).

Psychological screening of police applicants, minority recruitment efforts, the introduction of a community service officer in every police station, team policing, recreational programs for youth sponsored by police, assigning bilingual officers to certain neighborhoods, and a return to "walking the beat" are other ideas offered and sometimes tried to improve relations between police and a particular community.

Other "internal" solutions more readily adopted have been police professionalization, increased manpower, human relations training, expansion of intelligence-gathering and infiltration units, and the creation of heavily armed, para-military, special-weapons-and-tactics (SWAT) units, which practically give police unlimited retaliatory powers in the case of riots or other disturbance.

Obviously most of these programs are not directed at the root causes of minorities' frustration and anger. Their main purpose is to make the police more efficient in maintaining order and enforcing laws which the dispossessed and the ordinary citizen see as mostly protecting power, wealth, and property. Lynn Cooper aptly comments:

> Reformist reforms, decided upon and instituted by the ruling class, are not aimed at shifting or realigning the base of power, but are instead focused at leaving intact the existing distribution of power. The objectives of a reformist reform, whether in the schools, the prisons, the factory, or the police, are based on supporting the rationality of the existing system. The ideology and the system are not open for discussion and question. A structural reform (instead) questions the existing system. . . Needs and demands are defined outside of the context of the existing system. . . A structural reform has three fundamental elements:
> 1. the power to make decisions is decentralized;
> 2. popular power is expanded;
> 3. the powers of the state apparatus are restricted (1975:241–42).

A structural reform which has been proposed by more radical quarters is community control over the police, that is, community determination of how it is to be policed. The principle behind community control is obviously community self-government; the goal, making the police an integral part of the community they supposedly serve. Arthur Waskow describes three major approaches to the implementation of this idea:

> There are at least three major possible directions in which to go to achieve the kind of changes in police forces that seem necessary to restore democratic, civilian control over the police:
> 1. Formal restructuring of metropolitan police departments into federations of neighborhood police forces, with control . . . in the hand of neighborhood people through elections of commissions.
> 2. Creation of countervailing organizations (in effect, "trade unions" of those policed) responsible to a real political base, able to hear grievances and force change.
> 3. Transformation of the police "profession" and role so as to end the isolation of police from the rest of the community, and thus establish de facto community control by chiefly informal means (1969:4).

Improving Police-Community Relations

Obviously the idea of community control of the police has encountered heavy opposition and has generated heated controversy, particularly at ballot time. While the "establishment" and the police see it as a serious threat to the almost unlimited power of their apparatus, its proponents see it as only one part of the effort to take control of their own lives.

While the idea of community control may appear too radical or impractical to politicians and citizens alike, the controversy has attracted their attention to another sensitive and related issue, that of the residency patterns of members of cities' police forces. This issue has surfaced in recent times as more and more cities in America are being governed by elected black officials. It is a response to the often-heard complaint of city residents that they are being policed by an occupational army of suburbanites. Some data tend to confirm the city dwellers' perceptions. For instance, recent City Council's hearings in Washington D.C. revealed that only 22 percent of the police force in 1975 lived in the District of Columbia. Moreover, only 8 percent (21 of 272) of the lieutenants and higher ranked members lived in the city, although they should be able to afford to live in the city even more than their subordinates.

"Who Controls the Police?" prepared by the President's Commission on Law Enforcement and the Administration of Justice offers an overview of some of the traditional controls as administered by governmental institutions—that is, mayor, city council, prosecutors, judiciary—as well as suggestions for new approaches.

Robert Wintersmith reviews and evaluates police-community relations efforts. With the exception of the family crisis unit and the team policing effort, he rates all projects as not going beyond a superficial level. What is needed, he feels, is an approach that will allow the black citizenry to define its own style of order maintenance. Wintersmith also recounts and scrutinizes the strategies that black organizations have advocated in order to improve relationships with police. Here, too, he feels that most changes recommended have been mostly cosmetic and therefore short-lived in nature.

In her paper, "Increasing Community Influence over Police," Rita Kelly uses reference group theory as a general guide to assess how successful Washington D.C.'s Pilot District Project in police-community relations has been. The data presented were collected during an evaluation of the experiment.

Similarly, Kenn Rogers analyzes and evaluates four four-day intensive working seminars conducted under the aegis of the same Project, in the selection, "Group Processes in Police-Community Relations." The seminars were designed to enable participants to explore the nature of authority and the problems encountered in its exercise. They were attended by both police and citizens working or living in Washington's Third Police District.

James Levine proposes that to improve the quality of police work and to achieve the goal of police restraint, we ought to be taking advantage of the science of human behavior and of recent developments in conditioning through reinforcement, at the planning, recommendation, and implementation stages of policy making. He challenges the need for better "educated" police as if education were a panacea for all social ills. What is necessary, he claims, are systematically calculated programs which give police a vested interest in treating people like human beings.

A psychological solution to the problem is also offered by Terry Eisenberg and associates in "Action for Change in Police-Community Behaviors." Their analysis is modeled along a parallel they draw between the attitudes of American soldiers abroad toward foreign people and those of police toward minority groups and the poor. In other words, they accept as on target the minorities' perception of police as occupying forces and attempt to design a model for the improvement of police-community relations that draws upon the experience of American troops abroad.

Fred Broadaway instead advocates the use of administrative procedures as having the most potential for control over police misconduct in the selection, "Police Misconduct: Positive Alternatives." He proposes an expanded use of field tape recordings, peer group panels, supervisory responsibility, and procedural accountability for affecting the conduct of police officers. Thus, he more traditionally reflects confidence in the ability of law enforcement to compel standards of conduct without outside interference.

References

Advisory Commission on Intergovernmental Relations
    1971   State-Local Relations in the Criminal Justice System. Washington D.C.: U.S. Government Printing Office.
Cooper, Lynn
    1975   "Controlling the Police." In E. Viano and J. Reiman, The Police in Society. Lexington, Mass.: D.C. Heath and Co.:241–248.
Kreps, Gary and Jack Weller
    1973   "The Police-Community Relations Movement: Conciliatory Responses to Violence." American Behavioral Scientist 16 (January-February) 404–406.
President's Commission on Law Enforcement and the Administration of Justice
    1967   Task Force Report: The Police. Washington D.C.: U.S. Government Printing Office.
Waskow, Arthur
    1969   "Community Control of the Police." Transaction 7 (December).

CHAPTER 5-1

who controls the police?

PRESIDENT'S COMMISSION ON LAW ENFORCEMENT
AND ADMINISTRATION OF JUSTICE

The operations of the police, like the operations of any other administrative agency that exercises governmental authority, must be subject to effective legislative, executive, and judicial review and control. This is important when the police are called upon to carry out specific legislative, executive, or judicial mandates. It is doubly important in areas in which the police are left with discretion to develop their own policies within broad legislatively or judicially fixed limits.

Methods of External Control

While there is a very strong formal commitment to local control of law enforcement in this country, the actual means for exerting control has become quite obscure. To whom is a police agency responsible? By what means may citizens influence its functioning?

By City Councils and Mayors

Ultimate control, in local government, is normally exerted through the ballot box. But efforts to protect the police from partisan political influence have, in many jurisdictions, made the police immune from the local election processes. Early efforts to assure popular control of the police did include provisions in

Source: Task Force Report: The Police, The President's Commission on Law Enforcement and Administration of Justice, pp. 30–35. Published by the United States Government Printing Office, 1967.

some cities for the chief of police to be elected. In others, the police were made responsible to the local legislative body. It became quickly apparent, however, that such direct control led to a pattern of incompetence, lax enforcement, and the improper use of police authority. Elected office holders dictated the appointment and assignment of personnel, exchanged immunity from enforcement for political favors, and, in some cities, made use of the police to assist in the winning of elections.

In more recent times there has been a continuing effort to comprise the need for popular control with the need for a degree of operating independence in order to avoid the undesirable practices that have generally resulted from direct political control. Election and city council supervision of the police function gradually gave way to the establishment of administrative boards, variously constituted, in an effort to assure both independence and some semblance of civilian control.

These organizational patterns have, in turn, often led to an obscuring of responsibilities, resulting in a swing back to more direct control in the form of a movement for the appointment of a single executive, directly answerable to the elected major or, more recently, to a city manager who in turn is responsible to a city council. Variations of each of these arrangements, including some attempts at State control, continue to this day, with periodic shifting from one organizational pattern to another in response to a community's conclusion that its police force has too much or too little independence.

The record of involvement by elected officials in police operations, to the detriment of both the efficiency and effectiveness of the police establishment, has had a lasting and somewhat negative impact on the lines of control between the citizenry and the police. In cities in which the desire to isolate the police from political interference led to the adoption of special organizational patterns, the change in some instances has had the effect of making the police impervious to citizen demands of a legitimate nature. Although the organizational structure provides for direct control, the results have nevertheless been somewhat similar even in those cities in which the police administrator is directly responsible to an elected mayor.

Fear of being accused of political interference and an awareness of the sensitive nature of the police task have often resulted in the mayor abdicating all responsibility for police operations by granting complete autonomy to his police department. Indeed, the mayors of several of the largest cities, considering police department autonomy to be a virtue, have campaigned for reelection on a platform stressing the independence which they have granted to their police agencies. A mayor's apprehensions are created by his knowledge that any action on his part affecting the police, no matter how legitimate, may be characterized as political or partisan interference. The consequence is that we are now in a period of uncertainty as to the best relationship between police and the city government, the issue aggravated by the situation of unrest in large urban areas.

By Prosecutors

The prosecutor, State's attorney, or district attorney is designated as the chief law enforcement officer under the statutes of some States. However, despite this designation he is not generally conceived of in this country as having overall responsibility for the supervision of the police. His interest in police operations is usually limited to those cases likely to result in a criminal prosecution, thereby excluding the non-prosecution-oriented activities that constitute so high a percentage of the total police effort.

Practices vary significantly from one jurisdiction to another as to the degree of involvement on the part of the prosecutor in the review of police procedures and actions in those cases in which the police objective is prosecution. While some cases are subject to review prior to the effecting of an arrest, the vast majority of arrests by municipal police officers are made prior to consultation with the prosecutor. Some prosecutors establish procedures for the review of all arrests prior to their presentation in court, while others do not become involved until the initial hearing is begun before a magistrate. Systematic review of all cases prior to their presentation in court tends to result in the adoption of standards that are informally and sometimes formally communicated to the police agency. Police practices may be criticized or changes suggested, but such criticism and suggestions are not generally viewed as a form of control. Rather, they are seen as being primarily motivated by a desire on the part of the prosecutor to facilitate his task in the review and prosecution of cases. Where there is no prior review, the staff of the prosecutor in large cities often routinely presents in court cases in which the practices by the police were clearly illegal, apparently feeling no responsibility for reacting to the police practice, either in the form of a refusal to prosecute or in the form of a communication through appropriate superiors to the administration of the police force.

In general, instructions or guidelines issued by the prosecutor relating to procedures for the prosecution of criminal cases will be accepted and followed by the police, particularly if the prosecutor is viewed by the police as seriously interested in an effective presentation of the case in court. But neither the police nor the prosecutor assume that the prosecutor has the responsibility either to stimulate or to participate in the development of administrative policies to control the wide range of police practices.

By the Judiciary

In many jurisdictions the trial judge has acted as a sort of chief administrative officer of the criminal justice system, using his power to dismiss cases as a method of controlling the use of the criminal process. But except in those cases in which his action relates to the admissibility of evidence, this has been done largely on an informal basis and has tended to be haphazard, often reflecting primarily the personal values of the individual trial judge.

In contrast, the function of the trial judge in excluding evidence which he determines to have been illegally obtained places him very explicitly in the role of controlling police practices. However, trial judges have not viewed this role as making them responsible for developing appropriate police policies. Many trial judges, for example, when asked if they would explain their decision to the police, indicate that they have no more responsibility for explaining decisions to police than they have with regard to private litigants. When asked whether they would suggest to the police proper ways of acquiring evidence in the future, some judges assert that it would be unethical for them to do so unless they also "coached" the defense.

Occasionally a judge will grant a motion to suppress evidence in order to dismiss a case he feels should not be prosecuted because the violation is too minor or for some other reason. Use of a motion to suppress evidence in this manner serves to confuse the standards that are supposed to guide the police, and has a destructive effect upon police morale.

Most often, the process of judicial review is seen as a decision about the propriety of the actions of the individual officer rather than a review of departmental administrative policy. Judges seldom ask for and, as a consequence, are not informed as to whether there is a current administrative policy. And, if there is one, they seldom ask whether the officer's conduct in the particular case conformed to or deviated from the policy. As a result, police are not encouraged to articulate and defend their policy; the decision of the trial judge is not even communicated to the police administrator; and the prevailing police practice often continues unaffected by the decision of the trial judge.

The effectiveness of trial court review is further complicated in courts of more than a single judge by the disparity of their views about the propriety or desirability of given police practices. Ordinarily the prosecution has no opportunity to appeal adverse decisions. And where appeals are allowed, prosecutors seldom view them as a way of resolving conflict between trial judge rulings. As a result police often tend to ignore all of the decisions, rationalizing that it is impossible to conform to conflicting mandates. While increasing attention has been given to minimizing sentencing disparity through such devices as sentencing institutes, designed to minimize disparity, no similar attention has been given to disparity in the supervision of police practices.

Finally, the effectiveness of the exclusionary rule is limited by the fact that it deals only with police practices leading up to prosecution. Many highly sensitive and important practices are confined to the street and are not reflected in prosecuted cases.

Civil Liability of the Police Officer

One much discussed method of controlling police practice is to impose financial liability upon the governmental unit as well as the police officer who exceeds his authority. A somewhat similar approach is provided for under the Federal Civil Rights Act.

The effect of the threat of possible civil liability upon police policy is not very great. In the first place, plaintiffs are seldom able to sustain a successful lawsuit because of the expense and the fact that juries are not likely to have compassion for a guilty, even if abused, plaintiff. Insurance is also now available along with other protective methods that insulate the individual officer from financial loss.

The attitude of the police administrator is to try to protect his man or the municipality from civil liability even though he may privately be critical of the actions of the officer. Usually legal counsel will instruct the police administrator to suspend departmental disciplinary proceedings because they might prejudice the litigation.

Even in the unusual case where an individual is able successfully to gain a money judgment in an action brought against a police officer or governmental unit, this does not cause a reevaluation of departmental policy or practice.

In general, it seems apparent that civil litigation is an awkward method of stimulating proper law enforcement policy. At most, it can furnish relief for the victim of clearly improper practices. To hold the individual officer liable in damages as a way of achieving systematic reevaluation of police practices seems neither realistic nor desirable.

By Citizen Complaint

Complaints alleging police misconduct may relate to an isolated incident involving the actions of a specific officer or may relate to a formal or informal practice generally prevailing throughout a department. However, the citizen complaint process, like the civil action, is typically limited, in its effect, to the specific case which is subjected to review. Experience has shown that most complaints come not from the ghetto areas where there may be most question about police practice, but rather from middle income areas where an articulate citizen becomes irate over the actions of an officer which deviate from prevailing police practice in his neighborhood.

Most attention in recent years has focused upon the means for investigating such complaints, with public discussion concentrated upon the relative merits of internal departmental procedures versus those established by a form of citizen complaint board functioning in whole or in part outside the department. Whatever the method for conducting an investigation, there is no evidence that the complaint procedure has generally served as a significant vehicle for the critical evaluation of existing police practices and the development of more adequate departmental policies.

Proposed Improvements in Methods of External Control

The primary need is for the development of methods of external control which will serve as inducements for police to articulate important law enforcement policies and to be willing to have them known, discussed, and changed if change is desirable. There is obviously no single way of accomplishing this.

The task is complicated by the fact that popular, majority control over police policy cannot be relied upon alone. Often the greatest pressure for the use of improper police practices comes from the majority of articulate citizens who demand that "effective" steps be taken to solve a particular crime, to make the streets safe, or to reverse what is often seen as the trend toward an increase of lawlessness.

Effective response to crime is obviously a proper concern of police. But it is also apparent that police policy must strive to achieve objectives like consistency, fairness, tolerance of minority views, and other values inherent in a democratic society.

The creation of an institutional framework to encourage the development and implementation of law enforcement policies which are effective and also consistent with democratic values is obviously difficult. To achieve this requires a basic rethinking of the relationship between the police and legislatures, courts, prosecutors, local government officials, and the community as a whole.

The Legislature

Adequate external control over police policymaking requires first an explicit recognition of the necessity and desirability of police operating as an administrative policymaking agency of government. One, and perhaps the best, way to accomplish this is through legislative action which will delegate an explicit policymaking responsibility to police in areas not preempted by legislative or judicial action. Often it is neither feasible nor desirable for the legislature to prescribe a specific police practice; there is a need for administrative variation, innovation, and experimentation within limits set by the general legislative purpose and such legislative criteria as are provided to guide and control the exercise of discretion.

Legislative recognition of the propriety of police policymaking should encourage the development of means to develop enforcement policies and their subjection to adequate external control. It should also encourage flexibility and innovation in law enforcement while at the same time providing some guidance to police policy-making through the prescription of appropriate legislative standards or criteria.

Judicial Review of Police Policymaking

Given explicit legislative recognition of police policymaking, it ought to be possible to develop effective methods of judicial review which will not only serve to minimize the risk of improper police practices but will also serve to encourage the development, articulation, defense, and, if necessary, revision of police policies.

If there is legislative acknowledgment of the propriety of police policymaking, it would seem to follow that it would be appropriate for a person, with proper standing, to challenge existing policy, formal or informal, on the gound that it is inconsistent with general legislative policy. Where there is challenge, courts would have an opportunity to require the law enforcement agency to articulate its policy and to defend it, and, if the challenge is successful, to change the policy.

It is possible and certainly desirable to modify the current system of judicial control and to make it consistent with and, in fact, supportive of the objective of proper police policymaking. To accomplish this would require some basic changes in judicial practice:

(a) When a trial judge is confronted with a motion to suppress, he, and the appellate court which reviews the case, should request a showing of whether the conduct of the officer in the particular case did or did not conform to existing departmental policy. If not, the granting of such a motion would not require a reevaluation of departmental policy. However, it ought to cause the police administrator to ask whether a prosecution should, as a matter of police policy, be brought when the officer violated departmental policy in getting the evidence.

If departmental policy were followed, the judge would be given an opportunity to consider the action of the individual officer in the light of the overall departmental judgment as to what is proper policy. Hopefully, a judge would be reluctant to upset a departmental policy without giving the police administrator an opportunity to defend the reasons for the policy, including, where relevant, any police expertise which might bear upon the reasonableness of the policy. To do this will slow down the proceedings, will take judicial time and effort, but if judicial review of police policy is worthwhile at all, it would seem that it is worth doing properly.

(b) Trial judges in multijudge courts should develop appropriate formal or informal means to avoid disparity between individual trial judges in their decisions about the propriety of police policy. The Sentencing Council, created in the Eastern District of Michigan to minimize judicial disparity in sentencing, would seem to be a helpful model. This council uses a panel of judges to consider what is an appropriate sentence rather than leaving the decision entirely to a single judge. The panel serves to balance any substantially different views of individual judges, and results in a more consistent judicial standard. Again, this involves cost in judicial time.

(c) It seems obvious that judicial decisions, whenever possible, ought to be effectively communicated to the police department whose policy was an issue. Yet it is common in current practice for the police administrator to have to rely primarily upon the newspaper as a source of information about judicial decisions, even those involving an officer of his own department. One way of achieving effective communication might be through making the police officer commonly assigned by departments to regular duty in the courtroom responsible for reporting significant decisions to the police administrator. This would require a highly qualified, legally trained, court officer. In addition, trial judges would have to be willing to explain their decisions at least orally, if not in writing.

(d) If the exclusionary rule* is to be a principal vehicle for influencing police policy (as distinguished from disciplining an individual officer who acts improperly) then it seems apparent that the appellate process must be accessible to the prosecution as well as the defense so that inconsistent or apparently erroneous trial court decisions can be challenged. It is nonetheless often urged that allowing appeal in a particular case is unfair to the particular defendant. Moreover, where the authority to appeal does exist, prosecutors often limit appeals to cases involving serious crimes rather than systematically appealing all cases in which an important law enforcement policy is affected.

Other Forms of External Control Over Police Policymaking

Even with carefully drafted legislation and a more adequate system of judicial review, there will still be wide areas of police practice which give rise to very important issues which must be resolved by administrative action without specific legislative or judicial guidance. This is particularly true with regard to the wide range of police contacts with citizens on the street, contacts which usually do not result in criminal prosecution but which do have a major impact upon public order and upon the relationship between police and the community. It is very important that these practices be the subject of careful administrative policymaking and be subject to appropriate methods of external control.

It has been said that one of the major current challenges to our system of governmental control is to devise appropriate methods for safeguarding the

---

*In *Mapp v. Ohio*, decided in 1961, the Supreme Court held that evidence derived from an illegal search and seizure could not be admitted in evidence in state criminal proceedings.

exercise of discretionary power by governmental agencies in situations where judicial review is not feasible or not desirable.

Because there is no "best" answer to the question of control over the exercise of discretionary power, it seems obviously desirable to encourage a multifaceted approach, stressing innovation and experimentation, with the hope that, in the process, enough will one day be learned to afford an adequate basis for deciding what methods are best.

The basic need can be stated briefly, though at some risk of oversimplification. It is for giving police policymaking greater visibility, so that the problems and current police solutions are known to the community; to devise methods of involving members of the community in discussion of the propriety of the policies; and to develop in police a willingness to see this process as inherent in a democratic society and as an appropriate way of developing policies which are both effective and supported by the community.

There are some worthwhile alternatives which can be identified:

The Involvement of the Mayor or City Council in Policymaking

It may be helpful, in the long-range interest of law enforcement, to involve local officials in the process of developing enforcement policies, particularly those which have an impact upon a broad segment of the community. If, for example, a police agency is to adopt a policy to govern individual officers in deciding what to do with the down-and-out drunk, it would seem appropriate and helpful to report that policy to the mayor and city council in order to see whether there is opposition from the elected representatives. Where the issue is significant enough, a public hearing may serve to give an indication of the community response to the particular policy being proposed. Although this involvement of city government may give rise to concern over "political influence," the risk of improper influence is minimized by the fact that the involvement is open to view. The vice of political influence of an earlier day was that it tended to be of a personal nature and was secretive.

The Involvement of the Prosecutor and Trial Judiciary

Where a police policy deals with an issue such as investigative practices, which have impact upon the arrest, prosecution, and conviction of offenders, it would seem desirable to involve those other criminal justice agencies which also have policymaking responsibility.

This will require, in practice, a greater interest by the prosecutor who often today conceives of his role as limited to the trial and appeal of criminal cases rather than the development of enforcement policies which anticipate many of the issues before they arise in a litigated case.

The participation of the trial judge on an informal basis in policymaking raises more difficult questions. In theory, the judge is the neutral official not involved until an issue is properly raised in the course of the judicial process. In fact, some trial judges do act as if they are the administrative head of the criminal justice system in a particular community, and do deliberately try to influence policy with regard to when arrests are to be made, who is to be prosecuted, when charges are to be reduced, and other matters which vitally affect law enforcement.

Citizen Involvement in Policymaking

In some areas of governmental activity, there is increasing utilization of citizen advisory committees as a way of involving members of the community in the policymaking process. In some cases, the group may be advisory only, the governmental agency being free to accept or reject its advice. In other instances, the group is official and policies are cleared through the committee as a regular part of the policymaking process. The advantages of both methods are that they serve as an inducement for the police administrator to articulate important policies, to formulate them, and to subject them to discussion in the advisory group. How effective this is depends upon the willingness of the group and the police administrator to confront the basic law enforcement policy issues rather than being preoccupied with the much easier questions of the mechanics of running the department. Where there is a commitment to exploring basic enforcement policy questions, the citizens' advisory group or policymaking board has the advantage of involving the community in the decision-making process, thus giving a broader base than would otherwise exist for the acceptance and support of enforcement policies.

Official or Unofficial Inquiry Into
Police Practices

In some other countries of the world there is a greater commitment to continuing inquiry into governmental activity designed to learn and assess what is going on. Thus, in England a royal commission has, on several occasions, been based as a vehicle for helpful inquiry into the state of police practice there. In other countries, especially in Scandinavia, there has been reliance upon the ombudsman, not only as a way of handling complaints, but also as a vehicle for continuing official inquiry into governmental practice, including the practices of police.

There has been less tradition for systematic, official inquiry into governmental practice in this country. Where there has been inquiry into police practice it has commonly been precipitated by a crisis, has been directed toward finding incompetence or corruption, and, whatever the specific finding, has failed to give attention to the basic law enforcement issues involved.

It would be helpful to have systematic legislative inquiry into important police practices at the local, state, and federal level. If devoted to an effort to learn what the existing practices are and to give the police an inducement to articulate their policies and a forum for explaining and justifying them, the process of legislative inquiry can have a positive impact upon the long-range development of the police as a responsible policy-making agency. To achieve this objective, the short run price which police would have to pay in criticism and controversy would be well worth it.

Unofficial studies of law enforcement practices can also be helpful. For example, a bar association may make an important contribution by the maintenance of a standing committee with important law enforcement policies. The police field would, in the long run, be aided by the critical, but at the same time sympathetic, interest of the organized bar.

There is also need for greater involvement of universities and especially social science research into the basic problems which confront police. Continuing university interest is itself a form of inducement to confront some of the basic policy questions; and by reporting and critically evaluating current law enforcement practices research can serve as a method of review and control in the same way that law review comment has served this function with regard to the appellate judicial process. Greater involvement of the university would also serve as a basis for the development of badly needed social science courses which deal adequately with the tasks confronting police and the role which police play in our society. This in turn should increase the number of educated and articulate citizens who are knowledgeable about and interested in the important problems of law enforcement and who thus hopefully will constitute a support for proper police policies.

Establishing Communication With the Inarticulate Segments of the Community

One of the most important ways of asserting appropriate control over police practice is to have an informed and articulate community which will be intolerant of improper police practice. A difficulty in the law enforcement field is that the groups which receive most police attention are largely inarticulate, and no formal system for the expression of views will be utilized by the groups. There is need, therefore, for development within the minority community of the capacity and willingness to communicate views and dissatisfactions to the police.

Fulfillment of this need would not only be in the interests of the community, but is desirable from the police standpoint. If the minority community

could better articulate its needs, a more balanced com
role that the professional police administrator sees him
cratic society would be provided. A stronger minority
offset some of the pressures brought to bear upon th
and engage in practices that are of questionable nature.

Secondly, the police have a very practical reason for wanting to
formed about what is bothering the residents of an area. However narrow
a focus a police administrator may assume with regard to the development of
the police function, it seems apparent that if he is to take seriously his responsibility for preventing outbreaks of violence in his community, he must undertake
programs which will keep him informed of the basis for unrest.

There has been substantial progress toward meeting this need through the
establishment of a wide range of police-community relations programs. The
success of these is in large measure dependent on the degree to which they serve
as a vehicle for enabling the otherwise unorganized citizenry to make themselves heard. It seems apparent that programs which rely primarily upon contact with well established and organized interest groups, while of value in their
own right, do not serve to meet the kind of needs that are most critical. Properly
developed, police-community programs afford an opportunity for police to take
the initiative in soliciting the kind of insight into their own operations and the
way they affect a community, which should in turn contribute to the development of more adequate police policies.

Total dependence obviously cannot be placed upon the police to assist
the minority community in articulating its needs. Indeed, the lack of sensitivity
to the problem on the part of the police in some jurisdictions may place the
entire burden on other methods, such as the development of community action
programs and neighborhood law offices. Services of this kind, which are becoming increasingly available, are likely to bring demands upon the various governmental agencies, including demands that the police review some of their
policies for dealing with problems encountered in the ghetto area. A sensitive
police administrator ought to recognize that such groups can contribute to a
process of development and continuing evaluation of important law enforcement policies.

CHAPTER **5-2**

The police and the black community: strategies for improvement

ROBERT F. WINTERSMITH

It is sufficient to state that relations between the police and Black communities are, at best, strained, and fast deteriorating, without citing a long list of studies supporting this contention. Neither is it necessary to elaborate the finding that animosity is fast reaching very serious, critical stages that perhaps even threaten the fundamental principles of democracy as Black Americans have known it in the recent past.

Certainly national, state, and local leaders as well as police professionals have also recognized the seriousness of these poor relations; unprecedented amounts of resources have been allocated to redress the problem.[1] Some people advocate the provision of hardware and heavy artillery to police departments to deal with the problem, while others believe that tensions can be relieved by changing the attitudes and consequently the behavior of police officers and Black citizens in their contacts with one another. This section will review the various efforts of police departments to improve relations.

Police-community-relations efforts can be generally categorized into three models: Those that attempt to change public attitudes of the police by highlighting the many and varied responsibilities and services that officers perform on behalf of the public, and offering explanations for shortcomings in the name of human error; those that attempt to establish and deploy special human rela-

Reprinted by permission of the publisher, from *The Police and the Black Community* by Robert F. Wintersmith. (Lexington, Mass.: Lexington Books, 1974), pp. 71–77 and 112–114. ©1974, D.C. Heath and Co.

tions units in areas where relations are most strained; and those that attempt to change attitudes of police toward minorities on a wholesale basis.

The first model has taken the form of the establishment of citizens' committees, organized throughout various sections of the target cities. This particular approach to police-community relations (PCR) is not unlike a sophisticated Madison Avenue technique to improve faltering sales for a client's product. Having been personally involved in organizing these forums in one city, and having had the opportunity to observe their development in several others, I have seen them founder and have noted some of their inherent weaknesses. The PCR units were usually staffed by young, good-looking, articulate police officers. The caliber of PCR officers whom I met and got to know on a first-name basis was so drastically atypical of the average police officer assigned to the patrol bureau that it prompted one woman to announce in a meeting that the biggest problem the people in the community had with the police was that when they called for help none of the fine young men (police officers) that attended the meetings ever answered any of the calls. My second general reaction to the PCR neighborhood-council-forum approach was that those who participated were the same group of citizens who participated with the majority of other community organizations as well—if the PCR meetings had been adjourned and immediately called to order again it would have saved the participants a trip back the following evening for another organization's meeting. The cast of characters was organizationally interchangeable. These committees were comprised of persons who, without the efforts of the police department, were concerned about their community and wanted to make it a better place in which to live and raise their families. The committees never took any fundamental issue with the police over their practices. For the most part, the closest the citizens ever came to confronting the police on specific issues was when an occasional individual dominated the entire meeting to register a personal grievance. Those who participated were essentially propolice. The kinds of demands that were made gave impetus to more of what the police were already doing, under the banner of citizen input or the public will. This is exactly the kind of situation that Malcolm X referred to when he said, as one of his colleagues told me, "Any time you have two people who agree you don't need one of them."

The PCR committees were basically a vehicle for the police department to display some of its technology, outline the difficulties of its task without citizen support, and plead for understanding. Various police specialists made presentations with professionally prepared visual aids. And occasionally the police chief came and told the audience what good citizens they were for being there.

The PCR units maintained a speakers' bureau and dispatched their representatives into schools, churches, civic clubs, veterans' groups, business organizations, and any other place they were accepted. They toured groups of school children through police headquarters. Frequently narcotic and gun exhibits were taken into the neighborhoods for the citizens to see, self-defense demonstrations and K9 exhibitions were often performed as well. It was a hard sell and it was successful—but the success was not significant. The rest of the police department continued business as usual, and the rest of the community continued to feel alienated.

This early attempt to improve relations—which was the first approach for most departments—rested on the theory that relations were strained because the public had little or no insight into the problems that police departments face, and no knowledge of organizational workings and departmental resources. These efforts were externally directed. PCR units seemed less able and/or willing to cope with the citizen-forum model as the direction of the dialogue changed from external to internal. The direction of the discussion—that is, external when the police put on a program, or internal when citizens attending the meetings criticized police operations—was dependent on the socioeconomic, ethnic, and age characteristics of the citizens in attendance. Several studies of police-community workshops support my earlier contention that citizens will address themselves to their greatest area of vulnerability. The middle-class, upwardly mobile, and elderly citizens express concern for the vice and crime, while the young, poor minorities express concern for the disrespectful and inequitable treatment they receive from the police.[2] Wellman illustrates this latter point in a dialogue between a West Coast police chief and a group of young Black men who were participating in a job-training program.[3] One youth got the police chief to admit that an arrest would be made if one citizen smacked another, but that an investigation would be conducted if the same "interaction" took place between a policeman and a citizen. The youth's question was succinct: "How come we get arrested and you only get investigated?" The alienated segment of the community, not being satisfied with the direction of communications that reflected police theory (and contradicted community theory), and the police being uncomfortable in allowing that direction to change, for reasons that have already been elaborated, relations continued to be strained and tensions heightened. As Bittner has observed, committee members are chosen from among people considered "responsible" by the police. It becomes apparent that responsibility means agreement with police thinking.[4]

The second PCR model of dispatching selected police officers into alienated neighborhoods and strategically locating storefront mini-police offices to which the alienated segment of the population had access was, in varying degrees, more successful. The success of these police teams (in terms of gaining citizen confidence) was dependent on the extent to which they accepted and performed the roles and services as specified by their alienated constituency. Many of these units did not go into their respective areas with predetermined emphasis on law enforcement or order maintenance, but once they got there, there roles and functions began to crystallize. They worked with the unemployed, prostitutes, runaway and delinquent kids, derelicts, drug addicts, and a whole host of folk who don't attend meetings.[5] While the alienated communities defined an order-maintenance role for these police teams, they were successful mainly because the quality and nature of the order that was maintained was determined by those being policed, a completely different constituency than ordinarily dictates the quality and nature of order maintenance to the police department generally.

While members of these human relations teams were friendly and on a first-name basis with many residents, they nevertheless were police officers and their constituency knew this, but that apparently made little difference. The chances of an angry crowd gathering and turning on an officer when he is known to be both fair and concerned about the citizens he serves are significantly diminished. During the course of my data collection, I interviewed two young Black men who had had extensive formal contact with the police and were generally hostile toward them. They related the following incident: One evening while shooting craps with about fifteen other brothers they saw a cop walking toward them. As he got close enough they recognized him to be a PCR officer whom they all knew. As he reprimanded them, "one brother jumped up, pulled his knife and started at [name omitted]." The officer pulled his gun, and just then the entire group grabbed their companion, wrestled him to the ground, and disarmed him. When the officer explained to the group that he would have to arrest the knife wielder, the group verbally attacked their companion.

Police officers are forced to make a personal decision that is almost irreversible: To whom will their commitment be directed, the citizens they serve or the organization of which they are a part? The occupational characteristics and styles that must accompany these two constituencies are so inconsistent that coexistence is almost impossible. Community-committed police officers do not recognize departmental tenets of loyalty, solidarity, and secrecy because these principles are not in the best interests of their constituency, nor do they see all or the majority of their constituents as criminals or potential criminals. It is not surprising, then, that their colleagues who are committed to perpetuating the police organization see them as selling out the department. The tension between the two groups force "good" policemen to resign.[6] Unfortunately, officers who are community committed are far outnumbered by those committed to the organization.

It is argued by some students of the police, as well as by police officers, that social work should not be a police function. However, the Black community must have the same option to determine the nature and quality of order maintenance in their communities that middle-class whites have in determining that they will have the service style in theirs. Further, Edwards has noted that the police probably provide more essential services to lower-class residents than most other governmental service organizations. And Bordua has observed that although many police officers think of themselves as functioning to control the Black population, it is probably easier for a ghetto resident to obtain a needed service from the police than from a teacher, a social worker, a housing inspector, a psychiatrist, or a sanitation man.[7] Police officers have a very special, occupationally inherent opportunity on which to build and improve relations with the alienated Black community, but they are too often blinded by tradition and organizational chauvinism.

While this PCR model was overwhelmingly successful, ironically enough police-community relations probably deteriorated because of it, not to mention intradepartmental relations. These human relations teams forced their fellow officers to exhibit and act out their true feelings that for so long had laid relatively dormant.

The third model used by many police departments to improve relations with Black communities has been police-community attitudinal change. Departments have devised their own techniques, which for the most part have included sensitivity training, encounter group experiences, therapy-groups, role playing, and role reversal approaches. The more straightforward lecture, question-and-answer type attempts, usually conducted by social scientists, police scholars, and/or civil rights leaders with emphasis on interpersonal human and behavioral dynamics and police reform, have, for the most part, been rejected by the officers. The police perceive these efforts as attempts to further subvert them in enforcing the law, and in no small measure they have had the counterproductive effect of reinforcing those occupational characteristics that foster poor police-community relations in the first place—solidarity, loyalty, and secrecy. In two cities where I personally participated in these lecture series, police officers immediately shouted down speakers when they disagreed with a point being made. These series were so emphatically protested by the officers that they were discontinued. More recently, a social scientist who had just returned from a similar seminar in which only command level officers were involved related to me that he had "never felt quite so lonely" in all of his life. Not one of about seventy-five officers who were present publicly conceded that his argument could hold some validity.

Some progressive departments have reached out to alienated segments of Black communities in sincere efforts to relieve tensions. The police chief of Richmond, California has initiated police-youth discussion groups. He has instructed his officers to work small geographical areas at a time and seek out youth who have exhibited antisocial behavior, get them to a meeting, and encourage them to speak their minds, regardless of how hard it is on the police.[8]

In Houston, Texas a rather elaborate series of sensitivity and encounter groups was organized which lasted three hours a week for six weeks and involved about twelve members per group, equally divided between police and minority and/or dissident groups.[9] The Newark, New Jersey department developed a similar dialogue forum involving some thirty law-enforcement officers (including corrections officers, police officers, and officers of the court) and thirty poor citizens from Newark (including parolees and probationers).[10]

Similar programs have been initiated in Dayton, Ohio; Tampa, Florida; Des Moines, Iowa; Kansas City, Missouri; Minneapolis, Minnesota; Wauwatsa, Wisconsin; Detroit, Michigan; and St. Louis, Missouri, to name a few cities.[11]

One of the most exciting and perhaps most original of all of these police-sponsored projects was initiated by the Covina, California department. One unique aspect of the program was the unannounced appearance of a policeman from a nearby county who came into one of the class meetings and arrested, handcuffed, booked, and sentenced the entire class to spend three nights in jail. Another interesting aspect of this program required participants to spend one full day as skid-row bums. The one requirement of the field experience was that the officers were not to reveal their identify. One pair reported that they had got through the day without incident and had stopped in a parking lot to finish off their bottles of wine, when suddenly two uniformed policemen appeared and the "bums" were made to spread-eagle against a building and were searched. One of them panicked and revealed his identity. He later confessed that as he was being searched he thought of every negative thing he had ever heard about a policeman. He was afraid of the treatment that he would receive from a fellow officer, and even thought he might be shot.[12]

Many of these programs have been evaluated and deemed effective by some and ineffective by others. Many police officers and community participants reported a better understanding and appreciation for the feelings and roles of the other.

The underlying theory that supports police-citizen dialogue groups can be attributed to intergroup relations generally, whether it involves family members, college roommates, or nations. Once viewpoints are mutually pressed, a respect at least and an appreciation at most can reasonably be anticipated. Whether or not these attitudinal change attempts have succeeded or not becomes a moot argument, if the material presented thus far has merit. It is difficult, if not impossible, to argue convincingly that these police efforts to improve relations have met with no success if one judges from the level of attitudinal change, and this level is always easiest to identify. But if one concedes that the fundamental root of the problem of poor relations rests within the organizational nexus of occupational socialization, the occupational reward system, and the undifferentiated and ambiguous missions that departments and officers are charged with performing, then it can easily be understood why tensions continue to increase. None of the projects cited above get beyond the superficial level of discussing and sharing insights at the level of the problem that citizens feel, that is, the alleged brutality, disrespect, harassment, etc.; and at the level of citizen disrespect for police authority, that is, citizen uncooperativeness. The police milieu, by its very nature, quickly neutralizes whatever understanding or even empathy the officer brings from the classroom, the lecture, or the therapeutic field experience. These police projects could be more scccessful if they were not looked upon as solutions in themselves, but were supplemental to far more fundamental attempts to address modification of the organizational, psychological, and sociological characteristics of the occupation.

An excellent example of a fundamental approach to improving relations that modifies the police organization (personnel assignment and deployment), provides a different psychological and sociological orientation, and specifies the mission and tasks the officers are expected to perform is the family-crisis intervention project sponsored by the New York City police department. Some eighteen policemen were trained as family-crisis intervention specialists. They were relieved of the arrest and conviction expectation; rather, their effectiveness was measured by the number of persons that they did not have to arrest. The officers were taught the social skills involved in how to deactivate a potential family explosion calmly rather than to clumsily detonate it.[13]

This project possessed several characteristics that may offer new insights. No doubt the psychological make-up of the eighteen men selected for the family-crisis unit suited them for the task; that is, they were naturals, and were not forced to alter their perception of families in crisis. Second, their mission and purpose were explicit—to subdue the tension and not to arrest one of the marriage partners. And third, perhaps most significant, is that an order-maintenance function—concerning a factor that accounts for more murders (than persons unrelated by blood or marriage), that is, the family quarrel—is elevated to the level of a speciality, not unlike the various detective bureaus or law-enforcement specialities.

The extent to which Black citizens develop confidence in their police departments will have a very definite effect on the extent of cooperation the police can expect from the Black community as it relates to their law-enforcement role. The officer needs to learn the connection between good community relations (a style of order maintenance that is acceptable to the Black community) and greater effectiveness in crime deterrence, control, and criminal apprehension. Edwards has observed that Black law-breakers enjoy "a sort of racial brotherhood status" because police injustice has been so widespread. As a result, Black men more often than not give one another breaks when law-enforcement officers are involved.[14]

This lack of Black citizen confidence in their police has resulted in several demands in a number of cities across the nation. Perhaps the most popular demand is for a civilian review board, which reflects citizen distrust of so-called "fair and impartial" internal police investigation of citizen complaints against police officers. While an effective civilian review board may have merit as far as individual citizen redress is concerned—depending on who sits on the board— it has the counterproductive effect of hardening the organizational characteristics that are responsible for the problem in the first place. Skolnick describes the manner in which the police department became more solidified and even politicized in an effort to defeat the civilian review board referendum in the November 1966 election in New York City (which was in fact defeated).[15]

The Police and the Black Community: Strategies for Improvement

Further, the existence of a civilian review board could have the effect of more brutality and false arrest rather than less brutality.

If relations are to be improved between the police and the Black community it is necessary for the projects and programs to have some relationship to the problem, but only at its source. Except for the family crisis unit and the team policing effort, the focus has been at a very superficial level.[16] What is needed is an approach that will allow the Black citizenry to define its own style of order maintenance in such a manner as to consider the manipulation of those characteristics to which police officers must subscribe to remain in good favor, while at the same time continuing or even enhancing the effectiveness of the various police missions.

The strategies that Black organizations have advocated for realization of an improved relationship with police—more humane treatment and an increased rate of criminal apprehension—have not only been ineffective, but they have had no relationship to the problem at its source. In other words, it is unlikely that desired change would be realized even if all Black citizens' demands were implemented by police departments.

The order-maintenance style of policing bears directly on the unwillingness of Black citizens to cooperate with the police in law-enforcement matters. It is because of the discourteous, frequently brutal treatment that Black citizens receive from the police in their casual, day-to-day, routine contacts that they are not willing to assist and cooperate with them in law-enforcement matters. The Black community—or any other community, for that matter—cannot be expected to distinguish intellectually between police officers who specialize in enforcing the law and those who intervene initially when they are called. Citizens do not telephone the robbery division of the detective bureau to report a holdup—they call the one number provided for citizens to contact the Police. They make no distinctions between the various roles that police perform, and they naturally are not willing to cooperate with those whom they consider to be the culprits, even in a criminally related matter where it might be to their advantage to do so.

Attempts to improve relations between the police and the Black community have for the most part been by intervening at the level of the individual police officer—trying to make him understand the feelings of Black citizens, trying to encourage him to show more respect. These attempts have failed because the nature of the police organization, and the roles and functions that police perform, are in direct contradiction to these individualized attempts. The police award system is oriented to arrest and conviction—that is, police officers are considered for promotion on the basis of the number of arrests and convictions they have produced, not on the number of positive, trusting relationships they have stablished with the citizenry. Police, therefore, generally relate to the public in a manner that emphasizes their law-enforcement role and discounts their positive order-maintenance functions. For a police officer to be "successful" in his chosen career and make rank he must adjust his attitudes and behavior accordingly.

No doubt the same criteria are used in the selection of police recruits; but it is questionable whether the same criteria *should* be used. The roles and responsibilities to be performed must be analyzed, theoretically operationalized, and categorized. Then, and only then, can police officials be aware of the qualities that men must possess in order to carry out their specific tasks. Naturally, a recruit should be versatile, able to respond to any situation; but just as personal qualities, skills, and training—and above all, a suitable personality—are needed to become a specialist in vice or homicide, so are comparable qualities needed to intervene in domestic disputes, crowd control, etc.

As the order-maintenance functions become specialized, an appropriate award system should accompany them. Young recruits should be selected on the basis of their suitability to the specific tasks that they will be assigned to perform. They would therefore not be forced to adopt an attitude and a style of behavior with which they were uncomfortable, but instead would be appropriately rewarded for carrying out the assignments that best suited their personalities.

Just as the uniformed police generalist is distinguished from the plainclothes law-enforcement specialist, so too is it necessary to distinguish the generalist from the order-maintenance specialist. The public must know that the order-maintenance specialists are not primarily arrest and conviction oriented. The blue uniform has come to connote arrest rather than assistance. There should be little wonder that the sight of the uniform triggers citizen behavior that may or may not be appropriate. The police officer who intervenes in a domestic dispute is not perceived as a friend by an irate husband, because the public has come to expect no police action except arrest.

It is necessary to specialize the order-maintenance functions, to develop criteria for selection of police recruits to perform these specialized functions, to adjust the award system to enable promotion and recognition on criteria other than arrest and conviction. It is equally imperative that officers performing these roles be visually distinguishable from those wearing the traditional blue uniform. The public would soon become aware that, for these officers, individual success in their profession did not rest solely on arrest but on disposing of the matter in the fairest manner possible.

The extent of citizen cooperation with their police departments in crime deterrence and detection rests heavily on their day-to-day experiences with the police as they perform their routine duties. By expanding the traditional dual police system (patrolmen and detectives) into a tripartite police system (patrolmen, order-maintenance specialists, and detectives) virtually two promotional routes are created rather than the traditional single one. Police officers who enjoy working with and helping people, and who tend not to be authoritative, would no longer have to be passed over for promotion—there would be a bureau in the department where their personality traits would be more suitable.

Patrolmen will always be indispensible. Just as they perform a brokerage function for the detective bureau, the traffic bureau, and the juvenile division, for example, they would perform the brokerage function for the order-maintenance specialists as well.

The nature of assistance being requested by citizens upon calling the police is frequently identified, and this information is in turn radioed when a car is dispatched. It is just as easy to dispatch an order-maintenance car to the scene of a domestic dispute as it is a patrol car. The supervisory or command model that such a scheme would take could be similar to that now used for the detective bureau. Just as there is usually a chief of detectives, so too could there be a chief of order maintenance. It is not necessary to discuss the logistics of this tripartite model here, only the concept.

In view of the fact that the great majority of police-citizen confrontations have begun with a dispute between two citizens, and virtually every rebellion of the 1960s can be traced to a police officer's interventive actions in a noncriminal matter, it is of prime necessity that the order-maintenance role be scrutinized. Situations calling for an order-maintenance police strategy are for the most part by definition nonhostile—that is, the police are not initially the object of the hostility. The transference of hostility to them upon their interference in a situation is caused not only by the sight of the blue uniform and its accompanying citizen expectations. The style of order maintenance used by police officers is not the type desired by the Black community, but rather the brand that the white community (the system) wants imposed.

For relations to be improved, therefore, it is vital that Black citizens who are generally respected within the Black community sit in a policy-making or decision-making role within the police organization, especially to deal with the issue relating to the style of order maintenance that must be practiced in the Black community. While this may take on the form of community control, and while I am advocating a more professionalized police department, it must be understood that the role of a policy-maker is far different from that of an administrator. Black representation in the policy-making process would not specifically outline or tell police officers what to do and what not to do—that is the commanding officer's job. Rather, the role of policy-making would entail broad objectives to be achieved and general guidelines to be observed in operationalizing these objectives.

There can be no doubt that most attempts to improve police-community relations have failed. They have failed because the police officer's attitudes and behavior are a product of the police organization, rather than the organization being a product of the police officer's attitudes and behavior. It is crucial for Black individuals and organizations to understand this cause-and-effect relationship and to develop an agenda that will force lasting rather than cosmetic change in their attempts to improve police-Black-community relations.

References

1. For instance, just the President's Commission on Law Enforcement and the Administration of Justice, *Task Force Report: The Police* (Washington, D.C.: U.S. Government Printing Office, 1967) lists twelve different attitude surveys confirming the discrepancy in black-white attitudes toward the police.

2. For more elaboration on the audience variation and operation of these PCR programs *see* Charles Sklarsky, "The Police Community Relations Program" (Cambridge: Harvard University, Department of Government, 1968).

3. David Wellman, "Putting on the Poverty Program" (Ann Arbor, Michigan: Radical Education Project, no date).

4. Egon Bittner, *The Functions of the Police in Modern Society* (Washington, D.C.: U.S. Government Printing Office, 1970), p. 115.

5. For a more thorough account of a nationally acclaimed model PCR unit, see Mary Ellen Leary, "The Trouble with Troubleshooting," *Atlantic-Special Supplement: The Police and the Rest of Us* (March 1969), pp. 94–99.

6. Ibid.

7. Cited in Robert A. Mendelsohn, "Police Community Relations: A Need in Search of Police Support," *American Behavioral Scientist*, 13 (May-August 1970), 748.

8. Alan Coffey, Edward Eldefonso, and Walter Hartinger, *Human Relations: Law Enforcement in a Changing Community* (Englewood Cliffs, N.J.: Prentice-Hall, 1971), pp. 230–1.

9. L. McLean, "Psychotherapy for Houston Police," 23 *Ebony* (October 1968), 76–82.

10. Paul Lipsett and Maureen Steinbruner, "An Experiment in Police-Community Relations: A Small Group Approach," 5 *Community Mental Health Journal* (April 1969), 72–80.

11. For an excellent review of the projects see Deborah Johnson and Robert J. Gregory, "Police-Community Relations in the U.S.: A Review of Recent Literature and Projects," *The Journal of Criminal Law, Criminology and Police Science* 62 (March 1971), 94–103.

12. Fred R. Ferguson, Police Chief, "Creativity in Law Enforcement: Field Experiments in Preparation for the Changing Police Role," Mimeographed paper issued by Covina Police Department (Covina, California, 1968).

13. Morton Bard and Bernard Berkowitz, "Training Police in Family Crisis Intervention: A Community Psychology Action Program," 3 *Community Mental Health Journal* (1967), 315–17.

14. G. Edwards, "Police on the Urban Frontier," Bulleton #9 (New York: Institute of Human Relations, 1968), 77–78.

15. Skolnick, op. cit., pp. 278-81. Also see Algernon Black, *The People and the Police* (New York, Toronto, London, Sydney: McGraw-Hill, 1968).

16. The Neighborhood Police team consists of a group of officers who are all generalists but also have specialities in various phases of police work. They are assigned to a small geographical area where they can get to know the citizens better, but can also follow up initial contacts.

iNCREASiNG COMMUNiTY iNflUENCE OVER POliCE

RITA MAE KELLY

Results of Actual Efforts to Increase
Community Influence Over Police

In this chapter reference group theory will be used as a general guide to assess how successful Washington, D.C.'s partial implementation of the strategy of increasing the proportion of skilled minority group participation has been in increasing community influence over the police and in producing greater rank-and-file police-citizen agreement on critical issues. Once again, the assumption is that the greater this agreement is, the greater the informal *de facto* influence and control the community has over its policemen. The data presented represent empirical findings indicating how attached a sample of policemen are to the ghetto community they serve, and how politically potent they think their ghetto community is in influencing police activity in their area. Data is also presented revealing how ghetto residents and ghetto policemen compare in terms of: (1) their definitions of the police role and functions; (2) their definitions of the most critical problems facing the ghetto community and the police; (3) the extent to which they agree on which reference groups are most influential on the residents and the police in the area; (4) the extent to which they agree on the type of political action the ghetto community would use in efforts to change a police policy; and (5) the amount and type of influence and control appropriate for their community. To assess the results of this partial

Reprinted by permission of the author. An earlier version of this paper was presented at the 1972 Annual meeting of the American Political Science Association, Washington, D.C., September 1972. ©1972,The American Political Science Association.

implementation of the third strategy to citizen participation, the responses of the black policemen will be compared to those of the white policemen. The impact of race on the residents' responses will also be examined.

The Data, Samples, and Procedures Used

The data presented here was collected during an evaluation of an Office of Economic Opportunity (OEO)-funded experiment in police-community relations in a northwestern section of Washington, D.C. The ghetto area includes poor and middle-class blacks, Spanish-speaking immigrants, two black institutions of higher learning—the District of Columbia Teacher's College and Howard University—apartments for the elderly, white-owned businesses, white residents, and hangouts for hippies and other youthful groups. It was the site of the April 1968 riots in Washington, D.C., and contains within its boundaries the Washington headquarters of the Southern Christian Leadership Conference, the Black Panthers, the Black United Front, and several other locally based militant black self-help organizations.

In December of 1970, 165 of the slightly more than 400 policemen assigned to this ghetto area were surveyed as part of the OEO evaluation; in March-April 1971, 973 of the approximately 77,600 residents in this ghetto police district were surveyed. (For details on these surveys, see Kelly et al., 1972, Chapter 2 and Appendix A.)

Police Bonds of Attachment with the Ghetto Community

On the basis of reference group theory it appears likely that the greater the number of socioeconomic, demographic, physical, social, and communication bonds a person has in and with a community, the greater will be that person's sense of belonging and attachment to that community and the more susceptible that person is likely to be to the indirect as well as direct influence of that community.

The use of socioeconomic demographic variables as *reference classes* is important in the social sciences. On the basis of knowing the location of a person in a certain reference class, it is often possible to predict his position or views on another attribute (Hyman and Singer, 1968, p. 5). If the age of a person is known, so also is a quick assessment of the imminence of his death, barring unforeseen accidents.

In the police-community relations field, however, the extent to which some of the more typical socioeconomic demographic characteristics in and of themselves are likely to be helpful in predicting good relations would seem to be lower than in other fields. For example, almost all policemen are men, but over half of the U.S. population are women. Such a difference, while statistically significant, is also the norm; thus, it is not likely to be predictive of the quality of a community's relationship. (Sharp deviations from this norm might be worth examining, however.) Moreover, in communities other than homogeneous blue-collar working class ones socioeconomic disparities between the police and residents would be expected. In Montgomery County, Maryland suburbs of Washington, D.C., where police-community relations are not a problem and where an average single family dwelling costs more than $40,000, and the population is very highly educated, rank-and-file police suffer in comparison. In the Washington, D.C., ghetto that is being examined, the residents suffer in comparison, as they do in most ghetto areas. The majority of the residents in this area are black, over 34 years of age, have no high school diploma, are female, earn less than $150 a week, were born in the South, raised in an urban setting, are in an unmarried status, and live in northwest Washington, D.C. The police assigned to this ghetto area, however, are predominantly white, under 30 years of age, have at least a high school diploma, are male, earn at least $150 a week, were born outside the South, raised in an urban setting, are married, and live outside the city of Washington, D.C. (see Table 1, columns 1 and 5).

Considerable socioeconomic demographic differences exist among the residents in this ghetto as well (see Table 1, columns 2, 3, and 4). The internal racial-ethnic differences on these socioeconomic characteristics make it quite evident that one should not expect general agreement among the residents on important issues affecting the ghetto area. On the status type of variables, in particular, the whites are advantaged and the blacks disadvantaged, even in this predominantly black ghetto.

The racial-ethnic comparisons in Table 1 on the socioeconomic demographic characteristics point up several interesting phenomena that would perhaps not be expected. First, in terms of such variables as age, education, and rural-urban background, the distributions of the white policemen, though differing sharply from the black residents, is more similar to them than the black policemen are. Only on the variables of race and place of birth can it be said that the black policemen are more similar to the black residents than the white policemen are. To those familiar with police-community relations problems, such findings might be expected. In debates about police-community relations the presence or absence of the physical membership and location bonds are the ones most commonly discussed. Minority group leaders appear to assume that the physical bond of race in particular will be highly associated with the presence or absence of other socioeconomic, social, and communication bonds.

Like most socioeconomic demographic variables, the place of residence of a policeman need not be linked to his race. In the United States today, however, it does tend to be. As Table 2 shows, the ghetto police respondents, whether black or white, do not reside in the ghetto they serve. Only 4 percent of the 165 policemen sampled lived at addresses that could be identified as being in this ghetto area. Nonetheless, very sharp racial differences were found with regard to whether the police lived in Washington, D.C., or in a suburb in Maryland or Virginia. While 68 percent of the blacks live in the District of Columbia, only 15 percent of the white policemen do. Thus, although race does not seem to enhance the likelihood that a policeman will live within the ghetto community he is assigned to serve, it is related to his physical proximity to that community. The black policemen tend to have the bond of living within the same city as the residents they serve, while the white policemen tend not to have this bond.

Social bonds of attachment can often cut through the physical barriers of race, place of birth, and place of residence. Measures of such bonds examined here are the number of friends the police say they have in the ghetto and the amount of social contact they desire with people in the ghetto community.

Close to one-third (thirty-two percent) of the police state that they have no friends at all in the ghetto in which they work. None of the residents say they have no friends (see Table 2b). The majority of the residents, 52 percent, but only 26 percent of the police assert they have eleven or more friends. The race of a policeman is not directly linked with the number of friends he has in the ghetto he serves (see Table 2b).

It is plausible to assume that a person who desires social contact with a group or a person has a greater feeling of belongingness and/or would like to become more "attached" to that group or person than another individual who does not desire such contact. Hence, as an additional indicator of attachment the police respondents were asked to state whether they would like fewer, the same, or more social contacts with residents in their police district, this ghetto. As Table 2c shows, only 34 percent of the total 165 policemen sampled indicated that they would like more social contact. The analysis by race reveals that black policemen tend to be somewhat more inclined than white policemen (42 percent to 28 percent) to want more social contact.

The physical and social bonds are critical largely because they increase the probability that clear communication of ideas, values, and beliefs will take place. Three crude measures of existing communication bonds are the racial type of listening and reading habits of the police relative to those of the ghetto residents. Are the police getting the same news and information and interpretations of it as the residents are?

Tables 2d, e, and f reveal substantial differences between the police and community listening and reading habits as well as strong racial differences within the police and community groups. Among the three citizen subsamples, each group tends to listen to those radio stations especially programmed for it. Among the police respondents the black policemen do not follow this pattern. A majority of the black policemen listened to a combination of racial types of stations. Relatively few black policemen listen only to white stations. The white policemen as a group do not seem to make a comparable effort to listen to black or Spanish-speaking stations (see Table 2d).

Another way to learn of other people's beliefs and ideas is to read them.

TABLE 1. Socioeconomic Characteristics of the Ghetto Police and Residents* (In Percentages by Race)

Variable	Total (N = 973) (1)	Ghetto Residents Black (N = 765) (2)	White (N = 163) (3)	Spanish Speaking (N = 45) (4)	Total (N = 165) (5)	Ghetto Police Black (N = 69) (6)	White (N = 96) (7)
Race							
Black	79	100	–	–	42	100	–
White	17	–	100	–	48	–	100
Spanish-Speaking	5	–	–	100	0	–	–
Age							
Under 20	8	9	4	9	0	–	–
21–34	37	33	47	64	76**	73**	51**
35–49	21	23	13	16	22***	26***	48***
50–64	21	22	17	9	1****	1****	1****
65+	13	13	18	2	0	–	0
N.A., Refused	1	0	1	0	0	–	0
Sex							
Male	46	44	53	60	100	100	100
Female	54	57	47	40	0	0	0
Education							
No H.S. Diploma	55	64	17	40	12	3	18
H.S. Diploma	20	20	18	20	53	54	53
Some Higher Ed.	23	13	65	40	35	43	29
N.A.	2	2	0	0	0	0	0

Current Income (per week)							
None	33	37	17	16	0	0	0
Less than $150	38	35	40	70	0	0	0
$150–209	9	8	16	7	60	75	49
$210 plus	5	3	15	2	40	25	51
N.A., Refused	15	16	12	7	0	0	0
Birthplace							
Washington, D.C.	33	33	11	2	19	32	9
South	50	58	26	0	36	45	29
Non-South	10	5	53	0	44	21	59
Abroad	7	2	8	96	2	1	2
N.A., Refused	1	2	1	2	1	0	0
Rural-Urban Background							
Rural	26	28	23	9	27	20	31
Urban	62	61	58	78	66	71	63
Suburban	12	11	19	11	6	6	6
N.A., D.K., Ref.	1	0	0	2	1	3	0
Marital Status							
Single	33	30	47	36	20	35	16
Married	42	43	36	56	75	61	84
Other	25	23	17	8	4	1	0
N.A., Refused	0	0	0	0	1	3	3

*The police data comes largely from Police Department personnel files; the resident data is from the survey. The questionnaire is printed in Kelly, et al., 1972, Appendix B.

**29 years or under
***30 to 49 years of age
****50 years or more.

TABLE 2. Police Bonds of Attachment (In Percentages by Race)

	Ghetto Residents				Ghetto Police		
Variable	Total (N = 973) (1)	Black (N = 765) (2)	White (N = 163) (3)	Spanish Speaking (N = 45) (4)	Total (N = 165) (5)	Black (N = 69) (6)	White (N = 96) (7)
a. Place or Residence							
Maryland					47	28	62
Virginia					16	4	24
Washington, D.C.					37	68	15
(The Ghetto District)	(100)	(100)	(100)	(100)	(4)	(6)	(2)
b. Number of Friends in Ghetto							
No Answer	1	0	2	0	3	3	3
None	0	0	0	0	32	26	35
1–10	48	50	42	42	39	42	38
11 plus	52	50	56	58	26	29	24
c. Social Contact Desired with Residents							
No Answer					3	4	2
More					34	42	28
Same					52	46	55
Less					12	7	15

	1	2	3	4	5	6	7
d. Racial Type of Radio Station Listened to							
No Answer	8	6	22	13	4	1	6
Black (or SS) only	48	58	3	38	13	28	2
White only	25	16	67	33	53	13	81
Combination	19	21	14	16	30	58	10
e. Racial Type of Newspaper Read							
No Answer	6	6	4	4	6	4	7
Black (or SS) only	2	1	1	30	1	2	1
White only	81	81	92	42	77	64	87
Combination	10	11	4	24	16	30	5
f. Racial Type of Magazine Read							
No Answer	22	24	17	13	12	7	15
Black (or SS) only	19	22	2	24	5	13	0
White only	31	21	74	36	55	13	85
Combination	28	32	7	27	27	65	0

Columns 6, 7: x^2 = 50.69*; df = 2; p < .001

Columns 6, 7: x^2 = 1.164; df = 2; NS

Columns 6, 7: x^2 = 4.77; df = 2; p < .10

Columns 1, 5: x^2 = 82.95; df = 2; p < .001   Columns 2, 3, 4: x^2 = 257.52; df = 2; p < .001   Columns 6, 7: x^2 = 85.07; df = 2; p < .001

Columns 1, 5: x^2 = 4.76; df = 2; p < .10   Columns 2, 3, 4: x^2 = 157.77; df = 2; p < .001   Columns 6, 7: x^2 = 18.82; df = 2; p < .001

Columns 1, 5: x^2 = 33.92; df = 2; p < .001   Columns 2, 3, 4: x^2 = 169.92; df = 2; p < .001   Columns 6, 7: insufficient variation

*All chi square analyses reported here exclude the 'No Answer, Don't Know' categories.

The data in Table 2e indicate that the newspaper reading habits of the police and residents do not differ quite so sharply as the listening habits. The bulk of all racial-ethnic groups read the general "white" type of paper such as the *Washington Post* and the *Evening Star*. Both the resident and the police samples show marked internal racial-ethnic differences in their newspaper reading habits, however. Thirty percent of the Spanish-speaking sample read only their own newspaper. Ninety-two percent of the white resident sample and 87 percent of the white police sample read only general "white" newspapers. The blacks, whether police or citizens also tend to read these papers. Only one black respondent of the 765 residents sampled and one black policeman of the 69 sampled listed only black papers as their reading fare.

In addition to newspapers one can read magazines to obtain current news and interpretations of it. The findings here once again demonstrate that the white policemen are not using these readily available public media devices to increase their communication bonds with the community they serve (see Table 2f). Not one of the 96 white policemen sampled listed or checked one black or Spanish magazine. The majority of the black policemen (65 percent of the 69 sampled) said they read both racial types. The black resident population tends to be more racially oriented in their magazine reading than the black policemen, but less so than the white sample. Living in the ghetto does not seem to incline whites to read more black magazines.

On the basis of the indicators of police attachment to the ghetto community used here it is necessary to conclude that generally speaking race is a strong determinant of other physical, social and communication bonds between police and the black ghetto community. The data from the ghetto residents also show that very substantial racial differences exist within the ghetto community on many of these bonds as well.

In terms of the effectiveness of the approach of involving more minority group persons in law enforcement as a means of increasing community influence over the police, the data indicate that the addition of more blacks will increase the informal physical, social, and communication bonds serving as vehicles for transmitting and receiving community influence. The question is will an increase in these bonds bring about corresponding increases in the referent power of the black ghetto community among the rank-and-file policemen on police related matters?

Police-Citizen Definitions of the Appropriate Police Role and Functions

There has been much discussion about the disagreement that exists between the ghetto police and residents about the appropriate police role. Rather than being viewed as protectors, ghetto residents often are said to view the police as an alien occupying army, charged with controlling the community for outside interests rather than protecting it. If black policemen do indeed have more bonds with the ghetto community than the white policemen, then one should find the black policemen defining the police role and ordering the police functions more similarly to the way ghetto residents do than white policemen.

To determine if this hypothesis is correct, a set of activities policemen might identify as being important functions were examined. To obtain a measure of differences between the black and white policemen in terms of the relative importance with which they viewed the various items, the mean scores for each sample on each item were standardized into T scores with the standard mean of each sample being 50 and the standard deviation being 10. The lower the score, the higher the rating (see Table 3). The respondent could check one of the following for each item: important, somewhat important, I'm neutral, somewhat unimportant, unimportant.

Several differences between the black and white police samples exist. According to these scores, both black and white policemen place the greatest importance upon traditional law enforcement functions such as keeping the streets safe, apprehending criminals, preventing crime, keeping the peace, enforcing the law, protecting property, and being guardians of citizens' rights. The next most important group of police functions from this list for the black policemen are the counselor-social work ones: "helping people solve their problems," and "counseling troubled people." The white policemen do not place nearly so much emphasis upon the importance of either of these functions (see Table 3), but the difference in emphasis is statistically significant only for the "helping people solve their problems" item.

Both white and black police respondents place the items reflecting control for subgroups in society last in importance. Both racial groups were relatively similar in the importance with which they perceive enforcing accepted standards of decency and cracking down on immoral people. The black policemen placed significantly less importance on the "controlling militants and hippies" and the "seeing to it that suspects are convicted" items (see Table 3).

A general point of interest from this data is that if one takes the standard mean of 50 as a guide to the relative importance of these functions to the policemen, one finds that the black policemen rate the counselor-social work type of functions along with the more traditional law enforcement functions. The white policemen, however, have a much greater demarcation between the traditional functions and the social work type, rating the latter's importance at about the same level as controlling subpopulations. To illustrate, the white police sample's T score for "being a guardian of citizens' rights" is 44; the next T score is 58 for "cracking down on immoral people," with the two counselor-social work items coming next with a T score of 59 (see Table 3). In other words, the white policemen serving this ghetto community are much more strongly oriented toward the "crime fighter" role definition of the police pro-

TABLE 3. Police Function Items in Rank Order of Importance

| | Ghetto Police Respondents | | | | | | t-test result |
| | Black (N = 69) | | | White (N = 96) | | | |
	X̄	SD	T Score	X̄	SD	T Score	
1. Keeping the streets safe	1.04	.17	41	1.02	.15	40	.784
2. Apprehending criminals	1.03	.17	41	1.04	.20	40	.385
3. Preventing crime	1.06	.24	42	1.05	.34	40	.224
4. Keeping the peace	1.07	.31	42	1.07	.26	41	.000
5. Enforcing the law	1.13	.34	43	1.13	.39	42	.000
6. Protecting property	1.19	.60	44	1.13	.51	42	.674
7. Guardian of citizen rights	1.37	.79	47	1.19	.59	44	1.599
8. Helping people solve problems	1.47	.76	49	1.79	1.09	59	2.221**
9. Counseling troubled people	1.59	.97	50	1.82	1.08	59	1.432
10. Enforcing standards of decency	1.93	1.15	56	1.83	1.05	60	.571
11. Cracking down on immoral ind.s	2.01	1.15	57	1.77	1.03	58	1.381
12. Controlling militants/hippies	2.48	1.29	65	1.99	1.14	63	2.525**
13. Seeing that suspects are convicted	2.93	1.56	72	1.95	1.21	62	4.360**
Average mean (5 point scale)	1.56		50	1.44		50	
Average standard deviation		.61	10		.41	10	

**p < .05

fession than the black policemen; the black policemen are more inclined to incorporate what can be called an "armed social worker" definition, a concept encompassing both the traditional and the more social work type of functions. (This difference might well be more due to the race problem in general than to the white policemen's lack of willingness or interest in "social work" type of problems. A black policeman in a white suburb might change his order of importance as might white policemen.)

To gain some assessment of what type of functions the ghetto residents want their policemen to perform, the question "If you could tell policemen what to do, which jobs would you give them?" was asked. Racial-ethnic differences among the three resident samples is small (see Table 4). Approximately 59 percent of all samples said fighting crime and other traditional law enforcement functions were the ones they would stress. A considerably smaller proportion within each group said they would give the policemen social work type of jobs: 9 percent of the blacks, 15 percent of the whites, and 11 percent of the Spanish-speaking sample gave this type of response. Sixteen percent of the total 973 residents sampled wanted the police to leave them alone or thought so poorly of the police they would have them clean streets, chase dogs, or other such activities.

On the basis of these data, one would have to conclude that the majority of the citizens, as well as the police, believe that the traditional functions of enforcing the law and fighting crime are the most important ones to emphasize. Although there is no disagreement with the police on the importance of this crime fighting function, a great difference exists about the function of police control of various populations. Responses related to controlling hippies, militants, and other forms of noncriminal deviancy did not really appear for the citizens. The "Leave me alone, let them do their job, derogatory" category

TABLE 4. Residents View of Police Job (In Percentages by Race)

	Ghetto Residents			
Variable	Total (N = 973) (1)	Black (N = 765) (2)	White (N = 163) (3)	Spanish Speaking (N = 45) (4)
No Answer, Don't Know	14	14	13	18
Fight Crime, Other Law Enforcement functions	59	58	59	60
Social Work	10	9	15	11
Let them do their job; Leave me alone; Derogatory comments	16	17	12	11
Other	1	1	1	0

undoubtedly counterposes the police control function and is the source of major police-citizen conflicts. To the extent that the black policemen stress this possible police activity less than the white policemen, they are more similar to the residents they serve.

Police and Citizen Agreement on Existing Problems

To cooperate on solving problems it would seem best if agreement existed on what the most critical problems are. Thus, the respondents were asked to cite the most critical problems facing the police and the most critical problems facing residents. It is assumed that comparable definitions of problems by police and residents will lead to greater informal influence on police by the ghetto community and that greater cooperation between the two groups will be obtained.

The Most Critical Problem Facing Police

Sharp statistically significant differences in the responses to this issue exist not only between the police and community samples, but also among the racial-ethnic samples within each major group (see Table 5a). Generally speaking, the ghetto residents, regardless of ethnic-racial origins, viewed crime as being the worst problem facing the police. The police, however, placed almost equal emphasis upon crime, poor police-community relations, and internal problems within the police department, such as lack of education and interracial conflicts. The ghetto community as a whole tended to place much less emphasis upon poor police-community relations and internal police problems. A rather large nine percent of the residents said they did not perceive that the police had any critical problems at all. Not one policeman felt the police had no problems.

The racial-ethnic differences are basically black-white differences. The white residents place more stress on poor police-community relations, on internal police problems, and a smaller proportion say the police have no problems. The chief difference between the black and white policemen are the much smaller proportion of black policemen indicating crime is the most critical police problem and a much larger number of responses falling in an "other" category, which concerned evaluations, promotions, and so on. Even a quick glance at the data reveals that the black policemen differ even more than the white policemen from the residents on this question.

The Most Critical Problem Facing Residents

When the respondents identified the most critical problem of the residents, the police and citizens also answered differently. Sixty-two percent of the ghetto

TABLE 5. The Most Critical Problems Facing Police and Residents (In Percentages by Race)

Variable	Ghetto Residents				Ghetto Police		
	Total (N = 973) (1)	Black (N = 765) (2)	White (N = 163) (3)	Spanish Speaking (N = 45) (4)	Total (N = 165) (5)	Black (N = 69) (6)	White (N = 96) (7)
a. Facing Police							
No Answer, D.K.	17	19	10	20	16	20	14
Crime Problems	50	52	46	42	26	11	37
Poor PCR	14	13	26	13	25	27	24
Internal Police Problems, Interracial conflicts, Lack of Education, etc.	6	5	10	9	20	16	22
Other	2	2	4	4	13	25	4
None	9	10	3	11	0	0	0
b. Facing Residents							
No Answer	8	10	1	4	15	12	17
Crime, narcotics	62	58	75	58	38	38	38
Lack of trust, self-respect, education	0	0	0	0	17	18	15
Poverty	23	23	20	24	14	16	13
Other	3	2	2	9	17	17	18
None	5	6	3	4	0	0	0

Columns 1, 5: $x^2 = 284.67$; df = 4; p < .001   Columns 2, 3, 4: $x^2 = 31.77$; df = 8; p < .001   Columns 6, 7: $x^2 = 23.81$; df = 3; p < .001
Columns 1, 5: $x^2 = 260.99$; df = 4; p < .001   Columns 2, 3, 4: $x^2 = 15.46$; df = 6; p < .02   Columns 6, 7: $x^2 = 0.30$; df = 3; NS

citizen sample believed that crime, fear of the streets, juvenile delinquency, lack of police protection in general, and narcotics were critical problems for residents, but only 38 percent of the police felt this type of problem was the most critical. (Within this category about one-sixth of both the police and citizen samples tended to see drugs and narcotics as the most critical problems facing residents.)

Relatively large portions of all samples also saw poverty as a critical problem. Seventeen percent of the total 165 police respondents felt that lack of self-respect and trust in and by others and the lack of education were critical problems facing the ghetto residents. None of the citizens, however, felt these problems were the most critical. Five percent of this ghetto resident sample said they had no problems at all (see Table 5b).

The race of the policeman does not appear to be related to how the police respondents define the most critical problems facing residents (see Table 5b). Black policemen differ just as sharply from the residents' perception as white policemen do. Further, in contrast to the previous question regarding the most critical problems facing police, no significant statistical difference between the black and white policemen is found here.

Race does seem to make a difference in the responses of the residents to this question. The white ghetto-ites are substantially more concerned about the crime problems the community faces (75 percent of this group's responses fall here) than the black residents are. The blacks are more concerned about poverty than the whites. The Spanish-speaking residents are more similar to the black than the white residents, but they add concern for language problems, non-citizenship, and so on. It is of some interest that none of the Spanish-speaking respondents saw narcotics as a critical problem to their community.

The findings from these two questions on the comparability of police-citizen perceptions of problems to be solved reveals that the race of a policeman alone is quite insufficient to produce agreement. Perhaps the sharp income, education, status, and security differences between the policemen and the residents in general is too great for a bridging of the reference gap here, even for the black policemen. The fact that the ghetto residents differ from each other sharply on problem definitions suggests another source of the police-citizen disagreement.

Perceptions of Who Has Influence

The lack of police-community cooperation might stem from their having different reference groups and incorrect perceptions of who effectively represents and speaks for the other. To obtain insights on this question, the ghetto residents and police were asked identical questions about which individuals and which groups have influence on, first, community residents and, second, on police. From the pretest it was known that a high proportion of each sample would not respond to this question. Several black residents explicitly stated that they were afraid the F.B.I. or some other group would use the data to identify and destroy the power of persons and groups named. A very high proportion simply did not know. The reader should recall that the population is rather poorly educated and has in general those characteristics associated with non-involved alienated people (cf. Gerson, 1969, and Clinard, 1968).

A close examination and comparison of Tables 6 and 7 reveal that, when the police and community as whole entities are compared, the police and citizens disagree strongly on all the items, i.e., who has influence and how to rate them. A majority of the police who responded said the more militant self-help organizations such as the Black United Front, the Black Man's Liberation Army, and the head of a black manpower economic development firm, had the most influence on the residents and police. The individual leaders of such organizations were also named, by the largest proportion of policemen responding, as being influential with the residents. In contrast only a very small proportion of the residents (3 percent) identified such persons as having such influence on themselves (see Table 6a and 6b). The ghetto residents tended to feel that other civic, political, and religious leaders have the greatest influence on them.

Among the residents the blacks and whites tend to agree on who the critical reference individuals in the ghetto area are, but not on which organizations have influence. A higher proportion of the black respondents see self-help organizations as being influential with the police and residents. Among the white sample the highest proportion of organizations identified falls in the local civic, religious, business type of organizations in both instances. Very few whites said no organizations or self-help organizations influenced the police. Of the black respondents who answered this item concerning the police the largest proportion identified national organizations such as national civil rights groups. Next in relative importance for the black sample came the self-help organization category and the no organization has influence category.

A comparison of columns 6 and 7 in Tables 6 and 7 shows that the black and white policemen do not disagree significantly with each other as to which types of individuals and organizations have influence on the ghetto police and residents, but they do differ considerably over whether to evaluate that influence as being positive or negative. They differ most strongly in their evaluations of the effect of organizations. The white policemen are much more inclined to perceive the influence as being negative than the black policemen.

Although both groups of residents rate the influentials positively, a somewhat larger proportion of the white sample rates the perceived influence negatively than the black sample. As noted, however, even the bulk of white residents think the influence is positive in its outcome.

Given the possibility that black policemen might be more favorable because of greater contact with ghetto leaders, the policemen were asked if they had ever talked or written to a local community leader. Very little variation in

TABLE 6. Perceptions of Who Has Influence on Residents (In Percentages by Race)

	Ghetto Residents				Ghetto Police		
Variable	Total (N = 973) (1)	Black (N = 765) (2)	White (N = 163) (3)	Spanish Speaking (N = 45) (4)	Total (N = 165) (5)	Black (N = 69) (6)	White (N = 96) (7)
a. Type of Individual							
N.A., D.K., Refused	62	60	64	80	54	62	46
Self-help Militants	3	3	3	0	23	17	29
Other local and national leaders	30	32	31	20	18	17	19
None	4	5	2	0	5	3	6
b. Nature of Individual Influence							
N.A., D.K., Refused	63	62	64	80	56	65	47
Positive	29	30	28	18	24	25	23
Negative	3	2	7	2	16	7	22
Neither or both	4	5	2	0	5	3	8
c. Type of Organization							
N.A., D.K., Refused	63	60	70	87	44	43	43
Local	10	10	19	11	8	7	8
National	9	9	4	0	13	10	16
Self-help Local	14	17	4	2	29	30	28
None	3	4	4	0	7	9	5

	Col 1	Col 2	Col 3	Col 4	Col 5	Col 6	Col 7
d. Nature of Organizational Influence							
N.A., D.K., Refused	64	61	72	87	47	46	47
Positive	30	33	21	13	28	35	23
Negative	3	2	5	0	18	9	24
Neither or both	4	4	3	0	8	10	6
e. Have Written or Talked to Community Leader in District							
N.A., D.K., Refused					3	1	4
No					39	41	39
Yes, a few times					45	44	47
Yes, a lot of times					12	15	10

Columns 1, 5: $x^2 = 94.95$; df = 2; p < .001 Columns 2, 3: $x^2 = 3.11$; df = 2; NS Columns 6, 7: $x^2 = 1.05$; df = 2; NS
Columns 1, 5: $x^2 = 136.28$; df = 2; p < .001 Columns 2, 3: $x^2 = 11.90$; df = 2; p < .01 Columns 6, 7: $x^2 = 5.02$; df = 2; p < .10
Columns 1, 5: $x^2 = 13.66$; df = 3; p < .01 Columns 2, 3: $x^2 = 27.87$; df = 3; p < .001 Columns 6, 7: $x^2 = 1.77$; df = 3; NS
Columns 1, 5: $x^2 = 44.91$; df = 2; p < .001 Columns 2, 3: $x^2 = 7.49$; df = 2; p < .05 Columns 6, 7: $x^2 = 8.11$; df = 2; p < .02
Columns 6, 7: $x^2 = .661$; df = 2; NS

TABLE 7. Perceptions of Who Has Influence on Ghetto Police (In Percentages by Race)

	Ghetto Residents				Ghetto Police		
Variable	Total (N=973) (1)	Black (N=765) (2)	White (N=163) (3)	Spanish Speaking (N=45) (4)	Total (N=165) (5)	Black (N=69) (6)	White (N=96) (7)
a. Type of Individual							
N.A.; D.K.; Ref.	78	76	81	91	60	70	52
Police	3	2	4	0	14	9	18
Self-help militants	1	2	1	0	9	9	8
Other leaders	12	13	11	7	11	7	14
None	6	7	2	2	7	6	8
b. Nature of Individual Influence							
N.A.; D.K.; Ref.	79	76	82	91	62	71	54
Positive	13	14	12	7	22	16	25
Negative	2	2	4	0	9	7	11
Neither/Both	6	8	3	2	7	6	9
c. Type of Organization							
N.A.; D.K.; Ref.	75	72	81	100	52	46	54
Local groups	5	5	9	0	5	7	4
National groups	8	9	6	0	5	3	6
Self-help orgs.	6	7	2	0	30	36	25
None	6	7	2	0	10	7	10
d. Nature of Organization's Influence							
N.A.; D.K.; Ref.	76	74	82	100	54	51	56
Positive	13	14	11	0	13	22	6
Negative	4	4	5	0	24	20	27
Neither/Both	6	7	3	0	9	7	10

Columns 1, 5: $x^2 = 38.00$; df = 3; p < .001   Columns 2, 3: $x^2 = 1.03$; df = 3; NS   Columns 6, 7: $x^2 = 1.29$; df = 3; NS
Columns 1, 5: $x^2 = 12.46$; df = 2; p < .01   Columns 2, 3: $x^2 = 10.90$; df = 2; p < .01
Columns 6, 7: $x^2 = .001$; df = 2; NS
Columns 1, 5: $x^2 = 39.45$; df = 3; p < .001   Columns 2, 3: $x^2 = 12.94$; df = 3; p < .01   Columns 6, 7: $x^2 = 1.03$; df = 3; NS
Columns 1, 5: $x^2 = 39.22$; df = 2; p < .001   Columns 2, 3: $x^2 = 4.47$; df = 2; NS   Columns 6, 7: $x^2 = 8.37$; df = 2; p < .02

the proportion of responses saying yes and no to this question was found, indicating that the presence or absence of contact alone is not influencing, strongly at least, the differences found in the positive-negative ratings given (see Table 6e).

Although race does not appear to make the remarkable difference predicted by some minority group leaders (statistical differences still exist between black police and black residents), there is a general movement of the black policemen's responses in the direction of those given by the black residents. The black policemen do tend to take a more positive view of the influence of individuals and organizations perceived by them as having influence than the white policemen do. To the extent that this favorable view leads to the individual policeman actually being influenced by that person or group, the community will have increased its influence over the police.

Police View of Ghetto's Sense of Political
Efficacy and Potency

To obtain an indication of how the police respondents generally rated the community's sense of political efficacy and influence over the police, a series of questions were asked. The first of these was:

Suppose your commanding officer was considering a policy which the citizens of your district considered unjust or harmful. (a) How likely do you think it is that the citizens in your district would try to do something about the proposed policy?

The responses in Table 8a show that 64 percent of the policemen sampled believe that the residents would probably try to do something to counteract such a policy; only 14 percent think citizen action would be unlikely. The proportion of the black policemen (51 percent) who believe the citizens would act is smaller than the proportion of white policemen (74 percent) who believe they would (Table 8a, columns 6 and 7).

To obtain a measure of the police estimation of the actual political influence of the ghetto community over the police, a follow-up question was asked:

How likely do you think it is that these citizens could successfully prevent that (unjust or harmful) policy from becoming a police guideline?

Forty-two percent of the total 165 policemen believe the citizens could actually prevent the policy from taking effect. Once again, the white policemen (49 percent) considered the ghetto residents more influential than the black policemen (32 percent) (see Table 8b).

An important question for giving approval to political action is the legitimacy of the means by which a political effect is obtained. Both the ghetto resi-

454

TABLE 8. Perceptions of Citizens' Sense of Efficacy, Potency, and Fairness (In Percentages by Race)

Variable	Ghetto Residents				Ghetto Police		
	Total (N = 973) (1)	Black (N = 765) (2)	White (N = 163) (3)	Spanish Speaking (N = 45) (4)	Total (N = 165) (5)	Black (N = 69) (6)	White (N = 96) (7)
a. Likelihood of Citizen Political Activity							
N.A.; D.K.					2	1	2
Unlikely					14	19	12
Uncertain					19	29	13
Likely					64	51	74
b. Likelihood of Citizen Success in Changing Police Policy							
N.A.; D.K.					2	1	2
Unlikely					28	30	25
Uncertain					29	36	24
Likely					42	32	49
c. Action Citizens Would Take to Get Change in Police Policy							
N.A.; D.K.; Ref.	38	38	28	42	8	12	6
Organized Action in Formal Groups	27	27	31	20	27	38	20
Informal Action	27	25	35	36	21	16	24

Street Activity/
  Violence   4   3   0   39   29   47
  No Action   5   3   2   4   6   3

d. Treatment Expected
   if Citizens Hear Case
   of Police Brutality
   N.A.; D.K.   5   3   2   2   3   2
   Fair   10   17   4
   Unfair   48   33   59
   Don't Know   5   3   39   46   34

Columns 6, 7: $x^2 = 10.49$; df = 2; p < .01
Columns 6, 7: $x^2 = 5.31$; df = 2; p < .10   Columns 2, 3: $x^2 = 4.81$; df = 3; NS   Columns 6, 7: $x^2 = 9.88$; df = 3; p < .02
Columns 1, 5: $x^2 = 135.78$; df = 3; p < .001
Columns 6, 7: $x^2 = 14.34$; df = 2; p < .001

dents and police were asked to specify the type of action the citizens in that police district would be most likely to take in opposing a policy perceived to be unjust and/or harmful. As Table 8c reveals, 39 percent of the policemen believe the first action the residents would take would involve street activity or a violent protest. The percentage of white policemen giving the violent protest response first was higher than that of the black respondents (23 percent to 15 percent). The difference was not found to be statistically significant by a chi square analysis, however.

Most forms of political activity of citizens do not directly involve or concern a policeman on duty. Political activity taking place in the streets or involving masses of people do tend, however, to engage policemen while on duty. Further, such political activity could be viewed as a hazard or threat to policemen since they can lead to physical confrontations with citizens. In addition, such actions, in the 1960s at least, have shown great potential for harming police-community relations. For these reasons it would seem probable to assume that those policemen who believe the first political action of residents is likely to be some sort of street activity will be more inclined to dislike political activity of ghetto residents.

The data in Table 8c show that 39 percent of the police respondents believe the residents would immediately engage in street activity to oppose a police policy. The comparison by race shows that a considerable variation between white and black policemen exists. Forty-seven percent of the white policemen think street activity would be the first type of action, 24 percent think informal, *ad hoc* neighborhood activity would be first, and 19 percent think action based on some established, formal organization would be first used. In contrast, the highest proportion of black policemen (38 percent) believe the residents would engage in action revolving around established, formal organizations, particularly the newly formed and elected citizens' advisory board to the OEO-funded pilot police project. Twenty-nine percent of the black policemen, compared to 47 percent of the white policemen, believe street activity would be the first step taken to oppose the unwanted policy. Only 16 percent thought the residents would start with informal, *ad hoc* organization efforts in the neighborhood.

The 973 residents surveyed by the American Institutes for Research (AIR) were asked a comparable, but open-ended question on this topic as follows:

> If the residents here wanted to oppose something the police wanted to do, how would they go about doing it?

A very high percentage of the respondents, 38 percent, said they did not know or refused to answer the question. Twenty-seven percent stated the residents would seek to change the policy by working through some established political institution in the city. Another 27 percent said they would engage in informal, *ad hoc* political activity; only 4 percent of the persons sampled said street activity and/or violent protest would be the most probable first action. Five percent said the residents would do nothing at all.

In addition to the fact that the ghetto residents surveyed did not stress mass demonstrations as a means to alter police policies and that only 4 percent mentioned violent protest as the step residents would take, other critical variations exist in responses between resident and police. Perhaps the most striking is the type of established formal organizations the residents said they would utilize to institute action to alter police policy. Twenty-five percent of the citizens who responded said the residents would go directly to the police chief or top officials in the department to get a change of policy. Less than one percent said they would go to the elected citizens' board mentioned by 15 percent of the total 165 police respondents. This difference is a function of the fact that all the police sample knew of the board, but only 12 percent of the resident sample did. The residents also did not mention political parties. This may [have been] a function of the lack of home rule in D.C. [at that time] and the consequent lowered importance of elected political parties in the nation's capital.

The tendency of white policemen to be more negative in their perceptions of community action toward the police is further substantiated by the responses to the item:

Suppose you had been charged with police brutality by a citizen and that a local citizens' group from your district had been elected to hear the case, what type of treatment would you expect?

While 59 percent of the white policemen believe the treatment they would receive would be unfair, only 33 percent of the black policemen do. Only 4 percent of the white and 17 percent of the black policemen think they would get fair treatment (see Table 8d). Thus, although the black policemen have somewhat more faith in the fairness of the ghetto residents than white policemen, a high proportion does not feel even they, black policemen, will be objectively and fairly treated.

On the basis of these data it appears that although the black policemen do not rate the likelihood of ghetto community action or its success as probable as the white policemen, a higher percentage of them have a more positive view of the legitimacy and acceptability of the action the community would take should it take any. Nonetheless, the black policemen also obviously differ substantially from the residents in their stated perceptions of what action residents would take. Simple membership in the same racial group and working in the area are insufficient means of bringing such agreement in perception. More "education-therapy" between even black residents and black policemen is needed.

Improving Police-Community Relations

Police-Citizen's Views of Community Control
Over the Police

This paper has been concerned with examining the impact of increasing skilled minority group participation as a way of increasing the ghetto community's influence over police. This strategy falls short of community control. The author's assumption has been that community control within subsections of cities is unlikely and unfeasible at present. Here the question of how the rank-and-file ghetto police and residents view this question is examined.

The police were asked to indicate whether they agreed, were neutral, or disagreed with the statement, "Community control over policemen is not appropriate." The racial comparison of the responses given (see Table 9a) show that although the majority in both racial groups agree with this statement, fewer black policemen agree or are neutral than white policemen are. The data suggest, but do not provide conclusive evidence, that black policemen are ideologically less inclined to oppose community control efforts of a ghetto community than white policemen.

The residents sampled responded to several questions about community control over the police. The first of these inquired whether the respondent wanted greater, some, or no citizen control over the police. As the data in Table 9b show, the majority think some control is desirable, while 34 percent want greater control. The black citizens' overwhelmingly desire an elected board (Table 9c).

In addition to the method of forming such a citizens' board, the residents were asked to indicate the scope of control they desired over the police. Do they want full control over hiring and firing of police personnel, control over day-to-day police activities, or do they want influence more than actual control, giving the police recommendations and suggestions in a simple advisory role? Thirty-seven percent of the respondents said they would recommend the simple advisory role; thirty-one percent wished full control over the hiring and firing of police personnel in their area; while 24 percent expressed the view that the citizens need control over the day-to-day police activities. Racial differences between the blacks and whites is not great (see Table 9d).

Summary and Conclusions

The question of community control over the police is one rising in many cities today. To have real community control in this context means decentralized accountability with active, reasonably sophisticated citizen participation. Yet relatively little minority group participation in police work has been evident. Given that a strong community power strategy of controlling the police is an unlikely development in the near future, the potentials of increasing minority

TABLE 9. Police-Citizens' View on Community Control Over Police (In Percentages by Race)

	Ghetto Residents				Ghetto Police		
Variable	Total (N = 973) (1)	Black (N = 765) (2)	White (N = 163) (3)	Spanish Speaking (N = 45) (4)	Total (N = 165) (5)	Black (N = 69) (6)	White (N = 96) (7)
a. Police Control Over Policemen is Not Appropriate							
No Answer	1	1	1	0		4	1
Agree	34	34	33	33		61	78
Neutral	50	49	55	42		20	10
Disagree	16	16	12	24		15	10
b. Amount of Control Citizens Want							
N.A., D.K., Refused							
Greater Control							
Some Control							
No Control							
c. Form of Control Citizens Want							
N.A., D.K., Refused	4	4	4	4			
Appointed	28	17	33	25			
Elected	68	79	63	71			
d. Scope of Control Citizens Want							
N.A., D.K., Refused	9	9	7	11			
Full control of hiring and firing	31	32	27	25			
Day-to-day control	24	23	26	33			
Advisory role	37	36	40	31			

Columns 6, 7: $x^2 = 4.91$; df = 2; p < .10

group representation on the police force as a means of increasing the bonds of attachment between the ghetto community and police, of bringing their reference groups closer together, and thereby increasing community influence and control over the police has been examined.

In the author's view one of the major goals of this approach to citizen participation is to change the reference groups of the police and the community so that a meeting of minds is more likely to occur. Using data from a ghetto in Washington, D.C., where this strategy to increasing community influence over police was more or less tried, the impact of race on the perceptions of policemen in several critical areas was analyzed and compared to those of the ghetto residents. In brief, black policemen tended to have what may be interpreted as a more favorable attitude toward the residents in terms of their perception and definition of the police role and in how they perceive the influence of individuals and organizations active within the ghetto. The black policemen also appear to have a more kindly view of the type of political action citizens might take to oppose a police policy and of how the citizens would treat them in a police brutality trial. A smaller proportion of the black policemen also agree that citizen control over the police is inappropriate. Nonetheless, the black policemen and residents obviously do not agree on the issues and problems confronting them. Therefore, although this approach to citizen participation in police work appears to increase the physical and communication bonds with the black ghetto community and to some extent raise the potential for informal community influence over the police, many refinements and changes are still needed. The data does indicate, however, that more involvement of minority group persons in police activities, both at the decisionmaking and implementation levels, is quite likely to increase the informal types of accountability actually available, and thus, to reduce the need for a total community power strategy. In broader terms, the data provide support for the hypothesis that both the quantity of persons having a skill and the levels or quality of the skill held will, at some point, combine to produce a "quantum jump" in not only the type of control and influence feasibile, but also the type actually needed and desired.

It should be noted in closing, that the matters of police efficiency, "professionalism," and so on have not been addressed here. There is no reason to believe that black policemen will be "better" on these dimensions than white policemen. Hence, direct control on these matters would be necessary even if the race of policemen and residents matched perfectly.

Bibliography

Clinard, Marshall B. *Sociology of Deviant Behavior.* New York: Holt, Rinehart, and Winston, Inc., 1968.

Dodge, William R. *Citizen Participation in the Model Cities Program.* Washington, D.C.: Department of Housing and Urban Development, 1971.

Fantini, Mario, Gittell, Marilyn, and Magat, Richard. *Community Control and the Urban School.* New York: Praeger Publishers, 1970.

Gerson, Walter M., (ed.). *Social Problems in a Changing World.* New York: Thomas J. Crowell Co., 1969.

Harmon, B. Douglas. *Urban Data Service,* Vol. 2, no. 7 (July 1970), International City Management Association.

Hyman, Herbert H., and Singer, Eleanor (eds.). *Readings in Reference Group Theory and Research.* New York: The Free Press, 1968.

Kelly, Rita, et al. The Pilot Police Project: A Description and Assessment of a Police-Community Relations Experiment in Washington, D.C. Washington, D.C.: Government Printing Office and American Institutes for Research, 1972.

Kelly, Rita, and West, Garmon, Jr. "The Racial Transition of a Police Force," in *The Urban Policeman in Transition.* Charles C Thomas Co., 1972.

Mast, Robert. "Police-Ghetto Relations: Some Findings and a Proposal for Structured Change, " *Race* (London: Institute of Race Relations) XI, no. 4 (1970).

The New York Times, October 3, 1968.

Radelet, Louis A. "Implications of the Professional Concept in Law Enforcement for Police-Community Relations," *Police-Community Relations,* edited by Norman E. Pomrenke. Chapel Hill, N.C.: University of North Carolina Press, 1966.

Seeman, Melvin, Bishop, James M., and Grigsby, J. Eugene, Ill.: "Community and Control in a Metropolitan Setting," in *Race, Change, and Urban Society,* edited by Peter Orleans and William Russell Ellis, Jr., Beverly Hills, Calif.: Sage Publications, Vol. 5, Urban Affairs Annual Reviews, 1971, pp. 423–424.

The Washington Afro-American, October 28, 1968.

Watson, Nelson A., and Sterling, James W. *Police and Their Opinions.* Washington, D.C.: International Association of Chiefs of Police, 1969.

GROUP PROCESSES IN
POLICE-COMMUNITY RELATIONS

KENN ROGERS

Across the country of America, there is a large gap between police and inner city residents. On the establishment side there is an opinion that police are justified in performing their duties by virtually whatever means necessary—on the nonestablishment side it is very widely understood that some police will do anything necessary whether justified or not. Washington D.C., a city of 70 per cent Blacks, the capital of the nation, the place where Congress and the President dwell, is no exception to the rule of police-citizen misunderstanding and alienation on both sides.

To this end there are two sides with no bridge between them. —WHERE DO WE GO FROM HERE? (*The Pilot District Project Newsletter*, Vol. 1, No. 1)

This paper describes efforts to build such a bridge and in the process to develop data pointing to where to go from there. It is an analysis and evaluation of four four-day intensive working seminars conducted by the District of Columbia Government Pilot District Project (PDP). Designed to enable participants to explore the nature of authority and the problems encountered in its exercise, each seminar was attended by police officers working and civilian citizens living in Washington, D.C.'s Third Police District. I served as consultant for each of the seminars.

It was accepted at the outset that the increasingly high density of population, the rapid and often uneven pace of social, technical and economic changes

Reprinted with permission from *Bulletin of the Menninger Clinic,* Vol. 36, no. 5, September 1972, pp. 515-533.

in America's urban communities fosters alienation, distrust, fear and even hatred between police and community. Minority groups—Blacks, Chicanos, Puerto Ricans, Mexican-Americans and others—in their struggle to share more equitably the opportunities of American life often look upon police as enforcers of a middle-class morality which they themselves see as difficult, if not impossible to live by.[1] Police, on the other hand, experience taunts, curses and even physical attacks from those whom they are professionally charged to protect. As a result, there prevails all too often an atmosphere of mutual distrust and even hatred which demands analysis and most likely alternative approaches for dealing with the suspicions and uncertainties rampant in police-community relations.[2]

Police academy training programs generally address themselves to the technical knowledge necessary for police work and tend to disregard the emotionally-affected uncertainties inherent in this work and their ensuing anxieties. Police-community relations programs more often than not rely rather heavily on traditional approaches, e.g., inspirational lectures, dissemination of so-called scientific principles and exhortative recommendations, stressing the "professionalization of the police." Many of these efforts seem to be designed to convey "improved" public images but, alas, essentially of a cosmetic nature.

Seminars such as those described here are based on the realization that technical knowledge of police work cannot be seen as adequate preparation for the effective discharge of the police force's professional responsibility, let alone for the development of good police-community relations. Participants meet not only as individuals but also on behalf of the institutions in which they work. This fact makes interpersonal and institutional dynamics a subject of major importance, especially when organizational authority structures and their roles are examined in terms of facilitating or hindering police-community efforts toward achieving declared goals and tasks. Therefore participants should have an intellectual grasp of management and related concepts about organizational and personality development. These seminars provide opportunities for learning these concepts and testing their validity in direct application. This kind of learning can enhance the ways people discharge their responsibilities and thereby improve police-community relations.

Understanding group processes and their effects on human behavior has in recent years become of increasing interest to professionals—therapeutic, educational and organizational—as well as to laymen. The application of these techniques has a potentially wide range. Communication with the group generally focuses on efforts to change the group participants' behavior. The techniques of communicating this understanding vary widely in their terminology and application, e.g., Sensitivity Training, T-Groups, Laboratory Training, Group Psychotherapy, Encounter Groups, Sensory Awareness Groups, Yoga Meditation, Body Movement Groups, Alcoholics Anonymous, Weight Watchers and many others.

The seminars described here employed the so-called "Tavistock Model" developed by Rice[3] to focus on learning about group processes. Based on a body of concepts developed by Bion[4] in his psychotherapeutic work, and on "open systems theory"[5,6] as applied to social and organizational systems,[7] this process is designed as a framework for facilitating the study of group behavior and its underlying dynamics. Certain assumptions about this process need to be stressed:

1. Although society has authority over individuals and groups in a number of ways, particular sanctions are exercised by the police. Therefore, it is important for this public service institution to have it members understand the impact of their exercise of authority as fully as possible.

2. Social learning of mature adults can be enhanced by their need to make decisions in new and unfamiliar situations. The seminar's self-study exercises, therefore, were stripped of conventional institutional structures such as agenda, external tasks, name tags, chairmen, secretaries, etc. Making decisions in the resulting unfamiliar situations aroused anxiety and discomfort among the participants. Yet it is unlikely that one can learn about anxiety in decision-making and in situations involving uncertainty in a meaningful way unless this anxiety is actually experienced.

3. In all working relationships there are various levels of behavior going on at the same time, some overt and conscious, others less so. Many persons are familiar with hidden processes in themselves and between two persons. It is, however, far more difficult to think of such processes and to be aware of them in larger working groups or in tense situations such as frequently occur in police-community relations. Increased awareness, therefore, of covert and unconscious group processes potentially enhances the understanding of group behavior including its irrationality.

4. Important roles within groups are those of leader and follower. Each of these roles may be embodied in more than one person, and in different persons at different times. Moreover, neither function can exist without the other. Therefore, it becomes important to learn about the forces which affect a person who assumes the role of a leader and what forces a leader can bring to bear on those he attempts to lead. In the process of experiencing what it feels like to be a leader or a follower, conflicts are likely to arise and can then be studied as they affect the group's task performance.

Structure of the Seminars

The seminars consisted of lecture-discussions, self-study group exercises, an application session, and a final review session. The first day was given to *lecture-*

discussions with emphasis on the following topics: (a) practical applications of system concept in organizations concerned with police-community work; (b) psychological and social implications of work and work contracts; (c) organizational structures and role relationships. (d) authority, power, and responsibility; (e) manager-subordinate and leader-follower relationships; and (f) personal growth and maturation from infancy through adolescence to adulthood.

The second and third days and the morning of the fourth were given to *self-study group exercises.* Each participant had opportunities to examine group processes as they unfolded, to study the effects of his behavior upon others in the group, and to explore the effects of the behavior of the group upon himself. In the process, members tried out different ways of establishing relationships and various problem-solving techniques in work settings. Treating the seminar room as an institution, they were able to learn from each other the effects of their attitudes towards police work and the community and the dynamics influencing effective functioning, innovative changes, resistance and dysfunction in organizational structures.

The consultant's task in this exercise was to help the group examine its own behavior. He intervened only when he believed he could facilitate the learning of the group. Indeed, there was no advocacy of beliefs of values on his part.

Having no set agenda, the members generated their own topics of discussion and thus explored their developing interpersonal relations in the "here and now." In the afternoon of the fourth day, a one-and-one-half hour *application session* was held in which the members, assisted by the consultant, considered the relevance of the seminar's learning to their own work settings.

A one-hour *review session* concluded the seminar. Here members examined the entire seminar in terms of content, the prevailing dynamics of the group, and the techniques used in this kind of learning process.

Primary Task and Philosophy of the Seminars

The primary task of the seminars was to educate mid-management officials of the Third Police District and other participants about group processes, particularly authority relations. The seminars, therefore, were designed to provide participants with a frame of reference in which they could experience the effects of authority upon themselves and others and, in the process, examine their own role behavior, perceptions, and attitudes as they manifested themselves within the different groups. Special attention was paid to understanding the influence of irrational on rational and of unconscious on conscious elements in decision-making while at work.

The seminars' underlying philosophy assumed that intelligent individuals, whether acting alone or in groups, do not behave irresponsibly or against their declared interests without cause. Therefore, they can be held responsible for the consequences of exercising their authority, i.e., doing their work. This responsibility, however, extends itself to actions and decisions that arise not only from overt and conscious processes but also covert and unconscious factors, which may include irrational and destructive expressions of frustration and aggression. Thus, it is assumed that insight into one's own motivations will enable one to redirect his or her energies into more constructive behavior in line with the avowed mission of one's institution.

Resistance of Police Officers to PDP

Throughout the seminars most officers expressed verbally and behaviorally a strong resistance to the Pilot District Project (PDP). There were specific complaints about compulsory attendance at seminars; about having civilian riders in patrol cars; about PDP members lounging around the station houses—all culminating in a bitter resentment against the PDP's very existence, at times scatologically expressed.

The dynamic matrix from which their attitudes evolved can be seen in the police officers' fear that PDP's Civilian Board (CB) would turn into a civilian control board of the Metropolitan Police, if PDP should become effective in establishing good police-community relations. During one session, this apprehension rose to the surface and, when it was interpreted was such by the consultant, some officers "lost their cool," in which they generally take great professional pride. It was the only occasion when more than one person spoke at a time and when nervous shouting occurred. Expressions such as "That'll be the day!" "It will never happen," and "Not while we are around," poured forth, and one officer suddenly found himself in the grip of apparently uncontrollable giggles.

Data from the various seminar sessions showed that while the police officers claimed they were not familiar with the aims and mission of the PDP, nevertheless, some "ventured guesses" as to what those aims might have been originally and how they might have changed since the advent of the CB. Curiously, these guesses and surmises reflected reasonably accurately the official mission of PDP as stated in the original Office of Economic Opportunity grant and as subsequently reworded by the CB. PDP's original mission was seen as an effort to break the vicious circle where on the one hand the police were perceived as an occupation army in enemy territory, displaying attitudes of hostility and brutality toward the ghetto black, even harassing black militants in a cold and vicious way while, on the other hand, they were trying to exert honest and concerned efforts at enforcing the law. These opposing views created serious blocks in police attempts to maintain peace and order, and called for a rehabilitation of good will and cooperation between community and police. However, for reasons they could not understand, the police officers and not the members of the community were expected to make the adjustments. The policeman was branded as the villain, while the community, left alone, appeared to be awarded "the seal of good and responsible citizenship." In the eyes of the officers, this rank discrimination represented a distortion of reality, since "a goodly portion of the population consists of criminals and those supporting them," with only the small remainder being viewed as "citizens," i.e., noncriminals. To make things worse, the officers recalled an election in the precincts to decide where the PDP was to be located. Although the Third Precinct had the lowest number of votes for PDP, it was, nevertheless, located there. These recollections brought back strong feelings of betrayal expressed in statements of "sell-out" and "political deals" between the PDP's director, the "politicians," specifically "the Mayor," and the top echelons of the Metropolitan Police. The latter reaped special bitterness as they were seen to have "shirked their responsibility of protecting their men."

When the CB was subsequently elected, it rephrased PDP's mission. To the best of the seminar participants' knowledge, the CB sees itself as "representative of the community to the police and as a mediator of police action." By pointing to the low voting participation in the community, the men roundly denied that the CB is representative of the community. Indeed, the large number of abstaining eligible voters were seen as "the real citizens," while those who did vote were depicted to be largely rabble. The mediator role of the CB was attacked on the grounds that the CB was not invited by the police officers, but rather brought in as a result of political collusion. Officers felt the CB had neither the approval of the community nor of the police, and that it is not qualified to mediate judgments since it is biased in favor of "the criminal element" and is "without knowledge of police work." One factor underlying these arguments is the clannishness and secretiveness of the police culture. It was stated in varying forms that "it is impossible to work by the book," that "rules are probably broken a hundred times a day." There were thinly veiled allusions to "pimps and dope pushers on the force" and to "goldbricking on disability examinations." There was also some brief mention of brutality.

In this context, PDP's citizen riders were seen as spies who write secret reports on the men, most likely distorting actual events and "accusing some of us of being corrupt when we get a cup of coffee." Moreover, not only are these civilian riders "slovenly," "ill-behaved," "illiterate liars," "often with a police record," but their conduct in the station house is especially objectionable because they frequently interfere with regular police work. When in one seminar a photograph was passed showing a PDP member asleep in the station house with his feet on a desk, the officers agreed that the employment of the PDP staff was nothing but a form of "dignified welfare," i.e., the PDP misuses Federal Office of Economic Opportunity (OEO) funds for welfare payment to unemployables under the guise of doing police-community work. In another group the same theme arose and CB members in this group expressed surprise at such occurrences as shown in the photo and the feeling of others that OEO funds were used for "rehabilitation of dudes."

In addition, the statement quoted from one of the PDP leaflets, that "police should not be afraid of anyone observing normal operations unless something is sly, slick or wicked. If nothing is improper then there is nothing to hide . . ." was felt by the officers to be "rubbing salt into open wounds." One higher-ranking officer resolved the anxiety caused by this statement to the satisfaction of the men by pointing out that there *was* "something sly, slick, or wicked," but that it was on the part of the citizen riders and the PDP in general and not on the part of the officers.

Causes for Officers' Resistance to Insight into Their Behavioral Dynamics

Resistance to the seminars is embedded in the officers' perception of their work roles. In the course of the seminars the civilian participants, the consultant, and occasionally some of the officers themselves, indicated how much a police officer's perception of his role was affected by personal fantasies. Indeed, the particular fantasied image of the police officer as a tight-lipped, heroic, two-gun frontier marshall arose time and again in the course of the discussions. The two-gun facet of this image seemed particularly real to police officers who, in addition to their service revolvers, had also carried a second private gun. This fact was discussed at length and defended as a survival aid in cases when an officer is held up and stripped of his service revolver. It emerged, however, that departmental regulations have effectively disposed of this two-gun phenomenon, although the recollection evoked considerable nostalgia among some officers in the group. During one such discussion a particular insight emerged, although initially at an unconscious level. It started with one of the men describing his job as "maintaining tranquility." Some of his colleagues added that "any person out of the ordinary is suspicious to an officer" and "if he is a deviant, he is potentially a threat to good order." Although prodded by the CB members, the officers never specified criteria for being either "deviant" or a "threat to good order." In fact, one officer strongly implied the question was a stupid one. He stated emphatically, "You know it when you see it. What's more, it is a challenge to the officer's authority." The considerable anger among the officers of this group was then released through their discussion of the charges on which "such a deviant threatening good order" might be arrested. These charges were: disorderly conduct, assault, and resisting arrest.

Since throughout the discussion no references was made to any actual incident, one was left with the impression that these charges existed only in the officers' fantasies. Fear of physical danger could not be admitted overtly by the officers; instead they deflected this fear of personal attack as an attack on their authority. At this impersonal level they permitted themselves to deal with their fears through verbal belligerence which they then "acted out" in the "here and now." In the process they reassured themselves they would bravely do their duty.

When the consultant interpretatively linked the material developed by the group, i.e., the references to "sly, slick, or wicked," to the fear of being personally attacked, and the thinly veiled allusions to arrests and charges for offenses which had not actually occurred, most officers in this group became furious. At this point in this and the other three groups, a ranking officer stepped in and advised the consultant "not to stir up dirt," "not to set the men against one another," and finally, resorting to secretiveness, stated that "we do not wish to talk about such things." When the consultant reminded the participants that they themselves had selected the topics to talk about, and that it was his task to interpret the meaning of their comments, the police officers expressed feelings of being "trapped." The consultant's knowledge represented "a theft of their private thoughts," "helped to create an atmosphere of hostility" and "was aimed at proving a theory other than making the seminar productive."

In one group, making the participants aware of the embarrassment and pain caused by an assertion they clearly knew to be untrue caused a ranking officer to instruct the consultant to "make the men stop that." Realizing that this "instruction conferred upon the consultant" implied that the consultant had authority superior to his own, he suddenly rose and left the room. Although the session was not finished, the officers followed him in rapid succession, thus indicating loyalty to their leader and the department. This dramatic incident was the only occasion in 43 sessions where the men did not adhere to schedule. This particular resistance to insight into their own behavior can be attributed to the officers' need to protect self-esteem, their own perception of their working environments and making their roles fit into personal needs for self-defense. However, the more one learns about his own fantasies regarding individual and organizational authority, the better he can check them against reality and be responsible for his work. Consequently, if these police officers were to recognize that their exercise of authority had been often characterized, for example, by unnecessary use of physical power, it would represent to them a degree of failure in their performance. Moreover, it would subject the entire police force to accusations of police brutality. This kind of situation, of course, is too painful for an individual to admit. Such pain was exacerbated by the presence of superiors, colleagues, subordinates and civilians in the seminars. Telling members of the force to "wash out your mouth with loyalty," i.e., to adhere to solidarity and secrecy, was ineffective. The group process revealed some characteristics of the police culture which it seemed the men would prefer to keep to themselves.

Subgroups and Their Characteristics

In the course of the seminars, four identifiable subgroups emerged. The police officers formed three subgroups, the civilian participants the fourth. On a surface level manifest attitudes differentiating the police subgroups were well expressed when the consultant, during a relaxed lunch-break conversation, asked the police officers at the table why they were on the force. One said, "It's a living"; another stated, more eloquently, that he saw himself "providing important services to the community and maintaining order and peace"; a third spoke, with considerable fervor, of his "mission as a crime fighter." All three were sergeants working in the same geographic area, at the same time, and with the same population of citizens. Each, however, perceived his work and emphasized his authority substantially differently from the others. A valid profile for each of the subgroups can be drawn from the seminars' "data."

The *"It's a Living" Subgroup* was reluctant to communicate about itself. Many of its members managed to remain silent during most of the sessions; reading newspapers; dozing off; and indicating in varying ways they had come to the seminars only because they were ordered to do so. They considered the exercises "a waste of the taxpayer's money"—which could be given usefully to them instead. They made it quite clear they "could not be bothered with relearning their ways and values" and "if change is necessary, let society change." Their view of the consultant's work was as "an attempt to rape their minds."

The main concern for this subgroup was "How do I survive until I am eligible for my pension?" There were discussions of their generous but nontransferable pension rights which made them captives of the department and unable to seek a job elsewhere without foregoing this pension. They acknowledged the possible need for change in the police force—"but not while I am around."

The *"Crime-Fighter" Subgroup* came to the police force in the main from the Deep South or from abandoned coal-mining towns in West Virginia, Kentucky or Pennsylvania. Their formal education did not extend beyond high school, if that far. Overtly, they saw themselves as "undereducated" and "inadequately prepared for their work." Invariably they gave the impression of being shrewd and capable of learning to adapt to changing conditions although impeded by a distrust of large sectors of the community seen as the "enemy." This perception at times seemed to border on group paranoia.

They seemed to have chosen police work largely for two reasons. Their education, both formal and informal, did not provide them with skills for earning a livelihood at the same level of pay in other professions. Moreover, police work afforded them a socially accepted authority position superior to that of a sizeable portion of the total population—the blacks. Having an available underdog in the blacks served to bolster a self-esteem which apparently had been shattered seriously during their own personality development.

Of course, they could have also chosen to lift up "the underdog" by providing helping services with a sense of sympathy. Whenever the discussions touched on this subject, the men presented well-formulated statements about being "policemen and not social workers," although upon further thought, whenever it occurred, there was a realization that police work is in fact providing social services. This point was then quickly dismissed. The attitudes of these officers suggest at least two reasons for denying the validity of the social service concept by this subgroup: (1) The culture of the police force, as they perceive it, is such that it looks upon "helping little old ladies across the street," "soothing a family quarrel," "having compassion with an addict who in the throes of withdrawal requires paraprofessional help" as "sissy stuff" and offensive to the masculine mystique of the law enforcer. (2) Having empathy with the unfortunate tends to vitiate the policeman's unconscious need to force the less fortunate in our society into the role of the underdog and thus inferior to himself.

They deplored their inadequate contact with "good citizens"; instead they were exposed to blacks spouting their hatred, malice, and hostility; to militants calling them "pigs" and accusing them of brutality and corruption; to courts and politicians, both within the police and outside, who make their work even more difficult than it is already. They stressed that "the ideal police system is the Gestapo," but then "it could not be done here." There was repeated mention of an occasional need for martial law.

Again and again they termed themselves as "creatures of habit." Their values were neatly arranged in simple dichotomies of good and bad, right and wrong. They saw parents in our society as irresponsible and, elaborating on this theme, they told tales of their own parents being rather irresponsible and of being viciously whipped by their fathers. In two instances there were systematic expressions of unconscious and strongly suppressed homosexuality, always followed by verbalized idealization of womanhood.

Their request was for the consultant to provide them with a "bag of tricks" for dealing with street people and with higher-ups in the department. They became angry when they were frustrated in this wish but rationalized their disappointment by terming the consultant a "do-gooder wanting to bring about a social system for which the American people are not yet ready." The more manifest hostility was expressed when one officer wondered "how some people escaped the gas chambers," only to tell the consultant later on that he "did not realize he was Jewish." Most officers of these two subgroups were white.

The third subgroup, *Oriented to Community Service,* was about evenly divided between whites and blacks, the former generally holding higher ranks, the latter being patrolmen or sergeants. They felt strongly that crime is not inherent in ghetto populations but most likely is the result of a "crazy-quilt of causes; social, psychological, economic, political and many others." This problem makes it necessary for more and different kinds of police education than that offered by either the Police Academy or the "practical college of the street," not to mention most of the training offered by the PDP. This group acknowledged that "much crime was neither solved nor even investigated." The officers also spoke of the difficulty of "doing effective police work without the cooperation of broad groups in the community" and without "occasionally bending some rules."

The group seemed firm in expressing the need to eliminate corruption and arbitrary acts adversely affecting the rights of citizens. They stressed the importance of noncrime-related service functions and pointed to the flaws in a policy that favors generalization and abolishes specialization in officers' roles.

The black police officers of this subgroup frequently consented to these views but in the main remained silent, displaying poker-faced expressions and, occasionally, turned sullen. Replying to their colleagues who teasingly invited them to express themselves more actively, they seemed to say: "Don't mock us! We are hep to it. We have watched your spiel too often. We have trusted some of you in the past and were tricked."

When other police officers deplored the entrance of "unqualified new recruits," obviously black, the black members of this third subgroup sat in stony silence which could have been either a confident "We shall overcome," or a menacing "Just you wait." However, it clearly was *not* passive indifference.

The entire subgroup made repeated efforts to use the consultant's interpretive comments in spite of the resentful attitude this effort evoked in many of their fellow officers. The consultant was also asked repeatedly to convey the gist of their complaints to higher echelon officers in the department.

The *Civilian Subgroup,* except for two members, displayed a common intent—selling PDP to the police officers. Members differed in their approach. Some lectured at the men, often overbearingly talking down to them or arguing legalistically, proving them "wrong." Others tried to pursuade them to cooperate with PDP, since they were "reasonable men of good will." Only two members straightforwardly addressed themselves to the issues discussed, inquiring, approving, or criticizing. Apparently they felt able to justify their beliefs and values.

All members of this subgroup, however, were frequently late or absent which the police officers felt expressed a belittling attitude. This impression was enhanced further when on occasions CB members tried to explain their absences or tardiness. Their reasons were "busy with the Mayor," other "important matters," or "seeing someone important in the Federal Government." The implications was clear—by comparison, police-community relations and the police officers themselves were less important. Generally, this subgroup suffered from a credibility gap; their rhetoric deviated sharply from the "reality of the street" as daily experienced by the police officers.

Some Dynamics Common to All Seminars

The early stages of the seminars were characterized generally by an attempt on the part of the officers to maintain a solid organizational front with most of the talking left to the senior officers who conveyed a tolerant party-line acquiescence in a matter of potential importance while at the same time condemning the exercise for its irrelevance when compared to the other important things they had to do, e.g. catching criminals. Lower rank officers did little talking. The presence of two CB members served only to unite the police officers in another common purpose: to attack PDP, to show its wastefulness, uselessness, and "support of the criminal element in the community."

At this time, hostility against the consultant and the exercise, both linked to the PDP, emerged. Expressions of anger were directed toward the police hierarchy, although the intensity and frequency were different in each of the seminars.

Frequently, the self-study exercise was initiated by officers in a series of ethnic jokes, indicating thereby that examination of police authority could be carried out successfully only via scapegoating, although with an overcast of jocularity, thereby removing the sting and avoiding any serious rifts within the department. When the consultant interpreted this approach, he and the CB members were generally met with attacks. Splits in the ranks of the police officers recurred when discussion turned to the tendency of white officers to live outside the city while the blacks stayed in the ghetto, or when it was mentioned that the white officers have "their friends among the white shopkeepers." If an officer sided with the consultant or with one of the CB members, the other officers in the group attacked his loyalty.

One approach for covering these overt rifts was initiated, often by the ranking officer, with a discussion of the police as a deprived minority—deprived of civil rights in not being allowed to engage actively in politics, in having to wear their guns at all times, and in being seriously hampered in developing an effective trade-union organization of their own. One example of such a difficulty was cited in the "real possibility" that the Policemen's Benevolent Association's telephone was tapped.

When dealing with the CB members the police officers frequently used the same tactic. The police officers never directed their critical questions at both CB members simultaneously, but only at one or the other. In fact, they used a proven police tactic in splitting the civilian crowd and dealing with each individual separately. In this approach they found the CB members' behavior playing right into their hands by letting themselves be split one from another. Although this maneuver was called to the attention of the entire seminar on several occasions, nevertheless it persisted without change.

There seemed to be at least two dynamics underlying this phenomenon. First, board members wanted to show their individual superiority by demonstrating they could stave off police attacks single-handedly; and second, they obviously did not care to support one another. However, there is also persuasive evidence that the CB members "acted out" the prevailing atmosphere at their own CB meetings: a disunity expressed in squabbles, which can hardly be seen as task-oriented but which apparently satisfies the personal needs of individuals. Some of the more determined personalities will finally come through as dominant and the others then sit back in apathy, manifesting the defense of pretended noninvolvement, barely hiding their rage.

Self-Image of Metropolitan Police Officers

The officers themselves, at various levels of consciousness, suffer a hurt self-esteem, in some instances almost to the degree of lacking self-respect. They work for low wages, especially when considering the high personal risks they take. They see themselves inadequately educated and prepared for fighting or preventing crime, which is growing in frequency, intensity, and complexity. The causes of this increase are largely unknown or not understood by them. Moreover, there is no clearly or operationally defined task description for a police officer's role. The result is they depend more and more on higher-level management whom they believe to be neither competent nor dedicated to police work or to the men themselves. They see the police department forced into a "shot-gun marriage with the PDP," a mismating of the disciplined with undisciplined, incompetent "street people" who interfere with professional work of vital importance to the community. It is this lack of operational clarity about the primary tasks of the police—tasks the department must fulfill to justify its existence—they believe to be the main cause of the system creaking along without much sign of change.

Another serious constraint is an unsatisfied need for approval from "the good citizens." The officers are disturbed about being alienated from "the good citizens," who themselves, in turn, are subjected to an atmosphere of violence, drug abuse, crime and mistrust and thus have become resentful of the police for failing to provide protection and security. Indeed, when police officers, directly or otherwise, examined their contacts with other people, these seemed to be the criminal element; their "friends" were "the bootleggers on the corner who inform on the dope pushers." Resentment toward the community is then linked to the police officers' poor pay and the circle seems locked.

Yet it is worse than that. Locked in a tight hierarchical authority system they have become dependent for promotion on higher level management's evaluation of their task performance. However, the men regard these higher level managers as rather thin-skinned bureaucrats, and any mention of their incompetence or any appeal to them to allow lower echelon officers to make major decisions is likely to end in unpleasant results. In cases where appeals had been made, the men cited experiences in which "the papers have been held up for six to 12 months" and by then the matter got cold and everybody lost interest in it." The reason for these delays was given by the men as simply: "Neither the Chief nor his immediate assistants like complaints. Who, then, will show appeals to them?"

They suggested with varying directness that improved training is withheld from the lower ranking officers because "if they were to become more competent, then some of the superiors would be shown up." This problem took bizarre dimensions when a CB member earnestly inquired about the city's illegal heroin traffic. He was given a lengthy defensive lecture laying the blame on the doorsteps of the law, the Supreme Court, the bail system, and Turkey. However, in the end, he was told the department suffered from a lack of personnel and "officers are needed to write traffic tickets and cannot be spared for other work," presumably the heroin traffic. The CB member found this incredible, and the police officers were suddenly considerably embarrassed but they had made their point—they had nailed bureaucratically motivated disorganization.

An additional complaint came almost as an afterthought—police officers are all too frequently shifted in their assignments "shortly after they get the hang of things"—a condition not contributing to efficiency.

The middle-level police officers saw themselves more often than not "between two millstones": one, higher level management, with an image as described before; the other, an increasing number of new recruits, black, less than qualified initially, inadequately trained, and vaguely suspected of political militancy.

Viewed on the surface level, the image of police officers may be quite impressive, especially when looking at uniforms, shiny buttons, silver shields, guns, and "the traditional image of the respected cop." At a deeper level, however, they see themselves as "niggers," poorly rewarded, facing high risks against survival, lonely, oppressed. To change this image requires, they believe, effective higher level leadership, but they have little hope it will emerge. In short, the policeman's job could be a good one. However, caught in the double bind of insufficient basic skills for other types of work and being captives of a good pension, they have lost their mobility; all they can look forward to is survival and retirement.

The Validity of the Report's Findings

The origin of the data and the method of their evaluation have been described. However, when examining the validity of the report at least three caveats should be entered here.

1. It is clearly impossible to claim any general validity for judging the attitudes of these police officers outside this specific sample of 52 men. Both the size of the sample and its selection—nonrandom— would militate against it. How-

ever, it is not likely that the data from these seminars are the result of pure chance and that they do not reflect in some way actual conditions as perceived by these police officers and by some of their colleagues who were not present.

2. In terms of the description of group personality profiles, a report like this one is inevitably a simplification since it selects those criteria and motivations seen as relevant to the understanding of the institution's problems. Clearly the complexity of human nature embraces a multitude of hopes and fears and attitudes. In selecting those relevant to this particular institution is not to deny the existence of others.

3. Quite often, perhaps in this instance, when behavior of groups within an institution is examined and compared, there is the danger that the comparison will appear as a simple contrast of right and wrong, or competence and incompetence, and that one course of action or pattern of behavior and its motivation is recommended and others are not. I wish to deny explicitly any intention to make such value judgments. My task in this instance was to describe, to understand, and to explain the material provided by the participants, so the involved institutions could derive suitable problem solutions. Moreover, the detection by one person of particular causes underlying an organizational situation does not mean others are expected to think likewise. Consequently, it should be stressed that I do not intend to press the invulnerability of my diagnostic hypotheses. Rather, my intent is to present observations and explanations for critical examination.[8]

Recommendations for Further Work on Police-Community Relations

The need for more intensive study of ways to improve police-community relations seems rather obvious. Yet simply to leave it at that seems not only unsatisfactory but also unnecessary and some recommendations can be suggested here. Indeed, this study produced insights which may be potentially useful for improving police-community relations not only in Washington, D.C., but perhaps even nationally.

First, it seems necessary to define in clear and operational terms the specific tasks and policies of programs designed to effect healthy and constructive police-community relations. Such specifications will provide not only a basis for assessing their feasibility when planned, but criteria for judging their accomplishment or failures, as the case might be, when instituted.

The lack of such clarity enables, perhaps even forces individuals to exert pressures in determining policies for such programs and for their implementation. Moreover, this absence of clarity nurtures a rigidity of operations that results, for example, in forcing officers to attend training sessions whether they want to or not in the hope they might become "better motivated." However, in the process, no attention is paid to their capacity to change their behavior and their underlying attitudes. As a result, police and broad sections of the community frequently become further polarized and alienated from one another. Indeed, this study indicates a great deal of looseness and individually-determined role behavior among civilians and police regardless of the potential consequences. Frequently, unnecessary conflicts arose, obviously satisfying individual or parochial desires, but in themselves destructive to either or both institutions (the police and the community), and even to the individuals themselves. Important areas of joint interest were neglected and vitally important changes in these relationships were difficult, even impossible, to achieve because they conflicted with individual interests.

Second, it seems useful, even essential for the task of improving police-community relations to define operationally the organizational authority structure of the police force in terms of its statutory contracted service to the total community, and then subject it to close scrutiny in its application. How effective is it, for example, in facilitating police work desired by the community? To the best of my knowledge, this task has not been undertaken anywhere in the country. Police manuals offer detailed descriptions about how to do police work. However, there is a marked lack of operationally defined aims and tasks, something in itself worth pondering.

References

1. Liebow, Elliott: *Tally's Corner*. Boston: Little, Brown, 1966.
2. Skoler, D.L.: There is More to Crime Control than the "Get Tough" Approach. *Ann. Amer. Acad. Political Soc. Sci.* Vol. 397, Sept. 1971.
3. Rice, A.K.: *Learning for Leadership*. London: Tavistock Publications, 1965.
4. Bion, W.F.: Experiences in Groups. New York: Basic Books, 1961.
5. Bertalanffy, Ludwig von: The Theory of Open Systems in Physics and Biology. *Science* 3:23–29, 1950.
6. ———, et al.; General System Theory: A New Approach to Unity of Science, *Human Biology* 23:302–61, 1951.
7. Miller, E.J. and Rice, A.K.: *Systems of Organization*. London: Tavistock Publications, 1967.
8. Rogers, Kenn: *Managers—Personality & Performance*. London: Tavistock Publications, 1963.

implementing legal policies through operant conditioning: the case of police practices

JAMES P. LEVINE

Introduction

One serious obstacle to the achievement of social change in America has been the intransigence of large bureaucracies toward changes in goals, procedures, and styles. Although programs *ad infinitum* to remedy evils such as poverty, segregation, crime, and pollution are proposed and even written into law, the day-to-day operation of our political institutions often fails to reflect these innovations. Thus we are unable to evaluate the merits of alternative solutions to such ills because they are never given the test of full-fledged implementation.

In this paper I am going to suggest various measures to modify the behavior of one important political institution which has been staunchly resistant to change—the police. Our understanding of police operations is still quite limited (due partially to the secretive nature of most departments), but as David Easton (1969) has argued, social scientists have an obligation to use whatever intellectual tools are at their disposal to obtain "quick, short-run answers" to questions of pressing social concern. To this end, what follows is an attempt to apply some principles of learning theory (developed largely in highly-structured psychology laboratories on infra-human subjects) to the chaotic environment of the cop on the beat.

Operant behavior is behavior controlled by its consequences, and operant conditioning is the molding of behavior by differentially rewarding behavior that

Reprinted by permission from *Law and Society Review*, Vol. 6, no. 2, November 1971, pp. 195–222.

is desired and/or punishing that which is unwanted. The power of positive and negative reinforcements in regulating human life is revealed by the successes of psychotherapists, educators, social workers, and other who have used conditioning to correct destructive or inadequate behavior. Lifelong stutterers have been cured, paralyzing phobias have been eliminated, autistic children have been "reached," and juvenile delinquents have been steered away from a life of crime.[1]

That we are all conditioned to act in certain ways from our earliest years is hardly news. However, the notion that our patterns of behavior can be systematically and radically changed by altering patterns of reinforcement has not been fully appreciated by political scientists. Our discipline seems to have been seduced by those psychologists who are convinced of the existence of deep-seated cerebral states—personality traits (e.g., authoritarianism), attitudes (e.g., toward civil rights), complexes (e.g., deprivation of affection)—which subconsciously govern much of our private and public behavior. Certainly much of the literature on political socialization portrays man as the captive of early childhood experiences which become almost irreversibly internalized. Contrary to these notions, I assume that human behavior is extremely malleable, even at later stages of life, and that individuals can adapt readily and sometimes abruptly to new circumstances that impinge upon them.

Reflection about American political leaders suggests as much. Lyndon Johnson, the Texas Congressman, repeatedly votes against anti-lynching laws; as President he pushes strongly for civil rights and concludes a State of the Union message with the words "We Shall Overcome." Charles Goodell, the upstate New York Representative is a Vietnam war hawk; as Senator he becomes a leading dove. Sam Yorty originally runs for Mayor of Los Angeles as a moderate leftist (promising to fire Police Chief William Parker); shortly thereafter he becomes a spokesman for the far right. If presidents, legislators, and mayors can change colors, so can the countless and nameless "line personnel" like police, on whom prescribed social change so vitally depends. For better and for worse, we are all chameleons.

The Goal: Police Restraint

One of the cardinal rules of conditioning is, simply, know what you want before you try to get it. Put otherwise, change agents must establish, with some precision, desired *behavioral outcomes* before mapping out strategies and tactics. This may sound obvious, but proponents of police reform are often quite vague about what they want to achieve. The Wickersham Commission, appointed by President Hoover to investigate police, opted for efficient law enforcement, i.e., prevention of crime and the capture of criminals—an image of police popularized for years by Hollywood producers (National Commission on Law Observance and Enforcement, 1931). On the other hand, social scientists studying the police in recent years have pointed up the significance of order-maintainance or peace-keeping (e.g., breaking up fights) as an important goal of police work (Wilson, 1970; Banton, 1964). Still others see the police largely as a social service organization, whose forte should be retrieving cats, writing traffic accident reports, and counselling adolescents (Berkeley, 1969).

What I am seeking is *police restraint* in dealing with citizens no matter which of the above goals predominates. This was one of the major objectives of the United States Supreme Court under Earl Warren, and our constitutional law is now replete with specific rules about police practices. Limits have been placed on the right of police to interrogate (*Miranda* v. *Arizona*, 1966; *Orozco* v. *Texas*, 1969), arrest (*Spinelli* v. *U.S.*, 1969), search (*Chimel* v. *California*, 1969; *Shipley* v. *California*, 1969), and subdue (*U.S.* v. *Price*, 1966) citizens; there is now an authoritative national policy guaranteeing the citizen "due process" in his contacts with police. An individual, whether bearded hippie, militant black, vicious mobster, or middle-class speeder, is now *entitled* to the benefit of regularized procedures and respect for his life, liberty, and property.

Although my primary concern is translating these legal rights into the "living law" of actual police behavior, the outcome I would like to see attained goes much farther. The "good cop," the end product which I would like to see fashioned, is the officer who treats and handles *all* as respectfully, decently, and justly as circumstances permit. Operationally this means that police do the following:

1. Refrain from verbal abuse of citizens;
2. Use only necessary force against those caught in the midst of a crime or those resisting arrest;
3. Restrict field interrogations to persons likely to be suspects or witnesses to major crimes;
4. Ignore race as a factor in deciding whether to stop citizens, arrest them, or use force;
5. Make arrests only when they witness misdemeanors or have probable cause to believe an individual has committed a felony;
6. Make arrests sparingly (and as a last resort) in quieting minor street disorders;
7. Respect the integrity of private homes by forcibly entering them only after obtaining a search warrant or when observing a felony in progress.

I urge these ends because I think they are intrinsically worthy, part and parcel of the democratic ideal of "self-respect for everybody" (Riker, 1965: 17). But such goals are instrumentally valuable as well, given the fact that so much civil disorder in this country has been precipitated by police-citizen confrontations and standing grievances against the police (National Advisory Commission on Civil Disorders, 1968: Ch. 1, 11). In the 1967 Newark and Detroit riots alone (both of which were triggered by police incidents), 68 persons were killed, 1,049 injured and over fifty million dollars of property destroyed (National Advisory Commission on Civil Disorders, 1968: 115, 162). Certainly the underlying causes of such holocausts are complex, but devoting attention to bettering police-citizen relations might well reduce the probability that the social kindling in our cities will be sparked.

There is a further reason for trying to restrain the police. Unlike most policy changes, little or nothing may be sacrificed by curbing police aggression. Although many argue that reducing police discretion will increase crime and diminish public safety, much crime by its very nature cannot be prevented by police (Wilson, 1969: 130). Since either stealth or impulsiveness are elements of most serious criminal activity, even the most vigilant police surveillance would only be minimally effective. In fact, the probability of criminals being appre-hended and punished should actually increase if police become more trusted by citizens since information about events in question is the most crucial ingredient of crime solution, and lack of cooperation from victims (which characterizes high-crime areas) makes investigation very difficult. In any case, recent theories of criminology and high rates of recidivism raise doubts about the efficacy of penal sanctions in deterring serious crime. Thus, if there are no clear-cut social benefits from a free-swinging police department, we might as well protect the innocent (and guilty) who suffer from police anarchy.

How serious is police malfeasance—needless intimidation of citizens? What is the "base line" behavior we are trying to correct? Although measures are woe-fully inadequate because most police-citizen interactions are out of public view, recent studies have produced evidence that police misconduct abounds. Forty-four citizens were improperly assaulted *before the very eyes* of Reiss's observers of Boston, Chicago, and Washington, D.C., police in the summer of 1966 (Reiss, 1968: 12), and the nationwide study of police conducted by the President's Commission on Law Enforcement and Administration of Justice (1967: 28) indicated that rules of restraint are "often disregarded in practice." Similar con-clusions have been reached by seasoned journalists who cover urban police, such as William Serrin (1969) of the *Detroit Free Press*, who entitled an article on the Detroit police "Gold Help Our City" to convey the peril and urgency of the present state of affairs.

Because patrolmen operate rather autonomously in hostile and unpredict-able environments, it is sometimes argued that police lawlessness is almost as inevitable as death and taxes. But the efficacy of police administrators in regu-lating the enforcement of substantive laws by the men on the beat belies this contention. Gardiner (1969) has shown how the level of traffic law enforcement is controlled at the top; he cites examples of ticketing rates in major cities jumping five and ten times from one year to the next when new chiefs take over or old ones crack down. Likewise, Wilson (1970: Ch. 3-7) explains the variance in the handling of misdemeanors such as public drunkenness or juvenile curfew violations by the eight police departments which he studied in terms of alternative preferences of high-ranking police officials. Naturally, the job itself does impose some constraints on police officers (one could hardly condition them to react nonchalantly to sniper fire), but restraint and judiciousness are reasonable expectations. Violence and brutality are *not* indispensable tools of police work and enlightened leadership can do much to curtail their use.

Notwithstanding the current public appeal of cries for tougher police methods ("law and order"), police departments have been and still are relatively immune from direct control of either voters or politicians. Pressure mounts when a ruthless killer prowls at large or when demonstrators take to the streets, but normally police operate with a minimum of community interference. Consequently, police administrators who opt for greater legality and sensitivity on the part of their men should be fairly free to pursue this goal.

What follows in the remainder of this paper is predicated on the assumption that the top police leadership that emerges in the near future will be more far-sighted than their predecessors. They will recognize that terrorizing or maligning citizens, even those who are reprehensible outcasts or willful lawbreakers, is likely to boomerang and intensify the fierce ordeal already facing police by inflaming the passions of the community. Some may scoff at this "new breed" as the "same old pigs" in more respectable apparel (most top cops have shed uniforms), who use sophisticated language and more genteel techniques to execute the same repressive policies. This kind of sweeping rejection is unwarranted. It *was* an event of significant proportions when in 1966 Thomas Reddin replaced the infamous William Parker as Chief of Police in Los Angeles; it promised a real tempering of police conduct and no amount of rhetoric about Fascist domination can obscure this fact.

Unfortunately, the "new day" never dawned in Los Angeles (Mathews, 1969)—a tale similar to that of other cities where progressive chiefs with the highest aspirations take over. Although a number of changes were instituted— popular Dodger catcher John Roseboro was hired as a liaison man with the black community, the community relations staff was increased from three to 120, police began playing baseball with kids, the department was decentralized— police-citizen relations continued to deteriorate. The reason is simple: Reddin was unable to control the behavior of the men on the beat, many of whom persisted in the forceful practices of the past. It is an uphill fight to sell a bad product.

So we come to one of the central points of this paper: remaking a police force, what it *does* and not how it looks, requires a stock-taking of the traditionally proffered methods to control police and a willingness to experiment with radically new approaches based on sound theories of human behavior. It is possible to renovate and salvage veteran police, but it involves more than relying on the commitment of the chief or the deference of the patrolman. What must be systematically exploited is the power of the payoff; police can be restrained—they will tame themselves—if it is made worth their while.

The Futility of Punishment

The gut reaction of most liberals after reading *Rights in Conflict* (Walker, 1968), the official government study of police violence during the 1968 Democratic National Convention in Chicago, is one of anger, indignation, and vindictiveness. The hue and cry goes up for blood—wholesale purging of the department, public hearings, instant dismissals, criminal prosecutions, prison sentences.

Ignoring all that we have learned about the limitations of punishment to modify behavior, we steadfastly cling to the idea that perfecting the disciplinary system used against wayward police will rid us of the forces of evil. Strange, indeed—we now recognize (at least in theory) that hard-bitten criminals are not often reformed nor violent crime deterred by threats of punishment, but somehow police do not get the benefit of our enlightenment. Almost to a man, the critics of the police focus on ways of devising mechanisms for insuring and intensifying the application of punitive sanctions against incorrigibles. Whether the demand is for civilian review boards or "community alert patrols" (to police the police), the rather singular emphasis on redressing grievances of victims as a means of restraining police is ill-founded and unfortunate. Theoretically it is untenable and practically it will not work.

The Ease of Escaping Punishment

To condition behavior, reinforcements, whether positive or negative, must be administered according to a systematic schedule. Of course not *every* response need be rewarded or punished to be established and maintained, but it must become clear to individuals that they cannot escape the consequences of their action. If reinforcement patterns are totally unpredictable it simply makes no sense to rely on the off chance that they might fortuitously materialize. This is particularly so concerning punishment (i.e., the presentation of aversive stimuli following an undesirable response) because there usually are simultaneous positive reinforcements which *do* occur with regularity. The skid-row alcoholic who is jailed now and then for public intoxication is more than compensated by the instant satisfaction of reduced mental stress and satiated physiological needs accomplished by drinking. Guaranteed pleasure is a more powerful influence than intermittant or problematic pain (Bandura, 1969:314).

Herein lies the fatal flaw of most discipline schemes against police. There are immediate rewards for roughing up citizens (peer group approval, feelings of superiority, self-protection) while the chances of getting caught are quite low.

Improving Police-Community Relations

Paul Chevigny, a lawyer who for two years headed a well organized and reasonably well financed "Police Practices Project" to seek redress of grievances against New York City police, concluded that it was virtually impossible to bring offending police to task (Chevigny, 1969:27). Police are usually able to legitimate or camouflage abusive conduct so most available remedies against them are totally useless. They can, quite literally, get away with murder. There are at least eight factors that explain why most guilty police escape discipline: 1) the lack of witnesses; 2) police secrecy; 3) police lying; 4) "bargains" made with victims; 5) the meaninglessness of the "exclusionary rule"; 6) the softness of police review boards; 7) the difficulty of suing police; and 8) the impotence of victims. Let us look at them in turn.

      1. Generally, there are no dependable and disinterested witnesses present to observe police brutality. The most brutal attacks against citizens usually occur in places of low visibility and are thus most difficult to verify; the squad car and the station house (particularly its inner recesses like the "lock-up") are ideal sanctuaries in which physical assaults can be rendered with impunity. As a result, most disputes concerning police abuse are nothing more than contests pitting the officer's word against the citizen's, so it is very difficult to prove the validity of the complaint in a legally acceptable manner. The aggrieved citizen claims he was pushed down a flight of stairs; the officer says the complainant tripped and fell; who is right? Without any outside corroboration, the benefit of the doubt normally goes to the cop.

      Even if bystanders observe police brutality, they are ordinarily reluctant to intervene or get involved; the public apathy of urbanites that destroyed Kitty Genovese (who was viciously murdered in New York while 30 onlookers watched) puts the victim of the police in a similarly helpless position. Of course the risks of intrusion are considerable; the good samaritan protesting police action frequently winds up getting molested himself, or at least being arrested on an "interfering with an arrest" charge. Furthermore, few observers sympathize with the citizen who usually is some kind of social pariah, often is clearly guilty of a crime, and occasionally is a quite despicable specimen of humanity. Thus, the biggest frustration of lawyers representing challengers of police actions is that essential witnesses continually disappear from sight, preventing the authentication of complaints (Chevigny, 1969: 128). When this happens, the officer almost inevitably gets off scot free.

      2. In most altercations, other police officers are around. But no norm is paid greater homage by police than the so-called "Brothers Code": you don't rat on a fellow cop. There is a strong obligation among police, enforced with stiff social sanctions, to protect each other from uncovering of malpractice. Westley's interviews with police in a large midwestern city showed that 73% would not report another officer for stealing $500 from a drunk and 77% would not testify against him (Westley, 1956: 255).

Implementing Legal Policies Through Operant Conditioning

Equally significant is the finding of the Reiss study: in more than half of all instances of undue police coercion that were observed, at least one non-participating policeman was present who stood by and refused to restrain the offender (Reiss, 1968: 18). A "do your own thing" philosophy permeates most large forces, and the officer who tries to embody the department's conscience seriously jeopardizes his standing with his fellow men. This mutual tolerance of rule-breaking, backed up by secrecy, is a thick shield that hides most police abuses.

3. A corollary of the secrecy ethic is that police will lie, if necessary, to protect themselves and each other. Police will almost invariably fabricate criminal charges against their victims to justify the force which was used. A typical scenario might begin with an officer stopping a group of unfamiliar men meandering along a deserted commercial street late at night and making nasty cracks as he questions them. Someone curses the officer, who then proceeds to throw the defiant one against the squad car and frisk him (perhaps getting a few jabs in as he does). An arrest is then made for disorderly conduct even though the men were peacefully minding their own business when initially approached.

Similarly, a harsh beating administered by police in the interrogation room resulting in the hospitalization of the victim will be followed up by the placing of a felonious assault charge against him; it will be alleged that the defendant physically attacked police while being questioned. Or, more commonly, a car is stopped for a traffic violation, a citation is issued, and the driver responds insolently or sarcastically; the officer then roughs him up and slaps him with a resisting arrest charge. All of these cases have a common thread: the officer *falsely arrests* a citizen to legitimate his own illegal behavior. The injury to the citizen is thus compounded; he has not only been physically accosted but he must defend himself in a criminal prosecution where the odds are stacked against him notwithstanding his innocence. Even if he wins in court he is stuck with a criminal record which is a terrible stigma in our society.

The "cover charge" provides the officer with almost invincible protection against punishment because authorities will almost always exonerate him if his use of force was necessitated by the citizen's obstreperous behavior. Since the latter is most persuasively demonstrated if the defendant is convicted of a crime, a two-fold *modus operandi* is standard procedure among policemen: 1) the intensity of violence used against defendants determines the seriousness of the charges preferred against them; 2) stories are contrived to support the charges. Short of administering sodium pentothal to accused police to get at the truth, it is almost impossible to break down the lies which excuse the officer's conduct.

4. In those few cases where defendants of these trumped-up charges are able to marshal a reasonably good case and counter the contentions of the police, prosecutors will often offer to dismiss the charges if the defendant will sign a waiver of claims for damages against both the city and the individual officer (Chevigny, 1969: 48–49). For most defendants who face

the aggravations, expense, and uncertainty of a trial, this is too tempting a bargain to pass up, even though it disables them from seeking compensatory or punitive damages in civil court for the injuries that were suffered.

5. The "exclusionary rule" (see *Mapp* v. *Ohio*, 1961) which prohibits the admission of illegally obtained evidence into court is not much of a threat to police. The worst that can result from an unjustified search or seizure is an acquittal of the defendant, which is no great tragedy for individual police (unless the case has been highly publicized). Besides, the police, in carrying out some of the most egregious invasions of privacy do not envisage prosecutions at all; the major purpose is to secure information or harass deviants.

6. We normally expect those who act as judges to be impartial and unbiased, but this is decidedly *not* the case with most police review boards which hear allegations of police abuse of citizens. These are generally manned by senior police officers who have risen through the ranks of the department and sympathize with the men on the beat. It is therefore not surprising that the percentage of citizen complaints sustained by these boards is uniformly low.

The record of the Los Angeles Police Department Internal Affairs Division (indicated in Table 1) is typical. The "excessive force" complaints almost always originate from outside the department while the "neglect of duty" charges are brought by superiors from within. Those who slough off job assignments (e.g., fail to answer radio calls, under-enforce traffic laws, show up with unpolished shoes at the Christmas parade, etc.) are dealt with harshly, but those who use force overzealously are likely to go unscathed. Chevigny (1969: 56) reached an identical conclusion after two years of dealing with the New York City Review Board, claiming that "it is an extremely fine sieve through which relatively few complaints are pure enough to pass." The message is clear: the departments do not welcome outside intrusion in the running of their affairs.

For all the political ballyhoo about civilian review boards in which outsiders take part in the disciplinary process, the few which have gotten off the ground have also failed to crack down on police offenders. For

TABLE 1. Complaints Sustained by the Los Angeles Police Department[a]

	Excessive Force			Neglect of Duty		
	received	sustained	% sustained	received	sustained	% sustained
1965	231	12	5.2	326	265	81.2
1966	301	16	5.3	288	232	80.6
1967	369	42	11.4	241	192	79.9

[a]The Table is taken from American Civil Liberties Union of Southern California (1969: 22).

example, from 1958 to 1965 the Philadelphia Civilian Review Board received 7.04 complaints and wound up recommending penalties in only 38 cases (President's Commission, 1967: 201). What probably happens is that the civilians, most of whom are middle- or upper-class community elites who are unlikely to have had personal run-ins with police, wind up getting co-opted by the departments they are supposed to be controlling; this is especially likely when police representatives sit on the board. As it turns out, then, the civilian boards seem to be symbols of community control rather than meaningful checks on police.

The limitations of civilian review boards are of little moment anyway since no chief with any political acumen would presently strive for this kind of disciplinary system. The public, interpreting the boards' actions as coddling criminals and appeasing blacks, will not tolerate it (in 1966 it was defeated by a two-to-one vote margin in "liberal" New York). More significantly, such proposals are anathema to the police who have mobilized their considerable political strength to fight against them (Skolnick, 1969: 276-286). A chief who favors civilian controls faces nothing less than a revolt from the ranks and a breakdown of his authority.

7. Judicial personnel usually side with the police so outraged citizens normally have no recourse in the courts. Juries normally empathize with police and often abhor alleged victims so they tend to overlook police transgressions. Judges have another reason for believing police as a general rule: it keeps the rate of guilty pleas high in criminal cases and reduces the strain on the trial docket which is often hopelessly overburdened. The police implicated in the Algiers Motel incident during the 1967 Detroit riots were acquitted by the jury. (New York Times, 1970), and the same good fortune befell eight Chicago police prosecuted by the federal government for wantonly attacking newsmen during the 1968 Democratic Convention (Hasman, 1969). If these seemingly iron-clad cases (the later including close-up photos of the assailants) were insufficient to convict, it ill behooves the run-of-the-mill victim of police misconduct to waste precious resources fighting a losing battle in the courts. The police surely have little to fear from those quarters.

8. The victims of police brutality are ordinarily marginal, lower-class men—e.g., drunks, migrants, the unemployed—(Reiss, 1968: 16-18) who lack the initiative, resources, fortitude, and skills to fight the injustices inflicted upon them. It is now common knowledge that these kinds of individuals have a low sense of political efficacy, especially regarding legal institutions from which they are so totally alienated. They are either unaware of the proper channels for redress[2] or entirely dubious about the chances of success. Rarely can they afford to hire legal counsel, and most court-appointed lawyers or public defenders are only concerned about getting their "clients" off with the lightest sentence. These people are social expendables and are thus left largely on their own.

Consequently we have the paradox that those who hate the police the most, the racial minorities in the ghettos, took less advantage of the presumably responsive Civilian Review Board in New York during its short existence than the middle-class whites (President's Commission, 1967: 201). If those who suffer most complain the least, guilty police are not likely to be apprehended. Punishment for abuse of authority, then, is a highly improbable event and no rational policeman would spend much time worrying about it.

Delayed Punishment

The more immediately punishment follows behavior to be modified, the greater its suppressive effects (Bandura, 1969: 295). The child who is spanked hours after he disobediently strays across the street has meanwhile received a plethora of positive reinforcements (satisfied curiosity, the ebullience of rebellion, etc.); punishment is too late in the day to do much good. Since most serious sanctions imposed on police result only after multiple investigations, ponderous hearings, and all sorts of bureaucratic rigamarole, their efficacy in restraining future conduct is diminished.

The Leniency of Punishment

Abundant experimental evidence shows that severe punishment is necessary to permanently suppress responses unless alternative behavior is being rewarded at the same time. Azrin's pigeons, when shocked with 50 volts or less after each pecking response (which were simultaneously being positively reinforced with food) stopped responding completely the first day of the experiment but eventually recovered to a rate of 900 responses per day (contrasted with 2,800 per day during trials prior to punishment). When shock was weak (30 volts or less), responding recovered quickly to the prepunishment rate, but when the initial shock was severe (100 volts), the pigeons gave up pecking altogether (Azrin, 1960). The passing effects of lenient punishment are predictable; present satisfaction is a more compelling force than the recollection or anticipation of mild distress.

This principle renders laughable the measly sanctions which are sporadically meted out against errant police. A typical book on police administration states that "the oral reprimand, although the mildest form of discipline, can be the most effective in correcting violations" (Pell, 1967: 60-61). This, as any parent knows, is palpable nonsense; but it is a precept followed by many departments. From 1960 to 1965, 150 Detroit police officers were held responsible for misconduct by the Citizen's Complaint Bureau, but not one discharge was ordered and fewer than ten men suffered any loss of pay (Serrin, 1969: 120). The ill-fated New York Civilian Review Board also used kid gloves; it relied heavily on a "conciliation program" which pointed out a "mistake" to an officer without penalizing him (Black, 1968: 222). The issuance of token punishments (demerits, a few extra duties, etc.) may rankle the offender but hardly deters future improprieties.

Although this kind of discipline, the slap-on-the-wrist, is pointless, most chiefs really have few options. They are hemmed in by civil service regulations which usually require full-blown hearings for penalties in excess of five days' suspension. Also, the understaffing of most departments (65% of all departments are between five and ten percent below preferred strength [President's Commission, 1967: 133]) and the increasing number of pre-retirement resignations put a premium on current personnel; lowering the boom on irreplacable police not only results in the immediate loss of available manpower but could inspire droves of other men to quit in disgust. A less tangible but equally important constraint on police leadership is the muscle being flexed by police organizations in defense of their membership (e.g., a petition signed by one-third of the St. Louis police force vehemently protesting the one-month suspension of two officers for using too much force in arresting two black militants [Skolnick, 1969: 280-281]). The price of cracking down is just too high and so the threat of serious punishment will continue to be hollow—a transparent bluff which can be easily ignored.

The By-products of Punishment

There is only one threat that has made a serious impact on police—the specter of community vengeance. The phony arrest, the sadistic shooting, the degrading public shakedown, all can, and do, trigger far worse counterattacks on police— rock throwing, sniping, riots, and the like. Although most departments saturate the ghettos with police, the latter are still outnumbered, and they know it. The community's underlying capability of escalated violence is a working reality to police with far more potency than Supreme Court mandates or rule book pieties (Nieburg, 1969: 152-153). The retribution of the vigilante is swift and stern— most effective from the standpoint of learning theory.

Nonetheless, even effective punishment of police, whoever inflicts it, is fraught with risks of untoward consequences. First of all, one effect of punishment is to evoke emotions such as fear and anxiety when individuals are in situations similar to those that were originally punished. These incapacitating emotions, partially physiological in nature (higher blood pressure, twitching, etc.), often cause individuals to panic and act irrationally when confronted with the threatening stimuli. Police officers disciplined for wrongfully shooting a fugitive might well find themselves paralyzed—"gun shy"—when they have to fire to protect their own or others' safety. Similarly, policemen who have been attacked by black revolutionaries would probably be chronically tense when patrolling any black neighborhoods, and nervous reactions to events are *not* likely to be restrained. Highly-charged emotions result in impulsive and unpredictable behavior.

Another dangerous side-effect of punishment is the phenomenon of "generalized inhibition"—the stifling of appropriate behavior along with the unacceptable. Disciplining an officer for making an invalid arrest may cause him to refrain from making many perfectly legitimate arrests; much-needed aggressiveness on patrol is deterred along with the needless aggression. In Mc-Namara's study of experienced New York City police, 62% of those interviewed agreed with the statement that "disciplining a patrolman usually has the effect of making him a less active cop," while only 12% disagreed (McNamara 1967: 238). Of course these police perceptions cannot be taken at face value, but others have alleged (including the FBI) that Philadelphia police, fearing the civilian review board, were so cautious during the 1964 riots that they allowed looters and burners to carry on unmolested (President's Commission, 1967: 148). This may or may not be true, but one can well imagine police exercising prudence to the point of impotence in order to ward off threats of impending punishment.

Closely related is the problem of avoidance or escape behavior—staying clear of situations where punishing agents are present. If blacks in the ghetto have been retaliating against police, the latter may simply fail to take any action if it places them in a precarious position. When coming upon a gang brawl they might just watch from the sidelines rather than risk a mob action in which the crowd turns against them. Or they may pay no attention when the radio announces a robbery in progress in a housing project thought to be infested with snipers. This will, in turn, just aggravate police-community tension because most slum-dwellers living in high-crime locations are more angry about non-enforcement of the law (i.e., the unresponsiveness of police to their calls for help) than they are concerned about police brutality.

Thus, strategies which emphasize confrontations between the police and the community will not succeed in moderating police conduct. Police will not be pounded into submission, and if they were, they would cease to be police. The negative approach to governing police, like so many attempts to force conformity and compliance, is a dead end.

The Potential of Positive Reinforcement

The cardinal tenet of operant conditioning is that positive reinforcement of behavior increases the likelihood of that behavior being repeated. Higher-order animals are to a great extent self-interested and future-oriented so they will conduct themselves in a manner conducive to receiving rewards (which are *anything* of value to them). They will engage in all kinds of miserable tasks if there is a reasonable expectation that something more gratifying will be forthcoming. The human species, in particular, chooses its actions in a largely purposeful manner. Therefore the goal of police restraint will be facilitated if the police are offered an irresistible temptation to act discreetly. By selecting powerful reinforcers and arranging reward schedules efficiently, police administrators can induce behavior that could never be coerced.

There is an old adage that money isn't everything but it's way ahead of whatever is in second place. While I would not want to vouch for the universal applicability of this proposition, it certainly seems valid for America in the 1970s. Actually, in almost any modern society the free marketability of money, which enables the owner to satisfy his own unique set of preferences, makes it a powerful incentive.

The remarkable power of the monetary reward has been demonstrated by Staats and Butterfield (1965) who have used it to remedy reading deficiencies in culturally deprived delinquent adolescents. One subject was a fourteen-year-old Mexican-American, the fifth of eleven children, who had a second-grade reading level and had never passed any subject in his eight and one-half years of school. He was a constant troublemaker who smoked and drank excessively and who had been referred to juvenile authorities nine times for various offenses, including burglary. The treatment involved teaching the boy first to read single words, then sentences, and finally entire stories. The vocabulary items were written on index cards and the boy received token rewards worth from one-tenth to one-half of a cent each when he correctly pronounced the words; additional tokens were given to him upon completion of more complex tasks. Figure 1 shows his exceptional progress in reading after four and one-half months and 40 hours of treatment; he also attained passing grades in *all* subjects. It is worth noting that the total cost was $20.31 for the token exchange items.[3]

It would seem that money would be equally effective in altering intractable police whose resistance to learning is probably no greater than that of the youth just described. Indeed, material benefits are the primary reason they are on the job; salary attracted them to police work (McNamara, 1967: 194–195)

FIGURE 1. Reading Achievement Test Scores as a Function of School Instruction and Training Using Monetary Reinforcement[a]

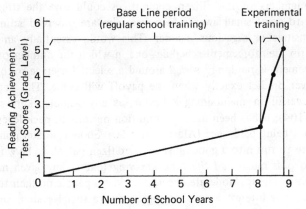

[a]The source is Staats and Butterfield (1965).

and security keeps them on.[4] Lipset (1969: 81) claims that notwithstanding the notoriety of the occasional right-wing political stands taken by patrolmen's benevolent associations, they are essentially trade unions whose members are concerned "with getting more for themselves."

Since the Samuel Gompers mentality seemingly prevails, the dangling dollar should be quite enticing to police.

But across-the-board salary increases, advocated by almost everyone, are most definitely not the answer to police failings because non-contingent reinforcement requires no special performance to merit the additional return. Rather, I suggest a novel approach—establishment of a substantial contingency fund out of which lucrative bonuses ($1,000? $2,000? $3,000?) would be granted to those officers who, over the year's time, won the respect of the community.

To make sure that awards go only to those who are deserving, who have dealt with citizens fairly and (when ever possible) humanely, neighborhood-based police advisory committees (which have already been created in some cities) should be authorized to select or recommend the recipients. Using various methods of gathering information (systematic observation of police, "inside dope" from trustworthy police, sample surveys of the community, "the grapevine," and so forth), the communities would separate the good eggs from the rotten.[5] Currently these committees, theoretically composed of a cross-section of community leaders, serve only a communications function; it is not surprising that they have generated minimal interest from the "grass roots" (President's Commission, 1967: 156-158). Giving them major clout would inspire more citizens to become involved in a constructive way in police-community relations, which itself should lessen some hostilities, and more importantly, it would be the most reliable way of evaluating the on-the-street judiciousness of police.

At the risk of sounding fanciful, let me suggest a more radical refinement of this basic plan which is consistent with learning theory. Since behavior is molded most effectively when reinforcement immediately follows correct responses, members of the citizen committees could rove the streets and be empowered to grant small awards to police who are observed acting in a particularly sensitive or sagacious manner. This would essentially amoung to a "variable ratio" reinforcement schedule—one in which the number of responses per reinforcement is randomly *varied* around a selected average so that the subject can never predict exactly when the payoff will come. This pattern is extremely powerful in maintaining behavior, as any gambler knows (Skinner, 1965: 102-104); it has been used to condition pigeons to peck levers 220,000 times without being paid once (Aldis, 1961: 60). Sooner or later police officers could be sure to run into a goody-dispensing citizen patrol, so he would rationally want to pass muster *all the time* knowing that at any given moment his number might come up. Moderate uncertainty keeps people on their toes.[6]

Because our interest is in changing an entire social system and not just isolated individuals, interdependent contingency systems might also be utilized. Under such programs, the payoffs shared by a group are dependent on the performances of individual members so a sense of social responsibility is an additional incentive to act correctly. In an experiment conducted by Wolf and Risley (1967) the disruptive classroom behavior of a child was more efficiently controlled when both she *and* her peers earned *one* point for every time period she behaved well than when she *alone* received *five* points for acting commend-ably; peer group pressures were quite effective. In like fashion, entire police "teams" (e.g., all the patrolmen in one precinct) could be rewarded upon re-ceiving good ratings by citizen boards with the booty to be divided equally among the police. Or, a city-wide competition might be held between precincts with honors (and greenbacks) going to the unit most appreciated by the com-munity it serves.[7] Peer approval is very important to police, who have greater camaraderie with each other than is true of other labor forces, so it makes sense to take advantage of this fact in trying to effect change. Those who object to such "collectivism" should remember that this is the identical principle used to promote excellence in the World Series and the Super Bowl—two of the nation's most venerated institutions.

This type of community control should not engender the intense police opposition which discipline-oriented proposals create because police would have much to gain and nothing to lose. Regardless of who receives pecuniary honors, all police would be receiving their guaranteed wage; these special allotments would be gravy on the mashed potatoes. The most significant cost might be the initial dissonance resulting from knowing that preferred work styles (e.g., knocking heads and cussing blacks) are no longer economically profitable, but this tension should be resolved if, as is hoped, police values change to match their new behavior. I would guess that most officers will find it easier to treat people decently, even if it is somewhat unpalatable at first, than to "moonlight" for extra cash.

Optimally the attraction of fiscal rewards would eventually be supple-mented by another kind of reinforcement—the gratification of relating to one's fellow human beings. Carl Rogers (1968) argues that men find it highly fulfilling to feel close to one another, and it is not inconceivable to imagine a "new breed" of cop who communicates in a meaningful way with many of the troubled citizens whose paths he crosses. Police who are tactful and understanding may actually become the benevolent stalwarts of the provinces in their charge. This is not romantic dreaming; success of the San Francisco Community Relations Unit in handling some of the city's most difficult social problems, like racial conflict and the drug scene, shows that police *can* be human and still come out alive.[8]

Playing a positive role in the community might in turn give police some-thing they sorely lack today—intrinsic satisfaction from police work itself.[9] A more powerful and durable reinforcer to maintain police restraint could not be found. Self-reinforcements—call it self-actualization, self-esteem, or plain old pride—are important regulators of human life (Bandura, 1969: 32–38).

Extinction of Preemptive Police Aggression

One common police practice to be eliminated is what I call preemptive aggression—the use of unnecessary force in speech or action to prevent the victim from himself initiating some defiant behavior. The officer "gets the jump on the draw" and shows the citizen who is really "in charge" of the situation. Instead of asking politely for an ordinary motorist's identification, the officer growls: "Let's have your license, bud." Or a group of seedy-looking blacks on a street corner are approached at gunpoint and frisked prior to any investigation about their purposes or business. Of the same ilk but with disastrous repercussions is the indiscriminate firing into a unruly but unarmed mob; this is Kent State. These actions are to be distinguished from legitimate self-defense where there is an objective danger to the officer.

A routinely effective way of terminating any undesirable behavior is "extinction"—discontinuance of the positive reinforcements which have maintained the behavior. But there are two barriers to extinguishing preemptive aggression. First, police culture approves of such conduct and constantly reinforces it. Second, the overuse of force at the outset of a confrontation is strongly reinforced by its usual success in averting assertiveness or resistance; the maltreated citizen silently and stoically takes it on the chin.

To break the hold of police culture is not easy, but some actions would seem to facilitate this end. The use of one-car patrols and single foot-beats abate the opportunities for police to "egg on" fellow officers who may be ambivalent or hesitant about using extra force but cannot resist this encouragement. Steering rookies on beginning assignments away from ultra-cynical veterans might insulate them somewhat from the prevailing ethos. Stimulating police to join outside organizations and privately associate with civilians should have the effect of whittling down the staunch and singular allegiance to their occupational group since they will occasionally find themselves subject to cross-pressures. However, this is easier said than done because police often face exclusion and rejection if they seek entry into the larger social world (Skolnick, 1967: 49–51).

The proven technique for getting rid of inappropriate defensive behavior like preemptive attacks is to introduce individuals to the aversive stimuli (in this case the potentially-antagonistic citizen) at non-threatening levels and to gradually increase the degree of threat until the most frightening conditions can be faced with equanimity. So, to extinguish police pugnaciousness we might first take an officer into a lily-white, high-income area and select a harmless-looking traffic violator (e.g., a mother with three kids) to be stopped and treated respectfully. When this is accomplished without dire consequences, a speeding sports car is stopped, then a hopped-up car driven by teenagers, and so forth. Not only do we gradually increase the suspiciousness of the encountered citizen, but we start moving into more dangerous neighborhoods with higher crime rates and greater resentment of police—while still requiring the officer to be calm and reserved. At the same time the natural tension of the police-citizen contact is raised; from the officer's beginning traffic stops he moves to noisy parties, marital fights, and on up to burglaries in progress and mass demonstrations. At each step of the training the officer is emphatically instructed to remain low-keyed; little by little, he learns that his generalized fear of being abused is unrealistic and a more subdued handling of citizens will not undermine his authority or endanger his life.

The key to this modification procedure is incrementalism—building self-confidence in the officer by slowly guiding him from trivial matters to greater challenges and finally to tasks that are very taxing. Although technically feasible (at least in large cities), it would be enormously costly because at any given time the officer's functioning would be seriously circumscribed, and many instructors would be needed to positively reinforce the new, non-aggressive posture being taken.[10] Thus, it *is* unrealistic now since a large burden of many chiefs is merely keeping enough men on the streets to deal with the daily business; but should the society at some future point make a full-scale commitment to control of the police, gradualized extinction of combativeness could be a very useful inservice training program. Indeed, it might also be a salutary way of introducing recruits into police services by extinguishing paranoic outlooks *before* they take their toll when the officer is on his own.

Reducing Police Emotionalism through
Counter-Conditioning

Jack Webb in many ways fits our image of the ideal police officer—calm, steeled, self-contained. Yet Webb is an actor and *Dragnet* is fiction; the real-life cop, taunted, tormented, and tried day in and day out, often responds with his heart instead of his head. This section suggests some classical conditioning processes to reduce this kind of emotional reaction to stress—to give police thicker skins and smaller mouths.

Numerous studies have shown that disrespect manifested toward police—the wisecrack, the contemptuous snarl, the filthy curse—precipitate more police infractions than any other cause (Westley, 1953: 38; Wilson, 1970: 130; Chevigny, 1969: 73; Walker, 1968). Police interpret such insolence as a personal affront and react in a hotheaded and disproportionate way. In short, they "blow their cool."

Desensitization through counter-conditioning is an ideal way of dealing with this problem, since it is a procedure in which disliked phenomena are repeatedly paired with artificially created positive experiences so that the threatening stimuli *lose* their aversive quality. Insults and epithets thrust at police are negatively valenced stimuli that seemingly could be neutralized by associating them with more felicitous circumstances.

Therapists commonly induce "muscular relaxation" to induce a pleasant and tranquil feeling in clients who are then presented with disturbing stimuli (e.g., snakes, heights, sex) in imaginary, symbolic, or real form. As with extinction, stimuli are introduced in graduated intensities, from mild to strong. But *any* means of relieving subjects of worries and anxieties can suffice, so similar results can be produced by presenting fearful objects in an ultra-relaxing physical and social environment.

To "de-fuse" disrespect toward the police of its emotion-arousing properties, officers might be placed in a congenial atmosphere (perhaps a specially constructed lounge or retreat with soft music, good food, comfortable furniture, and so forth), far removed from the turmoil of the throng on the streets. In this context police would be called a succession of foul names, starting with the innocuous "cop" and working up to the adrenalin-releasing "mother-fucking pig." Also films and tape recordings vividly portraying snide motorists, bellicose drunks, impudent gangs, and gesturing protesters would be presented, always, of course, building climactically to the really hated experiences.

Upon completing the sessions, officers will have been exposed to a plethora of obnoxious and unnerving events—but all taking place in a benign kind of setting. If the treatment works the officer, when faced with identical behavior patterns out on the beat, should be less distraught and consequently less inclined to retaliate. He might not grin, but at least he could bear it.[11]

Two unknowing applications of counter-conditioning theory by police have been made. Montgomery County (Maryland) police were involved in a crash training program shortly before the 1963 March on Washington to deal with interracial conflict that might spill outside the boundaries of the nation's capital. With the leadership of personnel from the National Institute of Mental Health, the officers engaged in lengthy discussions airing their fears and hatreds of assertive blacks. Subsequently they were able to eject picketers from private property in a restrained and even gentle manner, actually winning the praise of those who were arrested (Shellow, 1965).

The other example is the case of police in several cities who recently have adopted pigs as mascots and have started wearing "P.I.G." buttons, standing for pride, integrity, and guts. This was reported humorously in *Life* magazine (1970); but it follows desensitization principles to a tee. The disgusting pig is imbued with positive virtues, so when this particular invective is spewed at police they should be more able to shrug their shoulders and laugh it off.

The reverse kind of treatment, "aversive counter-conditioning," might have a place in keeping police from heaping indignities on citizens when there is no provocation. One of the deepest grievances of ghetto residents against the police is that they are spoken to, as a matter of course, in a discourteous and demeaning way. The first words they often hear when approached by an officer are, "Hey, nigger, get your fat ass over here" (President's Commission, 1967: 180-182). Although causing no permanent damage, this verbal needling is highly incendiary to people who have been disparaged and oppressed in hundreds of ways since birth. For police, however, expressing such insults is positively reinforcing; it enhances their feelings of superiority and feeds their need for power.

It is possible to develop conditioned avoidance of such behavior by contiguously associating it with exceedingly painful sensations. In psychotherapy, emetics and electrical shock are often the unconditioned aversive stimuli utilized to create repulsion to clients' debilitating cravings. Alcoholism, sexual fetishism, and drug use have been successfully controlled by counter-conditioning negative affect toward the formerly attractive objects (Bandura, 1969: 511-551).

For many officers, prejudice against non-whites and social deviants is deeply ingrained, so debasing the latter with racial slurs or profanities is habitual behavior which cannot be cured by departmental edicts prohibiting such speech. Aversive counter-conditioning might be used, obviously only with an officer's consent, to suppress this compulsive language. The method would be straightforward: apomorphine or emetine would be administered to the subject and as soon as nausea occurred, he would be required to viciously curse and berate blacks or "long-hairs" who were brought into view (either actually or on slides). The agony of the nausea should create negative feelings in the subject toward the kind of behavior in which he was engaging while undergoing the physical trauma, to wit, abuse of minorities. If the conditioning takes hold, future impulses to mock such individuals will be internally blocked; the nasty words are inextricably associated with the previous physical suffering so the officer will suppress the former to avoid the latter. Recollection of intense personal misery, although artificially induced, might deter socially destructive conduct by police.

Conclusion

There is a song from the early 1950s that starts out: "You've got to accentuate the positive and eliminate the negative." The central theme of this paper is just that: Both political actors and academic thinkers ought to be devising methods of making *good* police rather than concentrating attention on means of weeding out those who are bad. Strict discipline against abusive police is both impractical and unwise; the last thing this nation needs (white and black, young and old) is more bitterness on the part of police, which greater emphasis on punitive sanctions would undoubtedly engender.

Improving Police-Community Relations

To improve the quality of police work and achieve the goal of police restraint, we ought to be taking full advantage of the science of human behavior—which we are *not* doing now—at the planning, recommendation, and implementation stages of policy making. It is endlessly argued that what is needed is more "educated" police or more instruction on "human relations" in training programs; thus the Task Force on the Police urges that recruits be given "a much more solid foundation in the fundamental principles of democratic government and the society in which we live" (President's Commission, 1967: 37). This is vacuous balderdash; it is highly questionable whether and how sophistication in the liberal arts or additional civics courses would be translated into more acceptable on-the-job performance. My own guess is that some of our most animalistic patrolmen *already* possess the intellect and knowledge to behave in a more temperate way; it does not take the I.Q. of Einstein or mastery of sociology to be able to act fairly and dispassionately. What *is* necessary, and what I have suggested above, are systematically calculated programs which given police a vested interest in treating people like human beings.

On a broader level, my intent has been to demonstrate the potential utility of operant conditioning in modifying the operation of large-scale political institutions. Major legal changes usually require alteration in the practices of many individuals, both in and out of government, so a very important consideration in formulating new policies should be devising schemata to reverse the inertia of their time-honored routines. If some resources were set aside in the budgets of our multi-million dollar programs for *rewarding* those who comply with new directives, the number of massive policy failures might be lessened and more rapid social change accomplished. In shaking up bureaucracies, let us start using more carrots (green ones) and putting less faith in sticks.

One closing note is in order on a more philosophical plane. Some may raise objections to the use of technology—applied social science—to manipulate people for ends of which they disapprove. This concern about modern tendencies toward totalitarian control is legitimate; I too look with horror at the *Brave New World* (Huxley, 1932). But a critical problem today is that so many institutions seem totally *out of control*—the police, the military, the schools, even the family. What I favor is the more *rational* use of social controls that protect and promote individual dignity—the manifold controls attempted by many of us (Supreme Court justices, police chiefs, teachers, parents) which so often miss the mark and defeat their own purposes. Beyond all doubt counter-controls must also be encouraged so that choices of ends can be widely dispersed and precious freedoms guarded. But in an age where decrying "Big Brother" is becoming a rallying point for so many, it is sobering to recall the words of B.F. Skinner (1956: 1065): "Fear of control, generalized beyond any warrant, [can lead to] ... the blind rejection of intelligent planning for a better way of life."

References

1. Albert Bandura's definitive work on conditioning thoroughly reviews the varied therapeutic applications. See his *Principles of Behavior Modification* (1969).

2. It is often totally unclear where grievances can be registered since 75% of all departments lack formal complaint procedures (President's Commission, 1967: 195).

3. It is interesting to note how the boy converted the tokens. The items he purchased included "beetle shoes," hair pomade, a phonograph record, and a ticket to a school function; he also gave a cash gift to his brother. The diversity and uniqueness of these purchases attest to the beauty of money as a positive reinforcement.

4. Seventy-three percent of McNamara's respondents agreed with the statement: "It would be difficult to keep most patrolmen on the job if it weren't for the salary and other benefits connected with the job" (McNamara, 1967: 242).

5. Some department practices might be changed to accommodate this assessment procedure. Squad car numbers might be enlarged for easy identification at some distance; badge numbers could also be made more conspicuous.

6. At great inconvenience to himself, the enterprising real estate agent graciously consents to show homes to dozens of people who are not even in the buying market, because he cannot tell in advance when the iron will strike and he will have a serious customer on his hands.

7. It would only be fair to have different classes of competition depending on the level of crime, since the temptation to get out of line is greater in high than in low crime areas.

8. Journalist William Turner, a former F.B.I. agent, says that the unit "has earned the respect, trust, and confidence of even the most militant and police-suspicious elements in the city" (Turner, 1968: 159). See also Leary (1969).

9. More than half of McNamara's sample of New York police said they received little personal satisfaction in performing police duties (McNamara, 1967: 242).

10. There is some evidence, however, that self-managed extinction treatments can be successful if the individual's motivation to change is high. See Bandura (1969: Ch. 6).

11. The experience of Colin Barker (the fictitious name of one of the San Francisco police officers accompanied on the beat by journalist L.H. Whittemore) is relevant here. One evening while patrolling Haight-Ashbury, Barker was met with the usual profusion of derogatory and obscene comments ("Gestapo!" etc.) which he took in stride. Finally, however, one of the resident haranguers came up to him and, speaking right into his face, said "Fuck you, cop!" That sent Barker beyond the boiling point; he threw the young man against a wall and

began pummelling him. The youth was eventually arrested after a wild fight ensued, but had Barker been desensitized to this kind of vulgarity he might have just turned his back and walked away. The incident is described in Whittemore (1969: 225–232).

Cases

Chimel v. California 395 U.S. 752 (1969)
Mapp v. Ohio 367 U.S. 643 (1961)
Miranda v. Arizona 384 U.S. 436 (1966)
Orozco v. Texas 394 U.S. 324 (1969)
Shipley v. California 395 U.S. 818 (1969)
Spinelli v. U.S. 393 U.S. 410 (1969)
U.S. v. Price 383 U.S. 787 (1966)

Bibliography

Aldis, Owen (1961) "Of Pigeons and Men," 39 Harvard Business Review 59.
American Civil Liberties Union of Southern California (1969) Law Enforcement: The Matter of Redress. Los Angeles: Institute of Modern Legal Thought.
Azrin, Nathan (1960) "Effect of Punishment Intensity during Variable-Internal Reinforcement," 3 Journal of the Experimental Analysis of Behavior 123.
Bandura, Albert (1969) Principles of Behavior Modification. New York: Holt, Rinehart and Winston.
Banton, Michael (1964) The Patrolman and the Community. New York: Basic Books.
Berkeley, George (1969) The Democratic Policeman. Boston: Beacon Press.
Black, Algernon (1968) The People and the Police. New York: McGraw-Hill.
Chevigny, Paul (1969) Police Power: Police Abuses in New York City. New York: Pantheon Books.
Easton, David (1969) "The New Revolution in Political Science," 63 American Political Science Review 1055.
Gardiner, John (1969) Traffic and the Police: Variation in Law Enforcement Policy. Cambridge: Harvard University Press.
Hasman, Karen (1969) "Hanrahan Pondering New Assault Charge," 138 Chicago Daily News (June 12) 17.
Huxley, Aldous (1932) Brave New World. New York: Doubleday.
Leary, Mary (1969) "The Trouble with Trouble-shooting," 223 Atlantic Monthly 94.
Life Magazine (1970) "Parting Shots," 69 Life Magazine (July 31) 64.
Lipset, Seymour M. (1969) "Why Cops Hate Liberals—and Vice Versa," 223 Atlantic Monthly 76.

McNamara, John (1967) "Uncertainties in Police Work: The Relevance of Police Recruits' Backgrounds and Training," in David Bordua (ed.) *The Police: Six Sociological Essays*. New York: John Wiley.

Mathews, Linda (1969) "Chief Reddin: New Style at the Top," 223 *Atlantic Monthly* 84.

National Advisory Commission on Civil Disorders (1968) *Report*. New York: Bantam Books. [Kerner Commission]

National Commission on Law Observance and Enforcement (1931) *Report on the Police*. Washington, D.C.: Government Printing Office. [Wickersham Commission]

New York Times (1970) "Four in Motel Trial Freed in Michigan," 119 *New York Times* (Feb. 26) 1.

Nieburg, Harold L. (1969) *Political Violence: The Behavioral Process*. New York: St. Martin's Press.

Pell, Arthur (1967) *Police Leadership*. Springfield, Ill.: Charles Thomas.

President's Commission on Law Enforcement and Administration of Justice (1967) *Task Force Report: The Police*. Washington, D.C.: Government Printing Office.

Reiss, Albert Jr. (1968) "Police Brutality—Answers to Key Questions," 5 *Transaction* 10.

Riker, William (1965) *Democracy in the United States*. New York: Macmillan.

Rogers, Carl (1968) "Interpersonal Relationships: U.S.A. 2000," 4 *Journal of Applied Behavioral Science* 265.

Serrin, William (1969) "God Help Our City," 223 *Atlantic Monthly* 115.

Shellow, Robert (1965) "Reinforcing Police Neutrality in Civil Rights Confrontations," 1 *Journal of Applied Behavioral Science* 243.

Skinner, B.F. (1965) *Science and Human Behavior*. New York: Free Press.

—— (1956) "Some Issues Concerning the Control of Human Behavior: A Symposium," 124 *Science* 1057.

Skolnick, Jerome (1969) *The Politics of Protest*. New York: Simon and Schuster.

—— (1967) *Justice Without Trial: Law Enforcement in Democratic Society*. New York: John Wiley.

Staats, Arthur, and William Butterfield (1965) "Treatment of Nonreading in a Culturally Deprived Juvenile Delinquent," 36 *Child Development* 925.

Turner, William (1968) *The Police Establishment*. New York: Putnam's.

Walker, Daniel [Director, Chicago Study Team] (1968) *Rights in Conflict:* A Report Submitted to the National Commission on the Causes and Prevention of Violence. New York: New American Library.

Westley, William (1956) "Secrecy and the Police," 34 *Social Forces* 254.

—— (1953) "Violence and the Police," 59 *American Journal of Sociology* 34.

Whittemore, L.H. (1969) *Cop! A Closeup of Violence and Tragedy*. New York: Holt, Rinehart and Winston.

Wilson, James Q. (1970) *Varieties of Police Behavior*. New York: Atheneum.

—— (1969) "What Makes a Better Policeman," 223 *Atlantic Monthly* 129.

Wolf, M., and T. Risley (1967) "Analysis and Modification of Deviant Child Behavior." Paper read at the American Psychological Association meeting.

CHAPTER 5-6

ACTION FOR CHANGE IN POLICE-COMMUNITY BEHAVIORS

TERRY EISENBERG, ALBERT GLICKMAN, AND
ROBERT FOSEN

Loss of faith in the law enforcement establishment is increasingly manifested among the citizenry, especially minority group members, by increases in crime rates and riots; community indifference; charges of police prejudice, brutality, and disrespect for citizens; and complaints of lack of police protection.

On the other side, police officers frequently appear to have lost faith in the country's leaders and the public. They charge that they are subjected to strong political pressures and undue restraints, are held accountable for most social ills, are accorded low status and respect by the community, have little opportunity for redress of grievances, and must perform a tremendously complex job under conditions which, at best, are frustrating.

The escalation of antagonisms between police and citizens in certain sections of society has tended to induce the formation of two separate and distinct groups who communicate with and understand each other minimally, if at all.

These are harsh statements. To be sure, it must be recognized that the problem is complicated by inadequacies in housing, welfare, education, and employment. Yet, the magnification of these "opposing forces" is, in considerable part, a cause of the problems described. It threatens to undermine the basis of support from more temperate, sensitive, and rational people who constitute the essential communication links through which we can reclaim the

Reprinted with permission of the National Council on Crime and Delinquency, from *Crime and Delinquency*, Vol. 15, No. 3, July 1969, pp. 393–406.

middle ground necessary for the de-escalation of antagonisms and the resolution of differences.

Background

In order for any socio-political system to be effective, maintain its integrity, and survive, its established cultural values and traditions must be accepted by the people who are part of it. These values and traditions are formalized in laws, which are maintained by institutions of justice and law enforcement.

When significant segments of the population lose faith in the integrity of the system and its institutions (e.g., law enforcement), the self-disciplining value is destroyed. As a consequence, unacceptable behavioral acts increase in both frequency and intensity. The increase we have seen in crime rates, riots, and community indifference makes it appear that basic values have indeed deteriorated.

The attempted remedy in the form of more law enforcement personnel, better physical equipment, and implementation of a "crack-down" philosophy has been and will continue to be self-defeating; it produces only a vicious cycle. Violence generates more violence, and oppressive action sires hostile reaction.

As an interesting parallel, Americans overseas are likely to feel that their comparative wealth shows that they are smarter or somehow better than poor people. Because they feel superior, and because of prejudice or lack of knowledge, they are inclined to isolate themselves physically and psychologically, to behave with a lack of respect and sympathy toward foreign peoples, to overlook their real problems, and to derogate their values and aspirations.[1] The nationals are offended by this superior attitude and the arrogant behavior stemming from it.

Coming as they do from a comparatively wealthy, literate, and sanitary society, Americans tend to be confused, frightened, annoyed, and frustrated when they encounter poverty, illiteracy, stench and filth, and strange customs and values in poorer societies. The cultural shocks they experience with Koreans and Vietnamese, for example, are paralleled in their encounters with what Harrington has called "the Other America," the fifty million citizens who are without adequate housing, employment, education, and medical care.[2] Certainly, it must be recognized that one American may very well be ignorant of, feel discomfort with, and express hostility toward another American whose values and traditions differ from his own.

The disparity in attitudes between whites and Negroes has recently been described in a study conducted by the Lemberg Center for the Study of Violence.[3] Preliminary findings indicate that Negores and whites differ considerably on the perceived pace of integration, the causes of riots, and the prevention of riots. It is quite possible that the gap is at least partly attributable to the whites' ignorance of actual conditions in the ghetto. If this is so, the problem facing Negroes and whites is not a matter of pure and simple "racism" but rather unawareness of or indifference to the factual basis of Negro resentment and bitterness, and the inability of our social institutions to meet the need for change unless this need is demonstrated dramatically and painfully—e.g., by riots. The Lemberg report concluded that if white populations generally had a fuller appreciation of the just grievances of Negroes, they would give stronger support to their city governments to promote change and to correct the circumstances that give rise to the strong feelings of resentment now characteristic of ghetto populations.

The image of the law and the integrity of our system of justice are woven in the fabric of the police officer's uniform. The job of the policeman is difficult at best; it becomes tremendously complex when he misunderstands and is indifferent to variations in subcultural conditions, problems, aspirations, customs, and attitudes. Physical and verbal mistreatment of citizens contributes to the resentment against police. Citizens also misunderstand and mistreat police officers. The fact that there were 13.5 assaults per 100 officers in 1967 is evidence enough.

The similarity of attitudes of American military personnel toward foreign peoples and attitudes of American law enforcement personnel toward members of different American subcultures is obvious. The police are instruments of political power on the local scene just as the military are instruments of political power on the international scene. For the middle class, the police protect property, give directions, help old ladies, and are essentially necessary, constructive, and useful. For the urban poor, the police are aggressive and hostile, exerting arbitrary power and heaping indignity upon individuals. Almost every slum harbors a vast conspiracy against the forces of law and order. If a stranger approaches and asks for someone, no one will have heard of him, even if he lives next door. The outsider is cop, bill collector, investigator; in the Negro ghetto he is "the Man." The city jail is one of the basic institutions of the Other America; almost everyone in the "tank" is poor: skid-row whites, Negroes, Puerto Ricans, whose poverty is an incitement to arrest in the first place. "To be impoverished is to be an internal alien, to grow up in a culture that is radically different from the one that dominates the society."[4]

These resemblances between troop-community and police-community relationships suggested to us that the concepts and procedures that had been applied by the U.S. Army in Korea, in collaboration with the American Institutes for Research, had direct relevance and could be adopted with appropriate modification to the situation in large cities in the United States.

The program in Korea was successful in that desirable changes, measured in terms of both attitudes and observable behavioral acts, occurred among both American and Korean groups. A few examples of the changes in attitudes that occurred in the troop-community relations context are the following:

    1. The percentage of Americans holding the view that local people were to blame for anti-Americanism was reduced; e.g., Americans came to realize that they were, at least in part, to blame for anti-Americanism.

In the police-community relations context, it is reasonable to expect that policemen can come to understand that they are, at least in part, responsible for anti-police attitudes.

    2. The percentage of Americans holding the view that local people do not like Americans was reduced; e.g., more Americans came to realize that they are liked by local people.

In the police-community relations context, it is reasonable to expect that the proportion of citizens who are favorably disposed toward policemen is greater than policemen expect it to be.

    3. The percentage of Americans adhering to the opinion that the prime reason for poverty is the limitation of natural resources was increased; e.g., fewer Americans believed that personal shortcoming is the prime reason for poverty.

In the police-community relations context, it is reasonable to expect that policemen can perceive reasons for poverty other than, or in addition to, personal shortcomings of residents of the community.

It is expected that changes in attitudes, such as those just described, would substantially affect the manner in which policemen and citizens perceive and react to each other and that a climate of antagonistic confrontation keyed to stereotypes would give way to more moderate interactions based upon recognition of distinctions among individuals and better understanding of their problems.

In Korea, desirable changes in attitudes were accompanied by desirable changes in behavior. Thus, for example, the amount of U.S. Government property lost or stolen between 1964 and 1967 was reduced by approximately 20 per cent, and the number of offenses committed by host nationals against U.S. personnel was reduced by approximately 50 per cent. In translating these results to the police-community relations scene, we might expect, for example, less theft and destruction of police property and fewer assaults on police officers.

The Korean data are strongly indicative of the effectiveness of the education and action program, which has been expanded and adapted for use in Thailand, and is being considered for use in other countries.

General Approach

The proposed two-year action program has five essential elements: (1) selection of police districts from which information will be derived in order to develop, implement, and evaluate the education and action programs; (2) methods to be used in developing the educational curriculum, discussion materials, and the follow-up action program; (3) tentative general and specific contents of the educational program; (4) tentative dimensions of the action program; and (5) methods and procedures necessary for program management.

1. Selection of District Stations and Participants

The plan is to initiate the program in at least two police districts in each participating city—one in a main ghetto area and one in a secondary ghetto area. ("Main" and "secondary" refer to comparative intra-city crime and minority group areas.) All patrol and traffic officers in the selected districts will participate in the program regardless of rank.

The two selected districts (experimental) will be matched with two comparable districts (control) which will not be trained or involved in the program. The controls will provide a baseline for evaluation of the effectiveness of the program in the experimental districts. The same four districts will also function as sources of information in developing the educational materials. If necessary, additional districts will be used to develop the contents of training curricula.

Experimental and control districts will be matched on such variables as crime rates, police-to-citizen ratio, demographic characteristics of the residents, and biographic characteristics of the law enforcement officers. The two experimental districts can be similar on various relevant dimensions, or differentiated on the basis of crime rates, socio-economic factors, race, etc. (e.g., a predominantly Negro experimental district station matched with a predominantly Negro control district station, and a predominantly white experimental district matched with a predominantly white control district).

Data will be obtained from representative respondents of the districts involved, as well as from police personnel; political, educational, religious, economic, and civic leaders; children, adolescents, and adults; and those who have police records and those who do not.

Whenever possible, local residents will be selected and trained to conduct interviews and to use other information collection methods. The use of local people will help to insure the acquisition of candid responses, particularly from citizens in culturally and economically deprived neighborhoods.

2. Methods for Developing Curriculum
and Action Program

The problem is one of hostilities and resentments that build up in the minds of men. It concerns basic attitudes underlying how the police and various components of the community perceive, interpret, and react to each other. Consequently, to understand the problem, it is necessary to conduct objective studies of attitudes. Precise calculations of opinion percentages are not necessary. Rather, it is sufficient to ascertain that a large number of policemen or community residents are troubled about some particular source of friction.

A. Seven-Step Analytical Model

Described below is an analytical model, developed in the previously mentioned overseas studies, which has been adopted for the purpose of the proposed project. Included is an example of how the first two steps are applied to identify problems and uncover solutions.

Step 1: understanding how citizens regard policemen.—

The policeman serving the citizens of a particular community does not enter a situation where his actions alone bring success or failure to the law enforcement agency's mission. In various locales, he follows a course already charted by dozens of fellow policemen. The course is sometimes clear, sometimes vague. Moreover, stories in the press and on the radio and television, often accurate but at times distorted, have told the citizens about his way of life. Consequently, an impression of the policeman is already fixed in the mind of the individual citizen.

Impressions of policemen held by various elements of the community will be obtained through interviews in which individual citizens will be asked the following questions[5]:

What should policemen do or stop doing to promote better community-police relations?
What is your opinion of policemen?
What should citizens do or stop doing to promote better community-police relations?
Would it help police-community relations if policemen mixed more in social, cultural, athletic, and other functions with citizens? Or would more mixing hurt relations? And why?
What do you like or admire most about policemen?
What do you dislike most?

Studies conducted overseas among Koreans and Americans found that those groups having the least association with Americans had the highest opinion of them, while those having the greatest association were the most critical. A study conducted by the National Opinion Research Center concluded that "the same poeple who are most victimized by crime are most hostile to the police."[6] The responses of individuals who worked or lived in large American communities clearly confirmed that what they wanted was respect, not mere association. Association alone merely engendered resentment.

Step 2: understanding how policemen regard citizens. —

This component of the model is complementary to Step 1. The policeman must come to terms with residents of what is often for him a new and different environment. Groping, he will understandably accept the views of those who preceded him upon the scene. Since he must live with the struggle to understand what he observes, he tends largely to interpret what he sees as the inferiority of alien customs. Insofar as he cannot personally identify with it all, he develops feelings of insecurity and even fear of the local people. Each instance of subcultural shock, no matter how fleeting, reinforces a swarm of negative attitudes.

Impressions of citizens will be obtained through interviews in which individual policemen will be asked questions much like those above, plus the following:

> Aside from your feelings about the citizens, what do you dislike most about this area?
> If you have not already answered this question, what are the most harmful things to police morale in this district?

Step 3: analytical résumé. —

From the first two analytical steps, one can perceive what occurs in attitude development among police and community subcultures. Two persons, for instance, even though constructively inclined toward each other in the beginning, are surprised and shocked by some of the cultural differences they discover through contact. Soon the individual disappointments, hostilities, and frustrations cumulate as a generalized negative attitude. For policemen the hampering thought that members of subcultural groups are somehow basically different represents a failure of our ideological weapons—for example, the belief in equality. Until that ideological breakdown is repaired and until a generally constructive frame of mind toward different kinds of people is reestablished, the various individual culture-shock reactions toward specific cultural differences cannot be effectively counteracted through factual education about people and their subcultures.

The next three steps derive from an analysis of the ideological troubles that develop among Americans abroad. That the same problems exist among policemen and subcultural groups within the United States will become apparent.

Step 4: researching the concept of equality.—

A large part of the "revolution of rising expectations" represents the claim of millions of Americans to the recognition of their interests and individuality, to equal dignity of the individual in principle and in person-to-person relationships. Unless policemen are conditioned to grant the intrinsic human dignity and equality of the citizens with whom they live and serve, their working relationships will not effectively implement their objectives but will undermine them.

It is necessary, therefore, to study the American concept of equality to understand its meaning to policemen as they relate to citizens and to determine how a constructive meaning can be reinforced.

"Are all men created equal?" Previous studies have indicated that, among Americans, the response to the question is silence or a diversity of viewpoints. This suggests uncertainty and confusion or at least an inability to articulate a belief in the concept of equality. The next question, then, that one must ask is, "How can one promote respect among policemen for poverty-stricken peoples if the basic concept of equality is unclear?"

Answers to these questions designed to revitalize an articulate belief in the principle of equality were developed overseas. Similar discussion materials will be considered for use in the planned program.

Step 5: researching the concept of democracy.—

To some, democracy means simply that the people must have a voice in the selection of their leaders. To others it means more: free and frequent elections, equal voting power, representative bodies, a written constitution, separation of powers, federalism, judicial review, etc. In America, which has one of the highest standards of living in the world, democracy connotes free enterprise, liberty, freedom, and economic and social mobility. But when asked to help "the Other America" develop its embryonic democracy, the affluent America has been singularly clumsy in its efforts and has often, in despair, fostered undemocratic ideas and practices. If the idea of democracy is to serve as a bond of unity between policemen and poverty-stricken groups, the meaning of the term must be learned and understood by both elements. A strong, knowledgeable, articulate belief in the relevance of the fundamental principle of democracy is the foundation of a community relations program; without it, there can be little basis for a bond between the policemen and local citizens.

The discussion materials related to the concept of democracy developed overseas are to be adapted for use in the proposed educational program.

Step 6: researching policemen's views on the reasons for underdevelopment. —

There have always been privileged individuals, classes, and even nations that have lived in comfort or splendor. For most Americans, economic growth has been rapid and improvement of living standards has been persistent. But for most of mankind throughout most of its history the central problem has been survival. There have been periods of general economic advance, but improvement, in the perspective of history, has been slow and reverses have been common. For many people, life is sustained by long hours of hard work for a mere existence.

Poverty cannot be explained as the natural result of stupidity and laziness. Many individuals naïvely assume that the basic inputs for production (skilled) labor, natural resources, capital, equipment) are universally present or easily obtainable and that the sole requirements for developing a decent standard of living are organization, technical knowledge and know-how, and a strong will. If certain people have not developed their resources and do not have sufficient food and shelter and clothing, the conclusion arrived at by the innocent is that "It is primarily their own fault."

The problem, then, is one of promoting constructive humility: the policeman must be made aware of the magnitude of the resources possessed by the culture with which he identifies in comparison with the limited resources of the subcultures. The purpose is to eliminate unjustifiable disrespect for his handicapped fellow citizens.

Discussion materials, amenable to adaptation, revision, and extension as a consequence of initial attitude studies to be undertaken in this project, will be developed with reference to reasons for wealth and development.

Step 7: classifying and analyzing problem-attitudes pursuant to solutions. —

Problem-attitudes fall roughly into general and specific categories: (a) *General issues* are those involving a general state of mind, an ideological principle, or a philosophy of life (e.g., "some people are subhuman"), which makes it difficult for policemen to respect, or feel a sense of unity with, the poorer people in our society. (b) *Specific issues* are those concerned with particular customs of other people (e.g., the matriarchal family; "they are dirty") which frighten, annoy, disgust, or frustrate policemen. These are the familiar culture-shock causes encountered by policemen in relating to the public. One culture-shock phenomenon, the reaction to lower standards of cleanliness and sanitation, is so important that it must be considered as a general problem equal in importance to the ideological issues.

The educational curriculum and evolving action program must reflect both general and specific problem-attitudes, which constitute the foundation from which all subcultural differences are viewed. If these basic difficulties cannot be solved, the general attitude toward members of subcultural groups will continue to be one of fault-finding. If the basic difficulties, which become evident through attitude research, can be solved through educational and action programs, then attitudes will come to reflect tolerance and understanding.

B. Supplementary Methods

In addition to the implementation of various attitude studies comparable to those previously described, a number of other methods may be used to develop the educational curriculum and action program, including *Occupational Pair Comparison Scaling,* a *Social Distance Scale,* and the *Critical Incident Technique.*

The *Occupational Pair Comparison Scaling* technique may be used to assess the relative position of policemen within an occupational hierarchy. A selected group of occupations is presented to individuals in all possible pairs. The person judges whether one of the pair is of greater value than the other in some defined respect such as favorability, desirability, liking, respect, fear, etc. Judgments would be obtained from a number of different groups including law enforcement personnel, criminals, citizens varying in socio-economic levels, delinquents, school children, etc. Results would be compared among the different groups to yield insights relating to attitudes. Such information would be used to develop discussion materials and the action program. Approximately ten to fifteen different occupations would be used to form the pairs, tentatively including policeman, social worker, criminal, fireman, detective, dentist, mailman, etc.

The *Social Distance Scale,* an alternative method or one to be used in conjunction with the above technique, indicates the amount of difference between two persons or two groups in mores and ideals. Each respondent indicates the degree of intimacy that he would be willing to accept with a designated person or a representative of a social group. The scale has seven levels of acceptance: as close relation by marriage, as a member in a club or as a chum, as a neighbor, as an employee in one's place of work, as a citizen, as a visitor to one's country, and nonacceptance on any terms. This procedure may also be used indirectly to assess the effectiveness of the programs.

The *Critical Incident Technique,* developed by Flanagan,[7] can be adapted to studying attitudinal development relative to the law enforcement officer. One of the prime considerations in this component of the study would be chronological age, since it is believed that attitudes are formed early in one's life history and remain relatively intact. In this sense, studying the attitudes of school children could be significant in shedding light on attitudes toward law enforcement.

3. Educational Curriculum Contents

As was previously indicated, discussion and educational materials were developed essentially from extensive attitude studies conducted in Korea among Americans and the indigenous populace. The educational curriculum which would be applicable to police-community relations will be similarly built upon attitude studies. For instance, one of the problem topics isolated through attitude studies in Korea was the specific issue of foreign aid. American troops had many distorted views concerning the theory, distribution, and use of foreign aid. In the police-community context, the comparable specific issue may be welfare. Many citizens, including policemen, probably do not understand how our welfare system operates; yet, misconceptions of the system substantially affect our perceptions of welfare recipients. Objectification and clarification of this specific topic may enhance understanding and communication between police officer and citizen.

The main objectives of each discussion will be the following:

Establish the proper ideological and historical perspective.

Stress the points that local citizens probably want, or would be responsive to, genuinely friendly association with policemen and that a favorable reaction to such citizen response is important to policemen individually and collectively.

Help give real meaning to and belief in the principles of equality and democracy as they apply to residents of the communities.

Help correct the exaggerated conclusion of many policemen that some groups of people are poor (underdeveloped) mainly because they are stupid or lazy, and replace it with a realistic awareness of specific handicaps to their development.

Help correct the exaggerated conclusion of many citizens that policemen are intrinsically brutal and prejudiced.

Help policemen overcome subcultural shock by stimulating an understanding of the origins of local standards and concepts of cleanliness and sanitation.

Help eliminate the hostility of policemen toward citizens and citizens toward policemen over personal problems and other troublesome minor issues.

Ask each policeman and citizen to face his personal responsibilities in helping to win mutual respect and friendship.

Teach policemen to apply "the survival test" in search of understanding regarding strange customs in the subsistence economies.

Help policemen develop more political astuteness for constructive discussions with the local people.

Help citizens gain a better understanding of the policeman, his role in the community, the complexity of his job, and the frustrations and conflicts that characterize his daily activities.

Enlist the assistance of policemen and citizens in further analysis of local difficulties.

Re-establish the lost middle ground reflected in police and minority group feelings of abandonment by society in general.

Advanced approaches in educational technology will be utilized. For instance, the use of videotape presentations and video feedback would make it possible to record discussions separately among police and citizen groups and then play them back to the other group as a basis for discussion. Such an approach provides confrontation in a real but detached setting. The behavior of "antagonists" can be studied fairly objectively and one's own hostile reactions can be examined in a sympathetic climate and perhaps vented in some degree with reduced risk of mutually reinforced escalation that is almost inevitable in direct confrontation. Such training experiences can be used in preparation for direct confrontation.

Although much of the preceding material has made use of examples applicable to the education and orientation of policemen, it must be realized that comparable qualitative and quantitative efforts will be directed to citizens representing groups varying in age, socio-economic status, occupation, ethnic background, etc. The problems facing the law enforcement officer must also be appreciated in his attempts to strike the sensitive balance between protection and interference, between individual independence and social control, between personal liberty and social order.

4. Dimensions of an Action Program

If desirable attitude changes initiated through the education and discusssion processes are to be solidified, the performance or actions of both citizens and policemen must also be modified. These behavioral changes must reflect mutually sincere efforts to engage in constructive intergroup associations. The changes manifested in police and citizen actions must also be visible to each group.

The project does not terminate with success in changing the verbal attitudes of citizens and police; it continues with a behavioral modification phase. *It is this feature and the continuing concomitant accumulation of empirical evidence of changes that fundamentally distinguish the proposed program from most of those that have preceded it.*

Contents of the action program will be determined by a number of factors, including the establishment of priorities among behavioral change needs as perceived by police and citizen groups, financial considerations, results of attitude and city case studies, and discussion session information. The main objective in implementation of any element of the action program will be to enhance communication and understanding among the several segments of society most directly involved. As pointed out earlier, this gap in communication constitutes one of the chief problems in police-community relations today.

Behavioral modifications are reflected in overt and observable interactions between citizens and policemen. They consist of street corner conversations, increased police protection for citizens, increased cooperation with policemen, quicker response of police to calls in ghetto areas, and increased assistance from citizens when policemen request help. The action program is of critical significance to the success of the proposed project. It will require courage, sincerity, and commitment to the discussion of highly controversial, sensitive issues and to the resolution of conflicts and differences through implementation of action elements.

What might some of these action elements look like?

An effective response mechanism to citizen complaints.

A mechanism for policemen to express dissatisfcation with the establishment.

An objective and visible decrease in the response time in ghetto areas.

An increase in the amount of cooperation and information given the police.

A reduction in the number of assaults on police officers.

A reduction in the amount of abusive language used by both policemen and citizens.

Establishment of a liaison among school teachers and policemen.

Strong disciplinary measures for policemen who violate rules and regulations addressed to police-citizen interpersonal contacts.

Rewards and awards established for policemen and citizens who enhance police-community relations.

Recruitment of more minority-group officers.

Elevation of the importance of ability in promotion practices.

An objective and visible increase in police protection in ghetto or under-policed areas.

An increase in responsiveness to citizen complaints regardless of who the citizen is.

Assignment of a full-time public relations-communications specialist to the police department.

An increase in the number and type of police-community social, educational, or civic affairs.

A youth education program conducted by law enforcement personnel.

This last action element would appear to possess substantial and continu·

ing value. The effect of early experience on attitudes and attitude formation is extensive. Establishing effective communications and understanding between policemen and our youth as early as possible would expedite some of the project's operational objectives, although the effects may take some time to become visible. A "school resource officer" may prove to be extremely useful in educating youth about the police, their role in society, and their problems.

The action elements described above represent only a sample of both voluntary behaviors and city policy and procedural changes that can ultimately constitute the catalogue of police and citizen behavioral change needs. Other ideas will evolve as the project progresses. Some will be selected for implementation, while others may be rejected. Sensitivity to budgetary considerations will be evident in developing and implementing the action program. Many productive changes can be effected through minimal additional expenditures; many other elements will require no additional outlays for personnel, equipment, or physical facilities.

Some police and citizen behavioral change needs and the action elements that evolve to satisfy those needs can be expected to be controversial and offensive to some citizens, policemen, and city officials and to certain groups. At this critical point in the project a balance must be struck between the realities of the situation and the implementation of a proposed action element. Bargaining and compromise will be necessary but should not be allowed to nullify the effectiveness of an action element. In the past, overreaction to assumed offensiveness of proposed changes to both the majority and the minorities has negated implementation. Lack of courageous and deliberate risk-taking has significantly contributed to the state of police-community relations today. It is necessary to recognize polarized attitudes and behaviors as they exist. It is necessary to have an appreciation and sensitivity for the political and social milieu within which proposed changes are to thrive. Finally, it is necessary to have the knowledge and will to effect change. Hence, support of top-level leadership in local government and police as well as in key community groups will have to be obtained early and made clearly manifest to increase the probability of effective implementation of constructive changes.

5. Program Management

After completion of the four phases described above, the training and action program will be implemented. Program management in this phase includes evaluation, revision, and institutionalization.

A. Evaluation

Four classes of criteria can be utilized in evaluating the effectiveness of the training program:

1. Changes in police and citizen attitudes.
2. Changes in behavioral information including crime statistics, police agency or precinct effectiveness, and citizen and community behavior.
3. Nature of responses and opinions of policemen and citizens who have participated in the training program.
4. Mass media indicators, including radio and television news reports, press clippings, etc.

In the entire evaluation process, it will be necessary to collect baseline data available before the program is implemented as well as after it has been in existence for a period of time. If the program is effective, evidence of success should begin to become apparent within six to twelve months. Comparisons of data, which will consist of measurements of as many classes of criteria as are available, will be made between cities as well as between experimental and control districts within a city.

B. Revision

The curriculum will be revised according to initial evaluation of the training and action program and continuing attitude studies. A critical ingredient to be built into the educational and action program is flexibility. We are dealing with a complex problem with requires a dynamic approach. Continuous feedback about attitudes and about the effectiveness of educational materials and action elements will enhance the realization of operational objectives.

C. Institutionalization

The essential elements in institutionalizing the training and action programs include the following:

1. *Coordination of the program with existing police-community projects so as to provide interface, eliminate unnecessary redundancy, and initiate a uniform effort having specified, well-defined objectives.* This activity will be an extension of earlier efforts designed to enlist the co-operation and participation of interested and relevant parties in each city.
2. *Formation of police and citizen groups to whom the educational curriculum, discussion materials, and action program will be presented.* This element will also include refinement of specified experimental and control precincts necessary to evaluate the effectiveness of the program. The size and composition of these groups and the facilities necessary will also be considered.
3. *Training of discussion leaders.* The use of indigenous personnel for this function will be considered.

4. *Development of documentation necessary to provide city residents with the capability required to function in the absence of the outside professional organization that helped to get the program going, and to evaluate, revise, and expand the program themselves.* Such documentation will include research and information analysis, selection and training of discussion leaders and interviewers, coordination of the program with other community groups, educational system components, and the measurement of progress and effectiveness.

5. *Initiation of counter measures to cope with hostile, non-constructive opposition.*

Upon completion of the proposed two-year program, the American Institutes for Research will terminate its role, and continuity will be provided by the residents of each city who will have been involved in the program during the preceding two years. Program continuity is expected to follow success of the program during the first two years, with the realization that freedom and order can be complementary objectives to the extent that responsibility for their definition and achievement rests with the community as a whole.

References

1. R.L. Humphrey, *Fight the Cold War–Korean Supplement* (Washington, D.C.: American Institutes for Research, unpublished report, 1966).

2. Michael Harrington, *The Other America* (New York: Macmillan, 1962).

3. Lemberg Center for the Study of Violence, *A Survey of Racial Attitudes in Six Northern Cities–Preliminary Findings* (Waltham, Mass.: Brandeis University, 1967).

4. Harrington, *op. cit supra* note 2.

5. These questions are only a sample of those that will ultimately be used; additional questions will be developed during the initial stages of the project.

6. President's Commission on Law Enforcement and Administration of Justice, *The Challenge of Crime in a Free Society* (Washington, D.C.: U.S. Government Printing Office, 1967), p. 99.

7. J.C. Flanagan, "The Critical Incident Technique," *Psychological Bulletin,* July 1954, pp. 327–58.

police misconduct:
positive alternatives

FRED M. BROADAWAY

Human error—intentional or innocent—affects others. Error in the manufacturing of products may cause mechanical malfunctions which are repairable or replaceable. People-to-people contacts which are dysfunctional have a greater impact on those affected. These contacts may lead to physical or verbal affronts to individuals that influence their self-image or well-being. Error in agents of government dealing with other people derives its importance from the general expectations which United States citizens possess. In the realm of governmental services, citizens have a minimal right to be treated with dignity and fairness. We have witnessed a growing awareness of the abuses of governmental bureaucracy and resultant friction. Of special importance is the case of the police—the most visible symbol of the government—and human error. Human error by the police is generally termed police misconduct. For the purposes of this discussion, police misconduct is the transgression of some rule or improper behavior by a police officer as perceived by private citizens or fellow police officers.

Incidents of police misconduct may be illegal and/or improper. Complaints of misconduct may be categorized as excessive use of force, abuse of authority, discourtesy, ethnic slurs, theft, unsatisfactory service, and violation of codified or presumed departmental procedures. Table I summarizes the complaints of police misconduct received by the Kansas City, Missouri, Police Department

Source: Fred M. Broadway, "Police Misconduct: Positive Alternatives." Reprinted by permission of the *Journal of Police Science and Administration.* Copyright ©1974 by Northwestern University School of Law, Volume 2, Number 2.

during 1972. The number of substantiated complaints, 32 percent of the total complaints filed in 1972, is somewhat misleading as a measure of police misconduct. That is to say, no determination of misconduct is made when a complaint is not filed, or a complaint is filed but later withdrawn, or the complainant refuses to cooperate with the investigation.

The theme of this presentation is that police agencies in addressing themselves to citizen complaint procedures have failed to remain cognizant of the fact that police misconduct is at the crux of the problem. This discussion format is threefold: discussion of general policy requisites for programs dealing with police misconduct; analysis of selected programs in reference to the perceived policy requirements; and advancement of a proposed program for dealing with misconduct.

Policy

Police officers are capable of human error. The nature of police work requires that all error be minimized, especially error perceived as misconduct, because of its obvious effect upon community trust and professional image. However, in the past, misconduct has either been ignored, covered up or subject to disciplinary actions against individual officers on a sporadic basis. The author maintains that misconduct should be an organizational as opposed to individual officer responsibility. Among policy requisites for a positive program to affect police misconduct are: an emphasis on a corrective posture; the provision for external and internal identification of incidents of misconduct; and a procedure which maintains credibility.

A corrective posture requires that incidents of misconduct be utilized to change behavior. While it may be argued that disciplinary actions modify behavior through fear of suspension or other punishment, the realities are that incidents of misconduct resulting in reprimand are the exception rather than the rule. This situation results from a heavy reliance on an adversary proceeding. Generally, a charge of misconduct is filed as a citizen complaint against a specific officer or group of officers. The ensuing investigation, conducted by a unit outside the normal chain of command, centers on the specific officer and the specific complaint. If the complaint is withdrawn or the complainant refuses to cooperate, the process is stopped. If a preponderance of evidence of misconduct is not developed, the process is terminated because it is possible the case will eventually have to survive an adversary hearing. Some months later, if the complaint has survived, the specific officer may be tried and allotted punishment if "convicted". Of course, this occurs only if the complaint was filed in the first place.

The factual basis of complaints which have been eliminated through investigation or withdrawal are ignored. The setting of complainant versus the

TABLE 1. Summary of Citizen Complaints January 1, 1972 through December 31, 1972 Kansas City, Missouri Police Department

Unnecessary or Excessive Use of Force	114
Abuse of Authority	40
Discourtesy or Abusive and/or Insulting Language	35
Ethnic Slurs	4
Officer's Conduct	18
Missing Property	22
Police Service	8
Police Harassment	16
Operation Procedures and Other	32
Traffic Matters	8
Traffic: Tickets and Tow-ins	5
Traffic: Officer's Attitude	9
Total Complaints	311
Substantiated Complaints	96

Source: Kansas City, Missouri, Board of Police Commissioners, "Report of the Office of Citizen Complaints, January 1 through December 31, 1972", Kansas City, Missouri, 1973, pages 4, 6 and 7.

officer dissolves the officer's supervisors from any responsibility for their subordinate's acts. Also, the reliance on an "independent" investigation conducted by an internal affairs unit further removes the superior from any responsibility for serious evaluation of an incident. While an adversary process has value in protection of employee rights in a termination proceeding involving serious misconduct or situations where previous corrective steps have had no positive results on behavior, the adversary format has little corrective potential for effectively dealing with police misconduct.

The second policy requirement is a provision for internal and external identification of incidents of police misconduct. Sole reliance on external complaints of misconduct will only reveal the proverbial "tip of the iceberg". Regardless of the publicity given the existence of an external complaint mechanism, for a variety of reasons, such as ignorance, fear, lack of time and the like, relatively few formal complaints will be filed. This situation, combined with the adversary process which the filing of a complaint implies, stifles potential identification of misconduct.

The fear and implicit conflict involved in adversary proceedings prevent peer citation of occurrences of police misconduct. Peer identification is a reality and only needs channeling. Incidents of misconduct are informally discussed and evaluated—many times more critically than outsiders would believe. However, no formal mechanism exists which decisively exerts peer pressure to correct individual misconduct.

For a system of internal identification to be functional, the process must be corrective. Since everyone errs, one can hardly expect fellow officers to point out an incident which could result in official reprimand or suspension of a comrade. However, with the institution of an anonymous internal vehicle, identification and remediation of problem areas might be achieved. There is certainly nothing to lose from an emphasis on internal identification, since currently, most incidents of misbehavior receive little attention by the organization. At present, an external complainant would probably be surprised to find that the incident of misconduct which he wished to complain about had already been brought to the organization's attention internally.

Credibility as a policy criterion requires a procedure worthy of belief. The distinction is made between a process which is presumed credible because it is independent, and a process that is credible because it is capable of independent, logical examination arriving at the same conclusion. Credibility requires procedural sufficiency, which includes a central locator for control of incidents of misconduct to assure accountability, an explicit administrative procedure by which incidents of misconduct are processed, and provision of a review process by general government which would reexamine a complaint upon petition from competent parties if and only if the administrative procedure has been exhausted.

Programs

Administrative procedures present the most potential for control of police misconduct. Judicial remedies, either civil or criminal, have limited impact for correction of police misconduct.[1] Many forms of police misconduct are not violations of criminal law. In civil suits, which are costly and time consuming, if judgment is awarded, the financial capability of the officer limits recovery. Many times the government agency is immune from liability. In consideration of the foregoing policy criteria, the effect of judicial remedies would negate the espoused corrective requirement in their reliance on adversary hearings. Also, they make no provision for needed internal identification of acts of misconduct. A judicial remedy would, however, appear to be credible.

Judicial remedies have their place in dealing with specific acts which are illegal and can redress affronts to a citizen who has been the subject of police misconduct. However, they are not sufficient in frequency or approach to assist the police in dealing with misconduct on a day-to-day basis. Following is a discussion of three selected programs which are currently used to assist police departments in the identification and evaluation of acts of misconduct by their officers.

Peer Review Panel

The Kansas City, Missouri, Police Department has developed a peer review program which is currently in experimental stages. The program is financed through the assistance of the Police Foundation for the purpose of dealing with misconduct and potential misconduct. It has a corrective orientation and provides for internal identification of problems. The credibility of the program is attractive within the organization and demonstrated effectiveness over a period of time would enhance the overall acceptance of the program.

The Peer Review Panel consists of experienced officers from within each departmental element who receive training to assist them in identification and causes of stress from job and family related factors, identification of stress from correctable psychological disorders, and identification of personality characteristics that are not treatable which would potentially result in an undesirable law enforcement officer.[2] Officers come to the attention of the panel from referral by other officers, self-referrals and by accruing any combination of three incidents within 12 months from the following categories: citizen complaints, hindering and interfering with arrests, incidents involving discharge of firearms, and assaults on the officer.[3] Also, the Peer Review Panel conducts "Recruit Socialization Interviews", the content of which is described below:

> The interview will be intended to accelerate the feeling of peer acceptance on the part of the recruit. Other aspects of the interview are to expose the recruit to the combined experiences of panel members, pointing out the many common pitfalls a recruit faces and to impress upon him a code of conduct acceptable to his peers and the high standards of the department.[4]

Currently, one-fourth of the referrals are by fellow officers. Although there has not been sufficient time to assess the impact of the program on the conduct of those officers referred, the short-term results appear promising. In the interviews conducted incident to potential misconduct, the goal of the panel is to review and evaluate the actions of the officer and make recommendations relative to future incidents. The program manual states: "These recommendations will be reinforced with immediate and continuing peer pressure."[5] When review indicates that the officer was correct in his actions, his professional conduct will be commended and reinforced. The content of the interviews conducted by the Peer Review Panel is confidential, but the chief of police may receive upon request the number of times a particular officer has been interviewed.

The potential strength of the Peer Review Program results from the corrective stance of behavior modification through peer pressure. It provides a method for fellow officers to identify an individual who has demonstrated the capability to act improperly without subjecting the identifying officer to the resentment which the normal disciplinary process invokes.

Field Tape Recording

The Bakersfield, California, Police Department pioneered a field tape recording program in 1967. The original intent of the program of tape recording officer-citizen contacts utilizing compact recording devices resulted from citizen complaints alleging discourtesy. These complaints are particularly hard to adjudicate, and Bakersfield moved to provide the police administration with an additional tool for use in conflict resolution. The report of the Bakersfield study identifies the problem as they perceived it and offered an explanation of their decision to establish field tape recording:

> While the administrator may be satisfied in his own mind that the complaint was or was not justified, the party who was determined to be wrong is not satisfied. Usually there is no concrete evidence that the administrator can rely upon to give him the answer, and nothing he can offer the citizen or the officer to show that they were wrong.[6]

The Bakersfield report stated that citizen complaints against officers' speech and attitudes dropped to "practically nonexistence" after field tape recording was instituted. Of course, it is impossible to distinguish between the effect of officer awareness with resultant modification of approach and citizen awareness of availability of documentation of the incident. Bakersfield identified two auxiliary benefits achieved in the program. Supervisors routinely reviewed the field tapes to evaluate and improve the quality of their unit's performance, and the courts were requesting and admitting the tapes in criminal proceedings.

Obviously, the use of a field tape recording program would not be sufficient as a unilateral approach for dealing with officer misconduct. However, the program would be of definite value in combination with other approaches. The use of field tape recording complements the policy criteria discussed earlier. In October, 1973, the Kansas City, Missouri, Police Department initiated the field recording program on a limited basis for evaluation. The experiment was operational in November with the investigation bureau, the three patrol divisions, the special operations division and the traffic division participating. The unit cost of the miniature recording unit and accessories is about $130.

Citizen Complaint Boards

Citizen complaint boards had been advocated as early as the 1930s. In 1931, Zechariah Chafee, lawyer-professor, advocated creating in "each community an untrammeled body, not subject to political control, to which complaints of brutality and other official lawlessness can be brought, and by which complaints will be energetically and fearlessly investigated."[7] With the growth and influence of civil rights groups in the 1960s, increasingly "independent" review boards were demanded. Generally, a procedure exists, especially in major cities, for receipt and investigation of citizen complaints. Table II presents an overview of citizen complaint programs in 31 selected cities.

Many departments utilize special units to investigate complaints, but the independent review process does not generally exist. The Police Task Force of the Katzenbach Commission (1967) summarized the resolution of citizen complaints against police as follows:

> During the survey, approximately 300 departments were polled regarding their internal disciplinary proceedings. Of the 63 departments reporting, 5 percent found that 40 to 50 percent of the complaints they received had some merit and were sustained. In contrast, 50 percent of the departments found that less than 10 percent of the complaints they received were valid. Ten percent of the departments could not decide 70 to 100 percent of the complaints as true or not while 40 percent could decide in at least 90 percent of the complaint situations. A more detailed examination of excessive force complaints in five cities, based in part on confidential departmental records, also indicates a wide variation in the number of complaints sustained.[8]

As an effective tool for dealing with and correcting police misconduct, citizen complaint boards have serious pitfalls because the corrective possibilities are minimal. Beral and Sisk in their study of "The Administration of Complaints by Civilians Against the Police", state: "The department's interest is discipline, the complainant's is redress; both interests should be represented in a properly functioning complaint procedure."[9] This author maintains that the department's interest should be minimizing misconduct by modification of behavior. The redress of complaints should be accomplished on the complainant's initiative in civil suit. Mechanisms for accepting complaints by citizens should be a function of the general government body as well as the police department, since police officers are not the only agents of government subject to misconduct. The most positive element of citizen complaint boards is in the area of credibility. However, the implicit procedure in current review programs is not conducive to internal identification of acts of misconduct.

A Proposal

Although the author's proposal appears by implication throughout this article, what he advocates specifically is the use of field tape recording, peer group panels, supervisory responsibility and procedural accountability. The field recording tapes would be used to document incidents where misconduct was alleged and to provide a training tool for the supervisor on a continuing basis. Peer group panels would be specifically trained and exclusively utilized to correct apparent or possible deviant conduct. The exception would be cases of illegal acts or situations where previous corrective attempts had demonstrably failed. These exceptions would be referred to an adversary hearing for dismissal proceedings and/or to the prosecutor for criminal action. Referral to the peer group could be self-initiated, peer-initiated or supervisor-initiated.

Supervisory duties would entail attention to the performance quality of assigned men through internal identification of problems and responsibility for incidents of misconduct externally identified. The supervisor would work within a system of formal procedures providing central accountability of complaints and a policy for encouraging external identification of perceived instances of misconduct through reports to the police department or to the general government, which would defer to the police department. The internal affairs unit would observe the supervisor in his investigation of the complaints. The results of inquiries into instances of misconduct would be a finding of either "not substantiated" or "substantiated" with referral to the peer group panel. For clarification, consider how this proposal might function under the external and the internal identification of an act of police misconduct.

The external identification of purported misconduct would take the form of a complaint filed by a citizen with either the general government or the police department. When it is determined that the alleged act is not a violation of criminal law, the complaint would be forwarded to the supervisor of the officer against whom the complaint was made. The supervisor would conduct the complaint investigation with an internal affairs officer as observer and would be held accountable for both the thoroughness of the investigation and the findings. The subject of the investigation would be the entire police-citizen contact and not just the specific acts alleged in the complaint. The result of the supervisor's investigation of the complaint would be a finding of either "not substantiated" with appropriate explanation, or "substantiated" with a summary of acts constituting the misconduct.

The report of the supervisor's complaint investigation with an analysis by the internal affairs officer would be forwarded through the chain of command. The report would be accepted or remanded for correction of specific deficiencies. The report would then go to the general government, which would notify the citizen of the findings of the investigation. In the case of a "not substantiated" finding, the general government at its initiative or at the request of the complainant could elect to reinvestigate the complaint with its own personnel. If this should occur, the general government's report would be submitted to the police chief for action. When the police department's investigation has classified the complaint as "substantiated", the officer involved would be referred to the Peer Review Panel. If the Peer Review Panel refuses to act or if the officer refuses to cooperate with the panel, the case would be referred to the police chief for disciplinary action.

Internal identification of misconduct would employ a more informal

Improving Police-Community Relations

TABLE 2. Survey of Citizen Complaint Procedures

| | 1 | | 2 | | | 3 | | | |
| | Formal Procedure for Receiving Citizen Complaints | | Complaints Received at | | | Complaints Received | | | |
	Yes	No	Central Location	Any Police Facility	Other	In Person	By Mail	By Phone	All Methods
Baltimore	X			X					X
Birmingham	X			X					X
Boston	X			X					X
Buffalo	X			X	X*				X
Cleveland	X			X					X
Dallas	X			X					X
Denver	X		X						X
Forth Worth	X		X			X			
Honolulu	X			X	X*	X	X		
Houston	X		X						X
Indianapolis	X		X			X		X	
Kansas City, Mo.	X			X	X*				X
Long Beach	X			X					X
Memphis	X			X	X*				X
Newark	X			X					X
New Orleans	X		X						X
Norfolk		X		X					X
Oakland	X		X						X
Oklahoma City	X		X			X			
Omaha	X			X					X
Phoenix		X		X					X
Pittsburgh	X			X		X			
Portland	X			X					X
Rochester	X			X					X
St. Louis	X			X					X
St. Paul	X			X					X
San Antonio	X			X					X
San Diego	X			X					X
Seattle	X			X					X
Toledo	X			X	X*				X
Washington, D.C.	X			X					X

*2 Buffalo-Police Commissioners Investigating Unit
*2 Honolulu-a. Office of the Ombudsman, State of Hawaii-b. Office of Complaints and Information-c. Prosecutors Office
*2 Kansas City, Mo-Office of Citizens Complaints
*2 Memphis-Car dispatched to citizen's location
*2 Toledo-Human Relations Center
*5 Indianapolis-Human Rights Commission
*6 San Antonio-Effort is made to obtain notarized statement, but one is not necessary
*7 Baltimore-Prosecution depends on seriousness of complaint
*7 St. Louis-Allegations of law violations only
*8 Indianapolis-Follows recommendation of Human Rights Commission
*8 Washington, DC-Complaint Review Board reviews investigation conducted by police and makes recommendation, with City Commissioner as final authority
Source: Kansas City, Missouri, Police Department, "Survey of Citizen Complaint Procedures," Kansas City, Missouri, April 1971.

| 4 | | 5 | | 6 | | 7 | | 8 | |
| Anonymous Complaints Recorded | | Complaints Investigated by | | Complainant Required to Make Notarized Statement | | False Complaints Prosecuted | | Department Required to Follow Recommendation of Outside Agency | |
Yes	No	Police	Other	Yes	No	Yes	No	Yes	No
X		X			X	X*			X
X		X			X		X		X
X		X			X		X		X
X		X		X			X		X
X		X			X		X		X
X		X			X		X		X
X		X			X		X		X
X		X		X			X		X
X		X			X	X			X
X		X	X*	X		X		X*	
X		X			X		X		X
X		X			X		X		X
X		X			X		X		X
X		X			X	X			X
X		X			X		X		X
X		X			X		X		X
X		X			X		X		X
	X	X			X		X		X
X		X		X		X			X
X		X			X		X		X
X		X			X		X		X
	X	X			X		X		X
X		X		X		X			X
X		X			X	X*			X
X		X			X		X		X
	X	X			X*		X		X
X		X			X		X		X
X		X			X		X		X
X		X			X		X		X
X		X		X			X	X*	

Improving Police-Community Relations

procedure than the external complaint and would also include a procedure for self-referral and routine referral to the Peer Review Panel after logging a specified number of certain occurrences (such as resist arrests, assaults on the officer, *et cetera*). But, in the case of an act of noncriminal misconduct identified by a fellow officer or supervisor, the allegation would be referred directly to the Peer Review Panel. An information notice describing the incident of alleged misconduct would be forwarded to the unit responsible for receiving external complaints. An agent of the Peer Review Panel would contact the officer in question to either submit to panel examination of the case or request an investigation. In the instance of an investigation it would be conducted by the officer's supervisor, with an agent of the panel as observer, and would be completed to the satisfaction of the panel with the finding of either "not substantiated" or "substantiated." If the Peer Review Panel in considering a "substantiated" complaint refuses to act or the officer refuses to cooperate with the panel, the case would be referred to the police chief for discipline.

In a case which was internally identified but later an external complaint was filed, the internal identification procedure would continue and stand as the dispostion of the case unless the finding of the panel investigation was "not substantiated". The report of the "not substantiated" finding would be processed through the chain of command as provided in the above external complaint identification procedure with notification to the complainant by the general government.

This proposal for affecting the conduct of police officers relies on the ability of the law enforcement profession to compel standards of conduct. The law enforcement profession has experienced a dramatic change in tenor recently through college education, increased training and a national emphasis on upgrading standards, all of which have made the entire system more responsible. My proposal recognizes the abandonment of the former mark of quality in police organizations which held that the effective supervisor was the one who cleared his men of every transgression regardless of the circumstances. The void is already being filled with a professional concern for excellence, which, if effectively marshalled, can permeate the entire organization.

Bibliography

Bakersfield, California, Police Department. "Field Tape Recording." Bakersfield, Cal., 1973. (Mimeographed.)

Barton, Peter G. "Civilian Review Boards and the Handling of Complaints Against the Police." *University of Toronto Law Journal,* Vol. 20 (Winter, 1970), 448–469.

Beral, Harold and Sisk, Marcus. "The Administration of Complaints By Civilians Against the Police." *Harvard Law Review,* Vol. 77 (January, 1964), 449–519.

Black, Algernon D. *The People and the Police.* New York: McGraw-Hill, 1968.

Gellhorn, Walter. *When Americans Complain: Governmental Grievance Procedures.* Cambridge, Mass.: Harvard University Press, 1966.

"Grievance Response Mechanisms for Police Misconduct." *Virginia Law Review,* Vol. 55 (June, 1969), 909–951.

Harding, R.W. "Police Disciplinary Procedures in England and Western Australia." *University of Western Australia Law Review,* Vol. 10 (June, 1972), 195–222.

Hudson, James R. "Police-Citizen Encounters That Lead To Citizen Complaints." *Social Problems,* Vol. 18 (Fall, 1970), 179–193.

Hudson, James R. "Police Review Boards and Police Accountability." *Law and Contemporary Problems,* Vol. 36, (Autumn, 1971), 515–538.

Kansas City, Missouri, Advisory Commission on Human Relations. "An Evaluation of the Operation and Effectiveness of the Office of Citizen Complaints." Kansas City, Mo., June, 1972. (Mimeographed.)

Kansas City Missouri, Board of Police Commissioners. "Report of the Office of Citizen Complaints, January 1 through December 31, 1972." Kansas City, Mo., 1973. (Mimeographed.)

Kansas City, Missouri, Police Department. "Peer Review Panel Office." Kansas City, Mo., 1973. (Mimeographed.)

Kansas City, Missouri, Police Department. "Survey of Citizen Complaint Procedures." Kansas City, Mo., April, 1971. (Mimeographed.)

Locke, Hubert G. "Police Brutality and Civilian Review Boards: A Second Look." *Journal of Urban Law,* Vol. 44 (Summer, 1967), 625–633.

Naegele, Timothy D. "Civilian Complaints Against Police in Los Angeles." *Issues in Criminology,* Vol. 3 (Summer, 1967), 7–34.

National Center on Police and Community Relations, Michigan State University. *A National Survey of Police and Community Relations.* Field Surveys V. Washington, D.C.: Government Printing Office, 1967.

Schwartz, Louis B. "Complaints Against the Police." *University of Pennsylvania Law Review,* Vol. 118 (June, 1970), 1023–1035.

U.S. President's Commission on Law Enforcement and Administration of Justice. *Task Force Report: The Police.* Washington, D.C.: Government Printing Office, 1967.

References

1. For a comprehensive review of judicial remedies see "Grievance Response Mechanisms for Police Misconduct," Va. L. Rev., Vol. 55 (June, 1969), pp. 915–35. Also, see U.S. President's Commission on Law Enforcement and Administration of Justice, *Task Force Report: The Police* (Washington, D.C.: Government Printing Office, 1967) pp. 198–200.

2. Kansas City, Missouri, Police Department "Peer Review Panel Office," Kansas City, Mo., 1973, p. 13. (Mimeographed.)

3. Footnote 2, p. 9.

4. Footnote 2, p. 11.

5. Footnote, p. 1.

6. Bakersfield, California, Police Department, "Field Tape Recording," Bakersfield, Cal., 1973, pp. 1–2. (Mimeographed.)

7. Gellhorn, W., *When Americans Complain* (1966), p. 171, quoting from the Preface to Hopkins, E.J., *Our Lawless Police*, xii (1931).

8. U.S. President's Commission on Law Enforcement and Administration of Justice, *Task Force Report: The Police* (Washington, D.C.: Government Printing Office, 1967) p. 196.

9. Beral, H. and Sisk, Marcus, "The Administration of Complaints by Civilians Against the Police," *Harv. L. Rev.* Vol. 77 (January, 1964), p. 507.

PART VI.

CHANGE STRATEGIES

Introduction

We cannot be certain what the roles, goals, and priorities in law enforcement are or should be. Additionally, since we cannot properly and consensually define what a community is, it would appear to be impossible to develop appropriate change strategies for policing in contemporary America. Are we to change the police? Communities? Relationships? Or are we to change democratic values that permit policing and at the same time permit citizens to air their feelings about government services?

Earlier we pointed out that almost everyone agrees that some kind of policing is needed in contemporary America and that some kind of change is needed to enhance and preserve democratic values and society. We also know that most responsible citizens as well as law enforcement agencies recognize the need for change. But it is exactly at this point that agreement ceases. Who is to be the change agent, who is to change, and what precise changes are needed are the issues that beg resolution. Few are satisfied with allowing the police to decide what is to be changed without input from the "community." The police certainly have resisted all efforts, and perhaps rightly so, to permit complete control to be turned over to the community being policed. Even the community has rejected this, for a referendum in Berkeley, California on the issue of community control of the police a number of years ago was soundly defeated.

Change is defined by Webster as "to alter by substituting something else for, or by giving up for something else; to put or take another or others in place of; or to make different; or to convert." Therefore, any attempt to bring about change in contemporary law enforcement requires that we must know what it

531

is exactly we are substituting and what that something else is. While there is a great deal of rhetoric on the subject, there is minimal agreement. The consequence has led and may continue to lead to considerable inertia, for we know that change, of any kind and for any person or group, is generally resisted until that person or group recognizes the need for change or is forced to change. (See, for example, Coch and French, 1948; Etzioni and Etzioni-Halevy, 1973; Lewin, 1951; Toch et al., 1975; and Zaltman and Lin, 1971.)

Law enforcement agencies, as well as communities, however they may be defined, change slowly and, for the most part, incrementally. The move from agriculture to industry was slow in evolution. There was considerable time and bloodshed spent before unionization gained a foothold. Changing child welfare and labor legislation was an agonizing ordeal for many. Mechanizing police patrol was resisted by many police administrators and foot patrolmen for many years because it was thought that the policeman would lose meaningful contact with citizens on the streets (a concept being reconsidered again by some). The use of citizens as law enforcement employees has not been fully accepted by all departments. The development of actual police-community relations programs was not seen as a popular innovation by many police managers. The list of efforts to bring about meaningful and responsible change in policing and in community structure and services is endless, but, fortunately, attempts continue.

Insofar as policing is concerned, these change efforts and attempts seem to be on the increase. There have been numerous experiments in the last decade or so not only in the area of police-community relations, but in reorganizing police function priorities. It is not possible at this time to gauge how much community involvement there is in these efforts to bring about change, nor is there sufficient evidence yet to measure the impact such efforts have had in bringing about the kinds of changes groups have been asking for with regard to law enforcement practices. However, it appears to many that there not only is a greater willingness to experiment on the part of the police and responsible community groups, but to share feelings, beliefs, and values between and among police and citizens.

There also appears to be greater recognition that policing is indeed changeable and that the interactions between police and citizens have considerable significance for the relationships between the two groups. That is, it is the result of confrontations, whether they be positive or negative, that produces harmony or antognism; it is not simply the mere existence of the police or the community that leads to problems. In effect, it is what people do with and to each other that causes problems; therefore, the same people are really the only ones who can bring about meaningful change in their relationships. The police and the community, if they better understand each other and each other's needs and values, probably can bring about responsible change. But this will require continued efforts and willingness to experiment. It will also require some kind of commitment to study, research, and a genuine sharing of ideas. In the final analysis, that sharing of ideas, the commitment to engage in genuine dialogue, and the recognition that attitudes toward the police by the community and toward the community by the police are influenced by interactions between the two. The need for additional respect among and between each "side" will be influenced by additional recognition that police-citizen interactions are affected by the outcomes of such interactions. Respect for the meaning of such outcomes is what police-community relations really means.

In "The Kansas City Preventive Patrol Experiment," researchers George Kelling, Tony Pate, Duane Dieckman, and Charles Brown examine the meaning, routine, and significance of preventive patrol. Long held to be the backbone of police services, this experiment evaluated the results of changed operations. From 1972 to 1973, three kinds of patrol were initiated in order to test patrol impact on level of crime, citizens' attitudes toward police services, citizens' fear of crime, police response time, and citizens' satisfaction with police response time. The major finding of the study was that regardless of the amount of patrol, no significant differences could be established for any of the test issues. With the additional finding that approximately 60 percent of the patrolman's time was of a "noncommitted" nature, researchers and practitioners have the basis upon which to re-assess routine patrol and to come up with more meaningful activities for police operations.

The National Commission on Producitvity examined the nature and scope of law enforcement services and issued a report entitled "Opportunities for Improving Productivity in Police Services." From this report, we have extracted a selection, "Barriers to Productivity Improvement in Law Enforcement." The selection deals with such issues as apprenticeship, attitudes of police officials, lateral entry, budgets, and lack of commitment to innovation by police managers. Eight suggestions are made for overcoming impediments to innovations. Five suggestions are made by the Commission to help innovative programs succeed once they are introduced.

In "Resistance to Change," Goodwin Watson explores the meaning of change and why people and organizations tend to resist change so much. He discusses such topics as conformity to norms, systemic and cultural coherence, vested interests, those things and values that are viewed as sacrosanct, and the rejection of "outsiders." He also raises such questions as: Who brings the change? What kind of change? What procedures are needed to institute change? And, What is the climate for change?

Both the National Advisory Commission on Criminal Justice Standards and Goals and the American Bar Association Project on Standards for Criminal Justice express considerable concern over the need to bring about change in contemporary American policing. Both groups invested considerable efforts and funds in studying the issues associated with law enforcement, including operations, attitudes, procedures, and the relationships between the police and the policed. We have extracted from the Commission's *Police* a selection entitled "Police Service in America." This reading provides both an overview of the police role and function as well as a summary of the kinds of issues which need to be addressed if law enforcement is to change in the immediate future.

While the Commission issued 107 specific standards and 16 more general recommendations as guidelines for change in American law enforcement, we have cited in this selection only one standard, that relating to the "Police Function." It serves as the basis for understanding what it is that a policeman and his department should be doing and the areas where changes are thought to be indicated. The Commission also points out the need for prioritizing activities and functions according to shifting values and beliefs with the police department and the community. Finally, it advises against turning that which has been changed into something which itself becomes unchangeable.

From the ABA's *The Urban Police Function*, we have extracted a discussion concerning the contemporary police task and three related recommended standards. These deal with the complexity of the police task, how the police should be responsive to all the special needs for police services in a democratic society, and the need for experimental and evaluative police programs.

In the concluding article, Professor Irving Piliavin makes a dramatic recommendation for changing the manner in which the police are recruited. In "Police-Community Alienation: Its Structural Roots and a Proposed Remedy," he first describes the outcomes of various kinds of police-citizen interactions and some of the reasons who police-community relations has not improved as much as many people would have liked. He analyzes citizen criticisms of police and police views of citizens. Then, based on an assumption "that the basic operations of police cannot be drastically altered," he suggests the radical alternative of drafting young men to do police patrol work. He outlines both the recommended procedures and the pitfalls to such an alternative. He concludes that with such conscription, both the police and the community would benefit, for each "group" would learn from the other, carrying on positive images, beliefs, and understandings subsequent to tours of duty. Professor Piliavin states: ". . . the proposal of a draft is made because it is the only approach known . . . which has sufficient merit to suggest that it can cope with police-citizen alienation."

References

Coch, Lester and John R.P. French, Jr.
    1963   "Overcoming Resistance to Change." In Robert A. Sutermeister, ed. People and Productivity. New York: McGraw-Hill Book Co. 406–428.
Etzioni, Amitai and Eva Etzioni-Halevy
    1973   Social Change: Sources, Patterns, and Consequences. 2nd ed. New York: Basic Books.

Lewin, Kurt.
    1951   Field Theory in Social Science: Selected Theoretical Papers. 1st
            ed. New York: Harper.

Toch, Hans, J. Douglas Grant, and Raymond T. Galvin
    1975   Agents of Change: A Study of Police Reform. New York: John
            Wiley and Sons.

Zaltman, Gerald and Nan Lin
    1971   "On the Nature of Innovations." American Behavioral Scientist
            14 (May-June) 5:651–673.

CHAPTER **6-1**

THe kANSAS CiTY pREVENTiVE pATROl EXpERiMENT

GEORGE L. KELLING, TONY PATE, DUANE DIECKMAN,
AND CHARLES E. BROWN

Findings

Ever since the creation of a patrolling force in 13th century Hangchow, preventive patrol by uniformed personnel has been a primary function of policing. In 20th century America, about $2 billion is spent each year for the maintenance and operation of uniformed and often superbly equipped patrol forces. Police themselves, the general public, and elected officials have always believed that the presence or potential presence of police officers on patrol severely inhibits criminal activity.

One of the principal police spokesmen for this view was the late O.W. Wilson, former chief of the Chicago Police Department and a prominent academic theorist on police issues. As Wilson once put it, "Patrol is an indispensable service that plays a leading role in the accomplishment of the police purpose. It is the only form of police service that directly attempts to eliminate opportunity for misconduct. . . ." Wilson believed that by creating the impression of police omnipresence, patrol convinced most potential offenders that opportunities for successful misconduct did not exist.

To the present day, Wilson's has been the prevailing view. While modern technology, through the creation of new methods of transportation, surveillance and communications, has added vastly to the tools of patrol, and while there

Source: George L. Kelling, et al. *The Kansas City Preventive Patrol Experiment— A Summary Report.* Washington, D.C.: The Police Foundation. 1974, pp. 1-10, 48-49. Reprinted with the kind permission of the Police Foundation, Washington, D.C

536

have been refinements in patrol strategies based upon advanced probability formulas and other computerized methods, the general principle has remained the same. Today's police recruits, like virtually all those before them, learn from both teacher and textbook that patrol is the "backbone" of police work.

No less than the police themselves, the general public has been convinced that routine preventive patrol is an essential element of effective policing. As the International City Management Association has pointed out, "for the greatest number of persons, deterrence through ever-present police patrol, coupled with the prospect of speedy police action once a report is received, appears important to crime control." Thus, in the face of spiraling crime rates, the most common answer urged by public officials and citizens alike has been to increase patrol forces and get more police officers "on the street." The assumption is that increased displays of police presence are vitally necessary in the face of increased criminal activity. Recently, citizens in troubled neighborhoods have themselves resorted to civilian versions of patrol.

Challenges to preconceptions about the value of preventive police patrol were exceedingly rare until recent years. When researcher Bruce Smith, writing about patrol in 1930, noted that its effectiveness "lacks scientific demonstration," few paid serious attention.

Beginning in 1962, however, challenges to commonly held ideas about patrol began to proliferate. As reported crime began to increase dramatically, as awareness of unreported crime became more common, and as spending for police activities grew substantially, criminologists and others began questioning the relationship between patrol and crime. From this questioning a body of literature has emerged.

Much of this literature is necessarily exploratory. Earlier researchers were faced with the problem of obtaining sufficient and correct data, and then devising methodologies to interpret the data. The problems were considerable, and remain so.

Another problem facing earlier investigators was the natural reluctance of most police departments to create the necessary experimental conditions through which definitive answers concerning the worth of patrol could be obtained. Assigned the jobs of protecting society from crime, of apprehending criminals, and of carrying out numerous other services such as traffic control, emergency help in accidents and disasters, and supervision of public gatherings, police departments have been apprehensive about interrupting their customary duties to experiment with strategies or to assist in the task of evaluation.

It was in this context that the Kansas City, Missouri, Police Department, under a grant from the Police Foundation, undertook in 1972 the most comprehensive experiment ever conducted to analyze the effectiveness of routine preventive patrol.

From the outset the department and the Police Foundation evaluation team agreed that the project design would be as rigorously experimental as possible, and that while Kansas City Police Department data would be used, as wide a data base as possible, including data from external measurements, would be generated. It was further agreed that the experiment would be monitored by both department and foundation representatives to insure maintenance of experimental conditions. Under the agreement between the department and the foundation, the department committed itself to an eight-month experiment provided that reported crime did not reach "unacceptable" limits within the experimental area. If no major problems developed, the experiment would continue an additional four months.

The experiment is described in detail later in this summary. Briefly, it involved variations in the level of routine preventive patrol within 15 Kansas City police beats. These beats were randomly divided into three groups. In five "reactive" beats, routine preventive patrol was eliminated and officers were instructed to respond only to calls for service. In five "control" beats, routine preventive patrol was maintained at its usual level of one car per beat. In the remaining five "proactive" beats, routine preventive patrol was intensified by two to three times its usual level through the assignment of additional patrol cars and through the frequent presence of cars from the "reactive" beats.

For the purposes of measurement, a number of hypotheses were developed, of which the following were ultimately addressed:

> 1. crime, as reflected by victimization surveys and reported crime data, would not vary by type of patrol.
> 2. citizen perception of police service would not vary by type of patrol;
> 3. citizen fear and behavior as a result of fear would not vary by type of patrol;
> 4. police response time and citizen satisfaction with response time would vary by experimental area; and
> 5. traffic accidents would increase in the reactive beats.

The experiment found that the three experimental patrol conditions appeared not to affect crime, service delivery and citizen feelings of security in ways the public and the police often assume they do. For example,

> as revealed in the victimization surveys, the experimental conditions had no significant effect on residence and non-residence burglaries, auto thefts, larcenies involving auto accessories, robberies, or vandalism—crimes traditionally considered to be deterrable through preventive patrol;
> in terms of rates of reporting crime to the police, few differences and no consistent patterns of differences occurred across experimental conditions;
> in terms of departmental reported crime, only one set of diffences across

experimental conditions was found and this one was judged likely to have been a random occurrence.

few significant differences and no consistent pattern of differences occurred across experimental conditions in terms of citizen attitudes toward police services;

citizen fear of crime, overall, was not affected by experimental conditions;

there were few differences and no consistent pattern of differences across experimental conditions in the number and types of anti-crime protective measures used by citizens;

in general, the attitudes of businessmen toward crime and police services were not affected by experimental conditions;

experimental conditions did not appear to affect significantly citizen satisfaction with the police as a result of their encounters with police officers;

experimental conditions had no significant effect on either police response time or citizen satisfaction with police response time;

although few measures were used to assess the impact of experimental conditions on traffic accidents and injuries, no significant differences were apparent;

about 60 percent of a police officer's time is typically noncommitted (available for calls); of this time, police officers spent approximately as much time on non-police related activities as they did on police-related mobile patrol; and

in general, police officers are given neither a uniform definition of preventive patrol nor any objective methods for gauging its effectiveness; while officers tend to be ambivalent in their estimates of preventive patrol's effectiveness in deterring crime, many attach great importance to preventive patrol as a police function.

Some of these findings pose a direct challenge to traditionally held beliefs. Some point only to an acute need for further research. But many point to what those in the police field have long suspected—an extensive disparity between what we want the police to do, what we often believe they do, and what they can and should do.

The immediate issue under analysis in the preventive patrol experiment was routine preventive patrol and its impact on crime and the community. But a much larger policy issue was implied: whether urban police departments can establish and maintain experimental conditions, and whether such departments can, for such experimentation, infringe upon that segment of time usually committed to routine preventive patrol. Both questions were answered in the affirmative, and in this respect the preventive patrol experiment represents a crucial first step, but just one in a series of such steps toward defining and clarifying the police function in modern society.

What the experiment did not address was a multitude of other patrol issues. It did not, for example, study such areas as two-officer patrol cars, team policing, generalist-specialist models, or other experiments currently underway in other departments. The findings of this experiment do not establish that the police are not important to the solution of crime or that police presence in some situations may not be helpful in reducing crime. Nor do they automatically justify reductions in the level of policing. They do not suggest that because the majority of a police officer's time is typically spent on non-crime related matters, the amount of time spent on crime is of any lesser importance.

Nor do the findings imply that the provision of public services and maintenance of order should overshadow police work on crime. While one of the three patrol conditions used in this experiment reduced police visibility in certain areas, the condition did not withdraw police availability from those areas. The findings in this regard should therefore not be interpreted to suggest that total police withdrawal from an area is an answer to crime. The reduction in routine police patrol was but one of three patrol conditions examined, and the implications must be treated with care.

It could be argued that because of its large geographical area and relatively low population density, Kansas City is not representative of the more populous urban areas of the United States. However, many of the critical problems and situations facing Kansas City are common to other large cities. For example, in terms of rates of aggravated assault, Kansas City ranks close to Detroit and San Francisco. The rate of murder and manslaughter per 100,000 persons in Kansas City is similar to that of Los Angeles, Denver and Cincinnati. And in terms of burglary, Kansas City is comparable to Boston and Birmingham. Furthermore, the experimental area itself was diverse socio-economically, and had a population density much higher than Kansas City's average, making the experimental area far more representative and comparative than Kansas City as a whole might be. In these respects, the conclusions and implications of this study can be widely applied.

Description of Experiment

The impetus for an experiment in preventive patrol came from within the Kansas City Police Department in 1971. While this may be surprising to some, the fact is that by that year the Kansas City department had already experienced more than a decade of innovation and improvement in its operations and working climate and had gained a reputation as one of the nation's more progressive police departments.

Under Chief Clarence M. Kelley, the department had achieved a high degree of technological sophistication, was receptive to experimentation and change, and was peppered with young, progressive and professional officers. Short- and long-range planning had become institutionalized, and constructive debates over methods, procedures and approaches to police work were commonplace. By 1972, this department of approximately 1,300 police officers in a city of just over half a million—part of a metropolitan complex of 1.3 million—was open to new ideas and recommendations, and enjoyed the confidence of the people it served.

As part of its continuing internal discussions of policing, the department in October of 1971 established a task force of patrol officers and supervisors in each of its three patrol divisions (South, Central and Northeast), as well as in its special operations division (helicopter, traffic, tactical, etc.).* The decision to establish these task forces was based on the beliefs that the ability to make competent planning decisions existed at all levels within the department and that if institutional change was to gain acceptance, those affected by it should have a voice in planning and implementation.

The job of each task force was to isolate the critical problems facing its division and propose methods to attack those problems. All four task forces did so. The South Patrol Division Task Force identified five problem areas where greater police attention was deemed vital: burglaries, juvenile offenders, citizen fear, public education about the police role, and police-community relations.

Like the other task forces, the South task force was confronted next with developing workable remedial strategies. And here the task force met with what at first seemed an insurmountable barrier. It was evident that concentration by the South Patrol Division on the five problem areas would cut deeply into the time spent by its officers on preventive patrol.** At this point a significant

*The historical presentation should be viewed with care, since many episodes, concerns and problematic areas have been omitted in the interests of brevity. Chapter II of the technical report deals in greater detail with the events leading to the experiment, while Chapter IV discusses many of the technical and administrative problems experienced during that time. A comprehensive description of the experiment's development would require a volume in itself, and an analysis of the organizational dynamics involved in designing and administering the preventive patrol experiment will be published by the Kansas City Evaluation Staff at a later date.

**In this report, routine preventive patrol is defined as those patrol activities employed by the Kansas City Police Department during the approximately 35 percent of patrol duty time in which officers are not responding to calls for service, attending court or otherwise unavailable for self-initiated activities. (The 35 percent figure was a pre-experimental estimate developed by the Kansas City Police Department for use in determining officer allocation.) Information made available daily to patrol officers includes items such as who in their beats is wanted on a warrant, who is wanted for questioning by detectives, what criminals are active in their beats and type and location of crimes which have occurred during the previous 24 hours. The officers are expected to be familiar with this information and use it during their non-committed time. Accordingly, routine preventive patrol includes being guided by this information while observing from police cars, checking on premises and suspicious citizens, serving warrants, checking abandoned vehicles, and executing other self-initiated police activities. Thus routine preventive patrol in Kansas City is informed activity based upon information gathered from a wide variety of sources. Whether Kansas City's method of preventive patrol is typical is hard to say with exactness. Clearly, some thing happened. Some of the members of the South task force questioned whether routine preventive patrol was effective, what police officers did while on preventive patrol duty, and what effect police visibility had on the community's feelings of security.

Out of these discussions came the proposal to conduct an experiment which would test the true impact of routine preventive patrol. The Police Foundation agreed to fund the experiment's evaluation.

As would be expected, considerable controversy surrounded the experiment, with the central question being whether long-range benefits outweighed short-term risks. The principal short-term risk was seen as the possibility that crime would increase drastically in the reactive beats; some officers felt the experiment would be tampering with citizens' lives and property.

The police officers expressing such reservations were no different from their counterparts in other departments. They tended to view patrol as one of the most important functions of policing, and in terms of time allocated, they felt that preventive patrol ranked on a par with investigating crimes and rendering assistance in emergencies. While some admitted that preventive patrol was probably less effective in preventing crime and more productive in enhancing citizen feelings of security, others insisted that the activities involved in preventive patrol (car, pedestrian and building checks) were instrumental in the capture of criminals and, through the police visibility associated with such activities, in the deterrence of crime. While there were ambiguities in these attitudes toward patrol and its effectiveness, all agreed it was a primary police function.

Within the South Patrol Division's 24-beat area, nine beats were eliminated from consideration as unrepresentative of the city's socio-economic composition. The remaining 15-beat, 32-square mile experimental area encompassed a commercial-residential mixture, with a 1970 resident population of 148,395 persons and a density of 4,542 persons per square mile (significantly greater than that for Kansas City as a whole, which in 1970 with only 1,604 persons per square mile, was 45th in the nation). Racially, the beats within this area ranged from 78 percent black to 99 percent white. Median family income of residents ranged from a low of $7,320 for one beat to a high of $15,964 for another. On the average, residents of the experimental area tended to have been in their homes from 6.6 to 10.9 years.

Police officers assigned to the experimental area were those who had been patrolling it prior to the experiment, and tended to be white, relatively young, and somewhat new to the police department. In a sample of 101 officers in the experimental area taken across all three shifts, 9.9 percent of the officers

---

departments place more emphasis on pedestrian checks, car checks, and field interrogating than does Kansas City (experiments on some of these activities are now taking place elsewhere). Preventive patrol as practiced in Kansas City has some unique characteristics but for the most part is typical of preventive patrol in urban areas.

were black, the average age of the officers was 27 years, and average time on the force was 3.2 years.

The 15 beats in the experimental area were computer matched on the basis of crime data, number of calls for service, ethnic composition, median income and transiency of population into five groups of three each. Within each group, one beat was designated reactive, one control, and one proactive. In the five reactive beats, there was no preventive patrol as such. Police vehicles assigned these beats entered them only in response to calls for service. Their non-committed time (when not answering calls) was spent patrolling the boundaries of the reactive beats or patrolling in adjacent proactive beats. While police availability was closely maintained, police visibility was, in effect, withdrawn (except when police vehicles were seen while answering calls for service).

In the five control beats, the usual level of patrol was maintained at one car per beat. In the five proactive beats, the department increased police patrol visibility by two to three times its usual level both by the assignment of marked police vehicles to these beats and the presence of units from adjacent reactive beats.

Other than the restrictions placed upon officers in reactive beats (respond only to calls for service and patrol only the perimeter of the beat or in an adjacent proactive beat), no special instructions were given to police officers in the experimental area. Officers in control and proactive beats were to conduct preventive patrol as they normally would.

It should be noted, however, that the geographical distribution of beats (see Figure 1) avoided clustering reactive beats together or at an unacceptable distance from proactive beats. Such clustering could have resulted in lowered response time in the reactive beats.

It should also be noted that patrol modification in the reactive and proactive beats involved only routine preventive patrol. Specialized units, such as tactical, helicopter and K-9, operated as usual in these beats but at a level consistent with the activity level established the preceding year. This level was

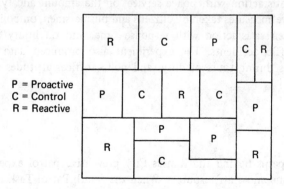

FIGURE 1. Schematic Representation of the 15-Beat Experimental Area

chosen to prevent infringement of these specialized units upon experimental results.

Finally, it should be noted that to minimize any possible risk through the elimination of routine preventive patrol in the reactive beats, crime rate data were monitored on a weekly basis. It was agreed that if a noticeable increase in crime occurred within a reactive beat, the experiment would be suspended. This situation, however, never materialized.

While the Kansas City experiment began on July 19, 1972, both department and Police Foundation monitors recognized by mid-August that experimental conditions were not being maintained, and that several problems had arisen. Chief Kelley then saw to it that these problems were rectified during a suspension of the experiment.

One problem was manpower, which in the South Patrol Division had fallen to a dangerously low level for experimental purposes. To correct this problem additional police officers were assigned to the division and an adequate manpower level restored. A second problem involved violations of the project guidelines. Additional training sessions were held, and administrative emphasis brought to bear to ensure adherence to the guidelines. A third problem was boredom among officers assigned to reactive beats. To counter this, the guidelines were modified to allow an increased level of activity by reactive-assigned officers in proactive beats. These revisions emphasized that an officer could take whatever action was deemed necessary, regardless of location, should a criminal incident be observed. The revised guidelines also stressed adherence to the spirit of the project rather than to unalterable rules.

On October 1, 1972, the experiment resumed. It continued successfully for 12 months, ending on September 30, 1973. Findings were produced in terms of the effect of experimental conditions on five categories of crimes traditionally considered to be deterrable through preventive patrol (burglary, auto theft, larceny—theft of auto accessories, robbery and vandalism) and on five other crime categories (including rape, assault, and other larcenies.) Additional findings concerned the effect of experimental conditions on citizen feelings of security and satisfaction with police service, on the amount and types of anti-crime protective measures taken by citizens and businessmen, on police response time and citizen satisfaction with response time, and on injury/fatality and non-injury traffic accidents. The experiment also produced data concerning police activities during tours of duty, and police officer attitudes toward preventive patrol.

Conclusions

The initial impetus behind the Kansas City preventive patrol experiment was the issue of time and staff resources. When the South Patrol Task Force began its deliberations, the concern was that any serious attempt to deal with priority problems would be confounded by the need to maintain established levels of routine patrol. Thus, in addition to testing the effect of various patrol strategies on such factors as crime, citizen fear and satisfaction, and response time, the experiment equally addressed the question of whether adequate time can be channeled to the development, testing and evaluation of new approaches to patrol.

From the beginning phases of this experiment, the evaluators formed hypotheses based upon certain assumptions. One primary assumption was that the police, as an institutionalized mechanism of social control, are seriously limited in their ability to both prevent crime and apprehend offenders once crimes have been committed. The reasons for these limitations are many and complex. But they include the very nature of the crime problem itself, the limits a democratic society places upon its police, the limited amount of resources available for crime prevention, and complexities within the entire criminal justice system.

As a result of these limitations, many have rightly suggested that we must now begin revising our expectations as to the police role in society.

Because there are programmatic implications in the findings of this experiment, several cautionary comments are offered.

During the course of the experiment a number of preliminary findings were reported initially and subsequently reprinted in and editoralized upon in many major newspapers. A weekly news magazine carried a brief and cryptic report on the experiment, suggesting that it had produced evidence that patrol officers were unnecessary. This was subsequently picked up by a television network and given further exposure. Public response to these stories was unfortunate, but predictable. Unfamiliar with the issues of the experiment, and yet highly sensitive to these issues, some saw the study as justification for limiting or reducing the level of policing. Many saw it as a justification for two-officer cars. Others, fearing some of the conclusions drawn above, simply rejected the study out of hand.

Such implications are unfortunate. Given the distinct possibility that the police may more effectively deal with the problems of crime if they work more closely and systematically with their communities, it may be that an increase rather than a decrease in the number of police is warranted. It may be that, given a different orientation and strategy, an increase in the number of police would increase chances for preventing crime. Those who drew manpower reduction conclusions from the preliminary findings assumed that if the crime prevention strategies currently being used did not work, no crime prevention strategies would work. This is not believed to be the case and such an implication is not supported by this study. Police serve a vital function in society, and their presence is of real and symbolic importance to citizens.

Nor does this study automatically lead to any conclusions about such programs as team policing, generalist-specialist models, minority recruitment, professionalization of the police or community relations programs. These are all package phrases embracing a wide variety of programs. While some recent works attempt to define the exact nature of these programs, most such terms remain ambiguous and for some, offensive.

These programs are attempting to deal with particular problems in the field of policing, including police and citizen alienation, the fragmented nature of police work, the inability to provide adequate supervision for police officers, the inability to coordinate the activities of officers in a variety of areas, the inability to adequately transmit information from officer to officer, from beat to beat, and from watch to watch, and the antiquated, quasi-military organizational structure in predominant use. These problems exist, but they were not the concern of this study.

The relevance of this study is not that it solves or even attempts to address many of these issues which admittedly are interdependent and central to the ability of the police to deal with crime. Rather, the experiment has demonstrated that the time and staff resources do exist within police departments to test solutions to these problems. The next step, therefore, will be to use that time and these findings in the development of new approaches to both patrol and policing.

CHAPTER 6-2

bARRiERS TO
pRoduCTiViTy iMPROVEMENT
iN LAW ENfORCEMENT

NATIONAL COMMISSION ON PRODUCTIVITY

The Impediments to Change

Most police departments are organized in what might be termed a "bottom-up" hierarchy that requires all new entrants to start at (or near) the lowest rank and move in a step-by-step fashion up the organizational ladder. "Promotion from within" is the cornerstone of most police personnel policies.

Bottom-up departments tend to become closed circles in which practices pass down from one closely knit group to another as new recruits are "taught the ropes" by oldtimers. There are, to be sure, advantages to such a structure. Police departments are closely knit paramilitary organizations that maintain their cohesiveness through the sharing of experiences and dangers. By insuring that all members of a department start at the same rank, close bonds are developed from common experience. The lengthy training program and "apprenticeship" faced by a new policeman equip him with a set of skills, and also instill in him a set of attitudes.

But while the attitudes developed by an officer reinforce solidarity with the force, they also discourage openness to outside ideas. Most officers have little exposure to policies and practices of other police departments. In time they tend to accept uncritically the methods they learn in their own department, and are likely to overlook a host of possible improvements that could be learned

Source: NCP. *Opportunities for Improving Productivity in Police Services.* 1973. pp. 65–70. Reprinted with the kind permission of the National Commission on Productivity and Work Quality, Washington, D.C.

from other police agencies or elsewhere in nonpolice circles. The potential influx of new ideas that could be brought into the department by experienced officers from other forces is impeded by the policy of promotion from within.

The discouragement of lateral entry also deprives the department of technical skills needed to select and evaluate innovations. New police recruits do not generally have the technical skills required for such evaluation. With rare exceptions, individuals with the requisite technical ability seldom are willing to enter a police department on the ground floor. Thus few departments possess the technical sophistication required to determine the relevance and value of new technologies and practices.

The bottom-up structure places in leadership positions men who have demonstrated excellent operating skills and abilities. Skill as an operating policeman, however, does not necessarily also insure skill in management or in the tricky business of introducing innovation. The more bottom-up an organization is, the more the skills and attitudes of the leadership derive directly from those of lower level personnel. External influences—the experience of other departments and ideas advocated by Federal assistance agencies, State and local criminal justice planners, and consultants—come into play here. But their impact is limited by the degree of receptivity of a police department's leadership.

The skills and attitudes produced at the top of a police department directly affect the leadership's aggressiveness in seeking innovations. A police chief who has worked his way up through a department over 25 years is not likely to be searching for, or perhaps even to be open to, new ways of operating. Also, he is not likely to risk the consequences of disrupting close personal relationships by introducing new techniques which will require major changes in established practices. As a consequence, too few police organizations have innovative leadership. There are, of course, some notable exceptions, but they are presently in the minority.

Budgetary constraints also affect a department's inclination toward innovation. Many small departments lack the resources to invest in experimentation. Many also lack the magnitude of operations to benefit from new techniques (e.g., computerization of dispatching). Even the large cities are severely constrained, in spite of the fact that they receive a large portion of the Federal assistance and private foundation funds. Often the only reason they try something new is that someone else will pay for it. The importance of union relations can also come into play here. For example, changes which affect the number of men or the skills required to perform a certain function may be tolerated in a pilot project but may encounter union opposition if the department attempts widespread implementation (e.g., one-man patrol cars, or changes in the organization of geographical units).

Finally, innovativeness of departmental leadership is also highly dependent on political considerations. As one large city police chief said: "You need to smell if something is going to be a winner before you get behind it." The risks are great because politicians and the general public do not let a police chief "win some and lose some." They are very unforgiving; a failure is hung around a chief's neck without much regard for his success. With this kind of pressure, it is important that an innovation show near-term results, i.e., before the next election. Experimentation is difficult, if not nearly impossible, under these conditions. For example, it may be more productive to use plainclothesmen or unmarked cars. But if the public *feel* less safe because the police are less visible, their reaction may well scuttle the experiment.

The interplay of all of these factors determines in large measure a department's innovativeness. In time, the character of a department's experience with innovation itself has a critical effect on departmental attitudes. If it has been positive, with "success building on success," the department's receptivity and the leadership's predisposition to try new things may thereby be heightened. If it has been negative, the department may mistrust new ideas and avoid trying innovations that may involve risks. Sufficient positive experience will tend to institutionalize innovation and make it a way of life—an important part of a department's self-image. This has happened in only a few cases. These departments attract more dynamic individuals at all levels; their programs are more "robust" and less susceptible to short-term political or constituent pressures.

The Determinants of Successful Innovation

In spite of the impediments discussed above, some departments have adopted innovative programs. The funds associated with the Safe Streets Act of 1968, disbursed by the LEAA, have undoubtedly been a major stimulus for the adoption of new programs. The need to seem "progressive" has also been behind the adoption of new programs by a number of departments. Others may have undertaken programs in a genuine attempt to increase effectiveness or minimize costs.

Once adopted, innovative programs may have difficulty in surviving. Whether they survive and prosper or fail and are rejected depends on a number of factors.

Newly introduced programs continue to face the same difficulties that may prevent them from being adopted in the first place. Political realities make it difficult for police management to support programs other than those that appear successful soon after their adoption. The lack of technical skills among most department personnel often makes it difficult to carry out innovative programs successfully and may lead to their early failure. Difficulties in evaluating the effectiveness of programs, especially as they affect the crime rate, may make it difficult to "prove" the effectiveness of a new program and sustain it against any opposition. Budgetary difficulties may render innovative programs vulnerable to cancellation if there must be a choice between them and a department's traditional activities. Programs that disrupt accepted patterns of operation, such as the adoption of one-man cars in a two-man car city, may be especially prone to creating resistance that will cause them to fail.

Innovative new programs are especially susceptible to rejection if they are felt to detract from the functions regularly expected of police departments. Two functions that are most visible to the public are response to calls for service and maintenance of a visible "presence" on the streets through patrol activities. Longer response times (even for nonemergency calls) and reduced visibility can contribute to a negative public reaction to police performance. If changes in regular service are associated with new programs, the latter are likely to be perceived as the cause of "lower" performance. If these reactions are strong and sustained over time, the department's management may respond by returning resources to the regular functions, in which case the innovative program may suffer or die. The degree to which the department's management responds to these pressures is largely dependent on the support of top management for the program and the store of political support and public confidence enjoyed by the force.

Some programs are especially vulnerable to this problem. Plainclothes patrol programs such as New York City's Anti-Crime Squad may divert officers from regular patrol and consequently reduce the visible police presence on the street. This anonymity, of course, is the principal strength of plainclothes patrol strategies and may more than make up in effectiveness what is lost in visibility. The reduced visibility, however, may be perceived by citizens as a reduction in police protection.

Public reaction to a program may depend as much upon the character of the program as upon its proven effectiveness. New York City's plainclothes Anti-Crime Squad has been especially successful because, in addition to its high effectiveness, it has seemed to capture the public's imagination with unusual tactics to foil and apprehend criminal perpetrators. Other cities' plainclothes squads, on the other hand, have alienated the public with such shortcomings as the excessive use of weapons, even while they are extremely effective in apprehending offenders.

Another factor affecting success or failure is the productivity of the resources invested in a new program, and the delay before an innovation becomes productive. If a program takes too long to get rolling, management may simply decide that it is inherently ineffective and scrap it. For example, the effectiveness of a team-policing program depends on the establishment of relationships between police teams and their communities, a process that necessarily takes a long time. If this lengthy delay is mistaken as an indication of intrinsic ineffectiveness, a potentially useful team-policing program may be eliminated before it has had a chance to prove itself.

Failure to enlist the cooperation of the department's personnel also can easily doom an innovative program to failure. Different programs will elicit different responses from a department's sworn personnel. A focused patrol program, for example, may create a negative reaction because officers believe it will entail more supervision than random patrol. In fact, random patrol may require greater supervision. Innovative mangement systems may be resisted because personnel resent the accountability required or feel that the system counts things that are easily countable (e.g., arrests) while ignoring the bulk of an officer's work. Resistance to these systems may often take the form of rendering their measures useless by such tactics as making many petty arrests merely to generate high arrest totals. Some programs, such as plainclothes patrol, may be extremely popular with the personnel directly involved, but are resented by other personnel.

The effects discussed so far do not occur in isolation from each other. Instead, they form a system of factors, all of which operate to determine whether a program will prosper and grow or will fail.

Dealing with one aspect of the system, such as enlistment of personnel cooperation, may not be sufficient to assure a program's success if, for example, it encounters a negative public reaction. The guidelines in the following section may be helpful in implementing innovative police programs.

Enhancing Innovation

There are a number of things that can be done to foster more successful innovation in police departments. These suggestions will deal, first, with ways to increase the inclination of departments to innovate; and, second, with ways to increase the likelihood that attempted innovations will be successful.

Increasing Innovation in Police Departments

Any action that would promote the acceptance of innovation by police departments at the expense of organizational cohesion and morale could well be counterproductive. Similarly, it is probably unrealistic to assume that deeply ingrained personnel policies, which represent an essential element of police department tradition, can be quickly altered. On the contrary, external attempts in that direction will be strongly resented and resisted.

Consequently, a "frontal attack" on the impediments to innovation is not recommended. Rather, a far less disruptive approach is to identify "leverage points" through which police department behavior can be affected. For example, if police leaders could be exposed to more ideas, accompanied by more honest and accurate evaluative information and precedents of successful implementation by other departments, they would probably become more flexible in their thinking. A department's leadership might thereby become more active in seeking better practices and more receptive to change. Another leverage point is the rate of successful innovation actually experienced. Better selection and management of innovative programs and more constructive relationships with outside "helpers" would increase the likelihood of success. That, in turn, would provide impetus for the "success building on success" phenomenon.

The following is one set of suggestions for overcoming impediments to innovations:

In general, there should be greater emphasis on incremental changes. Occasionally, too much time, effort, and money are spent on sweeping changes that are too great a departure from traditional operating procedures. While police departments should and can innovate, spending money on new ideas which have little relationship to present operating modes is foolhardy. Radical changes should be phased in through a series of evolutionary steps.

There currently exists no unbiased, readily available source of information regarding the performance of police innovations. This greatly increases the risks inherent in trying something new, and increases the skepticism with which outside ideas are received. An independent evaluation agency is badly needed in the police field. To be credible, it should be independent from governmental assistance programs and private equipment suppliers.

A regular survey of police innovations in major cities should be undertaken that describes the innovations and various departments' experiences with them. In this way, the "bandwagon" can be made more visible, the spread of successful innovations can be expedited, and the lesson of shortcomings more widely shared.

There should be joint funding of specialist positions in police departments using local, State, and Federal funds. Specialists to be "subsidized" should include technical personnel, people with special training in organizational development and change, and planners. This can provide the necessary skills to identify and support needs for change. These specialists should report directly to the police chief, possibly with a "dotted line" relationship to the mayor or city manager.

There should be more extensive use of interdepartment personnel rotation programs for periods of up to 2 years. Exchanging personnel is a way to exchange ideas, and the mere placement of an "outsider" in a department is a stimulus which can facilitate additional changes.

"Gatekeepers," i.e., those departments that tend to lead in the adoption of new ideas, should be identified. Their key role in the innovation diffusion process should be formalized by publicizing their activities and establishing personnel exchange programs between them and other departments. A study should be undertaken to determine what factors differentiate these departments and allow them to be "gatekeepers" so that other departments may follow suit.

Training programs for police officers should be established on the evaluation of new ideas, the management of change, and the concept of planned change. The idea of a national police academy should be seriously explored. Such an institution could have a great deal of prestige as a source of ideas. It could contribute to the professionalism of policemen and to their perception of themselves as professionals. And it could be an important source of badly needed managerial and technical skills.

LEAA grants could play an important role in encouraging and supporting increased police productivity. To date, LEAA programs have followed their legislative mandate to add strength to police departments to bolster the fight against crime. With greater stress on evaluation and improving the internal analytical capability of police agencies, LEAA programs could begin to foster an attitude that emphasizes the development of existing police resources to more effectively fight crime and provide other police services.

In general, there are two distinct governmental roles in fostering police innovation. The first, on the Federal level, is to identify and disseminate promising new innovations. This action will deal with a number of the barriers cited above. The second is at the State and local level where there is a need to recognize and revise the organizational, personnel, and financial policies and procedures that choke attempts to change.

Making Innovations Work

The following suggestions address the problems that keep innovative programs from succeeding once introduced. They are intended to increase the likelihood that new programs will succeed.

It is important to select programs that at least seem to be more productive in achieving a department's objectives than the normal police activities. This is especially true if the department is using some of its own resources rather than drawing on outside funds and capabilities.

Departments need to have a realistic idea of the time delays before new programs can become productive, and to protect these programs from raids on their resources before higher productivity is achieved.

The public must be educated about innovative programs so that it will be more tolerant of perceived reductions in regular activities due to a reallocation of resources. Otherwise, reduced visibility of police on the street, for example, may result in public pressures that will doom the innovative program.

A department's personnel must also be educated about the goals of innovative programs and the improvements they are expected to produce in the department's overall performance. This process of education should permit the personnel to provide feedback on the new programs and give them the opportunity to suggest modifications that will help the programs to be more effective.

New programs should be carefully designed and evaluated so that, whether they are permanently adopted or dropped, the department will still have gained some knowledge from the experience. Careful evaluations that explain why programs have succeeded or failed can help a department in the future selection and implementations of new programs. Care evaluation can also reveal the effectiveness of controversial programs and help to maintain them in the face of opposition.

CHAPTER **6-3**

RESISTANCE TO CHANGE

GOODWIN WATSON

The acceleration of technological change in all industrialized countries has led to growing recognition of, and concern to remedy, institutional lag. While speed of travel and power of destruction are multiplied by factors of ten or a hundred, family life, schools, communities, and nations tend to operate in traditional ways. Resistance to change is not uniform. While electric lights, telephones, automobiles, and television had to overcome some fear and suspicion at first, they quickly "caught on." New developments in the behavioral sciences, with implications for child care, schooling, business, race relations, and international affairs have been less welcome.

All forces which contribute to stability in personality or in social systems can be perceived as resisting change. From the standpoint of an ambitious and energetic change agent, these energies are seen as obstructions. From a broader and more inclusive perspective, the tendencies to achieve, to preserve, and to return to equilibrium are most salutary. They permit the duration of character, intelligent action, institutions, civilization, and culture.

Resistance to change has sometimes been misinterpreted as simple inertia in human nature. It is said that people are "in a rut," or "set in their ways." Actually, almost everyone is eager for some kind of change in his life and situation. He would like better health, more money, and more freedom to satisfy his

Source: Goodwin Watson, ed. *Concepts for Social Change.* Cooperative Project for Educational Development. Washington, D.C.: NTL Institute of Applied Behavioral Sciences. 1967. pp. 10, 18–22. Reprinted with the kind permission of the NTL Institute of Applied Behavioral Science, Arlington, Virginia.

desires. Excitement is more attractive than a humdrum existence. If people and organizations do not change, it must be because the natural drives toward innovation are being stifled or held in check by countervailing forces.

Resistance to Change in Social Systems

Conformity to Norms

Norms in social systems correspond to habits in individuals. They are customary and expected ways of behaving. Members of the organization demand of themselves and of other members conformity to the institutional norms. This is the behavior described by Whyte in *The Organization Man* (1956). It includes time schedules; modes of dress; forms of address to colleagues, superiors, and subordinates; indications of company loyalty; personal ambition to rise; appropriate consumption; and forms of approved participation in recreation and community life. Teachers, even more than businessmen, have been expected to exemplify certain proper behaviors.

Norms make it possible for members of a system to work together. Each knows what he may expect in the other. The abnormal or anomic is disruptive.

Because norms are shared by many participants, they cannot easily change. Above all, the usual individual cannot change them. He can get himself rejected for deviant behavior, but the norm will persist. A laboratory experiment (Merei, 1949) showed that even a child with strong leadership qualities was required, nevertheless, to conform to the established play norms of a small group of kindergarten children. An excellent teacher, who declined to submit the prescribed advance lesson plans for each week, did not alter the norm; he was fired.

When one person deviates noticeably from the group norm, a sequence of events may be expected. The group will direct an increasing amount of communication toward him, trying to alter his attitude. If this fails, one after another will abandon him as hopeless. Communication to him will decrease. He may be ignored or excluded. He no longer belongs (Festinger & Thibaut, 1951).

The famous experiments on altering norms of eating led by Lewin during the war indicated that changes are better introduced by group decision than by expecting individuals to pioneer a practice not being used by their associates (Lewin, 1952).

The evidence indicates that if norms are to be altered, change will have to occur throughout the entire operating system. The sad fate of experimental schools and colleges (in Miles, 1964) indicates the power of the larger system to impose its norms even on units which have been set apart, for a time, to operate by different standards and expectations.

Systemic and Cultural Coherence

The Gestalt principle that parts take on characteristics because of their relationship within the whole implies that it is difficult to change one part without affecting others. Innovations helpful in one area may have side effects which are destructive in related regions. For example, a technical change which increased the efficiency of pieceworkers in a factory enabled them to earn more than supervisors were being paid, so the new technique had to be abandoned. Electronic data processing in another company altered the size and relative responsibilities of related departments, generating considerable resentment (Mann & Neff, 1961). Studying change in a city YMCA, Dimock and Sorenson (1955) concluded:

> No part of institutional change is an "island unto itself": changes in program call for changes in every other part of the institution . . . and advance in one sector cannot proceed far ahead of change in other sectors. For example, program groups cannot be changed without officer training . . . which in turn is contingent upon advisor training . . . which in turn depends upon staff reeducation. Similarly, changes in staff goals and ways of working are dependent upon administrative procedures, policies, and budgets which in turn require changes in Boards and Committees.

A parallel statement for school systems might indicate that a change in teacher-pupil relationships is likely to have repercussions on teacher-principal interaction, on parent-principal contacts, on pressure groups operating on the superintendent, on board-member chances for re-election, and perhaps on the relationship of the local system to state or federal agencies. Any estimate of resistance which considers only the persons primarily and centrally concerned will be inadequate; the repercussions elsewhere may be even more influential in the survival of the innovation.

Our school systems are probably less cohesive and integrated than most business organizations. A teacher has more autonomy than a salesclerk or middle-manager. Considerable change can take place within one classroom and have relatively minor effects on what other teachers are doing. Yet, in the long run, the deviate is likely to be brought into line by his peer group, his supervisors, the pupils, or their parents.

Vested Interests

The most obvious source of resistance is some threat to the economic or prestige interests of individuals. A school consolidation which eliminates some board members and a principal is unlikely to receive their warm support, although such cases have occurred. The most common resistance to educational improvements which would cost money comes from organized or unorganized taxpayers. Mort (1941) found that desirable school innovations were most likely to be adopted by communities with high financial resources. Poverty has been—at least until the recent antipoverty programs—a block to educational experimentation. The writer (Watson, 1946) found likewise that YMCA's located in communities with a high volume of retail sales per capita were more likely to adopt recommended new practices.

A "vested interest" may be in freedom to operate as one pleases, quite as truly as in money-income or title on the door. Centralizing control of school decisions is usually unwelcome to the persons who would otherwise be making decisions in local school neighborhoods or classrooms.

Concern for school taxes and for positions on school boards is likely to center in the upper classes of the community. They are the people who have the most power and influence. Newspapers and broadcasting are more accessible to them than to the underprivileged. A few powerful political or financial interests can block programs desired by a large majority of ordinary citizens. The influence of upperclass families on school policies is vividly portrayed in Hollingshead's *Elmtown's Youth* (1949).

The Sacrosanct

Anthropologists have observed that, within any culture, some activities are easily changed; others are highly resistant to innovation. Generally, the technology is receptive to new ideas and procedures. The greatest resistance concerns matters connected with what is held to be sacred. Some women can become managers of businesses or presidents of colleges in our male-dominated society, but they find it almost impossible to become a priest, rabbi, bishop, or minister in a conservative denomination. Translations of Scriptures into the vernacular have met strong disapproval. The ritual reading of some verses from the Bible or the recitation of a prayer is held onto with far more fervor than is spent on retention of school texts or equipment. Traditional ceremonies are apt to persist despite doubts as to their educational impact. The closer any reform comes to touching some of the taboos or rituals in the community, the more likely it is to be resisted. Introduction of improved technology in underdeveloped countries runs into formidable obstacles if it seems to impinge on religious superstitions, beliefs, or practices (Spicer, 1952).

Cultures resist almost as stubbornly alterations which enter the realm of morals and ethics. Even when few live by the traditional code, it must still be defended as "ideal" (Linton, 1945). A well-recognized illustration is the expectation of sexual continence between puberty and marriage. Kinsey may find very few youths who practice it, but schools, churches, and courts must operate as if the prescription were unquestionable.

There is a clear connection between the operation of the superego in individuals and the taboos persisting in the culture. Both uphold impossibly high standards and react punitively to recognized infractions of the excessive demands.

Rejection of "Outsiders"

Most change comes into institutions from "outside." Griffiths, studying change in school systems, concluded, "The major impetus for change in organizations is from outside" (In Miles, 1964, p. 431).

Few psychological traits are so universal as that of suspicion and hostility toward strange outsiders. Kohler (1922) observed this kind of behavior among his chimpanzees on the Island of Tenerifa many years ago. Wood (1934) has explored, across different cultures, the mixture of curiosity and antagonism toward foreigners. A typical attack on any new proposal is that it doesn't fit our local conditions. Struggles to improve labor and race relations have commonly been discounted as inspired by "outside agitators" or "atheistic Communists." Research, development, and engineering units are familiar with the way in which a new project is hampered if it is seen as NIH (not invested here). Argyris (1952) has outlined common defenses against "outsiders."

The history of experimental demonstration schools is that they were often observed but seldom replicated: "This is fine, but it wouldn't work in our system." Differences in class of children, financial support, equipment, and tradition helped to rationalize the resistance. The genius of agricultural agents a century ago led them away from model farms run by state colleges and toward demonstration projects within the local neighborhood. Farmers would accept what was being done within their county, while they would not import new practices from far away.

A major problem in introducing social change is to secure enough local initiative and participation so the enterprise will not be vulnerable as a foreign importation.

Reducing Resistance: A Summary

Our observations on sources of resistance within persons and within institutions can be summarized in some concise principles. These are not absolute laws but are based on generalizations which are usually true and likely to be pertinent. The recommendations are here reorganized to answer three questions: Who brings the change? What kind of change succeeds? and How is it best done—by what procedures and in what climate?

A. Who brings the change?

　1. Resistance will be less if administrators . . . feel that the project is their own—not one devised and operated by outsiders.

2. Resistance will be less if the project clearly has wholehearted support from top officials of the system.

B. *What kind of change?*

3. Resistance will be less if participants see the change as reducing rather than increasing their present burdens.

4. Resistance will be less if the project accords with values and ideals which have long been acknowledged by participants.

5. Resistance will be less if the program offers the kind of *new* experience which interests participants.

6. Resistance will be less if participants feel that their autonomy and their security is not threatened.

C. *Procedures in instituting change*

7. Resistance will be less if participants have joined in diagnostic efforts leading them to agree on the basic problem and to feel its importance.

8. Resistance will be less if the project is adopted by consensual group decision.

9. Resistance will be reduced if proponents are able to empathize with opponents, to recognize valid objections, and to take steps to relieve unnecessary fears.

10. Resistance will be reduced if it is recognized that innovations are likely to be misunderstood and misinterpreted, and if provision is made for feedback of perceptions of the project and for further clarification as needed.

11. Resistance will be reduced if participants experience acceptance, support, trust, and confidence in their relations with one another.

12. Resistance will be reduced if the project is kept open to revision and reconsideration if experience indicates that changes would be desirable.

D. *Climate for change*

13. Readiness for change gradually becomes a characteristic of certain individuals, groups, organizations, and civilizations. They no longer look nostalgically at a Golden Age in the past but anticipate their Utopia in days to come. The spontaneity of youth is cherished and innovations are protected until they have had a chance to establish their worth. The ideal is more and more seen as possible.

Bibliography

Argyris, Chris. *Journal of Social Issues*. 1952. (Ann Arbor, Mich.: Society for the Psychological Study of Social Issues.)

Dimock, Hedley S., and Sorenson, Roy. *Designing Education in Values: A Case Study in Institutional Change.* New York: Association Press, 1955.

Festinger, Leon, and Thibaut, John. "Interpersonal Communication in Small

Groups." *Journal of Abnormal and Social Psychology* 46:92–99; January 1951. (Washington, D.C.: American Psychological Association.)

Hollingshead, August. *Elmtown's Youth.* New York: John Wiley & Sons, 1949.

Kohler, Wolfgang. "Zur Psychologie des Shimpanzen." *Psychologische Forschung* 1:1–45; 1922. (Berlin: Zeitschrift für allgemeine Psychologie, Ethologie und Medizinische Psychologie.)

Lewin, Kurt. *Field Theory in Social Science.* New York: Harper & Brothers, 1951.

——. "Group Decision and Social Change." *Readings in Social Psychology.* (Edited by G.E. Swanson, T.M. Newcomb, and E.L. Heartley.) New York: Holt, Rinehart and Winston, 1952, pp. 463–73.

Linton, Ralph. *The Cultural Background of Personality.* New York: Appleton-Century-Crofts, 1945.

Mann, Floyd C., and Neff, Franklin W. *Managing Major Change in Organizations.* Ann Arbor, Mich.: Foundation for Research on Human Behavior, 1961.

Merei, F. "Group Leadership and Institutionalization." *Human Relations* 2:23–39; 1949. (London: Tavistock Publications.)

Miles, Matthew B., editor. *Innovation in Education.* New York: Bureau of Publications, Teachers College, Columbia University, 1964.

Mort, Paul R., and Cornell, Francis G. *American Schools in Transition.* New York: Bureau of Publications, Teachers College, Columbia University, 1941.

Spicer, Edward H., editor. *Human Problems in Technological Change.* New York: Russell Sage Foundation, 1952.

Watson, Goodwin B. *A Comparison of "Adaptable" vs. "Laggard" YMCA's.* New York: Association Press, 1946.

Whyte, William H., Jr. *The Organization Man.* New York: Simon and Schuster, 1956.

Wood, Margaret Mary. *The Stranger: A Study in Social Relationships.* New York: Columbia University Press, 1934.

police SERVICE iN AMERICA

NATIONAL ADVISORY COMMISSION ON CRIMINAL JUSTICE STANDARDS AND GOALS

The police in the United States are not separate from the people. They draw their authority from the will and consent of the people, and they recruit their officers from them. The police are the instrument of the people to achieve and maintain order; their efforts are founded on principles of public service and ultimate responsibility to the public.

This chapter describes the way a productive relationship between the people and their police can be established. The standards propose broad functional objectives. The ultimate goal toward which all the standards are directed is greater public trust in the police and a resulting reduction in crime through public cooperation.

To a police officer, public service is more than a vague concept. When people need help, it is to a police officer that they are most likely to turn. He responds—immediately—without first ascertaining the status of the person in need. It does not matter if that person is rich or poor; he need not meet complicated criteria to qualify as a recipient of aid or as a potential client.

Decisionmaking

Police officers are decisionmakers. A decision—whether to arrest, to make a referral, to seek prosecution, or to use force—has a profound effect on those a

Source: NACCJSG. *Police.* Washington, D.C.: U.S. Government Printing Office. 1973. pp. 9–16.

police officer serves. Most of these decisions must be made within the span of a few moments and within the physical context of the most aggravated social problems. Yet, the police officer is just as accountable for these decisions as the judge or corrections official is for decisions deliberated for months.

The role the police officer plays in society is a difficult one; he must clearly understand complex social relationships to be effective. He is not only a part of the community he serves, and a part of the government that provides his formal base of authority, he is also a part of the criminal justice system that determines what course society will pursue to deter lawbreakers or rehabilitate offenders in the interest of public order.

Although the police service is a formal element of local government, it is responsible to the people in a more direct way. The specific goals and priorities which the police establish within the limits of their legislatively granted authority are determined to a large extent by community desires. These desires are transmitted to the police through the community and the governing body of the jurisdiction in which the police operate. For example, elements of the community might urge increased patrols around schools, stricter enforcement of parking regulations in congested areas, or reduced enforcement activities against violations of certain crimes. The priorities established by police agencies in such cases are often influenced more by the wishes of those policed than by any other consideration. The police officer is accountable to the people for his decisions and the consequences. The success of his mission depends to a great extent on the support of the people.

Police Responsibility

In the exercise of its police power, government enacts laws designed to protect the health, welfare, and morals of its citizens. Under this Nation's form of government, police power is exercised by the States and their political subdivisions in the promulgation of laws and regulations concerning building and safety, zoning, health, noise and disturbance, disorderly conduct, and traffic regulations. Repeated and willful violation of these regulations is generally considered criminal conduct.

Each State has developed a comprehensive criminal code defining crimes and providing punishments. Responsibility for the enforcement of these laws, however, has been largely delegated to local government.

Although local government provides many services the police are its most visible representatives. Because they are the agents of government who are most frequently in contact with the public, and because they are accessible around-the-clock, police are often contacted regarding services provided by other municipal, county, State, and Federal agencies.

Often the public does not differentiate between various elements of local government. An irate citizen is simply concerned that he is not receiving a service to which he feels entitled. If he is bewildered by the profusion of government divisions, he turns to the one most familiar and most recognizable—the police. Because their service to the citizen affects his respect for government in general and the police in particular, police should respond as helpfully as possible, even if the matter is outside their immediate jurisdiction.

Criminal Justice Process

Through the identification and arrest of a suspected offender, the police initiate the criminal justice process. The individual's guilt or innocence is then determined in the courts. If the individual is found guilty, an attempt is made to rehabilitate him through a corrections process that may include probation, confinement, parole, or any combination of these.

While each of the elements of the criminal justice system is organizationally separate, these elements are functionally interrelated. In most cases, for example, the police act before the other elements of the system. The subsequent release of an otherwise guilty person from custody because a court found the evidence necessary for his conviction to be unlawfully seized, the reluctance of a prosecutor to present a case for court determination, or the failure of corrections to reform a convict prior to his release, have a direct effect upon the manner and conditions in which the police must perform their tasks.

A very high percentage of police work is done in direct response to citizen complaints. This underlines the frequently unrecognized fact that members of the public are an integral part of the criminal justice system; in fact, the success of the system depends more on citizen participation than on any other single factor.

The police are the criminal justice element in closest contact with the public; as a result, they are often blamed for failures in other parts of the system. In like manner, public confidence in the criminal justice system depends to a large extent on the trust that the people have in their police.

The police, the criminal justice system, and government in general could not control crime without the cooperation of a substantial portion of the people. In the absence of public support, there would be little that an army could not do better than the police.

Community Relations

Currently, the relationship in most communities between the police and the public is not entirely satisfactory. Members of the public frequently do not notify the police of situations that require enforcement or preventive action. Often, they avoid involvement in averting or interfering with criminal conduct, and many are suspicious of the police, the criminal justice system, and the entire political process.

During the 20 years following World War II, the police became increasingly isolated from their communities. Reasons for this isolation include urbanization, rapidly changing social conditions, greater demands for police services, increased reliance by the police on motorized patrol, police efforts to professionalize, and reduced police contact with noncriminal elements of society. These factors, combined with public apathy, caused many police agencies to attempt to combat rising crime without actively involving their communities in their efforts.

Due in large part to the widespread riots in the sixties, and the report of the President's Commission on Law Enforcement and Administration of Justice, many police agencies reassessed their role and made changes that resulted in greater community involvement in crime control. Police agencies throughout the Nation have significantly improved their ability to deal with crime and disorder. They have also taken great strides in responding to the demands of their communities for greater service involvement and responsiveness. Perhaps more than any other institution, the police have advanced their ability to cope with rapidly changing social conditions.

In less than 10 years, the nature of debate in the police service has changed. The question no longer is, "Should we be involved in nonenforcement programs?" Now the question is, "How should we be involved in them?" As is usual during any time of great change, experimentation has resulted in both success and failure.

In attempting to reduce tension and improve their relationships with the public, the police have experimented with innovative programs. In some communities policemen wear blazers instead of the traditional military-type uniform, operate storefront offices, discuss local problems at neighborhood "coffee klatches," and engage in "rap sessions" with juveniles.

Inside and outside the service, there is little agreement on the role of the police. While one citizen group demands more nonenforcement programs, another demands that police devote all resources to direct protection and vigorous enforcement. Lack of manpower and fiscal resources has caused delay or abandonment of many programs to improve police-community relations, and the police have had to assign priorities to the delivery of direct protection services.

Programs

Attempts to involve the community in programs to prevent crime and improve police-community relations have often been met by both public apathy and resistance within police agencies. Middle managers and police officers, accustomed to taking public support for granted and dealing primarily with law violators, had little faith in nonenforcement programs. Members of the public, accustomed to relying upon the police to deal with crime, were slow to respond to public involvement programs. However, there are many successful programs, and relations between the people and the police have improved.

A program is defined as the planning, development, and implementation of specific solutions to identified problems. These solutions should take the form of organizational goals and objectives rather than specific activities. Where programs are constructed of specific activities rather than goals and objectives, implementation tends to be delegated to a specialized person or group rather than to all employees. Such programs tend to be uncoordinated with other agency efforts and are often, from the outset, destined for failure.

The broad objectives of most nonenforcement programs have been improved police-community relations, reduced tension, and greater mutual understanding between the police and the people. Functional objectives vary, however. Some programs appear to be primarily educational, while others are designed to prevent specific crimes or to improve communications.

The success of a nonenforcement program is often determined by the number of people involved or by the absence of unfavorable incidents. Programs that do not produce results that justify their cost may still be difficult to discontinue. In these cases, administrators may be reluctant to admit failure or they may fear the criticism that the program was merely window dressing. However, programs that were planned on a cost-effective basis with identified functional objectives, built-in methods for measuring effectiveness, and suggested alternatives in case of failure, have produced significant and lasting results.

The Police Function

Standard 1.1

Every police chief executive immediately should develop written policy, based on policies of the governing body that provides formal authority for the police function, and should set forth the objectives and priorities that will guide the agency's delivery of police services. Agency policy should articulate the role of the agency in the protection of constitutional guarantees, the enforcement of the law, and the provision of services necessary to reduce crime, to maintain public order, and to respond to the needs of the community.

1. Every police chief executive should acknowledge that the basic purpose of the police is the maintenance of public order and the control of conduct legislatively defined as crime. The basic purpose may not limit the police role, but should be central to its full definition.

2. Every police chief executive should identify those crimes on which police resources will be concentrated. In the allocation of resources, those crimes that are most serious, stimulate the greatest fear, and cause the greatest economic losses should be afforded the highest priority.

3. Every police chief executive should recognize that some government services that are not essentially a police function are, under some circumstances, appropriately performed by the police. Such services include those provided in the interest of effective government or in response to established community needs. A chief executive:

    a. Should determine if the service to be provided has a relationship to the objectives established by the police agency. If not, the chief executive should resist that service becoming a duty of the agency;

    b. Should determine the budgetary cost of the service; and

    c. Should inform the public and its representatives of the projected effect that provision of the service by the police will have on the ability of the agency to continue the present level of enforcement services.

    d. If the service must be provided by the police agency, it should be placed in perspective with all other agency services and it should be considered when establishing priorities for the delivery of all police services.

    e. The service should be made a part of the agency's police role until such time as it is no longer necessary for the police agency to perform the service.

4. In connection with the preparation of their budgets, all police agencies should study and revise annually the objectives and priorities which have been established for the enforcement of laws and the delivery of services.

5. Every police agency should determine the scope and availability of other government services and public and private social services, and develop its ability to make effective referrals to those services.

Commentary

If the overall purposes of the police service in America were narrowed to a single objective, that objective would be to preserve the peace in a manner consistent with the freedoms secured by the Constitution. The police alone do not bear the responsibility for preserving a peaceful society; that responsibility is shared by each element of society—each person, each institution, and each area of government. However, because crime is an immediate threat to the order of all communities, the police exist to overcome that threat and to reduce the fear of it.

Maintaining order requires far more than making arrests for violations of the law. The police must deal with many situations where, although a crime may not have been committed, the safety and order of a community may be threatened. Conflicts between individuals, the failures of other municipal or social services, accidents, and natural disasters are among the many events that can threaten a community.

The degree to which society achieves public order through police action depends on the price that its members are willing to pay. That price is measured, literally, in tax levies and the surrender of certain liberties. For example, if the people were willing to live in a totalitarian state where the police had unlimited resources and power, they might find their parks always safe to walk in but impossible to enjoy. Obviously, a balance must be struck that permits enough freedom to enjoy what is secured by sacrificing unlimited freedom. That balance must be determined by the people if a productive relationship with their police is to be achieved.

Concept of a Functional Police Role

Because the responsibility for law enforcement and the provision of police services to meet local needs are properly borne by local government, it would be unrealistic to establish rigid priorities for all police agencies in the United States. Priorities regarding the police role are largely established by the community the police agency serves.

The fundamental purpose of the police throughout America is crime prevention through law enforcement; however, enforcement priorities for every agency must be established locally. In certain cases, police must provide nonenforcement services, and they have a responsibility to aid persons in need or to refer them to the proper agency for aid. Nevertheless, duties that are not part of enforcement should be performed by other agencies, where possible.

Once established, an agency's police role should be put in writing so that police employees have a model, and members of the public have a standard by which to measure police performance. The subject of policy formulation is treated in greater depth in the standards on police discretion and goal implementation, where it is stressed that a written definition of the police role should be central to all written policy. The point is also made there as well as in this standard that the policies of the police must be based on the policy of the governing body that provides formal authority for the police function.

Basic Police Authority

Such ordinary police duties as taking suspected law violators into custody, investigating reported crimes, and using force when necessary are sanctioned by statute and by public opinion. However, when the police seek out unreported crime and deter its commission, or become involved in conflicts when no crime has been committed, citizens may disagree about what police activities are proper and necessary.

Most police agencies routinely deploy officers on conspicuous and irregular patrol to create an impression of police omnipresence and to discover crimes in progress. Certain public or street crimes may be deterred by the threat of immediate apprehension. Officers on patrol do happen upon robberies, burglaries, and other crimes in progress. Even the most intensive patrol, however, can do little to suppress crimes committed out of anger, by the mentally ill, or in private homes.

Patrolling officers observe and attempt to correct conditions that provide an opportunity for crime. In order to preserve the peace and to prevent crime, they regularly question persons behaving suspiciously even if there may not be legal cause to make an arrest. These inquiries frequently lead to arrests for outstanding warrants, possession of narcotics or concealed weapons, burglary, robbery, and other serious crimes. They also may lead to the recovery of stolen property. In addition, written reports of the contact may result in a subsequent arrest by placing the subject in the area of a reported crime and by providing descriptive data leading to his identification.

The true effectiveness of police patrol as a crime deterrent to gage. However, if patrols are conducted infrequently because of insufficient manpower, or if patrols are poorly deployed, whatever deterrent effect they may have is greatly diminished.

The police are frequently called upon to intervene in conflicts that, if unresolved, could result in crime. Such situations commonly include family, landlord-tenant, and businessman-customer disputes; control of unruly crowds; and quieting of loud parties.

Legal authority for police intervention is based upon their power to arrest for disturbing the peace or for disorderly conduct. Their effectiveness in restoring peace, however, frequently rests on their acceptance by the public as a neutral stabilizing influence or on the participants' belief that the police have more authority than they actually have.

The suggestion that a husband leave home for the night, that a landlord allow the removal of a tenant's furniture, or that a stereo be turned down is generally based more upon police experience than legal authority. However, mere police presence generally results in at least a temporary reduction in the possibility of crime. In addition, arrests are sometimes made for crimes committed prior to officers' arrival, or in their presence while attempting to mediate the situation.

The large-scale riots in major cities during the last 10 years have accentuated the role of the police in quelling civil disorders. The police have learned that these civil disorders are not restricted to large urban areas. Although the military or National Guard may be called in to support the police, original responsibility for suppressing civil disorder remains with the police, who must deal with those arrested as law violators.

Concern for the constitutional rights of accused persons processed by the police has tended to obscure the fact that the police have an affirmative obligation to protect all persons in the free exercise of their rights. The police must provide safety for persons exercising their constitutional right to assemble, to speak freely, and to petition for redress of their grievances.

Any definition of the police role must acknowledge that the Constitution imposes restrictions on the power of legislatures to prohibit protected conduct, and to some extent defines the limits of police authority in the enforcement of established laws.

Establishing Enforcement Priorities

The basic purpose of the police in any given jurisdiction is determined to a large extent by State and local law. Because there are innumerable Federal, State, and local statutes and ordinances to be enforced, and limited police resources to enforce them, full enforcement of all laws is not possible. Furthermore, it is not altogether certain that full enforcement, if possible, would be consistent with either legislative intent or the desires of those for whose benefit laws are enacted. That the police exercise considerable discretion is well recognized, and that the police do not and cannot enforce all the laws all the time is implicit in a definition of the basic purpose of the police.

Police administrators must make the difficult determination of which reported crimes will be actively investigated and to what extent, and which unreported crimes will be sought out and to what degree. A determination must be made as to whether a reported theft warrants the same investigative resources as a crime of violence. Police must also assess the extent to which police resources should be used to suppress gambling, prostitution, and liquor law violations.

The law provides only general guidance. In their sterile statutory form, laws define crimes; classify them as felonies or misdemeanors; and assess penalties for them. But the law does not provide sufficient criteria to guide enforcement resource allocation, particularly at the local level.

In determining enforcement policies and priorities, police agencies should identify and direct primary attention to those crimes which are "serious": those that stimulate the greatest fear and cause the greatest economic losses. Beyond that, police agencies should be guided by the law, collective police experience, the needs and expectations of the community, and the availability of resources.

Establishing the Full Extent of the Police Role and Determination of Service Priorities

The role of the police has expanded greatly as society has become more complex. Many and varied demands have been made upon the police because of their unique authority. Dealing with alcoholics and the mentally ill, providing ambulance service, handling stray animals, and controlling vehicular and pedestrian traffic are but a few examples.

Because police are usually the only government representatives available around-the-clock, and because they have investigative resources and the authority to use force, the police are frequently called upon to perform municipal services that could more appropriately be performed by another agency of government. However, particularly in small cities and towns, the police are used to accomplish municipal objectives that could not otherwise be performed efficiently.

The police role must be determined at the local level by the police chief executive. He should state policy assuring that the objectives, priorities, policies, and practices adopted by the agency are consistent with the law, the needs of local government, and the public. This policy will guide the operational decisionmaking of the police officers under his command.

The concept of a flexible police role, adjustable to local conditions, does not require police agencies to accept submissively the imposition of duties basically unrelated to their essential purpose. On the contrary, effective and efficient police management requires that police agencies restrict themselves as far as possible to the provision of services that directly or indirectly serve to achieve their basic objective of preserving the peace and protecting constitutional guarantees.

Thus, while it may be appropriate in certain instances for a police agency to perform a nonpolice function, such as providing ambulance service or collecting stray animals, it must be undertaken only after a full public examination of its effect on other and more basic services provided by the agency.

When a proposal is made that a police agency provide a service not directly related to its essential purpose, the chief executive should determine whether provision of the service would serve indirectly to achieve agency objectives. If so, he should determine if the resources necessary might be used more beneficially to expand existing programs or in some alternative program that achieves a similar objective.

If the proposed service does not relate directly or indirectly to the police agency's objectives, the chief executive should resist efforts to make it the agency's responsibility. In so doing, he should determine the budgetary cost of the service and the projected effect the provision of the service would have on the ability of the agency to continue its present level of service. He should then inform the public and legislative representatives of his findings and of any suggested alternatives.

If it is legislatively determined that a police agency is to provide a service, it should become a specific budgetary item, and resources necessary for its delivery should be detailed.

The services should be placed into perspective with all other services provided by the police agency, and considered as part of the local police role in determining objectives and priorities for the delivery of all police services.

Revision of Priorities

Once the police role has been established in a particular jurisdiction, there should be a regular review of it. As soon as the necessity for providing a nonenforcement and nonpreventive service is removed, there is no longer a duty to provide it. As a city grows in size, a newly organized municipal agency might feasibly take over certain duties which have been performed by the police. As other municipal agencies expand to provide 24-hour service, they may claim functions temporarily performed by the police.

Community Service Referrals

The nature of their duties regularly exposes police to circumstances of deteriorating social, psychological, and economic conditions. Under these conditions police frequently observe people in need of help that is customarily provided by some other community agency. Prompt and effective assistance for persons in need helps create public trust in government. To the extent that the police facilitate the delivery of community services, they develop good will and their tasks are performed more easily and effectively.

Police agencies routinely refer people in need of help to the agency providing the assistance. The police regularly notify juvenile and probation agencies of unfit home conditions or remove the children from such surroundings. Medical or psychiatric attention for chronic alcoholics, drug addicts, suicidal persons, or others who are no longer capable of caring for themselves, frequently results from their being taken into custody by the police.

A number of police agencies have undertaken a more direct role in seeking solutions to problems that are the concern of other departments of municipal government or of social support agencies. For example, the police in some cities operate storefront offices or deploy community service officers to receive and channel complaints and requests for government or social services, and to serve as a means of communicating with the public.

The extent to which police agencies engage in such referral services should be determined by local conditions. However, the indirect effect of such programs upon the achievement of agency objectives should be weighed against the community's need for crime prevention services, and a balance struck to most effectively serve both needs.

Many police agencies have provided personnel with information to refer persons in need to the proper agency. For example, since the initiation of the citywide "911" emergency number in New York City, telephone calls for non-police municipal services have dramatically increased. Officers in the communications section are provided with a list of telephone numbers to refer callers to the appropriate agency.

The Metropolitan Police Department in Washington, D.C., provides each field officer a Referral Handbook of Social Services that indexes available governmental and private services by problem and agency. The police in Milwaukee, Wis., have access to a comprehensive directory of almost 500 community agencies and organizations.

Every police agency telephone communications facility should be able to transfer calls for community service assistance to the proper agency, or to inform the caller how to contact the appropriate agency.

References

1. American Bar Association Project on Standards for Criminal Justice. *Standards Relating to the Urban Police Function*, tentative draft. March 1972.

2. Eastman, George (ed.). *Municipal Police Administration*. Municipal Management Series. Washington, D.C.: International City Management Association, 1969.

3. Etzioni, Amitai. *Modern Organizations*. Englewood Cliffs: Prentice-Hall, 1964.

4. Fisk, James G. "Some of the Dimensions of the Issue of Police Discretion." Unpublished Discussion Paper, University of California, Los Angeles, Institute of Government and Public Affairs, 1972.

5. Graham, Hugh Davis, and Ted Robert Gurr. *Violence In America: Historical and Comparative Perspectives*, A Staff Report to the National Commission on the Causes and Prevention of Violence. Washington, D.C.: Government Printing Office, 1968.

6. Niederhoffer, Arthur, and Abraham S. Blumberg. *The Ambivalent Force: Perspectives on the Police*. Waltham, Mass.: Xerox College Publishing, 1970.

7. President's Commission on Law Enforcement and Administration of Justice. *The Challenge of Crime in a Free Society*. Washington, D.C.: Government Printing Office, 1967.

8. President's Commission on Law Enforcement and Administration of Justice. *Task Force Report: The Police*. Washington, D.C.: Government Printing Office, 1967.

9. Reiss, Albert J. *The Police and the Public*. New Haven: Yale University Press, 1971.

10. Reith, Charles. *The Blind Eye of History*. London: Faber and Faber Limited, 1952.

11. Reith, Charles. *British Police and the Democratic Ideal*. London: Oxford University Press, 1943.

12. Sterling, James. *Changes in Role Concepts of Police Officers*. Washington, D.C.: International Association of Chiefs of Police, 1972.

13. Wilson, James Q. *Varieites of Police Behavior: The Management of Law and Order in Eight Communities*. Cambridge: Harvard University Press, 1968.

ThE URbAN policE fUNCTION

AMERICAN BAR ASSOCIATION PROJECT ON STANDARDS
FOR CRIMINAL JUSTICE

Introductory Note

The need for improvement in the quality of policing in our society has long been apparent. Study after study has documented—with almost monotonous regularity—the gross deficiencies to be found in the caliber and performance of police agencies. In recent years, police administrators themselves have been among the most vociferous in calling attention to the need for upgrading the quality of police services and police personnel.[1]

Positive change, to the extent that it has occurred, has been largely in response to sporadic demands for "reforming" the police. "Reform" has meant different things at different times in the history of policing. The first major efforts at improving police operations focused upon upgrading the caliber of personnel hired as police officers. Reform, in the early days, also called for isolating the police from partisan politics, giving police administrators tenure, and eliminating corrupt practices. During the 1930s and 1940s, emphasis in programs aimed at improving the police was upon the development of training, the adoption of mechanical aids, and the greater use of scientific methods for the investigation of crimes. In the 1950s and 1960s, emphasis was given to the centralization of police operations and to the increased use of technology—

Source: ABA. *The Urban Police Function.* 1973. pp. 27–46. Reprinted with the kind permission of the American Bar Association, which authored the standards and which holds the copyright.

especially communications and the motor vehicle. And, in the current decade, the most commonly advocated changes are those that call for college education for police personnel, use of the computer for police work, and the development of new techniques for improving relationships between the police and the community. Together, on a cumulative basis, these various proposals have come to be widely accepted as the established elements in any program aimed at improving police services.

There is, today, an increased sense of urgency regarding the need for improving both the caliber and the performance of the police. The unprecedented demands being made upon the police have served to point up the complexity and importance of the police function. They have also served to make more visible the inadequacies that have resulted from years of neglect. There appears to be widespread agreement that if the problems for which the police are held primarily responsible are to be dealt with more effectively, police agencies must be improved. But there is much less certainty as to the form such improvements should take.

Doubt as to the value of past efforts at improvement has arisen primarily as a result of the difficulties that have been experienced in coping with current-day crises by even those departments that have consistently been in the forefront in effecting change. Some of the specific proposals for change are being increasingly subject to question. Thus, for example, the appropriateness of organizational arrangements designed to insulate the police from political influence is now being challenged in the light of the demonstrated need for greater responsiveness on the part of the police to the needs of the community. Purposeful efforts to assure a degree of detachment, on the part of individual police officers, from the community they police (*e.g.,* prohibitions against police officers working in the neighborhoods in which they reside) are being abandoned in some jurisdictions in preference for a policy that encourages officers to reside in the neighborhoods in which they work. The view that almost all patrolmen should be assigned to squad cars is now being modified by the increased assignment of police officers to foot patrol. And the strong movement to a highly centralized form of control over police operations—especially in the larger cities—is being reversed by the establishment of storefront offices and by various other forms of decentralization intended in part to meet the kinds of complaints that give rise to demands from citizen groups for neighborhood control over the police.

These developments offer substantial support for the observation that some of the older "nonprofessionalized" police agencies that have been by-passed by the several waves of "reform" have been more effective in coping with the problems that police are currently experiencing than have those agencies that have consistently adopted all proposals advocated for the improvement of police operations.[2] Given the common lag between proposals for change and their implementation, the police field is experiencing the rather awkward situation today of having some police agencies aspiring to effect changes that are being substantially modified or abandoned by those agencies that have already adopted them.

The fact that so much of the effort to improve police operations appears to have been misdirected does not negate the importance of addressing such fundamental areas as police personnel, training, and management. Rather, what this realization suggests is that such efforts have been limited in their value because they have not gone far enough. They have been too narrowly conceived. They have in some instances been based upon questionable assumptions. And they have been developed without adequate regard for the overall nature and complexity of the police function.

In recognition of these shortcomings, this study departs significantly from what has become the traditional pattern for addressing the need for improvements in the police field. Primary emphasis has been placed upon examining the overall role of the police in an effort to clarify and, in some instances, hopefully to reach conclusions regarding some of the basic underlying issues that must be confronted as a prerequisite to effecting meaningful and lasting improvements in police agencies and in their operations. This study treats the more traditional areas of concern as well, but only to the extent that conclusions reached with regard to the more basic issues have direct implications for the form that programs in such areas should take.

1.1 Complexity of police task

(a) Since police, as an agency of the criminal justice system, have a major responsibility for dealing with serious crime, efforts should continually be made to improve the capacity of police to discharge this responsibility effectively. It should also be recognized, however, that police effectiveness in dealing with crime is often largely dependent upon the effectiveness of other agencies both within and outside the criminal justice system.

(b) To achieve optimum police effectiveness, the police should be recognized as having complex and multiple tasks to perform in addition to identifying and apprehending persons committing serious criminal offenses. Such other police tasks include protection of certain rights such as to speak and to assemble, participation either directly or in conjunction with other public and social agencies in the prevention of criminal and delinquent behavior, maintenance of order and control of pedestrian and vehicular traffic, resolution of conflict, and assistance to citizens in need of help such as the person who is mentally ill, the chronic alcoholic, or the drug addict.

(c) Recommendations made in these standards are based on the view that this diversity of responsibilities is likely to continue and, more importantly, that police authority and skills are needed to handle appropriately a wide variety of community problems.

Commentary

Section 1.1 (a)

It is hardly necessary to restate the dimensions of the problem of serious crime in America or its impact upon the lives of our citizens. This has been documented in an effective and frightening way by the Report of the President's Commission on Law Enforcement and Administration of Justice in 1967, and the scope of the problem is restated annually by the Federal Bureau of Investigation in its Uniform Crime Reports. These reports indicate not only that crimes in most categories are increasing at a disturbing rate, but also that clearance rates (the rates indicating the percentage of crimes which have been "solved" by an arrest of the alleged offender) remain low for most types of offenses.

It is obvious that the police as an agency of the criminal justice system have a major and central responsibility for dealing with serious crime. Concentrated efforts must be made, therefore, to identify and implement new approaches to improve the police response to serious crime. This may involve, among other things, developing new types of specialized preventive and investigative personnel; utilizing more scientific methods for allocating personnel and reducing the time for responding to calls for service; and improving crime laboratory and other supporting services for investigative personnel.[3]

It must be noted, however, that even with dramatic improvements in police resources, there are severe limitations on what the police alone can do about many types of serious crimes.[4] There are serious weaknesses in thinking about crime as essentially a "police problem."

> Although . . . it is understandable that major-city crime is thought of and dealt with essentially as a police problem, this narrowness of perspective cannot be afforded. Perception of crime as a police problem results in a failure to act to improve other components of the criminal justice system, such as the courts, prosecution and defense; correctional and youth service agencies and programs; other agencies that can and should become involved in working with potential offenders and offenders; and the community itself. In addition, this perception results in a failure to understand the system as a single process, composed of necessarily interdependent, although not effectively interrelated, elements—a process that flows from the community—where the causes of criminal behavior, criminal events, and the resources needed to respond to crime lie —through the police, the courts and correctional agencies, back once again to the community with the return of the offender.[5]

Thus, although it is most important to develop ways to improve the police capability to deal with serious crime, it is equally important to note that the police constitute only one part of a total system that must be improved if serious crime is to be contended with more effectively.

Section 1.1 (b)

Further, in thinking about needed comprehensive improvement in police effectiveness, it must be recognized that the police do far more than identify and
apprehend persons committing serious criminal offenses. Past efforts to improve
police operations have usually been based upon the widely held notion that
the primary responsibility of the police is that of combating crime and that
most of their work is directed toward this end. A number of recent studies
challenge this stereotype and point up the importance of recognizing the broader
role of the police.

The President's Commission on Law Enforcement and Administration of
Justice, which conducted the most comprehensive study of the police that has
been undertaken in recent years, reported that police department records "rarely
reveal what proportion of working time policemen spend on what activities."[6]
But in acknowledging the wide array of duties for which the police are responsible, the Commission made the following observation:

A great majority of the situations in which policemen intervene are not,
or are not interpreted by the police to be, criminal situations in the sense that
they call for arrest with its possible consequences of prosecution, trial, and
punishment. This is not to say that the police intervene in these situations
mistakenly. Many of them are clear public nuisances that the community wants
stopped: Radios blaring or dogs barking at 3 o'clock in the morning, more or
less convivial groups obstructing sidewalks, or youths throwing snowballs at
passing motorists.

Many situations involve people who need help whether they want it or
not: Helpless drunks out in freezing weather, runaway boys who refuse to go
home, tourists in search of exciting night life in a dangerous neighborhood.
Many of them involve conduct that, while unlawful, cannot be prevented or
deterred to any great degree by means now at the disposal of the criminal
justice system: Using narcotics, prostitution, gambling, alcoholism. Many situations, whether or not they involve unlawful conduct, may be threatening: A
sidewalk orator exercising the right of free speech in the midst of a hostile
crowd, a midnight street corner gathering of youths whose intentions are questionable, an offer by a belligerent drunk to lick any man in the house.

All of these situations could involve the violation of some ordinance or
statute. All of them could lead to a serious breach of public order, or for that
matter to a serious crime. Much of police work is seeing to it they do not lead
to this extreme. This means becoming involved in the most intimate, personal
way with the lives and problems of citizens of all kinds.[7]

Since publication of the Crime Commission's reports, there have been
several efforts to develop more detailed data descriptive of the police function.
In exploring the role of a patrolman, Professor James Q. Wilson undertook to
analyze citizen calls transmitted to police cars by the Syracuse Police Department for a period of one week. He reported:

About one fifth required the officer to gather information ("get a report") about an alleged crime for which no suspect was thought still to be on the scene. The patrolman's function in this case is mainly clerical—he asks routine questions, inspects the premises, and fills out a form. About a third of the calls were for services that could as easily be provided—and in many cities are—by a different government agency or by a private firm. Only about one tenth of the calls afforded, even potentially, an opportunity to perform a narrow law enforcement function by stopping a burglary in progress, catching a prowler, making an arrest of a suspect being held by another party, or investigating a suspicious car or an open window. In fact, very few of *these* will result in arrests—there will be no prowler, except in a woman's imagination, the open window will signify an owner's oversight rather than a thief's entry, the "suspicious" car will be occupied by a respectable citizen, and the burglar, if any, will be gone. Almost a third of all calls—and the vast majority of all nonservice calls—concern allegations of disorder arising out of disputes, public and private, serious and trivial.[8]

Somewhat similar findings were reported by several other studies. A survey of the Kansas City Department in 1966 revealed that patrol officers devoted only 32 percent of their time to criminal matters.[9] An analysis of calls received by the Chicago Police Department in a twenty-four-hour period from a section of the city containing approximately one twelfth of the city's population revealed that, of the 394 calls received, 16 percent consisted of reports of crimes in progress or crimes that had already occurred; 44 percent consisted of reports of incidents that could have involved a criminal action (*e.g.*, a disturbance or an intoxicated man), but which experience has indicated most frequently require no more than a warning, informally resolving conflict, or the providing of some form of assistance; and 40 percent consisted of requests for various forms of service and for information.[10]

In their studies of the police as a "support agent," Elaine Cumming, Ian Cumming, and Laura Edell found that more than one half of the calls made to the police appear to involve requests for help in personal and interpersonal matters unrelated to crime.[11] Raymond Parnas, exploring police handling of domestic disturbances, found that:

> The everyday police response to the minor family conflict probably exceeds the total number of murders, aggravated batteries, and all other serious crimes. For example, the Chicago Police Department publishes a Patrol Division Operations Report, not available to the public, one subcategory of which is "disturbances." Disturbances includes minor family conflict (domestic disturbances), teen disturbances, party noise, and the like. The report for the 11th Police Period, Oct. 13, 1966 to Nov. 9, 1966, shows a total of 134,869 calls for police service in the city of Chicago. Of this total of 134,869 calls, 17% are classified as "Criminal Incidents." This category includes crimes as serious as murder and as minor as bicycle

theft. The remaining 83% includes 12,544 traffic accident calls, 2,009 vehicle recovery calls, and 96,826 "Misc. Non-criminal" incidents. Hence, "Misc. Non-criminal" includes about 80% of *all* calls for police service during the period. One third of "Misc. Non-criminal" incident calls are "disturbances." Thus the non-criminal category of *all kinds* of reported disturbances exceeds *all* reported criminal incidents by almost 40%.[12]

From these studies and similar studies conducted in recent years, one commentator, Professor Gordon Misner, has observed that enough data have been collected to show clearly that "uniformed policemen in large urban areas typically spend less than 30 percent of their *working* time dealing with crime or other enforcement duties." Professor Misner concludes that the uniformed policeman is engaged for the most part in work which should properly be classified as "public service."[13]

Helpful as the various analyses of calls for police assistance have been in shedding light on the nature of police activities, it is important to recognize their inadequacies. Requests for police assistance must be categorized on the basis of information provided in a telephone call. Assignment of a police officer to contact the party from whom the call is received often results in the discovery of additional information that significantly changes the nature of the request for assistance as originally received. The absence of detailed information at the time a call is received requires that the initial categorization be in rather general terms. The resulting tabulations, therefore, lack the detailed kind of breakdown that would be more helpful for analyzing police activities. The most serious limitation on the data is the fact that such tabulations, in their entirety, do not begin to represent a comprehensive picture of the nature of all police operations, since matters about which the public typically calls the police account for but a portion of all police activity. Much of what the police do is self-initiated.[14]

In the light of these limitations on the data that have been developed up to this point, it is not possible to reach any precise conclusions regarding the nature of police services currently being provided. But, inadequate as they are, the data are sufficient to dispel the myth that police spend most of their time on crime-related matters. The above-cited studies and others make it clear that police also have responsibility for other complex tasks of municipal government which include protection of certain rights such as to speak and to assemble, participation either directly or in conjunction with public or private agencies in the prevention of criminal or delinquent behavior, maintenance of order and the control of pedestrian and vehicular traffic, resolution of conflict, and assistance to citizens in need of help such as the person who is mentally ill or the chronic alcoholic.

To continue to think about the police in terms of crime control only, therefore, ignores the problems and needs surrounding most of what the police do. This was noted quite clearly in a recent study made of Detroit and other major departments by Thomas E. Bercal:

[R]esearch [has] indicated that only 166,000 (16%) of all calls were "crime" related. As these data indicate, to study the police in the context of a para-military organization primarily concerned with the control and prevention of crime focuses attention on but a small portion of police work. Such an orientation has encouraged police to make major policy decisions on the weight of crime statistics and to overlook, and thereby fail to take sufficiently into account, the vast majority of its activities. Conversely, emphasis on the "crime problem" and "social unrest" have hidden the majority of police work from the public eye.[15]

Thus, attention must be given to the fact that any discussion of police improvements requires recognition that a substantial percentage of police time involves dealing with "abrasive conflicts that can be, and generally are, settled by a combination of counseling and exhortation,"[16] and dealing with "challenge for changes" in our society.[17]

The limited effectiveness of many of the improvements commonly advocated for police agencies is in large measure attributable to the failure on the part of both the police and the community to recognize the diverse nature of the functions performed by police personnel.

Section 1.1 (c)

Recognition of the true nature of the police function, while a major first step, does not by itself provide easy answers by which changes in police operations can be made more effective. Rather, confronting the true nature of police work forces an increased awareness of the incredibly complex nature of the police role—and makes all the more apparent the reasons why commonly-advocated proposals for improving the police have frequently not produced the results predicted for them.

Many of the individuals and official bodies that have studied and commented upon the police in recent years have acknowledged, in varying ways, the extent to which problems in the police field are traceable to the wide array of functions for which the police are held responsible. A number of the studies have gone on to suggest that the police be divested of certain functions on the assumption that there is no real question as to the primary role of the police; others, more modestly, have simply urged that the police function be more clearly defined. There is generally implied, in all such comments, the view that it ought to be possible—and it would certainly be desirable—to arrive at a more limited police role that could then be applied uniformly to the police field throughout the country. But reflection suggests that it is neither possible nor desirable to significantly narrow the police role and, furthermore, suggests that the implied hope that it can be done in itself reflects a gross oversimplification of the nature of police work.

It is significant that, while the hope has often been expressed for some kind of standard definition that would serve to narrow the police function, the only *specific* proposals that have been advanced relate to matters that are obviously peripheral to even the broadest concept of the police task. Thus, it has often been suggested that the police be relieved of such responsibilities as that involved in the collection of parking meter revenue and the repair of parking meters, in the licensing of dogs, and in the taking of a local census. The President's Commission on Law Enforcement and Administration of Justice came to no conclusion with regard to basic issues relating to the police function, but did urge that communities take a hard look at such police assignments as running the dog pound, tax collection, licensing, jail duty, and chauffeur duty.[18] And in supporting greater police involvement in community service-type activities, the National Advisory Commission on Civil Disorders joined with the Crime Commission's caveat that police should not become involved in service tasks which involve neither "policing nor community help."[19] Such proposals may serve some useful purpose, but they do not contribute significantly toward clarifying the police role.

Another approach to defining the police function has been through the advocacy of descriptive phrases intended to suggest relative emphasis and priority. Thus, at various times in the past and more frequently in recent years, it has been urged that the police view themselves primarily committed to "law enforcement," "crime prevention," "maintaining the peace," "maintaining order," or simply to providing "public service." The obvious difficulty with such terms is that they are much too broad to be helpful in an effort that requires, as a preliminary to setting priorities and emphasis, a taking apart of the mass of activity that currently occupies the police.

A third approach to defining the police function—somewhat negative in form—has consisted of various proposals for divesting the police of what are now substantial segments of their typical workload. Thus it has been suggested, for example, that the police be relieved of all responsibilities relating to traffic control; that the handling of intoxicated persons be transferred to some other governmental agency; that civil disorders be handled, as a matter of routine, by the National Guard; and that many of the miscellaneous emergency services that the police are called upon to perform be performed, instead, by other departments of municipal government or by private agencies.

The most common proposals for narrowing the police function contain a number of assumptions that, on examination, are subject to serious question.

(1) *An unwarranted judgment as to what should be the primary residual function of the police.* There is the implication in each of the above proposals that a narrowing of the police function will make it possible for the police to concentrate more directly on matters related to crime. Yet events in recent years have made it clear that those aspects of the police function that relate to minimizing the likelihood of disorder, for example, are equal in their importance to the police function in identifying and prosecuting wrongdoers. More-

over, there are a number of indications that the public wants the police to do much more than combat crime. They want the police to deal with all kinds of problems that endanger citizens—problems constituting an immediate threat or merely creating fears. The possibility that one's home may be burglarized may not be as threatening as the fear of being hit by a car, bit by a rabid animal, or harassed by a hostile crowd. If there is to be a narrowing of the police function, is it correct to assume that the "crime-fighting" role of the police is paramount and should be the activity around which the police are structured?

(2) *An assumption regarding the potential effectiveness of the police.* Implicit in the effort to make more time available for matters relating to crime is the assumption that there are proven ways by which the police can prevent and control crime. The President's Commission on Law Enforcement and Administration of Justice agreed with what many in the police field have long suspected—that there is great uncertainty as to the value of currently-employed techniques in deterring crimes and in apprehending those who commit them.[20] Given the limited impact that it appears the police can have upon crime, it has been persuasively agrued that, as a matter of national policy, the country errs in looking to the police for relief from the crime problem.[21] Would a more realistic assessment of the potential of the police to fulfill some of the functions commonly expected of them have any significant bearing upon a more rational definition of the police role?

(3) *As assumption that police activities as they now exist are in fact separable.* There are a number of practical problems in separating out substantial segments of police activity. Were a social agency, for example, to undertake to perform some of the functions now being handled by the police, it would be necessary for the agency to make a substantial staff available around the clock if the agency is to approximate the built-in, city-wide capacity of most police forces to handle such requests currently—putting aside, for the moment, the manner in which they are handled. Moreover, there is no easy way to determine, in advance of responding to a call for assistance, whether the principal need is for one trained as a social worker or for one having the authority and training of a police officer. A telephone report of a minor family argument may, on response, require that a police officer intervene in a physical struggle—often involving a knife or other weapon. The unique characteristics that are currently combined in the job of a police officer—twenty-four-hour availability, a capacity to handle potentially-dangerous situations, investigative skill, and the possession of general police authority—are not easily duplicated in others to whom portions of the police function might be assigned. This factor accounts, in part, for the continued assignment of police officers to work alongside other newly-hired personnel responsible for implementing the experimental programs aimed at diverting chronic alcoholics from the criminal system.[22]

(4) *An assumption that it is both desirable and feasible to reduce the conflict that arises by virtue of the police having to act in both a helping and a puni-*

tive role. Implied in some of the proposals is the assumption that a police officer can function more effectively as a control agent if he is not required, at the same time, to serve in a helping role; and, similarly, that he can be more effective as a "helper" if he is not required to be identified with punitive and coercive forces. Yet, as was previously pointed out, there are a number of indications that effectiveness in either role is at least to some degree dependent upon functioning in the other. A police officer, in other words, may be a more effective "helper" because he has control responsibilities; and he may be more effective as a control agent because he is also identified as a "helper." Thus it could be argued that efforts to eliminate some of the most obvious sources of conflict might be dysfunctional.

(5) *An assumption that private or other governmental agencies can perform some of the existing police functions more effectively than can the police.* The purpose in advocating that certain functions be transferred from the police in some instances is not only to reduce the magnitude and diversity of police responsibilities, but also to improve the quality of the service rendered. Thus it has been assumed by some that it would be preferable to have health personnel deal with alcoholics and narcotic addicts, social workers deal with juveniles, and military personnel cope with widespread rioting of the kind that has occurred in recent years. Inevitably, however, it would follow that adequate numbers of such personnel would have to be made available and that they be provided with the resources and training necessary to carry out their new responsibilities. Is there any reason to believe that the quality of the service subsequently rendered by these agencies would be superior to that which could be rendered by the police if they were similarly staffed, trained, and equipped? Would the problems involved in structuring new systems to regulate and control the exercise of needed authority be a factor in arguing in behalf of retaining such functions with the police who are already subject to such a system—ineffective as it may sometimes appear to be?

Given these considerations, it becomes obvious that, with limited exceptions, the wide diversity of current police responsibilities is likely to continue. The police must be recognized, therefore, as having an extremely complex function that will not be simplified in the future. Rather, it appears inevitable that the function will become increasingly more difficult. This recognition is essential in understanding the types of recommendations which are made within these standards. Even if other agencies and personnel with more appropriate skills were available to deal with certain social or health problems, would police officers still not be required to assist such personnel when potentially dangerous situations arose?

1.2 Scope of standards

To ensure that the police are responsive to all the special needs for police services in a democratic society, it is necessary to:

(i) identify clearly the principal objectives and responsibilities of police and establish priorities between the several and sometimes conflicting objectives;

(ii) provide for adequate methods and confer sufficient authority to discharge the responsibility given them;

(iii) provide adequate mechanisms and incentives to ensure that attention is given to the development of law enforcement policies to guide the exercise of administrative discretion by police;

(iv) develop a system of control to ensure proper use of police authority;

(v) develop an appropriate professional role for individual police officers;

(vi) provide police departments with human and other resources necessary for effective performance;

(vii) improve the criminal justice, juvenile justice, mental health, and public health systems of which the police are an important part;

(viii) gain the understanding and support of the community; and

(ix) provide adequate means for continually evaluating the effectiveness of police services.

Commentary

As noted in the introduction, these standards, for the most part, represent a new approach for identifying and dealing with the critical problems and needs confronting urban police agencies. Section 1.2 summarizes the major issues that must be faced in ensuring that the police are responsive to all the special needs of a democratic society.

1.3 Need for experimentation

There is need for financial assistance from the federal government and from other sources to support experimental and evaluative programs designed to achieve the objectives set forth in these standards.

Commentary

There has recently been a substantial increase in monetary support for programs designed to improve and strengthen the capacity of police organizations. Under the Omnibus Crime Control and Safe Streets Act of 1968, Congress has committed the federal government to providing substantial financial assistance to the police and other agencies in the criminal justice system through grants administered by the Law Enforcement Assistance Administration and by newly-created planning agencies in each of the fifty states.[23] Local governments have demonstrated their readiness to provide additional financial support to the police by substantial enlargements in police budgets—most of which have gone to support increases in manpower and increases in the salaries paid police personnel. As between the federal government and the local governments, therefore, there will, in the next several years, be a massive infusion of new funds into police operations. New support is coming from private sources as well. For example, in July, 1970, the Ford Foundation announced the creation of the Police Foundation, which was granted $30 million for a five-year period to assist experiments and pilot programs by police departments seeking to make basic changes in their operation and to upgrade their performance.[24]

But, if the country is to benefit from the increase in public spending in the criminal justice field, the programs for which funds are expended must be preceded by a careful analysis of goals and objectives. If, for example, substantial funds are to be invested in the development and expansion of training programs, it is becoming increasingly apparent that training programs must be related much more directly to the functions for which the police are or should be responsible. The same observation applies to efforts to improve recruitment standards, educational programs, staffing arrangements, and organizational efficiency.

Unfortunately, federal and state increases that have already been made in spending for police operations are, for the most part, proceeding without benefit of such consideration.

> [S]ince most cities have difficulty in meeting even day-to-day operational needs, such as police equipment, there is a strong temptation to use federal funds to supplant city expenditures. . . .
> [F]ederal funds should not now be used to reinforce the current way in which the criminal justice system operates. Rather they should be used to assist in analyzing the current defects of the criminal justice system, in setting new directions for the system, in developing and implementing new approaches to crime problems, and in testing the success or failure of such approaches.[25]

Because of the severe financial limitations on the ability of local government to experiment with basic changes or improvements in government service, there is significant need for financial assistance from the Law Enforcement Assistance Administration or from other souces to support and to stimulate the experimental and evaluative programs designed to achieve the objectives set forth in these standards. This is particularly true in areas of administrative policy-making and control over police misconduct.

References

1. Among the leading studies of the police in the last half century are R. Fosdick, American Police Systems (1920); L. Fuld, Police Administration—

A Critical Study of Police Organizations in the United States and Abroad (1910); National Commission on Law Observance and Enforcement, Report on Police, No. 14 (1931); and B. Smith, Police Systems in the United States (2d rev. ed. 1960). Most recently, the President's Commission on Law Enforcement and Administration of Justice completed its comprehensive review of the problem of crime and the provisions presently made for coping with it. President's Commission on Law Enforcement and Administration of Justice, The Challenge of Crime in a Free Society (1967) (hereinafter referred to as Challenge of Crime). See also President's Commission on Law Enforcement and Administration of Justice, Task Force Report: The Police (1967) (hereinafter referred to as Task Force Report: The Police). Much of the Challenge of Crime focused upon the police, with an emphasis upon needed improvements. Many of the problems which the Commission addressed are recognizable in somewhat different form in some of the earliest examinations of police operations.

2. See J. Wilson, *The Police and Their Problems: A Theory*, 12 Pub. Policy 189 (1963).

3. See generally recommendations made in Task Force Report: The Police, *supra* note 1; and President's Commission on Law Enforcement and Administration of Justice, Task Force Report: Science and Technology (1967).

4. See, *e.g.*, J. Wilson, Varieties of Police Behavior 295 (1968) (hereinafter referred to as Varieties of Police Behavior).

5. Krantz & Kramer, *The Urban Crisis and Crime*, 50 B.U. L. Rev. 343, 347 (1970) (hereinafter referred to as The Urban Crisis and Crime).

6. Challenge of Crime, *supra* note 1, at 98.

7. Challenge of Crime 91.

8. Varieties of Police Behavior 19.

9. Task Force Report: The Police, *supra* note 1, at 121.

10. H. Goldstein, *Police Response to Urban Crisis*, 28 Pub. Admin. Rev. 417, 418 (1968).

11. Cumming, Cumming, & Edell, *Policeman as Philosopher, Guide and Friend*, 12 Soc. Problems 276, 278–285 (1965).

12. Parnas, *The Police Response to the Domestic Disturbance*, 1967 Wis. L. Rev. 914 n.2.

13. Misner, *Enforcement: Illusion of Security*, 208 The Nation 488 (1969).

14. Some effort has been made to study self-initiated police activities. See, *e.g.*, D. Black & A. Reiss, Patterns of Behavior in Police and Citizen Transactions, Field Surveys Ill: Studies in Crime and Law Enforcement in Major Metropolitan Areas, Vol. 2 (A Report of a Research Study Submitted to the President's Commission on Law Enforcement and Administration of Justice, 1967); and Webster, *Police Task and Time Study*, 61 J. Crim. L., C. & P. S. 94 (1970).

15. Bercal, *Calls for Police Assistance*, 13 Am. Behavioral Scientist 681, 682–683 (1970).

16. Livermore, *Policing*, 55 Minn. L. Rev. 649, 683 (1971).

17. Murphy, *The Role of the Police in Our Modern Society*, 26 The Record of the Ass'n of the Bar of the City of New York 292, 295 (April, 1971).

18. Challenge of Crime, *supra* note 1, at 98.

19. Report, National Advisory Commission on Civil Disorders 167 (1968).

20. Challenge of Crime, *supra* note 1, at 95–96.

21. J. Wilson, *Crime and Law Enforcement,* in Agenda for the Nation 179 (K. Gordon ed. 1968).

22. See, *e.g.,* Vera Institute of Justice, The Manhattan Bowery Project 5 (1970).

23. The total appropriation to the Law Enforcement Assistance Administration for fiscal year 1969 was $63 million; for 1970, $268 million; for 1971, $468 million; and the figure for fiscal year 1972 will be $698 million.

24. The Ford Foundation, *A More Effective Arm* (1970).

25. *The Urban Crisis and Crime, supra* note 5, at 355. See also statement of Professor Sheldon Krantz, *Hearings Before the Subcomm. on Economy in Government of the Joint Economic Comm., on the Federal Criminal Justice System,* 91st Cong., 2d Sess., at 55–61 (Sept. 22, 1970).

police-community alienation: its structural roots and a proposed remedy

IRVING PILIAVIN

The Patrol Function and Citizen Alienation

Most discussions of police-community problems focus on police relations with lower class minorities and, more recently, college students. It is generally conceded in these discussions that police engage in many activities which demean, estrange, and promote violence among members of these groups. Accounts of police harassment and use of unnecessary force, in fact, indicate that officers at times intend that their actions attain these ends. On the other hand, police actions can demean and estrange citizens without being intended to do so. Such reportedly is the case when officers intervene in quarrels or make arrests. Whether or not intended to demean the citizen, the actions of police have been found to constitute 40 per cent of the prior incidents involved in the occurrence of civil disturbances studied by the National Advisory Commission on Civil Disorders.[1]

Some police are more likely than others to operate under conditions in which their actions give rise to citizen unrest. Personnel most often exposed to these conditions are the uniformed patrolmen. Those least likely to be exposed to these conditions are those belonging to the various investigative bureaus, that is, detectives.[2]

Detectives deal with crimes whose definition and seriousness have general agreement. They typically become involved after a crime has occurred and after

Source: MSS Modular Publications, Inc. New York. 1973. Reprinted with the kind permission of MSS Modular Publications, Inc., New York, N.Y.

a report to that effect—usually made by a citizen—has been filed. Thus, from the outset they operate in situations in which they can be seen as providing a service to citizens. Furthermore, these officers' definition of the situation—that a crime has or has not occurred and that some individual is a suspect—comes only after investigation. Their arrests, therefore, are typically buttressed by evidence which, if not convincing to everyone, is at least sufficient to obtain warrants. The arrests usually follow with relatively few exceptions from the assumption of guilt. Finally, the conditions under which detectives conduct their investigations are relatively private. Thus, their interrogation of hostile witnesses and suspects, their tactics, and the responses of those they interrogate are not likely to engender a public response.

In contrast to special investigators, uniformed patrolmen for the most part investigate crimes which are minor and whose definition is ambiguous. They often elect not to arrest after interrogation those they still suspect of committing such crimes. Patrolmen also have primary responsibility for carrying out the functions of maintaining order and preventing crime. Thus they frequently intrude in citizen affairs when no crime has been committed. The potential conflict inherent in the patrolman's job is thus readily seen. They interrogate and direct citizens when it is not clear either to them or to the citizens that a crime has taken place and, if it has, who has committed it. Thus, their actions, even their presence, is questioned. Furthermore, because patrolmen do not always arrest citizens in such situations, and because citizens are aware of this, decisions to arrest are subject to dispute. Finally, unlike the detective, the patrolman is not able to deal with these trying circumstances in private. His interventions are on the street or at the scene of disturbance. His decisions, his indecision, his disputes with suspects and complainants are all subject to civilian scrutiny. And because he must, in fact, make decisions without the opportunity to sift and weigh evidence—without the opportunity to conclude and justify that a "good case" can be made—this scrutiny may lead to a hostile, perhaps violent, citizen response.

Citizen Criticism of Police

Citizen complaints against police have been primarily of three concerns. First, allegations have been made that in their response to dispatches, as well as in their disposition of suspects, police discriminate against blacks, Puerto Ricans, and other racial and ethnic minorities. Secondly, and related to the first, police have been accused of unnecessary physical and verbal abuse of citizens, particularly those from minority groups. Third, and basic to both criticisms is the accusation that police are authoritarian, prejudiced against minorities, and unable to deal justly with citizens.[3] While data from several studies indicate that such charges have some basis, the studies also suggest that police practices and attitudes as well as citizens' views of police develop from a complex of factors whose mitigation or control poses serious difficulties.

...while the exercise of discretion by police in the making of dispositions leads to problems—not always assignable to the operation of prejudice—so too does the elimination of discretion. Among those who believe that discretion is inevitable, its deficiencies have been seen as amenable to two approaches: the development of policies directing its exercise and the improvement of police officers' abilities to employ it. Concerning the former, the President's Commission on Law Enforcement and the Administration of Justice has cited efforts in the State of New York and the City of Chicago to document that useful guidelines for police decision-making can and should be developed by law enforcement agencies.[4]

Even if police discretion in making dispositions could be brought under greater control, citizen complaints about its use might not be substantially reduced. Whatever guidelines are developed will necessarily call for subjective judgment and be based on impressionistic information. Thus, the consistency of decisions based on these guidelines is not likely to be apparent, and their legitimacy may continue to be questioned.

Police violence

Although the view is often expressed that police department recruits are disproportionally "violence prone," there are no data supporting this contention. In fact, the little research that has been concerned with the attributes of police recruits suggests that the personalities of those hired by law enforcement agencies are rather typical of the members of the social and economic groups from which these agencies draw their members.[5] Nevertheless, police have been found to engage in substantial mistreatment of citizens, ranging from verbal abuse to physical attack. The most comprehensive study of this practice, that recently undertaken by Reiss, found that policemen who operated in relatively high crime areas engaged in acts of clear brutality in 20 of an observed 850 eight-hour patrols, and that unnecessary force was used in 3 per cent of the police-suspect encounters which were observed.[6] Ten per cent of the policemen who were accompanied by observers utilized unnecessary force and, according to observers, their actions were tolerated, even encouraged, by other police.[7]

Aside from the fact that Reiss's data provide for the first time some specific information on the frequency and style of police use of force, they also reveal something about those against whom the force is applied. While the popular impression has been that police brutality is largely racial, with white police mistreating black citizens, this was not the case in the communities studies by Reiss. The "victim of force" rate among white suspects was 4-2/10 per cent while that among blacks was 2-3/10 per cent. Furthermore, police violence was largely intra-racial. Sixty-seven per cent of the citizens aggressed against by black policemen were black. Given that white policemen patrolled black and white areas about equally while black police largely patrolled black areas,[8] Reiss's data indicate that, relative to opportunity, whites were somewhat less likely to exercise unwarranted force across race than were blacks. In terms of total incidents, however, the use of force among police was about the same for whites (8-7/10 per cent) and blacks (9-8/10 per cent). As contrasted to this failure to find a strong cross-race effect in the use of force, Reiss did find a strong class effect. All of those against whom force was exercised were described as coming from the lower class, although 19 per cent of the suspects were identified as "white collar workers."

Unnecessary force was found by Reiss and his associates to be only one of the means by which police mistreated citizens. Verbal abuse was another. Officers ridiculed, became brusque with, or evidenced hostility toward citizens in 11 per cent of their observed encounters. The pattern of verbal abuse was similar to that found in the use of violence.[9] Whites were somewhat more likely than blacks to be insulted or ridiculed,[10] and suspects were much more likely than other citizens to be so treated.[11]

The patrolman's view of the citizen

Although one intent of this discussion has been to demonstrate that police decision-making and violence are not attributable simply to the character of those recruited for police work, there is ample evidence that police are, in fact, prejudiced. Piliavin and Briar report that two-thirds of the patrolmen they interviewed admitted disliking blacks. Black and Reiss report that 72 per cent of the white patrolmen and 18 per cent of the black patrolmen, whose encounters with citizens they studied, revealed in the course of their work negative views of lower class blacks.[12] And Bouma found evidence of prejudice toward blacks among 52 per cent of the police he interviewed in Grand Rapids and Kalamazoo.[13] Assuming that these data may well be somewhat conservative, it is evident that the great majority of white policemen dislike and disdain at least lower class blacks.

An important quality of this prejudice, indicated by some of the above studies, is that seemingly it increases as a function of contact with lower class blacks. Thus, Black and Reiss found that, while most of the white police they interviewed expressed prejudice toward blacks, this was more true among officers who patrolled predominantly black areas. Furthermore, although only a small percentage of black police voiced prejudiced views toward blacks, it was again those who worked in black communities who were most likely to express these views.[14] These findings, of course, may reflect the fact that the police departments observed by Reiss and his co-workers engaged in the self-defeating practice of assigning antiblack police to ghetto areas. Black and Reiss suggest otherwise, in contrasting their findings to those of Deutsch and Collins which indicate that intergroup communication reduces prejudice.[15]

It is apparent that any assumptions concerning the degree to which increased contact or association with Negroes decreases prejudice against

Negroes ... must take [the present] interpersonal contacts themselves and the roles of the persons involved as crucial conditions that affect the validity of such a hypothesis. Also policemen relate to Negroes as members of an organization, an organization with a belief system and goals of its own, rather than as individuals. This may be important in explaining their attitudes.[16]

Summary

The preceding extended discussion has sought to present support for the thesis that the problems of police operation and police-community relations inhere in certain crucial facets of the patrolman function, the conditions of patrolman-citizen interaction, and the character of police organization. Data used for some features of the argument are not fully adequate. Long-term panel studies of police patrolling different neighborhoods are necessary to determine whether and where the types of debilitation discussed here actually take place. Controlled invetigations of the attitudinal effects on citizens of their encounters with police are also needed. Nevertheless, the thesis has sufficient support to be taken seriously in assessing the feasibility of alternative proposals for mitigating police-community alienation.

Proposed Remedies

There are at least five broad (and traditional) classes of remedies put in operation or proposed for mitigating the problems between police and citizens. These include the following:

1. Recruitment of better qualified police.
2. Improvement in the capabilities of present personnel.
3. Development of community-police relations programs.
4. Provision of social services to community residents.
5. Increased citizen participation in monitoring of police activity and sanctioning of police misconduct.

A New Alternative

In the discussion to follow, an approach for mitigating police-citizen alienation will be presented which, it is believed, goes beyond efforts put forth to date. The approach assumes that the basic operations of police cannot be drastically altered. Thus, it seeks only to change the character of those who engage in these operations and to increase public trust in them. The approach also assumes that there are debilitating effects on patrolmen as a consequence of the tensions, hostilities, and dangers they encounter in patrol duty, and that these debilitating effects cannot be avoided. It therefore seeks to restrict the time which police must spend in this activity. While the approach is radical, it has precedent. It involves the drafting of young men to do police patrol work.[17]

The Conscription of Police Patrolmen

Some Administrative Requisites And Possibilities

No effort will be made to detail the mechanics of a police patrolman draft. There are several alternative approaches, each of which encounters certain problems. These problems would not be insurmountable if public and political support for the draft were present. In order to discuss the technical merits of the proposal, a brief overview is necessary.

As currently envisaged, the draft would apply at their 21st birthday to all males who meet normal police department qualifications with respect to physical and intelligence standards. While recent and serious offenders might be rejected, a past history of delinquency would not automatically disqualify an individual for service. In general, then, the characteristics of draftees would reflect those of their age group in the population. It is further assumed that the period of service would be approximately 30 months, with the first six months devoted to training. The draft would be conducted by the Federal Government and the tasks to which recruits would be assigned are those currently undertaken by patrolmen.[18] Obviously, the recruits will not be as experienced in patrol work as present personnel. We will shortly elaborate on the view that this may not be a serious problem. However, first we will discuss some major potential advantages of the system.

Training

One immediately apparent advantage of a police draft as outlined above is that police recruits will uniformly receive more training than is generally available to police recruits at the present time. Currently, reasonably adequate training is available for police recruits in only a relatively few law enforcement agencies. Within small jurisdictions particularly, staff training is either extremely limited or absent.[19]

Community Representativeness and Public Acceptance

A police draft—even one which excludes certain individuals because of their previous known delinquencies or crimes—should produce recruits whose racial and social class characteristics are far more representative of their age bracket than is currently true of police recruitment programs. Furthermore, the large size of the draftee pool, relative to the manpower needs of the military and law enforcement agencies, will permit the use of additional screening devices without destroying this representativeness. Thus, for example, only recruits who have whatever educational and personality attributes police administrators and public agree are important for police work would be assigned to it. Further, patrol areas can be assigned to recruits who represent the socio-economic character of the residents. This should help both to reduce black community criticism concerning bias in police recruitment and to insure that patrolmen are acquainted with and appreciate the norms and values found in the neighborhoods they patrol. Perhaps more important than these considerations, however, is the probable impact of recruitment by conscription on how the public will be *disposed* to view those who serve. Early in this paper the point was made that citizen critics view the shortcomings of law enforcement as due to the shortcomings of law enforcement personnel. These critics assume that certain personality types—the violence-prone, the bigot, the sadist—are attracted to police work and that, except in blatant cases, screening procedures are inadequate to weed them out. The second of these assumptions, as was noted earlier, is clearly true, and no strict evidence exists to deny the first. These considerations combine to permit suspicion of the fledgling policeman, whatever other redeeming features he might otherwise have. The fact that he *chose* to be a policeman is sufficient to cause doubt as to whether he could be a good policeman. Since patrolman recruits, under a draft system, would not be self-selected, a very strong basis for community suspicion of police would be removed.

Police Veterans and Public Relations

Inevitably, the great majority of police draftees will return to civilian life after their tour of duty. In time this will lead to a substantial number of police veterans among the general citizenry. As veterans they will be able to inform other citizens as to the problems, dilemmas, and compromises attending police work. As former draftees and current community members, they will have credibility. If police veterans come to regard their police experiences as worthy, the basis will exist to further community understanding and acceptance of police.

While it is impossible to estimate what percentage of police veterans have a favorable view of their law enforcement experience, two considerations suggest that this percentage will be greater than the percentage of service veterans who appreciate the merits of military duty. First the necessity of police work has been challenged less than that of making war, and second, the conditions attending police service are more desirable and comfortable than those accompanying military duty.

Limited Tours of Duty

The argument was made earlier in this paper that police patrol work, particularly in high crime areas, has debilitating effects on law enforcement personnel. These effects, in the form of increased prejudice and authoritarianism, were hypothesized to be the consequence of the adversarial and corrosive interactions police have with citizens. Several studies have been cited indicating similar effects in other settings among professionals whose jobs include responsibility for at times recalcitrant charges, and whose duties are not necessarily in the charges' perceived interests. In several of these studies, the point is raised that the mechanistic and punitive stance of workers might be altered, obviously enough, by reducing their work loads, relieving them of surveillance responsibilities, and increasing their service contacts with clients. None of these alternatives, however, is available to police patrolmen, whose primary responsibilities involve, and are seen to involve, control and the rendering of negative sanctions. One means for avoiding the long-term debilitating effects of policing a recalcitrant citizenry remains—that being to restrict the time during which individuals must perform this task. A police draft is obviously well suited to insure limited tours of duty. This is not to say that draftees would be prohibited from serving longer than the period of their conscription, a consideration we take up next.

Career Officers

At the present time police officers working in specialized bureaus or in supervisory jobs are recruited from the ranks of patrolmen. Under a police conscription system, these officers could be drawn out of the ranks of draftees who decide to make policing their career. This procedure would have three potential advantages. It would probably permit the selection of career officers from a much broader sample than is presently available. It would permit police administrators a longer period to scrutinize bottom-level personnel before approving their permanent status. And it would enable administrators to recruit for permanent duty individuals who meet more rigorous criteria than can be met by the average draftee, and which are met by few police under the present methods of recruitment.

Such personnel would be recruited in smaller numbers than are police patrolmen today. Furthermore, these personnel would have a substantially better opportunity for promotion than is the case for patrolmen today. Finally, for the above reasons, these personnel could receive at the outset, and could anticipate in the future, higher salaries than can patrolmen today. These considerations at least suggest that highly qualified personnel may be, more attracted to police work under a draft system than is true today.

A potential problem posed by the need to recruit permanent personnel should be noted. Such personnel might well remain in patrol work for some time as senior patrol officers, partners to inexperienced draftees, etc. To the extent that permanent personnel fill these roles, the less likely it is that the various possible advantages of the draft will be realized. Thus, the recruitment of permanent personnel must be carefully controlled.

Reducing the Isolation of Police

It was noted above that one probable consequence of a police draft will be to develop in time a group of police veterans in the community who can better interpret police problems and tasks to the citizenry. Conversely, another likely consequence is that the draft will help maintain the awareness and sensitivity of career personnel to the desires and concerns of the community. Career law enforcement personnel are relatively isolated from members of other occupational categories, and this fact has suggested to some analysts that police become unaware of and indifferent to the norms, values, and concerns of the general public.[20] The presence of short-term personnel in law enforcement whose ties are firmly rooted in the community may help break down this isolation and its attendant problems. In a recent essay supporting the drafting of patrolmen, Walinsky has noted that the draft has performed this function for the military.[21]

Problems of a Police Draft

Three major reservations of a short-term conscripted patrolman force can be identified.

Inexperience

The use of short job-tenure draftees might lessen the knowledge base of police in two ways. First, insofar as certain components of police patrol work can be perfected only through experience, conscripted police will be inevitably less than proficient in important skills. Second, insofar as quality police work requires intimate acquaintance with and knowledge about community residents, conscripted patrolmen will be saddled with the disadvantage of being essentially strangers.

The net effects of patrolmen operating under these presumed handicaps is not at all clear. The importance of experience for skill development is tempered, for example, by the fact that in several areas, the achievements of police are so limited that inexperienced police may do little worse. Thus, the arrest rates of patrolmen in New York City is less than one per month;[22] patrolmen's ability to provide special services is questioned by professionals;[23] and their understanding of the citizens they police is questioned by many, if not most, students of law enforcement. Furthermore, if there are measurable advantages of experience, they have not yet been clearly demonstrated. Thus, the validity and significance of the experience-skill link for patrol service may be overdrawn.

As for the argument that experience in a community provides patrolmen with knowledge crucial for the performance of their task, it is clear that if the thesis is valid, the conscripted, short-tenured recruit will be operating at a disadvantage. However, once again the argument is open to question. Reiss has written,

> The population in an area is often so large that no officer can know more than a very small proportion of its members . . . and then the high rate of mobility in urban populations—at least one in five changes his place of residence each year—similarly renders such knowledge less useful. . . . One can find other bases for questioning [this assumption] . . . . Thus, based on . . . Chicago data . . . beat cars are more likely to handle incidents outside their own area than within it.[24]

Furthermore, patrolmen generally spend little time outside their patrol cars; thus, they have little opportunity in any event to become acquainted with community residents. While some critics have argued that this problem can and must be dealt with by returning patrolmen to foot beats, this remedy has been questioned on the grounds that it would greatly lower the crime-fighting capacity of police. Again Reiss writes:

> There is good reason to believe that the foot patrolman responded primarily to citizen mobilizations [rather than radio dispatches]; he was relatively ineffective in dealing with crimes without citizen cooperation; he rarely discovered crimes in progress; and his capacity to prevent any crimes was extremely limited by his restricted mobility.[25]

Thus, while the drafted recruit may be limited in his knowledge of the community in which he patrols, much the same can be said of patrolmen today. And if Reiss' view is correct, there seems little chance that currently employed patrolmen can become more knowledgeable. The handicap of the conscripted patrolman again appears overdrawn.

Devotion to duty

A second question in the use of draftees as patrolmen concerns the degree to which they will be committed to performing the responsibilities of patrol work. In part this question is addressed to the willingness of draftees to take risks. But it also refers to their inclination to perform the routines of patrol work.

The possibility that conscripted patrolmen will not responsibly undertake these tasks stems from two considerations. First, since draftees do not voluntarily undertake their duty, they will lack the ideological commitment that some argue is required for carrying out the routine and dangerous tasks inherent in police patrol. Second, since draftees will not generally be interested in police careers, they will have little monetary and promotional incentives to adequately perform these tasks.

The problems posed by these considerations have serious implications. Again, however, the problems themselves may not prove to be so serious. Thus, military police are not generally expolicemen, volunteers, or highly experienced. Yet their patrol operations—admittedly somewhat simpler than those of urban police—are done with sufficient dispatch, thoroughness, and equity to avert the open and sustained criticism encountered by urban police. Second, the commitment to policing exhibited by patrolmen today is considerably less than that connoted by the premise giving rise to doubts about the operations of conscripted police. It has been noted, for example, that police patrolmen often avoid or limit performance in difficult circumstances when their actions cannot be observed.[26] Furthermore, according to Niederhoffer, police officers' commitment to patrol work and their service motivation is generally extinguished after five years of duty.[27] It is Niederhoffer's view that, while most police are initially committed to the goals of policing and to performing their duties, these requests for optimal performance are eventually erased by the problems and frustrations of patrol.

It should also be noted that while police draftees may engage in less than optimal performance, there are a number of inducements and sanctions available to insure, as in the case of present-day patrolmen, acceptable performance. These include increased pay for meritorious actions, the loss of post-service benefits for poor performance, and the array of punishments similar to those used by the military for failure to perform one's duty. The latter two sanctions have generally been sufficient to motivate draftees to perform duty under much more dangerous conditions than those encountered by police.

The legality of a police draft

A third major and in one sense the most crucial question to be raised regarding conscription for domestic police duty concerns its constitutionality. Military conscription has been challenged on the grounds that it violates the Thirteenth Amendment to the Constitution.[28] While the Supreme Court has denied these challenges, citing that *military* draft was a proper exercise of the delegated power given in Section 8 of the Constitution to raise and support an army, there is considerable doubt whether conscription for any other purpose would be found constitutional.[29]

There is, however, one approach to police conscription which may well be found constitutional. In a recent criticism of an early Twentieth Century Supreme Court decision supporting the constitutionality of a national military draft, Leon Friedman[30] has argued that while compulsory military service was intended by the framers of the Constitution, the sole draft authorized was into the states' militia. Furthermore, the early Congress, composed of many of the drafters of the Constitution, enacted the Militia Act of 1792, which provided for a state-regulated body in which "each free, able-bodied white male citizen" within certain age restrictions was required to serve. Each state could call upon its militia when necessary to quell disorder. Federal use of the various militia was provided for again in Article I, Section 8, of the Constitution.

> The Congress shall have Power to . . . provide for calling forth the Militia to execute the Laws of the Union, suppress insurrections and repel Invasions.

There is, then, some basis for assuming the constitutionality of a police draft structured under state militia powers.[31] The militia during the early years of the nation clearly utilized mandatory labor and was available to quell local disorders and, under the Constitution, to "execute the Laws of the Union." It is true that no full-time use of the militia was made in communities on an extended basis. However, expanding the militia obligation into full-time service for a set extended period would not seem to be any greater an extension of the states' power than was the federal draft into the regular army for fighting foreign wars. Establishing conscription for police duty at the state level would also be consistent with the present system of state and local organization and control of law enforcement agencies. It would, furthermore, be consistent with repeated court decisions that the police power belongs to the states.

Thus, the conscription of individuals for domestic police duty does not stand as clearly outside traditional practice in the United States as might be initially assumed. Either a national draft undertaken in behalf of the states or a state-by-state conscription might well be within the bounds of constitutionality.

Conclusion

The intent of this paper has been to show that police-citizen alienation will not be amenable to various currently suggested reforms because this alienation is itself a consequence of structural conditions not addressed by these reforms. An alternative reform proposed here admittedly represents a radical departure. It will be resisted by many patrolmen who will see their jobs threatened by the draft. It will be resisted by police generally, for the premises on which it is based are counter to those found among most law enforcement personnel, and because the current autonomy, power, and in-group solidarity of police will be lessened with the inclusion of draftees. While it will no doubt also encounter opposition from many police chiefs, a police draft does offer these administrators an alternative to the threats posed by the increasing unionization of police and, correspondingly, increased recalcitrance of law enforcement personnel to follow administrative direction. Others will also no doubt be unhappy with the draft; young people who now have an abiding antagonism toward police may well constitute, along with police, the most serious objectors.

Some groups may lessen their opposition as they become better acquainted with the concept of police conscription. The grandfather clause and the possibility of a supervisory position (along with a pay increase) may lessen the opposition of police. The recognition of the inevitable limitations of current remedies and the possible merits of a draft may bring about the support of youth. And the promise of increasing a police force at a comparatively low cost may bring about support from politicians and citizenry.

As noted earlier, it may seem untimely to advocate a program for conscripting policemen at a time when the federal government has phased out the military draft. Yet the merits and political acceptability of a police draft stand independently of those involved in military conscription. While police duty can be an alternative to military duty as suggested earlier, it need not be. Police conscription without military conscription only means fewer draftees. In any event, the proposal of a draft is made because it is the only approach known to this writer which has sufficient technical merit to suggest that it can cope with police-citizen alienation.

Radical remedies for social problems are not easily accepted and few are ever implemented. Nevertheless, when the conventional solutions have failed, only the radical remedies remain—unless, of course, we choose to live with our problems.

References

1. *Report of the National Advisory Commission on Civil Disorders* (New York: Bantam Books, 1968), p. 120.

2. Narcotics and vice squad personnel are exceptions to this. In other respects, however, the work of these officers is akin to that of other bureau personnel. For a more elaborate comparison of the working conditions of uniformed and nonuniformed police, see James Q. Wilson, *Varieties of Police Behavior* (Cambridge: Harvard University Press, 1968), pp. 7-10.

3. Report and Recommendations of the National Capital Area Civil Liberties Union. "A Police Department in Trouble: Racial Discrimination and Misconduct in the Police Department of Washington, D.C.," August 1, 1968, mimeo; Milton Rokeach, Martin G. Miller, and John A. Snyder, "The Value Gap Between Police and Polices," The Journal of Social Issues, 27, 2 (1971), pp. 155-171.

4. The President's Commission on Law Enforcement and the Admin-

istration of Justice—*The Challenge of Crime in a Free Society* (Washington, D.C.: Government Printing Office, 1967), pp. 103–106.

5. John McNamara, "Uncertainties in Police Work: The Relevance of Police Recruits' Backgrounds and Training," in David Bordua (ed.) *The Police* (New York; John Wiley & Sons, Inc., 1967), pp. 163–252; William A. Westley, "The Escalation of Violence Through Legitimation," *The Annals*, 364 (March, 1966), pp. 120–127; Arthur Niederhoffer, *Behind the Shield* (Garden City: Anchor Books, 1969), pp. 190–191.

6. Unnecessary force as used by Reiss includes such phenomena as assault by an officer and his subsequent failure to arrest; an officer's use of force in the absence of citizen resistance; an officer's use of force in response to resistance when alternative approaches were available, etc. A full listing is given in Albert J. Reiss, Jr. "Police Brutality—Answers to Key Questions," *Transaction*, 5 (July–August, 1968), pp. 10–19.

7. *Ibid.*, p. 18.

8. *Ibid.*, p. 17.

9. Donald J. Black and Albert J. Reiss, Jr., "Patterns of Behavior in Police and Citizen Transaction," in *Studies in Crime and Law Enforcement in Major Metropolitan Areas*, Vol. 2, pp. 132–139, (report submitted to the President's Commission on Law Enforcement and Administration of Justice, (undated), p. 32.

10. *Ibid.* Black and Reiss do not report the class position of those against whom verbal abuse was directed.

11. *Ibid.*, p. 55.

12. Black and Reiss, "Patterns of Behavior . . . ," *op. cit.*, p. 135.

13. Donald Bouma, *Kids and Cops* (Grand Rapids: William B. Eerdmans Publishing Company, 1969) pp. 103–104. Some of the variation in expressed prejudice found among these studies may be attributed to the manner in which data were collected. Bouma's findings in particular may be conservative in view of the fact that his data were obtained by questionnaire.

14. Black and Reiss, "Patterns of Behavior . . . ," *op. cit.*, pp. 135–137.

15. Morton Deutsch and Mary Collins, *Interracial Housing: A Psychological Evaluation of a Social Experiment* (Minneapolis: University of Minnesota Press, 1951).

16. Black and Reiss, "Patterns of Behavior . . . ," *op. cit.*, pp. 137–138.

17. Drafting young people for police patrol duty is practiced in at least two nations, Israel and Argentina.

18. It is probably a matter of some importance as to whether drafted police recruits should serve in their own or in other communities. There are apparent advantages and disadvantages in either alternative. If the drafting of police is thought to have sufficient merit to be considered for implementation, these alternatives might be compared empirically. Clearly alternatives in other aspects of implementation will also require testing.

19. The President's Commission on Law Enforcement and Administration of Justice—*Task Force Report: The Police* (Washington, D.C.: Government Printing Office, 1967), p. 36.

20. John D. Clark, "Isolation of the Police: A Comparison of the British

and American Situations," *Journal of Criminal Law, Criminology and Police Science,* 56 (September, 1965), pp. 307–319.

21. Adam Walinsky, "Proposal for a Fundamental Restricting of the Police," mimeo, undated.

22. Richard Reeves, "Police: Maybe They Should Be Doing Something Else," *New York Times—Week in Review* (January 24, 1971), p. 3.

23. Morton Bard, *Training Police as Specialists in Family Crisis Intervention* (Washington, D.C.: Government Printing Office, 1970).

24. Albert J. Reiss, Jr., *The Police and the Public* (New Haven and London: Yale University Press, 1971), p. 98.

25. *Ibid.,* p. 97.

26. *Ibid.,* p. 14.

27. Niederhoffer, *op. cit.,* p. 77.

28. I.e., "Neither slavery nor involuntary servitude, except as a punishment for crime whereof the party shall have been duly convicted, shall exist within the United States or any place subject to their jurisdictions."

29. The possibility that conscription for another purpose might be constitutional rests on the prior findings of the Supreme Court that various government-imposed duties such as jury duty, civilian work for conscientious objectors, and school attendance do not constitute involuntary servitude. See *Akers v. Handley,* 149 NE 2d 692, 238 Ind. 288 (1958); *In re Bacon,* 49 Cal. Reptr. 322, 339 (1966); and *U.S. v. Lebherz,* 129 F. Supp. 444 (DNJ 1955).

30. Leon Friedman, "Conscription and the Constitution: The Original Understanding," G7, *Michigan Law Review* (G493, 1969).

31. Barrett v. Richard, 124 N.W. 153 (1910).

Bibliography

Abbott, D.W., L.H. Gold, and E.T. Rogowsky. *Police, Politic, and Race: The New York City Referendum on Civilian Review.* Cambridge, Mass.: Harvard University Press, 1969.

Adams, Thomas F. *Law Enforcement: An Introduction to the Police Role in the Community.* Englewood Cliffs, N.J.: Prentice-Hall, 1968.

Ahern, James F. *Police in Trouble: Our Frightening Crisis in Law Enforcement.* New York: Hawthorne Books, 1972.

Aichorn, August. *Wayward Youth.* New York: Viking Press, 1969.

Alex, Nicholas. *Black in Blue: A Study of the Negro Policeman.* New York: Appleton-Century-Crofts, 1969.

Alinsky, Saul. *Reveille for Radicals.* Chicago: University of Chicago Press, 1946.

Allen, Rodney F., and Charles H. Adair. *Violence and Riots in Urban America.* Worthington, Ohio: Charles A. Jones, 1965.

Altshuler, Alan. *Community Control: The Black Demand for Participation in Large American Cities.* New York: Pegasus, 1970.

American Bar Association, Advisory Committee on the Police Function. *The Urban Police Function.* Chicago, 1972.

American Bar Association, Special Committee on Crime Prevention and Control. *Citizens Against Crime: A Crime Program for State and Local Bar Associations.* Chicago, 1968.

American Civil Liberties Union. *Secret Detention by the Chicago Police.* Glencoe, Ill.: The Free Press, 1959.

American Friends Service Committee. *Struggle for Justice: A Report on Crime and Punishment in America.* New York: Hill & Wang, Inc., 1971.

Anderson, Desmond L., ed. *Municipal Public Relations.* Chicago: International Managers Association, 1966.

Arnold, William R. *Juveniles on Parole: A Sociological Perspective.* New York: Random House, 1970.

605

606

Bibliography

Asch, Sidney H. *Police Authority and the Rights of the Individual.* New York: Arco, 1968.

Astor, Gerald. *The New York Cops.* New York: Scribner's, 1971.

Banfield, Edward C. *The Unheavenly City: The Nature and Future of Our Urban Crisis.* Boston: Little, Brown, 1970.

Banton, Michael. *Race Relations.* New York: Basic Books, 1968.

———. *The Policeman in the Community.* New York: Basic Books, 1964.

Barbour, Floyd B., ed. *The Black Power Revolt.* Boston: Porter Sargent, 1968.

———. *The Black Seventies.* Boston: Porter Sargent, 1970.

Bassiouni, M. Cherif. *Criminal Law and Its Processes: The Law of Public Order.* Springfield, Ill.: Charles C. Thomas, 1969.

———. *The Law of Dissent and Riots.* Springfield, Ill.: Charles C. Thomas, 1971.

Becker, Harold K. *Issues in Police Administration.* Metuchen, N.J.: Scarecrow Press, 1970.

———, and George T. Felkenes. *Law Enforcement: A Selected Bibliography.* Metuchen, N.J.: Scarecrow Press, 1968.

Becker, Howard S., ed. *Campus Power Struggle.* Chicago: Aldine, 1970.

Becker, Theodore L., and Vernon G. Murray, eds. *Government Lawlessness in America.* New York: Oxford University Press, 1971.

Bedau, Hugo Adam. *Civil Disobedience Theory and Practice.* New York: Pegasus, 1969.

Bell, Daniel, and Irving Kristol. *Confrontation: The Student Rebellion and the Universities.* New York: Basic Books, 1969.

Bellush, Jewell, and Stephen David. *Race and Politics in New York City: Six Case Studies in Policy Making.* New York: Praeger, 1970.

Bent, Alan Edward. *The Politics of Law Enforcement.* Lexington, Mass.: Lexington Books, 1974.

Berkley, George E. *The Democratic Policeman.* Boston: Beacon Press, 1969.

Bersani, Carl A. *Crime and Delinquency: A Reader.* New York: Macmillan, 1970.

Biderman, Albert D., L.A. Johnson, J. McIntyre, and A.W. Weir. *Report on a Pilot Study in the District of Columbia on Victimization and Attitudes toward Law Enforcement.* Washington, D.C.: U.S. Government Printing Office, 1967.

Bittner, Egon. *The Functions of Police in Modern Society.* Rockville, Md.: National Institute of Mental Health, 1970.

Black, Algernon D. *The People and the Police.* New York: McGraw-Hill, 1968.

Black, Donald J., and Albert J. Reiss, Jr. *Police and Citizen Behavior in Field Encounters: Some Comparisons According to the Race and Social Class Status of Citizens.* Ann Arbor, Mich.: University of Michigan Press, 1966.

Block, Herbert A., and Gilbert Geis. *Man, Crime, and Society.* New York: Random House, 1970.

Blumberg, Abraham S. *Criminal Justice.* Chicago: Quadrangle Books, 1967.

———, ed. *Law and Order: The Scales of Justice.* Chicago: Aldine, 1970.

Bonger, Willem (Abridged by Austin T. Turk). *Criminality and Economic Conditions.* Bloomington, Ind.: Indiana University Press, 1970.

———. *Race and Crime.* Trans. from Dutch by M.M. Hordyk. Montclair, New Jersey: Patterson Smith, 1969.

Bonjean, Charles M., Terry N. Clark, and Robert L. Lineberry, eds. *Community Politics: A Behavioral Approach.* New York: The Free Press, 1971.

Bopp, William J. *The Police Rebellion.* Springfield, Ill.: Charles C. Thomas, 1971.

Bordua, David J., ed. *The Police: Six Sociological Essays.* New York: John Wiley & Sons, 1967.

Boskin, Joseph. *Urban Racial Violence in the Twentieth Century.* Beverly Hills, Calif.: Glencoe Press, 1969.

Bouma, Donald. *Kids and Cops.* Grand Rapids, Mich.: William B. Eerdmans, 1969.

Bouma, Donald and James Hoffman. *The Dynamics of School Integration: Problems and Approaches in a Northern City.* Grand Rapids, Mich.: William B. Eerdmans, 1969.

Bragdon, Henry, and John C. Pittenger. *The Pursuit of Justice.* New York: Macmillan, 1969.

Brandstatter, A.F., and Louis A. Radelet. *Police and Community Relations: A Sourcebook.* Beverly Hills, Calif.: Glencoe Press, 1968.

Brennan, James, and Donald W. Olmstead. *Police Work With Delinquents: Analysis of a Training Program.* East Lansing: Social Sciences Research Bureau, Michigan State University, 1965.

Bristow, Allen P. *Effective Police Manpower Utilization.* Springfield, Ill.: Charles C. Thomas, 1969.

Brown, John, and Graham Howse, eds. *Police in the Community.* Lexington, Mass.: Lexington Books, 1975.

Brown, Michael. *The Politics and Anti-Politics of the Young.* Beverly Hills, Calif.: Glencoe Press, 1969.

Buckman, Peter. *The Limits of Protest.* New York: Bobbs-Merrill, 1970.

Buckner, H. Taylor. "The Police: The Culture of A Social Control Agency." Unpublished Ph.D. Dissertation, University of California, Berkeley, Calif., 1967.

Burpo, John H. *The Police Labor Movement: Problems and Perspectives.* Springfield, Ill.: Charles C. Thomas, 1971.

Caffi, Andrea. *A Critique of Violence.* New York: Bobbs-Merrill, 1970.

Cahalane, Cornelius and Frances. *The Policeman.* New York: Arno Press, 1970.

Cahn, Edgar S., ed. *Our Brother's Keeper: The Indian in White America.* New York: World Publishing Co., 1969.

California. Governor's Commission on the Los Angeles Riots. *Violence in the City: An End or a Beginning? Report on Watts Riot.* Sacramento, Cal.: Governor's Office, 1965.

California, University of, at Berkeley. *The Police and the Community.* Washington, D.C.: U.S. Government Printing Office, 1966.

Carlson, Ronald L. *Criminal Justice Procedure for Police.* Cincinnati: W.H. Anderson Co., 1970.

Carney, Frank J., Hans W. Mattick, and John A. Callaway. *Action on the Streets: A Handbook for Inner City Youth Work.* New York: Association Press, 1969.

Carter, Robert, and Leslie T. Wilkins. *Probation and Parole: Selected Readings.* New York: John Wiley & Sons, 1970.

Center for Research on Criminal Justice. *The Iron Fist and the Velvet Glove: An Analysis of the U.S. Police.* Berkeley, Calif.: Center for Research on Criminal Justice, 1975.

Challenge of Crime in a Free Society. President's Commission on Law Enforcement and Administration of Justice. Washington, D.C.: U.S. Government Printing Office, 1967.

Chambliss, William J. *Crime and the Legal Process.* New York: McGraw-Hill, 1968.

Chapman, S.G., and T.E. St. Johnston. *The Police Heritage in England and America: A Developmental Survey.* East Lansing, Michigan: Michigan State University, 1962.

Chappell, Duncan, and John Monahan, eds. *Violence and Criminal Justice.* Lexington, Mass.: Lexington Books, 1975.

Chevigny, Paul. *Cops and Rebels.* New York: Pantheon, 1972.

———. *Police Power.* New York: Pantheon, 1969.

Chicago Citizens' Committee to Study Police-Community Relations. *Police and the Public: A Critique and a Program* (A Final Report). Chicago, 1967.

Cicourel, Aaron V. *The Social Organization of Juvenile Justice.* New York: John Wiley & Sons, 1968.

Cincinnati, University of. *The Cincinnati Police-Juvenile Attitude Project.* Washington, D.C.: Office of Law Enforcement Assistance, 1968.

Civil Disorders After Action Reports. Washington, D.C.: International Association of Chiefs of Police, Professional Standards Division, 1968.

Cizon, Francis A., and William H.T. Smith. *Some Guidelines for Successful Police-Community Relations Training Programs.* Washington, D.C.: Office of Law Enforcement Assistance, U.S. Department of Justice, 1970.

Clark, Bernard J. *Police-Community Relations.* Huntsville, Texas: Sam Houston State University, Institute of Contemporary Corrections, 1969.

Clark, N. Terry. *Community Structure, Power, and Decision-Making: Comparative Analyses.* San Francisco: Chandler, 1968.

Clark, Ramsey. *Crime in America.* New York: Simon & Schuster, 1970.

Clift, Raymond E. *A Guide to Modern Police Thinking.* Cincinnati, Ohio: W.H. Anderson, 1970.

Coffey, Alan, Edward Eldefonso, and Walter Hartinger. *Human Relations: Law Enforcement in a Changing Community.* Englewood Cliffs, N.J.: Prentice-Hall, 1971.

———. *Police-Community Relations.* Englewood Cliffs, N.J.: Prentice-Hall, 1971.

Cohen, Bernard, and Jan M. Chaiken. *Police Background Characteristics and Performance.* Lexington, Mass.: Lexington Books, 1973.

Cohen, Bruce J., ed. *Crime in America.* Itasca, Ill.: Peacock, 1970.

Cohen, Nathan, ed. *The Los Angeles Riots: A Socio-Psychological Study.* New York: Praeger, 1970.

Cohn, Alvin W. *Crime and Justice Administration.* Philadelphia: J.B. Lippincott, 1976.

Commission on Community Interrelations. *Survey on Preparations for Urban Violence and Appendix: Special Study on Preparations for Urban Violence.* New York: American Jewish Congress, 1968.

Conant, Ralph W., and Molly Apple Levin, eds. *Problems in Research on Community Violence.* New York: Praeger, 1969.

Conklin, John E. *The Impact of Crime.* New York: Macmillan, 1975.

Connery, Robert H., and Caraley Demetrios, eds. *Governing the City: Challenges and Options for New York.* New York: Praeger, 1969.

Cray, Edward. *The Big Blue Line: Police Power versus Human Rights.* New York: Pantheon, 1969.

———. *The Enemy in the Streets: Police Malpractice in America.* New York: Doubleday Anchor, 1972.

Cressey, Donald R., and David A. Ward. *Delinquency, Crime, and Social Process.* New York: Harper & Row, 1969.

Crime Commission of Philadelphia. *Attack on Crime: Design of a Regional Approach to Law Enforcement in the Delaware Valley.* Philadelphia: Crime Commission of Philadelphia (mimeo), 1969.

Cromwell, Paul F., and George Keefer. *Police-Community Relations.* St. Paul, Minn.: West Publishing Co., 1973.

Cumming, Elaine. *Systems of Social Regulation.* New York: Atherton Press, 1968.

Curtis, Lynn. *Criminal Violence.* Lexington, Mass.: Lexington Books, 1975.

———. *Violence, Race, and Culture.* Lexington, Mass.: Lexington Books, 1975.

Dentler, Robert A. *American Community Problems.* New York: McGraw-Hill, 1968.

Denton, John H., ed. *Race and Property.* Berkeley, Calif.: Diablo Press, 1964.

Deutsch, Albert. *The Trouble with Cops.* New York: Cranon Publishers, 1954.

Detroit Urban League. *A Survey of Attitudes of Detroit Negroes After the Riot of 1967.* Detroit: The Detroit Urban League, 208 Mack Avenue, Detroit, Michigan, 1967.

Deutsch, Albert. *The Trouble with Cops.* New York: Cranon Publishers, 1954. *in the Process of Stigmatization and Societal Reaction.* New York: Oxford University Press, 1969.

Dinitz, Simon, and Walter Reckless. *Critical Issues in the Study of Crime.* New York: Little, Brown, 1968.

Douglas, William O. *Points of Rebellion.* New York: Random House, 1969.

Downs, Anthony. *Who Are the Urban Poor?* New York: Committee for Economic Development, 1970.

Drapkin, Israel, and Emilio Viano, eds. *Crimes, Victims, and Justice* (volume III in the series Victimology: A New Focus). Lexington, Mass.: Lexington Books, 1975.

Dressler, David. *Practice and Theory of Probation and Parole.* New York: Columbia University Press, 1970.

DuBois, W.E.B. *Dusk of Dawn: An Essay Toward an Autobiography of a Race Concept.* New York: Schocken Books, 1969.

Durham, Lewis E., Jack R. Gibbs, and Eric S. Knowles. *A Bibliography of Research—Explorations in Human Relations Training and Research.* Washington, D.C.: National Institute for Applied Behavioral Science, 1967.

Dynes, Russell R. *Organized Behavior in Disaster.* Lexington, Mass.: Heath Lexington Books, 1970.

Earle, Howard H. *Police-Community Relations: Crisis in Our Time*, 2d ed. Springfield, Ill.: Charles C. Thomas, 1970.
———. *Student-Instructor Guide on Police-Community Relations*. Springfield, Il'.: Charles C. Thomas, 1970.
———. *Police Recruit Training: Stress vs. Non-Stress*. Springfield, Ill.: Charles C. Thomas, 1973.
Eastman, George D., ed. *Municipal Police Administration*. 6th ed. Washington, D.C.: International City Management Association, 1969.
Edwards, George. *The Police on the Urban Frontier: A Guide to Community Understanding*. New York: Institute of Human Relations Press, The American Jewish Committee, 1968.
Eisner, Victor. *The Delinquency Label: The Epidemiology of Juvenile Delinquency*. New York: Random House, 1968.
Eldefonso, Edward. *Youth Problems and Law Enforcement*. Englewood Cliffs, N.J.: Prentice-Hall, 1972.
Eldefonso, Edward, Alan Coffey, and Richard C. Grace. *Principles of Law Enforcement*. New York: John Wiley & Sons, 1968.
Elliott, J.F. and Thomas J. Sardino. *Crime Control Team: An Experiment in Municipal Police Department Management and Operations*. Springfield, Ill.: Charles C. Thomas, 1971.
Ellis, William W. *White Ethics and Black Power: The Emergence of the West Side Organization*. Chicago: Aldine, 1969.
Empey, LaMar T. *The Silverlake Experiment: Testing Delinquency Theory and Community Intervention*. Chicago: Aldine, 1971.
Empey, LaMar T. and Steven G. Lubeck. *Delinquency Prevention Strategies*. Washington, D.C.: U.S. Government Printing Office, 1970.
Endleman, Shalom. *Violence in the Streets*. Chicago: Quadrangle Books, 1970.
Ennis, P.H. *Criminal Victimization in the United States*. Washington, D.C.: U.S. Government Printing Office, 1967.
Epstein, Charlotte. *Intergroup Relations for Police Officers*. Baltimore, Md.: Williams and Wilkins, 1962.
Etzioni, Amitai. *The Active Society: A Theory of Societal and Political Processes*. New York: The Free Press, 1968.
Etzkowitz, Henry, and Gerald M. Schaflander. *Ghetto Crisis: Riots or Reconciliation?* Boston: Little, Brown, 1969.
Fantini, Mario, Marilyn Gittell, and Richard Magat. *Community Control and the Urban School*. New York: Praeger. 1970.
Field, Arthur J. *Urban Power Structures: Problems in Theory and Research*. Cambridge, Mass.: Schenkman, 1970.
Fink, Joseph, and Lloyd G. Sealy. *The Community and the Police—Conflict or Cooperation?* New York: John Wiley & Sons, 1974.
Flacks, Richard, ed. *Conformity, Resistance, and Self-Determination: The Individual and Authority*. Boston: Little, Brown, 1973.
Flammang, C.J. *The Police and the Underprotected Child*. Springfield, Ill.: Charles C. Thomas, 1970.
Fleisher, Leslie A. *Police-Community Relations*. Chapel Hill, N.C.: University of North Carolina Institute of Government, 1967.

Fortas, Abe. *Concerning Dissent and Civil Disobedience—We Have an Alternative to Violence.* New York: Signet Books, New American Library, 1968.

Fosdick, Raymond B. *Crime in America and the Police.* New York: Century Corporation, 1920.

Freeman, Howard, and Norman R. Kurtz, eds. *America's Troubles: A Casebook in Social Conflict.* Englewood Cliffs, N.J.: Prentice-Hall, 1969.

Freeman, Linton C., and Morris H. Sunshine. *Patterns of Residential Segregation.* Cambridge, Mass.: Schenkman, 1969.

Friedman, Leon, ed. *Southern Justice.* New York: Pantheon, 1965.

Friendly, Alfred, and Ronald Goldfarb. *Crime and Publicity: The Impact of News on the Administration of Justice.* New York: Twentieth Century Fund, 1967.

Gagnon, John H., and William G. Simon, eds. *Sexual Conduct: The Social Sources of Human Sexuality.* Chicago: Aldine, 1973.

——. *The Sexual Scene.* Chicago: Aldine, 1970.

Galvin, Raymond, and Louis Radelet. *A National Survey of Police and Community Relations.* East Lansing, Mich.: Michigan State University, 1967.

Gans, Herbert J. *Levittowners:* Ways of Life and Politics in a New Suburban Community. New York: Pantheon, 1967.

——. *The Urban Villagers.* New York: The Free Press, 1962.

Ganz, Alan S., et al. *The Cities and the Police.* Chicago: The University of Chicago Round Table, 1968.

Garabedian, Peter G., and Don C. Gibbons, eds. *Becoming Delinquent: Correctional Process and Delinquent Careers.* Chicago: Aldine, 1970.

Gardiner, J.A. *The Politics of Corruption: Organized Crime in an American City.* New York: Russell Sage Foundation, 1970.

——, and Michael Mulkey. *Crime and Criminal Justice: Issues in Public Policy-Making.* Lexington, Mass.: Lexington Books, 1975.

Gardner, Erle Stanley. *Cops on Campus and Crime in the Streets.* New York: William Morrow, 1970.

Geary, David P., ed. *Community Relations and the Administration of Justice.* New York: John Wiley & Sons, 1975.

Germann, A.C. *The Problem of Police-Community Relations: A Report Prepared for the Task Force on Law and Law Enforcement.* Washington, D.C.: National Commission on the Causes and Prevention of Violence, 1968.

——, Frank D. Day, and Robert G. Gallati. *Introduction to Law Enforcement,* rev. ed. Springfield, Ill.: Charles C. Thomas, 1969.

Gibbons, Don C. *Delinquent Behavior.* Englewood Cliffs, N.J.: Prentice-Hall, 1970.

——. *Society, Crime, and Criminal Careers: An Introduction to Criminology.* Englewood Cliffs, N.J.: Prentice-Hall, 1968.

Glaser, Daniel, ed. *Crime in the City.* New York: Harper & Row, 1970.

Gold, Martin. *Delinquent Behaviors in an American City.* Belmont, Calif.: Brooks-Cole, 1970.

Goldsmith, Jack, and Sharon Goldsmith. *The Police Community.* Pacific Palisades, Calif.: Palisades, 1974.

Goldstein, Herman. *The Police Function in an Urban Society.* Proceedings of the September 1965 conference of the International City Managers' Association, 1965.

Gourley, G. Douglas. *Effective Municipal Police Organization.* Beverly Hills, Calif.: Glencoe Press, 1971.

———. *Public Relations and the Police.* Springfield, Ill.: Charles C. Thomas, 1953.

Grimshaw, Allen D., ed. *Racial Violence in the United States.* Chicago: Aldine-Atherton, 1971.

Grupp, Stanley E. *Theories of Punishment.* Bloomington, Ind.: Indiana University Press, 1972.

Hadden, Jeffrey K., et al. *A Time to Burn? An Evaluation of the Present Crisis in Race Relations.* Chicago: Rand McNally, 1969.

Hahn, Harlan. *Police in Urban Society.* Beverly Hills, Calif.: Sage, 1970.

Halpern, Stephen. *Police-Association and Department Leaders.* Lexington, Mass.: Lexington Books, 1974.

Hannerz, Ulf. *Soulside: Inquiries Into Ghetto Culture and Community.* New York: Columbia University Press, 1970.

Hansen, David A., and Thomas R. Culley. *The Police Leader.* Springfield, Ill.: Charles C. Thomas, 1971.

Harris, Richard. *Justice: The Crisis of Law, Order and Freedom in America.* New York: E.P. Dutton, 1970.

———. *The Fear of Crime.* New York: Frederick A. Praeger, 1969.

———. *The Police Academy: An Inside View.* New York: John Wiley & Sons, 1973.

Hazard, Geoffrey C. *Law in a Changing America.* Englewood Cliffs, N.J.: Prentice-Hall, 1969.

Headley, Joel T. *The Great Riots of New York: 1712–1873.* Indianapolis: Bobbs-Merrill Co., 1970.

Hewitt, William H. *British Police Administration.* Springfield, Ill.: Charles C. Thomas, 1965.

———, and Charles L. Newman. *Police-Community Relations: An Anthology and a Bibliography.* Mineola, N.Y.: Foundation Press, 1970.

Hirschi, Travis. *Causes of Delinquency.* Berkeley: University of California Press, 1969.

Hodge, Robert W. *The Public, the Police, and the Administration.* Chicago: National Opinion Research Center, 1965.

Hofstadter, Richard, and Michael Wallace, eds. *American Violence: A Documentary History.* New York: Alfred A. Knopf, 1970.

Holcomb, Richard L. *The Police and the Public.* Springfield, Ill.: Charles C. Thomas, 1964.

Holmgren, R. Bruce. *Primary Police Functions.* New York: William Capp, 1962.

Hopkins, Ernest, Jr. *Our Lawless Police: A Study of the Unlawful Enforcement of the Law.* New York: Viking, 1931.

Hormachea, C.R., and M. Hormachea. *Confrontation: Violence and the Police.* Boston: Holbrook Press, 1971.

Horwitz, John J. *Team Practice and the Specialist: An Introduction to Interdisciplinary Teamwork.* Springfield, Ill.: Charles C. Thomas, 1970.

Howard, John R., ed. *Awakening Minorities: American Indians, Mexicans, Puerto Ricans.* Chicago: Aldine, 1970.

Huenfeld, John. *The Community Activist's Handbook.* Boston: Beacon Press, 1974.

Hunter, Floyd. *Community Power Structure.* New York: Doubleday, 1963.

Iannone, Nathan F. *Supervision of Police Personnel.* Englewood Cliffs, N.J.: Prentice-Hall, 1970.

Inbau, Fred E., and James R. Thompson. *Administration of Criminal Justice.* Mineola, New York: Foundation Press, 1970.

International Association of Chiefs of Police. *Current Approaches: Police Training and Community Relations: Survey Supplement.* Washington, D.C., 1965.

——, and U.S. Conference of Mayors. *Police-Community Relations, Policies and Practices: A National Survey.* Washington, D.C., 1965.

International City Managers Association. *Police-Community Relations Programs.* Washington, D.C., 1967.

Jackson, Bruce. *In the Life: Versions of the Criminal Experience.* New York: Holt, Rinehart and Winston, 1972.

Jacob, Herbert. *Urban Justice: Law and Order in American Cities.* Englewood Cliffs, N.J.: Prentice-Hall, 1973.

Jacobs, Paul. *Prelude to Riot: A View of Urban America From the Bottom.* New York: Random House, 1968.

Janowitz, Morris. *Social Control of Escalated Riots.* Chicago: The University of Chicago Center for Policy Study, 1968.

Jeffrey, C. Ray. *Crime Prevention through Environmental Design.* Beverly Hills, Calif.: Sage Publications, 1971.

Jemilo, Robert F. *A Ten Point Program on Police-Community Relations: Planned Aggressive Prevention.* Chicago: The Young Men's Christian Association of Metropolitan Chicago, 1966.

Jenkins, Robert. *Keeping the Peace.* New York: Harper and Row, 1970.

Johnson, Elmer Hubert. *Crime, Correction and Society.* rev. ed. Homewood, Ill.: Dorsey Press, 1969.

Johnston, Norman, Leonard Savitz, and Marvin E. Wolfgang, eds. *The Sociology of Punishment & Corrections.* New York: John Wiley & Sons, 1970.

Jordan, Philip D. *Frontier Law and Order.* Lincoln, Neb.: University of Nebraska Press, 1970.

Juris, Hervey A., and Peter Feuille. *Police Unionism.* Lexington, Mass.: Lexington Books, 1973.

Justice, Blair. *Assessing Potentials for Racial Violence.* Houston: Rice University, 1968.

Kain, John F. *Race and Poverty: The Economics of Discrimination.* Englewood Cliffs, N.J.: Prentice-Hall, 1969.

Kavolis, Vytautas. *Comparative Perspectives on Social Problems.* Boston: Little, Brown, 1969.

Kay, Barbara A., and Clyde B. Vedder. *Probation and Parole.* Springfield, Ill.: Charles C. Thomas, 1969.

Keller, Oliver J. Jr., and Benedict S. Alper. *Halfway Houses: Community-Centered Correction and Treatment.* Lexington, Mass.: D.C. Heath, 1970.

Keller, Suzanne. *The Urban Neighborhood.* New York: Random House, 1968.

Kenney, John P. *Police Administration.* Springfield, Ill.: Charles C. Thomas, 1972.

Kenney, John P. and Dan G. Pursuit. *Police Work With Juveniles.* Springfield, Ill.: Charles C. Thomas, 1969.

Killinger, George G., and Paul F. Cromwell, Jr. *Issues in Law Enforcement.* Boston: Holbrook Press, 1975.

Klein, Herbert T. *The Police: Damned If They Do—Damned If They Don't.* New York: Brown Publishers, 1969.

Klein, Malcolm W., and Barbara G. Myerhoff, eds. *Juvenile Gangs in Context: Theory Research and Action.* Englewood Cliffs, N.J.: Prentice-Hall, 1967.

Klonoski, J.R., and R.I. Mendelsohn, eds. *The Politics of Local Justice.* Boston: Little, Brown, 1970.

Klotter, John C. *Constitutional Law for Police.* Cincinnati: W.H. Anderson, 1970.

Knapp, Whitman. *The Knapp Commission Report on Police Corruption.* New York: George Braziller, 1973.

Knopf, Terry Ann. *Youth Patrols: An Experiment in Community Participation.* Waltham, Mass.: Brandeis University, the Lemberg Center for the Study of Violence, 1969.

Knudten, Richard D., and Stephen Schafer. *Juvenile Delinquency: A Reader.* New York: Random House, 1970.

Kobetz, Robert W. *The Police Role and Juvenile Delinquency.* Gaithersberg, Md.: International Association of Chiefs of Police, 1971.

Kooken, Don L. *Ethics in Police Service.* Springfield, Ill.: Charles C. Thomas, 1957.

Kotler, Milton. *Neighborhood Government: The Local Foundations of Political Life.* Indianapolis: The Bobbs-Merrill Co., 1969.

LaFave, Wayne R. *Arrest: The Decision to Take a Suspect into Custody.* Boston: Little, Brown, 1965.

Lambert, John R. *Crime, Police and Race Relations.* New York: Oxford University Press, 1970.

Landesco, J. *Organized Crime in Chicago.* Chicago: University of Chicago Press, 1968.

Lane, R. *Policing the City: Boston, 1822–1885.* Cambridge, Mass.: Harvard University Press, 1967.

Lansberry, J. Robert. *Introduction to Criminal Justice.* Santa Cruz, Calif.: Davis Publishing Co., 1968.

Larson, Richard C. *Urban Police Patrol Analysis.* Cambridge, Mass.: MIT Press, 1972.

Law-Medicine Institute, Boston University. *Police-Community Relations Proj-*

ect: Pilot Project. Boston: Boston University, Law-Medicine Institute, Training Center in Youth Development, 1966.

Lawler, Irvin D. *Training Program in Human Relations for Cadet and In-Service Officers.* Detroit: Detroit Police Department, 1952.

Lawyers' Committee for Civil Rights Under Law. *Proceedings: Planning Sessions on Police-Community Relations.* Washington, D.C. 1967.

———. *Police-Community Relations: Selected Bibliography.* Washington, D.C., 1968.

———. *An Experiment in Using Legal Skills to Reduce Police-Community Hostility.* Washington, D.C., 1970.

Lee, Alfred McClung, and Norman D. Humphrey. *Race Riot: Detroit, 1943.* New York: Octagon, 1968.

Lefcourt, Robert, ed. *Law Against the People: Essays to De-mystify Law, Order, and the Courts.* New York: Vintage, 1971.

Leinwand, Gerald. *The Police.* New York: Pocket Books, 1972.

Leonard, V.A. *Police Crime Prevention.* Springfield, Ill.: Charles C. Thomas, 1971.

———. *The Police Enterprise: Its Organization and Management.* Springfield, Ill.: Charles C. Thomas, 1969.

———. *The Police, the Judiciary, and the Criminal.* Springfield, Ill.: Charles C. Thomas, 1969.

———, and Harry W. More. *Police Organization and Management.* 3rd ed. Mineola, New York: Foundation Press, 1971.

Lerman, Paul, ed. *Delinquency and Social Policy.* New York: Praeger, 1970.

Liebert, Lisa. *Police-Community Relations and the Role of the Non-Professional.* New York: New York University, New Careers Development Center, 1968.

Liebow, Elliot. *Tally's Corner: A Study of Negro Streetcorner Men.* Boston: Little, Brown, 1968.

Lincoln, James. *Anatomy of a Riot.* New York: McGraw-Hill, 1968.

Lindenfeld, Frank. *Radical Perspectives on Social Problems.* New York: Macmillan, 1973.

Lipset, Seymour Martin, and P.G. Altbach, eds. *Students in Revolt.* Boston: Houghton Mifflin, 1970.

Lipsky, Michael, ed. *Law and Order: Police Encounters.* Chicago: Aldine, 1970.

Lofland, John. *Deviance and Identity.* Englewood Cliffs, N.J.: Prentice-Hall, 1969.

Lohman, Joseph D. *The Police and Minority Groups.* Chicago: Chicago Park Police, 1947.

———, and Gordon E. Misner. *The Police and the Community: The Dynamics of Their Relationship in a Changing Society; Field Surveys IV.* Vols. 1, 2. Washington, D.C.: U.S. Government Printing Office, 1967.

Lowenthal, David, ed. *Environmental Perception and Behavior.* Chicago: University of Chicago, Geography Research Paper No. 109, 1967.

Mack, Raymond W. *Prejudice and Race Relations.* Chicago: Quadrangle Books, 1970.

MacNamara, Donald E., and Marc Riedel. *Police: Perspectives, Problems, Prospects.* New York: Praeger, 1974.

Marx, Gary T. *Protest and Prejudice.* New York: Harper and Row, 1967.

——, and Dane Archer. *Community Police Patrols: An Exploratory Inquiry.* Cambridge: Harvard University and MIT, 1972.

Masotti, Louis H., and Don R. Bowen. *Riots and Rebellion: Civil Violence in the Urban Community.* Beverly Hills, Calif.: Sage Publications, 1968.

Masotti, Louis H., and Jerome Corsi. *Shoot-Out in Cleveland: Black Militants and the Police, July 23, 1968.* New York: Praeger, 1969.

Matza, David. *Becoming Deviant.* Englewood Cliffs, N.J.: Prentice-Hall, 1969.

McCall, George, ed. *Social Relationships.* Chicago: Aldine Press, 1970.

McGehee, A. Lee. *Police Literature: An Annotated Bibliography.* Athens, Ga.: Institute of Government, University of Georgia, 1970.

McLennan, Barbara N. *Crime in Urban Society.* New York: Dunellen, 1970.

McPherson, James Alan. *Hue and Cry.* New York: Fawcett World Library, 1970.

Mendelson, Wallace. *Discrimination.* Englewood Cliffs, N.J.: Prentice-Hall, 1962.

Methvin, Eugene H. *The Riot Makers.* New Rochelle, N.Y.: Arlington House, 1970.

Meyerson, Martin, ed. *The Conscience of the City.* New York: George Braziller, 1970.

Michelson, William. *Man and His Urban Environment.* Reading, Mass.: Addison-Wesley, 1970.

Michigan State University at East Lansing. *A National Survey of Police and Community Relations.* Washington, D.C.: U.S. Government Printing Office, 1967.

Milio, Nancy, *9226 Kercheval: The Storefront That Did Not Burn.* Ann Arbor, Mich.: University of Michigan Press, 1970.

Miller, Martin G. *A Bibliography on Police and Community Relations.* East Lansing, Michigan: National Center on Police and Community Relations, School of Public Administration and Public Safety, Michigan State University, 1966.

Mills, James. *Report to the Commissioner.* New York: Pocket Books, 1973.

Misner, Gordon E. *The Development of "New Careerist" Positions in the Richmond Police Department.* Walnut Creek, Calif.: Contra Costa Council of Community Services, 1966.

Mitchell, J. Paul. *Race Riots in Black and White.* Englewood Cliffs, N.J.: Prentice-Hall, 1970.

Momboisse, Raymond M. *Blueprint of Revolution: The Rebel, The Party, the Techniques of Revolt.* Springfield, Ill.: Charles C. Thomas, 1970.

——. *Community Relations and Riot Prevention.* Springfield, Ill.: Charles C. Thomas, 1970.

——. *Riots, Revolts and Insurrections.* Springfield, Ill.: Charles C. Thomas, 1970.

More, Harry W., ed. *Critical Issues in Law Enforcement.* Cincinnati: W.H. Anderson, 1972.

Morris, Joe Alex. *First Offender: A Volunteer Program for Youth in Trouble With the Law.* New York: Funk & Wagnalls, 1970.

Morris, Norval,. and Gordon Hawkins. *The Honest Politician's Guide to Crime Control.* Chicago: University of Chicago Press, 1970.

Moynihan, Daniel Patrick. *Maximum Feasible Misunderstanding: Community Action in the War on Poverty.* New York: The Free Press, 1969.

———. *Toward a National Urban Policy.* New York: Basic Books, 1970.

———. *Violent Crime: The Challenge to Our Cities. The Report of the National Commission on the Causes and Prevention of Violence.* New York: George Braziller, 1970.

Munro, Jim L. *Administrative Behavior and Police Organization.* Cincinnati: W.H. Anderson, 1974.

Murphy, Jeffrey G., ed. *Civil Disobedience and Violence.* Belmont, Calif.: Wadsworth, 1971.

Murphy, Thomas P., and F. Gerald Brown. *Emerging Patterns in Urban Administration.* Lexington, Mass.: Heath Lexington Books, D.C. Heath Co., 1970.

Myren, Richard A. *The Role of the Police.* Submitted to the President's Commission on Law Enforcement and Administration of Justice. Washington, D.C.: U.S. Government Printing Office, 1967.

———, and Lynn D. Swanson. *Police Work with Children: Perspectives and Principles.* Washington, D.C.: U.S. Department of Health, Education, and Welfare, Children's Bureau, 1962.

Nagel, Stuart S. ed. *Law and Social Change.* Beverly Hills, Calif.: Sage Publications, 1970.

National Advisory Commission on Civil Disorders. *Report* (A Bantam Book: Z4273). New York: New York *Times* Company, 1968.

National Advisory Commission on Criminal Justice Standards and Goals. *A National Strategy to Reduce Crime* and *Police.* Washington, D.C.: U.S. Government Printing Office, 1973.

National Center on Police and Community Relations of the School of Police Administration and Public Safety. Michigan State University. *A National Survey of Police and Community Relations–Field Surveys V.* Washington, D.C.: U.S. Government Printing Office, 1967.

National Commission on Causes and Prevention of Violence. See under U.S. listings.

National Council on Crime and Delinquency. *Juvenile Justice Confounded: Pretentions and Realities of Treatment Services.* Paramus, N.J.: National Council on Crime and Delinquency, 1972.

National Institute of Law Enforcement and Criminal Justice, U.S. Department of Justice, LEAA. *Police Training and Performance Study.* Washington, D.C.: U.S. Government Printing Office, 1970.

Negro and the City. (Adapted from a Special Issue of *Fortune* on: "Business and the Urban Crisis.") New York: Time-Life Books, 1968.

Neighborhood Youth Corps. Washington, D.C.: U.S. Government Printing Office, 1969.

Nelli, Humbert S. *The Italians in Chicago.* New York: Oxford University Press, 1970.

New Jersey. *Governor's Select Commission on Civil Disorder: Report for Action.* Trenton, N.J., 1968.

New Jersey Police Training Commission. *Survey of Community Expectations of Police Service: A Pilot Survey.* Trenton, 1969.

Newman, Oscar. *Defensible Space: Crime Prevention through Urban Design.* New York: Macmillan, 1972.

Niederhoffer, Arthur. *Behind the Shield: The Police in Urban Society.* Garden City: Doubleday, 1967.

——. *The Police Family.* Lexington, Mass.: Lexington Books, 1975.

——, and Abraham S. Blumberg. *The Ambivalent Force: Perspectives on the Police.* Waltham, Mass.: Ginn & Co., 1970.

——, and Alexander Smith. *New Directions in Police Community Relations.* San Francisco: Rinehart Press, 1970.

Nielsen, Swven C. *General Organizational and Administrative Concepts for University Police.* Springfield, Ill.: Charles C. Thomas, 1971.

Nisbet, Robert A. *Community and Power.* New York: Oxford University Press, 1962.

——. *The Quest for Community.* New York: Oxford University Press, 1953.

Norman, Sherwood. *The Youth Service Bureau: A Key to Delinquency Prevention.* Paramus, New Jersey: National Council on Crime and Delinquency, 1972.

Norrgard, David L. *Regional Law Enforcement.* Chicago: Public Administration Service, 1969.

Norris, Donald F. *Police-Community Relations: A Program that Failed.* Lexington, Mass.: Lexington Books, 1973.

O'Connor, George W., and Charles G. Vanderbosch. *The Patrol Operation.* Washington, D.C.: International Association of Chiefs of Police, 1967.

——, and Nelson A. Watson. *Juvenile Delinquency and Youth Crime, the Police Role, An Analysis of: Philosophy, Policy, Opinion.* Gaithersburg, Md.: International Association of Chiefs of Police, 1965.

Operation Open City, New York Urban League. *Enforcing Open Housing.* New York: Friends of Operation Open City, 1970.

Oppenheimer, Martin. *The Urban Guerilla.* Chicago: Quadrangle Books, 1970.

Oppenheimer, Martin, and George Lakey. *A Manual for Direct Action.* Chicago: Quadrangle Books, 1969.

Ostrom, Elinor, et al. *Community Organization and the Provision of Police Services.* Beverly Hills, Calif.: Sage Publications, 1973.

Park, Robert E. *On Social Control and Collective Behavior.* Chicago: University of Chicago Press, 1967.

——, Ernest W. Burgess, and Roderick McKenzie. *The City*, 4th ed. Chicago: University of Chicago Press, 1967.

Patrick, Clarence H. *The Police, Crime and Society.* Springfield, Ill.: Charles C. Thomas, 1971.

People of Watts. *The Aftermath.* New York: Grove Press, 1969.

Peper, John P. *Public Relations for Law Enforcement Officers.* Sacramento, Calif.: California State Department of Education, 1965.

Perry, David C., and Paula A. Sornoff. *Politics at the Street Level: The Select Case of Police Administration and the Community.* Beverly Hills, Calif.: Sage Publications, 1973.

Pilisuk, Marc, ed. *Poor Americans: How the Poor White Live.* Chicago: Aldine, 1970.

Platt, Anthony, and Lynn Cooper. *Policing America.* Englewood Cliffs, N.J.: Prentice-Hall, 1975.

Police and the Civil Rights Act. Gaithersberg, Md.: International Association of Chiefs of Police, 1965.

Police, the Community, and You. Washington, D.C.: Women's International League for Peace and Freedom, 120 Maryland Avenue, N.E., 20002, 1968.

Pomrenke, Norman E., ed. *Police-Community Relations.* Chapel Hill, N.C.: University of North Carolina Institute of Government, 1966.

Portune, Robert G. *Changing Adolescent Attitudes Toward Police.* Cincinnati: W.H. Anderson, 1971.

Poston, Richard W. *The Gang and the Establishment.* New York: Harper & Row, 1971.

Preiss, J.J., and H.I. Ehrlich. *An Examination of Role Theory: The Case of the State Police.* Lincoln, Neb.: University of Nebraska Press, 1966.

President's Commission on Law Enforcement and Administration of Justice. *Task Force Report: The Police.* Washington, D.C.: U.S. Government Printing Office, 1967.

Quinney, Richard. *Crime and Justice in Society.* Boston: Little, Brown, 1969.

———. *The Problem of Crime.* New York: Dodd, Mead, 1973.

———. *The Social Reality of Crime.* Boston: Little, Brown, 1970.

Radano, Gene. *Walking the Beat.* Cleveland: World Publishing Co., 1968.

Radelet, Louis A. *The Police and the Community.* Beverly Hills, Calif.: Glencoe Press, 1973.

———. *The Police and the Community: Studies.* Beverly Hills, Calif.: Glencoe Press, 1973.

Radzinowicz, Leon, and Marvin E. Wolfgang, eds. *Crime and Justice.* 3 vols. New York: Basic Books, 1972.

Raine, W.J. *The Perception of Police Brutality in South Central Los Angeles.* Los Angeles: University of California Institute of Government and Public Affairs, 1967.

Rainwater, Lee. *Behind Ghetto Walls: Black Family Life in a Federal Slum.* Chicago: Aldine, 1970.

Rapoport, Roger, and Laurence J. Kirshbaum. *Is the Library Burning?* New York: Random House, 1970.

Reasons, Charles E., and Jack L. Kuykendall, eds. *Race, Crime and Justice.* Pacific Palisades, Calif.: Goodyear, 1972.

Rechy, John. *City of Night.* New York: Grove Press, 1963.

Reiss, Albert J., Jr. *The Police and the Public.* New Haven: Yale University Press, 1971.

———. *Studies in Crime and Law Enforcement in Major Metropolitan Areas.* vols. 1 and 2. *Field Surveys III.* Washington, D.C.: U.S. Government Printing Office, 1967.

Report of the National Advisory Commission on Civil Disorders. Washington, D.C.: U.S. Government Printing Office, 1968.

Richardson, James F. *Urban Police in the United States.* Port Washington, N.Y.: Kennikat Press, 1974.

Risso, Peter H., ed. *Ghetto Revolts.* Chicago: Aldine, 1970.

Rose, Arnold. *The Power Structure.* New York: Oxford University Press, 1967.

Rose, Thomas. *Violence in America.* New York: Random House, 1969.

Rosenquist, Carl M., and Edwin I. Megargee. *Delinquency in Three Cultures.* Austin, Texas: University of Texas Press, 1969.

Rossi, Peter, ed. *Ghetto Revolts.* Chicago, Ill.: Aldine Pub. Co., 1970.

Rubin, Sol. *Crime and Juvenile Delinquency.* 3d ed. Dobbs Ferry, N.Y.: Oceana Publications, 1970.

Rubin, Ted. *Law as an Agent of Delinquency Prevention.* Washington, D.C.: U.S. Government Printing Office, 1971.

Rubington, Earl, and Martin S. Weinberg. *Deviance: The Interactionist Perspective.* New York: Macmillan, 1968.

Rubinstein, Jonathan. *City Police.* New York: Farrar, Straus and Giroux, 1973.

Ruchelman, Leonard. *Who Rules the Police?* New York: New York University Press, 1973.

Saint Louis Council on Police-Community Relations. *Police Community Relations 1966–1967 Program.* Saint Louis: Saint Louis Metropolitan Police Department, 1967.

Sanders, Irwin T. *The Community.* New York: Ronald Press, 1966.

Saunders, Charles B. *Upgrading the American Police.* Washington, D.C.: Brookings Institution, 1970.

Schafer, Stephen. *Compensation and Restitution to Victims of Crime.* rev. Montclair, N.J.: Patterson Smith, 1970.

———. *Juvenile Delinquency: An Introduction.* New York: Random House, 1970.

Scheuer, James H. *To Walk the Streets Safely.* Garden City, N.Y.: Doubleday, 1969.

Schnore, L., and H. Fagin, eds. *Urban Research and Policy Planning.* Beverly Hills, Calif.: Sage Publications, 1967.

Schorr, Alvin L. *Slums and Social Insecurity.* Washington, D.C.: Social Security Administration, 1963.

Schur, Edwin M. *Narcotic Addiction in Britain and America.* Bloomington, Ind.: Indiana University Press, 1970.

———. *Our Criminal Society: The Social and Legal Sources of Crime in America.* Englewood Cliffs, N.J.: Prentice-Hall, 1969.

Schwartz, Louis B., and S.R. Goldstein. *Law Enforcement Handbook for Police.* Saint Paul, Minn.: West Publishing Co., 1970.

Schwartz, Richard D., and Jerome H. Skolnick. *Society and the Legal Order.* New York: Basic Books, 1970.

Selznick, Gertrude J., and Stephen Steinberg. *The Tenacity of Prejudice: Anti-Semitism in Contemporary America.* New York: Harper & Row, 1969.

Servin, Manuel. *The Mexican-Americans: An Awakening Minority.* New York: Macmillan, 1970.

Shaw, Clifford, and Henry D. McKay. *Juvenile Delinquency and Urban Areas: A Study of Rates of Delinquency In Relation to Differential Characteris-*

tics of Local Communities and American Cities. rev. Chicago: University of Chicago Press, 1969.

Shecter, Leonard. *On the Pad: The Underworld and Its Corrupt Police.* New York: Putnam, 1973.

Sherman, Lawrence W. *Police Corruption: A Sociological Perspective.* New York: Anchor Books, 1974.

——, C.H. Milton, and T.V. Kelly. *Team Policing.* Washington, D.C.: Police Foundation, 1973.

Short, James F., Jr., ed. *Modern Criminals.* Chicago: Aldine, 1970.

——, and Fred L. Strodtbeck. *Group Process and Gang Delinquency.* Chicago: University of Chicago Press, 1965.

Siegel, Arthur I., Philip J. Federman, and Douglas G. Schultz. *Professional Police-Human Relations Training.* Springfield, Ill.: Charles C. Thomas, 1963.

Simon, Rita J. *Women and Crime.* Lexington, Mass.: Lexington Books, 1975.

Skolnick, Jerome H. *Justice Without Trial: Law Enforcement in Democratic Society.* New York: John Wiley & Sons, 1966.

——. *Professional Police in a Free Society.* New York: National Conference of Christians and Jews, 1968.

Skolnick, Jerome H., and Elliott Currie. *Crisis in American Institutions.* Boston: Little, Brown, 1970.

Smith, Alexander, and Arthur Niederhoffer. *Police-Community Relations Programs: A Study in Depth.* Washington, D.C.: U.S. Government Printing Office, 1970.

——, and Harriet Pollack. *Crime and Justice in a Mass Society.* Waltham, Mass.: Xerox College Publishing Corp., 1972.

Smith, Bruce. *Police Systems in the United States.* New York: Harper, 1940.

Smith, R. Dean, and Richard Kobetz. *Guidelines for Civil Disorder and Mobilization Planning: Prepared for the President's Advisory Commission on Civil Disorders.* Gaithersberg, Md.: International Association of Chiefs of Police, Research, Development, and Planning Division, 1968.

Smith, Ralph Lee. *The Tarnished Badge.* New York: Crowell, 1965.

Sowle, Claude R. *Police Power and Individual Freedom.* Chicago: Aldine, 1962.

Spiegel, John P. *The Tradition of Violence in Our Society.* Waltham, Mass.: Lemberg Center for the Study of Violence, Brandeis University, 1968.

Stark, Rodney. *Police Riots: Collective Violence and Law Enforcement.* Belmont: Wadsworth. 1972.

Steadman, Robert F., ed. *The Police and the Community.* Baltimore, Md.: Johns Hopkins University Press, 1972.

Steinfield, Melvin. *Cracks in the Melting Pot: Readings in Racism and Discrimination in American History.* New York: Macmillan, 1970.

Sterling, James W. *Changes in Role Concept of Police Officers.* Gaithersberg, Md.: International Association of Chiefs of Police, Research, Development and Planning Division, 1968.

Stratton, John R., and Robert M. Terry. *Prevention of Delinquency: Problems and Programs.* New York: Macmillan, 1968.

Strecher, Victor. *Cyclopedia of Policing.* 2 vols. Los Angeles: Loyola University of Los Angeles, School of Law, 1973.

———. *The Environment of Law Enforcement: A Community Relations Guide.* Englewood Cliffs, N.J.: Prentice-Hall, 1971.

Summers, Marvin R., and Thomas E. Barth. *Law and Order in a Democratic Society.* Columbus, Ohio: Charles E. Merrill, 1970.

Sutherland, Edwin H., and Donald R. Cressey. *Principles of Criminology.* 9th ed. Philadelphia: J.B. Lippincott, 1974.

Suttles, Gerald D. *The Social Construction of Communities.* Chicago: The University of Chicago Press, 1973.

———. *The Social Order of the Slum: Ethnicity and Territory in the Inner City.* Chicago: University of Chicago Press, 1968.

Sykes, Gresham M., and Thomas E. Drabek. *Law and the Lawless: A Reader in Criminology.* New York: Random House, 1969.

Tannenbaum, Frank. *Crime and the Community.* New York: Columbia University Press, 1938.

Taylor, Karl K., and Fred W. Soady, Jr., eds. *Violence: An Element of American Life.* Boston: Holbrook Press, 1972.

Thurow, Lester C. *Poverty and Discrimination.* Washington, D.C.: Brookings Institution, 1969.

Tiffany, Lawrence P., Donald M. McIntyre, Jr., and Daniel L. Rotenberg. *Detection of Crime: Stopping and Questioning, Search and Seizure, Encouragement and Entrapment.* Boston: Little, Brown & Co., 1967.

Toch, Hans, J. Douglas Grant, and Raymond T. Galvin. *Agents of Change: A Study in Police Reform.* New York: John Wiley & Sons, 1975.

———., *Violent Men: An Inquiry Into the Psychology of Violence.* Chicago: Aldine, 1969.

Towler, Juby E. *The Police Role in Racial Conflicts.* 2d ed. Springfield, Ill.: Charles C. Thomas, 1969.

Trasher, Frederick. *The Gang.* Chicago: University of Chicago Press, 1927.

Treanor, Gerald F., Jr. *Riots and Municipalities.* Report No. 152. Washington, D.C.: National Institute of Municipal Law Officers, 1968.

Trubowitz, Julius. *Changing the Racial Attitudes of Children—The Effects of an Activity Group Program in New York City Schools.* New York: Praeger, 1969.

Tucker, Sterling. *Beyond the Burning: Life and Death of the Ghetto.* New York: Association Press, 1970.

———. *Black Reflections on White Power.* Grand Rapids, Mich.: William B. Eerdmans, 1969.

Turk, Austin. *Criminality: A Sociological Perspective.* Chicago: Rand McNally, 1969.

Turner, William W. *The Police Establishment.* New York: G.P. Putnam's Sons, 1968.

Urban Outlook, Bibliography of Films, Filmstrips, Etc. Washington, D.C.: U.S. Government Printing Office, 1969.

U.S., Advisory Panel Against Armed Violence. *Report of the Advisory Panel Against Armed Violence.* Washington, D.C.: U.S. Government Printing Office, 1969.

U.S., Commission on Civil Rights. Reports listed are available from the U.S. Government Printing Office, Washington, D.C.

Racism in America and How to Combat It, 1970.

The Unfinished Education: Outcomes for Minorities in Five Southwestern States. Mexican-American Education Series Report 2, 1971.

U.S., Commission on Human Rights. *To Continue Action for Human Rights: Federal Report.* Washington, D.C.: U.S. Government Printing Office, 1969.

U.S., Congress. House Select Committee on Crime. *Juvenile Justice and Corrections.* Washington, D.C.: U.S. Government Printing Office, 1971.

U.S., Department of Health, Education, and Welfare. National Institute of Mental Health. Reports listed are available from U.S. Government Printing Office, Washington, D.C.

Civil Commitment of Special Categories of Offenders. Public Health Service Publication no. 2131, 1971.

Community-Based Correctional Programs: Models and Practices. Public Health Service Publication no. 2130, 1971.

Diversion From the Criminal Justice System. Public Health Service Publication no. 2129, 1971.

Graduated Release. Public Health Service Publication no. 2128, 1971.

U.S., Department of Housing and Urban Development. *The Model Cities Program: A History and Analysis of the Planning Process in Three Cities: Atlanta, Ga.; Seattle, Wash.; Dayton, Ohio.* Washington, D.C.: U.S. Government Printing Office, 1969.

U.S., Department of Justice.

Psychological Assessment of Patrolman's Qualifications in Relation to Field Performance. Report Prepared by Melanie E. Baehr, John E. Furcon, and Ernest C. Froemel, Industrial Relations Center, University of Chicago, for the Office of Law Enforcement Assistance, November 1968.

A Look at Criminal Justice Research (Technological). Law Enforcement Assistance Administration, 1971.

Police Training and Performance Study, PR 70-4. National Institute of Law Enforcement and Criminal Justice, Law Enforcement Administration, 1971.

U.S., National Advisory Commission on Civil Disorders. Reports listed are available from U.S. Government Printing Office, Washington, D.C.

Report of the National Advisory Commission on Civil Disorders, 1968. (Kerner Report.)

Supplemental Studies for the National Advisory Commission on Civil Disorders, 1968.

U.S., National Commission on Causes and Prevention of Violence. Reports listed are available from U.S. Government Printing Office, Washington, D.C.

Assassination and Political Violence, 1969.

Criminal Justice, 1969.

Mass Media and Violence, 1969.

Miami Report, 1969.

Political Assassination, 1969.

The Politics of Protest: Violent Aspects of Protest and Confrontation, 1969.

Progress Report of the National Commission on the Causes and Prevention of Violence, 1969.

Rights in Concord: The Response to the Counter-Inaugural Protest Activities in Washington, D.C., 1969.

Shoot-out in Cleveland, 1969.

Shut It Down! A College Crisis (San Francisco State College, October 1968–April 1969), 1969.

To Establish Justice, To Insure Domestic Tranquility, 1969.

Violence in America: Historical and Comparative Perspectives, vols. 1 and 2, 1969.

U.S., President's Commission on Law Enforcement and Administration of Justice. Reports listed are available from U.S. Government Printing Office, Washington, D.C.

Challenge of Crime in a Free Society, 1967.

Field Surveys IV. The Police and the Community: The Dynamics of their Relationship in a Changing Society, 1967.

Field Surveys V. A National Survey of Police and Community Relations, 1967.

Task Force Report: The Police, 1967.

Task Force Report: Science and Technology, 1967.

U.S., President's Council on Youth Opportunity. *Manual for Youth Coordinators.* Washington, D.C.: U.S. Government Printing Office, 1969.

U.S., President's Task Force on Prisoner Rehabilitation. *The Criminal Offender— What Should Be Done?* Washington, D.C.: U.S. Government Printing Office, 1970.

Van Allen, Edward J. *Our Handcuffed Police: The Assault upon Law and Order in America and What Can Be Done About It.* Mineola, N.Y.: Reportorial Press, 1968.

Vedder, Clyde B. *Juvenile Offenders.* Springfield, Ill.: Charles C. Thomas, 1969.

——, and Barbara A. Kay. *Penology.* Springfield, Ill.: Charles C. Thomas, 1969.

——, and Dora B. Somerville. *The Delinquent Girl.* Springfield, Ill.: Charles C. Thomas, 1970.

Vera Institute of Justice. *Police-Community Relations: A Survey Among New York City Patrolmen.* Princeton, N.J.: Opinion Research Corp., 1968.

Viano, Emilio, ed. *Criminal Justice Research.* Lexington, Mass.: Lexington Books, 1975.

——, and Alvin W. Cohn. *Social Problems and Criminal Justice.* Chicago, Ill.: Nelson Hall, 1975.

——, and Jeffrey Reiman, eds. *The Police in Society.* Lexington, Mass.: Lexington Books, 1975.

Vidich, Arthur, Joseph Bensman, and Maurice Stein, eds. *Reflections on Community Studies.* New York: John C. Wiley & Sons, 1964.

Viteritti, Joseph P. *Police, Politics, and Pluralism in New York City: A Comparative Case Study.* Beverly Hills, Calif.: Sage Publications, 1973.

Vollmer, August. *The Police in Modern Society.* Berkeley, Calif.: University of California Press, 1936.

Voss, Harwin L. *Reader in Juvenile Delinquency.* Boston: Little, Brown, 1970.

Wade, Richard C., et al. *Urban Violence.* Chicago: Center for Policy Study, University of Chicago, 1969.

Walker, T. Mike. *Voices from the Bottom of the World: A Policeman's Journal.* New York: Grove Press, 1970.

Wambaugh, Joseph. *The New Centurions:* A novel about police work as an intimate social function. Boston: Little, Brown, 1970.

——. *The Blue Knight.* Boston: Little, Brown, 1972.

Warren, Roland L. *The Community in America.* Chicago: Rand McNally, 1963.

——, ed. *Perspectives on the American Community.* Chicago: Rand McNally, 1966.

Wasserman, Robert, Michael Gardner, and Alana Cohen. *Improving Police-Community Relations.* Washington, D.C.: U.S. Government Printing Office, 1973.

Watson, Nelson A. *Attitudes—A Factor in Performance.* Gaithersburg, Md.: International Association of Chiefs of Police, Research, Development and Planning Division, 1968.

——. *Human Relations Training for Police: A Syllabus.* Gaithersburg, Md.: International Association of Chiefs of Police, Research, Development and Planning Division, 1968.

——. *Improving the Officer-Citizen Contact.* Gaithersburg, Md.: International Association of Chiefs of Police, Research, Development and Planning Division, 1968.

——. *Issues in Human Relations: Threats and Challenges.* Gaithersburg, Md.: International Association of Chiefs of Police, Research, Development and Planning Division, 1969.

——. *Police-Community Relations.* Gaithersburg, Md.: International Association of Chiefs of Police, Research, Development and Planning Division, 1966.

——. *Police Procedures in the Handling of Juveniles.* Address before the American Bar Association, Family Law Annual Meeting, 1966.

——, ed. *Police and the Changing Community: Selected Readings.* Gaithersburg, Md.: International Association of Chiefs of Police, Research, Development and Planning Division, 1965.

——, and Robert N. Walker, eds. *Juvenile Delinquency in Police Education: Proceedings of Workshop for Police Professors, Michigan State University, 1966.* Gaithersburg, Md.: International Association of Chiefs of Police, 1966.

Webster, John A. *The Realities of Police Work.* Dubuque, Iowa: Kendall Hunt, 1973.

Weckler, J.E., and Theodore E. Hall. *The Police and Minority Groups.* Chicago, Ill.: The International City Managers' Association, 1944.

Westley, William A. *Violence and the Police.* Cambridge, Mass.: MIT Press, 1970.

Weston, Paul B., and Kenneth M. Wells. *Law Enforcement and Criminal Justice: An Introduction.* Pacific Palisades, Calif.: Goodyear Publishing Co., 1972.

Wheeler, Stanton, ed. *Controlling Delinquents.* New York: John Wiley & Sons, 1968.

Whisenand, Paul M. *Police Supervision: Theory and Practice.* Englewood Cliffs, N.J.: Prentice-Hall, 1971.

———, and R. Fred Ferguson. *The Managing of Police Organizations.* Englewood Cliffs, New Jersey: Prentice-Hall, 1973.

Whitaker, Ben. *The Police.* Baltimore, Md.: Penguin Books, 1964.

Whittemore, L.H. *Cop.* New York: Fawcett World Library, 1970.

Who Will Listen If You Have a Civil Rights Complaint? Washington, D.C.: U.S. Government Printing Office, 1969.

Whyte, William F. *Street Corner Society.* Chicago: University of Chicago Press, 1943.

Wilson, James Q. *City Politics and Public Policy.* New York: John Wiley & Sons, 1968.

———. *Varieties of Police Behavior: The Management of Law and Order in Eight Communities.* Cambridge, Mass.: Harvard University Press, 1968.

———, ed. *The Metropolitan Enigma.* Garden City, N.Y.: Doubleday, 1970.

Wilson, O.W., and Roy C. McLaren. *Police Administration.* 3rd ed. New York: McGraw-Hill, 1972.

Wintersmith, Robert F. *Police and the Black Community.* Lexington, Mass.: Lexington Books, 1974.

Wolfgang, Marvin E. *The Culture of Youth.* Washington, D.C.: U.S. Government Printing Office, 1968.

Wolfgang, Marvin E., and Bernard Cohen. *Crime and Race: Conceptions and Misconceptions.* rev. New York: Institute of Human Relations Press, The American Jewish Committee, 165 E. 56th St., 1970.

Wolfle, Joan L., and John F. Heaphy. *Readings on Productivity in Policing.* Washington, D.C.: Police Foundation, 1975.

Wright, R. Gene, and John A. Marlo. *The Police Officer and Criminal Justice.* New York: McGraw-Hill, 1970.

Yablonsky, Lewis. *The Hippie Trip.* New York: Pegasus, 1969.

Young, Whitney. *Beyond Racism: Building an Open Society.* New York: McGraw-Hill, 1970.

Yuan, D.Y. *The Chinese-American Population: A Study of Voluntary Segregation.* Morristown, N.J.: General Learning Press, 1972.

Zarr, Melvyn. *The Bill of Rights and the Police.* rev. ed. Dobbs Ferry, N.Y.: Oceana Publications, 1970.

Zimmerman, Joseph F. *Subnational Politics: Reading in State and Local Government.* 2d. ed. New York: Holt, Rinehart & Winston, 1970.

iNdEx

627